Psychological Anthropology

Blackwell Anthologies in Social & Cultural Anthropology

Drawing from some of the most significant scholarly work of the 19th and 20th centuries, the *Blackwell Anthologies in Social and Cultural Anthropology* series offers a comprehensive and unique perspective on the ever-changing field of anthropology. It represents both a collection of classic readers and an exciting challenge to the norms that have shaped this discipline over the past century.

Each edited volume is devoted to a traditional subdiscipline of the field such as the anthropology of religion, linguistic anthropology, or medical anthropology; and provides a foundation in the canonical readings of the selected area. Aware that such subdisciplinary definitions are still widely recognized and useful – but increasingly problematic – these volumes are crafted to include a rare and invaluable perspective on social and cultural anthropology at the onset of the 21st century. Each text provides a selection of classic readings together with contemporary works that underscore the artificiality of subdisciplinary definitions and point students, researchers, and general readers in the new directions in which anthropology is moving.

Series Board

Psychological Anthropology

A Reader on Self in Culture

Edited by

Robert A. LeVine

WILEY-BLACKWELL

A John Wiley & Sons, Ltd., Publication

Registered Office
John Wiley & Sons Ltd, The Atrium, Southern Gate, Chichester, West Sussex, PO19 8SQ, United Kingdom

Editorial Offices
350 Main Street, Malden, MA 02148-5020, USA
9600 Garsington Road, Oxford, OX4 2DQ, UK
The Atrium, Southern Gate, Chichester, West Sussex, PO19 8SQ, UK

For details of our global editorial offices, for customer services, and for information about how to apply for permission to reuse the copyright material in this book please see our website at www.wiley.com/wiley-blackwell.

Library of Congress Cataloging-in-Publication Data

Psychological anthropology: a reader / edited by Robert A. LeVine.
  p.   cm. – (Blackwell anthologies in social and cultural anthropology)
  Includes bibliographical references and index.
  ISBN 978-1-4051-0575-0 (hardcover : alk. paper) – ISBN 978-1-4051-0576-7 (pbk.   )
  1. Ethnopsychology. I. Levine, Robert A.

GN502.P753 2010
302–dc22
2009052088

A catalogue record for this book is available from the British Library.

Set in 9/11pt Sabon by SPi Publisher Services, Pondicherry, India.
Printed in Singapore

01   2010

I dedicate the book to the memories of six major contributors to psychological anthropology:

Takeo Doi (1920–2009); Alan Dundes (1934–2005); Robert I. Levy (1924–2003); John Uzo Ogbu (1939–2003); Beatrice Blyth Whiting (1914–2003); and John M. Whiting (1908–1999).

Contents

Acknowledgments

The editor and publisher gratefully acknowledge the permission granted to reproduce the copyrighted material in this book:

1   W. I. Thomas and Florian Znaniecki, The Polish Peasant in Europe and America: Monograph of an Immigrant Group, Volume I Primary-Group Organization; Boston, Richard G. Badger, The Gorham Press (1918). © 1918 Richard G. Badger, pp. 20–24, 44–45, 68–69; Volume III; Boston, Richard G. Badger, The Gorham Press (1919), © 1919 Richard G. Badger, pp. 5–6.

2   Edward Sapir, The Psychology of Culture: A Course of Lectures, reconstructed and edited by Judith T. Irvine, Mouton de Gruyter, Berlin, New York, 1994, a division of Walter de Gruyter & Co., Berlin © 1993 by Walter de Gruyter & Co., pp. 175–207. Reprinted with permission of Walter de Gruyter GmbH & Co.

A. Irving Hallowell, Psychological Leads for Ethnological Field Workers in *Personal Character and Cultural Milieu: A Collection of Readings*, Revised Edition, compiled by Douglas G. Haring, Syracuse University Press, Revised Edition © 1949 by Douglas G. Haring; 1937 Psychological Leads for Ethnological Field Workers, prepared under the auspices of the Committee on Personality in Relation to Culture, Edward Sapir, Chairman, Division of Anthropology and Psychology, National Research Council, mimeographed, under the title, "Introduction: Handbook of Psychological Leads for Ethnological Field Workers" previously unpublished, reproduced by courtesy of D. Hallowell, pp. 329–333.

3   Extract from "The Self and Its Behavioral Environment" by A. Irving Hallowell from *Explorations II*, (April 1954) *Culture and Experience* by A. Irving Hallowell. © 1955 by University of Pennsylvania Press, 1988, pp 390–395. Reprinted with permission of University of Pennsylvania Press.

4   Jean L. Briggs, Emotions Have Many Faces: Inuit Lessons, paper presented at 18th Annual Interdisciplinary Conference of the International Federation for Psychoanalytic Education, The Reach of the Mind, October 19–21, 2007. © Jean L. Briggs. Reprinted with kind permission of the author.

5   Geoffrey M. White, Moral Discourse and the Rhetoric of Emotion from *Language and the Politics of Emotion*, ed. Catherine A. Lutz and Lila Abu-Lughod,

Cambridge University Press, Cambridge, New York, Port Chester, Melbourne, Sydney and Editions de la Maison des Sciences de l'Homme, Paris. © Maison des Sciences de l'Homme and Cambridge University Press, 1990, pp. 46–68. Reprinted with permission of Cambridge University Press.

6   Usha Menon and Richard A. Shweder, Kali's Tongue from *Emotion and Culture: Empirical Studies of Mutual Influence*, ed. Shinobu Kitayama and Hazel Rose Markus, American Psychological Association, Washington, DC. © 1994 by the American Psychological Association, pp. 241–284. Reprinted with permission of the American Psychological Association.

7   Takie Sugiyama Lebra, Shame and Guilt: A Psychocultural View of the Japanese Self from *Ethos*, Vol. 11, No. 3, Self and Emotion (Autumn, 1983), pp. 192–209. Published by Blackwell Publishing on behalf of the American Anthropological Association. ©1983 by the Society for Psychological Anthropology. Reprinted with permission of the American Anthropological Society.

8   Arthur Kleinman and Byron Good, Introduction to Culture and Depression from *Culture and Depression: Studies in the Anthropology and Cross-Cultural Psychiatry of Affect and Disorder*, ed. Arthur Kleinman and Byron Good, University of California Press, Berkeley, Los Angeles, London. © 1985 by The Regents of the University of California, pp. 1–8. Reprinted with permission of the University of California Press.

9   Robert A. Paul, Psychoanalytic Anthropology from *Annual Review of Anthropology*, 1989, vol. 1, pp. 177–202. © 1989 Annual Reviews Inc. www.annualreviews.org. Reprinted with permission.

10   Anne Parsons, Is the Oedipus Complex Universal? from *The Psychoanalytic Study of Society*, III, ed. Warner Muensterberter and Sidney Axelrad (New York: International Universities Press, 1964), pp. 278–328. Copyright © 1964 International Universities Press. Reprinted with permission of International Universities Press, Inc.

11   Waud H. Kracke, Kagwahiv Mourning: Dreams of a Bereaved Father from *Ethos*, Vol. 9, No. 4, Dreams (Winter, 1981), pp. 258–275. Published by Blackwell Publishing on behalf of the American Anthropological Association. © 1981 by the Society for Psychological Anthropology.

12   Waud H. Kracke, Kagwahiv Mourning II: Ghosts, Grief, and Reminiscences from *Ethos*, Vol. 16, No. 2 (June, 1988), pp. 209–222. Published by Blackwell Publishing on behalf of the American Anthropological Association.

13   Amy L. Richman, Patrice M. Miller, and Robert A. LeVine, Cultural and Educational Variations in Maternal Responsiveness from *Developmental Psychology*, 1992, Vol. 28, No. 4, pp. 614–621. © 1992 by the American Psychological Association, Inc., received January 3, 1992, accepted January 5, 1992. Reprinted with permission.

14   Peggy J. Miller, Heidi Fung, and Judith Mintz, Self-Construction Through Narrative Practices: A Chinese and American Comparison of Early Socialization from *Ethos*, Vol. 24, No. 2 (June, 1996), pp. 237–280. © 1996 American Anthropological Association. Reprinted with permission of the American Anthropological Association.

15   Vanessa L. Fong, Parent–Child Communication Problems and the Perceived Inadequacies of Chinese Only Children from *Ethos*, Vol. 35, Issue 1, pp. 85–127.

© 2007 American Anthropological Association. Reprinted with permission of the American Anthropological Association.

16 Thomas Gregor, *Mehinaku: The Drama of Daily Life in a Brazilian Indian Village.* © 1977 by The University of Chicago, The University of Chicago Press, Chicago, The University of Chicago Press, Ltd., London, pp. 177–223. Reprinted with permission.

17 Gilbert H. Herdt, Sambia Nosebleeding Rites and Male Proximity to Women from *Ethos*, Vol. 10, No. 3 (Autumn, 1982), pp. 189–231. Published by Blackwell Publishing on behalf of the American Anthropological Association, © 1982 by the Society for Psychological Anthropology. Reprinted with permission of the American Anthropological Association.

18 Douglas Hollan, Cross-Cultural Differences in the Self from *Journal of Anthropological Research*, Vol. 48, No. 4 (Winter, 1992), pp. 283–300. Published by University of New Mexico. Reprinted with permission of the *Journal of Anthropological Research*.

19 Joseph D. Calabrese, Clinical Paradigm Clashes: Ethnocentric and Political Barriers to Native American Efforts at Self-Healing from *Ethos*, Vol. 36, No. 3, pp. 334–353. © 2008 by the American Anthropological Association. Reprinted with permission of the American Anthropological Association.

20 Carola Suárez-Orozco and Marcelo M. Suárez-Orozco, The Psychosocial Experience of Immigration reprinted by permission of the publisher from *Children of Immigration*, ed. Carola Suárez-Orozco and Marcelo M. Suárez-Orozco, pp 66–86, 173–174, 185–201, Cambridge, MA: Harvard University Press. Copyright © 2001 by the President and Fellows of Harvard College.

21 Robert A. LeVine and Sarah E. LeVine, The Schooling of Women: Maternal Behavior and Child Environments from *Ethos*, Vol. 29, No. 3, pp. 259–270. © 2002 by the American Anthropological Association. Reprinted with permission of the American Anthropological Association.

22 Anthony F. C. Wallace, Revitalization Movements from *American Anthropologist*, New Series, Vol. 58, No. 2 (April 1956), pp. 264–281.

23 Charles Lindholm, Culture, Charisma, and Consciousness: The Case of the Rajneeshee from *Ethos*, Vol. 30, No. 4, pp. 357–375. © 2003 by the American Anthropological Association. Reprinted with permission of the American Anthropological Association.

Thanks to my research assistants, Chelsea Shields Strayer and Arianna Fogelman for helping me comb the voluminous literature of this field an to participants in my Spring, 2008 seminar at the University of Chicago, "The Quest for a Psychological Anthropology," especially Ray Fogelson and George Stocking, for setting me straight on many historical points. I am of course solely responsible for the book as it stands.

Introduction

Psychological anthropology is the study of the behavior, experience and development of individuals in relation to the institutions and ideologies of their sociocultural environments, across all populations of the human species. As anthropology, it expands that discipline's reach to the inner experience and psychological development of individual participants in social systems. As an interface with psychology and psychiatry, it extends the scope of those disciplines beyond the confines of Western societies to all cultures in the world. Psychological anthropology is based on the premises that the inclusion of psychological and psychiatric topics in anthropology and of all world cultures in the psychological sciences is *necessary* for those disciplines to make valid contributions to human understanding. In other words: "All anthropology is psychological. All psychology is cultural" (Bock, 1988) – a rebuke to social anthropologists who claim their field needs no psychology (and use "psychologizing" as an epithet) and to psychologists and psychiatrists who base their generalizations about humans exclusively on Western evidence. Thus psychological anthropology continues to present a radical challenge to established thinking within the social and biomedical sciences. And it continues to shed interdisciplinary light on problems of fundamental significance that are otherwise neglected.

Research in this field addresses three classes of questions:

(a) *Questions of variation:* Do human populations vary in their psychological make-up, and if so, how? We now know, from evidence gathered by anthropologists, that there have long been significant cross-population variations in culture and behavior, within and between all major regions of the world, and that peoples differ in cultural practices that are morally and emotionally significant to them. In psychological anthropology we study how those significant psychological variations affect their behavior – in domains ranging from sexuality and parenting to social interaction and religion – and how their behavior affects the social contexts in which they live.

(b) *Questions of ontogeny*: What factors in individual development account for such variations? What is the course of psychological development in childhood and throughout the life cycle in human populations: its evolutionary basis, its cross-cultural diversity, its role in shaping differences in adult behavior at the population level, its ecological relationships? Anthropologists have uncovered wide variations in childhood environments – including parental care of infants, sibling caregiving, peer groups, language socialization, learning patterns – and explore the ways in which these experiences play a formative role in the acquisition of culture and the development of individual psychological dispositions.

(c) *Questions of change*: How are the developmental pathways and adult motivations of individuals related to the macrosocial forces of institutional stability and change? Psychological anthropologists find that the human motivations involved in maintaining and changing social institutions cannot be reduced to the few elemental drives (e.g. sex and aggression), needs (food, wealth) or capacities (rational choice) presumed by many generalizing theorists but take varied forms and symbolic contents in particular times and places. We seek generalizations based on evidence but we are keenly aware that simplistic theories cannot predict the variability of human behavior.

Anthropologists have been pioneers in field research on child rearing, gender, sexual behavior, language acquisition, mental disorder, psychodynamics, aging, alcoholism and drinking behavior, initiation ceremonies, religious movements and many other topics that form the heritage of this field and are represented in this reader. Research in psychological anthropology sheds light on issues, some of them controversial, like the following:

- *Universal vs. Culture-Specific Psychology*. Can human behavior be understood in utilitarian terms as universally shaped by environmental incentives (+) and disincentives (−): rewards and punishments in childhood, positive and negative sanctions in adulthood, selection pressures in evolution creating a universal human genome? Or must valid models of human behavior take account of more complex and culture-specific symbols, scripts and narratives, as publicly and privately interpreted, that produce a field of wide psychological variations across and within populations? Universal psychologies (utilitarian and otherwise) have presented many challenges to a cultural viewpoint: Universals of language, cognitive development, facial affect expression, sex and reproduction, parental behavior, brain function, have been posited by a great array of theories from those of Freud, Piaget and Chomsky to recent formulations in evolutionary psychology and neuroscience. At the same time, anthropology has developed concepts of the motivational force of cultural meanings compatible with new knowledge of universal capacities – concepts of processes operating in the human individual like the diverse software programs that realize the potentials of a computer's hardware. If cultural software gives direction to neurological hardware, both universals and cultural variations can be seen as parts of the same psychology.

- *Psychoanalysis vs. Psychometrics*. Has Freud's psychoanalytic approach to the human mind been eclipsed by psychological testing? Academic psychologists have long regarded Freud's clinical approach (and other clinical approaches derived from psychoanalysis) as unscientific, while accepting the validity of psychometrics, the science of psychological tests and measurements. Psychological anthropologists remain divided on this issue, however. Many are reluctant to accept psychometrics due to the difficulty and artificiality of testing nonliterates and to doubts about the validity of using tests devised in one culture in another with drastically different linguistic, social and cultural contexts. Some psychological anthropologists embraced the use of "projective" tests; others have devised new clinical approaches for use in ethnographic fieldwork. The Freudian legacy has been extensively revised but it remains influential in psychological anthropology.

- *Nature vs. Nurture.* Are the psychological development of the child and its adult outcomes best understood as the effects of child-rearing practices or the expression of hereditary tendencies determined by genes? The early research of Margaret Mead in Samoa (1928) and New Guinea (1930), was addressed to such questions, and psychological anthropology became known as challenging hereditarian or innatist proposals from a strongly environmentalist perspective. As genetics, neuroscience and evolutionary biology flowered in the late 20th century, it was widely expected that environmentalism in general and the cross-cultural study of child rearing specifically, would be correspondingly rejected. To a surprising extent, however, biological advances have shown that the door to environmental influence is open at many points in ontogeny, helping to specify the role of such influences, and psychological anthropologists have demonstrated the effects of culture-specific environments on children in diverse settings across the world.

- *Mental Health: Culture vs. Psychiatry?* If definitions of normal and abnormal behavior vary across cultures, as anthropologists have shown, are psychiatric theories, diagnoses and treatments applicable everywhere or only in our own society? This question has generated debate since the 1930s, but the problem itself has been reformulated and refined by medical and psychological anthropologists taking account of the biology of a mental disorder even as they study the sociocultural contexts in which it develops, is expressed and responds to treatment.

- *Ritual and Change: Macrosocial vs. Psychosocial Analyses.* Can social life and its major transformations be understood entirely in terms of societal processes outside the person or must their explanation involve a psychological dimension? Social theorists following Emile Durkheim (1982 [1912]) have opted for social-structural explanations, including the institutionalization and transformation of moral norms that enforce different types of social solidarity, while social theorists following Max Weber (1958 [1904]) have favored ideological explanations that explicitly address the issue of motivating individual behavior in a particular historical context. From the very beginning, psychological anthropologists have objected to models of social life and social change that left out the individual (Sapir, 1917; Thomas and Znaniecki, 1918), and they have formulated person–environment interactions in terms (closer to Weber than to Durkheim) of the psychosocial or "psychocultural" processes that account for social stability and change.

In their approaches to these and other issues in the social sciences, psychological anthropologists tend to focus on *psychocultural processes*: e.g. human adaptation, learning and development, integration and disintegration at individual and societal levels, viewed from cultural, biological, psychological and sociological perspectives.

They observe and raise questions about complex processes accessible only to ethnographic and clinical description as well as processes amenable to statistical analysis.

Psychological anthropology is a long-term project, analogous to the natural history of Darwin, to record the varieties of human behavior and experience. Like Darwin, we are also searching for principles of order that will explain the variations and regularities observed in the field. Anthropologists have conducted psychocultural fieldwork on every continent and among peoples who live in foraging, agricultural and urban-industrial societies; they have also sought to establish generalizations through comparative studies. The volume of research and publications has increased greatly since I last published a reader like this one 35 years ago (LeVine, 1974). The founding in 1973 of *Ethos*, now the official journal of the Society for Psychological Anthropology, has been a central factor in this expansion, providing not only an outlet for articles that might not otherwise have become part of the field's dialogue but also a stimulus and inspiration for further research.

The worldwide coverage of psychological anthropology is represented in this reader: In the Americas, for example, studies have been carried out in areas from the Canadian Arctic to the Amazon basin. The distribution has been uneven: There have been more studies in Oceania, fewer in sub-Saharan Africa, a growing number in East Asia. This book samples this diversity as well as the theories psychological anthropologists have devised to make sense of them.

Our field encompasses varied theoretical positions, and it sometimes seems especially split between universalists and relativists, but there is an ironclad consensus that universals must be based on empirical evidence as well as theoretical considerations and that exceptional cases cannot be ignored. The readings in this book represent somewhat different theoretical perspectives but share a commitment to empirical research and a framework or paradigm that is spelled out in Part I.

Outline of the Reader

The book is divided into six parts:

Part I: Constructing a Paradigm, 1917–55, presents a new view of the history of the "culture and personality" movement as the first phase of psychological anthropology, creating a framework of assumptions – a *paradigm* – that remains central to thinking and research in the field. In the introductory essay, I present an historical sketch that clarifies the development of the movement and its legacy. This is illustrated in the readings from the works of W. I. Thomas and Florian Znaniecki, Edward Sapir, and A. Irving Hallowell, presenting materials that have been overlooked in earlier histories and mythologies of the movement.

Part II: Emotion and Morality in Diverse Cultures, contains a set of articles published in recent decades portraying the cultural relativity of emotional experience and moral concepts among diverse peoples. The introductory essay begins with the separation of culture from bodily form and language in the anthropology of Franz Boas as establishing a context in which observed variations in the emotional and moral meanings of customary practices around the world could be related to the psychology of individuals. The chapters show examples from the Canadian Inuit, Melanesia, Hindu India, Japan and other cultures. They include different approaches to the evidence of cultural relativity and questions of universals, but taken as a whole, they demonstrate some of the indisputable starting points for a cultural psychology.

Part III: Psychoanalytic Explorations through Fieldwork, displays examples of post-Freudian anthropology. The quest for a depth psychology revealing unconscious motives and mental processes – but revised and enhanced by knowledge of cultural variation – has never been fully relinquished by psychological anthropologists. There have been periodic revivals of interest in building a psychoanalytic anthropology. The long-term trend has been toward fieldwork that captures the unconscious meanings of individual thought and action in social contexts defined by cultural symbolism: family relationships, religious imagery, ritual performances, dreams. The chapters by Robert Paul, Anne Parsons and Waud Kracke – three anthropologists with formal training in psychoanalysis – show the concern with clinical method, continued interest in problems and phenomena first identified by Freud, and willingness to go beyond Freud's theory and methods – characteristic of recent psychoanalytic anthropology. In Part V, the chapters by Gregor, Herdt, and Hollan, show more of the Freudian influence, combined with the ethnography and comparative study of the self.

Part IV: Childhood: Internalizing Cultural Schemas, presents works from the comparative study of child rearing, through which psychological anthropology has always studied *enculturation*, the culture shaping of psychological development. The introductory essay reviews the topic of *communicative socialization*, a process that has long received attention from linguistic anthropologists and which has emerged as providing some of our best evidence of the child's acquisition of culture.

Part V: The Self in Everyday Life, Ritual, and Healing, presents a broad array of topics united by an ethnographic focus on the self as portrayed in rituals (of interaction, personal transition and collective occasions), in adult situations of self-reflection and distress, and in healing or therapeutic intervention. Cultural narratives of self–other interactions that arouse and reduce emotions are presented as the means through which individuals seek and restore emotional comfort and prevent and alleviate anxiety. The case of male sex identity is offered as a psychocultural problem that has been studied through the analysis of ritual symbolism and practices.

Part VI: Psychosocial Processes in History and Social Transformation, includes a few diverse examples of how psychological anthropology illuminates social change: through examining the effects of immigration, global institutional diffusion (the case of women's schooling) and revitalization. In each example a specific process is in focus and the effects of personal responses to changing environments are shown. This final section displays ways in which psychological anthropology contributes to social theory and brings us back to the field's roots in Boasian historical anthropology, research on European immigration to the United States and questions of culture change among the Native Americans.

REFERENCES

Bock, Philip K.
   1988   Rethinking Psychological Anthropology. New York: W. H. Freeman.

Durkheim, Emile
  1982 [1895]   The Rules of Sociological Method and Selected Texts on Sociology and its Methods. New York: The Free Press.
LeVine, Robert A. (ed.)
  1974   Culture and Personality: Contemporary Readings. New York: Aldine.
Mead, Margaret
  1928   Coming of Age in Samoa. New York: William Morrow.
  1930   Growing Up in New Guinea. New York: William Morrow.
Sapir, Edward
  1917   Do We Need a Superorganic? American Anthropologist 19:441–447.
Thomas, W. I. and Florian Znaniecki
  1918   The Polish Peasant in Europe and America. Boston: Gorham Press.
Weber, Max
  1958 [1904]   The Protestant Ethic and the Spirit of Capitalism. New York: Scribners.

Part I

Constructing a Paradigm, 1917–55

(9-17) (22-28)

(33-46)

(60-67) (102-110)

(83-100) (112-116)

(124-127) (131-152)

(192-211) (309-321)

(329-340) (365-376)

Introduction

Invisible Pioneers: "Culture and Personality" Reconsidered

As the social sciences of anthropology, sociology, and psychology emerged from philosophy and became separate academic disciplines in the decades before and after 1900, several *inter*disciplinary movements, including "social psychology" (within both psychology and sociology) and "culture and personality" (largely within American anthropology roughly 1930–55), sought to explore the connections and interactions between the individual and society. There is no full or accurate history of the culture and personality movement, and it has been shrouded in misconceptions, but new evidence has enabled us to understand the movement as the first phase of psychological anthropology, one in which a unifying theoretical framework or paradigm was constructed that continues to inform contemporary theory and research.

The culture and personality movement was founded by three anthropologists – Edward Sapir, Ruth Benedict, and Margaret Mead – around 1930. All three had been students of Franz Boas at Columbia University and had published articles and books in the late 1920s intended to promote and illustrate research that combined psychological and cultural perspectives in the study of diverse peoples of the world. Sapir had been teaching a course on "the psychology of culture" at the University of Chicago since 1926. An interdisciplinary movement called "culture and personality" (or "the study of personality and culture") took shape at the Social Science Research Council in 1930, with the sociologist W. I. Thomas (see Chapter 1), the psychiatrist-psychoanalyst Harry Stack Sullivan, and the psychologist Mark A. May joining with Sapir and other anthropologists in a series of discussions directed toward setting a research agenda. In 1935, Abram Kardiner, a psychoanalyst who had studied with Boas but became a physician and was analyzed by Freud in 1921, began a seminar at the New York Psychoanalytic Institute, inviting anthropologists to present their findings and develop an integrated theory. There were also research and training activities in culture and personality during the 1930s and 1940s in the anthropology departments at Columbia, Yale, the University of Pennsylvania, and Harvard.

By the 1940s, culture and personality had become established in anthropology: The American Anthropological Association elected four of the movement's leaders (Ralph Linton, Ruth Benedict, Clyde Kluckhohn, and A. Irving Hallowell) to its presidency, and the discipline's quasi-official handbook, *Anthropology Today*, edited by A. L. Kroeber (1953), contained five chapters on culture and personality. But this favored position was short-lived. After 1950 there was a steep decline in the movement's reputation, and by 1960 it was widely reported to be dead. The name "psychological anthropology" was adopted to signal a fresh start (Hsu, 1961). In retrospect, these reports were exaggerated, as significant new projects were launched and established investigators continued their research and publication. Yet culture and personality was marginalized within anthropology, and doctoral students were discouraged from specializing in the field. By the later 1960s a revival had begun, followed by the publication of a journal, *Ethos*, in 1973 and the founding of the Society for Psychological Anthropology in 1977, which became a recognized unit of the American Anthropological Association. The field has never lost its vitality, as this book of readings shows, but it needs a new history.

The culture and personality movement was neither centralized nor coordinated; it was not a "school of thought" like the structural-functional anthropology of A. R. Radcliffe-Brown, since it lacked an acknowledged leader, an institutional center, and an explicit consensus on theory and method. In fact, culture and personality was a field of exploratory thinking and research, with many viewpoints and divisions; its participants often disagreed with each other on important issues and even disparaged the movement itself without leaving it. Some members of the movement became well known to the general public, while others of equal or greater importance were virtually invisible except in anthropology. The reactions that brought about the movement's sudden decline after 1950 were focused largely on a few parts without even recognizing that there were others.

Two projects at Columbia University were severely criticized for flaws of scholarship that were widely and inaccurately generalized to the culture and personality movement as a whole. One was Ruth Benedict's project on the national character of contemporary East European peoples, studied "at a distance" (i.e. through documents and *émigré* testimony), particularly *The People of Great Russia*, in which Geoffrey Gorer (her former research associate) proposed that a Russian preference for authoritarian rulers was connected to their being swaddled as infants (Gorer and Rickman, 1949). This proposal set off a storm of derision in Soviet studies and the social sciences, and, in any event, most anthropologists disapproved of studying cultures without fieldwork and of generalizing from ethnographic descriptions to the national character of large, complex societies like Russia and Poland. Ruth Benedict had died in 1948, and Margaret Mead, who took over direction of the project, defended Gorer's "swaddling hypothesis" (Mead, 1954), national character research (Mead, 1953), and "the study of culture at a distance" (Mead and Metraux, 1953). Her arguments convinced few anthropologists but may have fostered confusion between the Columbia project (run by Benedict, then Mead), and the culture and personality movement, of which Mead and Benedict had been two of the three founders (the other was Edward Sapir) some 20 years earlier. Thus the scandals of the Columbia project were soon attributed to the culture and personality movement as a whole, even though most participants in the movement were not supporters of the project's approach.

The second Columbia project was that of psychoanalyst Abram Kardiner (1939, 1945), whose seminar of 1937–45 resulted in two books that, though pioneering efforts to create a post-Freudian psychoanalytic anthropology open to social and cultural influences, were flawed by a failure to acknowledge the importance of individual differences in personality and by speculations about the impact of child rearing on personality that many social scientists found unbelievable. The first flaw would fuel the charge that the culture and personality movement assumed "the replication of uniformity" (Wallace, 1961); the second fallacy (like Gorer's swaddling hypothesis) was derided as an absurd "diaperology" characteristic of the movement as a whole.

But the two Columbia projects were not the whole movement, only the most visible and vulnerable parts of it. We now know that Edward Sapir had long been developing a different line of thought that, though much of it was unpublished at the time, influenced three anthropologists who were constructing an empirical approach to culture and personality: A. Irving Hallowell, Clyde Kluckhohn, and Ralph Linton.

Invisible Pioneers: Building a Theoretical Paradigm

Edward Sapir (1884–1939) has long been recognized as the original theorist of the culture and personality movement, but he died at the age of 55 without completing his book on the psychology of culture. His lectures at Yale and Chicago that were to be chapters of the book were published in 1994, 55 years later. The excerpts reprinted as Chapter 2 of this reader reveal the basic elements of his theoretical framework, forged through disagreements with other pioneers and embodying crucial ambiguities that were passed down to those who sought to translate the theory into field research. That Sapir did not do psychocultural research himself is only one of several limitations that must be recognized in identifying his role in this history: he spent most of his career in linguistic studies, and focused on psychiatry rather than psychology as the partner for an interdisciplinary nexus with anthropology. Yet Sapir's thought is the indispensable starting point for understanding the promise of psychological anthropology as well as its unsolved problems.

Sapir was by all accounts an exceptionally talented, sophisticated, and original thinker – many called him a genius – whose work on Native American languages helped bring linguistic anthropology into being. By the time he turned his attention to culture and personality, around 1926, he had already made fundamental contributions to linguistics and published a general book on language (Sapir, 1921) full of theoretically significant ideas for the social sciences. His interest in psychology was evident in publications dating back to 1917, but in 1926 he began a friendship with Harry Stack Sullivan, the psychiatrist and renegade psychoanalyst, which played an important part in his theory-building efforts. By that time Sapir was already teaching a lecture course on the psychology of culture at the University of Chicago, which he would bring to Yale and last taught there in 1936–37.

In Sapir's lectures on the psychology of culture and his published essays on culture and personality, a framework of assumptions can be found that entails the following propositions:

- **Plasticity.** The plasticity of the human organism permits variation in cultural patterns (symbolic codes like language) to develop, distinguishing one human population from another.
- **Cultural patterning, mediation, and communication.** Culture-specific codes mediate between external realities and individual experience by permeating all communication in the population, including the *interpersonal relations* of children from birth onwards.
- **Internalization.** From their communicative experience in *interpersonal* contexts, children internalize cultural meanings as normative standards influencing their conduct and their psychological tendencies. As they become socialized, their behavior is culturally patterned.
- **Individuality.** The culturally patterned psychological tendencies of the individual combine with the person's innate dispositions and specific environmental conditions to create individual differences in how cultural patterns are realized in behavior.
- **Individual differences.** The variability of individual psychological tendencies within a population is critical to understanding the processes of social stability and change.

This is the initial framework for culture and personality studies. Many of these points are not original with Sapir: Plasticity in human development had been emphasized by Boas (and borrowed from Rudolf Virchow, the Berlin biomedical pioneer, with whom Boas worked in 1883); cultural mediation of reality was another Boasian point (derived from phenomenological philosophy); cultural patterning was developed as a concept by Ruth Benedict as well as Sapir; communication, an important focus for Sapir, was also basic to the philosophy of George Herbert Mead; internalization as a conceptual metaphor for social-psychological development seems to have been invented several times (G. H. Mead, L. S. Vygotsky, James Mark Baldwin); and W. I. Thomas and Florian Znaniecki had published versions of the last two points in their "methodological note" to the first volume of *The Polish Peasant in Europe and America* (1918), excerpts from which are reprinted as Chapter 1 of this reader. Yet Sapir put these and the interpersonal psychiatry of Sullivan together into a framework for anthropological research in his lectures.

Sapir's emphasis on the individual as the locus of culture and on individual variability within a population put him at odds with, and critical of, other former students of Franz Boas: A. L. Kroeber, who treated culture as "superorganic" (disconnected from the individual) on the one hand (Sapir, 1917), and Ruth Benedict and Margaret Mead, who treated culture as "personality writ large" (suggesting a group personality) on the other. His aversion to reducing either personality or culture to elementary traits that could be aggregated numerically, and his passionate preference for identifying indissoluble "patterns" like the *gestalten* of the German psychologist Koffka or Jung's "psychological types" (or his own sound patterns in language), set Sapir apart from Boas, whose passions included measurable traits and statistical analysis, and put Sapir closer to Benedict.

Sapir's rift with Benedict, his close friend and ally in the culture and personality movement until her formulation of culture as personality writ large in the manuscript of *Patterns of Culture* (1934), was a crucial moment in the history of culture and personality studies (Darnell, 1990). Benedict's book became a best-seller that epitomized cultural anthropology for the American reading public, while Sapir's position – as represented in Chapter 2 – was known only to his graduate students at Yale and those postdoctoral anthropologists who had participated in conferences and seminars with him. Among the latter were Hallowell, Kluckhohn, and Linton, who sided strongly with Sapir in their publications of the late 1930s, echoing his criticisms of Benedict. Though they were not his students, all three had contacts with Sapir between 1930 and 1936 that influenced their own theoretical positions. In their research projects and publications Sapir's theoretical framework found its realization and its elaboration as a scientific paradigm (LeVine, 2007).

Sapir's framework raised a question he did not answer: If individuals are the loci of culture, and their psychological patterns reflect cultural influence in varying personal patterns, how does the anthropologist describe the distribution of psychological patterns within a population or their variations across populations? Sapir looked to Sullivan's psychiatry's for the answer, but that meant case studies or life histories of individuals who might be unrepresentative of the population. Sapir categorically rejected quantitative methods or statistical models, but he offered no coherent alternative.

Hallowell, Kluckhohn, and Linton, however, were keenly aware of the problem and proposed quantitative solutions, including sampling and frequency distributions. Their contrasting attitude toward quantification may reflect the influence of Boas, who used and contributed to modern statistical analysis in his pioneering work on physical growth (Howells, 1959; Tanner, 1959; Xie, 1988; Camic and Xie, 1994). Boas required his doctoral students to take his rigorous seminar on statistics, though Sapir managed to avoid it. Since Hallowell and Linton had studied with Boas at Columbia, and Kluckhohn considered himself a Boasian, they did not adopt Sapir's attitude to quantification when faced with a problem his framework neglected to solve. Instead, their research and theoretical statements of the 1930s and after provided examples of how personality characteristics (Hallowell, 1938, 1945), religious behavior (Kluckhohn, 1938), child development (Kluckhohn, 1939; Leighton and Kluckhohn, 1947), and mental disorders (Linton, 1936, 1945, 1956) could be approached through statistical methods. By adding this methodological dimension to Sapir's framework, Hallowell, Kluckhohn, and Linton prepared the ground for empirical research in psychological anthropology that owed as much to Boas's empiricism as it did to Sapir's theoretical vision.

Each of these three anthropologists also added to the paradigm for research. Linton added a sociological dimension, arguing that the social experience of individuals in a population was differentiated by their statuses and roles, leading to varying personalities (Linton, 1936, 1945). Kluckhohn added an ideational dimension by re-conceptualizing culture as a "blueprint for action" (Kluckhohn and Kelly, 1945), an idea later elaborated (without the psychology) by his student Clifford Geertz (1973). And Hallowell, writing in the 1950s, added a focus on the self (Chapter 3 of this reader), a concept that would eventually eclipse personality in psychocultural research (Part V of this reader).

Thus the paradigm for psychological anthropology was largely developed by Sapir, originally with Benedict, and later (after 1934) without her, and completed by three anthropologists influenced by Boas as well as Sapir. A fuller history of the period up to 1955 would include the contributions of Kardiner (1939, 1945) and Whiting and Child (1953), who devised more specific theoretical models consistent with what I have described as the Sapir line of influence. This line of influence contributed the basic ideas in terms of which most psychological anthropologists then and now, despite their theoretical and methodological divisions, frame their research and interpret their results. In the next section I identify some of the sources of this intellectual tradition in anthropology.

Sources of Culture and Personality Theory

Culture and personality was a distinctively American movement, born of conditions that marked it off from British explorations at the boundaries of anthropology with psychology and psychoanalysis by W. H. R. Rivers, C. G. Seligman, Bronislaw Malinowski, and F. C. Bartlett and from the Soviet Russian development of "socio-historical psychology" by L. S. Vygotsky and A. R. Luria. These peculiar cultural and historical conditions include:

- *Native American cultures*. Boas and most of his students, including Sapir, Benedict, and Hallowell, were dedicated to the study of the Native North Americans and concerned with questions concerning the diversity of their cultural traditions, the vulnerability of those traditions to social change, and their transmission to new generations (Darnell, 2001).
- *European immigration*. The influx of Eastern, Central and Southern Europeans into the United States between 1880 and 1924 made cultural heterogeneity an inescapable social fact for social scientists. Boas and Sapir were immigrants themselves, and Boas studied immigrant parents and children to detect the effects of environmental change on physical growth (Boas, 1912). As a beginning graduate student in 1923, Margaret Mead followed Boas's advice to study Italian-American children in her hometown of Hammonton, Pennsylvania, correlating their intelligence test scores with the amount of Italian spoken in their homes (Mead, 1959:131). W. I. Thomas and Florian Znaniecki had published their five-volume work on immigrants from Poland to Chicago (Thomas and Znaniecki, 1918), excerpts from which appear in Chapter 1 of this reader. The grounding of culture and personality theories in the immigrant experience was clear from the start.
- *Language*. Boasian anthropology (unlike its British counterparts) included the study of language, and Sapir introduced Indo-European linguistic methods into research on unwritten Native American languages (Darnell, 2001, p.51). His argument that language is central to the social experience of the individual as well as an aspect of culture became a fundamental tenet of the culture and personality movement (Sapir, 1921).
- *Pragmatism*. The culture and personality movement developed in a milieu of social thought that had been shaped by the American philosophers known as pragmatists: Charles Saunders Peirce, William James, John Dewey, Josiah Royce, and George Herbert Mead. Although the intellectual history remains to be spelled out, it is clear that the founders of the culture and personality movement were directly and indirectly influenced by these pragmatist philosophers. Echoes of Peirce on meaning, James on the self, Dewey on learning, and Mead on the internalization of social interactions as symbolically mediated self – resonate throughout the theorizing of the culture and personality movement.

- *Neo-Freudian psychoanalysis.* The founders of the culture and personality movement were acquainted with, but critical of, Freudian psychoanalysis. In the 1930s, European refugees in New York joined American colleagues in the "Neo-Freudian" movement of cultural revisionism in psychoanalysis led by Karen Horney, Erich Fromm, and Harry Stack Sullivan, who directly influenced Mead, Benedict, and Sapir. At the same time, Kardiner's seminar on culture and psychoanalysis moved from the New York Psychoanalytic Institute to the Department of Anthropology at Columbia, with Linton as a participant. From these efforts, the culture and personality field embraced a psychoanalysis purged of biological universals and open to social and cultural influences.

Thus the culture and personality movement arose from research on cultural diversity and intergenerational transmission among Native Americans and European immigrants to the United States and was built on premises derived in part from philosophical pragmatism, linguistics, and revised forms of psychoanalysis during the first half of the 20th century.

Chapter 1: *The Polish Peasant in Europe and America,* a five-volume work published in 1918, anticipated the culture and personality movement in its attention to individuals and families undergoing social and psychological change as they migrated from Poland to Chicago. Thomas, who had studied with G. H. Mead and would later work with Sapir in initiating culture and personality studies as a movement, was the leading theorist of the Chicago School of Sociology, which conducted ethnographic studies of urban life. In the "methodological note" from which the selections come, he and Znaniecki (a Polish philosopher of neo-Kantian inclinations) formulate a distinction between the social and the psychological and their adaptive interactions that influenced American social scientists – including the culture and personality movement – for generations to come.

Chapter 2: These selections from Sapir's lectures on the psychology of culture, delivered in 1936 and earlier but not published until 1994, reveal a conception of culture and personality, including his critique of Benedict, that remains the central framework of psychological anthropology.

Chapter 3: The first selection, from Hallowell's *Psychological Leads for Ethnological Field Workers* of 1938, shows his early effort to translate the ideas of Sapir and others into an empirical research program for culture and personality studies. The second selection, written about 15 years later, is from his now-famous essay, "The Self and its Behavioral Environment," a foundation-stone for contemporary psychological anthropology.

REFERENCES

Benedict, Ruth
  1934   Patterns of Culture. Boston: Houghton Mifflin.
Boas, Franz
  1912   Instability of Human Types. *In* G. Spiller, ed., Papers on Interracial Problems Communicated to the First Universal Races Conference Held at the University of London, July 26–29, 1911. Boston: Ginn & Co.

Camic, Charles and Yu Xie
  1994   The Statistical Turn in American Social Science: Columbia University, 1890 to 1915.
  American Sociological Review 59:773–805.
Darnell, Regna
  1990   Edward Sapir: Linguist, Anthropologist, Humanist. Berkeley: University of
  California Press.
Darnell, Regna
  2001   Invisible Genealogies: A History of Americanist Anthropology. Lincoln: University
  of Nebraska Press.
Geertz, Clifford
  1973   The Interpretation of Cultures. New York: Basic Books.
Gorer, Geoffrey and John Rickman
  1949   The People of Great Russia. London: The Cresset Press.
Hallowell, A. Irving
  1938   Fear and Anxiety as Cultural and Individual Variables in a Primitive Society.
  American Sociological Review 7:869–881.
  1945   The Rorschach Technique in the Study of Personality and Culture. American
  Anthropologist 47:195–210.
Howells, W. W.
  1959   Boas as Statistician. In W. Goldschmidt, ed., The Anthropology of Franz Boas:
  Essays on the Centennial of his Birth. Memoir No. 89. Washington, DC: American
  Anthropological Association.
Hsu, Francis L. K., ed.
  1961   Psychological Anthropology. Homewood, IL: Dorsey Press.
Kardiner, Abram
  1939   The Individual and His Society. New York: Columbia University Press.
  1945   Psychological Frontiers of Society. New York: Columbia University Press.
Kluckhohn, Clyde
  1938   Participation in Ceremonials in a Navaho Community. American Anthropologist
  40:359–369.
  1939   Theoretical Bases for an Empirical Method of Studying the Acquisition of Culture
  by Individuals. Man 39: 98–103.
Kluckhohn, Clyde and W. H. Kelly
  1945   The Concept of Culture. In R. Linton, ed., The Science of Man in the World Crisis.
  New York: Columbia University Press.
Kroeber, A. L.
  1953   Anthropology Today. Chicago: University of Chicago Press.
  Leighton, Dorothea and Clyde Kluckhohn
  1947   Children of the People: The Navaho Individual and His Development. Cambridge,
  MA: Harvard University Press.
LeVine, Robert A.
  2007   Anthropological Foundations of Cultural Psychology. In S. Kitayama and D. Cohen,
  eds., The Handbook of Cultural Psychology. New York: Guilford Press.
Linton, Ralph
  1936   The Study of Man. New York: Appleton-Century-Crofts.
  1945   The Cultural Background of Personality. New York: Appleton-Century-Crofts.
  1956   Culture and Mental Disorders. Springfield, IL: Charles C. Thomas.
Mead, Margaret
  1953   National Character. In A. L. Kroeber, ed., Anthropology Today. Chicago: University
  of Chicago Press.
  1954   The Swaddling Hypothesis: Its Reception. American Anthropologist 56:395–409.

1959   Blackberry Winter. New York: William Morrow.

Mead, Margaret and Rhoda Metraux
1953   The Study of Culture at a Distance. Chicago: University of Chicago Press.

Sapir, Edward
1917   Do We Need a "Superorganic"? American Anthropologist 19:441–447.

1921   Language: An Introduction to the Study of Speech. New York: Harcourt Brace & Co.

1994   The Psychology of Culture: A Course of Lectures. Berlin and New York: Mouton de Gruyter.

Tanner, J. M.
1959   Boas' Contributions to Knowledge of Human Growth and Form. *In* W. Goldschmidt, ed., The Anthropology of Franz Boas: Essays on the Centennial of his Birth. Memoir No. 89. Washington, DC: American Anthropological Association.

Thomas, W. I. and Florian Znaniecki
1918   The Polish Peasant in Europe and America, Vols. 1–5. Boston: Gorham Press.

Wallace, Anthony F. C.
1961   Culture and Personality. New York: Random House.

Whiting, John W. M. and Irvin L. Child
1953   Child Training and Personality: A Cross-Cultural Study. New Haven: Yale University Press.

Xie, Yu
1988   Franz Boas and Statistics. Annals of Scholarship 5:269–296.

1

The Polish Peasant in Europe and America

W. I. Thomas and Florian Znaniecki

Now there are two fundamental practical problems which have constituted the center of attention of reflective social practice in all times. These are (1) the problem of the dependence of the individual upon social organization and culture, and (2) the problem of the dependence of social organization and culture upon the individual. Practically, the first problem is expressed in the question, How shall we produce with the help of the existing social organization and culture the desirable mental and moral characteristics in the individuals constituting the social group? And the second problem means in practice, How shall we produce, with the help of the existing mental and moral characteristics of the individual members of the group, the desirable type of social organization and culture?[1]

If social theory is to become the basis of social technique and to solve these problems really, it is evident that it must include both kinds of data involved in them namely, the objective cultural elements of social life and the subjective characteristics of the members of the social group and that the two kinds of data must be taken as correlated. For these data we shall use now and in the future the terms "social values" (or simply "values") and "attitudes."

By a social value we understand any datum having an empirical content accessible to the members of some social group and a meaning with regard to which it is or may be an object of activity. Thus, a foodstuff, an instrument, a coin, a piece of poetry, a university, a myth, a scientific theory, are social values. Each of them has a content that is sensual in the case of the foodstuff, the instrument, the coin; partly sensual, partly imaginary in the piece of poetry, whose content is constituted, not only by the written or spoken words, but also by the images which they evoke, and in the case of the university, whose content is the whole complex of men, buildings, material accessories, and images representing its activity; or, finally, only imaginary in the case of a mythical personality or a scientific theory. The meaning of these values becomes explicit when we take them in connection with human actions. The meaning of the foodstuff is its reference to its eventual consumption; that of an instrument, its reference to the work for which it is designed; that of a coin, the possibilities of buying and selling or the pleasures of spending which it involves; that of the piece of poetry, the sentimental and intellectual reactions which it arouses; that of the university, the social activities which it performs; that of the mythical personality, the cult of which it is the object and the actions of which it is supposed to be the author; that of the scientific theory, the possibilities of control of experience by idea or action that it permits. The social value is thus opposed to the natural thing, which has a content but, as a part of nature, has no meaning for human activity, is

W. I. Thomas and Florian Znaniecki, The Polish Peasant in Europe and America: Monograph of an Immigrant Group, Volume I Primary-Group Organization; Boston, Richard G. Badger, The Gorham Press (1918). © 1918 Richard G. Badger, pp. 20–24, 44–45, 68–69; Volume III; Boston, Richard G. Badger, The Gorham Press (1919), © 1919 Richard G. Badger, pp. 5–6.

treated as "valueless"; when the natural thing assumes a meaning, it becomes thereby a social value. And naturally a social value may have many meanings, for it may refer to many different kinds of activity.

By attitude we understand a process of individual consciousness which determines real or possible activity of the individual in the social world. Thus, hunger that compels the consumption of the foodstuff; the workman's decision to use the tool; the tendency of the spendthrift to spend the coin; the poet's feelings and ideas expressed in the poem and the reader's sympathy and admiration; the needs which the institution tries to satisfy and the response it provokes; the fear and devotion manifested in the cult of the divinity; the interest in creating, understanding, or applying a scientific theory and the ways of thinking implied in it all these are attitudes. The attitude is thus the individual counterpart of the social value; activity, in whatever form, is the bond between them. By its reference to activity and thereby to individual consciousness the value is distinguished from the natural thing. By its reference to activity and thereby to the social world the attitude is distinguished from the psychical state. In the examples quoted above we were obliged to use with reference to ideas and volitions words that have become terms of individual psychology by being abstracted from the objective social reality to which they apply, but originally they were designed to express attitudes, not psychological processes. A psychological process is an attitude treated as an object in itself, isolated by a reflective act of attention, and taken first of all in connection with other states of the same individual. An attitude is a psychological process treated as primarily manifested in its reference to the social world and taken first of all in connection with some social value. Individual psychology may later re-establish the connection between the psychological process and the objective reality which has been severed by reflection; it may study psychological processes as conditioned by the facts going on in the objective world. In the same way social theory may later connect various attitudes of an individual and determine his social character. But it is the original (usually unconsciously occupied) standpoints which determine at once the subsequent methods of these two sciences. The psychological process remains always fundamentally a *state of somebody*; the attitude remains always fundamentally an attitude *toward something*.

Taking this fundamental distinction of standpoint into account, we may continue to use for different classes of attitudes the same terms which individual psychology has used for psychological processes, since these terms constitute the common property of all reflection about conscious life. The exact meaning of all these terms from the standpoint of social theory must be established during the process of investigation, so that every term shall be defined in view of its application and its methodological validity tested in actual use. It would be therefore impractical to attempt to establish in advance the whole terminology of attitudes.

But when we say that the data of social theory are attitudes and values, this is not yet a sufficient determination of the object of this science, for the field thus defined would embrace the whole of human culture and include the object-matter of philology and economics, theory of art, theory of science, etc. A more exact definition is therefore necessary in order to distinguish social theory from these sciences, established long ago and having their own methods and their own aims.

This limitation of the field of social theory arises quite naturally from the necessity of choosing between attitudes or values as fundamental data that is, as data whose characters will serve as a basis for scientific generalization. There are numerous values corresponding to every attitude, and numerous attitudes corresponding to every value; if, therefore, we compare different actions with regard to the attitudes manifested in them and form, for example, the general concept of the attitude of solidarity, this means that we have neglected the whole variety of values which are produced by these actions and which may be political or economical, religious or scientific, etc. If, on the contrary, we compare the values produced by different actions and form, for example, the general concepts of economic or religious values, this means that we have neglected the whole variety of attitudes which are manifested in these actions. Scientific generalization must always base itself upon such characters of its data as can be considered essential to its purposes, and the essential characters of human actions are completely different when we treat them from the stand-point of attitudes and when we are interested in them as values. There is therefore no possibility of giving to attitudes and values the same importance in a methodical scientific investigation; either attitudes must be subordinated to values or the contrary. ...

And thus social theory is again confronted by a scientifically absurd question. Assuming that individual activity in itself is the cause of social effects, it must then ask: "Why does a certain action produce this particular effect at this particular moment in this particular society?" The answer to this question would demand a complete explanation of the whole status of the given society at the given moment, and thus force us to investigate the entire past of the universe.

The fundamental methodological principle of both social psychology and sociology the principle without which they can never reach scientific explanation is therefore the following one:

The cause of a social or individual phenomenon is never another social or individual phenomenon alone, but always a combination of a social and an individual phenomenon.

Or, in more exact terms:

The cause of a value or of an attitude is never an attitude or a value alone, but always a combination of an attitude and a value.[2]

It is only by the application of this principle that we can remove the difficulties with which social theory and social practice have struggled. If we wish to explain the appearance of a new attitude whether in one individual or in a whole group we know that this attitude appeared as a consequence of the influence of a social value upon the individual or the group, but we know also that this influence itself would have been impossible unless there had been some preexisting attitude, some wish, emotional habit, or intellectual tendency, to which this value has in some way appealed, favoring it, contradicting it, giving it a new direction, or stabilizing its hesitating expres-

sions. Our problem is therefore to find both the value and the pre-existing attitude upon which it has acted and get in their combination the necessary and sufficient cause of the new attitude. We shall not be forced then to ask: "Why did this value provoke in this case such a reaction?" because the answer will be included in the fact in the pre-existing attitude to which this value appealed. Our fact will bear its explanation in itself, just as the physical fact of the movement of an elastic body *B* when struck by another elastic moving body *A* bears its explanation in itself. We may, if we wish, ask for a more detailed explanation, not only of the appearance of the new attitude, but also for certain specific characters of this attitude, in the same way as we may ask for an explanation, not only of the movement of the body *B* in general, but also of the rapidity and direction of this movement; but the problem always remains limited, and the explanation is within the fact, in the character of the pre-existing attitude and of the influencing value, or in the masses of the bodies *A* and *B* and the rapidity and direction of their movements previous to their meeting. We can indeed pass from the given fact to the new one ask, for example, "How did it happen that this attitude to which the value appealed was there?" or, "How did it happen that the body *A* moved toward *B* until they met?" But this question again will find its limited and definite answer if we search in the same way for the cause of the pre-existing attitude in some other attitude and value, or of the movement in some other movement. ...

The situation is the set of values and attitudes with which the individual or the group has to deal in a process of activity and with regard to which this activity is planned and its results appreciated. Every concrete activity is the solution of a situation. The situation involves three kinds of data: (1) The objective conditions under which the individual or society has to act, that is, the totality of values economic, social, religious, intellectual, etc. which at the given moment affect directly or indirectly the conscious status of the individual or the group. (2) The pre-existing attitudes of the individual or the group which at the given moment have an actual influence upon his behavior. (3) The definition of the situation, that is, the more or less clear conception of the conditions and consciousness of the attitudes. And the definition of the situation is a necessary preliminary to any act of the will, for in given conditions and with a given set of attitudes an indefinite plurality of actions is possible, and one definite action can appear only if these conditions are selected, interpreted, and combined in a determined way and if a certain systematization of these attitudes is reached, so that one of them becomes predominant and subordinates the others. It happens, indeed, that a certain value imposes itself immediately and unreflectively and leads at once to action, or that an attitude as soon as it appears excludes the others and expresses itself unhesitatingly in an active process. In these cases, whose most radical examples are found in reflex and instinctive actions, the definition is already given to the individual by external conditions or by his own tendencies. But usually there is a process of reflection, after which either a ready social definition is applied or a new personal definition worked out. ...

The social system which develops on this basis naturally tends to reconcile, by modifying them, the two originally contradictory principles – the traditional absorption of the individual by the group and the new self-assertion of the individual against or independently of the group. The method which, after various trials proves the most efficient in fulfilling this difficult task is the method of conscious cooperation. Closed social groups are freely formed for the common pursuit of definite positive interests which each individual can more efficiently satisfy in this way than if he worked alone. These organized groups are scattered all over the country in various peasant communities, but know about one another through the press. The further task of social organization is to bring groups with similar or supplementary purposes together for common pursuit, just as individuals are brought together in each particular group.

The more extensive and coherent this new social system becomes, the more frequent, varied and important are its contacts with the social and political institutions created by other classes and in which the peasants until recently had not actively participated (except, of course, those individuals who became members of other classes and ceased to belong to the peasant class). The peasant begins consciously to cooperate in those activities by which national unity is maintained and national culture developed. This fact has a particular importance for Poland where for a whole century national life had to be preserved by voluntary cooperation, not only without the help of the state but even against the state, and where at this moment the same method of voluntary cooperation is being used in reconstructing a national state system. The significance of such a historical experiment for sociology is evident, for it contributes more than anything to the solution of the most essential problem of modern times – how to pass from the type of national organization in which public services are exacted and public order enforced by coercion to a different type, in which not only a small minority, but the majority which is now culturally passive will voluntarily contribute to social order and cultural progress.

Elsewhere we have outlined the standpoint that a nomothetic social science is possible only if all social becoming is viewed as the product of a continual interaction of individual consciousness and objective social reality. In this connection the human personality is both a continually producing factor and a continually produced result of social evolution, and this double relation expresses itself in every elementary social fact; there can be for social science no change of social reality which is not the common effect of pre-existing social values and individual attitudes acting upon them, no change of individual consciousness which is not the common effect of pre-existing individual attitudes and social values acting upon them. When viewed as a factor of social evolution the human personality is a ground of the causal explanation of social happenings; when viewed as a product of social evolution it is causally explicable by social happenings. In the first case individual attitudes toward preexisting social values serve to explain the appearance of new social values; in the second case social values acting upon pre-existing individual attitudes serve to explain the appearance of new individual attitudes.

NOTES

1 Of course a concrete practical task may include both problems, as when we attempt, by appealing to the existing attitudes, to establish educational institutions which will be so organised as to produce or generalize certain desirable attitudes.

2 It may be objected that we have neglected to criticize the conception according to which the cause of social phenomenon is to be sought, not in an individual, but exclusively in another social phenomenon (Durkheim). But a criticism of this conception is implied in the previous discussion of the data of social theory. As these data are both values and attitudes, a fact must include both, and a succession of values alone cannot constitute a fact. Of course much depends also on what we call a "social" phenomenon. An attitude may be treated as a social phenomenon as opposed to the "state of consciousness" of individual psychology; but it is individual, even if common to all members of a group, when we oppose it to a value.

2

The Psychology of Culture

Edward Sapir

Psychological Aspects of Culture

The difficulty of delimiting a boundary between personality and culture

[If the psychologists' study of personality is deficient because] they persist in studying only fragmentary psychological processes, [omitting the cultural dimension,] the same is true in culture. There too we study fragmentary data. [As I have said,] we [anthropologists] are obtuse about the implications of data [that pertain to] personality. [The trouble is that both psychologists and anthropologists generally draw a sharp line between their disciplines and fail to recognize the overlap, even identity, of the problems they study.]

The failure of social science as a whole to relate the patterns of culture to germinal personality patterns is intelligible in view of the complexity of social phenomena and the recency of serious speculation on the relation of the individual to society. But there is growing recognition of the fact that the intimate study of personality is of fundamental concern to the social scientist.[1] [Indeed,] there is no reason why the culturalist should be afraid of the concept of personality, which must not, however, be thought of, as one inevitably does at the beginning of his thinking, as a mysterious entity resisting the historically given culture but rather as a distinctive configuration of experience which tends always to form a psychologically significant unit.[2]

[Thus the psychiatric view of personality as a configuration in which experience is organized in a system of psychological significance might also be applied to the problem of culture. So, for example, when we propose that] distinctions in nuclear attitudes are due to a difference in one's concept of a thing, [we might be speaking about personality or we might be speaking about culture. The attitude comprised in the individual's nuclear personality has an analogue in a cultural attitude, or what we might call] cultural loyalties – loyalties imbibed from your own culture which make you a little insensitive to the meanings in different cultures. You are obtuse to meanings that are not welcome, that do not fit into the old scheme of things.

From the personalistic point of view, the whole field of culture can be regarded as a complex series of tests for personality – tests of ways in which the personality meets the environment. All cultures have the potentiality of psychological significance in personal terms. That is, the totality of culture offers endless opportunities for the construction and development of personality through the selection and reinterpretation of experience. [Conversely, too,] the totality of culture therefore is

Edward Sapir, The Psychology of Culture: A Course of Lectures, reconstructed and edited by Judith T. Irvine, Mouton de Gruyter, Berlin, New York, 1994, a division of Walter de Gruyter & Co., Berlin © 1993 by Walter de Gruyter & Co., pp. 175–207. Reprinted with permission of Walter de Gruyter GmbH & Co.

interpreted differently according to the kind of personality that the individual has. [Consider what happens to a person upon] entering a new cultural environment. The essential invariance of personality makes one alive and sensitive to some things and obtuse to others, [depending upon how the] new environment [matches up with] pivotal points from the old. [Your] awareness of certain things in a new cultural [setting] is a test of the old one, [a test of what the old one's pivotal points in fact were.]

The study of etiquette is [another] good way to [approach the relationship] between personality and culture, for it is a field that unites the field of culture and the field of personality. Its conventional forms [are clearly] goods of a highly cultural kind, [yet these forms are manipulated by individuals for the most personal purposes.] How should we delimit the boundary between personality and culture [here] – between the cultural form and the individual attitude? [When the same forms evince both] the permanence of cultural dogma, on the one hand, and the expressiveness of the individual, on the other, it is difficult to know just what you are dealing with. [The study of] family relations, or of clothing, [would be other good examples of fields with similar problems.] There is nothing vainer than to classify [such cultural] organizations unless you know their psychological correlates. Some organizations may divide up into quite different segments.

The relation between personality and culture – [that is, on the level of observable behavior, between] behavior [expressing the personal concerns of the] individual and behavior [expressing] cultural [forms – has become] my obsession.

Culture as "as-if" psychology

[Before we continue with our discussion of psychological aspects of culture, a note of caution must be sounded.] The term "cultural psychology" is ambiguous, and there has been much confusion between two types of psychological analysis of social behavior. The one is a statement of the general tendencies or traits characterizing a culture, such as the pattern of

self-help in our culture; [as we have pointed out,] different cultures do have certain delineating factors, [including attitudes and] psychological standards about emotional expression. The other is a statement of certain kinds of actual behavior, [by actual individuals,] related to these cultural patterns. [In other words it is a statement of] the individual's psychology, and the problem of individual adjustment [to a cultural setting.] (This confusion is to be found, for instance, in the seven articles by psychiatrists about to be published in the *American Journal of Sociology*.[3] Alexander and Sullivan keep level-headed in their attempts to relate psychiatry and the social sciences, but some of the others are rather confused.)

These two kinds of psychology are not the same thing, but are in intimate relation with each other. [Moreover, the second kind has a further ambiguity, which perhaps we can see if we consider the notion of the individual's] integration. What do we mean by [this concept?] An adjustment to society, on the one hand – or the [coherence of the] thought, ideas, etc. of a man as seen by him, on the other hand? The same things can integrate or dis-integrate two different men.

[If the idea of a "cultural psychology" is so tangled, ought we to speak of such a thing at all? In a sense perhaps we ought not. Strictly speaking,] culture, in itself, has no psychology; only individuals [have a psychology. On the cultural plane] there is only [what I call] the "as-if psychology". That is to say, there is a psychological standard[4] in each culture as to how much emotion is to be expressed, and so on. This is the as-if psychology which belongs to the culture itself, not with the individual personality. [If we call this a psychology we are speaking] *as if* this scheme of life were the actual expression of individuality. The danger of [too literal an interpretation of this process] in the social formulations of the anthropologist and the sociologist is by no means an imaginary one. Certain recent attempts, in part brilliant and stimulating, to impose upon the actual psychologies of actual people, in continuous and tangible relations to each other, a generalized psychology based on the real or supposed psychological implications of cultural forms, show clearly what confusions in our thinking are likely to result when social science turns psychiatric without, in the process, allowing its own historically determined concepts to dissolve into those larger ones which have meaning for psychology and psychiatry.[5]

Ruth Benedict's book, *Patterns of Culture*, is a brilliant exposition of as-if psychology, but with confusion about the distinction made here. She is not clear on the distinction between the as-if psychology she is discussing and the psychology of the individual.[6] A culture cannot be paranoid. [To call it so suggests] the failure to distinguish between the as-if psychology and the actual psychology of the people participating in the culture.[7] The difficulty with *Patterns of Culture* is that certain objective facts of culture which are low toned are given huge significance. [I suspect that individual] Dobu and Kwakiutl are very like ourselves; they just are manipulating a different set of patterns. [We have no right to assume that a given pattern or ritual necessarily implies a certain emotional significance or personality adjustment in its practitioners, with-out demonstration at the level of the individual. Perhaps] the Navajo ritual can be considered as just their way of chewing gum. You have to know the individual before you know what the baggage of his culture means to him.

In itself, culture has no psychology. It is [just] a low-toned series of rituals, a rubber stamping waiting to be given meaning by you. The importance of cultural differences for individual adjustment [may well be] exaggerated, [therefore, for we may equally well suppose that culture means nothing until the individual, with his personality configuration, gives it meaning. In other words,] the apparent psychological differences of cultures are superficial – although they must be understood, of course, to know how to gauge the individual's expressions of his reactions.

[What I want] to bring out clearly [here is] the extreme methodological importance of distinguishing between actual psychological processes which are of individual location and presumptive or as-if psychological pictures which may be abstracted from cultural phenomena and which may give significant direction to individual development. To speak of a whole culture as having a personality configuration is, of course, a pleasing image, but I am afraid that it belongs more to the order of aesthetic or poetic constructs than of scientific ones.[8] [It is a useful metaphor for cultural patterning, but it loses its usefulness if it is taken literally.]

[For this very reason – that one is dealing with aesthetic constructs –] it is easier to apply a thing like Jung's [classification of] psychological types to cultures than to individuals. If you take the way of life of a community as a "psychology", it is easy to classify your cultures. On this basis, [one might speak of extraverted and introverted cultures: thus] American culture[9] of today on the whole is extraverted, recognizing no efficacy in unexpressed or only subtly expressed tendencies. We are willing to court private ill-will so long as it does not gain public expression. The Chinese and Japanese cultures seem definitely more introverted, [emphasizing] internal feeling (note, [for example, the Japanese custom of] hari-kiri, and the Chinese [type of] suicide [committed] so as to haunt one's enemy). But this [characterization of the culture] does not mean that the individual is extravert or introvert.

The Adjustment of the Individual in Society

The problem of individual adjustment: The general view

[Let us turn now to] the problem of individual [adaptation] to the requirements of society: the tacit adjustment between the psychic system of the individual and the official lineaments of the [social and cultural environment.] The discussion of personality types that we have [engaged in] heretofore, [with reference to Jung's psychiatric approach, on the one hand, and with reference to its metaphorical extensions on the plane of culture, on the other,] is important not so much [for the types] in themselves as from the point of view of personality adjustment within and to a culture. INFJ

[You will recall our suggestion that] the psychology of culture has [two quite distinct dimensions:] (a) the as-if psychology, or the meaning given by culture [to one's behavior;] and (b) the actual, and much more intricate, psychology of personal action. [What we must now ask is, what is the influence of the one on the other?] What is the effect of these cultural casts on the individual, whose avenues of expression are provided by society?

[If personality were but the consequence of one's racial inheritance, or if there were no variability of temperament among the members of a society, our interesting problem would not arise. There would be little reason to distinguish between the two dimensions of the psychology of culture in the first place.][10] I believe, however, that the differences in personality are fundamental and that the variation [of personalities] is about as great in one culture as another, the variation only taking different forms in different cultures. [I find myself somewhat skeptical, therefore, about certain recent works on culture and temperament, such as Margaret Mead's writings on Samoa.] Mead's work is pioneering in the sense that she realizes that different cultures result in different personality transformations. She is entirely oblivious, however, to the play of personality differences within a primitive culture, and treats primitive personalities as being all alike on the same dead level of similarity. For example, it is likely that in actual fact there are personality misfits among Samoan adolescents brought up under the old free Samoan pattern, yet Mead has nothing to say of this and assumes all personalities developed according to one type.

Probably we have in all cultures [individuals of] the same basic personality types to deal with, such types, for example, as Jung depicts in his [book.] The problem, then, is to show the way those basic types are transformed or re-emphasized or re-aligned according to the master idea[s] of each diverse culture. This is an immense problem, [for whose solution the usual methods of anthropological work are scarcely adequate; it presents us, therefore, with] the difficulty of acquiring new techniques. The broad program would involve:

(1) A thorough study and knowledge of the cultural patterns of a group;

(2) An attempt to study personality types of selected individuals against or in terms of this background, perhaps by keeping a day-to-day diary, or [through a] case study of selected personalities in their relation to each other and in reaction to key cultural situations. But the culture must be analyzed beforehand with special reference to its master ideas. Only then can one begin the task of understanding personality transformations that occur through the impact of culture contact on native personality configurations.[11]

Defining the process of adaptation to a culture thus involves a definition both of the personality type and of the demands of the culture. [Moreover, in order to define the personality type and understand its adjustments we must remember that] there is a difference between the psychological constitution of an individual – his real characteristics – and that of his group behavior or appearance in the society as a whole.

[For example,] the group may admire male aggressiveness toward women, and demand of its male members such clearly masculine characteristics. These are socially suggested and approved in that given culture, and the different individuals reflect this pattern in a variety of forms and degrees. Of course, the prior outlines of the [person's] individuality have the utmost significance. These must be taken into consideration, [but] in order to find the true personality of the individual we have to [go through] an enormous amount of elimination of certain aspects of traits. (The more we know about the culture, the more adequately we shall be able to [speak] about the individual's real personality.) [Thus this culturally-patterned] aggressiveness appears differently in different individuals. [This is not only because individuals' nuclear personalities differ, but also because] it is in relation to others' aggressiveness in the milieu that one has to organize one's social behavior.

[In so organizing their behavior] people act symbolically and not individually. The intellectual general in the army who is an engineer or perhaps a physician is not primarily concerned with, or interested in, aggressiveness and the war affairs of his group. He is perhaps looking for new symbols for his own satisfaction, but he cannot break the social patterns that are required of him. This behavior [(the behavior that conforms with his group's aggressiveness and interest in warfare)] is an indirect expression of group loyalty. He behaves so, not in harmony with his own desires, but accommodating himself to the preferred as-if [personality dictated by the] cultural patterns of his society. Thus, [in a case like his] there is a conflict with the preferred psychological patterning of the society and the psychological patterns of society are unreal to the personality[12] in such circumstances.

[For this reason,] no adjustment [defined simply] on the basis of an as-if psychology can be acceptable to the psychology of personal feelings. The problem of individual adjustment in society [may involve a variety of] methods of adjustment, successful and unsuccessful. [Moreover,] the energy spent in the process of adjustment to the preferred social patterns differs very much among individuals. The individual, to the extent of the difficulty he encounters, is abnormal in assimilating the psychological aspect of his culture.

[Now, suppose that a person has especially great difficulties of adjustment. The aggressiveness we were just speaking about may also arise as a consequence of this. His difficulty would display itself as] unusual aggressiveness, which is [really] cowardice. [For example, consider] an individual who, with a [wish for a] childish [form of] intimacy, wants a considerable hearing; but he cannot [have it] with every single individual member of the group. So, he hates the group and becomes excessively aggressive. He is not, therefore, normally aggressive, [only derivatively so as a result of his difficulties of adjustment. The particular nature of his aggressiveness reveals itself in his unusual acts: for instance,] he may enter the presence of a dignified and respectable elderly professor in a Napoleonic manner, making rationalizations of his own. He continues to be effectively aggressive [only] as long as his behavior is not repudiated by the group, [which it may well be. His case is different from] real aggressiveness, which belongs to the real personality, and receives some recognition among the members of the society.

[But it may be the case that the personality's adjustment to a social environment takes a different form, such as sublimation. For example,] to lie [to someone] for [reasons of] good manners is [a form of] sublimation of an original anxiety of circumstances. [One might say that because cultural patterns dictate what good manners are and when a lie is appropriate,] culture gives the key to the problem of sublimation. But individuals do not arrive at this end-point by the same means. [Moreover, some sublimations will go unnoticed because cultural patterns are available to handle them; but this is not the sum total of the sublimations effected by all the individuals in a society. We label as] perversions [those sublimations] without a cultural background into whose patterns the sublimation may be made, for those are [the sublimations] that stand out, while culturally handled perversions are absorbed. Culture gives the terrain of normal sublimation effected by the individuals [in the society, and as cultures differ so do the forms of sublimation normal to them. The introduction of] peyote and the Ghost Dance could take [hold] in the Plains but not in Pueblo [culture, therefore, since these forms of sublimation were consistent with normal cultural patterns in the one case and not the other.]

[The psychology of culture thus includes two distinct questions.] What are the general psychological roots of any culture pattern and of the as-if psychology? What is the personal psychology of [those] individuals who tend to follow the first [(the patterned as-if psychology),] and [what is the personal psychology which,] when divergent [from the cultural prescription,] will be envisaged as a morbid, obvious tendency?

[Perhaps we can say something more about] the personal world of meanings, [if we consider] the field of child development. As soon as we set ourselves at the vantage-point of the culture-acquiring child, [with] the personality definitions and potentials that must never for a moment be lost sight of, and which are destined from the very beginning to interpret, evaluate, and modify every culture pattern, sub-pattern, or assemblage of patterns that it will ever be influenced by, everything changes. Culture is then not something given but something to be gradually and gropingly discovered. We then see at once that elements of culture that come well within the horizon of awareness of one individual are entirely absent in another individual's landscape.[13]

[If we are to understand the transmission of culture, or indeed the whole problem of culture from this developmental point of view,] the time must come when the cosmos of the child of three will be known and defined, not merely referred to. The organized intuitive organization of a three-year-old is far more valid and real than the most ambitious psychological theory ever constructed. [Yet, our three-year-olds are not all the same.] Our children are fully developed personalities very early. [We do not quite know how this comes about, but it depends considerably on] the interactions between the child and his early environment up to the age of three.[14] [Even within the same family, each child's] world is a different kind of a thing because the fundamental emotional relationships were differently established [depending on his status] as first or second child.

In the child's cosmos, patterns of behavior are understood emotionally, [in terms of a particular constellation of relationships].[15] The genetic psychology[16] of the child will show specific emphases of meanings of patterns which are used to handle and control the people and events of the social world. [Thus words and other symbols do not have exactly the same meaning for the child as they will for the adult, for in the child's world] various words have special values and emotional colorations, [taken on through their] absorption [in the child's] emotional and rational [concerns]. Later additions of meanings must be seen in the light of the nuclear family complex and its effect on personality development. It is obvious that the child will unconsciously accept the various elements of culture with entirely different meanings, according to the biographical conditions that attend their introduction to him. It may, and undoubtedly does, make a profound difference whether a religious ritual comes with the sternness of a father's authority or with the somewhat playful indulgence of the mother's brother.[17] [So it is only through patient studies of child development, concerned with a limited number of specific individuals, that we may really begin to understand the connections between] childhood constellations and religion, between infantile *apperceptions-masse* [and the meaning of] adult activities, [between the child's] hunting in

closets and [the adult's] scientific interest in crystallography.

It has been suggested by Dr. Sullivan that studying a limited number of personalities, for about ten years, by different representatives of the fields of social science will, no doubt, be of great help to understand more clearly the problem of personality. [The same is true for the problem of culture.] This study will take the individual as early as possible in life and follow him through for quite a considerable period of time with utmost care and with cooperation and mutual aid of each system and method of approach involved.

Study the child minutely and carefully, from birth until, say, the age of ten, with a view to seeing the order in which cultural patterns and parts of patterns appear in his psychic world; study the relevance of these patterns for the development of his personality; and, at the end of the suggested period, see how much of the total official culture of the group can be said to have a significant existence for him. Moreover, what degree of systematization, conscious or unconscious, in the complicating patterns and symbolisms of culture will have been reached by this child? This is a difficult problem, to be sure, but it is not an impossible one. Sooner or later it will have to be attacked by the genetic psychologists. I venture to predict that the concept of culture which will then emerge, fragmentary and confused as it will undoubtedly be, will turn out to have a tougher, more vital importance for social thinking than the tidy tables of contents attached to this or that group which we have been in the habit of calling "cultures".

NOTES

1 The preceding two sentences are quoted from Sapir (1934b), "Personality".

2 The preceding sentence is quoted from Sapir (1934a). The sentence continues, in the 1934 publication, as follows: "... and which, as it accretes more and more symbols to itself, creates finally that cultural microcosm of which official 'culture' is little more than a metaphorically and mechanically expanded copy. The application of the point of view which is natural in the study of the genesis of personality to the problem of culture cannot but force

a revaluation of the materials of culture itself." Though the idea that both personality and culture can be viewed as symbolic systems lending a distinctive configuration to experience is quite consistent with Sapir's 1937 statements, the notion that culture might be just a mechanically expanded copy of personality seems not to be.

3   *American Journal of Sociology* 42 (6), May 1937, an issue of papers from a symposium of psychiatrists and social scientists discussing "social disorganization". The psychiatrist contributors were Alfred Adler, Franz Alexander, Trigant Burrow, Elton Mayo, Paul Schilder, David Slight, and Harry Stack Sullivan (see bibliography for full references). Sapir's paper, "The Contribution of Psychiatry to an Understanding of Behavior in Society", comes immediately after the psychiatrists' and comments upon them. The issue continues with articles by sociologists Herbert Blumer, William F. Ogburn and Abe Jaffe, and Mark May (see Bibliography).

4   Later writers on culture and personality used the term "norm" for a similar concept.

5   The preceding two sentences are quoted from Sapir (1937).

6   Sapir seems also to have suggested that Mead and Benedict projected their own values onto the cultural patterns they describe in psychological terms. One notetaker (M. Rouse) adds: "Benedict [assesses] Zuni from emot. evaluation | sensory type would ev. Zuni from sensory pt. of view – [emphasizing] forms – color – ritual – ..." Sapir's distinction between emotional and sensory personality types derives from Jung; see Chapter 8.

7   A notetaker adds: "(this is Mead)".

8   The preceding two sentences are quoted from Sapir (1980), a letter to Philip Selznick (October 25, 1938). The passage I draw upon begins thus: "I judge from a number of passages in your essay that you share my feeling that there is danger of the growth of a certain scientific mythology in anthropological circles with regard to the psychological interpretation of culture. I believe this comes out most clearly in Ruth Benedict's book, 'Patterns of Culture'. Unless I misunderstand the direction of her thinking and of the thinking of others who are under her influence, there is an altogether too great readiness to translate psychological analogies into psychological realities.

I do not like the glib way in which many talk of such and such a culture as 'paranoid' or what you will. It would be my intention to bring out clearly, in a book that I have still to write, the extreme methodological importance of distinguishing ..."

9   One notetaker has "society" throughout this passage.

10   See Sapir (n.d. [1926]) on the "mentality of races", and Chapter 13's statement (from the concluding lecture of the Rockefeller Seminar): "To study the problem of the relations of 'culture' and 'personality' means that one does not consider personality as the mere unfolding of a biological organism."

11   See also the various research proposals Sapir wrote, or to which he contributed, for the Social Science Research Council and the National Research Council; for example Sapir (1930).

12   I.e., not native to it?

13   The preceding passage, starting from "the field of child development", is quoted from Sapir (1934a).

14   This passage comes from the Rockefeller Seminar. Notes on the discussion period of this seminar session further show that "Mr. Dai raised the question of the development of Personality types. Dr. Sapir answered in brief the three stages: 1. Heredity, the somatic implications may mould the character. (Not so important from our point of view.) 2. The maturing period, we do not know quite about, but very important. 3. Interactions between the child and his early environment up to the age of three."

15   The notetaker actually has, "In the child's cosmos, Chinese patterns of behavior are understood emotionally." Sapir presumably contrasted the emotional outlook with the ethnological here, as in Sapir (1934a) and in the Lecture to the Friday Night Club, which begins, "I cannot be ethnological and be sincere in observing my little boy play marbles. I cannot watch a Chinese mandarin and be psychological." The child does not understand a particular mode of behavior as representative of a culture, Chinese for instance, but in terms of its emotional significance for him or her.

16   I.e., developmental psychology.

17   The preceding two sentences are quoted from Sapir (1934a). On this point see also Malinowski (1927), *Sex and Repression in Savage Society*.

3

Culture and Experience

A. Irving Hallowell

Psychological Leads for Ethnological Field Workers (1937)

While it has been assumed from time to time that little, if any variability in individual behavior was characteristic of the so-called primitive peoples, closer observation inevitably has disclosed the fact that even in these relatively homogeneous cultures variability in personality traits, as well as in talent, thought and behavior occurs.[1] Individuals are not completely moulded to a common pattern despite the forces at work which tend to produce this result. Perhaps a state of thoroughgoing regimentation of thought and action is impossible. It may conceivably be approached but never completely realized. Gross similarities must not be allowed to obscure the minutiae of genuine differences in thought and conduct. A great deal depends upon how our observations are scaled. The handwriting expert will detect individual peculiarities that escape the untrained eye, while the casual observer may be content to note generic similarities in styles of handwriting.

Indeed, the very nature of culture allows for such variations. It is not a die which stamps out succeeding generations of individuals indistinguishable in all their habits and beliefs. It defines ends for which individuals strive and at the same time provides correlative means for accomplishing them, for gratifying human desires within traditional limits. Even speech with all its established formalisms permits a certain amount of variability, provided that its functions of communication and social control can be served, within the context in which it is operative. As Allport[2] has shown, even the highly ritualized and repetitive act of crossing one's self with holy water, performed by Roman Catholics upon entering a church, varies widely among individuals. The significant thing here, as in many other aspects of culture, is the *purpose* of the act. Its form is subordinate to the end which it serves. Indeed, culture patterns as they actually function must be considered with reference to ends as well as means. For the individual to whom these ends are of primary

A. Irving Hallowell, Psychological Leads for Ethnological Field Workers in *Personal Character and Cultural Milieu: A Collection of Readings*, Revised Edition, compiled by Douglas G. Haring, Syracuse University Press, Revised Edition © 1949 by Douglas G. Haring; 1937 Psychological Leads for Ethnological Field Workers, prepared under the auspices of the Committee on Personality in Relation to Culture, Edward Sapir, Chairman, Division of Anthropology and Psychology, National Research Council, mimeographed, under the title, "Introduction: Handbook of Psychological Leads for Ethnological Field Workers" previously unpublished, reproduced by courtesy of D. Hallowell, pp. 329–333.

Extract from "The Self and Its Behavioral Environment" by A. Irving Hallowell from *Explorations II*, (April 1954) *Culture and Experience* by A. Irving Hallowell. © 1955 by University of Pennsylvania Press, 1988, pp. 390–395. Reprinted with permission of University of Pennsylvania Press.

importance, considerable latitude in ways of accomplishing them is often possible, unless the culture itself strongly emphasizes the formal aspects of act and thought. This is often the case in magic and ritual, and our own conscious emphasis upon grammatical speech is a further example. Emphasis upon strict tenets of established religious belief, as, e.g., the Trinity, is another instance, but on the other hand in many religious systems such precise formulations are unemphasized so that more variability in the conceptualization of deity may be expected, yet culturally determined notions of a characteristic form will no less prevail. Considered from the standpoint of the individual believer, the ends which religous behavior serves are important no matter what aspects of ritual or belief are traditionally emphasized. The same is true in the technological sphere, in economic life and in social life.

But since the attention of ethnologists has been principally centered upon the typical (or modal) aspects of group life and thought, as abstracted in terms of culture patterns, the problems connected with variability in individual behavior, the role of the individual as such in different societies and the extent to which its institutions serve his personal needs have been indifferently treated, if at all. No wonder, then, that investigators in other fields who dipped into older ethnological literature in order to discover something about the psychology of primitive man discovered a "group mind," a "pre-logical mentality," or came to the conclusion that myths could be equated with dreams, and neurotic compulsions and avoidances with primitive rites and taboos.[3] There was scarcely anything about the behavior of flesh and blood individuals and the degree to which their behavior conformed to, or departed from, the abstract culture patterns of the group. Individual and culture were practically identical. There were no dreams of individuals to be found, or, if so, they conformed to conveniently determined dream patterns. Hence, myths, having so many characteristics of the dreams of individuals in western civilization, became the dreams of a "group mind" or primitive mentality. Incest taboos likewise became exaggerated in their prohibitory incidence, since successful infractions were not ordinarily recorded and the severe penalties characteristic of some peoples were generalized into a generic horror of incest typical everywhere of primitive man. Consequently, the operation of exogamy was likewise overstressed since deviations were not systematically investigated. In the collection of myths Professor Boas was probably the first to insist that series of variants from the same people be collected rather than what was assumed to be a typical version by the investigator.

Nevertheless, the characteristic emphasis upon the typical behavior of different human groups among ethnologists led to the recognition of how profoundly different the cultural configurations of different human populations actually were, and to the exposure of specious generalizations about primitive man, primitive mind and primitive culture as unitary entities. Indeed, the task of accurately recording the culture patterns of innumerable human communities, to say nothing of determining the chronology of culture changes and the interrelation between peoples with different culture patterns, has been an enormously difficult one. For the purposes of inter-group comparisons and gross chronological relations, generalizations in respect to typieal modes of life, technologies, beliefs, etc., were sufficient. In this frame of reference the individual as such could be conveniently ignored, as could also variations in the significance of beliefs for different individuals, the infraction of custom by deviant individuals, to say nothing of variations in personality traits, dreams or psychic strains and stresses related to particular culture patterns or connected with specific situations arising under purely native conditions or as a result of acculturation processes and cultural change.

It is interesting to note that during the period when ethnologists were building up more and more detailed and comprehensive descriptions of the typical behavior patterns of human communities and paying little attention to the differential behavior of individuals, there arose in Psychology, with Galton, a profound interest in individual differences themselves, which led to systematic inquiries that have grown to such marked proportions in recent decades of psychological investigation.

Due to the fact that such investigations at first gave almost exclusive emphasis to physiological and psychological variables,[4] dissociated for the most part from their social significance even in western civilization, no link seemed discernible between such inquiries and the culturally oriented studies that were being undertaken.

Contemporaneously, however, in one field of anthropological investigation, data on individual differences were accumulating. These were observations on the variations in bodily traits which had racial significance. But such anthropometric observations were inevitably undertaken to provide the basis for making *group* comparisons. Whether intra-community or tribal variations in the physical or physiological characteristics of individuals had any psychological, sociological or economic significance in terms of the culture patterns of the people, was a question not considered. Today it still remains a problem open for investigation. Yet in westtern civilization physique is a recognized qualification for certain occupations (policemen, soldiers), and perhaps an unformalized qualification for others.[5] Herskovits' study of the role of skin color differences in negro mating,[6] that is the tendency for dark men to marry light women, is an example of the social significance that individual variability within a racial type may possess.

Group differences in specific psychological capacities or general level of intelligence have likewise been the focus of attention in many investigations rather than inquiries into the possible functional significance of these differences in terms of the life histories, occupations and social adjustments of individuals in societies with different culture patterns.

Do measurable differences in general – musical ability, for example – act selectively in the emergence of prominent singers and drummers in primitive societies? Or is a good memory (the capacity to remember a large repertoire of songs) or some other quality more important? Is a high level of general intelligence actually a *sine qua non* for leadership in certain enterprises, for chieftainship, ceremonial leadership, etc.? Is there any correlation between sensory acuity or special abilities and success in any particular occupation or craft?

The investigation of such problems would require an adaptation of techniques and methodologies not yet even fully perfected for use in western civilization. But a specialized field for investigation lies open here which might be more fruitful than the gross comparison of group differences, as well as proving another angle of attack upon the functioning of the human individual in relation to the varying culture patterns of different societies.

While individual variations in discernible anatomical and physiological traits and in abilities of various kinds may have positive negative or indifferent significance in relation to the culture patterns of different societies, a factor which M.A. May[7] has called an "integral variable," is perhaps of even greater importance. Individuals differ (a) in the degree and manner in which their respective organic traits, native capacities and acquired behavior patterns are organized, and (b) in the way they function as personalities in relation to the other members of the society in which they live. The former aspect of integral variability is one which only exceedingly intimate, detailed and prolonged studies of individuals can elucidate. The latter is open to more general observation.

It has already been pointed out that the culture patterns of a given society tend to engender certain personality traits which are favored to the exclusion of others. But it must be likewise recognized that the modes of personal integration stressed in different societies and the type of behavior demanded are by no means equally congenial to all individuals. Deviational behavior must consequently be taken into account to round out realistically the total picture of human behavior in a society. Data on deviational behavior also help to throw the typical behavior patterns of the society into stronger relief, and help to expose the functioning of social institutions. The relation of individual deviants to cultural change is a further problem.

The data on deviational behavior range all the way from idiosyncrasies in speech, dress, personal mannerisms, foibles, etc., through cases of immorality, crime, and religious heresy to pathological behavior. But the frame of reference to be kept in mind is always the culturally defined series of norms of a particular society, not those derived from the scale of values of some other society (that of the observer in particular) or some ideal norm.

The Self and Its Behavioral Environment (1954)

Basic orientations provided by culture

From this standpoint culture may be said to play a constitutive role in the psychological adjustment of the individual to his world. The human individual must be provided with certain basic orientations in order to act intelligibly in the world he apprehends. Such orientations are basic in the sense that they are peculiar to a human level of adjustment. They all appear to revolve around man's capacity for self-awareness. If it be assumed that the functioning of *human* societies depends in some way upon this psychological fact, it is not difficult to understand why all human cultures must provide the individual with basic orientations that are among the necessary conditions for the development, reinforcement, and effective functioning of self-awareness. It is these orientations that may be said to structure the core of the behavioral environment of the self in any culture. Whereas cultural means and content may very widely, common instrumental functions can be discerned.

Self-Orientation. – Animals below man, for instance, even though they may be highly capable of acting in a complex behavioral environment that includes many classes of objects other than themselves, including other animals of their species, do not have to become self-oriented in order to function adequately in a social group. On the other hand, one of the common functions of culture is to provide various means of self-orientation for the human being.

It is quite generally recognized that language plays an essential role in this self-orientation. But only certain features of language have been emphasized, to the exclusion of others, while the generic function of all languages in providing linguistic means of self-orientation has not been sufficiently stressed.

Despite wide variations in linguistic structure Boas called attention years ago to the fact that "the three personal pronouns – I, thou, and he – occur in all human languages" and emphasized that "the underlying idea of these pronouns is the clear distinction between the self as speaker, the person or object spoken to, and that spoken of."[8] If this be accepted, we have an unequivocal indication that languages all have a common sociopsychological function. They provide the human individual with a linguistic means of self-other orientation in all contexts of interpersonal verbal communication. A personal existence and sphere of action is defined as a fundamental reference point.

Although we do not have parallel investigations in other societies, in Western culture we have had a number of studies which indicate the mastery of our system of personal and possessive pronouns at a very early age. According to Gesell, for example, the child begins to use self-reference words – mine, me, you, and I, in that order – at two years, whereas at eighteen-months self and "not self" are not clearly differentiated.[9]

As compared with the mastery of a pronominal system we know very little about the acquisition and use of kinship terms in ontogenetic perspective. In many nonliterate societies such terms are among the major linguistic means that orient the individual in a self-other dimension in relation to his roles in the social order.

Then there is the universal phenomenon of personal names. These are related to self-orientation in so far as they are personal and serve as a linguistic device for self-identification and unequivocal indentification of the self by others. The fact that in some cultures the individual knows his name although it may not be customary for him to use it freely for self-identification indicates the need for more detailed studies of the variable aspect of personal naming in relation to self-orientation. But the ubiquitous fact of personal naming must be considered to be in the same functional category as the pronominal pattern.[10]

In this connection it would also be interesting to know more about the role which personal names play in the sexual orientation of the self. Certainly in may cultures – although how widespread the custom is I do not know – the panel of names available for boys is not the same as for girls. Names are sex-linked.

Under these circumstances, knowing one's own name is equivalent to knowing one's own sex. Awareness of one's sexual status is likewise implied in the use of certain kinship terms in many cultures, so that, in acquiring the proper use of kinship terms, the child likewise becomes sexually oriented. There are other aspects of language that should be considered in relation to self-orientation, but these illustrations must suffice.[11]

Whatever the idiosyncratic content of the self-image may be and whatever weight it may be given in psychodynamic analysis, the content of the self-image is, in part, a culturally constituted variable.[12] While one of the constant functions of all cultures therefore is to provide a concept of self along with other means that promote self-orientation, the individuals of a given society are self-oriented in terms of a provincial content of the self-image.

This by no means implies that we should expect to find a single linguistic term or a concept even roughly equivalent to "self," "ego," or "soul" in all cultures. The absence of any such single term and the correlative fact that the self-image may present subtleties foreign to our mode of thinking is one of the reasons such a topic, approached from outside a culture, poses inherent difficulties. On the other hand, there are analogies familiar to the anthropologist. Art, religion, and law, for example, have been investigated in societies in which abstract terms for such phenomena do not exist. It also has been found that too rigid a priori definitions and concepts, consciously or unconsciously modeled after those of our own intellectual tradition, may even lead to a denial that comparable phenomena exist in other cultures, only because the phenomena observed fail to meet all the requirements of the definitions and concepts employed by the observer. In any case, we must not expect to find concepts of the self among nonliterate peoples clearly articulated for us. To a certain extent it is necessary to approach the whole subject naïvely, to pursue it obliquely from different angles, to attack the conceptual core of the problem in terms of its pragmatic implications and in the full light of related concepts in a single cultural matrix. We already know from available data, for instance, that such concepts as reincarnation,

metamorphosis, and the notion that under certain circumstances the "soul" may leave the body, must be relevant to variations in the self-image which different peoples have. But we know much less about the way in which such concepts become psychologically significant for the individual in relation to his motivations, goals, and life adjustment.

Object Orientation. – A *second* function of all cultures is the orientation of the self to a diversified world of objects in its behavioral environment, discriminated, classified, and conceptualized with respect to attributes which are culturally constituted and symbolically mediated through language. The role of language in object-orientation is as vital as in self-orientation. The late Ernst Cassirer laid special emphasis upon this point. "Language," he said, "does not enter a world of completed objective perceptions only to add to individually given and clearly delimited objects, one in relation to the other, 'names' which will be purely external and arbitrary signs; rather, it is itself a mediator in the formation of objects. It is, in a sense, the mediator par excellence, the most important and most precise instrument for the conquest and the construction of a true world of objects."[13] It is this objectifying function of speech that enables man to live and act in an articulated world of objects that is psychologically incomparable with that of any other creature.

Object orientation likewise provides the ground for an intelligible interpretation of events in the behavioral environment on the basis of traditional assumptions regarding the nature and attributes of the objects involved, and implicit or explicit dogmas regarding the "causes" of events. A cosmic and metaphysical orientation of the self supplies a conceptual framework for action in an orderly rather than a chaotic universe. It is not necessary, of course, that the individual be aware of the underlying metaphysical principles involved, any more than it is necessary that he be aware of the grammatical principles of the language that he speaks. But the former are as open to investigation as the latter. It is for this reason that considerable confusion has been created by the application of the natural-supernatural category to non-literate peoples in approaching their religion or world view.[14] This dichotomy simply reflects the outcome of metaphysical speculation in latter-day thought in Western culture. Instead of assuming a priori that this dichotomy is really meaningful in other cultures, it might be more profitable to discover the metaphysical principles that actually exist. At any rate, if we assume the outlook of the self as culturally oriented in a behavioral environment with cosmic dimensions and implicit metaphysical principles, a great deal of what is ordinarily described as "religion" is seen to involve the attitudes, needs, goals, and affective experience of the self in interaction with certain classes of objects in the behavioral environment. These classes of objects are typically *other* selves – spiritual beings, deities, ancestors. The relation of the self to them may, indeed, be characterized by the same patterns that apply to interpersonal relations with other human beings. In any case, the individual must be quite as aware of his status in relation to other-than-human beings, as he is in relation to his human associates. He must learn to play his proper role in response to their roles as culturally defined.

In other words, the "social" relations of the self when considered in its total behavioral environment may be far more inclusive than ordinarily conceived. The self in its relations with other selves may transcend the boundaries of social life as objectively defined.[15] This is a fact of some psychological importance since it is relevant to the needs, motivations, and goals of individuals under certain circumstances. At the same time, the social relations of the self in this more inclusive sense may not be directly relevant in a sociological frame of reference where the aim of the observer is to define the lineaments of "social structure" in the usual sense. That is, the social structure, defined as a result of such an investigation, may not be the phenomenon apprehended by the self, nor represent the most salient aspects, for the individual, of the greater society of selves apprehended in the behavioral environment. In some cultures the social orientation of the self may be so constituted that relations with deceased ancestors or other-than-human selves become much more crucial for an understanding of the most vital needs and goals of

the individual than do interpersonal relations with other human beings.

Spatiotemporal Orientation. – Since the self must be prepared for action, a *third* basic orientation that all cultures must provide is some kind of spatiotemporal[16] frame of reference. Animals have to find their way about in space, but they do not have to be oriented in an acquired schema that involves the conscious use of culturally constituted reference points and the awareness of one's position in space.[17] Just as a culture provides the means that enable the individual to identify himself and to define his position with reference to his behavior in a scheme of social relations, it likewise provides him with the means for defining his position in a spatial frame of reference that transcends immediate perceptual experience.[18] Getting lost or becoming spatially disoriented is apt to be an emotionally distressing situation for an individual in any culture. The capacity to move freely and intelligently from place to place, to conceptualize the spatial location of one's destination, and to be able to reach it, as well as to be able to return back home, is a commonplace of everyday human living.

Just as personal names mediate self-identification and personal reference, in the same way names for places and significant topographical features are a universal linguistic means for discriminating and representing stabilized points in space which enable the self to achieve spatial orientation. Place names become focal points in the organized directional schema made available to the individual through knowledge and experience. Such stable points of reference are not only a guide to action, once known they can be mentally manipulated in relational terms at a more abstract level, as in maps for example. Place names likewise become integrated with the temporal orientation of the self. For self-awareness implies that the individual not only knows where he *is*, but where he *was* at some previous moment in time, or where he expects to be in the *future*. The identification of the self with a given locus – be it a dwelling, a camp, a village, or what not – also depends upon the linguistic discrimination of place. Other selves, living or dead, and selves of an other-than-human category likewise can be assigned a characteristic spatial locale through the device of place-naming. Place-naming is another, common denominator of cultures.

Orientation in time is coordinate with spatial orientation and, however simple the means or crude the temporal intervals discriminated may be, the self is temporally as well as spatially oriented in all cultures.[19] Temporal disorientation is abnormal in any culture if judged in relation to the traditional temporal schema. Of course, in a culture without names for days of the week self-orientation in time is not possible in terms of this particular schema. On the other hand, if "moons" are named it is assumed that the individual knows his "moons."

What we know all too little about are the earliest phases of temporal orientation in the child – a sensed relationship of experienced events in time – at a period before traditional cultural concepts are learned and consciously employed, and even before a concept of self is fully developed. L. K. Frank directed attention to this problem many years ago, indicating how what we have called motivational and normative orientations became integrated with the beginnings of temporal orientation and a growing sense of self at an early age:

> Here then begins the characteristically human career of man who, not content to be ruled by hunger and other physiological functions, transforms them so that hunger becomes appetite, bladder and rectal pressures become occasions for modesty, cleanliness, etc. and later sex becomes love. This transformation of naive behavior into conduct involves the acceptance of values, or, more specifically, necessitates value behavior and time perspectives wherein we see the individual responding to present, immediate situation-events (intraorganic or environmental) as point-events in a sequence the later or more remote components of which are the focus of that conduct.

The deeper psychological implications of the relation between temporal orientation and the emergence and functioning of self-awareness in the human being are nowhere more clearly apparent than in the integral connections between memory processes and the development of a feeling of self-identity. This integral relation is one of the necessary conditions required if any sense of *self-continuity* is to become salient. Human beings maintain awareness of self-continuity and personal identity in time through the recall of past experiences that are identified with the self-image. If I cannot remember, or recall at will, experiences of an hour ago, or yesterday, or last year that I readily identify as *my* experiences, I cannot maintain an awareness of self-continuity in time. At the lowest functional level, however, recall neither implies volition nor any capacity to organize the memory images of past events in any temporal schema. Even if we should grant animals below man a very high capacity for recall, without some symbolically based and culturally derived means, it would be impossible to organize *what* is recalled in relation to a temporal schema, on the one hand, and a self-image, on the other. Consequently, in order for a sense of self-continuity to become a functionally significant factor in self-awareness, the human individual must be temporally oriented as well as self-oriented. If we wish to postulate a sense of self-continuity as a generic human trait, a culturally constituted temporal orientation must be assumed as a necessary condition. This seems to be a reasonable hypothesis in view of the fact that self-identification would have no functional value in the operation of a human social order if, at the same time, it was not given a temporal dimension. *Who* I am, both to myself and others, would have no stability. It would make it impossible to assume that patterns of interpersonal relations could operate in terms of a continuing personnel. From this standpoint, I believe it can be deduced that psychopathological phenomena that affect the maintenance of personal identity and continuity must of necessity be considered abnormal in any society.[20] For in order to play my designated roles I not only have to be aware of who I am today, but be able to relate my past actions to both past and future behavior. If I am unable to do this there is no way I can assume moral responsibility for my conduct. I am not quite the same person today as I was yesterday if the continuity of my experience is constricted through the impairment of memory or, as in the case of some individuals with "multiple" personalities, different sets of memory images become functional as a "new" personality manifests itself. Fugue states, in some instances, are unconsciously motivated devices for breaking the sense of self-continuity, for disconnecting the self from past actions felt to be morally reprehensible.

There is still another important aspect of the relation between the temporal orientation of the self and the maintenance of self-continuity. This is the time-span of recalled experiences that become self-related. Cultural variables are involved here. What we find in certain instances is this: not only is a continuity of self assumed, self-related experiences are given a retrospective temporal span that far transcends the limits beyond which we know reliable accounts of personal experience can be recalled. The earliest experiences of the human being cannot become self-related and recalled as such because the infant has not yet become an object to himself, nor has he incorporated any working temporal schema which makes possible the differentiation of experiences of this period from later ones. Besides this, past experience as recalled implies a spatial as well as a temporal frame of reference. Dudycha and Dudycha, as a result of systematic investigation, state that the "average earliest memory is somewhere in the fourth year."[21] But one of my Ojibwa informants referred to memories in his mother's womb (spatial locale), and he knew *when* he would be born (consciousness of *future* time).[22]

From modern observation, we also are aware of the distortion of early memories that can occur through repressive amnesia[23] and the phenomena of pseudo-memory. One instance of the latter, in the form of *déja vue*, turned up while I was collecting Rorschach protocols among the Northern Ojibwa. Having been presented with Card I this subject hesitated a long while before he would say anything at all. Then he went into a long disquisition the main point of which involved the statement that when he was a baby and still on a cradle board (i.e., long before he was able to talk) he had once looked up through the smoke hole of the wigwam and seen exactly what he now saw before him on the Rorschach card.

Facts such as these indicate plainly enough that self-related experience as recalled need not be true in order to be psychologically significant for the individual or his associates. Since reliable knowledge regarding the vagaries of memory is such a recent acquisition in our own culture, it is easy to understand how, through the long span of human history, the door has been left wide open to varying emphases in different cultures upon the nature and the time span of past experiences that can be self-related.[24]

One common type of past experience that may become particularly important when integrated with certain concepts of the nature of the self is dreaming. Once we recognize the fact that self-awareness is a generic human trait, that a self-related experience of the past depends upon a memory process (recall) and that the human individual is at the same time exposed to some culturally constituted self-image, there is nothing psychologically abstruse about the incorporation of dream experience into the category of self-related experiences. Self-awareness being as phenomenally real in dreams as in waking life there is no inherent discontinuity on this score. Assuming an autonomous soul separable from the body under certain conditions, as in sleep, it is possible to interpret dream experiences as personal experiences, even though in retrospect the experiences undergone by the self in this phase may far transcend the self-related experiences of waking life in unusual spatial mobility, or in other ways. This by no means implies, however, that the individual ignores or is unaware of any distinction between self-related experience when awake and when asleep.[25] A sense of self-continuity conceptually integrated with a self-image, provides the necessary connecting link. Dream experiences become integrated through the same kind of memory process through which other experiences become self-related. But this integration of experience from both sources does mean that the content of self-related experiences may in different cultures assume qualitatively distinctive attributes.

A dream of one of my Ojibwa informants will serve to document several of the foregoing points in a concrete form.

As I was going about hunting, with my gun in my hand, I came to a lake. A steep rock rose from the lake shore. I climbed up this rock to have a look across the lake. I thought I might sight a moose or some ducks. When I glanced down towards the water's edge again, I saw a man standing by the rock. He was leaning on his paddle. A canoe was drawn up to the shore and in the stern sat a woman. In front of her rested a cradle board with a baby in it. Over the baby's face was a piece of green mosquito netting. The man was a stranger to me but I went up to him. I noticed that he hung his head in a strange way. He said, "You are the first man (human being) ever to see me. I want you to come and visit me." So I jumped into this canoe. When I looked down I noticed that it was all of one piece. There were no ribs or anything of the sort, and there was no bark covering. (I do not know what it was made of.)

On the northwest side of the lake there was a very high steep rock. The man headed directly for this rock. With one stroke of the paddle we were across the lake. The man threw his paddle down as we landed on a flat shelf of rock almost level with the water. Behind this the rest of the rock rose steeply before us. But when his paddle touched the rock this part opened up. He pulled the canoe in and we entered a room in the rock. It was not dark there, although I could see no holes to let in any light. Before I sat down the man said, "See, there is my father and my mother." The hair of those old people was as white as a rabbit skin. I could not see a single black hair on their heads. After I had seated myself I had a chance to look around. I was amazed at all the articles I saw in the room – guns, knives, pans and other trade goods. Even the clothing these people wore must have come from a store. Yet I never remembered having seen this man at a trading post. I thought I would ask him, so I said, "You told me that I was the first human being you had seen. Where, then, did you buy all of these articles I see?" To this he replied, "Have you never heard people talking about *pägítcïgan* (sacrifices)? These articles were given to us. That is how we got them." Then he took me into another room and told me to look around. I saw the meat of all kinds of animals – moose, caribou, deer, ducks. I thought to myself, this man must be a wonderful hunter, if he has been able to store up all this meat. I thought it very strange that this man had never met any other Indians in all his

travels. Of course, I did not know that I was dreaming. Everything was the same as I had seen it with my eyes open. When I was ready to go I got up and shook hands with the man. He said, "Anytime that you wish to see me, this is the place where you will find me." He did not offer to open the door for me so I knew that I had to try and do this myself. I threw all the power of my mind into opening it and the rock lifted up. Then I woke up and knew that it was a dream. It was one of the first I ever had. (The narrator added that later he discovered a rocky eminence on one of the branches of the Berens River that corresponded exactly to the place he had visited in his dream.)

My informant W. B. narrated this dream as the equivalent of many other personal experiences he had told me about that were not dream experiences. The phenomenal reality of self-awareness is as evident here as in his other narratives, but he distinguishes this narrative as a dream. It is noteworthy, too, that the behavioral environment of the dreamer is spatially continuous with that of waking life. This is unequivocal, not only because the narrator starts off by saying he was out hunting and because the topographical features of the county conform to ordinary experience, but particularly because of the comment in parentheses at the very end. He recognized later when awake the *exact spot* he had visited in the dream. He could go back there at anytime in *the future* and obtain the special kind of medicine that the *mèmengwéciwak*, the beings he met, are famous for. Had he been a pagan, this is what he would have done, he told me. For he received a special blessing – this is the implication of what they told him on parting, and of the fact that he was able to "will himself out" of their rocky abode. The fact that W. B. thought he could act in the future with reference to a dream experience of the past shows an implied temporal continuity of the self in a behavioral environment with a unified spatiotemporal frame of reference for *all* self-related experience. The anthropomorphic characters that appear in the dream are of particular interest because they are not human (*änicinábek*), yet they are well-known inhabitants of the behavioral environment of the Northern Ojibwa.

What is of special theoretical importance for our discussion is that whereas most nonhuman beings of the behavioral environment of the Ojibwa can *only* be met in dreams, it is otherwise with *mèmengwécīwak*. These beings reputedly have been seen or heard singing in ordinary life by a number of Indians. This "equivocal" status also demonstrates the unified structure of the behavioral environment of the Ojibwa. It is impossible to dichotomize it in our terms and make psychological sense from the anecdotal accounts of the Ojibwa themselves. *Mèmengwécīwak* are not human beings (Indians); nor are they "spiritual" entities in the sense of being perceptually intangible beings dwelling in a spatial region remote from man. From the Ojibwa point of view they are inhabitants of the same terrestial region as men and belong to the same class of perceptually apprehensible objects as a moose, a tree, or a man. And, like them, they may be "perceived" in dreams as well as in ordinary daily life.

Consonant with this conception of these beings anecdotes are told about Indians who sometimes have met *mèmengwécīwak* while out hunting. One of these stories has an interesting climax. After following some *mèmengwécīwak* to one of their rocky dwellings an Indian, according to his own account, attempted to follow them in. But the rocks closed as soon as *mèmengwécīwak* had gone through. As the prow of his canoe bumped hard against the rocks, the Indian heard *mèmengwécīwak* laughing inside. On the other hand, an old man once told me that he had seen his father enter the rocks. What the Ojibwa say is that it is necessary to receive a blessing from *mèmengwécīwak* in a dream first. This is the significance that W. B. attributed to his dream experience, although, being a Christian, he never took advantage of it to become a *manao* (i.e., an Indian doctor who uses medicine obtained from *mèmengwécīwak*).

It would be possible to demonstrate from other dream material how the horizon of self-related experience is enormously broadened through the integration of this kind of experience with that of waking life. The range of mobility of the self in space and time may likewise be extended throughout the limits of the behavioral environment. In the case of the Ojibwa, human beings share such mobility with the nonhuman selves of their behavioral environment. Furthermore, the psychological fact that the individual actually does experience such phenomena (in dreams) is one of the main reasons the events of mythological narrative can assume reality in the context of the same behavioral environment. Experientially, the world of the self and the world of myth are continuous. How far this is actually the case in any culture is, I believe, open to empirical investigation.

In the past decade or so the "personal document" approach in anthropology has begun to yield a new dimension to ethnography.[26] A number of autobiographies of individuals in nonliterate societies have appeared. But one point has been overlooked. If concepts of the self and the kind of experiences that become self-related are culturally constituted, then the content of autobiographical data must likewise be considered in a variable framework. This content in some cultures will not be in accord with the kind of self-related experience that we consider autobiographical in Western culture. It may contain a great deal of the fantasy material that we exclude from autobiography and relegate to dreams or visions. The anthropologist may collect dreams, it is true; but such data may be separated from autobiographical data on an a priori basis and never considered as integrally related to a self-image. In recent years, the aim of collecting dreams has been principally inspired by their value for the analysis of personality dynamics.[27] At another level, however, dreams or other fantasy data may be relevant to autobiography, if we consider that autobiography involves a retrospective account of the experiences of the self. It would be interesting to know what a systematic phrasing of autobiography with relation to the self-image of a culture might bring forth. One thing the investigator would then encourage would be the searching of the subject's memory and the recall of *all* experiences that were interpreted by him as self-related.

Temporal orientation is not only an important means through which past experience can be organized in a self-related manner; a temporal schema is directly related to future conduct, to contemplated action, to the destiny of the self. This implies the notion of self-continuity as one of the ubiquitous aspects of self-awareness. The self not only has a past and a present, but a long future existence. Murdock lists eschatology as a common denominator of culture. The self may be conceived to be immortal, indestructible, or eternal. Such grandiose attributes of the self-image necessitate a spatio-temporal frame of reference since deceased selves, if they continue to exist, must exist somewhere. Frank says that

It has been the great office of culture, and specifically of religion to provide the major time perspective of conduct by insisting upon the relative dimensions of the immediate present as seen in the focus of eternity. Culture, as transmitted by parents and other cultural agents, prevents man from acting impulsively and naively, as his needs, urges, and desires might dictate, and so compels him to regulate his conduct towards the opportunities around him, which he sees in the time perspective of life after death or other forward reference. The Hindu belief in reincarnation and endless striving toward perfection is probably the most attenuated and compelling time perspective that sets every event and human action in this ever-receding perspective from which there is no escape. Each culture and each religion presents its own time perspective and emphasizes the necessity of patterning human conduct in its focus, so that one culture will repress and another foster sexual functioning, one will favor and another repress aquisitiveness, and so on. Thus asceticism, continence, and all other virtues may be viewed as responses to the dimensions imposed upon the presently religious, ethical time perspectives, many of which reduce the present to insignificance except as a preparation for the future in which this asceticism will be rewarded. To insist then upon time perspectives in human conduct is to recognize the ages-old significance given to the future, but to bring that future into the manageable present and give it an operational meaning by showing that *the future is that name we give to the altered dimensions of the present.*[28]

To understand the orientation of the self in its culturally constituted behavioral environment, future time and a cosmographic dimension cannot be ignored.

Motivational Orientation. – A *fourth* orientation with which a culture must provide the self may be characterized as motivational.[29] Motivational orientation is orientation of the self towards the objects of its behavioral environment with reference to the satisfaction of its needs. This is why the self must be groomed for action. The satisfaction of needs requires some kind of activity. A world of objects is not only discriminated; objects of different classes have specific attributes that must be taken into account in interaction with them; even the valence they have for the self is culturally constituted. Some classes of objects may have highly positive attributes; others may, on occasion, or even characteristically, be threatening to the security of the self. Consequently, any sort of activity must be given purposeful direction in order that the pursuit of appropriate goals may contribute to the needs of the self.[30] Since the motivational structure of individuals includes the entire range of needs, interests, wants, and attitudes that underlie the functioning of a human social order, a motivational orientation is as necessary for the maintenance and the persistence of traditional culture patterns as it is for the psychological adjustment of the individual.

Motives at the human level are peculiarly complex because they are essentially acquired rather than innately determined.[31] In consequence, their range and variety is very great. Many attempts to reduce human motives to constant biological attributes of the organism, or physiological determinants, have proved inadequate. By this means we can, at best, only speak in terms of a common denominator of needs. In doing so we not only ignore the most characteristic feature of human motives, but also the relation of needs to the self as culturally constituted.

If in approaching the problem of human needs we take into account the needs of the self, then it would seem necessary to investigate variant needs of the self in its behavioral environment. In this way we may be able to identify and discriminate motivational patterns in the psychological field of the individual that may escape us entirely if we rely exclusively upon any reductionistic approach.

It has been frequently pointed out that in the process of self-objectification the self becomes an object of value for the human individual. Sherif and Cantril, e.g., write, "A characteristic fact that holds for any individual in *any culture* [italics ours] is that experience related to ego-attitudes, ego-experiences, are felt by the individual with a peculiar warmth and familiarity."[32] Accepting this generalization, I believe that a further point needs special emphasis. This positive evaluation of the self represents the keystone of the characteristic motivational structure that we find in man. This is due to the fact that cultures not only share a common function in mediating self-objectification, it is one of their concomitant functions to constitute the self as a primary object of value in a world of other objects. While self-love when considered in terms of the psychodynamics of the individual may have its own idiosyncratic patterns and while there are undoubtedly cultural variables to be considered, it seems difficult to escape the conclusion that some *positive* rather than negative evaluation of self is one of the conditions necessary for a human level of normal psychological adjustment. Neither the principle of homeostasis nor an "instinct of self-preservation" accounts for the needs of the human individual at this level of adjustment. Motivations that are related to the needs of the self as an object of primary value in its behavioral environment are not in the same category as the needs of animals whose behavior is motivated in a psychological field in which any form of self-reference is lacking.

With this fact in mind, concepts such as self-enhancement, self-defense, aspiration level[33] become more meaningful in cross-cultural perspective. The same is true for a deeper psychological understanding of concepts such as selfishness, self-love, self-interest. That there are important cultural variables involved and that an examination of them is pertinent to motivation is implied by Fromm.[34] From the standpoint of motivational orientation the phenomena characterized as "ego-involvement," the identification of the self with things, individuals, and groups of individuals, is likewise of great importance. The range and character of "ego-involvements"[35] as constituted by variations in the structure of different behavioral environments need detailed examination.

By way of illustration, a brief consideration of some of the foregoing concepts in relation to the interpretation of the motives of individuals in a nonliterate culture may serve to highlight some of the essential problems.

Among the Ojibwa Indians, a hunting people, food-sharing beyond the immediate family circle might appear to suggest unselfishness, generosity, affection, kindness, and love. Without denying altogether motives that such terms may suggest, I believe that any immediate interpretation of this sort is misleading. Nor can it be assumed that food-sharing is an indication that the individual has become so closely identified with other members of his group that there is an inseparable coalescence of interests. It is demonstrable that one of the most potent motivations in food-sharing and hospitality is apprehension or fear of sorcery. Food-sharing is an act of self-defense against possible aggression, for sorcery is a potential danger that is always present, it is necessary to be continually on the alert. Conequently, food-sharing cannot be interpreted motivationally without further knowledge of relevant cultural facts.

Even from an economic point of view, food-sharing may be interpreted as a defense against a very realistic threat – starvation. In the aboriginal period and even in this century, there are vicissitudes inherent in Ojibwa economy and ecology that are potent with anxiety. While I may be very lucky in my hunting or fishing today, I am also likely to be periodically faced with starvation. For try as hard as I may, I cannot secure enough to feed my family. Thus a system of mutual sharing of food bridges lean periods for everyone. When considered in relation to sorcery it is not difficult to see how malevolent motives may be attributed to any individual who refuses to share food, or who fails to be hospitable. If I don't share what I have with you, when you need it, I must be hostile to you. At any rate, you may in turn become angry and attack me by means of sorcery. On the other hand, if I always share what I have no one will have reason to sorcerize me on that score, and I will suffer from much less anxiety. At the same time, by playing my expected role, any anxiety that I may have about what may happen to me in lean periods is allayed. The psychological reality of this motivational picture is supported by a case in which an Indian overlooked another man when he was passing around a bottle of whiskey. Later when this Indian became ill, he was certain that the man he overlooked got angry and sorcerized him. His illness was a revengeful act in retaliation for not sharing the whiskey. This pattern of sharing is so deep-seated that I have seen very small children, when given a stick of candy, immediately share it with their playmates.

If we consider motives to be intervening variables which, since they cannot be directly observed,[36] must always be inferred, it is even more apparent why the self must be given some motivational orientation. As observers of the behavior of people in another cultural setting, it is almost inevitable that we go astray unless we have some understanding of this orientation. While the positive evaluation given the self implies the basic importance of self-defense in relation to motivation, the discrimination of the actual motives that have self-defense as their goal requires some understanding of culturally constituted threats to the self. The fact that the Ojibwa live in a behavioral environment where the threat of sorcery exists inevitably gives a characteristic coloring to their motivational patterns related to self-defense. The need for some means of defense against sorcery becomes highly salient for them so that activities such as food-sharing, hospitality, and lending, which in another culture might be placed in another motivational category, must here be considered in relation to self-defense.

There is another side to this picture, however, which required parallel emphasis. A more ultimate goal than self-defense is what the Ojibwa call *pīmådazīwin*: Life in the most inclusive sense. One hears them utter this word in ceremonies over and over again. It means a long life and a life free from illness or other misfortune. To them it is far from a banal or commonplace ideal. Their daily existence is not an easy one and there are many things that threaten life. Motivational orientation toward this central goal involves a consideration of culturally constituted means that assist the individual in reaching it. Among these, the help of other selves – entities that are willing to share their power with men – is the most important. These are the *pawáganak*. They exist in the behavioral environment and they become primary goal-objects of the self in achieving *pīmådazīwin*. An essential aspect of the motivational orientation of the self involves an attitude of dependence upon these *pawága-nak*. Human beings are conceived of as intrinsically weak and helpless, so far as what we would call "natural" abilities are concerned. Consequently, it is essential that assistance be secured from other-than-human selves. This assistance is concretely conceived in the form of special blessings from the *pawáganak* that confer power upon human beings to do many things that would be otherwise impossible for them to do. The desire for such power thus constitutes the primary need of every Ojibwa man. For it is only by securing such power that he can be a successful hunter, practice curing, resist sorcery or retaliate in kind, and so on. It makes him feel that he can achieve Life.

The existence of such goal-objects as the *pawáganak*, towards which they are so highly motivated, influences much of the conduct of the Ojibwa. The fact that from the standpoint of the outside observer such objects are not in the geographical environment makes no psychological difference. Goal-objects, through symbolic representation, can mediate the satisfaction of certain needs as well as material objects can. If we wish to translate the need that is satisfied into psychological terminology we can say that the *pawáganak* are the major means of self-enhancement in the behavioral environment of the Ojibwa. They are the mainstay of a feeling of psychological security. This is why their native religion meant so much to the Ojibwa. Largely because of the way in which sorcery was conceived to operate, and for other reasons, the self could not achieve a basic sense of security through interpersonal relations with other human beings alone. Relations with and dependence upon the *pawáganak* were more vital. The crucial nature of this focus of Ojibwa needs, goals, and motivations for an understanding of the dynamics of personal adjustment is heightened by knowledge of what has happened to them in the course of their contacts with white men and Western culture. Under these conditions the structure of their behavioral environment has been radically modified and the primary needs of the self can no longer be met in the traditional way. Nor has any substitute been found. Acculturation in certain groups of Ojibwa has pushed their personality structure to the farthest limits of its functional adequacy under these newer conditions, with dire results.[37]

I have tried to indicate that the motivational orientation that Ojibwa culture structures for the self includes dynamic relations with other-than-human beings. This must be the case in other cultures, too, although the psychological significance of the nature of these relationships requires examination. But once we assume the standpoint of the self rather than the viewpoint of an outside observer, the motivational orientation of the self throughout the entire range of its behavioral environment must be considered. This is why I have emphasized the importance of the *pawáganak* as goal-objects in relation to the satisfaction of needs of the self that cannot, in *this* behavioral environment, be met through human contacts. Once this fact is recognized, we can deduce the "isolation" of the Ojibwa self which, in turn, is consonant with the "atomistic" character of their society. Especially among males, there is a latent suspicion based on the potential threat of magical attack that operates as a barrier to genuine affective ties, even among blood relatives. This barrier does not exist in relations with the *pawáganak*. For even though superhuman in power, they are not the sources of hostility or punishment. The only real danger from them is when they are in the service of some human being who may invoke their aid against *me* because they have conferred power on *him*. On the other hand, I am in the same position in relation to him, through my own blessings. My *pawáganak* are my best and most loyal "friends." Who they are and how much power I have is my secret, as it is every other man's, until matters are put to a pragmatic test. Women do not customarily acquire power in the same way as men, although stories are told of what women have been able to do when the occasion has arisen.

Normative Orientation. – A normative orientation is the *fifth* orientation with which a culture provides the self. Values, ideals, standards are intrinsic components of all cultures. Some of these may be implicit others explicit. In any case, neither the psychological nor the sociological importance of this orientation of the self can be minimized.[38] On the one hand, motivational orientation in man cannot be fully understood without normative orientation, since values are an integral aspect of needs and goals. On the other hand, without normative orientation, self-awareness in man could not function in one of its most characteristic forms – self-appraisal of conduct. For the individual would have no standard by which to judge his own acts or those of others, nor any ideals to which he might aspire.

As pointed out earlier one of the most typical features of a human social order is that it is likewise a moral order. There is always the presumption that an individual is not only aware of his own personal identity and conduct in a spatiotemporal frame of reference, but that he is capable of judging his own conduct by the standards of his culture. Thus normative orientation is a necessary corollary of self-orientation. Among other things the individual must be motivated to consider whether his acts are right or wrong, good or bad. The outcome of this appraisal is, in turn, related to attitudes of self-esteem or self-respect and to the appraisal of others.

Implicit in moral appraisal is the concomitant assumption that the individual has volitional control over his own acts. This leads directly to the affective aspects of self-judgment – "In man," as Hilgard says, "anxiety becomes intermingled with *guilt-feelings*. The Mowrer and Miller experiments with animals carry the natural history of anxiety through the stages of fear and apprehension, but not to the stage of guilt-feelings. In many cases which come to the clinic, the apprehension includes the fear lest some past offense will be brought to light, or lest some act will be committed which deserves pain and punishment. It is such apprehensions which go by the name of guilt-feelings, because they imply the responsibility of the individual for his past or future misbehavior. To feel guilty is to conceive of the self as an agent capable of good or bad choices. It thus appears that at the point that anxiety becomes infused with guilt-feelings, self-reference enters."[39]

The fact that the human individual not only is motivated to become the moral judge of self-related acts, but reacts emotionally to this judgment is peculiarly human. At the conscious level, what the self feels guilty about or what particular acts arouse apprehension is one of the consequences of normative orientation. (As for the unconscious aspects of this same orientation and the processes through which values incorporated in a superego become an integral part of the self, any discussion of this problem would divert us into an aspect of the psychodynamics of human adjustment that is not our primary concern here.[40]) It is now clear that, in relation to this adjustment process, differential value systems are one important variable and that the orientation of the self in relation to these is of great importance. One broad conclusion seems inescapable. If the self were not motivated towards *conscious* self-appraisal, rationalization, repression, and other unconscious mechanisms of self-defense would have no ostensible purpose. On the one hand, the individual is self-oriented through cultural means in a manner which leads to the evaluation of the self as an object of primary value. Any kind of self-depreciation, loss of self-esteem, or threat to the self impairs the complex motivational systems that focus upon the self and its needs. At the same time, self-evaluation through culturally recognized norms is inescapable. Awareness of these is necessary because the individual has to take account of explicitly formulated or institutionalized social sanctions. This imposes a characteristic psychological burden upon the human being, since it is not always possible to reconcile, at the level of self-awareness, idiosyncratic needs with the demands imposed by the normative orientation of the self. For animals without the capacity for self-awareness no such situation can arise. In man, therefore, unconscious mechanisms that operate at a psychological level that does not involve self-awareness may be viewed as an adaptive means that permits some measure of compromise between conflicting forces.[41] They may relieve the individual of part of the burden forced upon him by the requirements of the morally responsible existence that human society demands. Hilgard points out that in addition to the role which

such mechanisms may play as defenses against anxieties experienced by the self, they likewise permit the "bolstering [of] self-esteem through self-deception."[42] "The need for self-deception arises because of a more fundamental need to maintain or to restore self-esteem. Anything belittling to the self is to be avoided. That is why the memories lost in amnesia are usually those with a self-reference, concealing episodes which are anxiety- or guilt-producing. What is feared is loss of status, loss of security of the self. That is why aspects of the self which are disapproved are disguised." There seems to be little question that one of the crucial areas of human adjustment of necessity turns upon the tolerance with which the self views its own moral status and the sensitivity of the self to feelings of anxiety and guilt. A comprehensive understanding of this whole matter requires a better cross-cultural knowledge of the self-image and of the manner in which the self is normatively oriented with reference to the values, ideals, and standards of different cultures.

If we view normative orientation as one of the major orientations of the self in its behavioral environment, there are some novel areas of inquiry that suggest themselves. Just as, in terms of a given self-image, naturalistic time and space may be transcended in self-related experience and the self may interact socially with other-than-human selves, so in the moral world of the self the acts for which the self may feel morally responsible may not all be attributed to waking life, nor to a single mundane existence, nor to interpersonal relations with human beings alone. For the selves of this latter category may be only a single class of beings that exist in the total behavioral environment as constituted for the self. Consequently, one fundamental question that arises is the actual dimensions of the area within the behavioral environment to which the normative orientation of the self is directed and the consequences of this in the observable behavior of the individual. What does a consideration of the normative orientation of the self in its *total* behavioral environment contribute to our understanding of the role of values, ideals, and recognized standards to the needs and motivations of the self?

We have some reports in the literature, for example, where the moral responsibility of the self in dreams is viewed as continuous with waking life. Lincoln[43] refers to Ashanti dreams of adultery which subject the individual to a fine, and to the Kai where adultery dreams likewise are punishable. But much more detailed inquiry into these phenomena would be desirable.

A case of suttee that occurred in India at the beginning of the nineteenth century and was reported by Sleeman[44] is of particular interest because it brings to a concrete focus all the orientations of the self that have been discussed here.

The essential facts are these: A married man, a Brahman, died and his widow was persuaded not to join her husband on the funeral pyre. But on hearing of the death of this man a married woman of about sixty years of age, of lower caste, who lived with her husband in a village about two miles away, presented herself to members of the Brahman's family. She said she wished to burn on the pyre with the deceased man. This was because she had been his wife in three previous births and "had already burnt herself with him three times, and had to burn with him four times more." The Brahman's family were surprised to hear this and said there must be some mistake, particularly in view of the difference in caste. The old woman had no difficulty in explaining this. She said that in her last birth, at which time she resided in Benares with the Brahman, she had by mistake given a holy man who applied for charity salt instead of sugar in his food. He told her that, in consequence, "she should, in the next birth, be separated from her husband, and be of inferior caste, but that, if she did her duty well in that state, she should be reunited to him in the following birth." The Brahman's family would not, however, accede to her request. Among other things, the widow insisted that "if she were not allowed to burn herself, the other should not be allowed to take her place." What happened was this. Despite the fact that the Brahman's family at this time was not fully convinced of the old woman's claims and denied her plea, she carried out her intentions nonetheless. She stole a handful of ashes from the pyre of her "former" husband and prevailed upon her present husband and

her mother to prepare the pyre upon which she immolated herself.

This had all happened twenty years before the youngest brother of the Brahman told the story to Sleeman. The latter requested his frank opinion. It turned out that, partly in view of a prophecy the old woman made at the pyre and other circumstances, the family of her "former" husband were, in the end, absolutely convinced that her claim was true. They defrayed all her funeral expense and the rites were carried out in accordance with her "real" social status. They also built her a tomb which Sleeman later visited. He found that everyone in her village and all the people in the town where her "former" husband had lived were thoroughly convinced of her claims.

It is perfectly clear that the motivation of the old woman of lower caste cannot be separated from a culturally constituted self-image which involves the conviction of reincarnation. Consequently, she could appeal to experiences in a former existence, through recall, to make her plea intelligible. From the standpoint of normative orientation her motives were of the highest in terms of the values of her culture. Suttee is a noble and divinely sanctioned act on the part of a wife. Although suttee, if viewed from outside this behavioral environment, may be considered as suicide in the sense of self-destruction, from the standpoint of the self-related motivational structure of the old woman, any self-destruction was literally impossible. She had already lived with her "former" husband during three births; she had only been separated from him during her present birth because of an error for which she had now paid the penalty; she had still other births ahead of her. The time had now come to rejoin her "husband." What suttee offered was an occasion for *self-enhancement* and self-continuity in thorough harmony with the continued maintenance of self-respect reinforced by the deeply rooted approval of her fellows.[45] Their behavioral environment was psychologically structured like hers so that their motivations and behavior could be very easily coordinated with hers in terms that were meaningful to them.

The role that normative orientation may play in giving moral unity to the relations of the self with *all* classes of animate beings throughout its behavioral environment is illustrated by the Ojibwa. In the case of certain central values, considered them from the standpoint of the Ojibwa self, it is completely arbitrary to isolate the relations of human beings with each other from the relations of the self to other-than-human selves. And from the standpoint of psychological understanding it is likewise unrealistic to ignore the significance of the dimensions of the normative orientation of the self.

It has been said that the grammatical distinction between animate and inanimate gender in Ojibwa speech is arbitrary and hard to master. It only appears so to the outsider. Actually, it is precisely these distinctions which give the Ojibwa individual the necessary linguistic cues to the various classes of other selves that he must take account of in his behavioral environment. It is also significant that he is not an "animist" in the classical sense. There are objects – an axe, a mountain, a canoe, a rainbow – that fall within the inanimate class. In addition to human beings and *pawáganak* all animals and most plants are classified as animate. So are Thunder, the Winds, Snow, Sun-Moon (*gizis*, luminary), certain shells, stones, etc. I once asked an old man whether all stones were alive. His reply was, "Some are." Another old man is said to have addressed a stone; another thought that a Thunder Bird spoke to him.

Many examples could be cited to show that on the assumption that animals have a body and a soul like man they are treated as if they had self-awareness and volition. Bears may be spoken to and are expected to respond intelligently; the bones of animals that are killed have to be disposed of with care. Although the Ojibwa are hunters and depend upon the killing of wild game, nevertheless cruelty is not only frowned upon but may be penalized by subsequent sickness.[46] Gigantic cannibal monsters exist in the behavioral environment of the Ojibwa. They have been seen and even fought with. To kill a *wíndĩgo* is a feat of the utmost heroism; it is a sure sign of greatness because it is impossible to accomplish without superhuman help. But cruelty to a *wíndĩgo* is not permitted, and in one case I have recorded this was the reputed source of a man's illness.

Greed is not only disapproved of in human relations. There is a story told of a boy who in his puberty fast wanted to dream of "all the leaves on all the trees." He was not satisfied with the blessing that had already been given him by the *pawáganak*, but insisted on more power. He did not live to enjoy the blessings he had been given.[47]

The psychological significance of considering the normative orientation of the Ojibwa throughout its total range rests upon the fact that in relations with animals or "spiritual" beings *departure* from traditional standards is subject to the same sanctions that apply in human relations. Any serious illness is believed to be a penalty for wrongdoing. The individual is encouraged to confess anything wrong he may have done in the past in order to facilitate recovery.[48] Consequently, it is possible to find out what the individual actually feels guilty about. It is demonstrable that, in addition to guilt based upon interpersonal relations with human beings, self-related experiences that transcend these and involve relations with nonhuman selves may likewise be the source of guilt.

Conclusion

[Here] I have advanced the hypothesis that by giving primary consideration to the self and its behavioral environment all cultures will be seen to share certain central functions. In order for self-awareness to emerge and function in human societies, the individual must be given basic orientations that structure the psychological field in which the self is prepared to act. Thus, while the content of the behavioral environment of man may differ greatly and intermesh with the geographical environment in various ways, there are common functions that different cultural means must serve in order for a human level of psychodynamic adjustment to be maintained. At this level self-awareness is a major component of the personality structure of man. If we assume the point of view of the self in its behavioral environment, it is likewise possible to gain a more direct insight into the psychological field of the individual as *he* experiences it than a purely objective cultural description affords.

NOTES

1 E. Sapir, "The Emergence of the Concept of Personality in a Study of Cultures," *J. of Social Psych.*, vol. 5, 1934, R.H. Lowie, "Individual Differences and Primitive Culture," *Schmidt Festschrift*, 1928; W. Koppers, "Individual forschung unter den Primitiven in besonderen unter den Yamina auf Feuerland," *ibid.*; C.G. Seligman, "Temperament, Conflict and Psychosis in a Stone-Age Population," *Brit. J. Med. Psych.*, vol. 9, 1929, pp. 189–190; the discussion and bibliography in G. Van Bulck, *Beitrage Zur Methodik Der Volkerkunde*, 1931, pp. 122–131; and J.H. Barnatt, "Personality in Primitive Society," in *Character and Personality*, vol. 2, 1933.

2 F. Allport, "The J-curve Hypothesis of Conforming Behavior," *J. Soc. Psych.*, vol. 5, 1934, p. 141–183.

3 Róheim records the following impressions in his latest book, *The Riddle of the Sphinx*, London: Hogarth Press and the Institute of Psychoanalysis, 1934, p. 238, *after* having come in personal contact with primitives: "My first impression during my field work was that savages are not nearly so savage as the anthropologists; or, in other words, that they are not nearly so mysterious as one would think from reading Tylor, Frazer, Levy-Bruhl and Róheim. Because we read so much about animism and magic, totemism and demons, we come to identify primitive people with these things unintentionally and to imagine them as always plagued by demons, or running into taboos, and passing their lives in a chronic state of terror. Similarly, if we only knew Europe from the Catechism, the Talmud, and the books of Folklore, we might easily imagine that the main occupations of the inhabitants of this continent were confessing, fasting and telling fairy tales and legends. No savage occupies himself as much with primitive religion as the anthropologist."

4 e.g., sensory activities, motor responses, difference in the so-called higher mental processes such as imagery, association, etc., and general capacities such as intelligence, musical and mechanical abilities.

5 Cf. May's M.A. May, "The Adult in the Community," in *The Foundations of Experimental Psychology*, C. Murchison, ed., Worcester, Mass.: Clark University Press, 1929, p. 766. reference to Gowin's study of the height and weight of senators, governors, bishops, etc. The average height of the 1,037 eminent men studied was nearly 3 inches greater than that of life insurance applicants, and the average weight 16 lbs. greater than the latter class.

6 M.J. Herskovits, *The American Negro*, New York, A.A. Knopf, 1928, pp. 62–66.

7 May, M.A. May, "The Adult in the Community," in *The Foundations of Experimental Psychology*, C. Murchison, ed., Worcester, Mass.: Clark University Press, 1929, p. 766. p. 750.

8 Franz Boas, *The Mind of Primitive Man* (New York, 1911). Ernst Cassirer, *op. cit.*, p. 250, calls attention to Wilhelm von Humboldt's opposition to the view, current in his time, that since in the traditional classification of the parts of speech the pronoun was said to be a substitute for a noun, it could not be considered autonomous in development. According to Cassirer, Humboldt insisted "the pronoun cannot possibly be the latest part of speech: for the first element in the act of speech is the personality of the speaker himself, who stands in constant contact with nature and in speaking must inevitably express the opposition between his I and nature. 'But in the I [says Humboldt], the thou is automatically given, and through a new opposition the third person arises, which, now that language has gone beyond the circle of those who feel and speak, is extended to dead things.'"

9 A. Gesell, *The Psychology of Early Growth* (New York, 1938). It is worth noting Cassirer, although he was not a psychologist, was well aware of the subtle relations between the development of self-feeling, on the one hand, and linguistic reference, on the other. Following his reference to Humboldt's theory (see footnote 40) he goes on to say (*op. cit.*, pp. 250–51), "The philosophy of language would indeed reduce itself to the narrow, logical grammatical view which it combats, if it strove to measure the form and configuration of the *I-consciousness* solely by the development of the pronoun. In the psychological analysis of children's language, the mistake has often been made of identifying the earliest phonetic expression of I with the earliest stage of I-feeling. Here it is overlooked that the psychological content and the

linguistic expression never fully coincide and above all that unity of *content* need not be reflected in *simplicity* of expression. Language has many different means of expressing a specific fundamental intuition, and we must consider them as a whole in order to see clearly the direction to which they point. The formation of the I-concept is not bound up exclusively with the pronoun, but proceeds equally through other linguistic spheres, through the medium of the noun, the verb, etc." Cassirer's discussion of the role of possessive pronouns (p. 259 seq.) as mediating the self–not-self relation contains ideas for further cross-cultural exploration.

10 M. Sherif, *The Psychology of Social Norms* (New York, 1936), p. 174, quotes W. McDougall as saying that one's name "becomes a handle by the aid of which he gets hold of himself and acquires facility in thinking and speaking of himself as an agent, a striver, a desirer, a refuser."

11 G. A. Pettitt, *Primitive Education in North America* (University of California Publications in American Archeology and Ethnology, XIII [1946], 1–182), Chap. 6, has discussed other functions of names among the North American Indians, such as "stimulating self-development and achievement through ridicule, as a type of prestige reward for specific achievements or general good behavior and popularity; as the principal medium for transference of readymade personalities."

12 D. Snygg and A. W. Combs, *Individual Behavior: A New Frame of Reference for Psychology* (New York, 1949), p. 82, appear to be among the few who have given this fact explicit recognition. They write, "To this point we have spoken of the development of the phenomenal self only in terms of the child's reactions to his physical surroundings. As a matter of fact, the culture into which the individual is born is a far more potent factor in the development of the phenomenal self. While the child is born into a world of physical objects, even these are subjected to the particular interpretations of the culture so that the phenomenal self becomes overwhelmingly the product of the culture. For most of us, the phenomenal self we develop is a direct outgrowth of the cultural matrix of our parents and early guardians."

13 E. Cassirer, "Le langage et la construction du monde des objets," *Journal de la psychologie normale et pathologique*, XXX (1932), p. 23.

14 David Bidney, *Theoretical Anthropology* (New York, 1953), emphasizes the point that the fact that "natives do differentiate between secular, everyday experience and sacred, superhuman tales and traditions about gods and spirits, since they have special terms to designate the different categories of narrative and tradition ... does not mean that they distinguish clearly between the sphere of the natural and that of the supernatural, since gods and spirits are just as much a part of the order of 'nature' as are men and animals." "The dichotomy of the natural and supernatural," he goes on to say, "implies a scientific epistemology and critical, metaphysical sophistication which must not be assumed without reliable evidence" (pp. 165–66).

15 From a psychological point of view this is by no means a peculiarity of primitive peoples. Krech and Crutchfield, *op. cit.*, p. 471, point out that "our social world does not consist only of "real" people but also characters of literature, history and fable."

16 Gibson (*op. cit.*, p. 157) emphasizes the fact that "the abstractions which we call space and time are not as distinct as they have been assumed to be, for space cannot be apprehended except in time."

17 The remarkable spatial mobility and directional orientation of bees described by Von Frisch, for example, in no way depends upon the self-awareness and self-reference that we assume in man. The mechanics of their spatial orientation are of a completely different order. G. Revez, "The Problem of Space with Particular Emphasis on Specific Sensory Space," *American Journal of Psychology*, I (1937), 434 *n.*, has pointed out that "although the experience of space and perception of objects of animals seem to agree with that of our own, the theory of a general phenomenal agreement between animal and human perception is highly disputable from a logical and theoretical angle. ... Because of lack of language and ideas, all animals must have a different space concept ... their objects must be perceived in a fundamentally different configuration and order than ours. ... This

must be the case regardless of their particular stage of evolutionary development and their biological relationship to man." Sherif and Cantril (*op. cit.*, pp. 93–94), while accepting William Stern's emphasis upon the fact that "the personal world of every individual becomes centered around himself," and that "in making judgments of 'space' and 'time' the individual inevitably uses himself as a central point of reference," do not emphasize the dependence of the individual upon cultural means in order to achieve spatio-temporal orientation.

18 With reference to locomotion, Gibson (*op. cit.*, pp. 229–30) differentiates a simple type, which is "oriented directly toward the goal" and where "the body movement is a function of optical stimulation which yields the perception of a visual world with the goal-object in it" from a more advanced form which involves the "act of going to an object or place beyond the range of vision." In the latter case "one must know both where he is going and where he is now. It requires, over and above the visual world, a frame of reference or a topographical schema. The individual must perceive the space which surrounds him on all sides ... and must also apprehend the world beyond the visible scene – the layout of the building, of the city and its streets, of the region, and of the country with its highways and cities. He is then said to be oriented in space – actually, in a series of more and more inclusive spaces of which the most general is the astronomical universe. The conception of an objective world, independent of the standpoint of any observer, rests upon this type of orientation." Thus, a culturally constituted orientation in a world of objects other than self must be integrated with a spatial orientation of the self that provides a frame of reference for activities in this world. Redfield, "The Primitive World View" (p. 31), remarks: "I suppose that every world view includes some spatial and temporal dimensions, some conceptions of place and past and future. Man is necessarily oriented to a universe of extension and duration."

19 Murdock, *op. cit.*, 1945, lists calendars among the common denominators of culture. Since the chapter on Ojibwa temporal orientation included in this volume was

published (1937) E. E. Evans-Prichard, *The Nuer* (Oxford, 1940); Meyer Fortes, *The Dynamics of Clans-ship among the Tallensi* (London, 1945); and Paul Bohannon, "Concepts of Time among the Tiv of Nigeria," *Southwestern Journal of Anthropology*, IX (1953), 261–62, have dealt with the topic among African groups. S. N. Eisenstadt has analyzed the perception of time and space among oriental Jews in Jerusalem in "The Perception of Time and Space in a Situation of Culture-Contact," *Journal of the Royal Anthropological Institute*, LXXIX (1949), 63–68 (published 1951). See also P. Sorokin, *Socio-cultural Causality, Space, Time* (Durham, North Carolina, 1943).

20 See M. Abeles and P. Schilder, "Psychogenic Loss of Personal Identity: Amnesia," *Archives of Neurological Psychiatry*, XXXIV (1935), 587–604; G. W. Kisker and G. W. Knox, "The Psychopathology of the Ego System," *Journal of Nervous and Mental Diseases*, XLVI (1943), 66–71; M. Sherif and H. Cantril, *The Psychology of Ego-Involvement* (New York, 1947), Chap. 12, "Breakdown of the Ego"; D. Rappaport, *Emotions and Memory* (Baltimore, 1942), pp. 197 ff. According to Rappaport, Abeles and Schilder "were the first to recognize that the loss of personal identity is a specific disturbance."

21 G. J. Dudycha and M. M. Dudycha, "Childhood Memories: A Review of the Literature," *Psychological Bulletin*, XXXVIII (1941), 668–82; p. 681.

22 The emphasis laid upon the recall of prenatal memories, memories at conception, and even memories of deaths in previous incarnations by those practicing dianetics, is an interesting anomaly in American culture. In one case a patient reported what her mother said while she was still an unborn foetus. See J. A. Winter, *A Doctor's Report on Dianetics. Theory and Therapy*, Introduction by F. Perls, M. D. (New York, 1952).

23 Sometimes these may assume a symbolic form and be derived from actual events of a previous period even though the individual is not conscious of them as recalled memories. Freud discovered early in his investigations that what he first took to be authentic early memories were not so in fact.

24 Further inquiries are needed. How widely prevalent in nonliterate cultures is the idea

that memories from early infancy or the pre-natal period can be recalled? What is their content and under what conditions is the individual motivated to recall them? Where the notion of reincarnation is present, answers to the same questions might be sought.

25 J. S. Lincoln, *The Dream in Primitive Culture* (London, n.d.), p. 28, e.g., remarks that "Tylor and early anthropologists used to speak of the primitives' inability to distinguish dream and reality. Although cases of such confusion do occur, the description is not altogether accurate as a universal generalization. . . . Most cases show that in spite of regarding the experience of the dream as real, primitives do distinguish between dreams and the perceptions of waking experience, yet often the dream experience is rgarded as having a greater value than an actual experience."

26 Clyde Kluckhohn, "The Personal Document in Anthropological Science," in L. Gottsschalk, C. Kluckhohn, R. Angell, *The Use of Personal Documents in History, Anthropology and Sociology*, prepared for the Committee on Appraisal of Research, Social Science Research Council (New York, 1947); "Needed Refinements in the Biographical Approach," in S. S. Sargent and M. Smith, *Culture and Personality* (New York, 1949). Georg Misch remarks in *A History of Autobiography in Antiquity* (London, 1950) that "as a manifestation of man's knowledge of himself, autobiography has its basis in the fundamental – and enigmatical – psychological phenomena which we call consciousness of self or self-awareness. . . . In a certain sense the history of autobiography is a history of human self-awareness."

27 G. Roheim, "Dream Analysis and Field Work in Anthropology," in *Psychoanalysis and the Social Sciences*, I (New York, 1947).

28 L. K. Frank, *op. cit.*, p. 345; cf. Smith, *op. cit.*

29 Hadley Cantril, *The Psychology of Social Movements* (New York, 1941), pp. 45–46: "For only by understanding the development of the ego can motivation be put into its proper *social* context, and only by understanding the relation of needs, derived drives, frames of reference, and attitudes to the ego can motivation be placed in its proper *per-sonal* context. If we leave the ego out of account, our picture is inadequate and we deal only with some abstract or incomplete man."

30 Krech and Crutchfield, *op. cit.*, p. 64, point out that "Since the nature of the preferred goals depends largely upon the pattern of past experiences to which the individual has been exposed, it is to be expected that typical goals will differ from individual to individual and from culture to culture. The physical and social environment of the person limits and shapes the goals he may develop." Stagner devotes a chapter to "A Cultural Interpretation of Motivation."

31 Cf. T. M. Newcomb, *op. cit.*, p. 131 et seq.

32 Sherif and Cantril, *op. cit.*, p. 119; Newcomb, *op. cit.*, p. 327 says: "One's self is a value – a supreme value to most persons under most conditions"; Krech and Crutchfield, *op. cit.*, p. 52: "Among society's most pervasive effects on the individual is the development in him of self-regard. Self-regard, essentially, is the social in man. Self-regard is related to one's conception of himself; his proper role in life; his ideals, standards, and values. And in connection with self-regard some of the most potent demands and needs of the individual develop." E. R. Hilgard, "Human Motives and the Concept of the Self," *American Psychologist*, IV (1949), p. 378, likewise emphasizes the point that the "self of awareness is an object of value."

33 See Murphy, *op. cit.*, particularly Chap. 22; Snygg and Combs, *op. cit.*, p. 58, define "the basic human need as: the preservation and enhancement of the phenomenal self."

34 Fromm, *op. cit.*, pp. 119, 135–36.

35 Sherif and Cantril, *op. cit.* Krech and Crutchfield, *op. cit.*, p. 70, write: "The normal processes of growth and socialization of the individual is one of development and multiplication of various self-involvements with objects, people, groups, and social organization in the world about him. The involvements of the self in these more and more complex social relationships give birth to new needs, new demands, and new goals as the horizons, interests and concerns of the individual continuously expand." Cf. Sherif, *Outline of Social Psychology* (New York, 1948), Chaps. 11 and 12.

36 See Newcomb, *op. cit.*, p. 31, for a paradigm of motives conceived as intervening variables.

37 See Chaps. 19, 20 and Hallowell, 1951a.

38 E.g., Sherif, 1936, *op. cit.*, pp. 185–86, writes: "Values are the chief constituents of the ego ... these values are the social in man ... the values set the standards for the ego ... the violations of the standards of the ego and ego-misplacements are painful; they produce conflicts or feelings of guilt." Cf. Krech and Crutchfield, *op. cit.*, p. 68. See also Clyde Kluckhohn, "Values and Value-Orientations," in Talcott Parsons and Edward A. Shils (eds.), *Toward a General Theory of Action* (Cambridge, 1951).

39 Hilgard, *op. cit.*

40 See Chap. I and Spiro, *op. cit.*, p. 34 et seq.

41 The nature of this conflict stated in terms of personality structure may be construed differently. With reference to normative orientation as discussed in the context of this paper, it is worth noting that O. H. Mowrer, "Discipline and Mental Health," *Harvard Educational Review*, XVII (1947), pp. 289–90, contends "anxiety, guilt, depression, feelings of inferiority, and the other forces of neurosis stem, not from an id-ego conflict, but from an ego-super ego conflict. The trouble, in other words, is between the individual's conscious self and the values implanted in him by his social training, rather than between the conscious self, or ego, and the biologically given impulses, of lust and hostility," Cf. Mowrer, *Learning Theory and Personality Dynamics: Selected Papers* (New York, 1950), Chap. 18, "Learning Theory and the Neurotic Paradox." Furthermore, Mowrer (1950, *op. cit.*, p. 445) points out that "Freud has repeatedly remarked that repression of an impulse or memory characteristically occurs when it arouses affects which are so strong that they threaten to overwhelm the "ego." To this extent repression is definitely a "defensive" mechanism, but the resulting advantages usually prove to be achieved at a great cost. Repression is effected by excluding the symbolic representative of certain impulses from consciousness, i.e., from the dominant integrative center of the personality. Although repression thus brings a temporary peace, the process is likely to be pathogenic for the reason that

energies which formerly submitted themselves to the management of, and thereby strengthened, the "ego" are now withdrawn and left free to seek – through those habits called "symptoms" – their own irresponsible, nonintegrative paths to gratification. This is why Freud has characterized repression as a reversion from the "reality principle" to the more primitive "pleasure principle," from the "ego" (consciousness) to the "id" (unconsciousness)."

42 I.e., "by *denial* of impulses, or of traits, or of memories ...," or "through *disguise*, whereby the impulses, traits or memories are distorted, displaced or converted, so that we do not recognize them for what they are." Hilgard, *op. cit.*, p. 376.

43 Lincoln, *op. cit.*, p. 29.

44 Sleeman was an Anglo-Indian administrator who had thirty-five years' experience when his book was first published in 1844. (Major General Sir W. H. Sleeman, *Rambles and Recollections of an Indian Official*, [2 vols., Westminster, 1918].) I am indebted to Dr. Dorothy Spencer for this reference.

45 If suicide is *only* viewed in an "objective" or "naturalistic" frame of reference, it seems to contradict the "instinct of self-preservation," and thus present a paradox. On the other hand, if it be assumed that the constitution of the self in its behavioral environment may pattern the motivational system of the human individual in various ways, it does not seem paradoxical to say that the individual may come to view himself in terms of a self-image that makes it possible to transcend *bodily* destruction. A culturally constituted self-image makes it possible to make use of a conceptual dichotomy that not only permits the individual to maintain a positive attitude towards the self as an object of value but, at the same time, to rule out self-destruction as a consciously motivated act, since the self may be thought to be essentially indestructible. Consequently, it is possible to be highly motivated towards self-enhancement even if this involves bodily destruction. Where such an ideology prevails, any concept of "self-destruction" must be completely reduced to an unconscious level of motivation. In order for bodily destruction to involve self-destruction at the level of self-awareness, there must be a

self-image that conceives the body as a necessary substratum of the self. The so-called "instinct of self-preservation" is really a misnomer. For the biological forces that operate to preserve the life of the individual organism are not equivalent to, nor do they explain, all of the acquired drives that may become self-related in man.

46   E.g., stretching a snake until it breaks in two; cutting off an animal's leg while alive and letting it go; pulling all the feathers from a live bird.

47   Radin, *op. cit.*, p. 177, has called attention to the fact that "throughout the area inhabited by the woodland tribes of Canada and the United States, over-fasting entails death." For the Winnebago he elaborates this point by analyzing three tales, showing in each case how one of the cardinal virtues of these Indians, a sense of proportion, is violated by over fasting. Other Ojibwa cases are found in the literature. In one of them the bones of a boy who had over fasted were found by his father.

48   Hallowell, 1939a; Chaps. 16 and 14.

Part II

Emotion and Morality in Diverse Cultures

Introduction

Human Variations: A Population Perspective
on Psychological Processes

Humans vary more widely from population to population in their patterns of behavior (social organization, communication, and parental care) than any other animal species (Wilson, 1975). This poses a problem of understanding for humans and for the science dedicated to them: How are these intra-specific variations in behavior patterns related to other variations at the population level, e.g. in visible bodily features such as stature, skin color, or hair form? Should we assume that body form, language, and behavior are inherently related, that peoples who look and sound different must behave differently because of mental and moral characteristics that are inherited along with their bodily appearance and language? Or should we assume that, since an individual can become multilingual, undergo religious conversion, and learn to enjoy foreign food that once disgusted her – all while remaining the same in skin color, hair form, and body build – the connections between these aspects of human variation are loose or non-existent? There were no empirically grounded answers to these questions until the 20th century, though speculative and pseudo-scientific answers were abundant.

Most European and American speculations on human differences in the 19th century were cast in evolutionary terms: There were simple or primitive peoples like the natives of Africa, Australia and the Americas, and complex or civilized societies like our own. The languages, cultures, and appearances of the primitives were correlated, it was claimed, with inferior abilities to think and communicate, and might be hereditary. Other theories posited a wide variety of racial types, with hereditary differences in mental and moral characteristics as well as physique among diverse peoples.

Franz Boas (1859–1942), a young German anthropologist who came to the United States in 1884, considered all of these theories inadequate in terms of their empirical support and was determined to set the record straight with better data. Thirty years later, that is, by about 1914, he had done so. He and his students had shown that race, language and culture vary independently, a point that now seems obvious, and that there are no "primitive" languages in terms of basic features of phonology, grammar, etc. His work on physical growth in immigrant children demonstrated a degree of environmental influence that was inconsistent with fixed racial types, suggesting that the social environments of children might influence their development in a wide variety of ways. Through empirical research Boas not only freed anthropology from misconceptions of the past but also laid foundations for Sapir's construction of a theoretical framework for culture and personality (Chapter 2).

The work of Boas also laid foundations for future research in biological and linguistic anthropology. His demonstration of plasticity in physical growth, bolstered by later biomedical research on the nutritional processes involved, led to a mature science of human growth (Bogin, 2001). For example, Bogin and Loucky's (1997) demonstration that the Mayans of highland Guatemala, once known as the "pygmies of the New World", quickly grow in stature when they migrate to the United States, replicates Boas's (1912) study of immigrants in New York, but with better measures and more knowledge of the processes, lending additional credibility to an outcome predicted by Boas. The history of language development research is similar, in that a concept of environmental influence like that of Boas, bolstered by later identification of critical periods for language acquisition in childhood, has led to a far better understanding of the processes and outcomes of language socialization in diverse cultures (see Part IV).

The theory of culture and personality, as Sapir and the others mentioned in Part I constructed it, is not so easily broken down into measurable parts as physical growth and language development and could not be as easily integrated into the human population sciences. There were many easily criticized explorations and false starts in culture and personality research during the 1930s and 1940s, and this may be why Boas never commented on its value or promise. (He was equally quiet about psychoanalysis after hearing Freud's lectures at Clark University in 1909.) From Boas's point of view as a radical empiricist (and a prescient population scientist) there may have been too many unresolved concerns about what should be measured, how it should be measured, and the validity of measurement procedures. And as he might have predicted, some of the earlier starts using life histories, Rorschach testing, and other personality assessment procedures proved inadequate and were largely abandoned by anthropologists, as research in personality psychology itself came under empirical attack from psychologists in the 1960s.

Thus specific aspects of human variation like physical growth and language development have proved more amenable to the observation, measurement, and recording of a strict empirical approach than the psychological orientations and dispositions that were the foci of culture and personality studies. But those psychological orientations and dispositions remain in focus in contemporary psychological anthropology, and with good reason: they are the wellsprings, the controlling factors, that motivate human action. The methods for assessing them cannot simply be borrowed from another discipline but have had to be developed from within anthropology through ethnographic approaches.

Ethnography as we now know it came to American anthropology from Britain, partly through Malinowski's (1922) work on the Trobriand Islands, rather than through the Boasian tradition. It involves the fieldworker's synthesis of interviews, observations, anecdotes, and personal experiences gathered over an extended period to describe the beliefs and practices prevalent in a community and interpret them in organizational, semiotic, adaptive, and motivational terms. The investigator uses her own judgment and empathic understanding to construct this synthesis, and thus ethnography is not an exact and fully replicable record of a community's culture. It does not satisfy radical empiricist criteria for assessment, but it answers a need that raw transcriptions of interviews (which might satisfy such criteria) do not: Ethnography provides the contexts of individual experience.

Without knowing the contexts in which individuals experience their lives, we can make no valid assessment of their psychological patterns, orientations, or dispositions. One of the fatal flaws of psychometric assessment across cultures is misapprehension of context. Experiments of the 1930s and 1940s with "blind" scoring of Rorschach (inkblot) test responses of non-Western persons by "experts" who knew nothing of their culture showed that there is no psychological method analogous to an x-ray or blood test that can identify an underlying state, trait, or disposition without interference by intervening conditions. A person's response to an inkblot reflects the visual and social conventions to which he is accustomed as much as it does his own psychological tendencies. In our own culture we are familiar with the context and share it with the respondent; elsewhere we are bound to make mistakes without ethnography.

The key contexts revealing personal experience in a community always involve emotions and morality. An ethnographic description provides the norms, rules, and conventions for thinking, feeling, and acting in a community, revealing the moral weight that is given to doing something one way rather than another. In an ethnographer's entry to a community, she must learn how to greet those prepared to meet her and how to eat food that is offered according to local practices. This is her initiation into the moral order of that community, from which she will learn the first lessons, almost like a child, in what counts as good behavior and what does not. As fieldwork progresses, more will be learnt about the more abstract conceptions of the desirable of that community and how they affect individual preferences and aversions.

An individual's conventional behavior can conceal his actual motivations; that is, his conformity may disguise the psychological tendencies the ethnographer seeks to describe. This is where emotion comes in, as the fieldworker observes and interviews about the feelings, positive and negative, evoked or avoided by conventional or nonconventional behavior. As the articles in this section show in vivid detail, expression of emotions and interpretation of others' emotional expressions are themselves subject to the conventions and rules of a community's normative order. In fact, to understand the emotional responses of persons in another culture, it is necessary to know their conventions for emotional expression, and the ethnography of emotion becomes a pathway to deeper psychological understanding.

Taking a culture-specific approach to emotional experience does not deny that there are universal categories of human emotional expression. Darwin (1955 [1872]) proposed such categories in considerable detail, and Ekman revived Darwin's approach and has made it the basis for psychological research. In Ekman's view (as in that of Izard, 1994) there are six or seven basic emotions that hold for all humans and "cultural display rules" that govern their expression (and suppression) in a particular human society (Ekman and Davidson, 1994). The linguist Anna Wierzbicka

(1999) has proposed that the culture-specific emotion terms of all languages can be translated into a universal meta-language that preserves the contexts from which they derive meaning. There is some controversy over whether cultural meanings are lost in such translations (Shimizu, 2001), but on the whole Wierzbicka's approach represents a step forward toward a science of human emotion that might comprehend culture-specific meanings within a common framework for all humans.

An alternative approach from psychological anthropology was developed by Robert I. Levy (1973, 1984), who – on the basis of his research in Tahiti – formulated the concepts of *hypocognized* and *hypercognized* emotions, thus distinguishing emotional states and feelings that are unlabeled, suppressed, or denied (hypocognized) from those that are linguistically recognized and given emphasis in speech and interaction (hypercognized). This formulation raises the question of how you know people experience an emotion if it is hypocognized. The answer is through ethnographic fieldwork, clinical interviewing, and accounts by ethnographers of *their own* cultures, like that of Takie Sugiyama Lebra in Chapter 7.

Samples of ethnographic studies of emotion appear in this section of the *Reader*. There have been many such studies of high quality in recent decades (many more than I could reprint here). Their diversity and depth demonstrate not only human variability in emotional expression and experience but also the unpredicted cultural variations different peoples have wrung on what may be universal themes. In reading these accounts, one sees the empirical turn that many psychological anthropologists took in the later 20th century, shifting from the aim, derived from Freud, of plumbing the depths of the psyche to that of clarifying the surface of conscious experience through ethnographic research.

If we find it surprising how peoples of other cultures experience emotions, it is due in part to the relationships of emotion with morality and religion. Each one of the chapters that follow, Chapters 4–8, makes a connection between feelings, their public and private expressions, and the moral norms that range from the conventional to the sacred – or that are both conventional and sacred. Through the emotions it evokes, we learn the deeper meanings of normative behavior, but through the moral evaluations of emotions we learn how central they are in personal experience. By looking at emotions in the context of morality, and moral norms in emotional context, we can begin to understand personal experience in another culture.

Chapter 4: Jean Briggs provides powerful examples of how the ethnographer's experience can be used to reveal the emotional expectation of her hosts, the Inuit of eastern Canada.

Chapter 5: Geoffrey White analyzes morality and emotion with illustrations from his fieldwork in Melanesia.

Chapter 6: Usha Menon and Richard Shweder use the understanding of a single religious symbol from India to demonstrate how an important symbol in one culture (involving facial expression of emotion) can be opaque to bearers of another, while it is also variable in its meanings within the community in which it is part of a powerful religious narrative.

Chapter 7: Takie Sugiyama Lebra, an American anthropologist who grew up in Japan, provides the insights of an insider and outsider on moral feelings in a culture that has often been misconstrued and incompletely understood by outsiders.

Chapter 8: Medical anthropologists Arthur Kleinman and Byron Good, in the introduction to a landmark volume of 25 years ago, show the connections between cultural and psychiatric investigations of emotion. This chapter and Chapter 19 by Calabrese provide glimpses of the relevance of contemporary medical anthropology to psychological anthropology. (A Wiley-Blackwell reader on medical anthropology by Byron Good and MaryJo Del Vecchio Good is in progress.)

REFERENCES

Boas, Franz
1912   Instability of Human Types. In G. Spiller, ed., Papers on Interracial Problems Communicated to the First Universal Races Conference Held at London University, July 1911. Boston, MA: Ginn & Co.
Bogin, Barry
2001   The Growth of Humanity. New York: John Wiley & Sons.
Bogin, Barry and J. Loucky
1997   Plasticity, political economy and physical growth status of Guatemala Maya children living in the United States. American Journal of Physical Anthropology 102: 17–32.
Darwin, Charles
1955 [1872]   The Expression of Emotions in Animals and Men. New York: Philosophical Library.
Ekman, Paul and Davidson, R. J., eds.
1994   The Nature of Emotion: Fundamental Questions. Oxford: Oxford University Press.
Izard, Carroll
1994   Innate and Universal Facial Expressions: Evidence from Development and Cross-Cultural Research. Psychological Bulletin 115: 288–299.
Levy, Robert I.
1973   Tahitians: Mind and Experience in the Society Islands. Cambridge, MA: Harvard University Press.
1984   Emotion, Knowing and Culture. In R. A. Shweder and R. A. LeVine, eds., Culture Theory. New York: Cambridge University Press.
Malinowski, Bronislaw
1922   Argonauts of the Western Pacific. New York: E. P. Dutton.
Shimizu, Hidetada
2001   Introduction: Japanese Cultural Psychology and Empathic Understanding. In H. Shimizu and R. A. LeVine, eds., Japanese Frames of Mind: Cultural Perspectives on Human Development. New York: Cambridge University Press.
Wierzbicka, Anna
1999   Emotions across Languages and Cultures: Diversity and Universals. New York: Cambridge University Press.
Wilson, Edward O.
1975   Sociobiology: The Modern Synthesis. Cambridge, MA: Harvard University Press.

4

Emotions Have Many Faces: Inuit Lessons

Jean Briggs

In my work, the personal and professional are all tangled up together; and I learn best when I am personally, emotionally, involved in events – especially when I make mistakes. (I shouldn't be surprised if this were true of a great many other people, as well. Indeed, I have come to realize that Inuit – and other North American aboriginal people – are quite right when they say that one learns only from Experience.) In this paper I am going to focus on the most powerful learning experience I had as a novice anthropologist 43 years ago, and try to show you what insights grew out of it. I will wander a bit on my way to this goal in order to let you follow my learning process, because the *process* of my learning – my experiences of Inuit – determined very much *what* I learned about the concepts.

The experience in question was to be ostracized by an Inuit family in a remote and tiny camp of fishermen in the depths of the Canadian North in 1964 (Briggs 1970).² Like other anthropologists of that time, I was in search of an exotic world. I wanted to find that "human nature" was not the same the whole world over – that ways of thinking and being were profoundly different in different cultural worlds. More than that, I wanted more options for myself. I wanted to learn to belong in a different world – to learn to be an Inuk (an Esklmo). I liked what I had read as a child about Inuit life and myth; and I loved the wind, the cold, the snow, the silence, and the delicate plant life above treeline – all of which I had experienced as a child on the highest ridges of New Hampshire's mountains. So I arrived in the small Arctic settlement of Gjoa Haven and arranged with the kind help of the Anglican missionaries there – man and wife, both Inuit – to be adopted as a daughter into one of four families who lived in a camp 150 miles away, in a river mouth out in the middle of the tundra.

Unfortunately for my dreams, but fortunately for my professional life, I quickly discovered that it was hard to be an Inuit daughter. It took me a much longer time to discover that I was a Bad daughter from the all-important point of view of my Inuit parents and relatives. I was much more a creature of my own culture than I had realized. One never does realize things until one experiences contrast.

My badness took various forms: I was sometimes slow and ungracious in responding to requests that I stop writing and make tea; I sometimes preferred sitting at home to playing giggly games of tag; and was sometimes reluctant to share supplies if I feared they were being used up too fast. Worst of all, I showed in antisocial ways my displeasure, my anxieties, fatigue, unhappiness. I withdrew into silence; I snapped; I said "No" instead of "Yes". And after a year – thinking I was being Good this time and feeling very righteous about it – I committed the worst sin of all:

Jean L. Briggs, Emotions Have Many Faces: Inuit Lessons, paper presented at 18th Annual Interdisciplinary Conference of the International Federation for Psychoanalytic Education, The Reach of the Mind, October 19–21, 2007. © Jean L. Briggs. Reprinted with kind permission of the author.

I told some visiting American fishermen that my Inuit father didn't want to lend them his canoe. He had, in fact, earlier, in the privacy of his tent, instructed me to tell them that – but, it turned out, his instructions were wish-fulfilling fantasy. He wanted not to lend his canoe, right enough; he was afraid the fishermen would break it up, as they had broken the only other canoe in the camp. We needed the canoe. Our autumn and winter supplies were cached on an island; we had nothing to repair canoes with, and were cut off from the store in Gjoa Haven until the sea froze in December. But Inuttiaq would never in the world have actually refused the request of the *qallunaat*, the white men. Such a refusal would have violated Inuit rules of courteous, obliging behaviour. It would also have caused – it did cause – Inuit to fear reprisals. So, when the Americans left, next day – for quite other reasons (fear that new ice would freeze their float plane into the inlet) – the Inuit assumed they were angry with us – even though, in the end, they had gotten the canoe. The result was that not only my family but everybody in the Inuit camp ostracized me.

I suppose this reaction seems a bit extreme to you, and more than a bit puzzling. I hope it will become clearer, later, when I tell you more about how Inuit emotions are shaped. At the time this all happened, I didn't understand any better than you do what was going on.

I didn't understand that I was ostracized, either. It was so subtly done that, although I vaguely felt something was wrong, I blamed my malaise on having been too long "in the bush": fatigue; longing for my own world. Then I read the letters that two camp members had written to the missionaries in Gjoa Haven. The authors had given the letters to me to keep until the annual plane should come to pick up any children who might be going out to school. Perhaps they intended I should read the letters, perhaps not. In any case, reading them was a revelation. The letters said that I was unhappy, easily angered, incapable of learning the proper behaviour that Inuit had tried to teach me, and therefore ought not to be there, studying "real people", that is, Inuit. It was that experience, above all, that started me on the road to studying Inuit emotions. It attuned me to noticing the sorts of emotional behaviour that upset

Inuit, and the values they placed on proper emotional behaviour. It honed my observational abilities to an acute perception of the previously invisible, inaudible signals that something was wrong in a relationship. Most particularly, of course, I learned to see the subtle signs that I was ostracized. Finally, the experience motivated me to analyse the ways in which Inuit managed emotional deviance. That study became my dissertation: *Never in Anger*.

Nowadays, studying emotions is all the rage (so to speak). There's even an international, multidisciplinary organization for research on emotion. But at the time *Never in Anger* was published, anthropologists (with the fortunate exception of my thesis supervisor) did not consider emotions an appropriate subject for investigation. Anthropologists did recognize that emotions existed; that rules for their expression varied from society to society; that expressive style might profoundly "flavour" a society (Benedict 1946) or a period in the life cycle (Mead 1928); and that failure to infuse themselves with the right flavour might make individuals extremely uncomfortable. Nevertheless, the analytic lense tended to be focused on the situation, the behaviour, the belief that caused a given emotion, not on the emotion itself. And nobody considered the possibility that emotions might be constructed and construed differently in different worlds. Fear, resentment, trust, love might be felt more or less frequently, and with greater or lesser intensity in different societies, but fear was fear, resentment was resentment, trust was trust, love was love.

I think one reason why emotions got short shrift for a long time was that they were considered *infra dig.*, not a worthy subject of study. We see them as destructive of social order, opposed to Reason (with a capital R) and (alas) – even in our enlightened times – more characteristic of women than of men. Thinking of emotion this way is a little like thinking of fire only in the context of forest fires.

Nevertheless, in 1964 my attention, too, was initially focussed on emotion because of its destructive qualities. I wanted to know what had gone wrong in my relationships with my Inuit family, so that I could restore those relationships. The Inuit themselves conceptualized the problem in emotional terms: "She's not happy here"; "she gets angry easily". So, following their lead and my own predispositions, I too concluded that the difficulty was a matter of emotion. It seemed to me, initially, that the problem arose from the contrast between Inuit rules of expression and mine. Then, trying to understand why my improper expressive behaviour was so extremely upsetting to Inuit, I began to notice the social meanings and values they placed on emotions like happiness and anger – meanings and values that were different from mine. For them, a happy person was a good person, a safe person; anger was mindless, childish; also – in the hands of a strong man – dangerous: an angry person might kill. For Inuit, social order did not derive merely from following rules of expression, it depended on *feeling* the culturally appropriate emotions. As they saw it – and again I agree with them – emotions motivated behaviour.

Once my interest was piqued, I set about studying Inuit emotions in a variety of ways. I listened to everyday conversations and when I heard an emotion word (i.e., the name of an emotion) used, I recorded as much as I could of the context: the speakers, the topic, and the content of the speech. Then, in the context of learning the language, I asked people to tell me what the emotion words I had heard meant. Sometimes I also watched events that were clearly emotionally charged and, especially if one or more of the actors were children, I would ask an adult who had been present what (in their understanding) the children had been feeling: was the child feeling *kanngu-* [shy]? *ilira-* [afraid of being scolded]? *kappia-* [afraid of being injured]?

These investigations led to several insights. First I was struck by how differently Inuktitut (the Inuit language) categorized emotions, as compared with English. But at the same time I learned that emotion concepts are very shifty multifaceted "things" – almost kaleidoscopic – and that one can get very different impressions of a concept depending on how one gets one's information. Sometimes contradictory impressions. Formal definitions are only the tips of very large, and most often emotionally perilous, icebergs. I will use words for attachment feelings as an example.

In all known dialects of Inuktitut (and even proto-Eskimo), there are two quite distinct words [really word-*bases*][3] for what English-speakers call "love": *nallik-* and *unga-*; and they represent two very different concepts. When one asks what *nallik-* means, one is regularly told that it is a nurturant, protective attachment, rather similar to our notion of Biblical love, as in "love thy neighbour as thyself". There is "pity" in it, a feeling of concern for the unfortunate and helpless; a wish to help. The speakers I lived with considered *nallik* a mature emotion. Its presence defined a good person and a good parent. But when talking about their experiences of *nallik*-ing in the context of individual social relationships, people said it was undesirable, uncomfortable, to feel *nallik-*; they said they *nallik*-ed very unevenly – *nallik*-ing some of their children more than others, this one or that one "too much", and some not at all; and they said they didn't like to *be nallik*-ed, either. Strange ways to talk about the highest value? We'll come back to this.

Unga-, on the other hand, is a needy, dependent attachment; and the speakers I lived with considered it *im*mature. They always defined it as: "The way a small child feels toward its mother; it cries when mother is not there." Defining the word, people will tell you that only children feel *unga-*; that it's a childish and uncomfortable feeling, which adults outgrow. However, in the context of ordinary conversation, one discovers that *everybody* feels *unga-*. Adults feel it as well as children – not only toward other adults but also toward small children. People considered it strange – even unnatural – that I claimed not to feel *unga-* toward my mother at the age of 35. And once a young father predicted that when I left to go home, I would feel *unga-* for his three-year-old daughter, Maata, a child I was fond of, "because she has no understanding". (We'll meet Chubby Maata again in this paper.) I'm not sure why her lack of "understanding" should have made me feel *unga-*, rather than *nallik-*[pity], but it's possible that Jaani's remark points to a dimension that *nallik-* and *unga-*share in spontaneous usage: they both give rise to tenderness.

In Canadian Inuktitut there is no specific "love" word that refers to an egalitarian, reciprocal attachment and enjoyment of another's company. (One may ask "why not?" – and I have an idea – but I've written about that in another paper (Briggs 1995).) In the two dialects I studied in the '60s and '70s, if one wanted to talk about such a relationship one used a term *piu+gi-* (or *pitsau+gi-*, depending on dialect), which can be translated literally as: "consider [another person] good"; or "be in a good relationship with [a person]"; or: to "like [someone or something]". Simple enough so far. But the use of this concept contains dangerous pitfalls, both for children and for adults. I'll illustrate the child's pitfalls later.

These kinds of data taught me that (as I had hoped) the repertoire of emotions is not the same the world over. There is no universal "set" of emotion concepts. Of course it also confirmed the well-known fact that *attitudes* toward specific emotions vary culturally. But most interesting (to me) was the discovery that strong and troublesome ambivalences that characterize a great many – if not most – Inuit emotions (with the possible exception of anger, which is completely appalling) – and even later, the realization that the stability, the smooth functioning, of nuit society depended on those ambivalences.

My insights into the emotional plots of Inuit life followed from my suddenly noticing (after 10 years or so of close – but blind – acquaintance with Inuit) the emotionally powerful "playful" interactions – interrogations and "dramas" – that were regularly enacted with children of about three years old in the camp where I was living. Interrogations and dramas in which the children learned to *feel* the emotions, both rewarding and painful, that motivated Inuit social life; to *experience* their consequences in their social contexts; and so, most importantly, to *use* those emotions in living their lives. (That discovery is what my 2nd book is about.)

I use the word "play" in the senses of both game and drama, but most importantly the interactions are playful in that adult players perceive themselves to be "pretend-talking"; they don't intend to follow up with "serious" *action*, statements or questions that sound very serious, indeed. What the adults are doing is "causing thought" – a concept that fundamentally guides Inuit educational practice. Adults stimulate children to think by presenting them with emotionally powerful problems, which the children can't ignore.

One way of doing this is to ask a question that, if taken seriously, could raise alarming specters. And when the child experiments with various answers, trying to find a safe solution, the questioner points out, dramatically, the dangers in each one. In this way, adults raise to consciousness, or actually create, issues that the child will surely perceive to be of great consequence for his or her life. "Why don't you kill your baby brother?" "Why don't you die so I can have your nice new shirt?" "Your mother's going to die – look, she's cut her finger – do you want to come live with *me*?"

Questions like these are asked all the time in interactions between adults and all small children. The adult questioners quite consistently see themselves, and are perceived by other adults, to be good-humoured, benign, and playful. In fact, the dramas could not exist at all if they were not enacted in "play" mode, because their aggressiveness violates the rules that govern "serious" behavior. But the children who are played with don't know this. For the adult, the interaction is part idle pastime, part serious teaching device, part test of how much understanding the child has developed; and more often than appears to *our* ears, it is a celebration of a child's existence and dearness. It is also frequently a means by which adults can vicariously enact their own interpersonal dramas, expressing, and perhaps relieving, their own concerns and problems. And all these motives exist in continuously shifting combinations. Uninitiated children, who don't understand that adults don't mean exactly what they say, may be severely challenged by the questions, especially as the interrogations are often focussed on transitions, even crises, that a child may be going through: weaning; adoption (very common in Inuit society); or perhaps the birth of a new sibling. When children have learned to disentangle the playful from the serious in a particular drama, and when they can no longer be drawn into the trap that the adult is setting, adults will stop playing that game with them.

An important feature of these interrogations and dramas is that they rarely give children answers. They hint, they nudge, they load the dice – and if a child gets too upset they comfort: "I was only joking; have some tea"; or "Do you really imagine he doesn't *nallik-you?*" But they push children hard, and they don't make solutions easy. Indeed, usually there are no permanent solutions; salvation lies in being continually alert to multifaceted and shifting situations. One of my favourite interrogations illustrates this:

A three-year-old girl, whom I call Chubby Maata (Briggs 1998), was sitting on my lap, playing with my nose and the pens in my pocket. Her mother asked her: "Do you consider Yiini good?" Maata raised her brows: "Yes." Mother: "You do?! Do you know that she's a qallunaaq? Do you know that qallunaat scold? Do you know that she's going to go very far away to her country? Do you want to go with her?" Chubby Maata began to look at me solemnly and searchingly. Mother: "Do you consider Yiini good?" Maata wrinkled her nose: "No." Mother in a tone of surprise: "You don't?! Do you imagine she doesn't *nal-lik-* you? Who gives you tea? Who gives you bannock and jam? ... Do you consider her good?" Maata: "No." Her mother laughed.[3]

There are clues that children can use in their efforts to figure out what adults mean and where the dangers hide, but they aren't easy to read. One clue, I think, lies in resonance among what I call "key phrases" and recurrent themes. Children hear the same questions and suggestions over and over again: "Want to come live with me?" "Whose is it?" "Take it home." "Who's your daddy?" "Your daddy's no good; do you consider him good?" "Who *do* you consider good?" Tracking three-year-old Chubby Maata over a period of six months, I can see her attending to those key phrases or questions, and altering her behaviour as she learns more about their implications.

One day, for example, Maata was visiting me with her mother. Maata – who was very fond of tea with milk – made some comment about the milk on my food platform. Liila said, "Take it home." Chubby Maata smiled self-

consciously and ducked her head. Liila repeated several times, "Take it home". Maata as consistently refused. "Why not?" "Because I'm scared." Two hours later, Chubby Maata visited me with her doting father, who poured her a cup of tea and asked her tenderly: "Are you going to put milk in it?" Maata smiled self-consciously. He asked her again, and again she smiled – and this time she added: "I don't own it."[4]

Another kind of clue to adult meaning comes from tones of voice. Small children are often spoken to in a repertoire of emotionally exaggerated voices, which I have labelled: fear; disgust; saccharine persuasion; tendemess, and so on. But watch out! Voices sometimes convey messages very different from the verbal content that goes with them; or both voice and words may be opposite to what is really intended. A criticism can be delivered in a tender voice ("What a darling little intrusively persistent selfishly demanding child she is"); and a loving message can be said in a disgusted voice with disgusted words ("Aaaaq! You stink! Do you wrongly imagine you're good?"). Indeed, an Inuit child's job is not an easy one.

Nevertheless, little by little, as dangerous key phrases and puzzling voices resonate with one another, children build up webs of association, and meanings cumulate.

Many of the dramas enacted with Chubby Maata have to do with attachment. It seems to me that attachment entails danger in any culture, because, whatever its specific nature, it creates vulnerabilities. Bonds of some sort – always imperfect – must exist. But cultures colour those bonds in a great variety of ways, imbue them with qualitatively different kinds of fears and longings, as well as satisfactions and rewards; and they combine and weight these emotions in various ways. I will trace out some of the interlocking strands in the web of attachment that Chubby Maata was weaving at the age of three, with the help of playful dramas like the following.

In this drama she was invited to come and live with a neighbour, a young woman with whom Chubby Maata had a relaxed, friendly, playful relationship. The young woman's invitation was issued (repeatedly) in the saccharine persuasive tone. She pretended that the decision was entirely up to Maata; but when Maata consistently refused to come, her friend became more forceful and pretended to steal Maata's puppy so that Maata would follow her pet. Finally, Maata hesitated before refusing to come, then said aloud: "Ih! I almost agreed!" Immediately, the neighbour swooped on Maata, picked her up and turned toward the door, saying: "You agree!" Maata cried out, struggled out of her captor's arms and retreated to the lap of her uncle. From this position she initiated a game of her own: a race she ran with herself, to and from the door, saying each time she set off: "One, two, talee, GO!" I think she was re-enacting the neighbour's threatening game, but this time she was securely controlling her own fate.

But was she secure? Suddenly, the uncle slapped Maata's bottom, and pretended that it was I who had attacked her. When Maata looked at me suspiciously, her mother asked her whether she considered me good. Maata said she did not, whereupon all the adults present began to inquire systematically into her likes and dislikes: "Do you consider *me* good?" "What about *me*?" Maata rejected almost everybody, including the neighbour girl and even her mother, but when her uncle asked if she considered him good, she said yes. After all, he was her "protector" against the seductive neighbour – until he turned traitor; but Maata was not sure that he did play her false. Immediately, he said in a tender tone: "Just me alone, yes?" This time, his perfidy was clear to Maata. Exclusive attachment is disapproved of, except – within limits – in the case of spouses; and Maata sensed this. She rushed off to the door in a frenzied race with herself: "One, two, talee, GO!" (Let me out of here! says her frenzy.) There is much more, but I can't go into that now.[5]

Clearly, this drama tells Maata that attachment (unlabelled in the drama) has its dangers. Both being attracted to, and being attractive to, neighbours could cost her her home. So she says she doesn't like her erstwhile friend; she doesn't consider her good. Her mother is watching Maata's every move to see whether she feels appropriately *unga-* (dependently attached) to her and to home. Both mother and neighbour certainly approve Maata's decision to stay home – though they don't say so. On the other hand, they are amused at Maata's rejection of everybody, because rejection (like exclusive attachment) is outlawed in Inuit society. Both are signs that one doesn't feel *nallik-*; one is not a good person.

Maata is on a tightrope. Let me spell it out for you, drawing on other dramas in addition to this one. She has to know where she belongs and must feel strongly bound to that home, to the point where she unquestioningly rejects others' invitations, which often masquerade in *nallik-* clothing. Safety lies in *unga-*, because, if she doesn't feel *unga-*, she could be stolen or adopted. Or else the protector she doesn't feel *unga-*toward could be stolen. But at the same time, feeling *unga-*is a little childish. To unmask false *nallik-* Maata has to be watchful and suspicious of other people's intentions toward her. But she has to be sharp enough to recognize when false *nallik-* is playful and harmless, so she can react with equanimity and humour. She should never let mistrust and *unga-* cause her to reject others' real *nallik-*feelings for her, and she should *nallik-*others in turn, so that people will not resent her standoffishness or neglect, and retaliate by attacking or abandoning her. But (back full circle) she should not *nallik-*, or allow herself to be *nallik-*ed *too* much, or too exclusively, either, because then she could be stolen or adopted.

Are you hopelessly confused? Think of how confused Chubby Maata must be. I am showing you only one small (and very oversimplified) fragment of the tapestry that is Maata's world as she experiences it. Notice that the weaving of that tapestry generates very mixed – and mutually entangled – attitudes toward all forms of attachment: the highly valued *nallik-*; the devalued *unga-*; and the reciprocal *piugi-*, "considering good"; while at the same time, it makes all three indispensable to Maata's social and emotional life. Maata has to tread a treacherous path, in order to behave appropriately and keep herself out of trouble.

It is these playful (and at the same time serious) experiences with the plots of everyday life that teach Maata what *nallik-*, *unga-*, and *piugi-* – as well as the social fear called *ilira-* – feel like, and thus, what they mean. As we watch her learning, I think we can understand what people meant when they told me that these feelings made them uncomfortable.

Perhaps it is less clear why such tangled and ambivalent emotions – not to mention doubts about people's intentions – are *useful* to Chubby Maata and to her campmates. I can't give you a full picture, but let me remind you of just a few characteristics of Inuit hunting society. (1) Hunters had to be both autonomous in action and strongly motivated to come home and feed their families. Families had to help each other, too, because resources were limited and luck never fell evenly. (2) People were often lost, through accident or death or just moving away. (3) There were no law enforcement institutions; and forceful settlement of conflict was impossibly dangerous. People had to settle disputes by avoiding them. And one way to avoid them was to anticipate others' needs and fill them before they were expressed.

How do ambivalent emotions, suspicions, and fears of imaginary dangers contribute to such a social situation? In Inuit society, strong ties of both *unga-* and *nallik-* motivated extraordinary efforts to provide for one's family, even in case of famine. *Nallik-* ensured that responsibility was more widely exercised, too. At the same time, discomfort with attachment and fear of the imagined power of others – that is, *ilira-* – energized autonomous decision-making and action. People strongly wanted not to be interfered with; not to be controlled or told what to do, as someone who *nallik*-ed or *unga*-ed you might try to do. Ambivalence about attachment also helped people to defend against loss. Often, they simply withdrew, emotionally, when they feared catastrophe – sometimes to the point of rejecting a child who unexpectedly came home, cured, from the hospital: the child was already effectively dead. Finally, *ilira-* – fear of a power that was hardly ever exercised "seriously", but that (thanks to the dramas) was blown up to nightmare proportions in imagination – motivated people to be alert to the slightest sign of others' displeasure, and to quietly, autonomously avert trouble. If *I* had had this sort of sensitivity when I first went to live with Inuit, they might not have had to ostracize me.

Tracing out Chubby Maata's entanglements has led me to the conclusion that Inuit social life is experienced by Inuit as a mosaic of emotionally charged issues – a mosaic of dilemmas, which are never permanently resolved. Some issues may be latent at any point in time; but they can be evoked again in a moment by any small sign of trouble, or merely by a question that resonates with the questions one was asked in childhood – just as the question "Are you angry, Yiini?", asked by a 13-year-old on Baffin Island in 1979, made my stomach knot up in memory of ostracism in 1964 thousand miles away, before that 13-year-old was born.

Now I think you can understand better why Inuttiaq was so upset when I told the qallunaat he didn't want to lend his canoe. Inuttiaq's instruction to me not to lend the canoe, like the young neighbour's seductive threat to Chubby Maata, was a wish-fulfilling exercise of power in imagination. The neighbour, just married, was really looking forward to having a daughter of her own, and might have liked to adopt Maata, who was a charming child. Inuttiaq really disliked and feared the American fishermen and would have liked to refuse them his canoe. Chubby Maata and I both mistook fantasy for reality. Maata's interpretation frightened only herself; mine frightened Inuttiaq. At the same time, when I spoke to the qallunaat, in his presence, I deprived him of his legitimate stance of authority, the stance of an autonomous decision maker. I also deprived him of his goodness, which would have been manifested in the *nallik-* behaviour of lending the canoe; and I ran a risk of conflict with the dangerous qallunaat. I made him feel *ilira-*.

Well, that's a lot of very specific Inuit data. But of course I have not been talking only about Inuit society and culture. I have been talking about the constructive power of emotions in social life, and about social and psychological processes of meaning construction that are certainly widespread – if not, in one variant or another, universal. I did not find in the Arctic the utterly unique human nature that I originally, naively, hoped to find. But I did find a fascinating variation on human themes.

I also discovered – it seems obvious *now* – that thought – at least about social and psychological matters – is never abstract; meaning and the understanding of meaning are always based on real life experience in real life situations.

I have come to think – along with increasing numbers of other scholars – that the meanings of emotions are always inextricably embedded in – not only coloured but profoundly shaped by – the contexts in which they are used: the purposes of their users, and the associations and memories of their hearers.

This is why investigation of what emotion concepts mean to their users can tell one so much about those users: their social arrangements and personal relationships, their values, their ideas about human nature and proper behaviour, and in general, the emotional texture of life: what it *feels* like to be an Inuk (or another kind of person), living in a particular time and place, with particular associates.

NOTES

1   This paper is a slightly modified version of a paper that was delivered in a distinguished lecture series at the Memorial University of Newfoundland, March 1995. The series was designed to acquaint both the university at large and the general public with the work of individual scholars. The original version of the paper was published in *Anthropologica* XLII (2000), pp. 157–164.

2   This incident is described at length in Chapter 6 of *Never in Anger* (Briggs, 1970).

3   Inuktitut is a polysynthetic language, one in which elements that would be separate words in English are all strung together into one word. Thus, an Inuktitut verb usually translates as an English sentence. My favourite example is: qupannuaqpaarjuaqhiuqatigijumangngitaatigulluunniinnguuq [they said they didn't even want to come hunting little horned larks with us]. The 'base' of this sentence is 'little horned larks'. The 'base' of an emotion word is the name of the emotion.

4   Elements of this interrogation are found also in other dramas, some of which are recorded in Briggs 1998. See, for example, pages 97–98, 167, and 169.

5   These incidents in their entirety can be found in Briggs 1998:211–213. Variations on the same themes occur in an episode recorded on pages 167–168.

6   The drama described in the preceding two paragraphs is the subject of Chapter 4 of Briggs 1998. See pages 91–115.

REFERENCES

Benedict, Ruth
1946   *The Crysanthemum and the Sword.* New York: World Publishing.

Briggs, Jean L.
1970   *Never in Anger.* Cambridge, Mass.: Harvard University Press.

Briggs, Jean L.
1995   "The Study of Inuit Emotions: Lessons from a Personal Retrospective." In: J. A. Russell et. al. (eds.), *Everyday Conceptions of Emotion.* Dordrecht, The Netherlands: Kluwer Academic Publishers.

Briggs, Jean L.
1998   *Inuit Morality Play.* New Haven: Yale University Press and St. John's, Nfld.: ISER Books.

Mead, Margaret
1928 (1973)   *Coming of Age in Samoa.* New York: American Museum of Natural History.

5

Moral Discourse
and the Rhetoric of Emotion

Geoffrey M. White

Theories of emotion and theories of culture have not always acknowledged their mutual relevance. To the extent that relations have been explored, this has usually come under the rubric of "culture and personality" – with the former regarded as the domain of public symbols and shared cognitions and the latter as that of individual affects and motivations. As Lutz (1985) has noted, this compartmentalization, and the implied division of labor between anthropology and psychology, parallel neatly our folk model of the person, which tends to dichotomize worlds of thinking and feeling, of society and the individual. In this chapter I explore briefly some of the ways in which culture theory and emotion theory (or, more broadly, self theory) may enrich one another. I do this by arguing that discourse occupies a strategic place in the ethnographic study of emotion and culture, and illustrate my argument with an example of emotive discourse from a Solomon Islands society.

Parallel to such familiar dichotomies as competence-performance and language-speech, approaches to discourse and discourse analysis tend to be split between those that emphasize conceptual process (e.g., Holland and Quinn 1987) and those that are largely interactional (e.g., Gumperz 1982).[1] Whereas the former,

more textual approaches are concerned with interpretive models, the latter focus to a greater degree on situated practices and institutional structures. This chapter explores points of convergence between these approaches by searching out relations between ideology and praxis in a specific, culturally constituted discourse of emotion referred to as "disentangling" (*grau-rutha*). Beginning with a culturally defined and socially situated activity – disentangling – it is possible to ask, "What are people doing with talk of emotion in this context?" and "What are the presuppositions and social conditions necessary for the rhetoric of disentangling to have the pragmatic effects it does?" Noting that emotion talk in this context not only represents but creates social reality, the analysis identifies specific rhetorical moves that work to transform socioemotional reality – specifically, by transmuting emotions of divisiveness into those of solidarity.

Emotion Schemas, Inference, and Ambiguity

Attributions of emotion obtain much of their social meaning from ethnopsychological understandings about the role of emotions in

Geoffrey M. White, Moral Discourse and the Rhetoric of Emotion from *Language and the Politics of Emotion*, ed. Catherine A. Lutz and Lila Abu-Lughod, Cambridge University Press, Cambridge, New York, Port Chester, Melbourne, Sydney and Editions de la Maison des Sciences de l'Homme, Paris. © Maison des Sciences de l'Homme and Cambridge University Press, 1990, pp. 46–68. Reprinted with permission of Cambridge University Press.

mediating social action (Lutz 1987). Folk models of social process are frequently structured in terms of scenariolike schemata that represent emotions as arising in social situations and compelling certain types of response. At a general level, the chain of reasoning represented in emotion schemas takes the following from (see Lutz 1987:293–4):

SOCIAL EVENT
↓
EMOTION
↓
ACTION RESPONSE

This representational format captures only the broad, simplified outline of a highly generalized structure – a "prototypical scenario" of social and emotional process (Lakoff and Kovecses 1987).[2] But positing this type of structure is useful in directing attention to specific classes of inference likely to obtain in emotive discourse. Although not all emotional understanding adheres to the interpersonal character of the preceding schema, it is hypothesized that such structures occupy the heartland of emotional discourse across cultures.

Culturally defined emotions are embedded in complex understandings about identities and scenarios of action, especially concerning the sorts of event that evoke it, the relations it is appropriate to, and the responses expected to follow from it.[3] To the extent that these understandings are elaborated in a generalized model, talk of a specific emotional response implicitly characterizes an action or event as an instance of a general type. In most cultures, a limited number of key emotions encode such generalized understandings. Applying these conceptions to the great diversity of everyday happenings sets up a dialectic between structure and event in which particular events are assimilated to prior structures of understanding. At the same time, the conceptual models so used may themselves by modified as they are accommodated to the comprehension of ongoing events. Analysis of this type of accommodation, beyond the scope of this chapter, would deal with historical transformations in the institutionalized patterns of emotion.

As an example of the type of emotion schema outlined here, consider the English-language concept of "anger." Commonsense understandings of anger posit that it typically follows from a moral violation that infringes upon the self, leading to a desire for retribution (Lakoff and Kovecses 1987). More than any other English-language emotion term, "anger" has been frequently applied in ethnographic accounts of social and psychological processes across cultures (e.g., Briggs 1970; Harris 1978; Valentine 1963). For the most part, it is only those studies with a stated interest in ethnopsychological meaning that have examined directly issues of translation and cross-cultural relevance (see, e.g., Myers 1988; Poole 1985; Rosaldo 1980; Schieffelin 1983). These studies have much to say about the culturally specific ways in which angerlike emotions adhere to local contours of meaning. And yet, the English word "anger" remains a comparison point for these and other ethnographic studies. Allowing for the inevitable distortions that occur from the cross-cultural application of English-language terms, the reason such "translations" work to the extent that they do is that they rely on cross-cultural convergences in prototype scenarios used to conceptualize emotion. Thus, for example, core elements in the meaning of American English "anger" and Santa Isabel *di'a tagna*, to be discussed, may both be outlined in terms of the following action-emotion-response sequence.[4]

TRANSGRESSION (Other, Self)
↓
[*di'a tagna*, "anger"]
↓
RETRIBUTION (Self, Other)

Even in this simplified form, denuded of social contextual information, the prototype schema gives an indication of the types of inferential paths that make emotion talk a moral idiom (i.e., a mode of evaluating and constituting social reality). As a personal response mediating social action and reaction, specific emotions such as "anger" designate interactive scenarios with known evaluative and behavioral implications. The attribution of emotion brings to bear presupposed knowledge about the desirability or undesirability of generic courses of action on the interpretation of events. For example, prototypic "anger" represented in the preceding schema would be regarded as problematic because of the implied propensity for retribution and the harm to persons and the social order likely to result. In this manner, an expression of emotion becomes a pronouncement or claim (often implicit) about the way things are or, more significantly, the way they ought to be (Bailey 1983). To continue with the example of "anger", expressions of "anger" draw attention to an antecedent event as a moral breach (i.e., as a generic type of social action) while at the same time implying the need for corrective action. Some examples from the discourse of disentangling, which is centrally concerned with problems of conflict, transgression, and "anger", will illustrate.

In one disentangling meeting, where people are encouraged to "talk out" their bad feelings about conflicted events, an older man, a village catechist, recounted an incident in which he chastised one of his neighbors, Edi (also a catechist), for hitting several misbehaving children. The alleged hitting runs counter to a strong proscription on the physical punishment of children and against the generalized ethos of nonaggression (White 1985b). Reporting his own speech on the occasion when he confronted his neighbor, the old man quoted himself:

Catechists shouldn't hit, shouldn't be angry towards children and people, man. [They] should take care of them, just like chiefs, in order to be good. But you were hitting children. ... I was very angry with you, Edi. Because you are a catechist, you should be teaching people, not hitting.

Here the speaker's "anger" is attributed to a clear-cut violation of moral strictures – a widely shared proscription against physical punishment of children. As he began his narrative of this event, the speaker threatened to report his neighbor, implying that his own felt "anger" was inclined toward some kind of retribution. In this way, the speaker's "anger" mediated an antecedent event (hitting) with his own impulse toward a corrective response (reporting).

It may seem ironic that the speaker says that he got "angry" at Edi for getting "angry." The difference, and it is an important one, is that the two angers are differently contextualized: between adult catechist and child on the one hand, and between mature men on the other. In the A'ara view, sharp "anger" should not be expressed in relations marked by asymmetries of power; hence the speaker's analogy between Edi's relation to the children and a chief's relation to his followers. Talk of "anger", then, is not only an idiom of moral claims. It also indexes social relations. Another example illustrates the relational rhetoric of emotion even more clearly.

In one of the recorded meetings, a man claimed to be "angry" with his sister's son for stealing betel nut from one of his trees. But because he simply expressed "anger", without acknowledging either the asymmetry or the close relation of kinship between himself and his nephew, others saw his talk of anger as inappropriate. Two other participants responded not to the act of stealing but to the uncle's stated "anger" toward his maternal nephew. One of the listeners spoke to the uncle, saying:

This kind of talk that you are making is as if you are all separate [soasopa] people. It is better to speak to your nephew to teach him, like I do with my nephew. ... That kind of ["angry"] talk can be aimed at other people, but to our own nephews, our own children, it is very bad.

The speaker's reprimand mirrors that of the first example. Both focus on the social context of expressed "anger": one between adult and child, the other-between mother's brother and sister's son. This second example is more explicit about the primacy of the social component ("["anger"] can be aimed at other people"). Given these assumptions about emotion and morality, it can be seen that the experience of anger poses a dilemma here: Anger' expressed in the context of community relations is likely to be regarded as contrary to the ideals of solidarity, whereas suppressed "anger," according to the folk theory of misfortune, poses a danger to the self and others (see White 1985a for more on this).

As an arena for the sanctioned expression of emotion, disentangling would appear to be a culturally constituted solution to the dilemma of suppressed "anger". Yet, as the preceding examples indicate, this is not as straightforward as it might seem. In disentangling as in other contexts, talk of "anger" in close relations is likely to be disapproved. The disentangling context does not legitimate expressions of hostility that are not tempered by ideals of solidarity and the goal of repairing damaged relations. What it does provide is an opportunity for the creation of a social reality in which "angry" events are rhetorically transformed and damaged relations symbolically repaired.

Talk of "anger" is somewhat out of place in disentangling sessions, defined as they are as occasions for reestablishing community solidarity rather than uncovering transgressions or imposing sanctions. The examples cited account for most of the "anger" attributions in the recorded meetings. Instead, one finds numerous examples of talk about "sadness" (*di'a nagnafa*) and "shame" (*mamaja*). The following analysis suggests that these attributions are particularly well suited to the work of transforming "angry" events to fit the avowed aims of disentangling while at the same time promoting a particular point of view about those events. The effectiveness of emotion talk in accomplishing the pragmatic work of disentangling is enhanced by the fact that it is both indirect and ambiguous.

As a moral idiom, emotion talk is indirect because it relies on presupposition and implication to state interpretations and evaluations of contested events. The quality of indirection is particularly important in small-scale, face-to-face communities such as that considered here, where overt public statements about others' behavior are often proscribed. The rhetoric of emotions offers a remedy. Relying on shared models of socioemotional process, speakers may pose and counterpose statements about their own actions and emotions, leaving moral assertions about others unstated. The availability of an idiom with which to assert moral claims indirectly while simultaneously acknowledging the overt agenda of reestablishing solidarity is essential to successful disentangling.

Related to the indirect quality of emotion talk is the fact that emotions are susceptible to multiple moral readings. The potential for ambiguity arises from the complexity of conceptual and situational factors contributing to emotional meaning. A specific emotion attribution may have a range of potential entailments, and just which implications are brought to bear in a given interpretation may remain ambiguous. The following analysis pursues this point by examining the use of a particular emotion term, *di'a nagnafa* ("sad"), in disentangling discourse.[5] This concept is central to the disentangling activity because it is seen to follow from transgressions that threaten interpersonal relations, but at the same time gives rise to attempts to repair those relations. Represented schematically, basic elements of the *di'a nagnafa* scenario may be sketched as follows:

DAMAGE CLOSE RELATIONS (Other, Self)
↓
di'a nagnafa ("sad")
↓
REPAIR (Self, Other)

An important source of moral ambiguity in talk of "sadness" derives from the potential for focusing variously on the antecedent (transgression) or the implied response (attempt at repair). The former may constitute a challenge to the other, whereas the latter emphasizes reconciliation and relatedness.[6]

The following analysis shows that interpretive ambiguity in talk of emotions facilitates the rhetorical transformation of socioemotional reality – a transformation central to the task of disentangling. Specifically, narrative constructions of past events reformulate those events so as to transmute threatening and conflict-ridden "anger" rhetorically to solidarity-engendering "sadness". Both "anger" and "sadness" pertain to the sorts of problematic events in which the transgressions of others impinge on the self. Disentangling institutionalizes a speech event in which speakers reframe "angry" responses in terms of "sadness", "shame", and related emotions. In doing so, conflict events are narrated so as to highlight valued interpersonal relations and community solidarity. The analysis also raises questions about the experiential basis of rhetorical transformations accomplished in discourse.

The conceptualization of "Disentangling"

Santa Isabel is one of five major islands in the Solomon Islands, with a present population of more than 14,000. Half of the population speak an Austronesian language known variously as A'ara or Cheke Holo (White, Kokhonigita, and Pulomana 1988). People engage primarily in subsistence gardening while pursuing various agricultural schemes to produce cash crops. Prior to changes at the turn of the century, sociopolitical activity was organized largely by relations of descent and regional alignments in which local big men or "chiefs" (funei) were the focal point for intergroup feasting and raiding. The idiom of descent is distinctly matrilineal. In former times, the territorial locus of descent group identity was marked by shrines where propitiatory offerings were made to ancestral spirits.

Although economic changes have been slow in coming, cultural transformations associated with Western influence, especially Christianity, have been more dramatic (White 1988). Historically, the most significant agent of change was the Anglican Melanesian Mission (now the Church of Melanesia), which completed its work of converting the island population just after the turn of the century. The Isabel people, who had been severely victimized by marauding headhunters from the western Solomon Islands, eagerly received the mission at the end of the nineteenth century. Conversion entailed major shifts in residential patterns in which people formerly scattered throughout the mountainous interior migrated to coastal villages of unprecedented size (100–200 people), where ritual life was (and continues to be) centered on the village chapel. More importantly for this chapter, contemporary moral ideals are also cast largely in terms of Christian ideology.

A'ara-speaking people sporadically (and decreasingly; White in press) engage in a practice known as *graurutha*, or "disentan-

gling" (from *rutha*, "undo" or "untie"). Put briefly, disentangling is an activity in which family members or village mates meet together to talk about interpersonal conflicts and "bad feelings" (*di'a nagnafa*). The point of this talk is to make bad feelings public so as to defuse their destructive potential. The A'ara believe, as do people in many cultures (e.g., Harris 1978; Ito 1985; Strathern 1968) that negative emotions that remain hidden may cause illness and misfortune – ranging from personal injury to a poor catch of fish or failure to locate domestic pigs in the forest. Furthermore, bad feelings are not only potentially damaging to the self, they may harm others as well. It is therefore in the interest of the community as a whole to repair social discord and maintain emotional harmony. Disentangling is an institutionalized means for achieving those ends. It provides an occasion in which people are encouraged to talk about conflicts and resentments that would otherwise be difficult and even proscribed topics of conversation.

The significance of disentangling depends on a presupposed world of understandings about persons and emotions. As already stated, a central tenet of this world is that hidden "bad feelings" arising from interpersonal conflict may cause illness and misfortune for the self and others. The operative word here is "hidden". By implication, if negative emotions can be "talked out" and made public, they lose their potential for causing harm. But this "talking out" is not conceived of as catharsis in the sense of reexperiencing or releasing intense emotions "bottled up" (my metaphor) in the person, as would be expected, for example, in the American model of anger (Lakoff and Kovecses 1987). To the contrary, disentangling talk is conducted in a narrative mode of reporting on past events rather than enacting demonstrative displays of felt emotion. For A'ara speakers, public talk about conflict in this context is itself an act of reconciliation. Individuated "anger", hidden from the restraining moral judgments of the community, may, in the local view, give rise to a broad range of destructive behaviors (White 1985a, 1985b). By engaging in disentangling, speakers tacitly acknowledge the prior value of community solidarity, ritually closing the conflict episode as a source of disruptive thoughts and actions.

This interpretation of the local conceptualization of disentangling is evident in a range of conventional metaphors used to talk about the activity. These metaphors suggest that disentangling is thought about as a process of *revelation*, of moving personal thoughts and emotions into community awareness. By examining a range of interrelated linguistic expressions, it is possible to identify key images used to conceptualize the rationale of disentangling.

Presuming an image of the person as a container, two commonly used metaphorical expressions describe disentangling as either "talking out" (*cheke fajifla*) bad feelings or as "opening up" (*tora*) so that thoughts and feelings do not remain hidden. In the former expression, problematic feelings are described as moving from inside to outside the person so that they become visible or known to the community. The directional adverb *fajifla* ("out") signifies physical movement across a boundary, as in leaving a room or removing an object from a container. The second metaphor also builds on a sense of revelation – of becoming known by virtue of coming into view. The verb "open up", often used to describe opening a door or lifting the lid to a box, describes the sort of talk that "opens up" persons in the context of disentangling.

Metaphors of sight and visibility are further elaborated in a variety of expressions used in this context. For example, disentangling makes thoughts and feelings public by "bringing them to the surface", just as a turtle is spotted when it "surfaces" (*thagra*) for air. And, by removing covering layers, disentangling reveals feelings that have been "buried" (*fruni*) or "covered over" (*plohmo*) by problems and reluctance to talk about them.

Metaphors of concealment and revelation represent a local analogue of the opposition of "public" and "private." Disentangling presumes that the person is a bounded locus of experience that may or may not be communicated in discourse. The expressions mentioned previously are indicative of the local view that disentangling transforms personal thoughts and feelings by placing them in a wider field of knowledge circulation. Participants in disentangling invoke images of "talking out" and "opening up with talk" to remind one another that *just by talking* in a certain way, one may fulfill the overt agenda of disentangling, of making thoughts and feelings public. Disentangling performances are not only *seen* as efficacious, they *are* efficacious in transforming that which is "hidden", "inside", or "below the surface" to that which is "visible", "outside", and "above the surface". However, as anyone familiar with the family life of small communities might expect, there is more to disentangling than the overt agenda. A closer analysis of the practice of disentangling gives a more complex picture of the multiple social and emotional realities created in context.

The Practice of Disentangling

Local theories of misfortune reflect the indigenous rationale for disentangling as a desired and even necessary activity (White 1985a). These understandings (among others) constitute an intersubjective basis for its joint enactment. To some extent, a disentangling session achieves its purpose simply by taking place. By virtue of their coparticipation, people signal their mutual commitment to repairing community relatedness. However, beyond the simple fact of its performance, a disentangling session creates a communicative environment in which a certain type of discourse is possible – specifically, narrative reconstructions of problematic events.

Consider some of the ways in which the social organization of disentangling supports its communicative goals and facilitates the transformation of "angry" emotions. To begin with, the narrative mode is well suited to the avoidance of "anger" in the disentangling session itself. For an event that has as its goal the alleviation of hostility, it would not do to provoke further expressions of resentment. And, given that participants are expected to talk about interpersonal conflicts, the avoidance of hostility is a difficult problem. The organization of disentangling as a sequence of narratives minimizes or suppresses the kind of quick challenge-and-riposte that typically leads to confrontation and argumentation.

The social genius of disentangling is that the conversational organization of the event is managed through the joint participation of all present. No designated person or group leads the meeting. Rather, various participants take turns urging one another to speak and, where necessary, jointly direct conversation away from problematic topics or formats (White 1990).

Even the physical setting of disentangling works to defuse confrontational modes of interaction. The two meetings I attended were both held at night in a large house with people gathered in the shadows both inside and outside. (The nighttime format may be more characteristic of larger, village-level meetings than of smaller, family disentangling sessions.) Not only would the protagonists not address their speech to one another, they would likely not even see one another. Narratives are produced for a largely unseen audience. And yet, the unseen coterie of listeners is essential to the successful enactment of disentangling. Furthermore, disentangling participants are not just passive listeners. They actively collaborate to evoke narrative performances from those known to be involved in not-quite-resolved conflicts, and to orchestrate the interaction so as to minimize the potential for antagonistic confrontation.

Each narrative produced in this environment is an opportunity for reforming socioemotional reality. Given the avowed purpose of disentangling to "talk out" bad feelings, it is not surprising that the narratives are punctuated with overt talk of emotions – talk dense with moral significance. In light of the fact that each emotion concept entails specific interpersonal information (Levy 1984; Myers 1979), what sorts of emotion talk recur in disentangling sessions? In my limited sample of recorded sessions,[7] three emotions emerge as particularly salient: "sadness", "shame", and "anger".[8] For reasons that should now be apparent, the last term, "anger", appears less frequently than the former two. This finding is consistent with the hypothesis that disentangling is concerned with rhetorically transforming "anger" in relations where overt tensions are not easily voiced. The following discussion takes up this hypothesis in more detail.

A review of several conflict narratives recorded in two separate meetings indicates that statements to the effect that "Event x made me *di'a nagnafa* ("sad")" occur frequently as speakers seek to draw attention to the problematic nature of event x. In my analysis talk of "sadness" in this context, like talk of "anger", presupposes some sort of morally questionable action – an action that has harmed the speaker or someone identified with the speaker. At a generalized level of understanding, both of these emotions (*di'a nagnafa* "sad" and *di'a tagna* "angry") may be seen to derive from forms of transgression. It is at a more specific level of cultural knowledge that they are differentiated in terms of distinctions about particular types of transgression. Although both "sadness" and "anger" are evoked by rule violations, "sadness" pertains to social actions that damage relations, whereas "anger" is regarded as a response to actions that harm or threaten the self or significant others. These differing degrees of generality in cultural understandings of emotion reflect the hierarchical organization of knowledge such that models are nested within models, with reasoning about specific emotions drawing upon more global understandings about kinship obligations and the social order generally (see Quinn 1987:189). The nesting of cultural models allows speakers to range across varying levels of specificity in their narrative, thus leaving room for differing degrees of ambiguity in their moral assertions.

The possibility of finding both "sadness" and "anger" as plausible responses to the same events is the basis for their substitutability – a feature of A'ara understandings that lies at the crux of disentangling discourse. By relying upon generalized understandings about responses to rule violations to talk about "sadness" rather than "anger", a speaker may then draw out differing implications for his or her response – interpreted in terms of a scenario of repair rather than retribution. Combining the schemas outlined earlier, one may visualize the potential for attributing "anger" and "sadness" to the same eliciting event, with divergent implications for the type of reaction inferred.

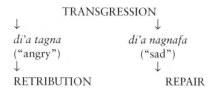

TRANSGRESSION

↓	↓
di'a tagna	*di'a nagnafa*
("angry")	("sad")
↓	↓
RETRIBUTION	REPAIR

A Case of Disentangling

An example of narrative drawn from a village disentangling meeting illustrates the process by which emotion talk is used to create an emergent social reality (a transcript of the entire meeting is given in White in press). The case summarized here was the second incident taken up in a meeting conducted one evening as people met to clear away possible unresolved conflicts that might interfere with preparations for an upcoming feast. (Hidden resentments might, for example, cause failure or injury to those going out pig hunting or turtle hunting.) The meeting, in fact, served two purposes. With the disentangling portion of the evening finished, villagers turned to a discussion of preparations for the upcoming feast.

Discussion of this case in the meeting consisted primarily of just one long narrative by one of the people principally involved in the incident (whom I refer to as Tom). Tom's narrative is then followed by a series of shorter statements. Several others who figure prominently in the story were not present at the meeting (a fact that was noted prior to Tom's speaking, as participants in the meeting attempted to get all the parties involved to speak before realizing that they were absent).

Tom's account focuses on the way he and others responded to the revealed transgressions of two young people (his younger brother and a young woman) who had been having an endogamous extramarital affair. His discussion is not concerned directly with the illicit relationship, but with the ways people reacted to it and the implications of those reactions for their relations with one another. In other words, his is a narrative of metaconflict – articulating conflicting views of conflict in the community.

When the mother of the young woman learned what was going on, she apparently told the young man to "never set foot" in her village (Paka) again. The young man then went off in a rage and at some point cut himself with his bush knife. Tom later encountered his younger brother in the bush and elicited his story about what had happened. After leading his brother back up to their village (Holo), Tom decided to return to Paka to see the people there and retrieve his brother's bag. Along the way, he encountered the young woman's father, Gata, and talked with him about what had occurred prior to his brother's injury. The father told him that his wife, Fala, had told Tom's brother not to set foot in their village again.

Tom then proceeded to Paka, where he found Fala's mother, Sukhi, and apparently told her that if that was how they were going to talk to his brother, then she and her family should not come up to his village, Holo, either. These mutual rejections had the potential to involve wider circles of people, since the planned Christmas feast was to be held at Holo. Tom's encounter with Sukhi was followed by a period of uncertainty as to who, if anyone, from Paka would participate in preparations for the upcoming feast. As in many such incidents in small communities, an initial transgression reverberated throughout the social order, threatening to ignite a wider conflict between others related to the antagonists.

Tom's narrative chronologically reconstructs his involvement in the events following his brother's self-inflicted injury, making extensive use of reported speech to give the account immediacy and validity. He punctuates his retelling of these events by describing his feelings during the episode. It is the emotions of "sadness" and "shame" that emerge most clearly in the account, serving to reinforce and amplify Tom's interpretations.

Tom begins speaking by distancing himself from the illicit affair and his brother's self-inflicted injury. He then proceeds to narrate the sequence of events leading to his first encounter with the young woman's father, Gata. In the course of his narrative, Tom twice emphasizes his younger brother's responsibility for his own injury. However, following this, he shifts attention to Fala's rejection of his brother, twice quoting her utterance "Don't set foot in Paka again!"

It is the moral significance of this rejection that becomes the focus of Tom's narrative. He brings Fala's act into moral scrutiny by placing his relationship with Fala in the foreground of his account. The evaluative implications of Fala's utterance are delineated most clearly by Tom's characterization of their relationship in terms of close kinship. He says that Fala is "like another mother" to him. (Tom and Fala are in fact related as maternal half-cousins. Fala's older age is the basis for Tom referring to her as "mother.") The idioms of kinship and food sharing are invoked to assert close relations among those involved in the entanglement. These images emerge clearly in Tom's narrative as he describes his encounter with Fala's husband, when he first heard about Fala's expulsion of his brother. The narrative establishes the incongruity between that act and the fact of kinlike relations:

Then he (Fala's husband) told about [the statement] "Don't set foot again in Paka."
[So I said] "Who said that man?"
"Fala."
"Fala! So, alright, [she] is just like another mother to me. You married her, but she was already [just like] my mother. There is water, there is food, there are sweet potatos there [for me to share]. "Don't set foot in Paka!" [she said to] my younger brother! He did do wrong before they started thinking like this, so alright," I said. But my thoughts became all confused ("knotted") about that.

Note that Tom uses a metaphor of entanglement ("knotted" *haru*) to express his response to the moral conflict created by his brother's transgression and his relatives' subsequent rejection of him. The image of entanglement effectively comments on the fact of a moral dilemma without committing to a specific interpretation pinpointing the agency and the responsibility.

Having established his sonlike relation with the woman Fala, Tom goes on to assert that her banishment of his younger brother made him *mamaja* ("ashamed") with her and, most immediately, with her husband, who reported the act of exclusion to him. Although a thorough account of A'ara "shame" is not possible here, it typically signifies some kind of mis-

match between context and event, usually involving a violation of appropriate social distance. In this instance, Tom's attribution of "shame" upon hearing of Fala's remarks implies that her act of rejection implicitly misread or undervalued the relations that should have obtained in that context. To underscore this point, Tom characterizes his relations with Fala in terms of potent symbols of food sharing, invoking a commonly used scenario of entering someone's house and helping oneself to their food.[9]

The juxtaposition of this characterization and the attribution of "shame" induced by Fala's rejection calls attention to her act as one that placed inappropriate distance between kin relations, thereby creating the need to repair the moral damage. This implication is then further reaffirmed by the attribution of "sadness" – just the emotion that would be expected in response to a transgression that damages close relations.

Each emotion attribution may be seen as a partial "filling in" or instantiation of a general schema such as those discussed previously. Once the emotion portion of a scenario is instantiated, the listener may draw inferences about how the events leading to or following from that emotion are to be interpreted. In other words, the listener fills in other portions of the schema through inference, even though the speaker has not been explicit about those aspects of the events.

Much of the "action" in emotion rhetoric involves the instantiation that results from giving an interpretation to precipitating events. Thus, when Tom asserts that the banishment of his brother made him "sad", he is implying, in this context, that the rejection is an instance of a certain *kind* of social action – one that damages close relations, that is, the sort of thing that evokes "sadness". And, even more importantly for his portrayal of the incident, he implicitly claims that *his* response of telling off the offending parties was an attempt at withdrawal rather than some kind of "angry" getting even.

The portion of Tom's narrative in which he talks most concertedly about his emotional responses is given subsequently so as to look more closely at the conceptual role of emotion rhetoric in building a desired interpretation. By combining Tom's overt statements about emotion with the hypothesized knowledge structures discussed earlier, the analysis seeks to identify implicit structures of emotional meaning. (For this analysis, only attributions of "sadness" are expanded in this way, but see White (1990) for a similar treatment of "shame".) Certain conventions are useful for depicting interpretation as a process of inference (Hutchins 1973; Quinn 1987). Borrowing from the standard format for representing syllogistic reasoning, the implications of emotion attribution are shown here as an inference drawn from a set of premises. As noted earlier, in many cases these inference pertain to instantiating a generalized schema. In the conventions adopted here, a specific proposition about emotion is shown in quotation marks and the hypothesized background schema is indicated by capital letters. The proposition implied by instantiating the schema is depicted below a horizontal line as follows:

GENERAL SCHEMA
+
"attributed emotion"
inferred proposition

Following the passage quoted earlier, Tom continues his narrative by recalling his thoughts and feelings at the time he encountered the young woman's father and heard him tell about the expulsion of his younger brother. He characterizes his feelings as a mixture of "sadness" and "shame":

It was the "Don't set foot in Paka" that made me ashamed with him. This man [the young woman's father] is like our father, we two [Tom and his younger brother] would go inside [their] house, these sweet potatoes were our food, these houses, these beds ... These feelings were probably with him [Tom's younger brother]. Because of this I was *sad*.

DAMAGE CLOSE RELATION → SAD
"Fala's remark → sad"
Fala's remark = damage close relation[10]

I was just ashamed from those ways, from the way "Don't set foot here." [So] I came to the old woman [Sukhi] up there.

Tom's talk of "shame" and "sadness" creates a context for rationalizing his own actions. Most problematic is his telling Fala's group (through a conversation with her mother, Sukhi) not to bother coming up to his village for the Christmas feast. The attribution of "shame" provides a motive for Tom's hasty words. The prototypical scenario for shame (not detailed here) entails a response of withdrawal. He here implies that his remarks to Sukhi were more of a response of avoidance in the face of the social distance created by Fala's rejection of his brother.

As Tom goes on with his narrative, he focuses more directly on his feelings and motives prior to making those remarks to Fala's mother. His talk of "shame" is embedded in attributions of "sadness". At this point in the narrative, the emotion rhetoric is oriented more to types of response than to characterization of antecedent events.

The hypothesis that much disentangling discourse is concerned with the transformation of scenarios of "anger" to a more desired reality is examined in the following passage. In this portion of Tom's narrative, as he continues describing his encounter with Sukhi, the anger-retribution schema can be seen to be lurking just behind the scenes. In fact, Tom here applies a tactic unusual to disentangling discourse: He explicitly poses the anger scenario as a possible alternative interpretation of his hasty words so that he can reject it from consideration (see Quinn 1987:185–6 for a similar example).[11]

It's just that when my real father said that [reported Fala's remarks] that I was *sad* and came and talked to the old woman [Sukhi] up here.

SAD → REPAIR DAMAGED RELATION
"sad → Tom's remarks to Sukhi"
Tom's remarks = repair damaged relation
I was just *ashamed* is all. It was not [I didn't mean], "You all don't come back up. Don't set food in my village, you all." I didn't [mean] that.

ANGER → RETRIBUTION
"Tom's remark not retribution"
not anger
That was just from my *sadness*, my own *shame*.

SAD → REPAIR DAMAGED RELATION
"sad → Tom's remarks"
Tom's remarks = repair damaged relation
Now I'm in front of my mothers and sisters [in
the village Paka]. These houses should be for
coming inside. These houses are for me to get
a drink. These houses should be for taking a
rest, so when my [fictive] father said that,
I was *sad* about it.
DAMAGE CLOSE RELATION → SAD
"Fala's remark → sad"
Fala's remark = damage close relation

In this passage, the attributions of "sadness"
and "shame" both contribute to an emerging
interpretation of Tom's response to his brother's rejection. "Sadness" is the emotion that
links Tom's reaction to the exclusion of his
brother with his own confrontation with Fala's
group – an emotion that follows from a concern for valued relations and is supposed to
lead to efforts at moral repair. Although Tom's
statements in the preceding passage emphasize
the types of action that follow from "sadness"
(and "shame"), he also reminds his listeners
about the source of those emotions in disrupted
social relations by reiterating images of kinship and food sharing. These images emphasize the social ties that are an essential element
of the interpretation that replaces a scenario of
angry confrontation with an awkward withdrawal motivated by "shame" and "sadness".
Whether this strategy works, of course, is
uncertain. But it is not so much the truth value
of his assertions as their coherence and force-
fulness in the disentangling context that constitute a successful performance.

This example, drawn from a single disentangling narrative, illustrates the ethnofunc-
tional beauty of disentangling as a predefined
social occasion in which people rhetorically
mend minor tears in the social fabric before
relations unravel further. In this context, direct
talk of "anger" that leads to retribution seems
to surface only in regard to minor incidents,
and even then it may be problematic (White
1990). Instead, disentangling discourse plays
on the inherent moral ambiguities of interpersonal conflict to characterize "angry" reactions as responses of "sadness" and "shame",
thereby reframing events that have been prob-

lematic for persons and communities alike. In
short, disentangling – as ideology and as social
institution – works (however imperfectly) to
bring conditions of divisiveness and individuated "anger" more in line with models of solidarity.

Conclusion

Disentangling institutionalizes an activity in
which community members ritually realign
skewed relations. Talk of emotions such as *di'a
nagnafa* is a culturally constituted means of
periodically re-creating these alignments while
simultaneously advancing more covert agen-
das of moral argumentation. The consistent
attribution of "sadness" and "shame" to problematic events (seen by many as having evoked
hostile responses) suggests that disentangling
discourse rhetorically transmutes "anger" to
"sadness". There is enough overlap in the
"anger" and "sadness" schemas so that they
may plausibly be applied to the same events,
with the effect of reconstruing conflict situations so as to emphasize reconciliation instead
of retribution. And, by implication, the likelihood of suffering any of the broad range of
damaging effects seen to follow from unresolved "anger" is reduced.

Without either the shared model of disentangling or the institutionalized context in
which to produce narrative accounts of conflict, neither the rhetoric nor the reality of
emotion manifest in disentangling would be
what it is. If one construes emotions as sociocultural *institutions* that depend on both the
cultural model and the interactive situation for
their meaning and effect, then analytic attention is directed more widely than a strictly
person-centered approach would suggest.[12] By
recognizing that emotions are not simply
expressed in social situations, but are in fact
constituted by the types of activities and relations in which they are enacted, ethnographic
attention may be given to the institutionalized
discourse practices that shape emotional meaning and experience (Lutz and White 1986).

Because of its evocative functions, emotion
discourse is especially relevant for theories of
social action. To talk about or express emotion

in context is to expect to evoke a certain type of response in both the self and the listening other. However, analysis of the socioemotional realities so created is complicated by the fact that the analysis is likely to go beyond the conscious awareness of the participants. In the case of disentangling, participants appear not to recognize or acknowledge the transformative effects of disentangling narrative, referring instead to the "talking out" aspect of disentangling. Even though participants acknowledge the attempts of narrators to replay past events to their moral advantage, the folk theory of disentangling does not encompass the act of re-forming specific emotions. In disentangling, as in many emotive institutions, the nature and degree of participants' awareness of discourse functions are important elements in the institution's ability to achieve its interactive ends.

Perhaps ironically, a discourse-centered approach such as that outlined here holds particular promise as a method for examining significances of emotional meaning unrecognized or unacknowledged by participants. It is usually taken for granted that the analysis of discourse is an avenue to identifying public constructions of socioemotional reality. To this we should add that analysis of patterns of unspoken meaning in emotive discourse may also provide a means of investigating less "visible" transformations of personal experience.

NOTES

This chapter is based on fieldwork in Santa Isabel carried out in 1975–6 and on more focused research on disentangling conducted during two months in 1984.

1 A third major thrust in anthropological approaches to discourse not addressed directly in this chapter is that represented in poststructuralist concerns with the historical and political conditions necessary for statements to obtain truth value and moral force (epitomized in the work of Foucault, e.g., 1981). I take the sociopolitical preconditions of knowledge and power that make a certain discourse possible to be different from the conceptual and communicative structures through which that dis-

course takes on cultural and experiential reality. However, approaching emotion as discourse opens up the former vantage point as a way of delineating the historical and institutional determinants of emotions as a culturally constructed political force.

2 As a prototype structure, the schema represents a typical or default course for socioemotional process, but not one that is seen as invariant or completely predictable. Ethnopsychological knowledge of persons and action may be elaborated in a great variety of ways and may still be consistent with the basic shape of the event-emotion-response scenario. For example, D'Andrade's (1987) discussion of the American folk model of the mind postulates a more detailed picture of conceptions of feelings and desires related to a range of mental and behavioral processes.

3 This chapter does not examine in detail the more specific sorts of relational information encoded in emotion concepts. Knowledge about the social contexts of emotions applies to the salience of certain emotions for certain relations, as well as to their appropriateness of expression in those relations. For example, "anger" in Isabel is widely regarded as a problematic response to conflict and transgression. Yet, according to cultural ideals, it is not appropriately expressed in relations that are either close (e.g., among family members) or sharply asymmetrical (e.g., between a "good" chief and his followers).

4 See Wierzbicka (1986) for a discussion of translation issues in the domain of emotion. She draws attention to the need to decouple the cross-cultural study of emotion from the unexamined semantics of English emotion terms. Although the type of semantics outlined by Wierzbicka is narrowly lexical (and ultimately limited by the absence of contextual and performative information), her suggestion that translation work may be advanced by the use of explicit metalinguistic models is consistent with the search for prototype structures in emotional meaning.

5 The vernacular term *di'a nagnafa* (literally, "bad heart" or "bad feeling") is not well translated by the English gloss "sad." For a more extended discussion of the local meanings of this emotion, see White (in press). English glosses such as "sad" and "angry" used in this

chapter for expository purposes should not be read as a claim of cross-cultural equivalence.

6   The "sadness" schema as sketched centers on the response of the experiencing subject. However, as Lutz notes in her discussion of Ifaluk emotion theory (1987:295–8), cultural models of emotion also encompass understandings about the evocative power of emotions to elicit specific feelings and responses from others. Thus, in the case of "sadness", not only does the self desire repair [REPAIR (Self, Other)], but so, ideally, does the other [REPAIR (Other, Self)]. Here the reciprocal quality of "sadness" implies a convergence in goals, with both self and other, according to the schema, seeking to reestablish mutual relations. By implication, then, talk of "sadness" may also assert implicit claims about the appropriate (or inappropriate) response of the other.

7   My "sample" of disentangling discourse is based on four particular sessions, two of which were tape-recorded.

8   Concepts of shame have received a great deal of attention in the cross-cultural literature on emotion (see, e.g., Epstein 1984, White and Kirkpatrick 1985). Although the A'ara term for "shame", mamaja, figures importantly in disentangling discourse, limitations of space preclude a detailed discussion here (but see White 1990).

9   In this instance, the entering-a-house-for-food scenario is stated with conditional past tense markers, indicating that the relations signified are contingent on their continuing acknowledgment by participants. Tom implies that Fala's exclusion of his brother constituted a failure of such acknowledgment, thus creating shame in contexts where none would be evoked if conditions for the scenario were in force.

10 For the sake of simplicity, the relation achieved by instantiating a generalized category with a specific action is indicated by an equals sign (=). This notation is intended as shorthand for the phrase "is an instance of" (not "is equivalent to"). It should also be noted that this sort of inference is not one compelled by the canons of propositional logic. The closest syllogism to that represented here would be something like: given $A \rightarrow B$, and B ("sad") is true, therefore A.

But, since reasoning from the consequent is not a move compelled by logic (not a "strong" inference), mathematicians and others have legitimized this sort of inference as "plausible" reasoning (see Hutchins 1980:56 for examples and discussion). This is the most common type of inference in the examples discussed here.

11 I'm grateful to Naomi Quinn for drawing my attention to this example of a discourse strategy in which a proposition is rejected, even as the schema necessary to its interpretation is invoked to do so.

12 This notion of "emotive institution" is well illustrated in recent work on suicide in Pacific societies. For example, Rubinstein's (1984) study of Trukese amwunumwun shows that the emotions implicated in suicide events are constituted in particular communicative forms and culturally patterned scenarios of conflict. The indigenous conceptualization of these responses appears to bridge categories of affect and action. The study of this and related practices in the Pacific (see, e.g., Freeman 1983:218–22 on Samoan musu) requires an ethnography of situated practices of talk and interaction, as well as an investigation of models of the person (Watson-Gegeo and White 1990).

REFERENCES

Abu-Lughod, Lila
   1986   Veiled Sentiments: Honor and Poetry in a Bedouin Society. Berkeley: University of California Press.
Bailey, F. G.
   1983   The Tactical Uses of Passion: An Essay on Power, Reason and Reality. Ithaca, NY: Cornell University Press.
Briggs, Jean
   1970   Never in Anger: Portrait of an Eskimo Family. Cambridge, MA: Harvard University Press.
D'Andrade, Roy
   1987   A Folk Model of the Mind. In D. Holland and N. Quinn, eds., Cultural Models in Language and Thought. Cambridge: Cambridge University Press, pp. 112–48.
Epstein, A. L.
   1984   The Experience of Shame in Melanesia: An Essay in the Anthropology of Affect.

London: Royal Anthropological Institute of Great Britain and Ireland, Occasional Paper No. 40.

Foucault, Michel
1981 The Order of Discourse. In R. Young, ed., *Untying the Text: A Post-Structuralist Render*. Boston: Routledge & Kegan Paul, pp. 48–78.

Freeman, Derek
1983 *Margaret Mead and Samoa: The Making and Unmaking of an Anthropological Myth*. Cambridge, MA: Harvard University Press.

Gumperz, John
1982 *Discourse Strategies*. Cambridge: Cambridge University Press.

Harris, Grave
1978 *Casting Out Anger: Religion Among the Taita of Kenya*. New York: Cambridge University Press.

Holland, Dorothy, and Naomi Quinn, eds.
1987 *Cultural Models in Language and Thought*. Cambridge: Cambridge University Press.

Hutchins, Edwin
1973 An Analysis of Interpretations of Ongoing Behavior. Unpublished manuscript, Department of Anthropology, University of California, San Diego. 1980. *Culture and Inference*. Cambridge, MA: Harvard University Press.

Ito, Karen L.
1985 *Ho'oponopono*, "To Make Right": Hawaiian Conflict Resolution and Metaphor in the Construction of a Family Therapy. *Culture, Medicine and Psychiatry* 9:201–17.

Lakoff, George, and Zoltan Kovecses
1987 The Cognitive Model of Anger Inherent in American English. In D. Holland and N. Quinn, eds., *Cultural Models in Language and Thought*. Cambridge: Cambridge University Press, pp. 195–221.

Levy, Robert
1984 Emotion, Knowing and Culture. In R. Shweder and R. LeVine, eds., *Cultural Theory: Essays on Mind, Self and Emotion*. Cambridge: Cambridge University Press, pp. 214–37.

Lutz, Catherine
1985 Ethnopsychology Compared to What? Explaining Behavior and Consciousness Among the Ifaluk. In G. White and J. Kirkpatrick, eds., *Person, Self and Experience: Exploring Pacific Ethnopsychologies*. Berkeley: University of California Press, pp. 35–79.

1987 Goals, Events and Understanding in Ifaluk Emotion Theory. In D. Holland and N. Quinn, eds., *Cultural Models in Language and Thought*. Cambridge: Cambridge University Press, pp. 290–312.

Lutz, Catherine, and Geoffrey M. White
1986 The Anthropology of Emotions. *Annual Review of Anthropology* 15:405–36.

Myers, Fred
1979 Emotions and the Self: A Theory of Personhood and Political Order Among Pintupi Aborigines. *Ethos* 7:343–70.

1988 The Logic and Meaning of Anger Among Pintupi Aborigines. *Man* (N.S.) 23:589–610.

Poole, F. J. P.
1985 The Surfaces and Depths of Bimin-Kuskusmin Experiences of "Anger": Toward a Theory of Culture and Emotion in the Constitution of Self. Paper given at the 84th Annual Meeting of the American Anthropological Association, Washington, DC.

Quinn, Naomi
1987 Convergent Evidence for a Cultural Model of American Marriage. In D. Holland and N. Quinn, eds., *Cultural Models in Language and Thought*. Cambridge: Cambridge University Press, pp. 173–92.

Rosaldo, Michelle
1980 *Knowledge and Passion: Ilongot Notions of Self and Social Life*. Cambridge: Cambridge University Press.

Rubinstein, Donald
1984 Self-Righteous Anger, Soft-Talk and *Amwunumwun* Suicides of Young Men. Paper given at the 83rd Annual Meeting of the American Anthropological Association, Denver, CO.

Schieffelin, Edward
1983 Anger and Shame in the Tropical Forest: On Affect as a Cultural System in Papua New Guinea. *Ethos* 11:181–91.

Shweder, Richard, and Robert LeVine, eds
1984 *Culture Theory: Essays on Mind, Self and Emotion*. Cambridge: Cambridge University Press.

Strathern, Marilyn
1968 Popokl: The Question of Morality. *Mankind* 6:553–62.

Valentine, Charles A.
1963 Men of Anger and Men of Shame: Lakalai Ethnopsychology and Its Implications for Sociopsychological Theory. *Ethnology* 1:441–77.

Watson-Gegeo, Karen, and Geoffrey M. White, eds.
1990 *Disentangling: The Discourse of Interpersonal Conflict in Pacific Island Societies*. Stanford: Stanford University Press.

White, Geoffrey M.
1985a Premises and Purposes in a Solomon Islands Ethnopsychology. In G. White and J. Kirkpatrick, eds., *Person, Self and Experience: Exploring Pacific Ethnopsychologies*. Berkeley: University of California Press, pp. 328–66.

1985b "Bad Ways" and "Bad Talk": Interpretations of Interpersonal Conflict in a Melanesian Society. In J. Dougherty, ed., *Directions in Cognitive Anthropology*. Urbana: University of Illinois Press, pp. 345–370.

1988 Symbols of Solidarity in the Christianization of Santa Isabel. In G. Saunders, ed., *Culture and Christianity*. Westport, CT: Greenwood Press, pp. 12–31.

1990 Emotion Talk and Social Inference: Disentangling in a Solomon Islands Society. In K. Watson-Gegeo and G. White, eds., *Disentangling: The Discourse of Interpersonal Conflict in Pacific Island Societies*. Stanford: Stanford University Press.

White, Geoffrey M., and John Kirkpatrick, eds.
1985 *Person, Self and Experience: Exploring Pacific Ethnopsychologies*. Berkeley: University of California Press.

White, Geoffrey, Francis Kokhonigita, and Hugo Pulomana
1988 *Cheke Holo Dictionary*. Canberra: Pacific Linguistics.

Wierzbicka, Anna
1986 Human Emotions: Universal or Culture-Specific? *American Anthropologist* 88:584–94.

6

Kali's Tongue

Usha Menon and Richard A. Shweder

This chapter is about an Oriya Hindu facial expression (biting the tongue) and the Oriya emotion that it conveys (*lajya or lajja*), and about the narrated meanings of a core Oriya cultural symbol, a particular iconic representation of the Great Mother Goddess of Hinduism. The Great Goddess, who is variously referred to in local South Asian discourse as Devi, Ma, Parvati, Durga, Kali, Chandi, and numerous other appellations, is [often] depicted [by an icon] in her manifestation as Kali, with eyes bulging and tongue out, fully equipped with weapons in ten arms, garlanded with skulls, wearing a girdle of severed arms and heads, grasping a bloody decapitated head, and poised with her right foot on the chest of her husband, the god Siva, who is lying supine on the ground beneath her (Siva is the reigning deity of the temple town of Bhubaneswar where our research in Orissa [India] was conducted).

The icon is a normative collective representation or core cultural symbol that is all about *lajya* and the meaning of the emotionally expressive act of biting the tongue. For the moment, we hazardously and inadequately translate *lajya* as shame (for a detailed discussion of the difficulties in translating *lajya* with any single term, such as *shame, embarrassment, modesty,* or *shyness,* from the English emotion lexicon, see Shweder, 1992; see also Parish, 1991). In the

Oriya language, the linguistic expression "to bite your tongue" is an idiom signifying *lajya.* In towns and villages in India where Oriya is spoken, it is a good and powerful thing for a woman to be full of "shame" (*lajya*). The icon of the Great Goddess, in her manifestation as Kali, is the key to understanding why.

Shame, happiness, and *anger* are three words for emotions in the English language. Were one to ask bilingual (Oriya–English) speakers for equivalent words in the Oriya language, they would most likely generate *lajya* (for shame), *sukha* (for happiness), and *raga* (for anger). When Anglo-American college students are asked to evaluate similarities and differences among shame, happiness, and anger using a triads test format (which of the three emotions is most different from the other two?), they typically respond in one of two ways. A majority say that happiness is most different. Many say that shame is most different. Almost no one says that anger is most different.

Those who say that happiness is most different have in mind some kind of hedonic component of comparison. They judge that it feels pleasant to be happy, but unpleasant to feel either shame or anger. Those who say that shame is most different have in mind that to experience happiness or anger is to feel expansive and full of one's self, whereas to

Usha Menon and Richard A. Shweder, Kali's Tongue from *Emotion and Culture: Empirical Studies of Mutual Influence*, ed. Shinobu Kitayama and Hazel Rose Markus, American Psychological Association, Washington, DC. © 1994 by the American Psychological Association, pp. 241–284. Reprinted with permission of the American Psychological Association.

experience shame is to experience a diminishment of the ego.

On the other hand, Oriyas frequently say that anger (*raga*) is most different from the other two. They say that anger is destructive of social relationships and of everything of value. They say that shame (*lajya*) and happiness (*sukha*) are the glue of social relationships. Armed with an appreciation of the cultural psychology of Kali's tongue in Oriya culture, it is to be hoped that the reader will understand why Oriyas typically judge the emotion of anger (and not happiness or shame) to be the most different from the other two, and why Oriyas in the temple town of Bhubaneswar believe that shame (*lajya*) is a feminine virtue that is both powerful and good.

The Cultural Psychology of Emotions

The aim of this chapter is to increase our knowledge of emotional functioning in a different cultural tradition by examining the stories told about a core cultural symbol. In recent years, a new interdisciplinary field of research known as *cultural psychology* has emerged on the interface of anthropology, psychology, linguistics, and philosophy, promoting theory and research on domains of psychological functioning, including the cultural psychology of the self, the cultural psychology of cognition, the cultural psychology of emotions, and so forth (see Bruner, 1990; Cole, 1990; D'Andrade, 1990; Jahoda, 1992; Markus & Kitayama, 1991, 1992; Miller, Potts, Fung, Hoogstra, & Mintz, 1990; Much, 1992; Shweder, 1990, 1992; Shweder & Sullivan, 1990, 1993; Stigler, Shweder & Herdt, 1990; Wertsch, 1992). Cultural psychology is the study of how culture and psyche make each other up (see Wiggins, 1991, for a philosophical discussion of psychological states and their objects as equal and reciprocal partners and of the necessity of softening received distinctions between inside and outside points of view). The aim of cultural psychology is to document and explain divergences in the way in which the psyche functions across different ethnic and cultural groups.

Among the many questions definitive of the research agenda of the cultural psychology of emotions, we focus on the following: What particular emotional meanings (e.g., Oriya *lajya*) are constructed or brought "on-line" in different ethnic groups and in different temporal–spatial regions of the world? How are these emotional meanings brought "on-line," socialized, or otherwise acquired? More specifically, what is the role of core cultural symbols (e.g., the icon of the Great Goddess and the storytelling norms associated with its interpretation) in the activation of emotional meanings (see Bruner, 1990; Garvey 1992; Lutz, 1988; Miller, Mintz, Hoogstra, Fung, & Potts, 1992; Miller, Potts, et al., 1990; Miller & Sperry, 1987; Shweder, 1992; Wierzbicka, 1992)? And perhaps more important, what evidence is there that the various meanings (psychological, metaphysical, social) narrated about a core cultural symbol such as the icon of Kali are *normative* meanings?

Narratives, Numbers, and Norms

We address the issues of narratives, numbers, and norms by examining the extent to which the various narrated meanings associated with the icon of the Great Goddess [as Kali] are organized into culturally sanctioned and enforced norms of correct meanings definitive of cultural competence or expertise in storytelling.

In this study, we infer the existence of a culturally sanctioned and enforced norm for generating correct meanings by relying on the logic of metric scaling, in particular Guttman scaling (Ghiselli, Campbell, & Zedeck, 1981; Gordon, 1977; Weller & Romney, 1990). If a local norm for generating culturally correct meanings exists, it is to be expected that it will exercise an influence not only on the likelihood of certain meanings being activated at all (e.g., that a protruding tongue bitten between the lips means "I am ashamed") but also on the distribution and pattern of sharing of those meanings across members of a single cultural community. We discovered that the distribution of meanings associated with the icon of Kali suggests the existence of a unidimensional scale or a cumulative hierarchy of normative meanings, which constrains the telling of a culturally correct story about the Goddess, organizes the order in which meanings unfold, and establishes a standard for differentiating levels of local cultural competence or expertise. Clearly, the very existence of such hierarchical levels of competence presupposes the reality and existence of a cultural norm that members of a community share in common even though they have mastered it to different degrees.

The Canonical Story of Kali's Tongue

The following is the canonical story about Kali's tongue as told in the temple town of Bhubaneswar. The expert narrator here is a 74-year-old Brahman man, the father of three sons and two daughters. A retired hotelkeeper, he spends his time these days keeping an eye on his grandchildren and going regularly to the Lingaraj Temple.

Q. Do you recognize this picture?
A. Kali.
Q. Can you describe the incident that is portrayed in this picture?
A. This is about the time when Mahisasura became so powerful that he tortured everyone on earth and heaven. ... He had obtained a boon from the gods according to which no male could kill him. All the gods then went to Narayana and they pondered on ways to destroy Mahisasura ... each contributed the strength and energy of his consciousness – his *bindu* – and from that Durga was created. But when Durga was told that she had to kill Mahisasura, she said that she needed weapons to do so and so all the gods gave her their weapons. Armed thus, Durga went into battle. She fought bravely, but she found it impossible to kill the demon ... he was too strong and clever. You see, the gods had forgotten to tell her that the boon Mahisasura had obtained from Brahma was that he would only die at the hands of a naked woman. Durga finally became desperate and she appealed to Mangala to suggest some way to kill Mahisasura. Mangala told her that the

only way was to take off her clothes, that the demon would only lose strength when confronted by a naked woman. So Durga did as she was advised to; she stripped, and within seconds of seeing her, Mahisasura's strength waned and he died under her sword. After killing him, a terrible rage entered Durga's mind and she asked herself, "What kinds of gods are these that give to demons such boons, and apart from that, what kind of gods are these that they do not have the honesty to tell me the truth before sending me into battle?" She decided that such a world with such gods did not deserve to survive, so she took on the form of Kali and went on a mad rampage, devouring every living creature that came in her way. Now, the gods were in a terrible quandary. They had given her all their weapons. They were helpless without any weapons, while she had a weapon in each of her 10 arms. How could Kali be checked and who would check her in her mad dance of destruction? Again, the gods all gathered and Narayana decided that only Mahadev (Siva) could check Kali, and so he advised the gods to appeal to him. Now, Siva is an ascetic, a yogi who has no interest in what happens in this world; but when all the gods begged him to intervene, he agreed to do his best. He went and lay in her path. Kali, absorbed in her dance of destruction, was unaware that Siva lay in her path, so she stepped on him all unknowing. ... When she put her foot on Siva's chest, she bit her tongue, saying, "Oh! My husband!" There is in Mahadev a *tejas*, a special quality of his body that penetrated hers, that made her look down, that made her see reason ... she had been so angry that she had gone beyond reason, but once she recognized him, she became still and calm. This is the story about that time.

Q. How would you describe the expression on her face?
A. She had been extremely angry, but when her foot fell on Mahadev's chest – after all, he is her own husband – she bit her tongue and became still; gradually, her anger went down.
Q. So is there still any anger in her expression?

A. Oh yes, in her eyes you can still see the light of anger shining.

Q. And her tongue? What is she feeling when she bites it?

A. What else but shame (*lajya*)? Shame ... because she did something unforgivable she is feeling shame (*lajya*).

What follows is our analysis of this story of Kali's tongue: a Guttman scaling of the distribution of narrated meanings across 92 informants and a discussion of the normative meaning of shame in Orissa, India.

The Icon of Kali: The Study

The study was conducted in the Old Town section of Bhubaneswar, Orissa, India in the neighborhood surrounding the Lingaraj Temple. Lingaraj is one of the many names of the Hindu god Siva (also spelled Shiva). The temple dates back to at least the 11th–12th century. It is an important pilgrimage site for Hindu wanderers (for a more detailed description of the community, see Mahapatra, 1981; Seymour, 1983; Shweder, 1991; Shweder, Mahapatra, & Miller, 1990; Shweder, Much, Mahapatra, & Park, in press).

The narrators

A total of 92 informants participated in the study: Seventy-three were Brahmans, and the remaining 19 were members of what are referred to locally as clean castes. Women outnumbered men: There were 66 women to 26 men in the sample interviewed. The narrators spanned an age range from 18 to 86 years: The average age of the male narrators was 58.8 years, and that for the female narrators was 42.1 years. Except for the two oldest men, who were widowers, and the two youngest, who were bachelors, all the men were married. Of the 66 women, 53 were married, 6 were still unmarried, 5 were widows, and 2 were separated from their husbands and had chosen to return to their fathers' homes. The mean length of education for the men was 9.6 years, whereas it was 6.5 for the women. Fifteen

women had no schooling at all, although no woman was completely illiterate. With one exception, all the men in the sample were literate: 15 had more than 10 years of schooling and 5 were particularly learned in Sanskrit. With the exception of the unmarried and separated women, all of the women maintained traditional female roles in their households or joint families as wife, daughter-in-law, mother-in-law, or widowed matriarch. Most of the men were civil servants, schoolteachers, shopkeepers, hotel owners, and small-time politicians. In spite of this involvement in nontraditional activities, their status in the community continued to be defined by their roles or by that of a family member's in the ritual activities of the temple.

The storytelling task

All interviews were conducted in Oriya by Usha Menon, coauthor of this chapter, at the homes of the narrators during the months of June through September, 1991. The interviews began with the interviewer showing to the informant the icon of the Great Goddess in her manifestation as Kali and consisted of a short series of probes.

The probes for the study had been designed so as to encourage every narrator to spontaneously generate his or her story about the icon. The first two probes were as follows: "Do you recognize this picture" and "Can you tell me the story that is associated with this picture."

After the narrator had told his or her story, there were additional follow-up probes, such as, "In this picture, how would you describe Kali's feelings?" "Have you seen this expression in everyday life?" If yes, "Who and under what circumstances?" "Is Kali merely stepping on Siva or is she dancing on him?" "Why do you think Siva is on the ground?" "Do you think that Siva is on the ground to subdue Kali?" "Whom do you see as dominant in this picture: Kali or Siva?" Additional probes or paraphrased variations of the probes were occasionally introduced in an effort to determine what the narrator knew about the icon, and whether the narrator had anything further to say.

The pragmatic context in which the narrators told their stories to Usha Menon is one in which we wanted to learn what they knew about their own cultural symbols, but the task was not constructed or presented as a test of knowledge. We imagine that the experience is much like asking a Christian to explain, to a seriously interested and persistent visitor, the meaning of the iconography of the Crucifixion scene. We do not know whether or in what ways the stories told by our narrators would be different if told within a different context or to a different interviewer.

We also cannot be certain about the cognitive status of absent meanings. Absent meanings are meanings that a particular narrator failed to produce in our interview context and in our follow-up probes. We do not know whether our informants would have incorporated those absent meanings into their narratives had we primed those meanings by making them readily available in the form of a true/false or recognition task.

Later in the chapter, we briefly survey several types of interpretations of the cognitive status of those meanings that a narrator does not mention while telling the story of the Great Goddess. Given the evidence at hand, we cannot know for certain whether an absent meaning is an indication of a lack of sufficient knowledge of normative meanings to support the verbal production of a story, or an indication of the repression of certain normative meanings (perhaps because they are too emotionally "hot" to handle consciously), or perhaps even an indication of a deliberate unwillingness to narrate particular normative meanings in the context of our storytelling task. For reasons that we shall discuss later in the chapter, we favor the lack of knowledge interpretation of the cognitive status of absent meanings, although further research is needed to settle this important issue and to sort out possible interpretations of the psychological significance of absent meanings.

What we do know with some confidence from our study is that the meanings that are narrated (or left out) in any particular narration are narrated (or left out) in a very systematic way, which is suggestive of the existence of a cultural norm for ascribing meanings to the icon of the Goddess in her manifestation as Kali.

Within the pragmatic context of our storytelling task, some of the older married women, though eager to chat and entertain, exhibited a certain reluctance to be interviewed. They would disclaim having any knowledge about the icon and would suggest that their husbands would make better informants. There is certainly a cultural aspect to this behavior pattern, in that women in the community are encouraged to be modest and self-effacing in such contexts, and such self-effacing behavior may even be an aspect of *lajya*. As we shall see, it is also possible that the task was especially problematic for some of those older married women because of their relatively limited mastery of available storytelling norms.

The interviews rarely lasted longer than half an hour. All were tape-recorded and later transcribed and translated into English. What follows is an interview with one of the more expert of our narrators. As can be seen, she adheres closely to the canonical story as it is told in the Old Town. This narrator (Narrator 78) was a married Brahman woman of 50, the mother of a grown-up son and daughter, who, although she had had no formal education, could read and write Oriya fluently. Two sections from her extensive narrative are given here.

Q. Do you recognize this picture?
A. Yes, of course. This is Kali.
Q. Can you tell me what is happening in this picture?
A. She has put her foot on Siva.
Q. Why has she done that? Has she done it deliberately?
A. No, Ma hasn't done it deliberately. When she came after killing Mahisasura, she was in a terrible rage, filled with the desire to destroy, and she was powerful – every god and goddess having given her their particular strengths, their particular weapons. Then, she took on the form of Ugra Chandi, the most destructive of Ma's forms and it is like this that she stepped on Siva. She didn't know what she was doing, and when she did, she asked herself, "What have I done? Have I stepped on my husband?" And she bit her tongue. When we have made mistakes and realize that we

have made them, don't we too bite our tongues? Don't we ask ourselves, "Eh, Ma, what have I done?" It is the same kind of *ma shakti* (mother power). Here, she is shown destructive and wild, but she has a peaceful form too, which she shows to the true believer. What we should do is close our eyes and pray to her without any fear or anxiety. She will then appear not as she is in this picture but otherwise. If I focus on you and pray to Ma, I will see her in you and if you focus on me and pray to Ma, you will see her in me. But we will neither of us see her as she is in this picture, fierce and bloodthirsty. What does this picture teach us? That none of us is free of her. She devours each one of us so that she can create more. Also, by standing with her foot on her husband, she shows that she doesn't pay heed to anyone. She is supreme. No one can question her.

Q. How would you describe Kali's expression here?

A. Kali here is frightening. She strikes terror. She is killing demons and so naturally she would look fierce. But once she recognized her husband lying under her foot, she bit her tongue and felt shame. She became calm and her anger began to go down.

Q. So there is both shame and anger in her face?

A. There is shame in her face. But can you look at her face alone? You can't. You look at everything else, the weapons she is carrying, the garland of skulls, her girdle of heads and arms, the way she is standing. And when you look at all that she doesn't look as though she is feeling shame. That is all part of her Ugra Chandi form.

Q. And her eyes? What do they show?

A. They too show how angry she has been.

Q. Is there a name or a way of describing this expression?

A. This is the way Kali is worshipped. She is a warning to all sinners. In this *kali yuga* (the fourth and final stage in the cycle of time) – I call it *korla yuga* (the age in which one has to work), one has to struggle to do one's *dharma* (duties of station). In other *yugas*, doing one's *dharma* came easily, but not in this *yuga*. And this way of portraying Kali is useful since it shows us which way we should not go.

Q. Have you ever seen this expression in everyday life?

A. I've told you already. All women, Ma included, bite their tongues when they feel they have not behaved properly. So to that extent, there is some similarity. But that is all. Kali is the mother of the world, and we may resemble her a little, but we are only weak shadows. Ma can take our forms, look like us if she wishes to because she likes to play with us, but we can never look like her.

Q. Who do you see as more dominant in this picture, Ma or Siva?

A. Here? Ma's strength is definitely greater. Why? Listen to me. What do the gods do? They give boons. They give boons to demons, but when it is necessary to destroy the demons they pray to Ma. And what sort of boons do they give these demons? That only when they see a naked *yoni* (female genitals) will they die. Like Ravana, he only became vulnerable to death because he desired Sita [the reference is to the Hindu epic, Ramayana]; and the Kauravas, would they have died but for the fact that they tried to strip Draupadi in public [the reference is to events in the Hindu epic, Mahabharata]? They are all instances of Ma Shakti (the power of the mother goddess). Similarly, here Ma took the form of Durga so as to kill Mahisasura, but her humiliation at the hands of the demon lead to the death of many more. All this can be found in the Chandi Purana.

The analysis of normative meaning

Initially, the interviews were analyzed into 60 elements of meaning (e.g., "This is Kali," "There was a demon named Mahisasura," "Mahisasura was given a boon by the gods that he could only be killed by a naked woman") that were mentioned at least once by any one of the 92 narrators. Of those 60 elements of meaning, 25 were mentioned by fewer (typically far fewer) than 15 narrators and were not included in our subsequent analyses (e.g., that "it was a voice from the sky who advised Kali that she had to strip," that "Kali was full of remorse"). We also decided to eliminate from the analysis all elements of meaning that were not narrations about the story of the icon per se but were propositions about side topics or the broader context of social life and morality in Orissa. Thus, some of the elements of meaning elicited by the probes ("Have you seen this expression in everyday life?" "Who and under what circumstances?") were not included in the Guttman scaling analyses (e.g., "that when a person is ashamed, he or she looks like Kali"; "that women rather than men feel shame"; "that a woman feels shame when she uncovers her face in front of an elder"; "that only those who are conscious of their duties – *dharma* – experience shame"). Such elements of meaning are, of course, relevant to any characterization of the nature of Oriya *lajya*, and we make use of them in the interpretation of our results.

We ultimately settled on 25 elements of meaning that were thematically relevant to telling stories about the icon per se and were mentioned by at least 15 of the narrators. These 25 elements of meaning are listed in Table 6.1 where they are presented as three packages or modules of meanings.

The first module (Kali's *lajya* as the antidote to her anger) involves 11 elements of meaning in which the narrator talks about Kali and Siva, their marital relationship, and the received hierarchy of domestic status relationships in which the husband is the social superior of the wife, while mentioning that Kali felt angry and accidentally stepped on Siva, but then experienced acute shame (*lajya*) at having been so outrageously inmodest and disrespectful, thereby restraining herself and cooling out her anger.

The second module (the destructive nature of female anger) involves nine elements of meaning in which the narrator elaborates on the magnitude and destructive nature of the Goddess's anger, mentions that the Goddess is a tremendously powerful force created by the male gods to kill demons, in particular a demon named Mahisasura (buffalo demon), but that after her battle with the demon, she was so enraged that she turned into Kali and lost awareness of her surroundings and her ability to discriminate right from wrong, which had disastrous implications for the very survival of the world. This required the male gods to enlist Siva to hatch a plan to bring the Great Mother Goddess back to her normal protective and nurturing sensibilities, which Siva carried out by deliberately positioning himself in Kali's path so that she might step on his chest and experience *lajya*.

The third module (men humiliate women and are the cause of their anger) involves five elements of meaning in which the narrator explains the source of Kali's anger. These elements of meaning link Kali's rage to a boon given by the male gods to the demon Mahisasura and to the ultimate humiliation experienced by the Goddess when she had to take off her clothes and stand naked before the demon to rescue the male gods from the demonic powers that they themselves had bestowed on him.

Captured in these three modules of meanings is a certain narrative logic for generating stories about the icon of the Great Goddess. The various meanings in Module 3 (the explanation of the Goddess's destructive rage and rampage by reference to the nakedness of the Goddess and the humiliating boon given to a demon by the male gods) seem to presuppose and build upon the various meanings in Module 2 (the elaboration of the nature and destructive implications of Kali's anger), just as the various meanings in Module 2 seem to presuppose and build upon the various meanings in Module 1 (the reality of Kali and Siva as divine characters, their social relationship, and Kali's basic moral and emotional attitudes).

The 25 elements of meanings in Table 6.1, analyzed either as 25 individual elements of meaning or as three modules or meta-meanings, form a transitive hierarchy of meanings suggestive of a unidimensional Guttman Scale. The stories told by different narrators unfold their meanings in a relatively fixed order so that the particular meanings narrated can be predicted by the number of meanings narrated, and the least frequently mentioned or distinctive meanings are narrated by precisely those informants who seem to know the most about how to ascribe meaning to the icon of Kali. The Guttman Scale seems to measure the degree to which a narrator exhibits competence or expertise in the norms for telling culturally correct stories about the Great Goddess.

Table 6.1 *25 Elements of meaning (listed as three modules)*

Module 1. Kali's *lajya* (shame) as the antidote to her anger.
1   This is the Goddess Kali.
2   All goddesses are incarnations of the Great Goddess.
3   That is the God Siva.
4   Siva is Kali's husband.
5   Kali stepped on Siva accidentally.
6   Males are superior to women in social status.
7   Kali is more dominant and powerful than Siva.
8   Kali's expression is one of anger.
9   Kali's expression is one of shame.
10 Kali exercises self-control/self-restraint.
11 To "bite the tongue" is an expression of Kali's shame.

Module 2. The destructive nature of female anger.
12 There once was a demon, called Mahisasura.
13 Durga was created by the male gods to help them fight the demon.
14 In her rage, the Great Goddess transformed herself into Kali.
15 Rage is a loss in the capacity to discriminate, a loss of awareness of one's surroundings.
16 As Kali, the Great Goddess threatened the survival of the world.
17 Kali destroys the world with her dance.
18 Siva lay in Kali's path at the request of the male gods or of mortal men.
19 Siva lay in Kali's path deliberately.
20 When she stepped on Siva, Kali became calm/still/statuesque.

Module 3. Men humiliate women and are the cause of their anger.
21 A boon was given by the male gods to the demon that he could never be killed except by a naked woman.
22 When the male gods were challenged by the demon, they were helpless to defend themselves.
23 Durga was helpless against the demon until she stripped naked.
24 Durga was humiliated at having to strip naked.
25 Durga's humiliation was followed by uncontrollable rage.

The four stages of cultural competence

On narrative and empirical grounds, we feel justified in characterizing the local normative meaning of the icon of Kali in terms of three modules of meaning and in characterizing local cultural competence in terms of four stages or levels of expertise.

The lowest level of expertise includes those who have not even progressed to the first stage of competence. The Old Town community of high caste narrators is a relatively well-defined community, yet even in our sample, approximately 21 narrators (23% of the sample) seemed to be either ignorant of the normative meanings associated with this core cultural symbol or else (in the case of two *Tantric* narrators, to be discussed later) narrated their stories under the influence of story telling standards that are not normative in the local Bhubaneswar community. Most of these 21 narrators may well be members of a subculture of (real or feigned) "ignorance": These narrators might be referred to as *cultural duds*. They are either unaware of or unwilling to reveal their knowledge of the storytelling norms of the community.

Correlates of expertise

Diversity in the production of a culturally competent story about the meaning of the icon of Kali clearly exists in our sample. The question that arises is, Does this cognitive diversity relate in any obvious way to the dynamics of the cultural system?

One aspect of our sample of narrators is that, at first blush, variations in degrees of cultural competence appear to be patterned according to differences in gender, with men more likely to exhibit a higher level of narrative expertise. Thus, if we divide the 92 narrators into two groups, the 33 Stage 2 or Stage 3 narrators (Guttman Scale score of 15 or greater) versus the 59 Stage 0 or Stage 1 narrators (Guttman Scale score of less than 15), gender is a significant correlate of expertise $\chi^2(1) = 5.06$, $p < .05$. However, upon closer examination, it turns out that this gender effect is significant when comparing relatively educated men (with 12 years of education or more) with relatively educated women, $\chi^2(1) = 12.45$, $p < .001$, yet, it disappears entirely when comparing less educated men (with less than 12 years of education) with less educated women. It is not gender per se that is a correlate of expertise in our sample, as we shall see.

A second aspect of our sample of narrators is that, for the men, cultural competence is patterned according to number of years of formal schooling. The educated men (with 12 years of education or more) were far more likely to be Stage 2 or Stage 3 narrators than their less educated male counterparts, $\chi^2(1) = 10.84$, $p < .001$. This was not the case for the women in the sample. The relatively more competent female narrators (Stage 2 or Stage 3, scale score of 15 or greater) were not more educated than the relatively less competent female narrators. In fact, the mean number of years of schooling among more competent female narrators was marginally lower than the mean number of years of schooling among the less competent women. The educated men may have been more competent than the less educated men in their ascriptions of culturally correct meanings to the icon, but this did not appear to be the case for the women.

Age seems to play no part in the distribution of cultural competence for either men or women. Those who were 50 years of age or older did not exhibit higher levels of cultural expertise (Stage 2 or 3) than those who were younger. There was no evidence of an age effect on narrative expertise.

In sum, neither age, nor education, nor gender per se was a correlate of cultural competence in ascribing meanings to the icon of the Great Goddess. However, there was an interaction effect between schooling and gender

such that education was associated with the enhancement of the narrative expertise of men but not of women. Thus, although there were female experts, it was the educated men in Bhubaneswar for whom a high level of cultural competence in ascribing meaning to the icon of Kali was most commonplace. Indeed, 85% of the men with 12 years or more of formal education were Stage 2 or Stage 3 experts, whereas this was true of only 23% of women with 12 years or more of education. Less educated men had no such advantage over their female counterparts; 23% of the men with less than 12 years of formal schooling were Stage 2 or Stage 3 experts, whereas this was true of 32% of the less educated women. Nevertheless, the intuition of some female informants that they knew less than their men folk about the icon may be justified, especially if they were married to an educated narrator.

Given the high levels of narrative expertise among educated men but not among educated women, it appears likely that the intracultural variation in cultural competence observed in the sample reflects more than just individual variability in native intelligence, although precisely what it reflects remains to be documented.

At best, our findings are merely invitations to further research on the sources of cognitive diversity in the production of a culturally correct story about the Great Goddess. Differences in social contexts of learning and in social identities (Boster, 1986) may account for some of the cognitive diversity, but the range of plausible accounts is vast. We have favored the view that the diversity in our sample regarding the culturally competent ascription of meanings to Kali is an index of differential mastery of local narrative norms. We would expect mastery of those narrative norms to be related to differential *exposure effects* that, in turn, we would expect to be related to the pragmatic contexts of storytelling in everyday life (e.g., the importance of both education and knowledge of the Gods for the social standing and prestige of high caste Hindu men, the socially sanctioned narration of the story of Kali on public ritual occasions run by educated male religious specialists, and the differential use of the story of Kali in familial contexts as an exhortation about feminine virtues).

Yet, given the limited evidence available, other views cannot be ruled out totally. It is conceivable that in Bhubaneswar everyone is well-exposed to the narrative norms of the community and that the diversity in our sample is an index of differential (conscious or unconscious) resistance to certain of the meanings of the icon. Psychoanalytically inclined theorists will have little difficulty generating hypotheses of this kind, for example, by postulating male identification and oedipal fascination with a demon whose fate is to be decapitated at the hands of a naked, tongue-wagging Mother Goddess, or female defensiveness against the recognition of one's own rage and potential to do harm.

It is even conceivable, given a slight stretch of the imagination, that everyone in the community really is a Stage 3 expert in the local narrative norms, but that in the context of our storytelling task, only certain informants were motivated or willing to reveal all that they knew. Some of the educated men might have wanted to show off their knowledge to an educated female interviewer. Some of the females might have been so devoted to the Goddess and afraid to talk about her that they decided to feign ignorance. However, on the basis of our experience in the community and with the narrators, these hypotheses feel a bit ad hoc and somewhat contrived. Yet, personal testimony is no substitute for more systematic evidence on cognitive diversity in the ascription of meanings to the Goddess and, at the moment, we cannot rule out absolutely any of the hypotheses.

Our various analyses were designed only to determine whether the pattern of sharing of ascribed meanings across informants in the temple town suggests the influence of a culturally defined standard of correctness for telling stories about the icon of Kali. We believe that they do. But precisely how the local cultural norm exercises its influence (e.g., via selective flow of symbols, differential rates of face to face interaction, hegemonic control over or differential access to education institutions, defensive identification with authority figures, etc.), we are not in a position to access.

There are other limitations to the study. It is perhaps worth reiterating that our study relied on evidence from a story production task not from a story recognition task. The failure by an informant to narrate (produce) certain meanings associated with the icon of Kali is not an index of his or her failure to acknowledge those meanings as culturally correct. It seems likely that some of our Stage 0 and Stage 1 narrators would have recognized and endorsed many of the meanings in Modules 2 and 3 had those meanings been made cognitively available to them by means of a true/false test.

Because our sample of narrators oversampled the female population of the temple town, we can only guess what the distribution of narrative expertise would have looked like for a sample more evenly balanced by gender. It seems likely that the proportion of expert Stage 3 storytellers would have been higher than 23%. Nevertheless, it seems clear that whatever the sample selected for study in Bhubaneswar, the normative meanings associated with Module 1 are going to be the most widely distributed meanings across the community. In our study, those meanings were narrated by 80% of the members of our sample.

Perhaps the most relevant finding of the study for a discussion of the cultural psychology of the emotions was that the meaning of *lajya* as a divinely sanctioned antidote to destructive anger expressed by biting the tongue (Module 1) was widely distributed across the community. We feel confident about making the following claim: that in the temple town of Bhubaneswar, a conception of *lajya* (shame) as a highly valued mental state is the local cultural norm.

Is there a canonical scriptural version of the story?

When asked about the icon of the Great Goddess in her manifestation as Kali, members of the Bhubaneswar temple community produced stories that suggested that the icon was a representation of events or scenes that could be found in the traditional corpus of medieval scriptural narratives, the *Puranas*, in particular the *Devi Mahatmya* and the *Devi Bhagvata Purana*, two texts that reflect on the nature of the Great Goddess and try to establish that ultimate reality is feminine in nature. Thinking that it might be instructive to compare the local contemporary versions of the story to a canonical version in the scriptures, we turned to the scriptural literature to locate an original, or at least an early official version, of the key events (the boon to the demon Mahisasura that he could be killed only by a naked woman, the striptease by the Goddess, the foot on Siva's chest) leading up to the moment of Kali's shame (expressed by her protruding tongue) as portrayed in the icon as told by Oriya narrators.

To our surprise, the most popular meaning of the icon (that the Goddess is full of shame and that her protruding tongue expresses this shame) cannot be found in the traditional scriptural narratives, neither Sanskritic nor Oriya. There are many classical Puranic variations of the stories about the Great Goddess, but none that matches precisely the version that is currently the local cultural norm for ascribed meanings to the icon of the Goddess in the temple town of Bhubaneswar. One can find variations in which the male gods beg the Goddess to become a celestial nymph and to seduce, weaken, and kill Mahisasura, although no boon is mentioned (O'Flaherty, 1975, p. 241). One can find variations in which the demon receives a boon that he will be released from all his sins by dying at the hands of the Goddess, although no mention is made of nakedness or shame (O'Flaherty, 1975, p. 242). One can find Puranic stories in which the Goddess behaves recklessly and indiscriminately and is overcome by shame, for example, when she curses her own son in a fit of anger (O'Flaherty, 1975, p. 260), but these do not occur in the context of a battle with demons or with a foot on Siva's chest.

In Tulsi Das's *Adhbhuta Ramayana*, Sita as Kali does step on Siva, but there is no boon, no stripping, no humiliation, and no rage. A fifteenth-century Oriya text, the *Chandi Purana*, is the only one that provides a story that comes tantalizingly close to the structure of meanings that is normative in the vicinity of the Lingaraj Temple in Orissa, India, but, in the end, it too fails because it makes no mention of the Goddess stepping on Siva or her sense of shame (*lajya*). We are now entertaining the alternative hypothesis that there is no single canonical scriptural version of the story of Kali's shame as told in the temple town, and

that the events and psychological attitudes narrated by our informants are imaginative synthetic constructions of the local folk mind, which is well-deserving of note and comment.

Shards of meaning reworked by the local Oriya imagination

The Oriya story of the Goddess as Kali does not match any of the canonical stories in the *Devi Mahatmya* or the *Devi Bhagvata Purana*. If the icon of the Great Goddess, which is today a core symbol in the temple town of Bhubaneswar and in other locations in Eastern India, does not have its source in the orthodox Puranic scriptural literature, where does it come from? If it is not a Puranic image, could it have its source in the more heterodox Tantric way of depicting the Great Goddess?

In Eastern India (and in nearby Nepal; see Levy, 1990), Tantra has long been the subaltern, heterodox voice of Hinduism, existing on the edges of mainstream Brahmanical culture, an exotic cult of dark fortnight sacrificial rites and magical powers. Tantrics are ideologically committed to the inversion of traditional orthodox values and conceptions. In Tantric rituals, menstrual blood is not polluting, it is sanctifying; in Tantric metaphysics, the world is run by women, not men. Men are passive and inert; it is female power, especially the erotic power of naked young women, that makes the world go round.

One particular Tantric text, *The Mahanirvana Tantra* (4.34), describes the Great Goddess as black skinned because she encompasses everything in the universe, "just as all colors disappear in black, so all names and forms disappear in her"; as naked because she is beyond all illusions; as having a red, lolling tongue because that represents the passion and creativity of nature; and as standing on the lifeless corpse of Siva, awakening him, because she is the giver of life and its destroyer. In his monumental study of Hinduism and Tantra in the Newar city of Bhaktapur in nearby Nepal, Robert Levy (1990) noted that, in Tantric imagery, Siva is represented as a corpse, and he mentioned a Newar representation of the Great Goddess in her manifestation as Mahakali in which her vehicle or mount is not the lion described in the Puranic scriptures but "an anthropomorphic male form, at or under her foot" (pp. 212, 251).

Jeffrey Kripal (1993), in his work on the nineteenth century Bengali saint Ramakrishna, discussed the Tantric meanings attached to Kali's tongue and described it as a "consumer of blood sacrifice, a provoker of horror." He also saw it as indicating the "goddess's erotic arousal": Her tongue is extended in passion, as she stands on her husband, Siva, engaged in "aggressive intercourse" (p. 12).

Curiously enough, though Tantrism is a rather exotic cult of the night and of nighttime fantasy, peripheral to local Brahmanical culture in the temple town of Bhubaneswar, it would appear that it is a Tantric icon that has become a core symbolic representation in the local community. Most informants had no difficulty in recognizing the icon as Kali because, in Bhubaneswar, it is a typical way of depicting the Great Goddess. Although it is impossible to offer a definitive explanation for the popularity of Kali's image, some insight into the core of the symbol may be gained by juxtaposing this icon against its social context.

In the patriarchal social world of Oriya Hindus, hardly anyone questions the superior position of the male. And yet in Eastern India (in Bengal, Orissa, and the Eastern border districts of Madhya Pradesh), there is a strong tradition of goddess worship as well as of Tantric belief that the power and energy of the universe is female. This particular combination of beliefs and practices makes the maintenance of the patriarchal social order more problematic than it would have been if the superiority of the male had been unabashedly acknowledged and celebrated.

It is in this context of conflicting cultural beliefs about superior male social status and supreme female divine power that the icon of the Great Goddess gathers its significance because it symbolizes, for Oriya Hindus, the essentially unresolvable nature of male–female relationships. The local narrators of the story of the Great Goddess, especially those who are most expert in the storytelling norms of the community, articulate these ambiguous and often contradictory themes as they interpret the icon.

By and large, the local narrators ignore the pure Tantric view that consistently subordinates men to female power. Instead, they prefer to integrate certain highly edited incidents from the second story in the *Devi Bhagvata Purana* about a battle between a demon named Mahisasura and the Great Goddess (which contains no mention of the Goddess as Kali or of the Goddess's nakedness) with the provocative imagery of the *Chandi Purana* story and certain key elements that have social significance locally to create a new and compelling narrative. This synthesis has produced the canonical story of the icon as it is told in the temple town of Bhubaneswar.

Apparently, one of the more striking features that the narrators felt the need to explain is the Goddess's nakedness in the iconic representation. In their search for a plausible explanation, they went back to the *Chandi Purana*, a fifteenth-century Oriya extrapolation of classical Puranic literature, in which Sārala Dāsa, the author, modifies the boon, making the conditions for the demon's death even more stringent than any condition to be found in the Puranas themselves. In his imagination, Mahisasura may be killed only by a naked woman. Thus, the Goddess's nakedness becomes part of the logic of the story and is used to make sense of the sequence of the narrated events.

It is fascinating that such an explanation tends to strengthen the Tantric view of the power of female sexuality. After all, none of the weapons provided by the male gods suffices to kill the demon. Ultimately the only weapon that the demon cannot withstand is that which is intrinsically the Goddess's own: her gendered anatomy, her female genitals.

An equally plausible non-Tantric explanation for the demon's death could be that he is undone by his own uncontrolled lust. Such an explanation shifts the emphasis from Tantric notions regarding the power of women to the more common Puranic view that desire, in and of itself, is evil and can have only disastrous consequences.

The Oriya narrators do not explicitly articulate one or the other interpretation, leaving it to the listener to sift through the ambiguous meanings of the demon's death. Unlike the

Tantrics who see in the Goddess's creativity and in her absolute destructiveness the ultimate meaning of life, the narrators with the broadest narrative reach (Stage 3) offer a moral justification for the devastation caused by her. They believe that having been, in a sense, set up by the gods in her battle with Mahisasura, she is not entirely unjustified or irrational when she goes berserk with rage. Finally, with great finesse and in clear contradiction to Tantric descriptions, the experts point to Kali's protruding tongue as the mark of her shame (*lajya*) at having stepped on her husband. They fashion an explanation that harmonizes perfectly with notions of male superiority inherent in the patriarchal social order.

Thus, it seems plausible to suggest that this contemporary way of telling the story of the Great Goddess in the temple town of Bhubaneswar represents a local Brahmanical synthesis of a Tantric icon with the moral requirements of a patriarchal social world. In trying to integrate the images of female power invoked by the Tantric icon with the idea that *lajya* (self-control, shyness, modesty, and a sense of shame) is an essential attribute of female virtue, the local folk imagination has invented a new and different story that has only the most tenuous associations with the canonical Puranic versions of the Goddess narratives.

We have no way to assess the creative historical role played by local experts in synthesizing or transforming local narrative norms. D'Andrade (1990) has suggested that not only do cultural experts know a great deal about their own particular domains, but more important, that they are adept at integrating more esoteric knowledge with meanings and understandings that are shared more commonly. It is also possible that the social recognition of the "expertise" of experts gives them a special authority to introduce new elements of meaning into their narratives and generate fresh interpretations of cultural symbols, which then become normative. We do not know whether this is the historical process that produced a distinctive local Oriya version of the story of the Great Goddess. We do know that a reworked and reconstructed story that has no direct parallel in either the Puranic or the Tantric scriptures is today culturally correct in

the wards of the old temple town of Bhubaneswar and lends definition to what it means to be an expert in that small, closeknit community of orthodox, Saivite (Siva worshipping) Brahmans.

Beyond the narrative norm: A Tantric story

Given all these ambivalent and conflict-laden themes about male-female relationships and the attempt by Oriya narrators in the temple town to reconcile them within a single narrative framework, it is instructive to examine what happens to the two pure Tantric narrators in our analysis of local Oriya norms. They end up looking like the cultural duds. However, unlike the cultural duds who seem ignorant of any storytelling norms, the problem for the Tantric narrators in the sample is that they narrated the meanings of the icon under the influence of a canon that is not normative in the Bhubaneswar community. They possessed heterodox specialized knowledge that is so esoteric and counterhegemonic that it was not shared by most local informants. Thus, pure Tantric stories about the (admittedly Tantric) icon of Kali have so little in common with the stories that are generally shared in the temple town that Tantric informants are identified as ignorant and grouped with those who know nearly nothing about the icon. In the context of local cultural norms, their stories are exotic and from out of the underground, making no concessions to commonly held notions about traditional hierarchy and social relations.

In the example of the Tantric narration presented below, the narrator (No. 21) is a 70-year-old Brahman man, married with two sons and two daughters. All his adult life, he has been a priest at the Lingaraj Temple. During the interview, he admitted having attended some Tantric ceremonies, although he claimed that he was not a true worshiper of the Goddess.

Q. Do you recognize this picture?
A. This is the Tantric depiction of Kali. Kali here is naked, she has thrown Siva to the ground and is standing on him. She

displays here absolute, overwhelming strength. She is in a terrible rage, wearing her garland of skulls and in each arm a weapon of destruction. Look, in this hand, the trisul; in this, the *chakra* (the disc); in this, the sword; in this, the sickle; in this, the bow and arrow. This is how Kali is shown in Tantric *pujas* where the devotee is praying to the goddess for perfect knowledge and awareness. All this kind of worship goes on in the Ramakrishna Mission. The monks there are all Tantrics and they know all about it. Sri Ramakrishna and Swami Vivekananda, both great sages, knew about such *sakti* pujas and Tantric rites.

Q. Can you tell me the story that is associated with this picture?

A. In all these Tantric pujas, the goal is to acquire perfect knowledge and ultimate power. The naked devotee worships Mother on a dark, moonless night in a cremation ground. The offerings are meat and alcohol. Ordinary people cannot participate in such worship; if they were even to witness it, they would go mad. I have attended such worship once, but I am not a true worshiper, and I have no special knowledge of Tantric worship.

Q. How would you describe Kali's expression here?

A. She is the image of fury.

Q. You mean she is angry? She is in a rage?

A. Yes … yes. You must understand that this is how she appears to her devotee. He has to have the strength of mind to withstand her fierceness. She is not mild or tender, but cruel and demanding and frightening.

Q. Do you think that she has put out her tongue in anger?

A. Yes, she has put out her tongue in anger. Kali is always angry, she is always creating and, at the same time, destroying life. Here you see her standing with her foot placed squarely on Siva's chest. When the time comes for the universe to be destroyed entirely, no one will be spared, not even the gods – whether Visnu or Siva – everyone will be destroyed.

Q. Some people say that she is feeling deeply ashamed at having stepped on her husband and that is why she has bitten her tongue. You don't agree?

A. People have different views. People believe whatever makes them feel comfortable and if they like to think that Kali is ashamed, then let them. What I have told you is what the special devotees of Kali believe. They believe that Mother is supreme. Even Brahma, Visnu, and Siva are her servants.

Q. Have you seen this expression, that is, Kali's here, in daily life?

A. No, if one was to see this expression on an ordinary human being's face, he would have to be mad, to have lost all his senses. Kali, in fact, is mad with rage, but her rage has nothing that is remotely human about it, it is a divine rage that only a human being who has completely lost his mind can duplicate.

Q. Can you tell me why Siva is lying on the ground?

A. Kali has thrown him to the ground and she puts her foot on him to make clear that she is supreme.

Q. So you don't think that he is lying on the ground to subdue Kali?

A. No, that is beyond Siva's capacity. If Kali becomes calm, it is because she wishes to, not because she is persuaded to be so. Even to her most faithful devotee, Kali's actions sometimes don't make sense, but life itself often doesn't make sense, so what can one say?

Q. Who would you say is dominant in this picture: Is it Kali or Siva?

A. Obviously, Kali. But it is also important to realize that while Sakti is absolutely necessary for the creation and evolution of the universe, by itself even Sakti cannot achieve anything. Sakti has to combine with consciousness for the process of creation to take place and so consciousness, as symbolized by Siva, has a unique position. Just as it is only through the union of a man and a woman that a child can be conceived, so too, only when Sakti and Cit (consciousness) come together does creation occur.

In many ways, this is an impressive informant, especially if one is not interested in the representation of local narrative norms. He is helpful and self-reflective and his narration is "juicy." His narration might even be informative for an investigation of Tantric meanings. Yet, he cannot be viewed as a local cultural expert, and it would have been a disaster for an anthropologist to rely on him as a key informant for the reconstruction of the meaning of this core cultural symbol in the temple town. From the perspective of the approach to the study of cultural norms developed in this essay, an expert or competent informant is not just a helpful member of another culture or even a helpful and highly self-reflective and imaginative member. An expert is a community member whose imaginative reflections are helpful in identifying locally sanctioned and culturally defined truths or canons of correctness. The Kali of Tantric lore is the antithesis of the model of domestic female restraint idealized in Bhubaneswar. The meanings of Tantra are in tension with the local narrative norm.

The moral of the story: The two castes of Orissa (male and female)

Interestingly, the Oriya norms for telling culturally correct stories about the icon of the Goddess explicitly affirm the view that all the goddesses, Kali, Durga, Parvati, and so forth, are but different manifestations of the Great Goddess Devi (see Kurtz, 1992, on the theme that all the goddesses are one). More than half the narrators insist that all the goddesses are lower embodied forms of the transcendental Goddess, merging, separating, and taking on different identities depending on the circumstances and on the particular action that has to be undertaken. They do not portray, as might Western psychoanalytic narrators, a splitting of the divine Mother, with Kali epitomizing the Bad Mother, whose identity is distinct from that of the Good Mother. Rather, for these indigenous storytellers, Kali is represented as one side or aspect of the Divine Mother who, just like any human mother, has her cruel as well as her tender aspects. As one of the women narrators said, "How can a mother be one and not the other? If she genuinely desires the best for her child now and in the future, she has to be both harsh and demanding as well as indulgent and forgiving; only then will her child come to know what the real world is like."

Also, unlike certain Western psychoanalytic narrators, our local Oriya narrators do not portray the female as an incomplete male. Tantric stories about the Great Goddess portray her as self-creating, autonomous, and capable of reproduction through her own emanations. She is parthenogenic. Even in those Puranic portrayals, where the Goddess is the creation of the male gods, she has the combined powers of the male gods and is greater than any one of them. In the stories of the local narrators, Devi's awesome potential for self-sufficiency is recognized even as she is called upon to renounce it and to acknowledge her cosmic interdependency with and social subordination to her husband for the sake of the social good. Unlike narrators in the West who are under the influence of psychoanalytic norms for storytelling, Oriyas do not construct a story about the female as a castrated male. The idea of the female as an incomplete male (a castrated male; an emanation from the rib of Adam) seems to be more characteristic of storytelling norms in the Judeo-Christian traditions, of which contemporary psychoanalytic storytelling may be a local variant.

Whereas the first Oriya module of meanings (Module 1) seems to be saying that the world is truly energized when women regulate, control, and rein in their power, the other two modules of meanings (Modules 2 and 3) offer somewhat ambivalent views regarding female power. At one level, there appears to be the notion that female power is, in and of itself, essentially dangerous because it is always in imminent danger of slipping out of control. At another level, there is the sense that men are often so treacherous, untrustworthy, and exploitative that women would be justified in destroying the world. Taken together, the different interpretations seem to reveal a deep set of ambivalences in the culture regarding the power and potency of the female.

One reason for the popularity of this particular iconic representation of the Great Goddess (as Kali with her tongue out and foot planted on a supine Siva) may well be because of the value that members of the community place on the meta-commentary that it provides on the problem of organizing and understanding a key existential issue or universal social existence theme: the issue of what is male and of what is female and the nature of male–female relations (Shweder, 1982, 1993). That the informants are aware of this interpretive function of the icon is made abundantly clear by the way in which they make pragmatic use of the icon and its narrative. When discussing the disastrous consequences of uncontrolled rage, or proper wifely conduct, or the kind of restraint and modesty valued in a daughter-in-law, the icon is used time and time again to prove points and support arguments. The story of Kali articulates the concerns of a patriarchal society that seeks to establish its own legitimacy.

At the same time, in a place like India where "the preferred medium of instruction and transmission of psychological, metaphysical and social thought continues to be the story" (Kakar, 1989, p. 1), the story of the Great Goddess does not merely reflect a preexisting sensibility but also creates and maintains such a sensibility in a positive manner. In most discussions about the icon, there is an effortless moving back and forth between the world of gods and that of humans, divine action being explained in terms of human needs and failings and standing as an ideal for mortal beings. Every time an informant discusses or interprets the icon, the story told generates and regenerates the very subjectivity that it seems to display.

The significance and popularity of this icon appears to lie in the way in which it crystallizes several themes important to the culture: female power and female shame, anger as socially disruptive and destructive the disjunction between a male dominated hierarchical social order and the potential power of women, and self-control and self-discipline as the only effective means of regulating destructive power. The stories about the Great Goddess in her manifestation as Kali give order to these themes within an encompassing narrative structure and represent them in such a way as to throw into relief a particular view of their essential nature.

As one female narrator put it: There are only two castes in the world, male and female.

All other caste barriers can be breached, but the one that divides men and women is so fundamental that it can never be transcended. Therefore, men and women are different and unequal, an inequality that is context sensitive (Ramanujan, 1989), moving in either way in favor of or against women depending on the circumstances. Thus, men, being more *sattvika* (pure), rank higher than women in ritual status, whereas women partake of the Great Goddess's power to create and destroy, and to nurture and deconstruct simply by virtue of being female and of having female bodies. As the Great Goddess creates and destroys the universe, so does every woman contain within herself the power to sustain or destroy her family.

Durga's ability to kill Mahisasura – the mere sight of her naked genitals (*yoni*) sufficing to destroy the demon – epitomizes the potency of female sexuality. Yet, as the icon displays so dramatically, uncontrolled power may have disastrous consequences. Kali's foot on Siva's chest symbolizes the most shocking reversal of traditional hierarchy. As the story goes, Kali's power, when unchecked, leads not only to death and devastation, but more important, to a complete collapse of family values. She forgets the respect that she owes her husband as his servant, she forgets her wifely duties, and she forgets her dharma.

In other words, the story articulates the fear that anger, when unchecked, could destroy the social order, and the belief that uncontrolled power is immoral. Therefore, power, although a natural consequence of being female, has to be controlled. Because the most effective and the most moral way to control one's power is through means that originate within oneself, Oriyas work to cultivate the emotion of *lajya*, imperfectly translated as shame, to achieve precisely such control.

Bite your tongue: The meaning of lajya

Everyday, Oriya Hindu morality requires self-regulation through sensitivity to the emotion of *lajya*. To have a sense of *lajya* is to be civilized; to know one's rightful place in society; to conduct oneself in a becoming manner; to be conscious of one's duties and responsibilities; to persevere in the performance of social role obligations; to be shy, modest, and deferential and not encroach on the prerogatives of others; and to remain silent or lower ones eyes in the presence of social superiors. *Lajya* is something that one shows or puts on display, just as one might show gratitude or loyalty through various forms of public presentation. Like gratitude or loyalty, *lajya*, which is a way of displaying one's continuing commitment to the maintenance of social harmony, is judged in Bhubaneswar to be a very good thing.

Because everyone concedes that women rather than men have natural power, it is primarily women who need to exercise control over it, and it is they who have to develop their capacity to experience shame. *Lajya* is analogized to a gorgeous ornament worn by women. *Lajya* is the linguistic stem for a local plant (a touch-me-not) that is so coy that it closes its petals and withdraws into itself at the slightest contact. Every time a woman covers her face or ducks out of a room to avoid affiliation with an "avoidance relative" (e.g., her father-in-law or husband's elder brother), she is displaying *lajya*, giving evidence of her civility and intimating that she has within herself the power to do otherwise and to wreck the entire social show. In Orissa, there is not only virtue in *lajya*; there is also terrifying power in it as well.

It is noteworthy that when narrators comment on the manner in which Kali is recalled to a sense of her wifely duties, nearly two thirds of them insist that it happens by her reining in her own power and not through any external control that Siva might exercise. They point to Siva's passivity and argue that Kali could have, if she had wished, trampled on him and gone on. That she chose to recognize him is a measure of her self-control and of her sensitivity to *lajya*. (For more on *lajya*, see Parish, 1991; Shweder, 1992.)

The ultimate message of the icon is to display the cultural truth that it is women who uphold the social order. The more competent narrators, both men and women, articulated this view. They described wives and mothers as the centripetal forces that hold families together. They contrasted those roles with those of husbands and fathers who contribute only financially to the welfare of the family, a contribution that most informants did not view as terribly significant to the family's well-being. Curiously enough, this view of women coincides with the Tantric one that also sees women as the power that upholds the universe. The difference is that although the Tantric view sees women as achieving this position through the unchecked exercise of power, the narrators in the sample saw it as being attained through the moral self-control of such power.

Conclusion

Our analysis demonstrates that expert knowledge about the icon of Kali is hierarchically structured, consisting of four different levels or stages of competence. The Stage 0 level is one of apparent or real ignorance of local narrative norms. The Stage 1 level of normative knowledge adduces female shame as an antidote to female anger. The Stage 2 level of normative knowledge encompasses that first stage of understanding and elaborates on the destructive nature of female anger. The Stage 3 level of normative knowledge offers, in addition to everything else, an explanation for the anger, a critique of male authority, and an appeal to women to control their awesome powers for the sake of social reproduction.

The set of meanings that is most frequently narrated across the community (Module 1 meanings) appears to postulate the view that women keep the world going by reining in their power and by regulating it through sensitivity to the emotion *lajya*. This message is within the competence of anyone with at least a Stage 1 level of expertise. Perhaps it is the most important message that the icon conveys in the sense that the greatest number of people mention it. They accept Kali as the embodiment of power but see in her expression and in the biting of her tongue in particular, the mark of her shame at not controlling her damaging force.

For Oriyas, female *lajya* is an antidote to anger. The icon of the Great Goddess freezes and commemorates a particular divine moment in which the Goddess realized her potential for destructiveness and chose to recognize the necessity for reining herself in. By biting her tongue, she gave expression to her sense of deep shame at having forgotten herself in the first place. The facial expression has become a culturally standardized expression of shame, one that is lexicalized in the Oriya idiom "to bite your tongue," which forms part of everyday discourse.

At the beginning of this essay we asked which emotion was most different from the other two: *sukha* (happiness), *lajya* (shame), or *raga* (anger). Perhaps the reader will no longer be surprised that for residents of the temple town of Bhubaneswar, it is *lajya* (shame) and *sukha* (happiness) that go together and *raga* (anger) that is judged most different from the other two. In Orissa, India, *lajya* is both powerful and good, and the icon of the Great Goddess in her manifestation as Kali is the key to understanding why.

REFERENCES

Boster, J. S.
(1986)   Requiem for the omniscient informant: There's life in the old girl yet. In J. Dougherty (Ed.), *Directions in cognitive anthropology* (pp. 177–197). Urbana: University of Illinois Press.

Bruner, J. S.
(1990)   *Acts of meaning*. Cambridge, MA: Harvard University Press.

Cole, M.
(1990)   Cultural psychology: A once and future discipline? In J. J. Berman (Ed.), *Cross-cultural perspectives: Nebraska Symposium on Motivation (1989)*. Lincoln: University of Nebraska Press.

D'Andrade, R. G.
(1990)   Some propositions about the relations between culture and human cognition. In J. Stigler, R. Shweder, & G. Herdt (Eds.), *Cultural psychology: Essays on comparative human development* (pp. 65–129). Cambridge, England: Cambridge University Press.

Garvey, C.
(1992)   Talk in the study of socialization and development. *Merrill–Palmer Quarterly, 38*, iii–viii.

Ghiselli, E. E., Campbell, J. P., & Zedeck, S.
(1981)   *Measurement theory for the behavioral sciences*. San Francisco: Freeman.

Gordon, R. L.
(1977)   *Unidimensional scaling of social variables*. New York: Free Press.

Jahoda, G.
(1992)   *Crossroads between culture and mind: Continuities and change in theories of human nature*. London: Harvester Wheatsheaf.

Kakar, S.
(1989)   *Intimate relations: Exploring Indian sexuality*. Chicago: University of Chicago Press.

Kripal, J.
(1993)   *Kali's tongue: Shame and disgust in a Tantric world*. Unpublished manuscript.

Kurtz, S. N.
(1992)   *All the mothers are one: Hindu India and the cultural reshaping of psychoanalysis*. New York: Columbia University Press.

Levy, R. I.
(1990)   *Mesocosm: Hinduism and the organization of a traditional Newar city of Nepal*. Berkeley: University of California Press.

Lutz, C.
(1988)   *Unnatural emotions: Everyday sentiments on a Micronesian atoll and their challenge to western theory*. Chicago: University of Chicago Press.

Mahapatra, M.
(1981)   *Traditional structure and change in an Orissa temple*. Calcutta: Punthi Pustak.

Markus, H. R., & Kitayama, S.
(1991)   Culture and the self: Implications for cognition, emotion, and motivation. *Psychological Review, 98*, 224–253.

Markus, H. R., & Kitayama, S.
(1992)   The what, why and how of cultural psychology. *Psychological Inquiry, 3*, 357–364.

Miller, P., Mintz, J., Hoogstra, L., Fung, H., & Potts, R.
(1992)   The narrated self: Young children's construction of self in relation to others in conversational stories of personal experience. *Merrill – Palmer Quarterly, 38*, 45–67.

Miller, P., Potts, R., Fung, H., Hoogstra, L., & Mintz, J.
(1990)   Narrative practices and the social construction of self in childhood. *American Ethnologist, 17*, 292–311.

Miller, P., & Sperry, L.
(1987)   Young children's verbal resources for communicating anger. *Merrill–Palmer Quarterly, 33*, 1–32.

Much, N. C.

(1992) Analysis of discourse as methodology for a semiotic psychology. *American Behavioral Scientist, 36,* 52–72.

O'Flaherty, W. D.

(1975) *Hindu myths.* New York: Penguin Books.

Parish, S.

(1991) The sacred mind: Newar cultural representations of mental life and the production of moral consciousness. *Ethos, 19,* 313–351.

Ramanujan, A. K.

(1989) Is there an Indian way of thinking? An informal essay. *Contributions to Indian Sociology, 23,* 41–58.

Seymour, S.

(1983) Household structure and status and expressions of affect in India. *Ethos, 11,* 263–277.

Shweder, R. A.

(1982) Beyond self-constructed knowledge: The study of culture and morality. *Merrill–Palmer Quarterly, 28,* 41–69.

Shweder, R. A.

(1990) Cultural psychology: What is it? In J. Stigler, R. Shweder, & G. Herdt (Eds.), *Cultural psychology: Essays on comparative human development* (pp. 1–43). Cambridge, England: Cambridge University Press.

Shweder, R. A.

(1991) *Thinking through cultures: Expeditions in cultural psychology.* Cambridge, MA: Harvard University Press.

Shweder, R. A.

(1992) The cultural psychology of the emotions. In M. Lewis & J. Haviland (Eds.), *Handbook of emotions* (pp. 417–431). New York: Guilford Press.

Shweder, R. A.

(1993, Winter) "Why do men barbecue?" and other postmodern ironies of growing up in the decade of ethnicity. *Daedalus, 122,* 281–310.

Shweder, R. A., Mahapatra, M., & Miller, J. G.

(1990) Culture and moral development. In J. Stigler, R. Shweder, & G. Herdt (Eds.), *Cultural psychology: Essays on comparative human development* (pp. 130–204). Cambridge, England: Cambridge University Press.

Shweder, R. A., Much, N. C., Mahapatra, M. M., & Park, L.

(in press) The "Big Three" of morality (autonomy, community and divinity), and the "Big Three" explanations of suffering. In P. Rozin, S. A. Brandt (Eds.), *Morality and health.* Stanford, CA: Stanford University Press.

Shweder, R. A., & Sullivan, M.

(1990) The semiotic subject of cultural psychology. In L. A. Pervin (Ed.), *Handbook of personality: Theory and research* (pp. 399–416) New York: Guilford Press.

Shweder, R. A., & Sullivan, M.

(1993) Cultural psychology: Who needs it? *Annual Review of Psychology, 44,* 497–523.

Stigler, J., Shweder, R., & Herdt, G (Eds.).

(1990) *Cultural psychology: Essays on comparative human development.* Cambridge, England: Cambridge University Press.

Weller, S. C., & Romney, A. K.

(1990) *Metric scaling.* Newbury Park, CA: Sage.

Wertsch, J.

(1992) Keys to cultural psychology. *Culture, Medicine and Psychiatry, 16,* 273–280.

Wierzbicka, A.

(1992). *Semantics, culture and cognition: Universal human concepts in culture-specific configurations.* New York: Oxford University Press.

Wiggins, D.

(1991) Truth, invention and the meaning of life. In D. Wiggins (Ed.), *Needs, values, truth.* Oxford, England: Basil Blackwell.

7

Shame and Guilt in Japan

Takie Lebra

In a previous paper (Lebra 1971) I attempted to analyze shame and guilt with a focus on the *social* mechanism underlying these emotions, shame being associated with status occupancy and guilt with the rule of reciprocity. The present paper supplements that paper by concentrating on the *psychocultural* dimension of shame and guilt. The Japanese case is taken, but I do not claim that the following discussion applies exclusively to Japan. Some attempts will be made, however, to differentiate the more culture-bound from the more culture-free aspects of both concepts.

Shame and guilt are defined here as two psychic channels for processing stress into self-punishment. "Stress" rather than "norm violation" is chosen in this definition because among the Japanese norm violation is not a necessary condition for giving rise to shame or guilt, as will be explained below.

Psychoculturally viewed, both shame and guilt are anchored in the individual's self, and yet they reflect concern with others. Both are thus allocentric in that they are based upon the actor's ability in empathy to "take the role of other" (Mead 1967) or to be aware of his self as an object of sanction. The "other" may be human or supernatural, specific or generalized, alive or dead. In the case of shame, others are visualized as audience or spectators, whereas in the case of guilt they appear as victims of or sufferers from one's action. This viewpoint is meant to be universally valid, but there may be cultural variation in the degrees of allocentric awareness especially with respect to guilt. In guilt as well as shame, I propose, the Japanese tend to be more aware of others than, for instance, those who have been socialized in the Judeo-Christian theistic tradition.

Shame

Benedict (1946), while wrong in characterizing Japan as a shame culture *in contrast to* a guilt culture, was nonetheless right in capturing the pervasiveness of shame in Japanese culture. Shame is pervasive partly because Japan, unlike culturally and ethnically diverse societies such as the United States, has its cultural norms well defined so that their violations are readily recognized, and partly because the Japanese individual is more surrounded by significant audiences to whom his action is exposed. In conjunction with these objective factors, I propose another, more subjective factor to explain the pervasiveness of shame, that is, the exposure sensitivity of the outer self.

Takie Sugiyama Lebra, Shame and Guilt: A Psychocultural View of the Japanese Self from *Ethos*, Vol. 11, No. 3, Self and Emotion (Autumn, 1983), pp. 192–209. Published by Blackwell Publishing on behalf of the American Anthropological Association. ©1983 by the Society for Psychological Anthropology. Reprinted with permission of the American Anthropological Society.

The exposure sensitivity of the outer self

Lynd (1958:27) identifies shame as the experience of "exposure of peculiarly sensitive, intimate, vulnerable aspects of the self." As she claims, shame is more intensely painful and irreversible than guilt, involving "the whole self." Similarly, Lewis (1971:30) describes shame as involving the self more directly than guilt does:

> The experience of shame is directly about the *self*, which is the focus of evaluation. In guilt, the self is not the central object of negative evaluation, but rather the *thing* done or undone is the focus. In guilt, the self is negatively evaluated in connection with something but not itself the focus of the experience. Since the self is the focus of awareness in shame, "identity" imagery may be evoked. [Emphasis in original]

This kind of intense shame, afflicting the total self, more painful than guilt, is by no means alien to the Japanese. It is indeed shared by a Japanese individual who is exposed to significant spectators when he seriously fails in living up to an expected level of ability, knowledge, performance, rectitude, propriety, or any other value. Inherent in this shame is the exposure of a distinct norm violation.

What sets the Japanese apart from Westerners seems to be their particular sensitivity to the surface-level shame affecting the outer self only, or what might be more properly called "embarrassment." The Japanese actor is embarrassed when he is exposed to an audience, no matter whether he has done anything wrong or not. Norm violation is not a necessary condition. It might be argued that embarrassment and shame are two distinct categories. But I think these are continuous for the Japanese under a single word *haji*. Furthermore, the prevalence of embarrassment-*haji*, in my view, makes the Japanese all the more vulnerable to shame-*haji*.

A culture-bound aspect of Japanese *haji* thus lies in the exposure sensitivity of the outer self. It is no coincidence that Sakuta (1967), a Japanese sociologist, criticized Benedict for her exclusive attention to "public shame" in disregard of "private shame." The concept of public shame alone, Sakuta contends, cannot explain why one feels *haji* when subjected not only to ridicule but to praise. What gives rise to *haji* here is the fact that one is exposed to the concentrated attention or "gaze" of others, whether it is malevolent or benevolent. Sakuta (1967:18) further attributes the Japanese *haji* to the failure of a social group to protect the privacy of its members from the gaze of external groups:

> Members of a group are often exposed simultaneously to the eyes of those within the group and the eyes of those outside the group. When a member engages in personal interaction with fellow members of his group, he feels *haji* because he becomes aware of outsiders' eyes focusing on him. [My translation]

Gaze as a stressor arousing physiological reactions has been experimentally demonstrated on the basis of an American sample (Mazur, Rosa, Faupel, Heller, Leen, and Thurman 1980). In the Japanese case it seems that stress aroused by gaze is processed foremost into *haji*. Furthermore, exposure sensitivity for Japanese is so intense that imaginary gaze alone tends to suffice to generate *haji*. This tendency is derived from the allocentric empathy with which the Japanese actor is prone to take the role of audience and to stare at his own action as if he were an object of attention.

The primacy of the exposure sensitivity of the outer self in Japanese *haji* may be illustrated by TAT responses. In 1969, a sample of residents of Eastern City[1] were asked to write stories in response to a Japanese version of the TAT (a selection from Rinsho Shinri Gaku Kenkyu Kai [1953]). The responses used here are from 35 women (33 to 59 years of age) who were participating in a PTA meeting and a women's club meeting, and from one class of high school students including 20 males and 18 females. The picture intended to elicit shame responses was of an adult male looking away from an adult female, with the female looking at the back of the male's head while placing her right arm upon his shoulder. In a corner of the background hung a tiny picture of a bikini-clad woman, which, however, could well be overlooked because of its peripheral location and the vagueness of its subject. A written instruction was given to insert in the story one of the words *haji, hajiru,* and *hazukashii,* which are the noun, verb, and adjective forms of shame/embarrassment. Because of the sample bias and stimulus bias (for a sexual overtone), the test result is undoubtedly limited in its generalizability but still may elucidate the above proposition regarding *haji* and exposure sensitivity.

An overwhelming majority of respondents identified the couple as husband and wife, and only a few saw them as lovers, as father and daughter, and the like. With negligible exceptions, shame was associated with one form of exposure or another, feared or actualized. Adult women in particular tended to project themselves into the woman in the picture. Some examples are given below (the number indicates the age of the respondent):

Woman 35: My husband came home from work. "Welcome home. You must be exhausted from your hard work."[2] So saying, I gently put my hand upon his shoulder as he sat down upon a chair. He felt *hazukashii* and looked away toward the children.

Woman 34: The woman, I think, is displaying herself to the man too daringly. Doesn't she feel *hazukashii* in front of me?

Female student 17: A young man and woman. They had been enjoying chatting until moments before, but one word she said upset him and made him turn away from her. At a loss, she wondered what to do. She felt *hazukashii,* but gathered up the courage to put her hand upon his shoulder and whisper, "I love you."

The most common theme across generations is the exposure – not only inadvertent exposure but voluntary disclosure and confession – of intimacy or love within a sexual dyad as it is expressed physically or verbally. The audience for the exposure is the sexual partner, a third party present, or a general, often invisible, public.

One might suspect that exposure sensitivity expressed in these responses is simply due to the sexual nature of the stimulus picture. Indeed, it is likely that the stimulus of sexual intimacy, because of its private nature, did

intensify exposure sensitivity. But this confirms, not negates, the proposed relationship between exposure sensitivity and *haji.* For another demonstration, I shall draw upon Barnlund's (1975) comparison of Japanese and American college students with respect to self-disclosure in communication. He tested the hypothesis that Japanese disclose themselves less than Americans. It was found that the tactic of nondisclosure is resorted to by Japanese even in defense against threats:

In threatening interpersonal settings some people relied heavily upon only one or two defensive tactics. In the case of the Japanese it was usually a preference for remaining silent, laughing, or replying ambiguously; in the case of the Americans it consisted of talking their way out of a situation or defending themselves through argument. [1975:128]

It appears that the Japanese individual makes himself vulnerable to embarrassment/shame by disclosing himself (e.g., his opinion), whereas the American does so through his inability to disclose himself. As a result, the "private self," that part of self that remains unexpressed and hidden, occupies a greater area of the total self for the Japanese, whereas the "public self," the part which is externally communicated, is greater for the Americans (1975:90).

It is understandable that Japanese reticence is often explained as a sign of *haji,* or more correctly, as a strategy for avoiding *haji,* and that a variety of typical Japanese gestures, behavior styles, or speech patterns are described as *tereru, hanikamu,* or other untranslatable equivalents of "shy." Further, the avoidance of exposure has much to do with the cultural emphasis on the expressiveness of the back of the body or what Aida (1970:21–26) calls *haigo-shugi* (the primacy of the back). Two actors in a kabuki play express their mutual love typically by attaching themselves back to back, and what people on earth, wonders Aida, would understand the expressions of a person's back as sensitively as the Japanese? Similarly, the woman's beauty has been, and somewhat still is, symbolized by the kimono which conceals rather than exaggerates its wearer's body curves (McCoy 1980).

The foregoing suggests that exposure sensitivity is not only a spontaneous response but a culturally desirable and even prescribed attitude. What underlies this is the modesty code whereby the self is supposed to remain hidden, unexpressed, or inconspicuous. One is thus expected, when exposed or about to be exposed, to behave as if one were embarrassed or shy. Viewed this way, self-exposure itself can be said to amount to a norm violation.

Perfectionism in display

Exposure sensitivity, while it encourages non-exposure, also motivates a Japanese actor to display himself, when he has to, in perfection as if he were on stage. What is required is a formally impeccable presentation of the self. To insure or facilitate such self-presentation, Japanese culture abounds with codes of formal communication,[3] verbal and nonverbal, to which Japanese are generally ready to conform their action: highly conventional forms of greetings for routine usage; status-congruous or occasion-appropriate rules of speech, gesture, facial expression, posture, and other display rules; coordinated or joint actions of group members as in singing and athletics; regimentation in the procedures of ceremonies, banquets, and the like. To make a staged self-presentation flawless, the predictability of the sequence of events is maximized, and personal, extemporaneous disruptions and variations are minimized.

In light of the cultural premium placed on formal display, it is not surprising that Japanese have cultivated and perpetuated what might be called formal arts. The tea ceremony is an outstanding example. One finds in the tea ceremony the actor's self-presentational performance in conformity to the fixed and elaborate rules for posturing, manipulating tea utensils, preparing and serving or accepting and appreciating tea. But tea rules encompass much more. In addition to teamaking and drinking, a participant must know, or must imitate a co-participant who knows, what to wear, what to take with him, how to go through the tea house gate, how to enter the tea room, how to bow and what to say while bowing, where to take his seat, how to comment on a wall picture, on the hearth,

and so on. One person's move or utterance serves as a signal for another person's action so that the whole event, if successful, looks like a well synchronized choreography (Mayuzumi 1976). It is against the background of the *haji* complex that one can understand why such a rule-bound self-presentation is accepted by Japanese as relaxing, therapeutic, or tranquility-inducing.

Anthropophobia

Exposure sensitivity and the pressure for perfectionism in display may augment one another to drive a person into a neurotic syndrome called *taijin kyōfushō*, anthropophobia or the fear of interpersonal contact, which has been designated by psychiatrists as characteristic of Japanese. It takes various forms including the fear of blushing, of body odor, of facial expression, saliva swallowing, etc., but the most typical symptom seems to be the fear of being stared at or of staring at another. The fear of eye-to-eye contact involves the worry that being overly conscious of another person's stare one would look unnatural, or the feeling that "I cannot look others in the face: if I force myself to look, my gaze would appear too intent and cause discomfort in others" (Iwai and Abe 1975:69). Implicit here is a morbid fear of self-exposure, as the self is localized in various parts of the body; eye, mouth, face, etc.

The fear of self-exposure may take the form of *hitomishiri*, the term identified by Doi (1969) as the Japanese version of "stranger anxiety." *Hitomishiri* usually refers to an infant who has begun to discriminate the familiar from the unfamiliar persons around it and to fear the latter, but is also used by psychiatrists to describe adult behavior (*Seishin Bunseki Kenkyū* 1969). Maeda (1969) applied this concept to the behavior patterns he observed in sensitivity-training sessions with normal adult participants who were mutual strangers. He noted that, even after several sessions, the members remained tense, nervous, and reticent, and would rather listen to what older members would say than discuss their own feelings. Fujita (1969) attributes the *hitomishiri* characteristic of Japanese to shyness arising from the clear demarcation line drawn between *uchi* (the psychically or socially internal domain) and *soto* (the external domain).

The anthropophobic Japanese has a dilemma: he fears self-exposure to the audience and thus is inclined to withdraw from social interaction; and yet, being aware of his oddness, he is driven to overcome this inclination and to present himself in a perfectionist manner. In this sense it may be safe to consider *taijin kyōfushō* a part of the shame complex.

Off-stage self-disclosure

Aversion to exposure and the desire for formally flawless display underlying the Japanese sensitivity to shame, act together to inhibit self-expression. These would cause a morbid hypertrophy of what Barnlund (1975) calls the private self unless there are some legitimate occasions for self-disclosure, or for releasing the excess of the private self into the public self. The truth of the matter is that Japanese set aside certain occasions or situations for free, personal, uninhibited self-disclosure.

Two persons, or a small group of persons, engage in "gut-level" communication by "splitting the *hara* (belly) open," or "becoming *hadaka* (naked)." It appears that the rhythm of the Japanese life represents cycles of alternation between on-stage inhibition and offstage shamelessness, or underexposure and overexposure. Same-sex peers, particularly those who have grown up together such as schoolmates, make an ideal group for an uninhibited mutual self-disclosure. Such occasions are marked off from the workaday life, as when two men meet at a bar and talk out their accumulated frustrations over their work experiences, social lives, and so on, in a state of inebriation. The occasion may involve around-the-clock contact, as in a group tour that permits not only the verbal but physical exposure of the participants to one another. An Eastern City woman says she looks forward to a reunion, once or twice a year, with several of her high school classmates at a local hotel where they usually stay overnight, enjoy co-bathing in the hotspring bath, and talk all night about themselves, their husbands, and in-laws, while lying in beds adjacent to one another.

Off-stage communication is an essential part of decision-making process in Japan. Japanese leaders in group decision making consider it absolutely necessary to go through *nemawashi* or *jinarashi* (off-stage communication to secure agreement or acquiescence) prior to a formal session which tends to be reduced to a ritual.

The cycles of the on-stage formality constrained by shame and the off-stage informality allowing for shamelessness are so well patterned in Japanese expectations that what is essentially an on-stage event tends to include an off-stage phase as an integral part. The wedding banquet I observed in Eastern City in 1978 is a case in point. A large tatami-matted banquet hall of a local hotel contained roughly two hundred people, sitting along the rows of tables where a full dinner was set for each guest. On one side of the room was a platform with a raised head table along which were seated the bride and groom, flanked by the formal go-betweens and parents, facing the assembled guests. The first phase was dominated by the extreme formality of the occasion, marked by a series of highly stylized speeches given by "important guests" such as the president of the company employing the groom and a prefectural assemblyman who had been invited primarily to render prestige to the whole ceremony. The participants looked serious, remained absolutely quiet, listened attentively to the lengthy, often boring speeches, and no one touched the dishes. When this phase was over exactly as programmed, the second phase was begun by toasting in unison. Now the master of ceremonies told the guests to start eating while listening to another series of speeches. This time, speakers stood up to speak at their own seats, unlike the previous speakers, who stepped forward to the head table to command the attention of the whole audience. Another contrast was that these speakers were less prestigious but more familiar with the groom or bride (the groom's schoolteacher, the bride's uncle) so that they could tell personal anecdotes, some of which drew laughter from the audience. The audience, however, was listening half-heartedly, dividing its attention between the auditory stimuli and palatal pleasure. The third and final phase, as announced by the master of ceremonies, was "entertainment." By this time, inebriation was making its progress, people were moving from table to table to exchange sake cups as a token of friendship, talking loudly, and some stretching out their limbs on the tatami floor, half asleep. In charge of "entertainment" were intimate friends of the groom and bride, and the center of action switched to a stage located at the opposite end of the room from the head table. Popular songs and dances were performed on the stage, their contents became increasingly indecent and obscene, and the performers presented themselves more as clowns. Middle-aged women in particular cracked erotic jokes and sang about copulation. The whole event may be described as "liminal" (Turner 1969), but it should be noted that liminality can thus range from the sacred to the profane, from extraordinary regimentation to a chaotic mess, from shame-sensitive underexposure to obscene overexposure. These opposite extremes, I believe, should be together considered inherent in the shame complex.

Guilt

Contrary to Benedict's (1946) designation of Japan as a shame culture, a keen sense of guilt has been recognized to prevail among Japanese (DeVos 1974). I even argue that the Japanese type of shame, as characterized above, intensifies, rather than precludes, guilt, because exposure avoidance embedded in the shame complex orients one inward. Paradoxical as it may sound, a strong concern about what one looks like outwardly in the eyes of audience preoccupies one with the state of his inner self. It is my proposition that, for Japanese, guilt is locked together with introspectiveness or self-reflection.

Self-reflection

Japanese are socialized to be self-reflective, and *hanseikai* (classroom session for self-reflection) is part of the school curriculum. Their self-reflective tendency can be demonstrated by the result of sentence-completion tests given to adult samples of urban Japanese and Hong Kong Chinese. As reported in Lebra (1973), nearly half (46%) of the Japanese sample (*n* = 201) responded to the sentence fragment, "If you are kind to others," with expectations for inner rewards: "your heart will be brightened," "you will feel good," "it will stay with you as a heart-brightening memory," and the like. Only 4% of the Chinese sample (*n* = 205) responded in this manner, and more than half (53%) showed expectations for direct, reciprocal repayment: "they, too, will be kind to you," "the kindness will come back to you," and so forth. In response to another sentence fragment, "After having committed all sorts of wrong-doing,"[4] the majority of both Japanese and Chinese respondents projected the efficacy of immanent justice: "he was ruined," "he was rejected by the world," "after death, he was not even admitted to Hell," and the like. Yet, such responses were 20% fewer among the Japanese (66% of 203 respondents) than among the Chinese (86% of 200). Conversely, more Japanese (23%) than Chinese (10%) referred to inner retribution, such as anxiety, repentance, confession, or reform, indicative of guilt feelings independent of external justice: "you feel uneasy at heart," "he will feel regretful and guilty," "he settled down to work seriously."

Compared with shame, guilt is more likely to be preceded by a definite norm violation and to involve a moral transgression, as will be illustrated by the TAT responses in the next section. Nonetheless, even guilt, when translated into a Japanese version, does not always presuppose a norm violation. The Japanese actor tends to, or is encouraged to, reflect upon himself when in trouble and to examine where he has gone wrong: he may come to realize that he has committed a moral transgression only after self-reflection and then to feel guilty. Again, it may be just stress rather than a clearcut norm violation that is processed, through self-reflection, into guilt. In the TAT responses summarized and analyzed by DeVos (1974) we find the theme of self-blame a typical Japanese response to a stressful situation: "A husband comes home very late at night; *the wife thinks it is for the lack of her affection* and tries hard; he finally reforms" (1974:128); "An elder brother did something wrong and is examined by the policeman; he will be taken to the police station, but will return home and reform. *The younger sister also thinks that she was wrong herself*" (1974:129; emphasis supplied).

Guilt is systematically aroused and intensified to cope with stress in many religious sects in Japan. The Gedatsu,[5] for example, insists that illness or any other kind of suffering is to be imputed to the sufferer's own fault such as negligence of his or her duty. Whatever adversity one encounters, one should reflect upon oneself in search for one's own wrongdoing. Moreover, the convert is supposed to blame another person's misery upon him or herself: A child's illness should arouse guilt in its mother. What appears clearly to be the other person's fault is to be blamed on oneself. The husband's infidelity should be taken as a sign of the wife's character defect. A child's rebellion should remind the mother of her own disobedience to her parents, her repentance being the key to the child's reform. If an alter aggresses against ego, it should be understood that the aggression originated from ego against the alter and now has returned to its origin. This kind of reasoning would not be persuasive unless the listener is susceptible to guilt arousal through self-reflection without necessarily having consciously deviated from a norm.

The allocentric self-blame

The Japanese sense of guilt ties in with the allocentric concern in that one's awareness of another as a victim of one's action or inaction is essential. Guilt is aroused or intensified through ego's vicarious sharing of alter's suffering. This will be illustrated again by the TAT responses (of the same sample as the "shame" respondents used above). The guilt-eliciting picture had a front view of an old man's face at the upper-right of the frame and a profile of a younger person – male or female – at the lower-left, looking up and close to the old man. The instruction was to use one of the common expressions equivalent to "guilty": *sumanai, mōshiwakenai,* and *ki ga togameru.*

The two persons in the picture were identified as a heterosexual pair, married or unmarried, more by adult respondents, whereas cross-generational relationships – father and son/daughter, grandfather and grandchild – were seen more by the students. The themes of norm deviation in association with guilt feelings vary more widely and are more serious than those with shame. Those who saw a heterosexual pair associated guilt with adultery, other forms of clandestine sexual engagement, and disregard of age imbalance; as many as 10 out of the 35 women explicitly mentioned adultery (and several more if implicit accounts are added). The respondents who saw a father-child or grandfather-grandchild pair tended to associate guilt with disobedience, runaway, unpaid debt, causing trouble/suffering/worry, inadequate parental care. Several respondents, in both the sexual and kin contexts, mentioned *wagamama* (selfishness, having one's way) as the cause of guilt. A few examples:

Woman 44: He falls in love with a married woman and, unable to keep it within himself, confesses his love. She, too, in time, finds herself, to her astonishment, in love with the *sensei.* This illicit love, while it makes her feel *sumanai* and *mōshiwakenai* toward her husband and children, cannot be curbed, and they continue to meet.

Male student 17: Father, why did you die before me? I am *mōshiwakenai* for having caused you so much hardship without a chance to repay you.

These and most other stories specify the persons toward whom guilt is felt as the victims of ego's action or inaction: a woman in adultery feeling guilty toward her husband and children, or toward the wife and children of her partner; a widow guilty toward her child for getting sexually involved with a man; a son guilty toward parents and siblings for causing trouble; a daughter guilty toward her father for abandoning him in order to marry, and so on. Such victim-consciousness, or more generally, allocentric empathy is what induces self-blame. It is not surprising that intense guilt is often associated with the death of the victim which makes ego's guilt unredeemable.

The allocentric aspect of guilt comes into focus when guilt is aroused more by the sight of an alter in pain than by ego's own action. It is not uncommon for Japanese to become sensitized to guilt-feelings when they see their kin or other significant persons suffer from illness, death, or other misfortunes, regardless of their responsibility for these sufferings. This point reinforces what was said in the previous section regarding a norm violation not always being involved in guilt. This also explains why some of the guilt-arousing transgressions, as shown in the TAT responses of Eastern City residents, tend to be diffuse and ambiguous, such as "causing trouble *(meiwaku)*," "causing worry *(shimpai)*," "being selfish *(wagamama)*," or having oneself "looked after *(sewa o kaketa)*."

The therapeutic method called Naikan (meaning "inner examination") intensifies guilt consciousness through self-reflection and allocentric self-blame. The client, under the guidance of a counsellor, is supposed to reflect in isolation upon his faults in relation to the most significant persons around him, his mother in particular. Specifically, he is to recall in detail how much he owes to the alter, how little he has repaid, and most importantly, what *meiwaku* and *shimpai* he has caused the benefactor instead. Unable to recall anything at first, the client begins in a few days to "recall" what wrong he has done against the person he is most indebted to (Yoshimoto 1965; Okumura, Sato, and Yamamoto 1972; Murase 1974; Lebra 1976c: 201–214). Again, the efficacy of this therapy may well be embedded in Japanese culture with its particular definition of guilt.

Guilt is so other-oriented that feeling guilty tends to amount to feeling apologetic to a specific person. Indeed the words for "guilty" such as *sumanai* and *mōshiwakenai* are expressions for apology; they imply the alter whom ego owes an apology. Given such an equivalence between guilt and apology, a person who is guilty and yet fails to apologize is extremely offensive to Japanese. In fact most Japanese are only too willing to offer an apology for the slightest annoyance they happen to create for others.

The last point calls attention to the fact that admitting guilt and apologizing is not only a spontaneous tendency, but, like shame, a matter of cultural style or social gesture as well. *Sumanai*, while expressive of deep guilt derived from one's empathy for another's pain, is also taken as a perfunctory ritual lacking sincerity or even as a strategic camouflage of rule breaking on the part of its user in presenting an apology. *Sumimasen*, the conversational form of *sumanai*, is thus detested by some Japanese. Both shame and guilt, then, cover a wide range of emotional intensity, from deep and serious to superficial and ritualistic. The point is that this variety makes guilt and shame all the more pervasive among Japanese.

The primacy of guilt

The allocentricity of guilt has a further implication. Although shame and guilt are perhaps equally pervasive, Japanese tend to stress guilt feelings in expressing their emotions. What is likely to be experienced as shame may therefore be talked about and thought about as guilt. A failure in expected performance may elicit a guilt response, as it happened in some TAT stories (of the above-cited Eastern City sample), rather than a shame response: an unsuccessful candidate for an entrance examination felt *sumanai* toward his parents. This particular point reconfirms DeVos's (1974) argument in refuting the equation, as proposed by Piers and Singer (1953), between ego ideal and shame. The Japanese data suggested to De Vos a closer relationship between the inability to achieve the parental expectation and guilt. To illustrate the primacy of guilt further, reference may be made to another result of my sentence-completion tests. The fragment, "If you do not know manners and etiquette," was meant to elicit shame responses, and, indeed, the majority of both groups (60% of Japanese, 71% of Chinese) anticipated the shame experience, either internal or external: "people will make fun of you," "you will be ashamed," "you will be called a barbarian." However, many more Japanese (33%) than Chinese (6%) gave responses like: "your parents will be criticized," "you will cause discomfort in the people around you," "you will cause trouble *(meiwaku)* for others." This group of responses indicates the allocentric awareness of the victims of ego's impropriety. Here it is not so much ego himself as alter who suffers, whereas the shame response shows ego as the sufferer.

The same point may be reinforced by the case of anthropophobic patients who often turn out to be more concerned with the discomfort they arouse in others by, for instance, staring at them than with losing face by being stared at. An extreme case involving the fear of "symptom contagion" was reported by Tsukamoto, Takagaki, and Yamagami (1973). This patient did not only worry that his nervousness and other defects would be revealed, but was much more afraid that his tenseness would hurt other persons, and that his symptom, which he was convinced was contagious, would appear in others. In a severe case like this, the guilt complex appears to overwhelm the shame complex.

The reason behind this relative primacy of guilt among Japanese may be the ultimate moral value associated with self-denial.[6] Shame, though it is also allocentric, still involves an egocentric concern for self-image. Egocentricity entailed in shame arouses a degree of ambivalence in Japanese regarding admission of shame, whereas guilt admission involves no such ambivalence. This explains why a few of the Eastern City TAT respondents denied that there was any feeling of shame in disclosing one's love while no respondent denied the existence of guilt feelings toward someone. Both shame and guilt are important moral sanctions for Japanese, but at the same time, Japanese tell one another to transcend shame-sensitivity although guilt-sensitivity is considered always desirable.

Given this primacy of guilt, the behavior patterns usually associated with shame may well be reinterpreted in light of the guilt complex. Exposure-avoidance, shyness, fear of eye-to-eye confrontation, the culturally stylized self-denigration and humility – all these may be attributed to the actor's thoughtfulness to avoid hurting or annoying others, that is, to avoid the Japanese version of guilt.

It might be concluded that guilt is anchored more firmly than shame in the Japanese moral system, and that shame emotions, therefore, are often translated into guilt terms. This conclusion reverses Benedict's position regarding Japanese emotions.

NOTES

1 A resort city in central Japan with a population of 70,000 where I have been conducting fieldwork periodically since 1968.

2 A common form of greeting that defies a meaningful translation.

3 By "formal" I mean all the four aspects of "formality" identified by Irvine (1979): code structuring, code consistency, invoking positional identities, and centrally focused communication.

4 This portion of the results of the sentence-completion-test project and another to be referred to below have not been reported yet in print.

5 Fieldwork was conducted on this cult, primarily on the activities of its Eastern City branches, in 1970–71. The results have appeared in Lebra (1974, 1976a, 1976b, and 1982).

6 Self-denial entails the sincerity, purity, cleanness, transparency, and ultimately "emptiness" or "nothingness" of the self. This logically links to the Japanese association of *tsumi* (sin or guilt) with *kegare* (pollution), the latter implying an impure, unclean, clouded state of the self.

REFERENCES

Aida, Yuji
   1970   *Nipponjin no ishiki kozo* (The structure of Japanese mentality). Tokyo: Kodansha.
Barnlund, Dean C
   1975   *Public and Private Self in Japan and the United States*. Tokyo: The Simul Press.
Benedict, Ruth
   1946   *The Chrysanthemum and the Sword: Patterns of Japanese Culture*. Boston: Houghton Mifflin.
DeVos, George
   1974   The Relation of Guilt toward Parents to Achievement and Arranged Marriage among Japanese. *Japanese Culture and Behavior: Selected Readings* (T. S. Lebra, and W. P. Lebra, eds.), pp. 117–141. Honolulu: The University Press of Hawaii.
Doi, Takeo
   1969   [Preface to] Shimpojumu hitomishiri (*Hitomishiri* as a Japanese concept of stranger anxiety). *Seishin Bunseki Kenkyu* (The Japanese journal of psychoanalysis) 15(2):12.

Fujita, Chihiro
1969   Hitomishiri to taijinkyofu (*Hitomishiri* and anthropophobia). *Seishin Bunseki Kenkyu* (The Japanese journal of psychoanalysis) 15(2):20–25.

Irvine, Judith T.
1979   Formality and Informality in Communicative Events. *American Anthropologist* 81:773–790.

Iwai, Hiroshi, and Toru Abe
1975   *Morita ryoho no riron to jissai* (The theory and practice of morita therapy). Tokyo: Kongo Shuppan.

Lebra, Takie Sugiyama
1971   The Social Mechanism of Guilt and Shame: the Japanese Case. *Anthropological Quarterly* 44:241–255.

Lebra, Takie Sugiyama
1973   Compensative Justice and Moral Investment among Japanese, Chinese, and Koreans. *The Journal of Nervous and Mental Disease* 157:278–291.

Lebra, Takie Sugiyama
1974   The Interactional Perspective of Suffering and Curing in a Japanese Cult. *International Journal of Social Psychiatry* 20:281–286.

Lebra, Takie Sugiyama
1976a   Ancestral Influence on the Suffering of Descendants in a Japanese Cult. *Ancestors* (W. H. Newell, ed.), pp. 219–230. The Hague: Mouton.

Lebra, Takie Sugiyama
1976b   Taking the Role of the Supernatural "Other": Spirit Possession in a Japanese Healing Cult. *Culture-Bound Syndromes, Ethnopsychiatry, and Alternate Therapies* (W. P. Lebra, ed.), pp. 88–100. Honolulu: The University Press of Hawaii.

Lebra, Takie Sugiyama
1976c   *Japanese Patterns of Behavior.* Honolulu: The University Press of Hawaii.
Lebra, Takie Sugiyama. 1982. Self-Reconstruction in Japanese Psychotherapy. *Cultural Perceptions of Mental Health and Therapy* (A. J. Marsella, and G. M. White, eds.), pp. 269–285. Dordrecht, Holland: Reidel.

Lewis, Helen B.
1971   *Shame and Guilt in Neurosis.* New York: International Universities Press.

Lynd, Helen M
1958   *On Shame and the Search for Identity.* New York: Harcourt, Brace.

Maeda, Shigeharu
1969   Hitomishiri. *Seishin Bunseki Kenkyu* (The Japanese journal of psychoanalysis) 15(2):16–19.

Mayuzumi, Toshiro
1976   *Watakushi no sado nyumon* (How I was introduced to the tea ceremony). Tokyo: Kobunsha.

Mazur, Allan, Eugene Rosa, Mark Faupel, Joshua Heller, Russell Leen, and Blake Thurman
1980   Physiological   Aspects   of Communication via Mutual Gaze. *American Journal of Sociology* 86:50–74.

McCoy, Sharon L.
1980   *Keikogoto*: The Study of Polite Accomplishments by Japanese Women. Unpublished ms. (in author's possession).

Mead, George H.
1967   *Mind, Self, and Society.* Chicago: University of Chicago Press.

Murase, Takao
1974   Naikan   Therapy.   *Culture-Bound Syndromes, Ethnopsychiatry, and Alternate Therapies* (W. P. Lebra, ed.), pp. 259–269. Honolulu: The University Press of Hawaii.

Okumura, Nikichi, Koji Sato, and Haruo Yamamoto, eds.
1972.   *Naikan ryoho* (*Naikan* therapy). Tokyo: Igaku Shoin.

Piers, G., and M. B. Singer
1953   *Shame and Guilt.* Springfield, Ill.: Charles C. Thomas.

Rinsho Shinri Gaku Kenkyu Kai
1953   *TAT Nihon-ban shian I, haiga tokaku kensa zuhan* (The Japanese tentative version of the thematic apperception test, No. 1). Tokyo: Kaneko Shobo.

Sakuta, Keiichi
1967   *Haji no bunko saiko* (Shame culture reconsidered). Tokyo: Chikuma Shobo.

Seishin Bunseki Kenkyu (The Japanese journal of psychoanalysis)
1969.   Special issue on *hitomishiri*. Vol. 15, No. 2.

Tsukamoto, Yoshihisa, Chuichiro Takagaki, and Masako Yamagami
1973   Taijin kyofu ni tsuite (On anthropophobia). *Seishin Igaku* (Clinical psychiatry) 15:237–242.

Turner, Victor W.
1969   *The Ritual Process: Structure and Anti-Structure.* Chicago: Aldine.
Yoshimoto, Inobu. 1965. *Naikan yonjunen* (Forty years of *naikan*). Tokyo: Shunjusha.

8

Introduction to Culture and Depression

Arthur Kleinman and Byron Good

Why should a group of anthropologists, psychiatrists, and psychologists devote a volume to culture and depression? Historians tell us that the Greek and Roman medical writers described "melancholic diseases" among their populations which are quite similar to those seen by psychiatrists today, and that the terms "melancholia," "depression," and "mania" have a long and relatively stable history in European thought. Although writers such as Robert Burton, whose compendious *Anatomy of Melancholy* (1621) summarized clinical lore of his day, sought causes for the disorder in the black bile and described subtypes of melancholia that ring strange today, there seems little question that the ancients suffered depression as do people today. Furthermore, psychiatrists practicing in Third World clinics and mental hospitals see patients who are recognizably depressed and treat them with medical regimens current in Western clinics, including antidepressant medications and supportive therapy. This apparent universality arouses no surprise among contemporary biomedical researchers, who believe depression is a disease that is found in all human populations and that we are just beginning to understand. During the past decade, enormous strides have been taken in unraveling the complex set of interacting biochemical and psychological processes which produces depression. Although the picture is not as clear as many researchers thought five

years ago, there is little question that neurotransmitters – bioamines involved in the transmission and regulation of neurological messages – and a set of hormones are implicated in depressive illness. So what is cultural about depression? What do anthropologists or cross-cultural psychiatrists have to offer to an understanding of such a disorder? Is there reason to believe that life in some societies is organized so as to protect their members from depressive illness? Is there evidence that the condition looks quite different in some cultures?

Growing evidence indicates the issues are not as clear as this picture of depression as a universal disease would suggest. First, the study of depression continues to be plagued by unresolved conceptual problems. Depression is a transitory mood or emotion experienced at various times by all individuals. It is also a symptom associated with a variety of psychiatric disorders, from severe and debilitating diseases such as schizophrenia to milder anxiety disorders. It is also a commonly diagnosed mental illness. Depression is thus considered mood, symptom, and illness, and the relationship among these three conceptualizations remains problematic. Is depressive illness a more severe and enduring form of depressed emotions, or is it an altogether different process? Are the boundaries between depressed mood and illness simply conventional, or are

Arthur Kleinman and Byron Good, Introduction to Culture and Depression from *Culture and Depression: Studies in the Anthropology and Cross-Cultural Psychiatry of Affect and Disorder*, ed. Arthur Kleinman and Byron Good, University of California Press, Berkeley, Los Angeles, London. © 1985 by The Regents of the University of California, pp. 1–8. Reprinted with permission of the University of California Press.

they related to more essential differences between them? Are depressive illnesses really discrete forms of pathology, separate from anxiety disorders, for example, or is depression a symptom – like fever – that may be associated with any number of disorders? These basic questions continue to bedevil researchers and preclude clear analysis of depressive illness.

Reading through the history of changes in conceptualization of the subtypes of depression does not give one confidence that such problems are about to be solved once and for all. The history of psychiatry is strewn with "nosologies," or systems of categorization of depression. Some are etiological categories, such as endogenous and reactive, reflecting interest in the underlying cause of a depression. Other distinctions, such as that between primary and secondary depressions, are relational, designating which is to be considered the illness, which the symptom. Other categories, such as neurotic and psychotic, are descriptive, indicating characteristics and severity of the disorder. The current wisdom, represented in the American Psychiatric Association's most recent Diagnostic and Statistical Manual (DSM-III), eschews cause altogether, treating psychiatric disorders as unitary diseases, precipitated by social precursors and superimposed on enduring personality characteristics. But is the depression of a basically healthy individual with unresolved grief over loss of a spouse or child the same disease as a depression of a more fundamentally troubled person? Anthropologists are not, of course, the first to raise questions such as these. They are debated regularly in the psychiatric literature. To the anthropologist, however, such disagreement over basic terms is a reminder that we are in the presence of culture. Psychiatric categories and theories are cultural, no less than other aspects of our world view. It seems reasonable, therefore, to ask to what extent depression itself is a cultural category, grounded both in a long Western intellectual tradition and a specific medical tradition.

Cross-cultural research offers evidence of cultural variations in depressive mood, symptoms, and illness which suggests the importance of pursuing this question. "Dysphoria" – sadness, hopelessness, unhappiness, lack of pleasure with the things of the world and with social relationships – has dramatically different meaning and form of expression in different societies. For Buddhists, taking pleasure from things of the world and social relationships is the basis of all suffering; a willful dysphoria is thus the first step on the road to salvation. For Shi'ite Muslims in Iran, grief is a religious experience, associated with recognition of the tragic consequences of living justly in an unjust world; the ability to experience dysphoria fully is thus a marker of depth of person and understanding. Some societies, such as the Kaluli of Papua New Guinea, value full and dramatic expression of sadness and grieving; Balinese and Thai-Lao, by contrast, "smooth out" emotional highs and lows to preserve a pure, refined, and smooth interior self. Members of such societies vary not only in how they express dysphoric emotion; they seem to experience forms of emotion that are not part of the repertoire of others. So dramatic are the differences in the cultural worlds in which people live that translation of emotional terms requires much more than finding semantic equivalents. Describing how it feels to be grieved or melancholy in another society leads straightway into analysis of different ways of being a person in radically different worlds.

What anthropological evidence we have indicates differences not only in depression as mood but also in symptoms of depressive illness. For members of many African societies, the first signs of illness are dreams that indicate a witch may be attacking one's vital essence. For members of many American Indian groups, hearing voices of relatives who have died is considered normal, not a sign of sickness. For members of other societies, hearing voices or dreaming of spirits may indicate a member of the spirit world is seeking a victim or demanding to establish a relationship with one who will become a follower and perhaps a healer. Dramatic differences are also found in expression of bodily complaints associated with depressive illness, indicating forms of experience not available to most members of our own society. Nigerians complain that "ants keep creeping in parts of my brain," while Chinese complain of exhaustion of their nerves and of their hearts being squeezed and weighed down. In few societies of the world is depression associated with overwhelming guilt and feelings of sinfulness, as it often is in the Judeo-Christian West. Because such differences are found in the symptoms associated with depressive illness, determination of whether one is studying the same illness across societies is essentially problematic. There is no blood test for depression. If there were one, it would indicate some physiological disorder, but not the fundamentally social illness we call depression. Since symptoms serve as the criteria for depressive illness, and since symptoms vary significantly across cultures, the difficulty of establishing the cross-cultural validity of the category "depression" must be faced.

The world's cultures have offered researchers of various disciplines a natural laboratory for investigating the relation between depression and contrasting systems of social organization and cultural meanings. Questions asked reflect the theoretical orientation of the discipline and period. For years, psychoanalytically oriented researchers attempted to test theories of depression as aggression directed against the self, and to maintain the theory in the face of evidence that depression is often not associated with feelings of guilt and self-depreciation, and that the anger experienced by those who are depressed is commonly expressed toward others. Cross-cultural epidemiologists have sought variations in rates of depressive illness across societies, then looked for aspects of social life and culture that would explain the variance. Clinical researchers have looked at differences in levels of somatic and psychological symptoms across patient populations, some offering explanations of these differences in terms of the evolution of societies.

Although questions of the role of social and psychological factors in placing individuals at risk or protecting them from depressive symptoms and illness have great currency and are appropriate to put to the cross-cultural evidence, this book is organized around a prior question: Does the concept of depression have cross-cultural validity? Do members of other societies experience what we call depressive emotions and major depressive illness? Do differences in cultural meanings significantly alter the experience of depressed mood and the symptoms of depressive illness? If so, how are we to translate between our emotional world and those of other societies; how are we to establish criteria for depressive illness in other societies which will be comparable to those we use in our own?

In a sense, the great advances in biological psychiatry provoke these questions. Discovery of effective antidepressant medications in the 1960s initiated the most active period in the history of research on depression. Identification of effective psychopharmacology allows researchers to follow a strategy of comparing individuals for whom the drug is effective with a normal population and of investigating physiological changes in the individual which result from the medication. Both of these strategies are aimed at discovering biological mechanisms that correlate with depressive illness. In order to undertake such research, however, reliable diagnoses of depression must be made to serve as a basis for identifying samples to be studied. By the mid-1960s, it was clear that basing diagnoses on the "clinical judgment" of psychiatrists was unreliable. The same patient was likely to be diagnosed schizophrenic in the United States and manic-depressive in Great Britain, for instance.

To facilitate such research, the National Institute of Mental Health sponsored a major effort to establish clear diagnostic criteria for psychiatric disorders. These efforts resulted in a dramatically new diagnostic manual and innovative epidemiological instruments designed to assign psychiatric diagnoses to individuals (as contrasted with older instruments designed to determine level of psychiatric symptoms). Because these new diagnostic instruments are proving reliable, and because they are useful in identifying individuals with particular physiological as well as psychosocial characteristics, there is growing consensus in the psychiatric community that the current criteria of depression are valid and represent criteria of a universal, biologically grounded disease. It is just such certainty that our Western categories, in this case disease categories, are universal rather than culturally shaped which provokes anthropological response. When medical researchers act on an assumption of universality by directly translating our own diagnostic criteria into other languages to determine who is mentally ill in another society, anthropologists may be expected to challenge the validity of the entire enterprise.

This volume is designed to examine these issues. It represents the editors' conviction that cross-cultural research is of extraordinary importance in advancing our knowledge of human behavior, psychiatric illness, and, in particular, depression. It also represents our belief that disciplinary boundaries have greatly impeded examination of the questions raised here. Anthropologists often have little or no clinical experience and consequently criticize the psychiatric literature based solely on their research with normal populations. Psychiatrists seldom have extended experience with non-Western populations and consequently *under-estimate* the great difficulty of translating between our Western analytic schemes, grounded as they are in our tacit cultural knowledge concerning emotion, interior experience, and psychological disorders, and the very alien psychological worlds of many of the societies studied by anthropologists. Epidemiologists so struggle to develop reliable approaches to measuring psychological disorders and social factors that they seldom seriously confront issues of validity. These great differences in perspectives have prevented the kind of serious scholarly exchange necessary to advance our understanding of depression in the context of cross-cultural studies.

This book is addressed to an interdisciplinary audience of researchers, scholars, and lay readers. We asked the authors – a distinguished group of anthropologists, psychiatrists, and psychologists – to present original data concerning depression in the societies they have studied, to address fundamental theoretical issues, to outline methodological issues raised by their work, and to engage members of other disciplines explicitly. Several common themes emerge from the contributions. The chapters submit the dominant psychiatric conceptualization of depression, in particular that represented by DSM-III, to sustained cultural analysis. Although there is no simple consensus about the cross-cultural validity of Western concepts of depression, the chapters document

how differently dysphoric affect is interpreted and socially organized in many societies and suggest that depressive illness takes culturally distinct forms in several of the societies studied. The authors thus challenge current conceptualizations as parochial, as a form of "local" knowledge, and attempt to reinterpret "emotion," "symptom," and "illness" in thoroughgoing social and cultural terms. However, they do not stop at anthropological critique. A number of the contributors go on to outline research programs and to provide data, at times based on joint ethnographic, clinical, and epidemiological work, that significantly advance our understanding of the role of culture in shaping dysphoria and depression. We believe these contributions lay the ground for a new anthropology of depression.

Orientations

Three distinctive disciplines dominate the cross-cultural study of depression: anthropology, psychiatry, and psychology. Though each has been interested in this subject for decades, they have gone about the descriptive and comparative tasks in separate ways, so that, as in the more general study of emotions and mental disorder cross-culturally, each discipline has constructed a more or less discrete literature. Theories have differed as much as methods, and within each discipline contributions have ranged along a spectrum of theory from materialist to idealist (Hahn and Kleinman 1983). So separate have these traditions become that one finds in each few references to recent work outside that tradition. If there ever was a situation accurately captured by the image of the blind men and the elephant, this would seem to be it.

This volume is an attempt to overcome the obvious and unavailing limitations that such splendid isolation creates. We have assembled papers from each tradition and asked contributors to deal with contributions from the other fields. Each contributor was also urged to set out fairly explicitly his or her theoretical paradigm and to illustrate it by working through empirical materials. The results vary, as they will in a large collection, but we the editors believe that taken together they portray (warts and all) both the present state of these distinctive disciplinary approaches to understanding culture and depression and the opportunities for and barriers to interdisciplinary colloquy and collaboration.

This volume is neither exhaustive nor truly representative. Rather, it reflects the chief preoccupations of the editors. We believe the biological component of clinical depression is important and cannot be disregarded, but we also share the view that biological studies divorced from clinical and ethnographic investigations have little to contribute to our understanding of the relation of culture and depression. Hence we have not sought to include a paper on this latter approach. During the preparation of the chapters, however, contributors were sent relevant reviews of the biology of depressive disorder, along with other papers on clinical, epidemiological, experimental, and ethnographic approaches, so that their discussions might include some attention to biology.

Similarly, because it is now so well known, we have not felt the need to include a strictly psychoanalytic account, though several of the contributions are informed by a psychoanalytic perspective. In place of a narrow experimentalist exposition, we have elected to have the relevant elements of this research tradition discussed in a more broadly based review of leading psychological research traditions. We

have also eschewed sociological accounts that treat depression totally as an ideological or moral phenomenon, since with William James (1981:1068) we hold that "a purely disembodied human emotion is a nonentity."

What have we chosen to emphasize? Because it is our view that the single most troublesome problem plaguing the cross-cultural study of affect and affective disorder is the failure to take an anthropologically sophisticated view of culture, we have emphasized anthropological accounts, especially those that regard culture as the intersection of meaning and experience. We believe the cross-disciplinary study of culture and depression will be best advanced by coming to terms with the analytic questions raised by these accounts, and by critically examining the ethnocentric bias of psychiatric and psychological research categories.

REFERENCES

Burton, R.
    [1621] The Anatomy of Melancholy. New York: Tudor Press. 1955
Hahn, R. A., and A. Kleinman
    1983 Biomedical Practice and Anthropological Theory. Annual Review of Anthropology, 12:305–333.
James, W.
    [1890] The Principles of Psychology. Vol. 2. Cambridge: Harvard 1981 University Press.

Part III

Psychoanalytic Explorations through Fieldwork

Introduction

After Freud: Dramas of the Psyche in Cultural Context

Why do some anthropologists continue to find inspiration in the ideas and methods of Sigmund Freud, after more than a century in which criticism has often outweighed acceptance? The answer is that psychoanalysis as created by Freud in Vienna beginning in the 1890s, was not like other psychologies then or now. Some of its most distinctive features brought it close to anthropology, while other features presented a problematic gap. Freud was, first of all, a medically trained neurologist and psychiatrist in private practice, not an academic psychologist with a laboratory, let alone an ethnographic fieldworker. His original concern was with the causes and treatment of neurotic disorders like hysteria, not the basic dimensions of the human mind. Yet out of his clinical inquiries and introspection came a comprehensive theory of mental processes, innovatively positing continuities between conscious and unconscious experience, dreaming and waking, childhood and adulthood, healthy and disturbed personalities. This was first offered in Chapter 7 of *The Interpretation of Dreams* (published in 1899) and elaborated over the next 25 years. Unlike experimental psychology, which focused on specific *capacities* for experience (e.g., perception, memory, emotion), psychoanalysis was concerned with the symbolic *contents* of the mind, particularly the *narratives* that (according to his theory) motivate and inhibit action, create neurotic symptoms, and form the basis of religious, aesthetic, and political symbols. The relevance of his theory to anthropology was evident to Freud and his early followers as well as to anthropologists in Britain and America.

Freud considered the Oedipus complex to be one of his major discoveries, made during his self-analysis in 1897 and presented in his publications of the next decade (especially Freud, 1905). This related the psychology of the developing child to family relationships dramatized in personal experience and powerfully affecting the symbolic imagery driving adult behavior and religion. Its basic idea is that young children have sexual drives and ideas, which in the case of a boy consist of sexual desire for his mother, jealousy of the father's privileged relationship with her, and fear that the father will castrate him. The boy's intrapsychic conflict is resolved by relinquishing his desire for the mother (adopting an incest taboo), as he "becomes the father" mentally, that is, he identifies with the imagined punitive father and internalizes the castration threats as a moral conscience. Freud thought of this course of child development in narrative terms, as indicated by his naming it for the protagonist in Sophocles' tragedy *Oedipus Rex* (after considering the possibility of naming it after Hamlet in Shakespeare's tragedy). Oedipus unintentionally kills his father and marries his mother, putting out his eyes when he understands what he has done, whereas the boy in the narrative of Freud's developmental theory *intends* to possess his mother and kill his father but does not do so, and his development resolves the conflict intrapsychically, driving the original intentions into his unconscious as he assumes the identity of the father he once hated and feared. Freud claimed this narrative to be a universal aspect of development, acquired in the course of human evolution, which explained the universality of the incest taboo and its appearance in disguised forms in the customs and folklore of many peoples.

Freud and his early followers eagerly analyzed the customs of peoples around the world, but they did no fieldwork. Instead, they depended largely on secondary accounts of ethnographic reports by missionaries and colonial administrators. When Bronislaw Malinowski (1922), whose fieldwork in Melanesia set a new standard for anthropology, published an article (1924) proposing that Freud's concept of the Oedipus complex required revision to fit the facts he had actually seen among the matrilineal Trobriand Islanders, it aroused a strong reaction in London. It was also noted in Vienna, by Freud himself, and in Paris by Princess Marie Bonaparte, his devoted follower there. At Freud's suggestion, she offered to fund fieldwork by Géza Róheim, the Hungarian folklorist and psychoanalyst, to set the record straight. Róheim spent almost three years visiting Australian aborigines, Melanesians, and the Pima Indians in Arizona. His preliminary results, published in the *International Journal of Psychoanalysis* (Róheim, 1932), argued with field data that those peoples, including the two matrilineal groups, were no less Oedipal than Freud's patients. That settled the matter as far as orthodox Freudians were concerned, and anthropology receded as an area of their interest.

In fact, however, Freud had to face other – until recently unknown – non-Western challenges to the universality of the Oedipus complex. In 1929, he corresponded with a Dr. Girindrasekhar Bose of Calcutta, who informed him of how different were his Indian male patients in their Oedipal conflicts and resolutions – no castration anxiety, strong desire to become the mother (Kakar, 1989, 1990) – and three years later Dr. Heisaku Kosawa of Tokyo visited Freud and proposed not only a modification in the Oedipus complex for Japanese patients but also that a narrative he called the *Ajase complex*, based on Buddhist scriptures, fitted their experience better (Blowers and Yang, 1997). Both Asian psychiatrists identified an intrapsychic drama in which the mother played a more important role than Freud had formulated for the Oedipal triangle.

The contemporary Indian psychoanalyst Sudhir Kakar says:

> In my own work, fifty years after Bose's contributions ... I am struck by the comparable patterns in Indian mental life we observed independently of each other, and this in spite of our different emotional predilections, analytic styles, theoretical preoccupations, geographical locations and historical situations.... My main argument is that the "hegemonic

narrative" of Hindu culture as far as male development is concerned is neither that of Freud's Oedipus nor that of Christianity's Adam. One of the more dominant narratives is that of Devi, the great goddess, especially in her manifold expressions as mother in the inner world of the Hindu son (Kakar, 1989, p. 356).

Similarly, Kosawa's Ajase complex was focused on "the mutual dependency that develops between mothers and children" in Japan and dramatically represents their guilt feelings (Blowers and Yang, 1997, p. 119).

Coincidentally, European psychoanalysts from Melanie Klein to Heinz Hartmann began to focus more on early mother–child relations during the 1930s, and by the time the late Japanese psychoanalyst Takeo Doi (1973), a former student of Kosawa, published his book on mother–child interdependency among Japanese, he could point to a theoretical precedent in the work of Michael Balint (1965), *within* European psychoanalysis. Surveying the psychoanalytic scene many years later, Bennett Simon (1991) noted the decline of the Oedipus complex, with a concomitant rise of interest in the pre-Oedipal development of the child (particularly mother–child relations) and its long-term impact. In the long run, then, the notion that psychodynamic development reflected the interpersonal conditions actually experienced by the child was confirmed by clinical experience with patients in Europe and the United States as well as in India and Japan. And though the dynamically active narratives varied by culture, they put mother–child relations in a more central place than had Freud's Oedipal drama. Anne Parsons' ethnographic portrait of the Madonna complex among Neapolitans in Chapter 10 provides a European example, differing from those of India and Japan but also contrasting with the Oedipal prototype. Parsons' article of 1964 anticipated the interest of psychoanalytic anthropologists later in the 20th century, when the cross-cultural validity of the Oedipus complex was widely debated, by Spiro (1982), Paul (1982), Spain (1992), Johnson and Price-Williams (1996), and many others.

From the 1960s onwards, some anthropologists sought a new relationship with psychoanalysis. The culture and personality movement had been largely hostile to the "psychoanalytic anthropology" typified by Róheim (1934), regarding it as an unfortunate holdover from 19th-century evolutionism combined with a highly speculative theory of sexual and aggressive instincts. The movement's leaders were, as mentioned in the introduction to Part I, closely allied with the "neo-Freudians" Sullivan, Horney, and Fromm, and they borrowed some of Freud's ideas, while rejecting many regarded as fundamental within the Freudian movement itself. In the new turn, anthropologists took a fresh look at Freud's work, partly through undertaking training at psychoanalytic institutes (as the three authors represented in Part III did), partly through reading the newly translated and published Standard Edition of Freud's psychological writings, and partly through examining aspects of psychoanalysis that previous generations of anthropologists had not considered.

One of these aspects was the clinical method and process of psychoanalysis, as Robert Paul mentions in Chapter 9 and as imported into fieldwork (though differently) by Anne Parsons and Waud Kracke in the following chapters. This sensitivity to the method of gaining knowledge about unconscious processes from individuals in a different culture was intensively discussed by Devereux (1967), LeVine (1973), and others reviewed by Paul. While no consensus has emerged about how to find such knowledge, the new psychoanalytic anthropology contributed a greater sophistication about the assessment of psychic dispositions in diverse cultural settings than we have previously had, and this is exemplified in some of the articles of Part V.

A major trend in the new psychoanalytic anthropology could be called *cultural psychodynamics*, and it includes the concepts of culturally constituted conflicts and defenses. Freud saw humans as tragically conflicted between their drives or wishes and their morality or prohibitions, with this intrapsychic conflict being played out in cultural dramas: taboos, rituals expressing both wishes and prohibitions in symbolic disguise, and ceremonies that dramatize a defensive resolution while censoring the underlying wish. This approach had attracted Gregory Bateson (1936; Bateson and Mead, 1942), a major figure in the culture and personality movement, though he may have come to an interest in cultural contradictions in ritual through a different route. But it was A. Irving Hallowell (1955) who formulated the concept of the culturally constituted behavioral environment and his former student Melford E. Spiro (1965) who defined and illustrated the *culturally constituted defense mechanism* as defining a critical interaction between the individual and the culture. The latter concept became central to the new psychoanalytic anthropology, indicating that cultural narratives provide individuals with the symbolic means of alleviating anxiety and tensions stemming from their intrapsychic conflicts (see also Obeyesekere, 1982, 1990).

Chapter 9: Robert Paul introduces what I am calling the new psychoanalytic anthropology, as part of a comprehensive review published in 1989 (but still instructive today).

Chapter 10: Anne Parsons examines family dramas and imagery among Neapolitans of South Italy, using the Thematic Apperception Test as well as ethnography to reveal salient religious and personal narratives in the context of a distinctive pattern of family life.

Chapter 11: Waud Kracke examines the process of mourning among the Kagwahiv people in the Amazon basin, using clinical observations with a survivor.

Chapter 12: Kracke continues his inquiry into what effects the Kagwahiv customs restricting public mourning have on individuals suffering the loss of family members.

REFERENCES

Balint, Michael
    1965   Primary Love and Psychoanalytic Technique. New York: Liveright.
Bateson, Gregory
    1936   Naven. Stanford, CA: Stanford University Press.
Bateson, Gregory and Margaret Mead.
    1942   Balinese Childhood: A Photographic Analysis. New York: New York Academy of Sciences.
Blowers, Geoffrey and Serena Yang Hsueh Chi
    1997   Freud's *Deshi*: The Coming of Psychoanalysis to Japan. Journal of the History of the Behavioral Sciences 32: 115–126.
Devereux, George
    1967   From Anxiety to Method in the Behavioral Sciences. The Hague: Mouton.
Doi, Takeo
    1973   The Anatomy of Dependence. New York: Kodansha International.

Freud, Sigmund
  1953 [1899]   The Interpretation of Dreams. In J. Strachey, ed., The Standard Edition of the Complete Psychological Works of Sigmund Freud, Vol. IV. London: The Hogarth Press.
  1953 [1905]   Three Essays on Sexuality. In J. Strachey, ed., The Standard Edition of the Complete Psychological Works of Sigmund Freud, Vol. VII. London: The Hogarth Press.
Hallowell, A. Irving
  1955   Culture and Experience. Philadelphia: University of Pennsylvania Press.
Johnson, Allen W. and Douglass Price-Williams
  1996   Oedipus Ubiquitous: The Family Complex in World Folk Literature. Stanford, CA: Stanford University Press.
Kakar, Sudhir
  1989   The Maternal-Feminine in Indian Psychoanalysis. The International Review of Psycho-Analysis 16: 355–362.
LeVine, Robert A.
  1973   Culture, Behavior and Personality. Chicago: Aldine.
Malinowski, Bronislaw
  1922   Argonauts of the Western Pacific. New York: E. P. Dutton.
  1924   Psychoanalysis and Anthropology. Psyche 4: 293–332.
Obeyesekere, G.
  1982   Medusa's Hair. Chicago: University of Chicago Press.
  1990   The Work of Culture. Chicago: University of Chicago Press.
Paul, Robert A.
  1982   The Tibetan Symbolic World: Psychoanalytic Explorations. Chicago: University of Chicago Press.
Róheim, Géza
  1932   The Psycho-Analysis of Primitive Cultural Types. International Journal of Psychoanalysis 13: 1–224.
  1934   The Riddle of the Sphinx. London: The Hogarth Press.
Simon, Bennett
  1991   Is the Oedipus Complex Still the Cornerstone of Psychoanalysis? Three Obstacles to Answering the Question. Journal of the American Psychoanalytic Association 39: 641–668.
Spain, David H.
  1992   Psychoanalytic Anthropology after Freud: Essays Marking the Fiftieth Anniversary of Freud's Death. New York: Psyche Press.
Spiro, Melford E.
  1965   Religious Systems as Culturally Constituted Defense Mechanisms. In M. E. Spiro, ed., Context and Meaning in Cultural Anthropology: Papers in Honor of A. I. Hallowell. Glencoe, IL: The Free Press.
  1982   Oedipus in the Trobriands. Chicago: University of Chicago Press.

9

Psychoanalytic Anthropology

Robert A. Paul

Introduction

Those who practice psychoanalytic anthropology assume that human life is meaningfully influenced by unconscious thoughts, affects, and motives and that anthropological understanding is deepened by investigating them. But how can one investigate such influences if they are unconscious? Here I discuss various approaches to this problem.

Psychoanalytic Clinical Technique

I begin with a brief description of the technique used by psychoanalysts to study unconscious phenomena (14, 30, 39, 40, 72, 83). A patient who has elected to undergo treatment for a neurosis [or for any personality disorder considered "analyzable" (86) i.e. a disturbance toward the "healthy" end of the mental illness scale] attends regular clinical sessions for hundreds of hours. The patient lies on a couch with the analyst behind him or her. The only instruction given is that the patient is to try to put into words whatever comes to mind, no matter how apparently trivial, meaningless, or offensive. In this highly artificial situation (62), the analyst gives a minimum of guidance, allowing free rein to the patient's flow of asso-

ciations; the analyst intervenes only to "interpret" conflict, that is, to point out when difficulties or resistances in the patient's freedom of thought indicate that unconscious wishes and fears have been aroused.

Enabled to regress, without feedback or social interaction from the analyst, the patient begins to "transfer" onto the analyst the patient's own unconscious fantasies. In other words, elaborating on inevitable hints and opportunities offered by reality – the analyst's office, the schedule, the bill, unforeseen events – the patient will unconsciously construct a deep and complex imaginary relationship with the analyst. This "transference" relationship (39, 60, 62, 87) will be organized around the habitual patterns of interaction and expectation the patient has used in previous significant relationships – most importantly, with the parents during early childhood.

These habitual patterns of thinking, feeling, and acting are reflections of unconscious fantasies (4, 6, 10, 17, 36, 75) – more or less elaborate, stable, concrete images or systems of ideas representing wishes and fears preserved from early life but kept out of awareness. Sandler and Rosenblatt's (73) concept of the "representational world" pictures the unconscious as a theater peopled with affectively charged representations of different aspects of the personnel of the person's infantile social

Robert A. Paul, Psychoanalytic Anthropology from *Annual Review of Anthropology*, 1989, vol. 1, pp. 177–202.

world. These fantasies are actively excluded from consciousness by means of defense mechanisms (34). When there is a difficulty in free association, a conflict is at work between a wish associated with an unconscious fantasy and a defensive psychic maneuver being used to avoid saying something about it to the analyst.

As the analysis progresses, these conflicts center more and more on the transference relationship itself. In many analyses, a "transference neurosis" develops (59) that is a new edition of the patient's neurotic disorder. The nuclear or "infantile" fantasy (35, 70) around which the patient's defensive operations have clustered is now enacted in the transference, and then interpreted along with a construction by the analyst of the childhood experiences that have led to the elaboration of the nuclear fantasy peculiar to that individual, his or her "personal myth" (57).

Thus, the technique for observing unconscious fantasies in analysis is attention to transference enactments repeated many times over the long period of the analysis. Validation of the analyst's understanding of the unconscious fantasies is provided by the patient's gain in freedom in the free associative process following a correct and well-timed interpretation: Memories, helpful associations, and insight previously held up by resistance now become available. (Many analysts today focus not on the unearthing of long-buried historical truth but on providing the patient with a more adaptive narrative of his or her life (74, 78).)

Dreams reported in analysis can exhibit, in condensed and disguised form, and in concrete imagery opaque to the patient's consciousness, those aspects of unconscious fantasy that are salient at any particular moment in the analysis (1, 41, 132). It must be emphasized that dreams are not interpretable in isolation or out of context. The length of the analysis allows dreams to be analyzed in series and in the setting of the developing transference relationship. Since dreams have a communicative function (46), those dreamed in analysis are usually about the analysis and directed at the analyst. This accounts, by the way, for the well-known phenomenon of patients in Freudian analysis dreaming Freudian dreams

and those in Jungian or Kleinian analysis dreaming Jungian or Kleinian dreams.

The unconscious fantasies of the analyst also play a role in the analysis. This is called the countertransference (60, 68). When it is merely the arousing in the analyst of his or her own unresolved conflicts by the patient, it is an obstacle to the process and must be dealt with as such. But the concepts of "trial identification" and "empathy" (6, 27, 40, 50) encourage the analyst to try, using a temporary regression in the service of the ego, to step into the patient's shoes and thus discover in his or her own feelings something about the patient's lived world.

More controversially, some analysts have suggested that the countertransference induced in the analyst by the patient is an important inroad into understanding the patient's mental life. If one assumes with Kernberg (47) that the building blocks of psychic structure are affectively charged self-object dyads, then one can suppose that through "projective identification," the patient is subtly able to make the analyst feel like one of the characters in the dyads of the patient's representational world (42, 48, 68). The analyst may be cast in the role of the self, in a "concordant" identification, in which case he or she feels the way the patient feels; but the analyst may also be cast as the object, in a "complementary" identification (68). Thus, for example, with a masochistic patient, an analyst may feel either an urge to be domineering in response to cues from the patient, or else reactively may attempt to be overly considerate, in an effort to ward off the urge to be domineering.

Anthropological Analogues to Psychoanalytic Clinical Technique

Only infrequently is it possible to carry out psychoanalyses or psychoanalytic therapy with people from non-Western cultures. Among the circumstances in which this can occur are those in which a researcher with both psychoanalytic and anthropological skills analyzes patients from ethnic minorities within the Western world (5, 25, 37); when the analyst is from a non-Western culture (2, 3, 28, 44, 45, 71, 76); or when a Western analyst is able to practice in another cultural setting (11, 31, 32, 71).

Because psychoanalysis is a therapeutic procedure not likely to be undertaken by people in non-Western cultures, one cannot hang out a shingle in another part of the world and expect customers to appear who can then become informants in psychoanalytic anthropological research. Doing psychoanalytic research in West Africa, Parin et al (64) attempted to solve this problem by paying seven individuals to undergo many hours of psychodynamic interviewing, thus approximating the analytic situation (but with obvious and important differences).

The similarities between the ethnographic interview and the analytic session or diagnostic interview (19, 38, 54, 69) have led some anthropologists (58) to recommend the clinical method as the most appropriate aspect of psychoanalysis to be exploited by anthropologists. One advantage of the clinical method is that it is processual. As Crapanzano (21) argues, the treatment of interview data as a fixed text is an error of which Freud himself was guilty, as when he treated Dora's dreams as "holy writ." Instead of being the secondary exegesis of an already existing primary text, Crapanzano argues, the ethnographic interview, like the psychoanalytic process, is an ongoing act of mutual creativity in which interviewer and interviewee dialectically constitute – rather than unearth and comment on – the reality being sought. In his presentation of his interviews with a Moroccan informant, Crapanzano (20) not only lets the informant speak but also recounts his own "countertransferential" movement from a neutral and "ethnographic" to a more empathic "therapeutic" stance.

Kracke (51, 56) devoted many months in the field to open-ended interviews with Kagwahiv, in the course of which he had ample opportunity to observe dreams, free association, and transference and counterteransference manifestations. Levels of dynamic meaning in his data became clearer to him only later, after his own training in psychoanalysis.

Herdt and Stoller (43, 82) resolved the problem of how to unite ethnographic and psychoanalytic expertise and research – each

so demanding of time and study – by bringing together Stoller's analytic experience and Herdt's ethnographic immersion in Sambia culture in joint interviews during short visits by Stoller to the field. Ewing (29) gained insight into informants' inner worlds by carefully attending to "transferential" aspects of interview material examined at close range. Briggs (15, 16) used her own feelings of making social mistakes in relations with Inuits as a guide to conceptualizing what exactly was distinctive about their interpersonal style and the organization of their affective lives. Works by Davidson (22), Kilborne (49), Maranhão (61), Riesman (69), Ticho (84), and Tobin (85) address the use of transference and countertransference as ways to understand the ethnographic dialogue between self and the other.

Devereux's influential book (24) examines the distortions introduced into social science research by the nature of the data, which are bound to arouse anxiety in the observer because what is being observed inevitably touches on conflicts also active in the observer. Devereux argues that scientific method often serves not as a tool for obtaining an undistorted view of the informant, but rather as a defense interposed between the researcher and conflictual material. Optimally, for Devereux, the ethnographer should confront rather than defend against the operative anxieties and defenses, in order to develop genuine empathic understanding.

In this vein, for example, Obeyesekere (63) makes it clear that his attention was drawn to the women devotees with matted locks who became the subjects of his research because of the anxiety they aroused in him at first.

Kracke (54) addresses countertransference issues by comparing his reactions in the field, as these are recorded in his journal, with stages of "culture shock" described by Caudill (18): After an initial euphoria followed by an experience of frustration, he underwent a prolonged dependent socialization, leading to a breakdown of his distancing, structured stance and culminating in his direct involvement in the personal tribulations of the people he was involved with. The illness of his informant's children and the unconscious conflicts this aroused found expression in the dreams of both ethnographer and informant, until finally

Kracke found himself redreaming dreams his informant had told him. The transference-countertransference entanglements here could hardly be denser, but they led to unusually deep understanding on Kracke's part.

Parin and his coworkers (64) made extensive use of transferential phenomena in discovering the fantasies of the seven Anyi individuals they interviewed intensively. Thus, one informant's elaborate report about a tyrannical European mine owner revealed a degree of hostility towards the European ethnographers that was otherwise masked by the informant's unaggressive demeanor.

Stein has investigated the countertransferential aspects of attitudes of American medical doctors toward their patients (80, 81). In a booklength study Wengle (88) reports interviews with returned ethnographers. He postulates a typical field experience centered around death anxiety and leading to a fantasy of death and rebirth.

Individual Portraits

Insofar as the ethnographic interview is analogous to the clinical interview as a setting in which unconscious fantasy may be brought into open discourse, the study of individuals, rather than of cultures or societies, becomes the appropriate genre for psychoanalytic anthropology. A sizable literature has by now accumulated in which individual cases are explored with sensitivity to both psychodynamic and cultural aspects (7, 8, 9, 11, 12, 13, 20, 23, 25, 26, 32, 33, 37, 52, 63, 64, 65, 66, 67, 77, 79).

REFERENCES

1. Altman, L. L.
   1975 *The Dream in Psychoanalysis*. New York: International Univ. Press.
2. Apprey, M.
   1981 Family, religion, and separation: the effort to separate in the analysis of a pubertal adolescent boy. *J. Psychoanal. Anthropol.* 4:137–58.
3. Apprey, M.
   1983 The black analyst in adolescent analysis and psychotherapy. *J. Psychoanal. Anthropol.* 6:647–54.

4. Arlow, J. A.
   1969 Unconscious fantasy and disturbances of conscious experience. *Psychoanal. Q.* 38:1–27.
5. Babcock, C. G., Gehrie, M. J.
   1986 The Japanese-American experience: an approach through psychoanalysis and follow-up. *J. Psychoanal. Anthropol.* 9: 373–90.
6. Beres, D., Arlow, J. A.
   1974 Fantasy and identification in empathy. *Psychoanal. Q.* 43:26–50.
7. Bilu, Y.
   1985 The woman who wanted to be her father: a case study of *dybbuk* possession in a Hassidic community. *J. Psychoanal. Anthropol.* 8:11–27.
8. Bilu, Y.
   1988 Rabbi Yaacov Wazana: a Jewish healer in the Atlas Mountains. *Cult. Med. Psychiatry* 12:113–35.
9. Bilu, Y., Hasan-Rokem, G.
   1990 Cinderella and the saint: the life story of a Jewish Moroccan female healer in Israel. *Psychoanal. Study Soc.* 15: In press.
10. Blum, H. P., Kramer, Y., Richards, A. K., Richards, A. D., eds.
    1988 *Fantasy, Myth, and Reality: Essays in Honor of Jacob A. Arlow, M.D.* Madison, CT: International Univ. Press.
11. Boyer, L. B.
    1979 *Childhood and Folklore: A Psychoanalytic Study of Apache Personality*. New York Library Psychol. Anthropol. Publ.
12. Boyer, L. B., DeVos, G. A., Boyer, R. M.
    1983 A longitudinal study of three Apache brothers as reflected in their Rorschach protocols. *J. Psychoanal. Anthropol.* 6:125–62.
13. Boyer, L. B., DeVos, G. A., Boyer, R. M.
    1985 Crisis and continuity in the personality of an Apache shaman. *Psychoanal. Study Soc.* 11:63–114.
14. Brenner, C.
    1976 *Psychoanalytic Technique and Psychic Conflict*. New York: International Univ. Press.
15. Briggs, J. L.
    1970 *Never in Anger*. Cambridge, MA: Harvard Univ. Press.
16. Briggs, J. L.
    1987 In search of emotional meaning. *Ethos* 15:8–15.
17. Burgin, V., Donald, J., Kaplan, C.
    1986 *Formations of Fantasy*. London/New York: Methuen.

18. Caudill, W.
    1961 Some problems of transnational communication: Japan–U.S. *Appl. Psychiatr. Insight Cross-Cult. Commun.* 7:409–21.

19. Cohler, B. J.
    Psychoanalysis and the human studies. Presented at Ann. Meet. Am. Anthropol. Assoc., 87th, Phoenix.

20. Crapanzano, V.
    1980 *Tuhami: Portrait of a Moroccan.* Chicago: Univ. Chicago Press.

21. Crapanzano, V.
    1981 Text, transference, and indexicality. *Ethos* 9:122–48.

22. Davidson, R. H.
    1986 Transference and counter-transference phenomena: the problem of the observer in the behavioral sciences. *J. Psychoanal. Anthropol.* 9:269–84.

23. Day, R., Davidson, R. H.
    1976 Magic and healing: an ethnopsychoanalytic study. *Psychoanal. Study Soc.* 7:231–92.

24. Devereux, G.
    1967 *From Anxiety to Method in the Behavioral Sciences.* The Hague: Mouton.

25. Deverenx, G.
    1969 *Reality and Dream: The Psychotherapy of a Plains Indian.* Garden City, NY: Doubleday.

26. DeVos, G. A.
    1982 An Apache woman's account of her recent acquisition of the shamanistic status. *J. Psychoanal. Anthropol.* 5:299–331.

27. DeVos, G. A.
    1989 Empathy to alienation: problems in human belonging. In *Personality in the Construction of Society*, ed. M. Swartz, D. K. Jordan. Tuscaloosa, AL: Univ. Alabama Press. In Press.

28. Doi, T.
    1973 *The Anatomy of Dependence.* New York: Harper & Row.

29. Ewing, K.
    1987 Clinical anthropology as an ethnographic tool. *Ethos* 15:16–39.

30. Fenichel, O.
    1941 *Problems of Psychoanalytic Technique.* Albany, NY: Psychoanal. Q. Publ.

31. Foulks, E. F.
    1973 *The Arctic Hysterias.* Anthropol. Stud. 10. Washington, DC: Am. Anthropol. Assoc. Press.

32. Freeman, D. M. A., Foulks, E. F., Freeman, P. A.

33. Freeman, D. M. A., Foulks, E. F., Freeman, P. A.
    1978 Pre-oedipal dynamics in a case of Eskimo Arctic hysteria. *Psychoanal. Study Soc.* 8:41–69.

34. Freud, A.
    1936/1966 *The Ego and Mechanisms of Defense.* New York: International Univ. Press Rev. ed.

35. Freud, A.
    1971 The infantile neurosis: genetic and dynamic considerations. *Psychoanal. Study Child* 26:79–91.

36. Freud, S.
    1915/1955 The Unconscious. *Standard Edition* 14:205–18. London: Hogarth.

37. Gehrie, M. J.
    1976 Childhood and community: on the experiences of third generation Japanese-Americans in Chicago. *Ethos* 4:353–83.

38. Gehrie, M. J.
    1989 Psychoanalytic anthropology: the analogous tasks of the psychoanalyst and the ethnographer. *Psychoanal. Study Soc.* 14: In press.

39. Gill, M. M.
    1982 *Analysis of Transference.* New York: International Univ. Press. 2 vols.

40. Greenson, R. R.
    1967 *The Technique and Practice of Psychoanalysis.* New York: International Univ. Press.

41. Grinstein, A.
    1987 *Freuds Rules of Dream Interpretation.* New York: International Univ. Press.

42. Heimann, P.
    1950 On counvertransference. *Int. J. Psycho-Anal.* 31:81–84.

43. Herdt, G. H., Stoller, R. J.
    1985 Sakulambai – a hermaphrodite's secret: an example of clinical ethnography. *Psychoanal. Study Soc.* 11:115–56.

44. Kakar, S.
    1978 *The Inner World: A Psycho-Analytic Study of Childhood and Society in India.* Delhi: Oxford Univ. Press.

45. Kakar, S.
    1985 Psychoanalysis and non-western cultures. *Int. Rev. Psycho-Anal.* 12:441–48.

46. Kanzer, M.
    1955 Communicative function of the dream. *Int. J. Psycho-Anal.* 260–65.

47. Kernberg, O. F.
1976 *Object Relations and Clinical Psychoanalysis.* New York: Jason Aronson.

48. Kernberg, O. F.
1987 Projection and projective identification: developmental and clinical aspects. *J. Am. Psychoanal. Assoc.* 35:795–819.

49. Kilborne, B.
1987 Alterité et contratransfer. *Nouv. Rev. Ethnopsychiatr.* 7:135–47.

50. Kohut, H.
1977 *The Restoration of the Self.* New York: International Univ. Press.

51. Kracke, W. H.
1978 Dreaming in Kagwahiv: dreams, beliefs, and their psychic uses in an Amazonian Indian culture. *Psychoanal. Study Soc.* 8:119–71.

52. Kracke, W. H.
1978 *Force and Persuasion: Leadership in an Amazonian Society.* Chicago: Univ. Chicago Press.

53. Kracke, W. H.
1981 Kagwahiv mourning: dreams of a bereaved father. *Ethos* 9:258–75.

54. Kracke, W. H.
1987 Encounter with other cultures: psychological and epistemological aspects. *Ethos* 15:56–79.

55. Kracke, W. H.
1987 Myth in dreams, thought in images: an Amazonian contribution to the psychoanalytic theory of the primary process. See Ref. 287, pp. 31–54.

56. Kracke, W. H.
1988 Kagwahiv mourning II: ghosts, grief, and reminiscences. *Ethos* 16:209–22.

57. Kris, E.
1956 The personal myth. *J. Am. Psychoanal. Assoc.* 4:653–81.

58. LeVine, R. A.
1982 *Culture, Behavior, and Personality: An Introduction to the Comparative Study of Psychosocial Adaptation.* New York: Aldine.

59. Loewald, H. W.
1980 The transference neurosis: comments on the concept and the phenomenon. In *Papers on Psychoanalysis*, ed. H. W. Loewald, pp. 302–14. New Haven: Yale Univ. Press.

60. Loewald, H. W.
1986 Transference-countertransference. *J. Am. Psychoanal. Assoc.* 45:275–88.

61. Maranhão, T.
1986 *Therapeutic Discourse and Socratic Dialogue.* Madison, WI: Univ. Wisconsin Press.

62. McAlpine, I.
1950 The development of the transference. *Psychoanal. Q.* 19:501–59.

63. Obeyesekere, G.
1981 *Medusa's Hair: An Essay on Personal Symbols and Religious Experience.* Chicago: Univ. Chicago Press.

64. Parin, P., Morgenthaler, F., Parin-Matthey, G.
1980 *Fear Thy Neighbor As Thyself: Psychoanalysis and Society among the Anyi of West Africa.* Chicago: Univ. Chicago Press.

65. Paul, R. A.
1988 Fire and ice: the psychology of a Sherpa shaman. *Psychoanal. Study Soc.* 13:95–132.

66. Poole, F. J. P.
1987 Personal experience and cultural representations in children's "personal symbols" among Bimin-Kuskusmin. *Ethos* 15:104–35.

67. Rabkin, L. Y.
1986 Longitudinal continuities in the personality of a kibbutznik. *J. Psychoanal. Anthropol.* 9:319–38.

68. Racker, H.
1957 The meaning and use of countertransference. *Psychoanal. Q.* 26:303–57.

69. Riesman, P.
1977 *Freedom in Fulani Social Life: An Introspective Ethnography.* Chicago: Univ. Chicago Press.

70. Ritvo, S.
1974 Current status of the concept of infantile neurosis. *Psychoanal. Study Child* 29:159–81.

71. Roland, A.
1988 *The Expanding Self: Psychoanalysis in India and Japan.* Princeton: Princeton Univ. Press.

72. Sandler, J.
1973 *The Patient and the Analyst.* New York: International Univ. Press.

73. Sandler, J., Rosenblatt, B.
1967 The concept of the representational world. *Psychoanal. Study Child* 17:128–45.

74. Schafer, R.
1983 *The Analytic Attitude.* New York: Basic Books.

75. Segal, J.
1985 *Phantasy in Everyday Life: A Psychoanalytic Approach to Understanding Ourselves.* Harmonds-worth, England: Penguin.

76. Sinha, T. C.
1966 The development of psychoanalysis in India. *Int. J. Psycho-Anal.* 47:430–39.

77. Slote, W. H.

1986   Metaphor, imagery and fantasy: the symbolic world of the Vietnamese. *J. Psychoanal. Anthropol.* 9:285–318.

78. Spence, D. P.
1982   *Narrative Truth and Historical Truth: Meaning and Interpretation in Psychoanalysis.* New York: Norton.

79. Spindler, G. D.
1982   Joe Nepah, a "schizophrenic" Menominee peyotist. *J. Psychoanal. Anthropol.* 10: 1–16.

80. Stein, H. F.
1985   *The Psychodynamics of Medical Practice: Unconscious Factors in Patient Care.* Berkeley: Univ. Calif. Press.

81. Stein, H. F., Apprey, M.
1985   *Context and Dynamics in Clinical Knowledge.* Charlotteaville, VA: Univ. Virginia Press.

82. Stoller, R. J., Herdt, G. H.
1982   The development of masculinity: a cross-cultural contribution. *J. Am. Psychoanal. Assoc.* 30:29–59.

83. Stone, L.
1961   *The Psychoanalytic Situation.* New York: International Univ. Press.

84. Ticho, G.
1971   Cultural aspects of transference and countertransference. *Bull. Menninger Clin.* 35:313–34.

85. Tobin, J. J.
1986   (Counter)transference and failure in intercultural therapy. *Ethos* 14:120–43.

86. Waldhorn, M.
1960   Assessment of analyzability; technical and theoretical observations. *Psychoanal. Q.* 29:478–506.

87. Watt, D. F.
1986   Transference: a right hemisphere event? An inquiry into the boundary between metapsychology and neuropsychology. *Psychoanal. Contemp. Thought* 9:43–77.

88. Wengle, J. L.
1977   *Ethnographers in the Field: The Psychology of Research.* Tuscaloosa, AL: Univ. Alabama Press.

10

Is the Oedipus Complex Universal?

Anne Parsons

In the 1920s a famous debate took place between Ernest Jones and Bronislaw Malinowski which set forth some outlines of theoretical differences between psychoanalysis and anthropology which are still unresolved today. On the basis of fieldwork in the matrilineal Trobriand Islands, Malinowski drew the conclusion that the Oedipus complex as formulated by Freud is only one among a series of possible "nuclear complexes," each of which patterns primary family affects in a way characteristic of the culture in which it occurs. In this perspective, Freud's formulation of the Oedipus complex as based on a triangular relationship between father, mother, and son appears as that particular nuclear complex which characterizes a patriarchal society in which the most significant family unit consists of mother, father, and child. The alternative nuclear complex which he postulated for the Trobriand Islands consisted of a triangular relationship between brother, sister, and sister's son, this in function of the nature of matrilineal social structure in which a boy becomes a member of his mother's kin group and is subject to the authority of his maternal uncle rather than the biological father. One of his most important observations was that in the Trobriand Islands ambivalent feelings very similar to those described by Freud with respect to father and son can be observed between mother's brother and sister's son. Relations between father and son, on the other hand, are

much more close and affectionate; however, Malinowski felt that the father should not be considered as a figure in the kinship structure since the Trobrianders do not recognize the existence of biological paternity. The child is seen as conceived by a spirit which enters the mother's womb and later the father appears to him as the unrelated mother's husband.

In addition, Malinowski noted that the Trobrianders give a very special importance to the brother – sister relationship. While the brother has formal authority over the sister and is responsible for her support, their actual relationship is one of extreme avoidance, to the point that an object may be handed from one to the other by means of an intermediary. He characterized the brother–sister incest taboo as "the supreme taboo" from the Trobriand standpoint; while incest with other primary biological relatives and within the matrilineal kin group at greater biological distance is also forbidden, in no instance are the taboos as strict or surrounded by intense affects as in the brother–sister case. He also discerned, with his acute clinical eye, many evidences of the real temptations underlying the avoidance pattern, for example, in that while no Trobriander would admit to having such an incest dream, the questioning itself aroused a great deal of anxiety and often the assertion that "well, other people have such dreams, but certainly not me." He noted

Anne Parsons, Is the Oedipus Complex Universal? from *The Psychoanalytic Study of Society*, III, ed. Warner Muensterberter and Sidney Axelrad (New York: International Universities Press, 1964), pp. 278–328. Copyright © 1964 International Universities Press. Reprinted with permission of International Universities Press, Inc.

brother–sister incest to be a primary theme in Trobriand mythology, for example, in that love magic is seen as originating in a situation in which brother and sister actually committed incest and died as a result of it. He considered these variations from the European pattern of sufficient significance to uphold the view that the Oedipus complex is not universal.

Jones, in a 1924 paper,[1] upheld with considerable vehemence the classical psychoanalytic point of view that it is. Thus while he felt that Malinowski's field data were in themselves interesting, he came to the conclusion that they did not point to the need for any important theoretical revisions in the psychoanalytic framework. For the data on the Trobriand failure to recognize the biological relationship between father and son, he provided an alternative explanation, namely, that the non-recognition was a form of denial covering affects originating in the Oedipus situation.[2] Much to Malinowski's dismay, this argument was carried to the point of the assertion that matrilineal social organization can itself be seen as a defense against the father – son ambivalence universally characteristic of the Oedipus situation. He also pointed out that Malinowski's observations of ambivalence between mother's brother and sister's son concerned adolescent and adult life, so that, theoretically, it is possible to see it as a secondary displacement in that there is an initial Oedipal rivalry between father and son, but that in adult life the hostile feelings are displaced to the mother's brother. He also commented that similar patterns can be observed in Europe, for example, in that the hostile father figure may later be an occupational superior or rival, while the actual father remains a positive figure.

A re-examination of the debate in a contemporary perspective indicates that actually there are a number of intertwined issues. In the first place, it is characterized by a highly polemic character related to the newness and consequent defensiveness of both fields: for Jones "the" Oedipus complex appears as a kind of point of honor upon whose invariance psychoanalysis would stand or fall, and exactly the same is true of some elements of Malinowski's argument, in particular those which touch on the resemblance between Jones's views and those of the older evolutionary

anthropology which he himself did so much to overthrow. Thus, concerning the question of whether matrilineal social organization can be seen as a defense against Oedipal affects, it seems difficult now to see how a complex social pattern could be based on the "denial" of an affect which occurs in the individual. But on the other hand, one can regret that Malinowski, in his rebuttal, went into a tirade against the evolutionary implications of this view rather than attempting to answer Jones's much more cogent point, namely, that Freud's concepts concern infantile life, and in this perspective it is quite possible that the hostility toward the mother's brother observed in adolescent and adult Trobrianders might be displaced from hostility initially experienced toward the father. What is perhaps most regrettable of all, given his status with regard to the psychoanalytic theory of symbolism, is that Jones never discussed in detail Malinowski's observations concerning the special importance of the Trobriand brother–sister relationship and the integrally related material concerning dreams and mythology.

Some South Italian Cultural Complexes

At this point, I should like to attempt the description of a third nuclear complex, resembling neither the matrilineal one of the Trobriand Islands nor the patriarchal one described by Freud. The material concerns Southern Italy, but descriptions by other researchers indicate the existence of similar patterns throughout the Latin world and possibly even in pre-Reformation Europe. My own concrete observations were made primarily in the city of Naples where I carried out a study of working-class families; however, the basic pattern does not seem fundamentally different in other areas of Southern Italy or in other social class groups, though, of course, there are many variations in details. What I shall try to do is to bring together a number of facts from quite diverse areas – general cultural patterns, intrafamily behavior, and projective test material – in a way which depends on the framework sketched above.

The South Italian family system, similar in this respect not only to other Latin countries but also to much of the Mediterranean world, is in a certain sense intermediate between the kind of lineage system found in the Trobriand Islands and the discontinuous nuclear family characteristic of the industrial world. As we have seen in the Trobriand Islands, it is quite possible that units other than the biologically based mother–father–child one serve as the key axis of social structure; this is very often true of primitive societies where the latter unit usually is enclosed in some wider kinship unit which in turn defines patterns of social organization for the society as a whole. In industrial societies, on the other hand, it is often said that since there is such an elaboration of alternative non-kinship social structures (religious bodies, bureaucratic organizations, governments, etc.) the functions of the family have contracted to an irreducible minimum, i.e., the satisfaction of intimacy needs and the caring for small children. The family is discontinuous in the sense that it lasts only as long as particular individuals are alive; as children grow up they gradually move into a wider society and eventually form new families on their own rather than acquiring adult roles in a continuing social group. The world outside the family is seen in this perspective as a locus of positive achievement.

The South Italian family is an intermediate form in two senses. First, although there is no corporate lineage, since religious, economic, and political functions are handled by nonkinship organizations just as in any complex society, there is a rather loosely organized body of extended kin, the "parenti" which has some significance; one's "parenti," or relatives in a generic sense (usually meaning siblings of parents and their offspring), form the most immediate field of social relations and in theory at least are the persons on whom one can best count on for aid in time of trouble. Second, while the family unit is the immediate biological one (with monogamous marriage, no legal divorce, and co-residence of husband, wife and minor children), this latter tends to be centripetal rather than centrifugal. In other words, parents, or in particular the mother, bring up children in such a way as to strengthen loyalties toward themselves rather than to move increasingly

into a wider social context. This latter tendency is in turn associated with a definition of the world outside the family as hostile and threatening and very often as a source of temptations toward sexual or other forms of delinquency and dishonesty.

We can begin on the level of global culture patterns by examining a key complex of attitudes, namely, those surrounding the Madonna. The importance of the Madonna complex throughout the Latin world is evident to even the most casual observation; in the South Italian villages she stands in every church and along with the saints may be carried through the streets in procession, and in even the poorest quarters of the city of Naples she is likely to occupy some niche or other, decorated with the flowers or even gold chains brought by her children grateful for her favors. Moreover, every home has a private shrine, in which pictures or statues of the Madonna appear along with photographs of deceased relatives illuminated by a candle or lamp.

As a figure in Roman Catholic theology, the Madonna, of course, is only one element in a much wider religious complex. However, popular religion in Southern Italy does not always conform to theological doetrine, for example, in that it has a considerable admixture of magical beliefs and in that the Madonna and the saints are conceived of more as persons of whom one can ask a favor (Italian *grazia*, or a grace) than as ideal figures in a moralistic sense. The Madonna may also be seen in characteristic folk manner as a quite familiar figure who is very much part of daily life. One older woman has said, "The Madonna must have had a hard time when she was carrying the Savior, because people couldn't have known about the Holy Ghost and they always gossip about such things." Religion in general is seen in this concrete and living way, and religious vocabulary as exclamations, for example, *Madonna mia* and *Santa Maria*, are very much part of daily conversation.

The most important characteristic of the Madonna is that her love and tenderness are always available; no matter how unhappy or sinful the supplicant, she will respond if she is addressed in time of need. Acts of penitence may be carried out for her, for example, pilgrimages or even licking the steps of the church one by one and proceeding to the altar (today only in the most traditional rural areas). Even such acts of penitence, however, are apt to be conceived of as means of showing one's devotion in order to secure a favor, such as the recovery of a sick child. In this sense, the Madonna complex is based on an ethic of suffering rather than sin; the devotee seeks comfort for the wrongs imposed by fate rather than a guide for changing it.

The Madonna is quite obviously the ideal mother figure, and the relationship of the supplicant to her is conceived of as that of a child. The other family figures in the Christian pantheon are, of course, not lacking, that is, the father and the son. However, God the Father is usually conceived of as being so distant that he is unapproachable except through the intermediary of the Madonna or a saint; in Naples, the first-cause theory of creation is very common, according to which God set the world in motion and then let it run according to its own devices. Christ, on the other hand, is perceived not as in many Protestant denominations as a representative of moral individuality, or even as an alternative comforting figure, but rather either as the good son who is truly and continually penitent or else in the context of suffering; as dramatized in Lenten rituals, the Madonna weeps when he dies martyrized by a hostile world. Of the three figures, it is the Madonna who has by far the greatest concreteness in the popular eye. Moreover, of all her characteristics one of the clearest is her asexuality: she conceived without sin and so became mother without being a wife.

Not only is the most apparent deity a feminine one, but also religion is defined as a primarily feminine sphere. Thus, while small boys may attend mass regularly in the company of women, as they approach puberty most of them are teased out of this by their male peers or relatives. The level of participation in religious functions (except for those touching on the secular such as fiestas) is in general very low for adult males; but at every Sunday mass one can observe crowds of young men waiting outside the door. The reason they themselves give for being there is that the girls are inside; thus, at the courtship phase religious participation becomes an opportunity for escaping surveillance, but with the difference that the girl's overt devotion increases and the reverse is true for the boy. Moreover, Southern Italy is noted for its anticlericalism, but, along with some socioeconomic aspects, a major feature of this anticlericalism is a joking pattern whose main consequence is to raise doubts concerning the ideals of purity which religion represents. This joking pattern is an important part of interaction in the male peer group which crystallizes around adolescence. It thus seems as if religion and adult male sexuality are conceived of as incompatible with each other.

The oppositional or skeptical trend which is represented by anticlerical joking is seen in a number of other cultural patterns as well; first, in swearing and obscenity which are extremely widespread. The particular expressions used can be divided into four groups: those wishing evil on someone else (e.g., "may you spit up blood," from the extreme anxiety evoked by the idea of tuberculosis); those reflecting on the dead ("curse the dead in your family"); those reversing religious values (the most common oath being "curse the Madonna"); and those reversing the values of feminine purity. The latter group includes graphic expressions for a variety of possible incestuous relationships with mother or sister, anal as well as genital, and can also be linked with the horn gesture (index and little finger extended) implying infidelity of the wife. Cursing may be engaged in by women as well as men, but it is far more characteristic of the latter, particularly the last two types.[3]

The context and seriousness of insult and obscenity is extremely variable; one may curse the Madonna on the occasion of stubbing one's toe, but raising the possibility of the "horns" or using the incestuous expressions with enough seriousness may also lead to murder. It is this subtle distinction of style and context which differentiates Neapolitan patterns from those found in association with lineage systems where there are more formalized distinctions between those kin relationships which permit joking or obscenity, and those which do not because they are based on respect.[4] But the essential point is that the frequency of obscenity as used by men is such that one might talk of any positive value as reversible into a potential negative one; the reversibility relation is in turn confirmed by the particular content choices.

A second index of the same oppositional or skeptical trend is found in the style of masculine behavior and in social interaction within the male peer group. From adolescence on, an important segment of male life takes place on the street corner, at the bar, or in the club setting which at least psychologically is quite separate from either the home or the church. But in this setting in contrast to the other two, it is masculine values which predominate over feminine ones. Not only are swearing and anticlerical joking characteristic, but most social interaction has a particular style which is partly humorous and partly cynical in quality; many features of both language and gesture point in the direction of skepticism. Moreover, attitudes toward all forms of higher authority, secular as well as religious, are far more negative than positive in emphasis. Much of this style has a ritualized quality to it, but again we have a further index of the reversibility in the masculine setting of values defined as positive in the feminine context. In addition, many male peer-group patterns, in particular the emphasis on gambling and risk, are such that they provide a kind of counterpoint to the extreme emphasis on protection and security found in the Madonna complex.[5]

The second cultural complex which we will describe centers on courtship. Courtship is highly dramatized, and in the very important tradition of Neapolitan drama one can find over and over again the same plot: girl meets boy, this is kept secret from the family, or in particular from the father, father finds out (by catching them or by gossip from others), there is a big fight in which the girl or the fiancé stands up for the couple's rights against the father, father gives in at last, and here the play ends. Sometimes there are attempts on the part of the parents to marry a daughter to an old and ugly man for reasons of *interesse* or financial gain, but they are apt to be frustrated and never go without protest from the daughter. Says Rita in the early nineteenth-century play

Anella when her father tries to marry her off to a rich but effeminate rag dealer.[6]

You can cut me up piece by piece, but that Master Cianno, I'll never take him. Poor me! Even if I had found him while Vesuvius was erupting, I wouldn't have gone near him. If I weren't your daughter but your worst enemy, even then I wouldn't think of marrying that sort of man. What sort of life would it be?

The same play also serves to point up the very high degree with which courtship is romanticized and the particularly humble and supplicative position attributed to the young man. The following dialogue is addressed to Anella, standing in the balcony, by her suitor, Meniello:[7]

What sleep, what rest! What sleep, what rest can I have if I am in love, and the man in love is worse off than the man who is hanging on a rope and as soon as he gets a bit jealous, then the cord tightens. What sleep, the minute I close my eyes from exhaustion, jealousy makes me see my Anella up on her balcony surrounded by a crowd of lovers all looking up at her from below ... what sort of sleep can you look for. And the worst of all is that I haven't even any hope of getting out of torment because I can't even ask her mother to give her to me as a wife because my dog's destiny made it happen that just to make a baker's dozen her mother is in love with me, too. You see what terrible things can happen in this world to torment a poor man in love!
    (Anella appears) Oh, Menie, is that you?
    (Meniello) Oh, beautiful one of my heart!
    (Anella) What on earth is wrong? I haven't even dressed yet, and you are up already. Why on earth are you so early?

The dialogue continues between Meniello's supplications and Anella's much more self-assured and often more mundane reassurances against his jealousy.

Courtship is not only a theme of popular drama; it is also one of the major topics of conversation and joking in everyday life. In one sense, the social norms surrounding it are very strict, in that there are patterns of chaperonage, parents have many active rights of control, and the whole area is surrounded with an aura of taboo. Above all, it is considered highly important that the young girl keep her virginity until she is able to stand in church in the white veil which symbolizes it. Thus, there is a very sharp polar distinction between the good woman and the bad woman, the virgin and the prostitute. The assumptions underlying courtship are linked up in turn with a metaphorical image from which one can derive many specific customs and sayings: in a similar bipolar fashion, the home is defined as safe, feminine, and asexual, while the street is defined as inherently dangerous, tempting, and freely accessible only to men. Thus, a woman of the streets is one who has violated the taboos and in a sense has taken over masculine prerogatives. Coming into the girl's home is a very crucial step in legitimate courtship (popular terminology distinguishes between the often quite casual "so-so engaged" or "engaged in secret," and the more formalized "engaged in the house," i.e., with parental knowledge and approval), and the doorway occupies a particularly strategic intermediary position. Young girls usually become very excitable and giggly when they have the occasion for a promenade, and street phobias are a very common neurotic symptom in Italian women.

But a second aspect of the courtship complex is that in spite of the apparent strictness violations continually occur nevertheless, and the whole topic is treated with a particular kind of humorous ambiguity. Thus, while sexual matters are never referred to in serious or "objective" ways in everyday conversation, in a teasing or joking way they are an almost continuous focus of social exchange. The actual atmosphere or attitudes created by the strictness are far from puritan; it is rather as if the mothers and aunts and cousins who watch over the young girl with terrible threats about what will happen if she is "bad" are at the same time very much enjoying the possibility with her. One might by analogy to the many primitive societies in which there is a polar distinction between social relationships based on teasing or joking and those which are based on seriousness or formal respect, distinguish along the same lines between the Madonna complex and the courtship complex. For this reason, the distinction between the good woman and the bad woman is not as absolute as it might

seem; often these may be alternative asexual and sexual images for the same woman, as when a father in anger calls his daughter a prostitute because she has come in late.

However, there is one point at which the sacred and the profane come together, and this is at the point of marriage, which almost without exception is symbolized by a church ceremony. Thus, while courtship is a secular process and while the idea of violation of chaperonage norms is often treated with humor, its more serious aim is nevertheless that it should end up in church with the young girl being able to stand "in front of the Madonna" in the white veil.[8] At the same time, marriage for the man symbolizes a kind of capitulation to the feminine religious complex, whose importance is denied in the male peer group setting by the pattern of sarcasm and secularization. In contrast to the girl, whatever prior sexual entanglements he has had lack significance. Thus, while at least in peasant areas even today the girl's "honor" may be verified by relatives after the wedding night, the whole question is seen as simply irrelevant on the sexual plane as far as men are concerned: said one informant, "How would anyone ever know if a man had it or not?"

There is, nevertheless, a sense in which the idea of honor is relevant to masculine identity as well as feminine. This is that the task of chaperonage is seen by the father (or brother) as a matter of maintaining his personal honor as well as the collective honor of the family. Thus, if a girl falls into disgrace, it will be said that the family honor has been lost, or that her father is also a *disgraziato* or lacking in grace. Moreover, whenever insults are cast at female kin, as in the oaths which reflect on the purity of mother, sister, daughter, or wife, the man is expected to consider this as a violation of his own personal integrity and to immediately come to their defense – in some instances with a knife. There are areas where the violation of the honor of a daughter or sister can lead to socially approved homicide, necessary to the defense of the family honor. This pattern is particularly characteristic of Sicily, where the brother's role is more important than in Naples. In eighteenth- and nineteenth-century Naples the task of protecting the honor of slum women was taken over by the Camorra, the most highly organized form reached by the Neapolitan underworld, which was not averse to using knives in order to force a reluctant man who had violated virginity into marriage.

We can now try to sum up some of the respective implications of the courtship complex and the Madonna complex as two contrasting sides of a global cultural pattern. One of these we have seen as a joking pattern and the other as a pattern of serious respect and desexualization, although the two meet and cross each other both in the male peer-group rebellion against the Madonna and in the culmination of legitimate courtship in the church wedding. The symbol that unites them is that of virginity, or an initial asexual image of femininity that can only be violated in the appropriate social circumstances. These contrasting but interdependent patterns in themselves give us some of the elements of a distinctive nuclear complex; the two most important elements are that of the sublimated respect of children for the ideal mother and that of the game in which erotic temptations continually come into clash with this image of feminine purity. In the latter context, the most important actors, as Neapolitan drama would suggest, are the girl, her father, and the prospective son-in-law. The key value is that of virginity or honor, and the father seeks to preserve it against all comers; it is here that we can look for a distinctive triangular situation.

Family Structure

At this point, we can turn to the more direct consideration of the family. We noted earlier that the primary unit is the nuclear family but that it is embedded in a larger kin group, and there is a high degree of continuity to the mother-child tie. The family is close in a certain sense, at least in that family ties and obligations outweigh all others, but family life is also characterized by a great deal of aggression and conflict. One way in which conflict is handled is by various patterns for the separation of roles, a result of which is the extrafamilial male peer group. After marriage, as well as before, many of the man's needs for comradeship and

mutuality continue to be filled by the male peer group and much of the time he is out of the home. The woman, on the other hand, continues in close daily exchange with her natal family (perhaps less in the city than in the villages, and neighbors may also be important) so that many needs for mutual sympathy are fulfilled by mother and sisters or by other women. The division of the sexes is such that the marriage relationship is not often a focus of continuous intimate or reciprocal affective exchange. After the courtship phase and the honeymoon, it more often than not becomes very conflictual, principally because of the emotional ties which both partners retain to the natal family.

In actual fact, of course, there are a great many varied families as well as the noted regional variations; however, many of the observable norms and patterns can be interpreted from the above structural givens. For example, there is a variety of possible balances to the husband–wife versus primary family conflict. For Naples, the most common type of residence is in the vicinity of the wife's family, but the husband as an individual is likely to maintain important contacts with his own. Sometimes the couple together becomes assimilated into one family or another; women, for example, who have had particularly unfavorable relations with their own families, or who have lost a mother by death, are more likely to accept the mother-in-law as a mother surrogate, thus achieving a better relationship with her than is generally expected. The same may happen in the case of the man who marries into a fatherless family or one consisting of girls alone who may take over male roles in that family with relative success. This is unlikely if there are competing figures. Quarrels concerning where the couple should reside are very common, and they are accompanied by a great deal of mutual projection; thus, a man may complain that his wife is much too dependent on her mother and pays little attention to him, and then suggest as a solution to the problem that they move to the house next door to his mother. In extreme cases the two families may end up with quite violent feelings about each other; in studying schizophrenic patients, we found this to be common, and many marriages, while maintained in form, actually dissolved with each partner returning to his own home. The uncertainties of the conflict are intensified by the fact that in contrast to many simpler societies, there are no fixed rules of choice or subordination. A result of this uncertainty is that in situations of choice and conflict, it is more often the feminine point of view than the masculine one which prevails, since it is the woman who in daily life is most concerned with and most emotionally involved in matters pertaining to the family.

It is also the mother who is the primary personage in maintaining family unity, and many results of this can be observed; for example, ties with father or siblings are very likely to break up or become more distant on the death of the mother. Another consequence is seen in differential attitudes toward the remarriage of widows and in differing consequences of the death of parents. If a man is left without a wife, it is taken for granted that he will need a woman, and whether or not he has children, he is likely to find one, though often outside of legal sanction. Thus, many persons who have widower fathers simply state that they have drifted off somewhere, and the ties are no longer very real. On the other hand, a widow or a woman deserted by her husband may be condemned if she seeks alternative sexual attachments before her children marry; it is assumed that her primary loyalty is to them. Marriage, which in Naples is likely to take place either in the late teens or not until the late twenties or thirties, often in this latter instance follows very closely on the death of the parents. Remarriages when both partners have children are often conflictual on the grounds that each prefers his own offspring, and the stepmother is seen as in the Cinderella legend. She may do her best by the children, but even then the tie is never the same; the best possible solution to the loss of a mother is seen to be adoption by the mother's sister, who, because related by blood, will come much closer to fulfilling the maternal role. Marriage to the deceased wife's sister is not uncommon in the case of widowers, though practiced more in rural than in urban areas.

The importance of the mother-child tie as the axis of family structure is seen in some additional patterns characteristic of lower-class Naples. Where illegitimacy occurs, the child is legally recognized and brought up by the mother in about 50 per cent of the cases; such status is not formally approved but it does occur.[9] Fathers very rarely recognize illegitimate children, but there are, on the other hand, certain forms of semi-institutionalized polygamy, according to which a father may have two distinctive families, one of which is legal while the other is not. In contrast to the pattern of the affair where it is assumed that if the relationship is not socially sanctioned, precautions will be taken to avoid reproduction, it seems that aside from prostitution it is usually assumed that children are the necessary and wanted consequence of any sexual relationship; thus, the rapid multiplication which often characterizes monogamous families also characterizes polygamous ones.

The major requirement for a husband is that he be able to feed and support his family. However, in the urban working class, it very often happens that he is not able to fulfill this task; thus, one common source of arguments is that the husband has not brought in any money. It is also the case in urban areas where the married woman often works in her own right; for example, women may be street vendors, artisans, domestics, etc. At the lower socioeconomic levels it is often the woman who has a better opportunity of earning money than the man. She is more motivated to work since she more willingly accepts a low-prestige or low-reward position because of concern for children, while for the man, peer-group relationships or a kind of pseudo identification with the higher status groups offers a more immediately rewarding proof of masculinity. One of the primary symbols of peer-group belongingness in Naples is the ability to offer food or drink to others, so that the man is faced with an inherent conflict in that what he spends to gain status in relation to other men is bread lost out of his children's mouths. Thus, a vicious circle may be set in motion in which the wife accuses the husband of irresponsibility, and the husband in turn goes off in anger and tries to recapture his self-esteem by taking risks at cards or by treating his friends to coffee. It is, moreover, the way of dealing with this situation which differentiates male relationships with wives and mothers;

the mother, if she has anything at all, will give it to her son, but the wife expects the husband to hand everything over to her in the interests of the children. Thus, financial conflicts are one factor which can push a married man back to ask for support at home.

A second factor is the degree to which intra-family behavior is characterized by rivalry between husband and children for the attention of the mother in her food-giving role. One symbolization of the difference between South Italian society and the more truly patriarchal Victorian one can be found in the nature of eating patterns and their relation to family social structure; in contrast to the regular ritualized mealtimes of the Victorian epoch, with father taking a commanding position at the head of the table, there is a highly irregular eating pattern (space often makes a regular dinner table impossible) in which each member of the family may eat according to his own preference at his own time, but in which the mother is almost continually involved in the process of feeding. In this structure the superior position of the father, and of sons as they grow up, is symbolized by the right to demand what they want and the right to complain if not pleased. When a man complains, the woman will try to do what she can, and as long as she has anything at all, she will give it; but the pattern also puts the husband on an equal subordinate basis with his children.

Thus, the ties to the primary family, the high significance of the maternal role, and the very great difficulties in making a living which characterize most of the working-class groups are such that in spite of appearances the husband and father does not actually enjoy much prestige or authority in the home. From this standpoint the male peer group can be seen as an escape; the man who gets totally "fed up" always has the possibility of leaving. Likewise, many of the male rage reactions, which give the impression that the Italian family is patriarchal, though much more stylized, have the quality of the child who throws his plate on the floor when he has had enough. Moreover, many of the status-gaining activities of the peer group can be seen as identifications with the feminine feeding role, for example, the high importance attributed to offering food or coffee. However, a second

aspect of the masculine role in the home and its relations to sex segregation should not be neglected. This is that male rage may be seen as truly terrifying to women, so that kicking men out becomes necessary, and this goes with an image of masculinity as a kind of threatening force which is a disruptive factor in the feminine circle; images used in daily conversation clearly suggest the idea of phallic intrusion.

A few details on socialization can serve to round out the picture of family life. Children become a center of attention as soon as they are born and receive a great deal of physical handling which does not undergo systematic interruption; moreover, as they are weaned, substitute gratifications are provided so there is no significant discontinuity ending the oral phase of development. However, it would be a mistake to conclude from this that they simply receive that much more of the "security" and maternal warmth which are currently so highly valued in the United States. In the first place, the mother may give little attention to any individual child, being busy and often having many; moreover, maternal behavior (in the sense of giving food and physical caresses) is so widespread that in actual social reality the maternal attachment is far from being exclusive. Rather, one might say that the circle of maternal objects progressively widens to include the family as a whole and in many respects strangers; along with this goes the learning of certain kinds of politeness and formality having to do with eating and giving.

In the second place, handling of children is often rough and unsubtle and includes a very high aggressive component.[10] As physical motility appears, it can be systematically frustrated by anxious adults who immediately bring back the wandering or assertive child to thrust a cookie into his mouth; one can see here the beginning of the forced feeding pattern which characterizes moments of tension in the family throughout life. An illustrative example concerns a three-year-old son of a gardener who picked up his father's tools and was immediately called back by mother with the tacit support of father. Children at this age may show considerable diffuse aggressivity and put on an unnatural amount of weight. Later, most of them learn to "talk back" with verbal rhetoric and gesture; these important components of South Italian culture might be seen as developed in counterreaction to muscular inhibition in that they become a major means for expressing individuality. A second relevant example concerns an eighteen-month-old girl who seemed hardly interested in learning to walk and was not yet able to talk; yet, held by her father she was able to perform fairly complex symbolic operations with her hands, such as snapping her fingers ten times when asked to count to ten.

For these early phases there seems to be little difference between the handling of the small girl and of the small boy, with the single exception that the small boy is more likely to go unclothed from the waist down and to have his penis singled out for teasing admiration.[11] This open phallic admiration is characteristic of the behavior of mothers to sons, and in teasing intrafamily behavior the genital organs may be poked or referred to with provocative gestural indications. Children may also share beds with their parents or with each other even at advanced ages (crowding often makes this necessary)[12] though precautions are taken to prevent their observing parental intercourse. One young man was asked what he would do if he saw this; the answer was "I would kill them." Except for small children, modesty taboos are very strict, and while physical proximity within the family is very close with respect to anything except genital activity, this latter is surrounded with some secrecy.

There are, however, two crucial points at which sex difference is more prominent. The first is in the ritual of First Communion which ideally takes place at the age of six or seven. Around this age the growing attractiveness of the little girl is the focus of considerable teasing admiration from father or older brothers, uncles, etc., though these have not taken much interest in the very small child. One Neapolitan informant, for example, told me how his seven-year-old daughter had taken to getting into bed with him in such a seductive way that he finally had to slap her and kick her out. It did not surprise him in the least when I said that a famous Viennese doctor had made quite a bit out of this sort of thing. However, once the small girl's Oedipal affects have been excited

to this degree, it is also necessary that the culture find a resolution for them which it does in the ritual of First Communion; the small girl is dressed as a miniature bride, and at this point it must be impressed on her fantasy that she must delay fulfillment of her wishes until such a time as she can again appear in church in a white veil. Thus, a particularly elaborate cultural symbolization is provided for feminine Oedipal wishes.

For the boy, on the other hand, there is much less in the way of such cultural elaboration of the Oedipus crisis, nor for that matter is there any ritual symbolization of masculine status at adolescence, as there is in many other cultures where socialization at earlier stages is so exclusively in the hands of women. First Communion does take place, but masculine emphasis and degree of symbolization is simply less. Moreover, in many ways the boy's position at home is much more passive than that of the girl; the beautiful warm-eyed docility which one can observe in many boys in the Neapolitan slums might make for the envy of the American mother in the Hopalong Cassidy phase. The same degree of aggressive tension does not appear to be present, nor for that matter is there as much elaboration of the phallic "I want to be when I grow up" type of fantasy. What does differentiate the small boy from the girl is, first, the open admiration which may be shown for his purely sexual masculine attributes, and second, the fact that he has much less in the way of home responsibility and is in many ways favored by the mother; but since the father is so often out of the home, his socialization is placed in feminine hands almost as much as that of the girl.

In other words, while cultural ritual can be seen as providing a complex symbolic framework for feminine oedipal wishes, this is not true in the case of the boy, who may receive special privileges and an open acknowledgment of his physical masculinity, but no such elaborate social symbolization of it. Presumably, this should result in much stronger motivation for the delay of sexual wishes in girls than in boys. This kind of differential in turn becomes extremely important in adolescence, at which point the pattern of sex differentiation becomes a much sharper one, for it is then that chaperonage rules begin to apply to the girl, and the boy in turn acquires a special freedom to move out into the inherently dangerous and sexualized world of the street.[13] It is at this latter point that the prerogative of adult masculinity crystallizes, especially with respect to the quasi taboo on feminine inquisitions concerning masculine activities which take place outside the home.

Projective Test Material

One of our initial assumptions was that culture appears in the individual in the form of object representations which crystallize in the conscious mind at the time of the passing of the Oedipus complex. In this perspective, the norms of intrafamily behavior should be reflected on the psychological plane in the form of more or less uniform representations of the significant family figures in relation to the self. This dimension is one which can be measured through the use of projective tests. Such material will be presented as a supplement to the cultural and social observations which we have already made.

In two separate studies, a number of cards from the Murray TAT were presented to working-class informants in Naples. Four cards (6GF, 6BM, 7BM, 7GF) will be discussed here. They were presented to the informants with the specific directive that they represent family scenes (mother–daughter, father–son, father–daughter, and mother–son), and they were to describe the scene as it appeared to them. Though few very elaborate stories were given, the subjects saw the cards in an amazingly vivid way with a high degree of sensitivity to the immediate perceptual and gestural details of the figures.[14] The high degree of uniformity of response is in itself a proof of the psychological reality of culture. This uniformity was greatest for the mother–son and father–daughter scenes.

Mother–daughter card

The mother–daughter card was presented to twenty-six female informants with a specific directive: "The mother is advising the daughter, what do you think she is telling her?" Additional questions such as "How does the daughter feel about it?" were also asked. Thus, we purposely biased the situation in the direction of emphasis on maternal authority. However, only to a certain extent was this the major theme; rather, the responses fell into three distinct groups, of which the first is most directly relevant to the question of authority as such.

For eleven subjects, the mother appeared as giving some very definite form of censure or advice. In only one such instance is the reaction of the daughter to this seen as wholly positive; in one other instance the reaction of the daughter is openly rebellious, and in the remaining nine, the daughter accepts the advice as "for her own good" but with expressed resentment; however, the mother is finally vindicated since "things don't turn out well in the long run":

The mother is giving good advice to the daughter; the mother tells the daughter to behave well, not to go out much, to pay more attention to things at home. She has to help her mother to do the housework. The picture is beautiful because there is nothing bad in it.

The mother is yelling at the daughter because with the excuse of the child who is her little brother she goes out walking and comes in late. The daughter talks back to her mother saying "What do you want with me? You made this baby and now you go around finding out bad things about me."

The mother is moralizing. The daughter is a bit fed up with the mother's words. ...

The mother tells the little girl that she has to do housework and the daughter is not looking at the mother as if she had not heard and did not want to do this work. ... Things won't go very well because the daughter won't listen to the mother.

The first reaction is particularly interesting in that by implication it so clearly brings out the asexual nature of the home in contrast to the outside world where there may always be "something bad." The second is equally interesting in that where there is open rebellion on the part of the daughter, the mother is also portrayed as a sexual being. The remaining responses show a very classic pattern of internalized but ambivalently accepted authority; the mother is clearly a superego figure, but considerable rebellion and resentment are experienced toward her.

For the next group of subjects, the card itself provided a particular difficulty. The Murray card shows a girl in the latency period being read to by her mother and holding what could be either a doll or a live baby. The situation of a mother reading to the daughter is, of course, somewhat out of the ordinary in this group, but in addition a number of informants were led to comment from the girl's age that this could not actually be an authority situation since "the girl is too young to be given the most important advice."

Thus, these responses were limited to fairly factual and emotionally neutral kinds of advice ("the mother is telling the daughter how to bring up her little brother"), and more crucial attitudes of mother and daughter were not made clear. The responses are important principally for their value in pointing up just how crucial the courtship situation is as compared to any other area of performance with respect to the question of authority in general.

For the third group of three respondents this was true as well, but they simply ignored the age of the girl on the card and perceived the situation as involving a mother, her daughter, and the latter's illegitimate child:

The mother talks with the daughter that is married and has a child, no, I mean the daughter is not married. The mother tries to help her and get her married, the mother is good and does not throw her out of the house.

The girl is not married and it seems to me that her mother gives her advice on how to bring up the child. It seems that the mother has forgiven her and tells her to treat the child well. The mother gives advice to the daughter about how to behave and how not to fall a second time. Because the mother is understanding she says to the daughter to be careful because the mother should try not to say to the daughter that she is guilty because the girl could do something to hurt herself, she could commit suicide or fall into the same error again thinking that she doesn't have anyone who cares.

This is, of course, a crucial and dramatic situation where norms have actually been violated. The responses make clear that fear of loss of maternal love is a major threat preventing more frequent violations; but also in the actual crisis situation the mother may not really kick the girl out of the house. Another evidence of the internalized nature of maternal authority is seen in the respondent who conceived of suicide as a possibility in the event that such forgiveness did not take place.[15]

Father–son card

The father–son card was presented to ten men and ten women in a second study. No specific directives were given beyond the statement that the scene involved a father and a son. Authority, however, turned out to be the most important theme, found in the responses of seven men and three women, but in contrast to the mother-daughter responses the specific content of the advice or censure given by the father to the son was left indeterminate. However, there is no doubt but that fathers were seen by the majority of men as censuring figures.

… the father reproaches the son … the son is a delinquent, you can see from his face that he is not a nice person and I think he will not listen to the father's advice. . . .

The son is bitter and the father displeased because the son would like to talk about something and doesn't. During the family life, the father asks the son what trade he would like to have while the son takes the matter unhappily. He would like to be a chauffeur and the father makes him learn carpentry and the result is that he practices his trade against his own will and cannot succeed in it. After a few years he begins to hate the father and so he remains without any trade at all. The son on his side would like to be a chauffeur. As a result father and son fight, the son curses the father, the father says "you ought to listen to me."

The second response was stated to be an autobiographical one; the respondent was the son of an artisan and, as the result of having gambled away his youth and refusing to learn a trade, was at the time I saw him a very despondent man, father of eight children whom he tried to support as a street vendor. Moreover, while all the male respondents were themselves fathers with children, they seemed not to take the perspective of the father. The exceptions to the rule that both were seen negatively were only partial ones; one respondent did unconvincingly portray the father as affable while another (particularly intelligent and outward seeking) was the only respondent to think of the possibility of positive rather than negative assertion against the father:

> The son is affable and absolutely convinced of the father's counsels.
> The father is decided and authoritarian, ugly. The son *might* be bad, he has an independent spirit and does not want to listen to the father. The son follows something else, as if the father's wisdom were something annoying, not very important for him.

Two of the remaining three men saw the situation as one of shared sorrow for the death of a woman and the third presented an alternative comradely view of their relationship:

> There is a close friendship between the father and son, they confide in each other.

But for women it was themes of common sorrow and depression which took precedence over those concerning authority. Thus, three saw authority themes and three a common sorrow over death; but the remaining four show the two as sharing a common sense of helplessness with respect to the (primarily economic) external reality:

> They are desperate (for money) – they worry. Nothing more.
> They are worrying about something, the office, work, because they are melancholy.
> What a shame, the father is completely blind! Don't you see he has his eyes completely closed and an absent expression? The son is as if he were listening to something, it must be a radio, but the father has the look really of a blind man. (Don't they say anything to each other?) No, the father minds his own business,

really with the look of a blind man, and the son on the other hand is listening, he must be listening to the radio.

In this the women seem to be able to portray a socially very real aspect of their relationship, that it is hard for a man to be an effective authority when he cannot provide anything for his son, which the men themselves have to deny.

The most striking features of the responses to the father-son card are, thus, the lack of a clear social agreement concerning the nature of this relationship, and for the men the lack of effective internalization of paternal authority. By the latter, we mean that sons are simply seen as "bad" or "delinquent" in relation to the father, without, as was the case in the mother-daughter situation, there being a view of how the son ought to accept the authority for his own good. One might say that this provides further evidence that the society is not patriarchal, and masculinity is defined more in terms of rebellion than positive identification. In simplest terms, the conflict is that portrayed by one informant who says, "They seem against each other."

Father–daughter card

For a contrast with responses to the father–son scene, we might again quote the street vendor, who turned to this card with considerable relief and pleasure:

> This case here defines a father, he is sociable. Here it is no longer a job problem, the girl must know a man and he knew from the information that he has been a delinquent. He says "look for another path, there are millions of men." The father wants happiness for his daughter, he wants her to marry someone who will give her something to eat. (Q) The daughter answers "it's my business," no daughter ever listens to her father. (Q) They get bitter but then they make peace after a child is born.

Unfortunately, we do not have enough male answers to this card to analyze quantitatively; however, this one indicates that while the father does have authority over the daughter, its overthrow is to be expected even by the father himself and while they may "get bitter," the bitterness is nothing like the real hostility of the father–son antagonism. The same card was administered to thirty-two female respondents, and it was among these that the highest degree of uniformity was found. Twenty saw the situation as conflict between father and daughter related to courtship:

The father does not want the daughter to get engaged to a man he knows and does not want this man to marry his daughter. The father is making her ashamed. The father seems bad to me. He is jealous of the daughter and does not want her to get engaged. The daughter is a beautiful girl. She cares a lot about this man that her father doesn't want to give her to and she wants to get married at any price.

The father is mortifying the daughter. The father is having it out with the daughter because other people have told him something. He makes her ashamed and she remains surprised and amazed. The father wants to know the story of his daughter's engagement. She does not want to tell about her affairs and probably the father heard about this engagement from other people. The father wants to know if it is a good marriage for his daughter.

The daughter seems like an actress. The father is reasoning with the daughter. They are probably talking about the daughter's fiancé; the father wants to know how things are going in her engagement. The father is happy and the daughter is a bit fed up because her father wants to know many facts about her relationship with the fiancé. For this reason she is not answering spontaneously.

Nine of the remaining twelve respondents gave generally very inhibited answers or denied that the scene could actually be father and daughter in such a way as to suggest some neurotic inhibition.

I don't know how to say anything about this picture. The father is mad and the daughter is calm. They are talking about not very important problems that have to do with family life. (Informant says that the test seems a bit complicated here.) The father is upset because the daughter didn't do something in the house; she should have done some errand and didn't

do it. The father says to the girl, "You got dressed up to go out and didn't do the errands." The father doesn't let her go out but the relations between father and daughter aren't bad.

And finally three informants saw the scene as one in which the father was making seductive advances toward the daughter.

The father is looking at the daughter in a strange way, that is more like a man than like a father. She looks at him perplexed and almost struck dumb. The father will not succeed because the daughter has understood his intentions, she will control herself unless he attacks her. The father is not behaving very well; he has gone astray … maybe because the girl is attractive.

All three saw the girl as able to control the situation. An additional two among the above nine, while denying that the scene could be father and daughter, saw, respectively, a husband and wife, and an older Don Juan boss seducing a secretary.

As far as we know the incest responses were not given by seriously disturbed women and they show fewer signs of inhibition than the respondents who did not perceive any shame or conflict between father and daughter at all.

For the first group there was not a single informant who failed to perceive the situation as a conflictual one in which the conflict lay between the father's censure or possessiveness and the daughter's wish to have a boyfriend. Moreover, the card typically evoked a complex of affects which included pleasure (blushing and giggling), shame, and embarrassment. When we look for the outcome of the conflict, we find one element in common with the father-son card, namely, the tendency is in the direction of expected rebellion rather than internalized acceptance of paternal authority. In ten out of twenty instances the daughter is specifically stated to win the battle with father, while in only three does she concede; in the remaining cases the fact of conflict is simply stated. In other words, the TAT responses repeat the same dramatic pattern which we have already seen in the play *Anella* in which the courtship situation is a triangular relation between father, daughter, and prospective son-in-law, and the expected outcome is the ritual termination of the father's possessive relation to the daughter.

Mother–son card

The most important characteristic of these responses is the extent to which they show a close correspondence to the Madonna complex, just as the father–daughter card corresponds to the courtship one. One theme occurs over and over again, more frequent among male than female respondents, namely, that of the penitent son who is returning to the mother:

> … the son is asking forgiveness of the mother, repenting of the evil he has done. …
>
> The mother pushes the young man away and he asks for something insistently. Or maybe he did something very serious, probably he went away, and so now he has come back to ask her forgiveness and the mother no longer wants to receive him.
>
> The mother has a son she has not seen for many years … he returns after having done many bad things, stealing and other things. He returns to the family to ask forgiveness. Who knows whether or not the mother will give it to him but I think she will. The son is asking forgiveness for something … a mother would always forgive her son, even if he were an assassin, even if he were Chessman.
>
> The penitent son who returns to the mother and the mother cannot or does not know how to forgive him.

In comparison to the responses concerning the father, what is most striking is the extent to which the son places the burden of guilt upon himself, in that asking for forgiveness implies an internalized sense of wrongdoing.

There was some variation among the respondents as to whether the mother was seen as certain to provide forgiveness or not; the fact that some expressed doubt or uncertainty is evidence that maternal love is not conceived of as wholly unconditional. In two instances informants were known to have marked difficulties in their actual relationships with the mother. One of these is the informant who states that "the

mother cannot or does not know how to forgive" – but he portrays the son as the saint who forgives the mother unable to forgive. The second, recently kicked out of home, is the only one who saw the mother as acting aggressively ("The mother pushes the young man away," etc.), but after in a sense blaming the mother, he changes pattern and like the others puts the burden of guilt on the son.

For ten male and ten female respondents, what we call the penitence response was given by seven men and four women. Among the other responses, three portrayed simple sadness ("The mother is sad because the son will leave"), and three anger. All of the anger responses were given by women, who, on the whole, presented a less romanticized view of the relationship. One response given by a beggar is particularly interesting in that it shows a relation between psychic abnormality and open anger and sexual deviance on the part of the mother:

> As if he (she?) were all upset. You can see the son is arguing with the mother, he has turned his back, maybe they had a family fight. (About what?) Mama and son because the mama you can see made a lot of scandals and the son wants to find out something, who knows what, and so mama and son are arguing … because you can see that the mother is a bit off in the head because she turns her back on the son. (Yes, you can see that she is a bit angry. But how does the son feel about it?) The son has an enraged face, he has his nerves out of place too. (In response to further questions, she shifts subject.)

In many instances the fact that the American card portrays a mother looking away from her son was sensed as disturbing but that it could imply psychic distance was denied. Thus, while it may be perceived by women, there seems to be a taboo on perceiving anger in the mother–son relationship by men. In this respect there is a very clear contrast with respect to the father–son relationship.

Conclusions

We began, with reference to the Jones–Malinowski debate, by considering the possibility that each culture is characterized by a distinctive nuclear complex whose roots lie in its family structure. Our subsequent task has been to pull together various orders of data concerning Southern Italy in such a way as to portray such a nuclear complex which differs both from the brother–sister–sister's son triangle characteristic of the Trobriand Island and from the patriarchal complex isolated by Freud. In the South Italian data we have found that two cultural complexes, the sacred one centered on respect for the feminine Madonna figure and the secular joking pattern surrounding courtship and embodied in popular drama, also have their reflections in the actual patterning of family life and childhood experience and in the intrapsychic life of the individual as seen in projective tests. It is this continuity which has led us to the conclusion that it is possible to define a single global complex which can be perceived simultaneously either as intrapsychic or as collective, the representations which are passed on from generation to generation on the social level coming to be internalized in the individual in the form of representations of the self in relation to objects. The task which remains is the more precise summary of the outlines of the South Italian nuclear complex, comparing it with Freud's patriarchal one, and the drawing out of some more general implications with respect to research methodology and application.

Our principal supposition is that the two most significant among the biologically given family relationships are those between mother and son and between father and daughter. In the former instance the son occupies a subordinate position in the sense that authority stemming from the mother is fully internalized, and violations of it are subjectively sensed as inducing guilt, in comparison to the father-son relation where the son may openly express hostility or rebellion in such a way as to put the father in a negative light. In other words, respect for the mother is much stronger than respect for the father. We do not mean by this to say that women dominate in any simple sense, since it is evident that many other taboos, such as the barring of feminine interference in areas of activity defined as masculine ones, act against this result, not to mention the open admiration and permissiveness which women usually show toward the masculinity of their sons. However,

in many ways the mother-son relationship is qualitatively different from that of our own society or that of Freud, most notably in the continuation throughout life of what might be referred to as an oral dependent tie, i.e., a continual expectation of maternal solace and giving rather than a gradual or sudden emancipation from it.

It is this fact that might lead an American observer to speak of an "oral" culture, or one based on feeding as the dominant mode of libidinal interaction, in contrast to a hypothetical "anal" or "phallic" based one. However, this type of formulation we would consider quite inadequate both with respect to theory and the empirical facts. It is evident that types of interaction based on the exchange of gifts and food do have an extremely important role, though these result in very complex types of adult interaction which can by no means be derived directly from infantile roots. More important, however, is the theoretical postulate which would lead us to believe that the phallic phase of development nevertheless occurs. In other words, although he may not give up oral types of gratification, the boy nevertheless passes through a phase at which the wishes he experiences toward the mother are sexual and masculine in nature, and that, moreover, this phase will be associated with aggressive reactions against the subordinate feeding position. We can then trace some of the implications of these postulates rather than simply stopping with the "oral culture" formulation.

In this perspective we can better see some of the more general consequences of the fact that the masculine role is so little emphasized within the home and that cultural values center on the feminine image. From the genetic standpoint, we might say that while oral gratifications do not have to be renounced (although they do come to take more complex social forms), this is not true with respect to phallic and aggressive wishes toward the mother; these in fact must systematically undergo repression as they arise. In fact, to characterize the relation to the mother as one based on respect, in social language, is exactly the same thing as to say in psychodynamic language that sexual and aggressive wishes cannot be expressed directly. We then can ask what happens to these wishes, assuming that in some form they persist, and arrive at three kinds of formulation, each of which is relevant to the understanding of culture patterns. Through all of them the important contrast with Freud's formulation lies in the greater continuity of the relationship with the mother and the lesser continuity of that with the father.

First, referring back to the concept of the symbol as arising in precisely those areas where a culture both exploits (by actual affective closeness) and inhibits (by imposing of taboos) primary drives, we can say that the erotic wishes of the son toward the mother come to be sublimated, and it is precisely this fact which gives rise to the representation of the Madonna figure. Moreover, in her characteristics we can see both derivatives of the actual cultural reality, e.g., in that the dependent relationship of the penitent to the maternal figure is preserved, and some unrealizable aspects of fantasy, e.g., in that the Madonna became a mother without being a wife. This latter is, moreover, the characteristic which in itself represents oedipal repression, in that the Madonna is perceived as an asexual maternal figure. But in addition, and in contrast to the "oral culture" view which might say simply that mothers are more permissive, the Madonna is a "superego" figure; she could not be forgiving if she did not have a concept of sins which have to be forgiven. In this perspective we can say that oedipal wishes are repressed in such a way as to give rise to an internalized representation of the tabooed object, who then comes to play the role of conscience. However, the complication in this case is that the internalized object is in the case of men a feminine one; it is this which we mean by speaking of a matriarchal rather than a patriarchal "superego." What it leads to then is a masculine identification with a set of cultural values identifiable as feminine, or even as very concretely perceived according to a feminine body image. The most important of these is the respect for virginity, shared by men and women alike and manifested in the courtship taboos on entering the home of the girl who is sought before the relation is formalized. The identification of the girl who is legitimately courted with the idealized mother is seen in the similar submissive relation adopted by the male; the infantile wishes underlying the image of the pure woman are also seen in a sometimes extreme degree of defensiveness concerning the issue of whether or not the purity is real and to be believed.

Second, however, impulses which are repressed can also be dealt with by displacement. It is in this respect that the significance of the masculine peer group and the definition of the sphere of life outside of the home, i.e., the sum total of masculinity as defined by the rebellion pattern which we have discussed, become apparent. Many of the patterns of the outside peer group are distinctively phallic in nature. Moreover, in many more concrete senses one can conceive of the outside world as the focus for aggressive and phallic wishes which must be displaced outside the home, e.g., the common situation of the male in anger who simply picks up and leaves, or the great importance of cursing. Thus, aggression which arises within the home may be dealt with by displacement outside it. One characteristic of the Madonna is that she is an ideal figure; ordinary mothers of course rarely approach her, in that they may not forgive, they may very often get angry or impatient, or they may in fact dominate in a very aggressively matriarchal way and in this event the recourse of the male is the privilege of exit. Women in turn support this form of expression of masculinity by respecting the taboo on interference and often by direct admiration and encouragement of even delinquent extrafamilial activities. In addition, anger which arises in a mother-son relationship conceived of as exclusive in fantasy may also be dealt with in a complex series of intrafamilial rivalries and jealousies within which the affective consequence of reality frustration vis-à-vis the mother may be expressed with respect to other family objects. Thus, displacement both within and outside the family is used to deal with aggressive impulses whose direct expression toward the mother is tabooed.

Third, erotic wishes may be displaced as well as aggressive ones, and it is here that we can find the source of the bipolar distinction between the good woman and the bad woman. The contrary image to the Madonna is, of course, that of the prostitute, and the close intertwining of the two images is seen at a great many points, e.g., in the obscenity patterns that reverse the values of feminine purity and in the family quarrels where even closely associated women may be accused of promiscuous impulses. The persistence of the early sublimations in later life is manifested in two crucial assumptions: first, that the sexualized woman may be appreciated in a naturalistic way but she is always perceived as on a lower spiritual plane than the pure one; and second, the idea of sexuality is almost inevitably associated with the possibility of betrayal and pluralization of the relationship, i.e., in that wives, sweethearts, and mistresses are continually suspected by men of wanting other partners than themselves as soon as the idea of sexuality comes into play.

It is facts such as these which lead us to postulate an underlying and persistent fantasy of an exclusive maternal object as a theoretical assumption. Because of repression, we cannot, of course, acquire direct information concerning the sexual aspect in most cases. One particularly important area of research, however, is found in schizophrenic cases where one may see gross breakdowns of cultural sublimations. One of two South Italian schizophrenic men whom I have seen intensively showed the sexual aspect of the mother-son relationship and the associated Madonna complex in a very transparent form. He had many religious delusions; while praying to the Madonna he had open and bizarre erotic experiences and he was unable to distinguish consistently between maternal and erotic objects. The early history was probably one in which prolonged nursing merged into the awakening of genital feelings. However, the second case points up the need for care in separating local and individual variations from global patterns. Coming from a mountainous area where patriarchal patterns and a lack of sentimentality are more typical, the patient showed a much more autistic form of pathology of which the most conspicuous elements were warded-off homosexuality and an extremely submissive identification with the father. He rejected the breast of a wet nurse at an early age, and a crucial traumatic experience was a childhood seduction by an older brother.

One consequence of such a relationship, which fits many of the data we have concerning the South Italian family, is that it acts against social mobility in the broadest sense of the term by making for a very strong centripetal tendency. In other words, if a key axis of family structure is the relationship between mother and son, and if this relationship tends to maintain itself by the preservation of an infantile fantasy which is then dealt with by a complex series of social sublimations and displacements, rather than by attenuating its significance by dispersal or replacement by other objects, then we should have no theoretical basis for explaining the formation of new families. Rather we should expect each mother-son combination to simply continue until the death of the mother; the incest taboo alone does not seem sufficient for explaining the process of change, since nothing in South Italian norms prevents the adult son from obtaining immediate sexual gratification outside while continuing to occupy the emotionally more important position of son. It is at this point that we might turn to the examination of the father-daughter relationship, which can be seen as complementary to the mother-son one in defining a total structure.

The most important difference between these two lies in the dimension of continuity. The father is not continually and lovingly interested in his daughter as the mother is in her son, but rather his interest becomes particularly important at two points in the daughter's life history: the oedipal phase and the courtship phase. At both of these points the father is highly sensitive to the daughter's femininity, and the daughter is given considerable scope for exploiting this sensitivity in what is often a very active way. Moreover, while the taboo on incest between mother and son is as in all societies a very deep-lying one, it is very easy to come to the conclusion that the desexualization of the father-daughter relationship is not nearly as complete. Thus, in particular in instances where the mother has died, father-daughter incest is not an unheard of phenomenon and the possibility may be referred to even rather casually, as in the many stories about "that case in our village" that go around. We noted this on the TAT responses. In an American setting an openly incestuous perception might be taken as an indication of serious pathology, but we have no reason to believe this was the case for our informants. Their counterpart in the normal case where the taboo is preserved is found in the teasing behavior or embarrassed avoidance which characterizes the relation between the father and the sexually mature daughter or in the giggling embarrassment which women associate with the idea of being found out in their love relationships.

In other words, the incestuous impulses in the father-daughter relationship are quite close to the surface, in such a way that we might speak of a lesser degree of repression than is implied in Freud's concept of the Oedipus complex. There is of course a taboo but one might well speak of a persistence of the incestuous impulses on a preconscious level in such a way that they are openly expressed in cultural idiom, as in the frequent use of the word jealousy to describe the father's feelings about the daughter's suitors, and transformed into the joking pattern which is characteristic of the courtship complex.

The major significance of the triangle involving father, daughter, and prospective son-in-law, moreover, lies in the fact that it is to a much greater extent with respect to the daughter than to the wife or mother that the man plays an active role. When he himself is courting, he has to beg at the balcony for a well-protected woman whose virginity he has to respect, but in the case of his own daughter it is he who does the protecting and whose consent has to be sought by the prospective suitor. Thus, the most fully institutionalized masculine role in Southern Italy, one which is defined positively and not by rebellion, is that of the protection of the honor of the women who are tabooed. In turn, if the sexual affects felt toward these are quite close to the surface, considerable fantasy satisfaction must take place in a way which is active and masculine in contrast to the mother-son relationship, which in so many ways spreads into the marital one, where the male role is passive.

But in addition it is in the father–daughter relationship that we can find a mechanism of change which acts against the centripetal family tendency. The courtship situation not only gives the father an active role but also has a particular affective style, namely, that of a sudden explosion in which erotic impulses break out with a dramatic intensity which suggests some underlying dynamic force. Moreover, in spite of the chaperonage norms, the behavior of young women at this point is not such as to suggest much innocence or ignorance of sexuality; they just as well as the young men seem propelled to rebel against the taboos, and they are very often teasers. We have also commented at length on the ambivalent nature of the taboos themselves, in that while violations may be severely condemned explicitly, it often seems as if they were just as much encouraged. It almost seems as if the entire pattern of restriction and parental control were a kind of cultural fiction whose actual purpose is to cover something else; this is what we mean in characterizing it as a joking pattern.

In this perspective it is not at all difficult to postulate that much of the actual source of tension lies in the socially exploited incestuous tie between father and daughter. Thus, the South Italian girl does not appear as inhibited or naïve for precisely the reason that even though carefully kept away from outside men, she has in a great many indirect ways been treated as a sexual object by father (and brothers or other male relatives) both at puberty and during the oedipal crisis. Within the family the incestuous tension may be handled by joking (or avoidance[16]), but to the extent that the wishes generated seek a biological outlet, the daughter has to seek an object outside of the family – and the father has to rid himself of a woman whom he perceives as very desirable but cannot possess. We would then say that it is the strength of the incestuous wishes which accounts for the dramatic and explosive quality of the courtship situation; and the father–daughter relation, by accentuating incestuous tension and at the same time by imposing a taboo, acts as a kind of spring mechanism which running counter to the strong centripetal forces inherent in the mother–son tie has sufficient force as to cause the family unit to fly apart, resulting in the creation of a new one. In this context the insufficiency of the oral culture view again becomes apparent.

One can then see the father's role in defending the honor of the daughter as the masculine counterpart of the Madonna identification; the father's incestuous impulses are sublimated in the active role which he plays toward the daughter in competition with her suitor. Since the sexual wishes cannot be fulfilled, the symbolic assertion of authority is much more important than the actual outcome, a consideration which can explain the ritualized nature of the father's control over courtship and the gracefulness with which he eventually backs down. As the street vendor stated, his real wish is for his daughter's happiness, but in order to show that he is a man he has to be able to demonstrate the power he has over her, and over the still subordinate prospective son-in-law. The principal means he has at his disposal for doing this is by being obstinate in such a way as to increase the excitement of the drama – of which one could say the most important member of the audience for him is the daughter. Likewise, the complementary wishes of the daughter are sublimated in the pleasure which she experiences over the fact of being controlled, a pleasure which is evident in the courtship descriptions of women, however much they may verbally express resentment or rebellion. Moreover, just as the Madonna fantasy provides a feminine identity for men, so the courtship complex provides masculine modes of expression for women, in that in participating in an active teasing pattern the daughter may also identify with the father, as seen in the great importance which women attribute to their own capacity to make a stand in front of him which demonstrates that they really want a suitor.

In other words, while the mother–son tie acts primarily as a centripetal one, in that it maintains itself in such a way as to make for an unbroken continuity of the primary family, the father–daughter tie acts in the inverse sense in that the incestuous tension, being much closer to the surface, has to seek an external outlet so that a kind of spring mechanism is generated. The two together make up a viable structure which can be differentiated from our own on two counts: first, it emphasizes the romantic cross-sex ties within the family far more than same-sex identifications, and second, it preserves incestuous fantasies in such a way that they may never be fully replaced by the actually sexual husband–wife relationship. Thus, though courtship is based on the idea of individual romantic love, this latter does not appear as a prelude to an intimate emotional interdependence between husband and wife, but rather as a temporary suspension of an equilibrium in which intergenerational ties are in the long run more significant. One might say that after the wedding the supplicant suitor returns in fantasy to his own mother, and at the same time comes increasingly to resent the maternal aspects of his wife in such a way that he is again driven outside, much as in adolescence. The wife on the other hand may experience a parallel disillusion when she discovers that the husband is not the father of fantasy, and she comes increasingly to transfer her own affective needs to her son, and so the pattern repeats itself. The husband will of course have a reawakened interest in the family later, namely, when he has a daughter.[17] Thus, on both sides, it is having children, and in particular children of the opposite sex, which provides the principal affective source of commitment to the family.

We have up to this point given little systematic attention to the mother–daughter and father–son relationships, which we have conceived of as having a lesser cultural significance than the cross-sex pairs. This is, of course, not to say that they are inexistent or unimportant; but what we mean by a lesser cultural significance might come out more clearly if we draw a few brief contrasts with our own society and with the Oedipus complex as formulated by Freud.

The TAT responses for the mother–daughter card indicate a pattern that is quite classic in that the daughter appears to internalize maternal authority but she does so in an ambivalent way – contrasting with the romantic internalization found in the case of the son. Moreover, the actual mother–daughter relationship corresponds to that found in most societies; it is the mother who teaches the daughter the routine techniques of daily life. However, an additional feature of the TAT responses was that the informants themselves often stated that "these counsels are not very important," implicitly by comparison with those given during the courtship phase. But this comment gives us the possibility of tying together one global feature of South Italian values with the family nuclear complex: utilitarian accomplishments, notably in contrast to Protestant value systems, simply do not receive much emphasis. As our society sees the Oedipus complex, its outcome is that the child gives up the sexual fantasies centered on the parent of the opposite sex and then identifies with the parent of the same sex, whom he or she takes over as an ego ideal. Thus, the small girl wants to grow up to be a woman like her mother, and fantasies that when she is, then she too will have a husband, this depending on how well she learns to carry out womanly tasks. But in small girls or young women in Southern Italy there is remarkably little in the way of the ego ideal, or the superior person one hopes to emulate. The necessary tasks are taken for granted, but the affectively more important matter is not becoming something one is not yet but rather guarding something one has already, namely, virginity. This in turn can be related back to the fact that the infantile wish is dealt with to a greater extent by symbolic replacement (the First Communion enactment of the role of the bride) of the cross-sex fantasy than by identification with the same-sex parent. In other ways the mother–daughter relationship acts as a centripetal force in much the same way as that between mother and son, and the two go together in defining a somewhat static social tendency rather than an active accomplishing one.

The father–son relationship on the other hand seems to constitute an unresolved cultural problem, a fact which may have roots in economic conditions which make continuity of identity from father to son through occupational or social achievement very difficult to attain, though the nature of the family may in turn help to create such conditions. It is in examining the father–son relationship that the contrast between South Italian patterns and those described by Freud becomes clearest. The TAT responses do indicate that the father may be perceived by the son as a judging or condemning figure. However, when we have said that this does not give rise to an internalized paternal superego figure, what we meant was that on the whole our male informants did not present any social values going beyond their immediate relationship which the father represents, e.g., according to a pattern of "well he was tough but he did it to teach me to act like a man." Moreover, although they were adult men, they identified with the son figure

far more than the father, and they saw the outcome as a simple mutual antagonism in which the father accuses the son of delinquency but the son justifies himself and his own rebellion, rather than channeling the rebellious forces into any kind of sublimated form.

In other words, father–son hostility simply leads to fights and antagonism rather than being restrained in the interest of higher social goals or symbols. The clearest case in this respect was that of the street vendor, who very explicitly relates the kind of decreasing social energy with respect to occupation – for which he is one of a great many representatives – to a failure to solve the problem of antagonism with the father in any creative way. But for Freud, of course, the exact opposite is true: in perceiving the great importance which hostile wishes against the father on the part of sons may have in psychodynamics, he also provides a cultural resolution in his view of repressed father-son rivalry, and its many derivatives in adult life, as a dynamic which can underlie superior creative achievements – including his own creation of psychoanalysis which resulted from his reactions to the death of his father and the contemporaneous intellectual competition with Wilhelm Fliess.

In this perspective it is possible to look at Freud's formulation of the Oedipus complex in its wider cultural context in such a way as to bring out some of the contrasts with the South Italian complex. First we might sum up some of the essential characteristics of the latter in such a way as to make a comparison possible. We have seen the mother–son relationship as the primary axis of family continuity and emphasized the degree to which the son maintains a dependent position vis-à-vis the mother, dealing with sexual and aggressive feelings in a variety of ways among the most important of which is an identification with the feminine values of purity; we have also brought out the extent to which the father-daughter relationship provides a counterpoint pattern by a failure to repress deeply the incestuous element. We have also noted that cross-sex relationships are emphasized more than same-sex ones and have suggested that this may build both romantic and conservative elements into the social structure, in that the strength of intergenerational ties wins out over individually formed ones and in that the cross-sex emphasis acts against the creation of ego ideals which the individual seeks to achieve. Both the conservative and feminine emphasis are summed up in the importance given to virginity as a social symbol: virginity is something which is given and not acquired and it is given to women and not to men.[18]

But in discussing the Oedipus complex Freud is quite explicit about the fact that oedipal wishes are given up in such a way as to be replaced by identifications with the same-sex parent; where this does not take place the resulting phenomena are seen as pathological.

NOTES

1   Jones (1924) in a paper read before the British Psycho-Analytical Society first discussed three prior publications by Malinowski: "Baloma: The Spirits of the Dead in the Trobriand Islands" (1916) and two articles which were later published together as the first two sections of *Sex and Repression in Savage Society* (1927). The last two sections of this latter work were written in response to Jones's paper. For the most complete summary of the Trobriand field data, see Malinowski (1929).

2   Not all anthropologists have accepted Malinowski's observations on this at face value; however, the data he presents indicate that the Trobrianders had formulated a reasonably coherent and intelligent picture of the facts of biology for a people lacking in any scientific framework.

3   Women may in quarrelling with each other call each other prostitutes, but without reference to incest. They may also substitute euphemisms for actual curse words, such as *mannaggia alla marina*, literally "curse the seashore" for "curse the Madonna."

4   See Radcliffe-Brown (1952, pp. 90–116). For the Trobriand Islands, obscene jokes are freely exchanged with the father's sisters but not with the mother's brother, and there are obscene expressions referring to mother, sister, and wife. Of these the most serious insult refers to sexual relations with the wife, a fact which is not quite congruent with the emphasis we have placed on the brother-sister taboo (see Malinowski, 1927, pp. 104–108).

5   See Vaillant (1958), Whyte (1943), and Zola (1963) for descriptions of relevant patterns.

6   Davino, Gennaro: *Anella: Tavernara A Portacapuana*. In: Trevisani (1957), p.125.

7   *Op. cit.*, Trevisani (1957, pp. 118–119).

8   Voluntary abstention from public church ceremony sometimes occurs when wearing the veil would be a shame in front of the Madonna.

9   Of the illegitimate children born in Naples in 1956, 51 per cent were legally recognized by the mother alone, as compared with 9 per cent by the father alone, 10 per cent by both parents, and 29 per cent remaining unrecognized. See Office of Statistics of the Commune of Naples (1959, p. 22).

10 It is roughest among the poorest and here also may be quite erotically stimulating as well. I am indebted to Vincenzo Petrullo for the suggestion that this latter may be the case because when children have to go hungry, erotic stimulation may be a means of maintaining their interest in life.

11 This pattern is even more characteristic of Puerto Rico (see Wolf, 1952), where sex differences in modesty rules are also sharper.

12 I know of examples of mothers sharing beds with adult sons, and also of a case of a mother who lost a child in infancy whereupon she asked a thirteen-year-old son to take the milk from her breast; he, however, refused on the grounds that "she was my mother and I was ashamed."

13 Boys are of course outside earlier too, the actual age and amount of time depending on the specific social milieu. The street gang in the slums may include girls and in some groups much of the family income may come from small boys. The important fact is the lack of any very formalized masculine authority over the boy.

14 "Stories" more often took the form of "well, from the way his eyes are you can tell that ...," followed by a conclusion about motivation or feeling.

15 Low suicide rates are often taken as evidence of the lack of internalized superegos. However, material from Southern Italy, including the fact that depressive symptoms are not at all rare, might suggest that instead there are secondary social mechanisms (i.e., the possibility of forgiveness) which alleviate guilt whose subjective intensity may nevertheless be very great. The

high suicide rates found in modern industrial countries may result then from the lack of these, or what Durkheim (1897) calls anomie.

16 Casual joking and teasing between men and women within the family is characteristic of urban areas; in some country ones (where courtship taboos may be taken more seriously), there is more likely to be embarrassed avoidance, or *vergogna* (shame), between father and daughter.

17 The importance of the father-daughter relationship becomes particularly apparent when we contrast South Italian patterns with those seen in other cultural groups where the rule is the matrifocal family, in which there is no stable husband–wife attachment and the only constant relation is between mother and child. The matrifocal family (found throughout the Caribbean and among working-class American Negroes) seems regularly to appear where masculine identity cannot be easily maintained on the basis of some real occupational achievement. The same conditions hold in Southern Italy and should be seen as underlying the matriarchal trends which we have described; however, with a few exceptions the monogamous family is nevertheless maintained. But the active role which the father has vis-à-vis the daughter must be one of the primary reasons for this, a view which should be considered by social agencies that often too readily seek to save daughters from fathers whom they see as acting solely from cruelty.

18 At least from the South Italian perspective, where the body referent is very clear: as a humorous response to the assertion that Freud defines femininity in terms of a lack of masculinity, we could again refer to the Neapolitan informant who, when questioned about the double standard, replied, "But how could you ever tell if a man had lost it or not?"

REFERENCES

Durkheim, E.
(1897) *Suicide*. New York: The Free Press, 1951.

Jones, E.
(1915) *The Elementary Forms of the Religious Life*. New York: The Free Press, 1958.
Jones, E.
(1912) The Theory of Symbolism. *Papers on Psychoanalysis*. Boston: Beacon Press, 1961, pp. 87–145.
(1924) "Mother-Right and Sexual Ignorance of Savages," in *Essays in Applied Psychoanalysis*, 2: 145–173. New York: International Universities Press, 1964.
Malinowski, B.
(1916) Baloma: "The Spirits of the Dead in the Trobriand Islands," *J. Royal Anthropolog. Inst.*, 46:353–430.
Malinowski, B.
(1927) *Sex and Repression in Savage Society*. London: Routledge & Kegan Paul, 1953.
(1929) *The Sexual Life of Savages*. London: Routledge & Kegan Paul, 1953.
Office of Statistics of the Commune of Naples .
(1959) *Annuario Statistico del Commune di Napoli: Anno 1956, 21*. Naples: Stabilimento Tipografico Francesco Giannini & Figli.
Petrullo, V.
(1937) "A Note on Sicilian Cross-Cousin Marriage," *Primitive Man, 10*, 2:8–9.
Radcliffe-Brown, A. R.
(1952) *Structure and Function in Primitive Society*. New York: The Free Press.
Trevisani, G., ed.
(1957) *Teatro Napoletano dalle origini*, 2 Vols. Bologna: Tip. Mareggiani.
Vaillant, R.
(1958) *The Law*. New York: Knopf.
Verga, G.
(1953), *Little Novels of Sicily*. New York: Grove Press.
Whyte, W. F.
(1943) *Street Corner Society: Social Structure of an Italian Slum*. Chicago: Univ. of Chicago Press.
Wolf, K. R.
(1952) "Growing Up and Its Price in Three Puerto Rican Sub-Cultures," *Psychiatry, 15*, 4:401–433.
Zola, I. K.
(1963) "Observations of Gambling in a Lower Class Setting," *Soc. Prob., 10*, 4:353–361.

11

Kagwahiv Mourning I: Dreams of a Bereaved Father

Waud H. Kracke

It is sometimes averred that empathic understanding cannot be gained of the inner experience of a person of a culture very different from one's own, at least not deep enough to make possible depth interviewing of a psychoanalytic sort, either because the terms in which people in some other cultures conceive and talk about their inner life are so different from ours, or because empathy and mutual understanding are too difficult across the barrier of radical cultural difference. Rodney Needham, in one recent phase of his thought, has perhaps espoused this point of view most strongly of recent anthropological writers, arguing that:

If individual ideation is in part contingent on changeable cultural convention, there can be no prior guarantees that it will be comprehensible to men whose representations are framed by other cultural traditions. [1972:158]

But the question is at least implicit in many discussions of mental life in non-Western cultures (e.g., Geertz 1973:398–404; Rosaldo 1980), and positions not too different from Needham's seem implied at times in discussions of human nature with a relativistic emphasis (Geertz 1965).[1]

Such questions, as Needham points out, raise fundamental issues for anthropological investigation (cf. Hanson 1975, chap. 3); but they go especially to the heart of the enterprise of cross-cultural psychoanalytic investigation, which depends sensitively on empathic understanding. Robert LeVine has gone so far as to suggest (1973:220–224) that, to bridge the gap in understanding, every cross-cultural psychoanalytic investigation might best be carried out in collaboration with a psychoanalytically trained interviewer from the culture in question; but this in part merely shifts the locus of the problem, for the psychoanalytic training of the indigenous interviewer would itself require a cross-cultural psychoanalysis.

When this issue has been raised, it has generally been discussed primarily in abstract, philosophical terms[2] (although the anthropologists who discuss it of course draw on their own intercultural experiences) or in terms of methodological prescriptions for evading the barriers perceived. Yet as Needham (1972:158) justly observed, the question "falls ... within the scope of empirical determination," and it may be useful to present here the results of an attempt at achieving empathic understanding in an intercultural situation, in interviews that I carried out with Kagwahiv Indians in Brazil.

I found no such difficulty in establishing empathic rapport with some, at least, of my Kagwahiv informants. By establishing an atmosphere of relaxed, intimate communication in an interview situation predominantly à deux, it was possible to gain many glimpses of the inner life and experience of several

Waud H. Kracke, Kagwahiv Mourning: Dreams of a Bereaved Father from *Ethos*, Vol. 9, No. 4, Dreams (Winter, 1981), pp. 258–275. Published by Blackwell Publishing on behalf of the American Anthropological Association. © 1981 by the Society for Psychological Anthropology.

Kagwahiv and, to varying degrees, to understand their psychological processes. The main obstacle I had to overcome in order to begin these interviews, I found, was my own reluctance to abandon the relatively protected, semi-detached role of anthropologist, and enter the deeper emotional involvement entailed in depth interviewing.

The depth interviews I conducted often tended to focus around dreams, for I found that asking people about their dreams and childhood memories was a way to communicate an interest in their own personal experience (as opposed to the ethnographer's interest in more "official" beliefs of their culture), and led people in association to their dreams to open up fantasies and memories of a sensitive kind that were especially helpful in understanding how they felt about themselves and their current life. I will select one informant with whom I developed a particularly successful working relationship of this kind, to show the kind of mutual understanding that is possible.[3] The aspect of this man's psychic processes that was a central focus of my interviews with him was mourning.

The interviews I will describe were carried out in July through September, 1968. I did not begin such interviews at the beginning of my fieldwork, but delayed until I had accumulated some six months of contact with Kagwahiv, much of the time spent in the settlement where the interviews described here were conducted (cf. Langness 1965:35). I was able in that time to acquire some familiarity with Kagwahiv patterns of emotional expression, and a rudimentary knowledge of the Kagwahiv language (although I had to begin the interviews largely in Portuguese, shifting increasingly into Kagwahiv as I mastered it). When I altered my role from that of ethnographic investigator interested in "Kagwahiv life and customs," to the psychological interviewer expressing an interest in individuals and their dreams and fantasies, I experienced a dramatic shift in the aspects of themselves that my informants presented to me, opening up a range of personal fantasies of which I had not previously been aware.

It may be that my interviewing was facilitated by some aspects of the culture I was working in – the Kagwahiv Indians, who live

on the east bank of the Madeira River, a southern tributary of the Amazon. The fact that dreams are a focus of Kagwahiv cultural interest certainly helped to make it seem less strange to informants to be asked to relate them and discuss them; and the traditional interest of their shamanic curers (*ipají*) in dreams makes the telling of dreams potentially part of a succorant relationship, although I have no indication that they were used by the *ipají* of the past (none of whom survive) in anything like the way they are used in our therapy. The Kagwahiv are accustomed to tell their dreams to one another, individually or to the settlement in general, generally first thing in the morning, and discuss their dreams' meanings. They would be interpreted in terms of predictions about game or health, mediated by traditional dream symbols (to dream about a broken-down house means someone will die, for example, or a party means white-lipped peccary will be bagged in hunting), or in terms of other beliefs about dreams which I have described more fully elsewhere (Kracke 1979). Dreams are in general thought to be a continuation in sleep of the train of thought one was following while falling asleep.

Another helpful factor was the nature of Kagwahiv living arrangements. In their small local groups, of no more than 16 members each, anthropologists are much more direct participants in the daily life of the people than in an African village, say, where they may live in a separate compound. Under such close conditions, intimacy is much easier to achieve.

The cultural stress on dreams, and the Kagwahiv settlement pattern, *facilitated* my establishing such intimate interview relationships; but for informants to open their private thoughts and feelings to an anthropologist in depth interviews, they must have both a motivation to do so and a basis for trusting in the anthropologist's personal concern. The nature of an informant's motive and basis for trust in the ethnographer will of course shape considerably the aspect of the self that will be revealed in the depth interviews. In this paper, I will examine one informant's motives – what emotional satisfaction or relief he sought from the interviews – and some of the situational factors which I think contributed to his feeling free to confide in me. Then I will consider some of the implications of these observations for anthropologist-informant relationships in general. I will limit my discussion to one informant, a young headman whose interviews were perhaps the richest in the insights he gave into his emotional life – partly due to his own self-insight and natural psychological acumen and communicativeness, but partly also due to the strength of his motivation for talking about his feelings: Jovenil was a father who had lost two children three months before the interviews.

As background, I should say a bit about how Kagwahiv deal with death.[4] It is not usual to talk much about such a loss; the accepted thing is to avoid talking about it, because of the painful feelings it arouses. Crying is anathema, leaving one exposed to supernatural dangers. The way to deal with loss is to forget the deceased person as rapidly as possible: you give away all the person's belongings, or any utensils they have used that remind you of them. You dismantle the house you have lived in with the person, and even move your house, or the whole settlement, to a new spot, in order not to be reminded. The rationale for this in Kagwahiv belief is that the person's ghost (añang) might return to familiar spots and seek familiar objects, so that everything associated with the deceased person is pojý, super-naturally dangerous. But informants also say, as if it were synonymous with this: we move so as not to remember, because it makes us sad. New kin terms are used for deceased primary relatives: ji rúva, "my father," becomes ji poría, "my late father"; hy, "mother," becomes ymbóra; and so on. Everything is done to push away the memory of the deceased and the immediacy of the death. Under these conditions, mourning is all the more a problematic period.

In retrospect, the illness of Jovenil's two children was an important transition point in my relationship with Jovenil and the others of his group. For a few weeks, my research activities practically came to a halt as I spent most of my time giving what rudimentary medical attention I was able to give to the two children, and others in the settlement suffering from complications to a measles epidemic. Beforehand, I was a stranger, with a rather peculiar interest in Kagwahiv lifeways, and a

periodic source of relatively cheap trade goods. After the episode of illness, I became more a part of the group, or at least someone who cared, who valued their lives and had shown I shared some of their concerns and feelings. I also took on a more medical kind of role in the group from then on; I had been giving injections to one or two members of the group as part of a series of treatments for TB, but now this role became more a part of my identity in the group, and of my contribution to it. This, I think, made possible the kind of interviewing I was to carry on in my last three months of fieldwork that field trip.

The first time I arrived at Jovenil's settlement, I was welcomed quite hospitably as a visitor (in some contrast to a rather cooler reception on my initial contacts some months earlier with a neighboring group which a pair of missionaries made their center of operations when "in the tribe"); but I was strictly (and somewhat ambivalently) regarded as a transient guest. In a conversation the second evening I was there, Jovenil compared me with other American visitors who had come and enlivened things, showing their generosity by distributing fish they caught, but passed on. He forecasted that, like them, I would get married and never come back.

This visit grew into a period of mutual testing. For a time, I became the visitor who overstayed his welcome, with the distribution of my last food supplies at a time of sparse hunting and fishing becoming a rather focal issue toward the end of this initial one-month visit. My return a few months later (albeit still unmarried) impressed Jovenil with my commitment, and at the beginning of this second, longer visit, Jovenil negotiated with me the construction of a house for me in the settlement. It was only later in this visit, however, that the episode of illness occurred that was to more substantially alter my relationship with Jovenil and his group.

Several of Jovenil's children were sick when I arrived in November, 1967, for a three-month stretch of fieldwork, in the aftermath of a measles epidemic. But the climax came around Christmas, when his one-year-old daughter became extremely ill. He was at first reluctant to have me give her injections, fearing that in her weak state the strong medicine would be too much for her. At one point, she reached the unresponsive state the Kagwahiv call death, and her mother had started wailing. Antibiotics did pull her through that crisis, however, and with continued treatment she gradually improved. I also treated Jovenil's cherished five-year-old son, Alonzo, who had also gotten seriously ill, although not quite to the same extremity. Unfortunately, I had to leave to replenish my supplies at the end of February, before they had fully recovered; but both were definitely on the mend when I left, and seemed well on the way to recovery. A month or two later, however, both had relapses (or in their weakened state contracted new illnesses) and, one right after the other, they died.

It was in my next three-month stint of field-work, after a break of several months, that I began the intensive, psychologically oriented interviews. It was the last of four stints of field-work in 1967–1968, the first three of which were devoted to more general ethnography: participant observation primarily in Jovenil's settlement and a neighboring one and shorter visits to several others. The psychological interviews were saved for the last one, when I had some feel for Kagwahiv culture and modes of emotional expression, and a little grounding in their language.

I learned of the children's deaths as I was returning from the break in June, 1968. I went in with some trepidation, with vivid images of what their reaction to the deaths might be. My worst fantasies were not realized. But on arriving, I realized later, I did commit something of a faux pas in asking Jovenil's wife Aluza about the deaths, expressing sympathy – thus reminding her of the painful event she was trying to forget.

Jovenil was the first informant with whom I began the intensive interviews when I got up to his settlement. I established a pattern of daily interviews with him, varying in length from under an hour to more than two – "50 minutes" would of course have no significance whatever to a Kagwahiv – asking him to tell me whatever he felt like talking about, including dreams, childhood memories, or whatever thoughts he had. We sat either on a bench in the clearing in the middle of the settlement, or on

the open platform of the house in which I was staying – an uncompleted house without walls, affording much greater privacy than would any more secluded, walled spot, at which the children would indubitably gather to listen.

Jovenil did not mention the deaths of his children for the first week and a half of the interviews, with the exception of one indirect allusion: in telling me for the first time, in his fourth interview, about an incestuous affair he had had in adolescence with a parallel cousin, a woman of his own (Kwandu) patrimoiety, he observed that the consequence of such behavior is that "your child dies, or else your father." Except for that, he made no explicit reference to it until the ninth interview.

In the latent content of his dream, however, allusions to his children's death begin to appear much earlier. In the sixth interview, Jovenil told me a dream that was rather startling in its frankness. At first sight, it seems to have little to do with his loss, but closer examination reveals strong allusions implicit in it.

José Bahut [an older man, of the opposite moiety] was having intercourse with his wife [Camelia]. Everyone saw it. Suddenly his dick was very big. Patricio [Camelia's younger half-brother] grabbed his dick and pulled it, and it snapped. "Why did you break my dick?" "Because you were screwing my sister!" Patricio was fixing José's dick, with a vine thong, and it got real thin. – It's funny, my dream! – Aí, they said, "Did your dick snap?" Aí, a lot of blood came out, his dick got rotten. Patricio fixed his dick, it got real thin. Homero [Patricio and Camelia's father] scolded Patricio, "Why did you snap his dick? He'll die!" "No, he won't die," he said.

He followed the dream with a series of associations that underscored the danger to the dreamer of such a dream – "If you dream of a woman's genital, it's a wound you are going to get, you cut yourself" – suggesting that the wound represented in the dream may be his own.

I pointed out that this was the second time in two days he had mentioned to me a dream of José Bahut's big penis: in the previous interview, he had told me of a dream he had upriver that "José Bahut had a dick this long!" Could it be, I asked him, that he had sometime seen a grown man's big penis when he was little? Yes, he replied, he had. At five years of age, he saw José Bahut's penis, when he went swimming in the river as José was there bathing. He had asked José how he got such a big penis, and José responded: "I make my wife a lot, that's why it gets so big." Excitedly, Jovenil ran back to report his observation and new knowledge to his mother, only to receive a severe scolding: "When you see someone else's dick like that," his mother told him, "when you get older, you will go blind!" "She scolded with a stick, a belt," Jovenil recalled, "for me not to ask him any more."[5]

Further memories led him to recollections of a childhood phobia of pigs and cows: "It seemed as if they wanted to eat me." Sometimes he couldn't sleep at night for fear of ghosts, so he would go to sleep in his father's hammock.

All of this shows a remarkable access to memories of his own childhood phobias and conflicts; but so far we see little connection with his mourning of his children. A hint of some dream thoughts related to this mourning appears, however, when we note that the woman José Bahut was making love with in the dream – José's current young wife at the time of the dream, not his wife of the time of Jovenil's five-year-old memory – was the very same parallel cousin of Jovenil's with whom Jovenil had had an incestuous affair in adolescence. In Kagwahiv terminology, she was his "sister." If we put Jovenil himself, the dreamer, in the place of José Bahut in his dream, then some of the comments in the dream take on new significance: "Because you were screwing my sister!" may be an echo of Jovenil's own self-accusatory guilty conscience; and Homero's exclamation: "Why did you do that? Now he'll die!" may refer to the punishment for such incestuous activity, the death of a close relative – perhaps that of his child. The dream, then, is a self-accusation, saying that he himself was responsible for his young (*five-year-old*) son's death, represented in the dream as a castration. In the imagery of the dream, it was his own incestuous desires that brought about his "castration."

This guess is confirmed by the somewhat more open expression of the idea in a dream he reported in his interview the next day. Daniel Aguarajuv (a neighbor and close friend of Jovenil's) and his older Brazilian wife had a pet monkey which, since they were childless, was like a child to them. In the dream, Daniel went out hunting and shot what he thought was a wild monkey – but it turned out to be his own pet monkey, which had run away. Daniel's wife was furious when she found out, and chased him out of the house. Jovenil, this dream seems vicariously to aver, had inadvertantly killed his own child. Jovenil's associations, just to confirm this, went back to earlier losses, and finally to that of his first child, who had many years earlier died young, with his wife almost dying at the same time; they then focused on the various prohibitions that surround the birth of a child:

> When he is born, you don't go working ... If you do, the child won't grow up – he'll die.

He listed the animals one should not hunt – including monkey – to avoid bringing harm to one's infant, and recalled how another of his children was seriously ill in infancy because he was negligent in observing the taboos. The mood of the interview was sad, and it was clear that his thoughts were returning to his lost children, with allusions to his own sense of responsibility for their death.

The next day, he elaborated much more on his teenage affair with Camelia, who was then single, vividly describing the incident that terminated his relationship with her: the dog barked as he and his companion snuck into her settlement, and they were almost caught. In that interview, he also described a recent fight in which José Bahut almost killed a man who had slept with his wife – Camelia. And, toward the end of the interview, he commented on a dream he had reported in it:

> When you dream that your clothes are all torn, you dream your own death. ... You're afraid in the morning, because sometimes something can happen to you. Sometimes you can get sick. You get sad when you dream like that. If you dream of a house, it's a bad dream like that, a house full of holes, it's a child of yours that's going to die.

(The literal prediction of this dream element, a falling-down house, is that a close relative will die.)

It was the following day, in his ninth interview, that Jovenil finally brought up his son's death explicitly – through a dream. "I had a dream," he said right off. "A bad dream."

My son died. Alonzo. They drowned him in the deep – in the water. "Why did you guys kill my son?" "No, he died." "Where did you bury him?" "In the bank." They buried him in the bank.

He elaborated that it was three Brazilians who had drowned him, then revised it: they hadn't drowned him, it was that Alonzo went out in a canoe with them and the canoe turned over.

The drowning in the "deep water" is a punning reference to the sin Jovenil felt he was being punished for. When he first told me of his incestuous relationship with Camelia, he had used a Kagwahiv word for "incest" – typyowý – whose literal meaning is "deep green/blue water." But what of the three Brazilians in the dream? They could refer to the thought that came out toward the end of the interview, his suspicion that a woman jealous of his healthy family had hired a Brazilian sorcerer. But they may also be an allusion to my treatment of the children, holding me responsible (in the end) for not saving them. ("Three" may include the two SIL missionaries, who had a part in the treatment.)

In the rest of this interview, he went on to describe the children's deaths in detail, with deep affect. It was the first time, with me at least, that he had fully experienced and expressed his grief – an important step in his mourning. It would seem that he had to deal with his conflicts over it, his sense of guilt and remorse over having, as he felt, caused his own children's death – and, in this last dream, his anger at me for not saving them – before he could go on with the mourning.

In the rest of the interviews, he went on to mourn further, and deal with other facets of these conflicts. In the next (tenth) interview, in association to a dream with a theme of being lost in the jungle, he acknowledged another contributory to his guilt over Alonzo's death: some ambivalence toward the child. I suggested that some planks he was carrying in the

dream might be for a coffin, which he agreed was a conventional interpretation of that dream image; and I suggested that they might refer to Alonzo's death, to which he replied: "I dreamed of Alonzo, too."

He went to the Festa with me. "Ah, Alonzo, there you are, after so much time!" Alonzo said, "I died at first, now I came alive again."

The Brazilians [Jovenil went on] say it is God who gives the orders. If you scold your child too much, He kills him. If you scold your child too much, God is watching and says, "He doesn't like his son. I'm going to kill him, to see if he will be sad." (Did you feel you scolded him too much?) I scolded him a lot. Afterwards, Papa said to me: "One doesn't scold one's son."

First I thought one's children didn't die. That's why I married, to have children. A single woman doesn't have children. It happens a lot when you are married: If your wife doesn't die, your child dies.

Here, he remarked on a plane passing over: "Puxal One after another, the airplanes!" and a moment later, returning to this theme, observed: "From Porto Velho, you took a plane to Rio." This referred to my movements after I left his settlement in February; so, his train of thought went from Alonzo's death to my departure a couple of months prior to it. If I had not left, he may have been thinking, I might have been able to save his children's lives with my medicines. By leaving, I let them die. In addition, a week hence I was to go to a neighboring settlement where I was doing other interviews – the first interruption since I had started these interviews with Jovenil – and there awaited a small SIL float plane that would take me out for a two-week sojourn in Porto Velho. It would be just a three-week interruption (after three intense weeks of interviews), but it no doubt reminded him of my permanent departure planned for two months later, as well as of my previous absence that had been so disastrous for him. He felt he was about to be deserted.

In casual conversation later that morning, he mentioned that Maria, a Kagwahiv girl who had flirted with me in earlier field trips and was jokingly regarded as my amour and bride-to-be, had gotten married. *Opohí he nde-huguí*, he said: "She discarded you." But this husband of hers was very jealous, and she left him to go to Porto Velho, at which he cried piteously. "He was old and crippled, that's why she didn't like him." These spontaneous remarks, though not in the interview itself, may be taken as further free associations. They again express the theme of abandonment and anger – perhaps a fear that his anger, like the husband's jealousy, might drive me away, as it had led to Alonzo's being taken away.

All these feelings Jovenil had to work through as part of the emotional process of mourning the loss of his children. The sense that one might in some way have caused the death of someone with whom one is close, even in our culture which does not have concepts of supernatural retribution rationalizing such ideas, is a normal part of the reaction to bereavement (Pollock 1961). So is anger at others for not preventing it. We tend to rationalize these ideas in medical terms – one should have called the doctor sooner, or recognized the symptoms earlier, or the doctor was not competent; Jovenil rationalized them in terms of breach of taboo.

These interviews, a situation decidedly out of the ordinary in Kagwahiv society (as it would be in ours), seem to have given Jovenil significant help in carrying through the mourning process (although that was not their intent, nor was I fully aware to what degree Jovenil was using the interviews in this way until I reviewed the interviews in the perspective of later psychoanalytic training). That his uncompleted mourning had been affecting his life was suggested by a remark he had made to me early in July, before we started the interviews: "I don't want any more children," he said. For Jovenil, usually immensely proud of his prolific family, this was a very unusual remark. I asked him why, but he only said: "It seems I already have enough." The source of these feelings in discouragement and anger over the loss of a favorite son comes out clearly in the remarks just quoted: "If your wife doesn't die, your child does." His depression over the death thus interfered with his full emotional involvement with his children, and his pleasant anticipation of having more. By the end of the

summer, he had recovered some of his good spirits and enjoyment of life. After I left, Aluza became pregnant again, and has since had three more children.

But it was not only the conflicts immediately pertaining to the loss of his child that he had to work through before he came to directly experiencing the loss in his interviews. The first dream alluding to the loss – the castration dream – was one directly modeled on a childhood memory: seeing José Bahut's big penis, and learning that its size (erectness, presumably) had something to do with "making his wife." The conflicts he needs to work out over his current loss are related, then, to interests and feelings he had when he was five years old. His guilt feelings about his incestuous experimentation in adolescence may be derivatives of guilt over childhood curiosity in the same area, perhaps related to the blindness threatened by his mother in punishment for his curiosity. The loss of his child in punishment for incest is represented in his dream as castration – the loss of that about which he was so curious at five. Perhaps the threat of loss of eyesight for his visual curiosity may have suggested the loss of another member in punishment for illicit pleasures involving it. Perhaps, too, this representation suggests why he felt with special intensity the loss of his *male* child.

The exact nature of his five-year-old conflicts need not concern us here – just what response he wished from his mother when he approached her with his new discovery, and why in the dream the young boy, Camelia's brother, literally pulls off José's erect penis. The details of this did come out in a later dream,[6] but the point here is that he had to work through these conflicting feelings from childhood that were stirred up by the loss of his child, as well as the adult guilt feelings about having caused his child's death that were closer to consciousness, before he could really begin to experience the grief he felt over his children's deaths. It was only after recalling these conflict-laden childhood experiences that he had the first dream directly expressing his sense of being to blame for his children's death, the dream of shooting the monkey. It would seem, then, that his childhood conflicts interfered with his mourning process; articulating them helped him to sort them out, separating past fantasy from current reality, and freed him to face the present mourning task. It was his needs in mourning, then, that prompted his relating to me these deep childhood conflicts; this is why his interviews are so rich in childhood memories.

I have presented in great detail what was going on in the interviews with one informant, down to the infantile conflicts that were engaged in the interviews, in order to suggest the depth and complexity of the motives an informant may have for participating in interviews. The interviews were of course not carried out for therapeutic purposes. Yet every informant who engaged in them – not just Jovenil – used them to express and sort out conflicting feelings, and to work out (and seek some help with) personal problems.

I should make it clear that I was not aware of all of these themes and conflicts during the interviews. Some of the connections only became clear to me as I went over the materials after coming back from the field (as is of course the case with other more straightforward anthropological data), and some of the important themes only became evident to me during my subsequent training in psychoanalysis. In particular, it was not until much later that I realized how much Jovenil was dealing with the mourning of his son throughout these interviews, although in retrospect it seems obvious that he was skirting the issue through several interviews before he finally explicitly brought it up.

Various circumstances make Jovenil's case a special one – as any single case is. Mourning a loss, particularly the loss of one's own child (Pollock 1961), is an emotional task which calls for much support from others. While Kagwahiv beliefs facilitate the *articulation* of certain frequent emotional conflicts surrounding mourning – such as blaming oneself for the death, or someone else – Kagwahiv norms do not give much opportunity or communal support for recalling and working through grief and the attendant conflicts, although they do provide support for separation and forgetting. For these reasons, the interviews came at an especially opportune time for Jovenil's needs.[7] Yet all the other informants I interviewed had

some personal crisis they were facing or had recently undergone and were working through, or some adaptation they had to make, which provided a motive for talking to someone willing to listen. For Jovenil, and for all informants, a strong motive to participate is the opportunity to talk to a sympathetic listener about things that are disturbing them.

The nature of the crisis or adaptation facing each informant as they came to the interviews must have made some difference as to what aspects of their personality came to the fore, which childhood memories surfaced, or generally what they talked about and how they saw it. Awareness of an informant's personal motives for participating must help anthropologists evaluate the information they get from the informant, not only when the information is of such a personal nature as what I was looking for, but even when it is more abstract social and cultural data.

There are other preconditions for such interviews as these, however, besides motivation. The subject of the interview must have confidence in the trustworthiness of the interviewer not to abuse one's confidences. My involvement in the treatment of Jovenil's children I think played an important part not only in my relationship with Jovenil, but in preparing the way for these interviews with *all* the informants, in demonstrating that I was a person who could be trusted to be concerned personally. Such a point of transition, where one becomes a person who can be trusted with confidences and to respect personal feelings, must be a significant one in the field experience of any anthropologist with a group that he or she gets to know reasonably well. Doubtless there is not one but many such points in any field sojourn, at different levels or in different domains.

The issues of mourning his children were intertwined for Jovenil, especially in the later interviews, with the issue of impending separation from me. Owing to the transitory nature of fieldwork, and at the same time to the intensity of relationships that are built up during it, the issue of separation from anthropologists and mourning them after their departure[8] (as well as anthropologists' mourning of their informants)[9] must be, as Edgardo Rolla suggested to me in a personal communication, a general one in ethnographer – informant relations.

The anthropologist's involvement with an informant includes not only the anthropologist's personal needs and professional goals (not discussed here), but also the personal needs of the informant that are fulfilled (or frustrated) in the interviews, and the personal gratifications the informant seeks. Understanding these processes that go on in the relationship with one's informants should be of help not only in conducting the interviews, but also in evaluating the nature of the information communicated in them – and in tuning in to levels of information that are present in all interviews (or conversations) but that are not usually made use of in anthropological interviewing. It enables us to see more clearly some of the gratifications and aids that we are, knowingly or unknowingly, offering our informants – for better or for worse – in exchange for being our collaborators in research. Being aware of what we may be offering an informant, and what the informant may be seeking from us, may help make the exchange more rewarding for both parties.

But the more fundamental point demonstrated here is that cultural difference is not an insuperable obstacle to communication and to the understanding of psychological states in another person. Jovenil, at least, was able to verbalize his feelings and fantasies to me clearly enough that I could achieve a psychoanalytic understanding of the mourning process that he was engaged in and the conflicts that blocked it, and even to help him surmount that blockage. This is not to say that I could communicate as easily with every Kagwahiv I interviewed as I did with Jovenil; some were far less communicative than he, others less able to put their thoughts and feelings into words, and still others beset with conflicts far more severe and crippling than his, which would have required a longer and more difficult series of interviews to unravel. Such variations and difficulties of course exist just as much in our own culture. But all of the individuals I interviewed worked on some inner problems in the interviews, and in doing so revealed some of the psychological processes involved in grappling with their problems (Kracke 1978, 1979). If the investi-

gator is willing to make the additional effort of understanding the cultural world of the person being interviewed, as well as being receptive to the subtle, implicit, and not always culture-syntonic messages which the person interviewed conveys about his or her emotional state, psychological understanding can be both possible and beneficial.

NOTES

1 When discussing the issue most specifically. Geertz takes the middle position – but one still rendering cross-cultural psychoanalysis a highly tenuous enterprise – that "the Ethnographer does not, and in my opinion, largely cannot, perceive what his informants perceive. What he perceives – and that uncertainly enough – is what they perceive 'with' or 'by means of,' or 'through' or whatever word one may choose" (1975:48).

2 Two notable exceptions are Kenneth Read's account of his poignant communication with Makis in *The High Valley* (1965:84–88) and Paul Riesman's perceptive thoughts on empathic intuition in his fieldwork with the Fulani (1974:151–153). Intercultural communication has been a central theme of some noted works of fiction (Bowen 1954; Forster 1949), but only in Devereux's classic *From Anxiety to Method* (1967) did it become the subject of a systematic theoretical discussion in anthropology.

3 Interviews with this and other individuals I interviewed are presented and discussed more fully in Kracke 1978 and 1979.

4 Although much has been written about mortuary ritual in anthropology, to my knowledge there is rather little research on the mourning experience in non-Western societies. In a later publication which will focus more specifically on Kagwahiv mourning I will discuss the literature on this topic more fully, but some brief comments are apposite here. Of special relevance here is Lewis's (1575) interesting report of a "Culturally Patterned Depression in a Mother after Loss of a Child" among the Trio of Surinam. A particularly important contribution is Pollock's (1972) article discussing mourning ritual as a culturally constituted defense mechanism that articulates the psychological process

of mourning. I am somewhat skeptical of Goldschmidt's (1973:98) contention that the Sebei do not experience a loss deeply enough to mourn, but clearly, as among the Kagwahiv, their grief is vigorously suppressed. This and other important contributions (Matchett 1974; Woodward 1968) will be discussed more fully elsewhere.

5 Kagwahiv modesty forbids a man to be seen without his penis sheath, so Jovenil's mother may have been simply giving him a lesson in modesty.

6 In Interview 11, Jovenil reluctantly recounted to me a frightening dream: he was watching a family of forest spirits (añang) from behind a tree, while the father-añang was making love to the mother-añang, teaching his five-year-old son how it was done. Terrified at the sight, Jovenil ran back to the settlement, and told about it. Another man in the settlement was all for going out to hunt the añang family and kill the father; Jovenil tried to dissuade him, but he went ahead and did it.

This dream is a blatant portrayal of a childhood fantasy which, to judge by the age of the onlooking child, Jovenil must have had at the age of five – the same age as the earlier reported childhood memory, which also involved watching and learning about sex. The fantasy was a little *too* openly expressed for Jovenil's comfort; even the last-ditch distancing mechanism of presenting the action, as it were, "on the stage" (Jovenil was *watching* the scene take place before him) was not enough to allay his anxiety. Not only was he afraid in the dream, but he did not at first want to tell it to me.

If we regard this as a second edition of the first dream that referred to memories at the same age, the child's intent in pulling off José Bahut's penis becomes clearer. If the two dreams are parallel, then Jovenil's fantasy was of *borrowing* José's penis (or his father's) for his own use, just as in the second dream he learned from his father how to use it.

The theme of learning in the añang dream also has a reference to me, for I had, just two days earlier, suggested in casual conversation, that he *learn to give injections* (note possible analogies) so that he could continue the tuberculosis treatment I was giving *to his wife*.

7 It is an interesting but perhaps unanswerable question whether Jovenil would have resolved his conflicts in the same way without having these interviews with me, or whether my interviews offered him a support for his mourning process that would have been unavailable in his own culture. This raises further questions about the part that anthropologists play in the lives of the people they study, and how their contributions to their lives affect the data and image of their culture, as well as about the question of the degree to which any culture provides satisfactorily for all the needs of people in it. In any case, though, Jovenil was quite ready to use the interviews with me to his own benefit in working out his conflicts over mourning, and it seems not unlikely that he might have worked out some, though perhaps not all, of these problems in conversations with some other person.

8 Dorothy Eggan's informant, Don Talayesva, expressed this issue very neatly in the dream image of his "white wife" who was eager to watch Hopi rituals, but who "gets homesick" and wants to leave (Eggan 1949:182–183).

9 The idealization that one often sees in an anthropologist's memories of his or her principal informants (cf. Casagrande 1960) may be a consequence of mourning them, for the mourning process often results in some idealization. I am indebted for this observation to Laura Kracke.

REFERENCES

Bowen, Elenore Smith
1954 *Return to Laughter*. New York: Natural History Press 1964.
Casagrande, Joseph B., ed
1960 *In the Company of Man*. New York: Harper.
Devereux, George
1967 *From Anxiety to Method in the Behavioral Sciences*. The Hague: Mouton.
Eggan, Dorothy
1949 The Significance of Dreams for Anthropological Research. *American Anthropologist* 51:177–198.
Forster, F. M.
1949 *A Passage to India*. New York: Harcourt Brace.
Geertz, Clifford
1965 The Impact of the Concept of Culture on the Concept of Man. *New Views of the Nature of Man* (J. Platt, ed.), pp. 93–118. Chicago: University of Chicago Press. Reprinted

in *The Interpretation of Cultures*, New York: Basic Books, chapter 2.

1973   Person, Time and Conduct in Bali. *The Interpretation of Cultures*, New York: Basic Books, chapter 14.

1975   On the Nature of Anthropological Understanding. *American Scientist* 63:47–53.

Goldschmidt, Walter

1973   Guilt and Pollution in Sebei Mortuary Ritual. *Ethos* 1:75–105.

Hanson, F. Allan

1975   *Meaning in Culture*. London: Routledge & Kegan Paul.

Kracke, Waud H.

1978   *Force and Persuasion: Leadership in an Amazonian Society*. Chicago: University of Chicago Press.

1979   Dreaming in Kagwahiv: Dream Beliefs and Their Psychic Uses in an Amazonian Indian Culture. *Psychoanalytic Study of Society* 8:119–171.

Langness, Lewis L.

1965   *The Life History in Anthropological Science*. New York: Holt, Rinehart and Winston.

LeVine, Robert

1973   *Culture, Behavior and Personality*. Chicago: Aldine.

Lewis, Thomas N.

1975   Culturally Patterned Depression in a Mother after Loss of a Child. *Psychiatry* 38:92–95.

Matchett, William Foster

1974   Repeated Hallucinatory Experiences as a Part of the Mourning Process among Hopi Women. *Culture and Personality*. (Robert LeVine, ed.), pp. 222–231. Chicago: Aldine.

Needham, Rodney

1972   *Belief, Language and Experience*. Chicago: University of Chicago Press.

Pollock, George H.

1961   Mourning and Adaptation. *International Journal of Psychoanalysis* 42:341–361. Reprinted in *Culture and Personality*, (Robert LeVine, ed.), pp. 65–94. Chicago: Aldine, 1974.

1972   On Mourning and Anniversaries: The Relationship of Culturally Constituted Defensive Systems to Intrapsychic Adaptive Processes. *The Israel Annals of Psychiatry* 10:9–41.

Read, Kenneth

1965   *The High Valley*. New York: Scribners.

Reisman, Paul

1974   *Freedom in Fulari Social Life*. Chicago: University of Chicago Press.

Rosaldo, Michelle

1980   *Knowledge and Passion: Ilongot Notions of Self and Social Life*. Cambridge, England: Cambridge University Press.

Woodward, James A.

1968   The Anniversary: A Contemporary Diegueño Complex. *Ethnology* 7:86–94.

12

Kagwahiv Mourning II: Ghosts, Grief, and Reminiscences

Waud H. Kracke

A basic question that psychoanalysis asks of anthropology, and to which Weston LaBarre has devoted considerable attention throughout his writings, is to what extent the configurations of emotional experience that we consider essentially human are indeed constant across mankind.[1] How profoundly may emotional responses to events be influenced by the different concepts of human nature held by different cultures? A particularly dramatic emotional phenomenon, one which is certainly fundamental in the psychic processes of individuals in our culture, is the grief felt over the death or loss of someone loved, along with the adaptive process of mourning which gradually attenuates the grief and reconciles us to the loss (Pollock 1961). Two questions may be posed: first, are grief and mourning universally human responses to loss? (Are they, at least, typical of the average makeup of most members of any society?) And second, how do cultural beliefs, norms, and patterns of relationship influence the expression of grief and the process of mourning?

The first question was partially addressed a few years ago. In an earlier article in *Ethos* (Kracke 1981a) exploring the emotional response of an Amazonian Indian father to the loss of two young children, I demonstrated that even in a culture that condemns the open expression of grief and encourages putting the deceased

out of mind, a bereaved father experienced strong grief and underwent a mourning process. But I did not there address the other question: how do cultural values and the culturally provided ritual surrounding death shape the experience of grief and mourning? That is the question I would like to take up briefly for Kagwahiv Indian culture of the Brazilian Amazon.

This latter question is in turn linked with a broader one to which Weston LaBarre has devoted considerable writing: are religious beliefs and rituals a kind of collective neurotic maladaptation as LaBarre suggests (1970:21–24 and *passim*, 1978a:51–57)? Or can they be valuable and psychologically helpful guides for the individual in dealing with an emotional crisis (Pollock 1972)? (In a brief but thoughtful piece in 1978 (1978b) LaBarre seems to move somewhat closer to the latter position).

A number of comparative studies of mourning have focused on cultures in which the response to death is regulated by extensive and elaborate ritual. In these cultures, it is frequently argued, the ritual serves as a sanction permitting the individual to withdraw temporarily from society and engage in the work of mourning, or what Freud (1917) called the "work of remembering,"[2] especially in cultures with memorial rites that close a several-month period of mourning (Carneiro da Cunha

Waud H. Kracke, Kagwahiv Mourning II: Ghosts, Grief, and Reminiscences from *Ethos*, Vol. 16, No. 2 (June, 1988), pp. 209–222. Published by Blackwell Publishing on behalf of the American Anthropological Association.

1978:54–56; Levak 1980; Mandelbaum 1959; Reid 1979). George Pollock (1972) suggests that such rituals may constitute part of a kind of "culturally constituted defensive system" (Spiro 1961 [1972]:598–604, 1965), helping the bereaved person to deal with a universally experienced personal crisis.

If this is true, then it implies the converse proposition: that cultures that restrict grieving and minimize ritual articulation of the mourning process may make the experience of grief more difficult for their members and the process of mourning more problematic and difficult to carry through to a successful resolution. No cultures of this type, to my knowledge, have been studied with this question in mind outside our own European orbit. It has frequently been argued, however, that northern European and American values discouraging the open expression of grief inhibit the mourning process for us (Bateson 1968; Gorer 1965; Krupp 1962). There are a few studies that focus on extreme manifestations of grief in cultures suppressive of open expression, though the studies themselves do not draw the connection. Matchett (1972) argues that hallucinations of the deceased are so frequent in Hopi culture that they are to be regarded as normal for Hopi, and Daniel Freeman (Freeman, Foulkes, and Freeman 1976) notes a high incidence of "ghost sickness" among his Kiowa Apache psychiatric patients. Other sources indicate that Hopi (Kennard 1937) and Apache (Opler 1946; Mandelbaum 1959) mourning customs strongly promote suppression of grief. Both the Hopi hallucinations of people who have just died and the Apache cases of ghost sickness – epileptic-like spasms that come on after having been attacked from behind by a ghost, usually happening to someone in mourning – could be seen as pathology of mourning. Although these two instances do not prove the hypothesis that norms inhibiting the expression of grief tend to impede and prolong the mourning process, they at least lend circumstantial support to it.

In addition, clinical experience with mourning has shown that one of the most difficult issues to deal with in mourning is the acceptance of angry feelings toward the deceased, either feelings that were already present in the relationship, or unconscious anger provoked

by the "abandonment" of death (Bowlby 1980; Pollock 1961; Volkan 1981). An additional hypothesis, then, would be that cultural disapproval of the face-to-face expression of anger would heighten the problematic nature of unresolved anger in mourning. Such inhibition exacerbates feelings of guilt over anger toward the dead person, and further increases the difficulty of reaching a resolution of the mourning process and abatement of grief.

The Suppression of Grief

Both of these characterizations apply to the Kagwahiv of the Amazon: the expression of grief is discouraged except for the immediate moment of death, when keening and wailing are permitted at least to women; and in general terms, despite the headhunting heritage of the Kagwahiv, the expression of anger (or even aggressive self-assertion) in face-to-face relationships is strongly disapproved.

I witnessed only one death among the Kagwahiv, that of a three-year-old child. The initial shock of grief was freely expressed, with the mother wailing aloud and women gathering around to comfort her, speculating on reasons for the death. (One explanation was that the missionaries had left that day and taken their protective healing power with them.) But after this initial reaction, the ritual and customary regulation of mourning prescribed the muting of emotion and avoidance of memories of the deceased.

The funeral ceremony for the child was brief and simple: the grave was dug by two men of the opposite patrilineal moiety from the dead child, although classificatory fathers of the child helped their affines fill in the grave.[3] The child's body was carried prone in a hammock from the house he had died in and buried wrapped in it.

In the past, before the influence of Brazilian burial customs, burials took place in the floor of the longhouse (ongá) in which the person lived. An adult man would have been buried in full ceremonial dress, with his headdress on and with valued possessions such as a bow and arrows, or his best seed corn (Betts 1967:42). The face would have been painted with urucu-berry paint by a sibling, father's sister, or other member of the deceased's own moiety, and "tied up" (-*ñimongarungwár*) with a piece of cloth (in recent times) to prevent the spirit from escaping or being able to see its way out. The corpse would be buried flexed with its legs drawn up, with the hands palm-to-palm between the thighs (according to one informant, Paulinho; or with the arms around the knees and the wrists crossed – *ojopoapí* – according to Aruká, who also added that only a man of substance was buried this way – a lesser person would be buried lying flat in his hammock). The body was wrapped in the hammock and tied at the ankles, knees and waist and placed in the grave with the head pointed upriver, Paulinho said[4] – the reverse of the way the Brazilians do it – in order to keep the *añang* from leaving the body.

For four or five days after the death, the bereaved (*poñi'ím*) observe certain avoidances. One should not eat much, but just sip small amounts of water; and one should not bathe or go swimming. (These are the same restrictions that apply during the ceremony for a boy's receiving his first penis sheath or a girl's menarche ceremony, and for the ritual observed after killing any enemy.) Also, except for old people who are considered resistant to many noxious influences – they can eat many foods tabooed for younger people, for example (Kracke, 1981b:100) – a mourner does not decorate his or her own body with urucu or sing. On the first night after the burial, one stays up all night weeping and grieving (*ojehe'ó, ogwahí*), while keeping the fire lit to keep the *añang* at bay. In these ways, the acute stage of mourning – the initial shock and the subsequent reaction of intense pain and grief (Pollock 1961:72–73; 1972:14–15) – is given ritual recognition. These observances may, in some cases, extend beyond to the chronic stage of mourning (Pollock 1961:73, 76). Jovenil, even several months after the death of his children, felt he should not eat much and refrained from going to festas, for fear his other children might also die.

Immediately after the burial, steps are taken to distance the memory of the dead person. The family of the deceased give away, destroy, or discard any belongings of the dead person not buried with him or her, along with any household utensils frequently used by the person when alive, or in any way associated with that person. Other people may ask the surviving spouse or children of the deceased to give them some of the deceased's *mbateruéra*, "former possessions." In particular, the immediate and classificatory siblings of the person who died are entitled to make such demands on the widow or widower, their brother- or sister-in-law: *oporandú ojombateruéra itairo'ihugui* ("demand each other's former possessions from their brother-in-law") in exchange for the sibling who has been lost. These payments to clan siblings of the dead person may be other things besides the dead person's possessions – a new bow, for example.

Not only personal effects, but the very house in which the dead person lived, are disposed of. Nowadays, for the most part, the person's house is taken down and re-erected in another spot – or at the very least (for a child's death) the house is completely stripped of its thatch and rethatched. In the past, on the death of the headman, the longhouse in which he and his followers lived would be burned, along with his bows and arrows. The entire settlement would then be relocated.[5] Even in recent times, when the headman Jovenil's two young children died of illness during the period of my fieldwork in 1968, Jovenil decided to dismantle all the village houses but one and move them to an altogether different location, to a site where he had lived when younger. (The one not moved had been built for me, and was subsequently occupied by Jovenil's brother's father-in-law).

Two different rationales are given for these practices, yet so interchangeably that it almost seems as if they are different ways of phrasing the same thing. One is that the ghost (*añang*) of the person who has died is likely to remain around the home where he or she lived, using the familiar utensils and lifetime belongings, so that for the survivors to continue living in the same house or using the same utensils the dead person used would be to invite dangerous contact with the *añang* or *ra'úv* of the dead person – which might tempt a survivor to wander off and join it in the *ongá* (house or village) of the dead. Old, abandoned settlements are considered haunted by the people who died there, and the living sometimes encounter their ghosts there. Objects associated with the deceased, and places that the dead person frequented, become *pojí*, "frightening-uncanny" or "supernaturally dangerous" (a term conveying both intense anxiety, such as the vertigo experienced in a tree by someone with a fear of heights, and the actual danger of encounter with a malevolent supernatural force).

The other reason given by the Kagwahiv for avoiding these objects and places is that they hold painful memories of the dead person and are sad reminders of one's loss. One puts them away or gives them away so as not to be reminded. Such explanation is given for putting the hammock, arrows, and headdresses in the grave with the body – "because they make one sad [*ogwahí*]. … When the things are there, you cry. When you put them in the grave, you stop crying because you don't see them any longer."

In general, the Kagwahiv avoid reminding a bereaved person of the loss, or being reminded of it. A bereaved mother carefully asked me, before looking at pictures I brought back, whether they included any of her child who had recently died. If they did, she didn't want to see them. I am not aware of any taboo on the names of recently deceased persons as among the Yanomamo (Lizot 1973) and other Lowland South American cultures, but mention of the name is tactfully avoided in the presence of the bereaved. When the name of any person who has died is mentioned, it is thereafter – from the day of death on – modified by the suffix *-ve'e*, which is otherwise used to nominalize adjectives or verbs referring to inanimate objects (such as: an airplane is *ovevé-ve'e* a "flying-thing"). Thus the dead person's name is de-animized.

The system of kinship terminology and the pronoun system both draw a sharp separation between the living and the dead. Kin terms for a dead person are replaced by a totally new set of terms for deceased relatives: a dead father is no longer *ji rúva* ("my father") but *ji poría* ("my deceased father"), and *ji ihẽ* ("my mother") becomes *ji imbóra*. When I referred to someone's long-dead father as *nde rúva*, I was not understood until I corrected it to *nde poría*. A dead husband or wife is no longer *ji rembirekó* ("spouse," literally "one who I possess," "one I am married to") but *ji pohije'ím*. A man refers to his dead child as *ji rekovíar*, and a woman to

hers as *ji japikár* (instead of *ji ra'ír* for either a man or a woman speaking of a living child). A dead son (of either a man or a woman) is *pia-jihú*, and a man's dead daughter is *ji rembia-vikár*. Other terms for deceased relatives are simply formed by adding to the relationship terms the de-animizing suffix *-ve'e*.

Even the pronoun used to refer to the person is no longer the sex-differentiated personal pronoun (*ga*, "he," or *hẽ*, "she"), but a single neutral pronoun *ahé*, used for ghosts or for anyone no longer living. Other grammatical forms also shift to the nonhuman forms used for animals, plants, or inanimate objects. The dead person is grammatically depersonalized and distanced from the living (cf. Carneiro da Cunha 1978).

Yet in the derivations of some of the relationship terms used for dead relatives, deep feeling does seem to be implicit. The man's term for a dead daughter, *rembiavikár*, may be derived from the verb *-vig*, "disconnect" (the prefix *rembi-* plus *vikár*, "person who is disconnected from one") – or possibly from *-aví*, "to hit the mark" (with an arrow). *Japikár*, the woman's word for a dead child, could come from *-pig*, "to hold onto, trap," but the close similarity to the verb *-japiaká*, "think, ruminate," may not be accidental, and is certainly relevant to its connotations. Even more clearly, *poría* ("deceased father") is closely related to *mboría*, an exclamation of sympathy or of distress ("What a shame! Alas!"). And finally, *pohije'im*, "late spouse" (literally, "not heavy" – the negative nominal suffix *-e'im* added to the adjective *pohii*, "heavy") is a synonym of the adjective *ndipohii* (literally, "not heavy"), which refers to emotions of deep sadness – grief, regret, and guilt.

Other than such implicit recognition of affects, however, Kagwahiv values encourage the muting of expression of strong sorrow. Such muting is supported and justified by belief: weeping, at least excessive weeping, is considered to expose a person to supernatural dangers. Homero attributed his adult daughter's death to her having cried too much when her younger half-brother was flown to a hospital in Porto Velho. The consequence of the breach of certain food taboos – taboos imposed on parents during pregnancy and the early months of infancy – is that the taboo-breaker's infant will "cry, go crazy, and die." Understandably, given these beliefs about crying, great pains are taken to keep children from crying by distracting them, and to soothe them when they break into tears. Older children are frequently admonished to stop crying. And, of course, adults are not encouraged to express their grief in tears, after the initial shock. Such suppression of grief might be expected to inhibit the "work of remembering" in the mourning process.

Kagwahiv norms also strongly condemn face-to-face expression of any kind of antagonistic feelings – a stricture on interpersonal relationships that tends to promote accumulation of anger and periodic ruptures and flare-ups. Since, as discussed earlier, feelings of anger about the person who has died – whether pre-existing feelings of anger or anger about being left – are among the most difficult to deal with in bereavement, one would expect that the dammed-up anger in Kagwahiv relationships, and the resultant guilt, would add further to difficulty in mourning.

Here another aspect of Kagwahiv funerals is pertinent. Many of the traditional prescriptions of the burial and postmortuary ritual are explained by my informants as precautions to hamper the mobility of the ghost (añang) or to keep the ghost at bay. The eyes of corpses used to be closed and the face "tied up" with cloth before burial to prevent the ghost from being able to see, and the body oriented with the head upriver to keep the ghost from coming out of the grave. The face of the corpse was painted with urucu to keep the ghost from leaving the body – or, according to other reports (Betts 1967:42), so that it could not see to find people if it did leave the body.

The days after the burial are a time of special precautions against añang. "When the burial is over, that night people are afraid of añang," Aruka recounted. "They do not put out the fire. They don't sleep, they weep and grieve. A long fire [tatá pukú]. ... If you don't put out the fire, the añang will not come." The reason one does not bathe for five days after a death, he said, is that "the añangwéra doesn't like it if one bathes right away – it will drag one into the water."

These precautions reflect a strong fear of ghosts – a fear that is intimately associated with the feeling of grief itself, to judge by the frequent interchangeability of explanations for customs that refer to either feelings of grief or fear of añáng. In addition, Kagwahiv often report vivid encounters with people who have died. Some of these are reported as vivid dreams (which, if they are nightmares, could be taken as actual encounters with añáng – see Kracke 1979), but others as waking visions. Could this preoccupation with ghosts and these visions of the departed be taken as an indication that the norms of Kagwahiv culture tend to inhibit the completion of mourning, leaving the mourning process uncompleted so that the bereaved does not fully accept the reality of the death?[6]

Personal Experience of Mourning

This analysis is all very well on a *cultural* level, and seems plausible. But as a psychological hypothesis about the influence of cultural norms on the personal mourning process it must be examined not only on the level of cultural practices, but through direct access to the psychological experience of individuals. For this examination I conducted in-depth interviews with several Kagwahiv who had lost close relatives fairly recently. They ranged from some who had lost parents, spouses, or children within the past few years, to one woman who only learned of her father's death during the course of the interviews. (The last gave me the opportunity to see and participate in one person's first reactions to a loss, from the initial disbelief with which she received the news to her gradual assimilation and acceptance of the reality of it.) Although the transcription and analysis of these interviews is still in progress, the preliminary results are *not* consistently in accord with the analysis I have given. It is not that the emotional conflicts I have discussed above are absent from the cases – in many instances they are present – but rather that most of these individuals do not show such conflicts or defenses to an inordinate degree, or more than one would expect from the situation of the death and of the bereaved.

It is true that all of the kinds of conflicts and difficulties in mourning that I have mentioned do appear in the interviews. Some of the individuals with whom I worked, such as the woman who had just learned of her father's death, do show some degree of denial of the reality of the death, at least initially. Others show some manifestation of guilt and conflict over their anger at the person they have lost – as did Jovenil, the bereaved father of my first article on Kagwahiv mourning (Kracke 1981a). But for the most part these reactions do not seem more intense or problematic than in the normal mourning process in our own culture. Jovenil had some intense conflicts aroused by the death of his two children that partly blocked his mourning of them, but these seemed at least partly resolved – enough to allow him to proceed with his mourning – during the 15 interviews I had with him (though the interviews were not intended for therapeutic purposes, nor was I fully aware at the time that he was experiencing them so). In fact, when I presented my interviews with Jovenil to an audience of psychoanalysts, an analyst who had lost a child of his own recognized in Jovenil the same emotions and conflicts he himself had experienced in mourning his child.

A few Kagwahiv mothers who had lost children showed prolonged reactions to their deaths. A woman helping me to treat a sick child, her brother's daughter, had a consistent and rather vehemently pessimistic outlook on the child's chances for survival, to a degree that I sensed was overdetermined. One day she talked at length with me about the death many years before of her only child. After that, she seemed more free to express hope about the child we were treating, and more able to be involved in the effort to save the child's life. Shortly thereafter, she adopted that child's newborn younger sister. The incident suggests that she had not fully resolved the mourning of her child; but what mother can? Another bereaved mother, Jovenil's wife, said five years after her son's death, "Every day I think about Alonzo. I don't forget him." As George Pollock observes, "The loss of a child can never be fully integrated and totally accepted by the mother or father" (Pollock 1961:82–83).

One old woman, Gabriela, exemplifies particularly well a number of the cultural patterns I have discussed (although she spent part of her childhood living with a Brazilian family). She, more than anyone else, greets me when I return with circumstantial accounts of the deaths that have taken place; and she recounted a waking experience of seeing her father after his death. Her account of this vision clearly expressed ambivalence. On the one hand, in the interview in which she first mentioned it, she went on to recall her father's near delusional jealousy of her mother, and the parental quarreling that resulted from it, which disturbed her greatly as a child. On the other hand, however, she described the vision in almost ecstatic terms, emphasizing how beautiful her father was with his long hair (the mark of a ghost), describing him as a *santo*. The vision occurred shortly after her father's death and thus may be regarded as a part of the mourning process; she never mentioned it recurring.

Gabriela has suffered all her life from sleeplessness that has some roots in her parents' nocturnal quarrels during her childhood. I have not, at this stage of analyzing my interviews with her, however, uncovered strong evidence that she has specific difficulty with mourning. She did describe at length the death of one of her adult sons and has dreamed at times of deceased relatives; but these are not necessarily indications of a generalized difficulty with mourning. Final conclusions await a fuller analysis of her interviews, but my impression is that the culturally sanctioned vision of her father may have itself been a beneficial step in her mourning process.

Matchett (1972) finds Hopi visions of the dead frequent enough to be normal for them. Bowlby in his book on mourning (1980) stresses that such visions are not at all uncommon in our own culture, and should not be regarded as pathological. My informant Jovenil had a vivid dream of talking with his parents some years after his father's death, which he did not interpret as a real encounter, although he might have. This seems to be a relatively normal part of the mourning process in many cultures.

At least two of the Kagwahiv people I interviewed *did* have great difficulties in mourning – one a man who had lost his father fairly early in life, and the other a young man who reacted extremely to his mother's death when he was in his twenties. Interestingly enough, both of these men seemed to embody or embrace with special intensity the pattern I have described for Kagwahiv mourning. The first, Sérgio, frequently had extremely anxious dreams of encounters with *añang*, sometimes in the form of identifiable people who had died, at other times as generalized forest spirits (Kracke 1978:178–181, 1979:155–157). Sérgio had lost his father at a critical time in his childhood, and did not seem to have received much support from his mother in mourning him. He never adequately mourned his father's death. The second, Francisco, embodied the cultural style of restraint in face-to-face self-assertiveness to the point of personal inhibition, and was especially distressed at the possibility of losing self-control. He was, when I interviewed him, still bound up with the death of his mother five years earlier, a trauma whose repetition he brought upon himself by marrying a woman who was dying of the same illness that had been fatal to his mother. He, too, had frequent and vivid encounters with *añang* (Kracke 1979:148–149).

I will not go into the personalities and conflicts of these two men, which I have analyzed elsewhere (Kracke 1978:148–166, 169, 184, 1979:148–160), but both are atypical in the disabling intensity of their conflicts. Yet it is precisely these *atypical* individuals who most closely approximate the kind of pathology of mourning that I suggested in the cultural analysis.

Conclusions

Based on these cases, I suggest that the kind of pathognomic analysis of culture patterns in which many psychoanalytically oriented anthropologists have engaged in the past is not incorrect, but is misplaced in its emphasis. Many of the culture patterns I have described seem, when appropriately used by the average member of the culture, to facilitate mourning, or at least not to completely inhibit the mourning process. The giving away of objects – ostensibly in the service of forgetting the deceased – may itself be cathartic, and purge or assuage feelings of guilt arising from the inevitable ambivalence marking close relationships. Cultural acceptability of visions of the deceased make it easier to

experience and accept in oneself what some psychoanalysts are beginning to regard as a normal part of the mourning process, or at least a frequently occurring part of it in our own culture. But the conflicts of at least some individuals whose personal difficulties correspond most closely to ritualized cultural patterns – who, perhaps, embody those patterns too well for their own good may – at least sometimes, suggest the pathognomic implication of rituals referred to by LaBarre. One must examine individual differences in the specific meaning of a personal relationship to comprehend how a culture pattern is utilized or not in given cases.

NOTES

1 This paper is a revised version of one first presented in the symposium: "Symbol, Insight and Fieldwork," organized by Benjamin Kilborne and George DeVos in honor of Weston LaBarre at the 80th annual meeting of the American Anthropological Association in Los Angeles, December 2, 1981.

2 The psychological work of mourning consists in going through one's memories of the lost person, painfully recognizing the finality of the loss in the context of each memory (Freud 1917). One may hypothesize, then, that the suppression of expression of grief and the avoidance of memories of the person who has died would not promote the work of mourning but, instead, interfere with it.

3 My informant, Paulinho, at one point asserted that the burier should be of the same moiety as the deceased, but most instances I know of support the more frequently voiced rule that it should be someone of the opposite moiety.

4 Or away from the river, according to another informant.

5 Before the Kagwahiv adopted the Brazilian pattern of separate dwellings for each nuclear family, a settlement consisted of a single longhouse.

6 At a cultural level, this idea would seem to be confirmed by another pattern of the Kagwahiv, which was noted by Metraux (1947:40) among the ancient Tupinambá as well: when one returns after a long absence, one is often greeted with a litany of all those who have died since one was last there (or even before), together with a circumstantial account of the deaths.

REFERENCES

Bateson, Mary Catherine
1968 Insight in a Bicultural Context. *Philippine Studies* 16:605–621.

Betts, Lavera
1967 Anthropological Check List. Typescript prepared for the Technical Studies Department, Summer Institute of Linguistics, Brasilia.

Bowlby, John
1980 *Less: Sadness and Depression. Attachment and Loss* Vol 3. New York: Basic Books.

Carneiro da Cunha, Manuela
1978 *Os Mortos e os Outros: uma Anâlise do Sistema Funerario e da Noção de Pessoa entre os Índios Krahó*. São Paolo: Editora Hucitec.

Freeman, Daniel M. A., Edward Foulks; and Patricia A. Freeman
1976 Ghost Sickness and Superego Development in the Kiowa Anache Male. *Psychoanalytic Study of Society* 7:123–171.

Freud, Sigmund
1917 *Mourning and Melancholia. Standard Edition* (J. Strachey, ed.). vol. 14, pp. 243–260. London: Hogarth.

Gorer, Geoffrey
1965 *Death, Grief and Mourning in Contemporary Britain*. New York: Doubleday.

Kennard, E. A.
1937 Hopi Reactions to Death. *American Anthropologist* 29:491–494.

Kracke, Waud H.
1978 *Force and Persuasion: Leadership in an Amazonian Society*. Chicago: University of Chicago Press.
1979 Dreaming in Kagwahív: Dream Beliefs and their Psychic Uses in an Amazonian Indian Culture. *Psychoanalytic Study of Society* 8:119–171.
1981a Kagwahív Mourning I: Dreams of a Bereaved Father. *Ethos* 9(4):258–275.
1981b Don't Let the Piranha Bite Your Liver: A Psychoanalytic Approach to Kagwahív (Tupi) Food Taboos. *Food Taboos in Lowland South America* (K. M. Kensinger and W. H. Kracke, eds.). Working Papers on South American Indians No. 3. Bennington, VT: Bennington College.

Krupp, George R.
1962 Bereavement Reaction: A Special Case of Separation Anxiety. Sociocultural Considerations. *The Psychoanalytic Study of Society*. 2:42–74. New York: International Universities Press.

Labarre, Weston
1970 *The Ghest Dance: Origins of Religion*. New York: Delta.
1978a Anthropological Perspectives on Hallucination, Hallucinogens and the Shamanic Origins of Religion. *Culture in Conflict*, pp. 37–92. Durham, NC: Duke University Press.
1978b Psychoanalysis and the Biology of Religion. *Culture in Context*, pp. 269–275. Durham. NC: Duke University Press.

Levak, Milena Masselli
1980 Motherhood by Death among the Bororo Indians of Brazil. *Omega* 10(4):323–334.

Lewis, Thomas H.
1973 A Culturally Patterned Depression in a Mother after Loss of a Child. *Psychiatry* 38:92–95.

Lizot, Jacoues
1973 Onomastique Yanomami. *L'Homms* 13(3):61–70.

Mandelbaum, David G.
1959 Social Uses of Funeral Rites. *The Meaning of Death* (H. Feifel, ed.), pp. 189–217. New York: McGraw-Hill.

Matchett, William Foster
1972 Repeated Hallucinatory Experiences as a Part of the Mourning Process among Hopi Indian Women. *Psychiatry* 35:185–194. Reprinted (1974) in *Culture and Personality: Contemporary Readings* (R. A. LeVine, ed.) pp. 222–231. Chicago: Aldine.

Metraux, Alfred.
1947 Mourning Rites and Burial Forms of the South American Indians. *America Indigena* 7(1):7–44.

Opler, Morris E.
1946 Reactions to Death among Mescalero Apache. *Southwestern Journal of Anthropology* 2:454–467.

Pollock, George
1961 Mourning and Adaptation. *International Journal of Psychoanalysis* 42:341–361. Reprinted (1974) in *Culture and Personality: Contemporary Readings* (R. A. LeVine, ed.) pp. 65–94. Chicago: Aldine.
1972 Mourning and Anniversaries: The Relationship of Culturally Constituted Defensive Systems to Intrapsychic Adaptive Processes. *Israel Annals of Psychiatry* 10:9–39.

Reid, Janice
1979 A Time to Live, a Time to Grieve: Patterns and Processes of Mourning among the

Yolngu of Australia. *Culture, Medicine and Psychiatry* 3:319–346.

Spiro, Melford
1961 An Overview and a Suggested Reorientation. *Psychological Anthropology* (F. L. K. Hsu, ed.), 1st edition. Homewood Illinois: Dorsey Press. 2nd edition (1972), pp. 573–607. Cambridge, MA: Schenkman.

1965 Religious Systems as Culturally Constituted Defense Mechanisms. *Context and Meaning in Cultural Anthropology* (M. E. Spiro, ed.), pp. 100–113. New York: The Free Press.

Volkan, Vamik D.
1981 *Linking Objects and Linking Phenomena: A Study of Complicated Mourning.* New York: International Universities Press.

Part IV

Childhood: Internalizing Cultural Schemas

Introduction

Childhood Experience: The Role of Communication

Franz Boas's landmark study of physical growth among European immigrants in New York, completed in 1911, introduced environmental influences on child development into anthropology as a serious topic of empirical research. Boas referred only to "social and geographical influences" without further specification, but he left little doubt that he was proposing influence on the mental as well as skeletal development of children. Boas was not an extreme environmentalist who believed the child to be a blank slate or denied the importance of genetics; on the contrary, he had met with Francis Galton, the pioneering British scientist, statistician and genetic determinist, and took Mendelian genetics (rediscovered in 1900) into account in his conception of human development. Boas's environmentalism was intended to contradict the doctrines of fixed racial typologies and recapitulationism (the theory that the development of each human recapitulates the stages of human evolution) that were still widely believed in the first decade of the 20th century. (G. Stanley Hall, founder of child psychology in the United States, was a proponent of recapitulationism.)

Boas's conviction that cross-cultural research would be crucial to the understanding of human development found its realization in the fieldwork of his student Margaret Mead in Samoa and Melanesia. Mead's *Coming of Age in Samoa* (1928) and *Growing Up in New Guinea* (1930) were best-selling books that introduced the American public, as well as scientists, to the idea of cultural influence in development. Her work was also a foundation-stone of the culture and personality movement and its theoretical paradigm. She went on to work in Bali (Bateson and Mead, 1942) and to write extensively on child rearing and child development in diverse cultures. Other anthropologists followed in her footsteps during the rest of the 20th century, describing the course of childhood throughout the world (LeVine, 2007; LeVine and New, 2008).

Yet neither Mead nor her followers could resolve the problems raised by trying to conceptualize childhood experience: What does it consist of, what are its constituents, what events are memorable, what pushes it in one direction or the other, how long lasting are its effects? For this, a developmental psychology was needed, and when anthropologists turned to psychology and psychiatry, they received conflicting – sometimes misleading – answers over the years: Freud's psychosexual stages suggested the observation of feeding practices in infancy, toilet training in toddlerhood, the Oedipal triangle thereafter. Behavioristic psychology dictated looking at rewards that "reinforced" behavior and created habits during childhood. Jean Piaget's cognitive stages recommended examination of the logical and numerical concepts children attained at different ages and whether their sequence of attainment resembled that of children in Geneva, Switzerland. These and other developmental formulations came into and went out of fashion during the 20th century, leaving an ethnographic description based on one classified as "obsolete" a decade later.

Thus the study of childhood experience and its impact on psychological development did not enjoy the success of human growth research in biological anthropology, which was able to link Boas's early work on bone growth among immigrant families with the science emerging from later biomedical studies of nutritional processes. Psychology did not approximate the phenomenal progress of biology in the 20th century, leaving anthropologists of child development late in the century still seeking to understand the processes by which childhood experience affects psychological development.

With help from biological studies of parental care, language acquisition research and cognitive anthropology, however, the anthropology of child development did make progress in the late 20th century, as shown in our companion volume *Anthropology and Child Development: A Cross-Cultural Reader*, edited by Robert A. LeVine and Rebecca S. New (2008). Of particular note were the studies of language socialization in a wide variety of cultures published during the 1980s and 1990s, showing the way toward an understanding of childhood as the acquisition of cultural meanings in children aged two to five. Edward Sapir (Chapter 2, this book), though he never studied childhood in another culture, had advocated studying the world of the three-year-old child over time, in and before 1936, and his theory entailed (without specifying) a process by which interpersonal relations in context were transformed into culture-specific psychological dispositions. It would take almost 50 years after Sapir's lectures at Yale before fieldworkers demonstrated that language mediates cultural meanings in the experience of young children of different cultures (Schieffelin, 1986; Ochs and Schieffelin, 1987); language socialization research continues to provide some of the most interesting insights into the processes by which children acquire meanings from their environments.

Meanwhile, the development of schema theory in cognitive anthropology provided another conceptual tool for comprehending childhood experience and its impact in different cultural environments (D'Andrade, 1995). Although the British psychologist F. C. Bartlett had formulated a schema theory in cultural context in 1932, it was ignored during the behaviorist ascendancy (1935–60) and only re-emerged later. A schema is a mental representation or image of experience in a given environment that becomes established in memory. It can be verbal or pictorial, emotional as well as cognitive, an action sequence or a story. It is not simply a habit or a fixed concept and is responsive to features of the experience like repetition and emotional arousal; it affects one's expectancies in a particular setting or one resembling the original. In the anthropological writings of D'Andrade, Naomi Quinn (2005), and Claudia Strauss (Strauss and Quinn, 1997), it is associated with the parallel distributed processing (PDP) model of brain function formulated by Rumelhart, McClelland and the PDP Research Group (1986), but the focus is on cultural meanings and their acquisition. Quinn (2005) has taken an important step toward applying a schema perspective to the comparative study of childhood by attempting to specify universal features of child rearing that give experience meaning, including repetition, emotional arousal, and instructive moral suasion. Her proposal is not developmental in the sense of specifying age levels or stage sequences in development, but it can be used by empirical researchers to explore the patterns of childhood experience that become part of the memory and behavior repertoire of children in a particular culture. Schemas represent a promising approach to the internalization process that is central to the interests of psychological anthropologists in childhood.

The selections in this section are focused on parent–child communication, not because it is all or most of the childhood experience that drives or facilitates the internalization of culture, or even that it represents more than a fraction of the child's learning, but because it has been studied in various settings across the world with illuminating results.

Chapter 13: Amy Richman, Patrice Miller, and Robert LeVine show with observational data how different are the patterns of mother–infant communication across distinct cultures and, within a Mexican sample, across mothers of differing levels of school attainment.

Chapter 14: Peggy Miller, Heidi Fung, and Judith Mintz compare the narrative practices of Chinese (in Taiwan) and American mother–child pairs, suggesting the patterns through which narratives are internalized in early childhood.

Chapter 15: Vanessa Fong shows with older children and adolescents in a city of mainland China that parents of a particular culture can communicate conflicting messages to their growing children, inadvertently sacrificing one set of strongly held cultural values for another.

REFERENCES

Bartlett, F. C.
  1995 [1932]   Remembering: A Study in Experimental and Social Psychology. Cambridge: Cambridge University Press.
Bateson, Gregory and Margaret Mead
  1942   Balinese Character: A Photographic Analysis. New York: New York Academy of Sciences.
D'Andrade, Roy G.
  1995   The Development of Cognitive Anthropology. New York: Cambridge University Press.
LeVine, Robert A.
  2007   Ethnographic Studies of Childhood: A Historical Overview. American Anthropologist 109: 247–260.
LeVine, Robert A. and Rebecca S. New, eds.
  2008   Anthropology and Child Development: A Cross-Cultural Reader. New York: Wiley-Blackwell.
Mead, Margaret
  1928   Coming of Age in Samoa. New York: William Morrow.

1930   Growing Up in New Guinea. New York: William Morrow.
Ochs, Elinor and Bambi Schieffelin, eds.
1987   Language Socialization Across Cultures. New York: Cambridge University Press.
Quinn, Naomi
2005   Universals of Child Rearing. Anthropological Theory 5: 475–514.
Rumelhart, David E., James L. McClelland and the PDP Research Group, eds.
1986   Parallel Distributed Processing: Exploration in the Microstructure of Cognition, Vol. I: Foundations. Cambridge, MA: MIT Press.
Schieffelin, Bambi and Elinor Ochs
1986   Language Socialization. Annual Review of Anthropology: 163–246.
Strauss, Claudia and Naomi Quinn
1997   A Cognitive Theory of Cultural Meaning. New York: Cambridge University Press.

13

Cultural and Educational Variations in Maternal Responsiveness

Amy L. Richman, Patrice M. Miller,
and Robert A. LeVine

Child development research in the United States has often shown maternal responsiveness to infants to be predictive of their subsequent cognitive and emotional behavior (Ainsworth, Blehar, Waters, & Wall, 1978; Bornstein, 1989; Clarke-Stewart, 1973; Martin, 1981). In some studies, socioeconomic and cultural factors are deliberately controlled through sample selection so that their effects will not be confounded with those of maternal responsiveness. Other studies have shown maternal behavior during infancy to be associated with variations in culture, ethnicity, socioeconomic status (SES), and maternal education (e.g., Bornstein, Tamis-LeMonda, Pecheux, & Rahn, 1991; Cohen & Beckwith, 1976; Field, Sostek, Vietze, & Leiderman, 1981; Leiderman, Tulkin, & Rosenfeld, 1977; Richman et al., 1988), though only a few (e.g., Dixon, Tronick, Keefer, & Brazelton, 1981; Field & Widmayer, 1981) have examined the mother's contingency of response to infant signals. On the whole, the literature to date suggests that social and cultural factors influence maternal responsiveness in humans, but specific evidence on the amount and kind of influence, and the mediating processes, is largely lacking.

The concept of maternal responsiveness as usually used in the literature includes varied forms of behavior contingent on a variety of infant signals; vocalization is included along with other maternal and child behaviors. The literature referred to in the preceding paragraph indicates variation across socially and culturally defined populations in the particular infant signals (e.g., distress vs. nondistress) responded to as well as in the types of maternal behaviors (e.g., distal vs. proximal) elicited by those signals. In this article we consider two hypotheses: (a) that maternal responsiveness is affected by cross-cultural differences in conventions of conversational interaction, particularly as specified by scripts governing the mother-infant relationship, and (b) that maternal responsiveness is affected by within-culture differences in mothers' levels of formal education.

Hypothesis 1: Maternal responsiveness is affected by cross-cultural differences in local conventions of conversational interaction, particularly as specified by cultural scripts governing the mother-infant relationship. Populations vary in their conventions of normal adult conversation, that is, in the locally dominant norms for mutual gaze, turn taking, affective expression, intonation, and their organization in the

Amy L. Richman, Patrice M. Miller, and Robert A. LeVine, Cultural and Educational Variations in Maternal Responsiveness from *Developmental Psychology*, 1992, Vol. 28, No. 4, pp. 614–621. © 1992 by the American Psychological Association, Inc., received January 3, 1992, accepted January 5, 1992. Reprinted with permission.

canonical scripts that influence all conversations (except as qualified by more specific situational or relational norms). This means that even if some form of "proto-conversational" interaction between mother and infant were universal among human societies, the actual conversational behavior would be differentiated by local conventions of adult speech and by whether or not the language provides a special, simplified register (baby talk) for speaking to infants. But proto-conversation between mother and infant is not a universal cultural script, and mother–infant interaction is further differentiated by a variety of culture-specific norms that exempt babies from verbal interaction altogether, prescribe formulaic routines such as lullabies that are not overtly designed to initiate a communicative exchange, direct the mother to attend to crying and ignore babbling, or specify the variable terms of what Schieffelin and Ochs (1986) called "communicative accommodation" to the infant's capacities. The ethnographic and sociolinguistic evidence reviewed by Schieffelin and Ochs (1986) leaves little doubt that the varying normative contexts of conversation in general and the mother–infant relationship in particular influence the observable interaction of the mother with her prelinguistic infant.

This is generally confirmed by observational studies yielding quantitative data. For example, Konner (1977) found variations in frequency of caretaker vocalization to infants 7-to-12-months-old across samples drawn from the Kalahari San, Guatemalans, the Boston working class, and the Boston middle class. Dixon et al. (1981), in their microanalysis of videotaped face-to-face interaction of young infants with their mothers among the Gusii of Kenya and the Boston middle class, found that the Boston mothers attempted more frequently to elicit a reciprocal exchange with their infants, whereas the Gusii mothers more frequently averted their gaze when their infants became visibly excited, reflecting different interactional goals and suggesting the influence of culture-specific conventions on mother–infant interaction.

The question of whether the mother's level of responsiveness is affected by the conventions of conversation and their application to the infant care situation, however, remains a matter of debate, and it has been suggested that where reciprocal vocalization is rare in

mother-infant interaction, tactile or other forms of responsiveness may play an equivalent role in the infant's psychological development (Trevarthen, 1989). Thus in testing Hypothesis 1, our aim is not only to examine the influence of cultural scripts on observable interaction but also to explore the extent to which this influence has implications for the psychological development of the child.

Hypothesis 2: Maternal responsiveness within a culturally similar population is affected by the mother's level of school attainment, that is, by the number of years she has attended school. The association between a mother's formal education and her behavior to her preschool children is a familiar one in research on child development in the United States (e.g., Laosa, 1980, 1982), though only a few of these studies concern maternal behavior during infancy (e.g., Crockenberg, 1983). In a longitudinal study of 156 children, Feiring and Lewis (1981) found that

> the child's development of cognitive and language skills at 24 months is related to the mother's language use at earlier age points. Mothers characterized here as upper-middle SES, i.e., college educated or more, tended to employ a greater amount of verbal interaction as compared to middle SES mothers and had children who performed better on language measures at 24 months. The amount of verbal interaction a child receives at an early age is important and is probably related to the mother's education level. … [T]here is a tendency at 3 months for upper-middle SES mothers to vocalize more to their infants. At 12 months, although both SES groups vocalize a similar amount, upper-middle class mothers were more responsive to their children's vocalization. (pp. 87–88)

These findings concerning verbal interaction are typical of the U.S. literature, but it is noteworthy that the educational variation in Feiring and Lewis's (1981) study was between a college-educated group of mothers and a group educated to the high school level and described as middle class, rather than the working-class versus middle-class comparisons that have more commonly yielded such results (e.g., Tulkin & Kagan, 1972). Maternal schooling was confounded with other socioeconomic factors in the comparison of the two groups, because the aim of the study was to identify the effects of SES rather than to isolate the impact of maternal education itself. Such a comparison is interpretable as revealing subcultural differences in the conventional scripts and styles of interaction of different social strata rather than the effect of school experience as an individual variable on maternal behavior. To isolate that effect, it is necessary to control other socioeconomic and cultural factors through sampling or multivariate analysis or both.

In the research reported here, we examine the first hypothesis by comparing samples drawn from the Gusii of Kenya and suburban Boston (LeVine, Miller, & West, 1988) and the second hypothesis through a study of individual differences in low-income neighborhoods of a Mexican city (LeVine et al., 1991).

The Gusii–Boston Comparative Study

Method

Subjects. The first study compared mother-infant interaction in two samples, one from a rural Gusii community of southwestern Kenya, the other from suburban Boston, Massachusetts. The Gusii are an agricultural people with a distinctive language and culture who number more than 1 million and inhabit the highlands east of Lake Victoria in the southwestern corner of Kenya, East Africa (LeVine & LeVine, 1966). Their total fertility rate in 1979 was 8.7 children per woman, one of the highest in the

world. Twenty-eight Gusii infants and their caregivers were studied over a 17-month period (from February 1975 to July 1976) with a variety of biomedical, behavioral, and developmental assessment procedures (Dixon, LeVine, Richman, & Brazelton, 1984; Dixon et al., 1981; Keefer, Tronick, Dixon, & Brazelton, 1982; LeVine et al., in press-a). The Boston area sample consisted of 20 infants and their mothers, white middle-class Americans, studied in 1979–1980 for comparison with the Gusii (see Richman et al., 1988). A subgroup of each of these larger samples is examined here: 12 Gusii and 9 Boston mother-infant pairs.

In each community, women were contacted in the last months of pregnancy or shortly after giving birth and were invited to participate in a study of child development. The Gusii mothers were recruited through a local census carried out by the research team, the Bostonians through contacts with privately practicing pediatricians in the Boston area whose patients were largely middle class. All infants who met basic criteria of health, age, and sex and whose families fell within the normal range of socially acceptable family organization within each community were included in the sample. In addition, because hardly any of the Gusii children were firstborns, we restricted the Boston sample to non-firstborn children so that the comparison would not be one of firstborn Bostonians with laterborn Gusii. Table 13.1 presents some basic demographic information about the two samples and their respective subsamples. In general, the subsamples from each culture are representative of their respective larger samples.

Table 13.1 *Characteristics of the Gusii and Boston samples*

Characteristic	Gusii (n = 28)			Gusii subsample (n = 12)			Boston (n = 20)			Boston subsample (n = 9)		
	M	SD	Range	M	SD	Range	M	SD	Range	M	SD	Range
Mother's age	29.2	6.4	20–41	29.7	6.3	23–41	31.4	3.2	27–38	29.8	2.4	27–33
Mother's education	2.9	3.3	0–10	2.5	2.9	0–7	14.0	2.2	9–18	15.1	2.0	12–18
Father's age	37.4	11.5	20–66	36.3	8.4	28–58	33.9	4.3	29–42	32.3	3.9	29–41
Father's education	5.6	3.5	0–11	6.2	3.3	0–11	14.9	3.5	6–20	16.1	3.3	12–20
Birth order of infant	4.3	2.4	1–10	5.2	2.3	3–10	2.6	.69	2–4	2.4	.53	2–4

Two noteworthy differences between the Gusii and American samples have to do with maternal schooling and parity. The Boston mothers averaged 14–15 years of schooling and 2–3 children, whereas the Gusii mothers had 2–3 years of schooling and 4–5 children on the average. (The Gusii mothers were continuing to bear children and would end up with 10 or more before they stopped.)

Procedure. Infants were observed in their normal home environments at 3–4 months and at 9–10 months. The procedures followed in the Gusii setting and in Boston were somewhat different, but produced roughly equivalent information, as will be described.

Three bodies of naturalistic home observations were collected on each child in the Gusii longitudinal sample: spot observations of the care situation by a local assistant, precoded observations of mother and child by another Gusii assistant (for 6 months of the study), and narrative observations of mother and child by a foreign investigator fluent in the Gusii language and experienced in child observation, Sarah LeVine. The findings from all three approaches are presented elsewhere (LeVine et al., in press-a). Because the narrative observations were the only ones that permitted sequential analysis of mother-infant interaction throughout the study period, they were selected for intensive analysis, and the coding system developed for them provided the basis for the comparative research presented here. The narrative observations were conducted at the infant's home in the daytime for 1 hour every 3 months; mothers and other caregivers were instructed to carry on with their usual activities. The observer recorded each interactive behavior by mother and infant in sequence and noted the time at 1-min intervals. The pace of interaction was so slow that it was possible to record gross behaviors with accuracy and even to inscribe every utterance in full.

These observations were then coded using categories of behavior developed from Clarke-Stewart's (1973) system for coding social interaction. The coding consisted of translating the verbal record into numeric codes without further inference by the coders. This coding scheme contained 47 codes for describing infant behavior and 48 codes for describing caregiver

behavior. Some of these codes were the same for infant and caregiver. Categories of behavior shared by infants and caregivers included facial expressions (smiles, frowns, miscellaneous facial expressions), gestures (head and hand gestures), object-mediated behaviors (looking at objects, touching objects, showing objects, etc.), looking at another person, and noninteractive behaviors. Both caregiver and infant could be coded as vocalizing, but specific vocalizations were somewhat different for each. For the infant, vocalizations coded included cry, fret, miscellaneous noise, laugh, vocalize, imitate, talk, sing, and any noise. For the caregivers, vocalizations included talk, sing, imitate, miscellaneous noise, declarative, interrogation, imperative, laugh, praise, reprimand, threaten, or any noise. Both infants and caregivers were coded as engaging in various physical behaviors, but again somewhat different sets were appropriate (only caregivers were coded as holding or jiggling the infants; only infants could be coded as rooting; both could be coded as touching, hugging, or kissing). Finally, a few categories were unique to either the caregiver or the infant. For example, caregiving behavior was something that was only coded for caregivers and included such behaviors as physical caregiving, washing/cleaning, grooming, dressing, offering food or the breast, and so forth. General locomotion was coded only for infants, although either infants or caregivers could be coded as approaching the other.

Observations in the Boston sample were collected with a portable event recorder called the MORE (Micro-Processing Observation Recording Equipment). In order to generate comparable data, the coding categories were the same ones used in the Gusii study. There were some differences between the Gusii and Boston data collection: (a) The use of the MORE enabled event-level recording with the added feature of marking, in this case, 5-s time intervals as they occurred. (b) Certain categories were added for those behaviors or contextual variables that did not occur during the Gusii observations – for example, baby equipment such as walkers or infant seats or gestures such as peek-a-boo. (c) Seven observers, rather than one, rotated as collectors of data. (d) Infants were observed in interaction with their mothers for a total of four 1-hr periods at each age point. As with the Gusii study, mothers were asked to go about their normal activities while the observers were present. See Richman (1983) for more details on the methods.

Although the slow pace of the Gusii interaction and the relatively low level of inference involved in the coding provide confidence in the data, we further reduced the threats of observer and coder bias by collapsing the codes into a small number of crude categories with a high degree of face validity: talk, look, touch, hold, and feed/nurse for the mothers, and vocalize, cry, and look for the infants. In the American study, the graduate student observers were trained by watching videotapes of mothers and infants from the community who were comparable to the subjects in the study. Observers watched tapes in pairs and discussed their coding in order to reconcile any differences. This training and the MORE technology enabled the observers to deal with the sometimes faster-paced Boston interaction, and the coded data were eventually collapsed into the same eight categories used for the Gusii. Thus both bodies of data used the same simple categories, involving a minimal amount of inference in observation and coding and a maximum amount of face validity in their interpretation.

Results

Table 13.2 shows the rank orders by their frequencies of the five maternal behaviors among the Gusii and Boston mothers. As reported elsewhere (Richman et al., 1988), Gusii mothers most often hold and touch their infants at both age points. American mothers also hold their 3–4-month-olds the most, but by 9–10 months their predominant mode of interaction is talking and looking at their infants. We interpret this as showing that the Gusii mothers seek to quiet and soothe their babies, whereas the American mothers pursue a style in which verbal interaction and stimulation of the infant play an important part.

The rank ordering by frequency of the infant behaviors within each sample (not shown) is as follows: for the Gusii at 3–4

Table 13.2 *Rank ordering by frequency of the maternal behaviors for Gusii and Boston mothers to infants at 4 and 10 months of age*

4 months		10 months	
Gusii	*Boston*	*Gusii*	*Boston*
HXold	Hold	Hold	Look
Touch	Look	Touch	Talk
Talk	Talk	Talk	Hold
Look	Touch	Look	Feed/nurse
Feed/nurse	Feed/nurse	Feed/nurse	Touch

months – cry, vocalize, look; for the American infants at the same age – vocalize, look, cry. At 9–10 months, Gusii infants are vocalizing the most, crying the next most, and looking the least. Boston infants continue their earlier pattern: They vocalize and look much of the time, with crying being much less frequent.

How does the evidence from the Gusii–Boston comparison bear on Hypothesis 1, that mothers of different cultures respond differently to comparable infant behaviors? Table 13.3 displays the mean proportions of maternal responses to three infant behaviors (vocalize, look, and cry) among the Gusii and Boston mothers. For this analysis, a behavior of the mother was defined as a response to an infant behavior if it was recorded as occurring immediately after the infant behavior (Gusii) or in the next interval after an infant behavior (Boston). These numbers are conditional probabilities in which the number of responses that the mother made to a particular infant behavior is divided by the raw frequency of that infant behavior; that is, they show the number of responses that the mother made, given the number of opportunities she had to respond. (In the Gusii observations, the response would be immediately following the infant behavior but in a slightly varying time frame, whereas in the Boston study the response would be the maternal behavior[s] occurring in the next 5 s.)

As Table 13.3 indicates, the Gusii and Boston mothers show different patterns of responsiveness to the infant behaviors of nondistress vocalization, looking, and crying at 3–4 and 9–10 months of age. Gusii mothers most

Table 13.3 *Mean proportions of the maternal behaviors as responses to infant vocalizations, cries, and looks in the Gusii and Boston samples*

Maternal behavior	Infant behavior					
	Vocalize		Look		Cry	
	Gusii	Boston	Gusii	Boston 3	Gusii	Boston
	4-month-old infants					
Talk	.10	.19	.19	.25	.10	.21
Look	.04	.31	.19	.37	.03	.22
Touch	.09	.05	.28	.04	.20	.08
Hold	.51	.26	.88	.18	.44	.30
Feed	.04	.02	.01	.02	.09	.02
	10-month-old infants					
Talk	.05	.20	.12	.25	.07	.29
Look	.02	.29	.07	.29	.05	.29
Touch	.08	.02	.22	.02	.20	.03
Hold	.18	.10	.31	.08	.33	.23
Feed	.01	.01	.01	.04	.03	.07

frequently respond to all of the infant behaviors, whether by 3–4 month-olds or 9–10-month-olds, by holding and other physical behaviors. Boston mothers most frequently respond to infant looking and crying by holding at 3–4 months, but they respond most frequently to all three infant behaviors at 9–10 months by talking and looking. For mothers in both cultures, these response patterns are similar to the overall frequencies of their behaviors. Furthermore, the more frequent talking and looking of the Boston mothers in response to infant vocalization at both ages suggest that they are treating the baby's babbling as incipient speech, thus creating the "proto-conversations" that have been described elsewhere for American white middle-class mother-infant interaction (Ochs & Schieffelin, 1984).

Both groups of mothers are responsive to infant signals, but their different behaviors indicate divergent goals and styles. The responsiveness of the Gusii mothers is directed toward soothing and quieting infants rather than arousing them, as was also noted by Dixon et al. (1981) in their analysis of the videotaped face-to-face interaction of these mothers with their babies in a structured situation. The

responsiveness of the Boston mothers, especially as their infants become more communicative later in the 1st year, is designed to engage the infants in emotionally arousing conversational interaction. Gusii mothers see themselves as protecting their babies, not as playing with or educating them. From their point of view, emotional excitement should be avoided, and verbal communication can wait until the child is capable of speech.

These differences in the goals and styles of maternal responsiveness can be interpreted in a variety of ways, given the many differences between the cultural traditions and socioeconomic situations of the Gusii and Bostonian mothers. Gusii conventions of adult conversation involve much less mutual gaze and affect expression than their Boston counterparts, so it is possible that this canonical script for conversation has influenced observable mother-infant interaction. Furthermore, there is a specific prescription of emotional restraint for parents with their mature children that may have even greater force in this situation, and older Gusii mothers tend to ridicule the idea of talking to children before they are capable of speech, which they estimate at about

2 years of age. Although Gusii informants do not formulate an explicit concept of good mothering, it is abundantly clear from what they say and do that their concept of requisite responsive care during infancy entails comforting distress but not engaging the baby in conversational interaction.

It is also possible to attribute the greater emphasis on verbal communication among the Boston mothers to their much longer average exposure to schooling, but the confounding of maternal education with so many other variables makes this untestable with such small and homogeneous samples. The cross-cultural comparison brings out divergence in patterns of maternal responsiveness across human societies, but a more controlled study is needed to explore the impact of specific variables.

The Mexican Study

Method

To test Hypothesis 2, we selected a country with recently expanded female school enrollments, where wide variations in maternal school attainment could be found within relatively homogeneous local populations – namely, Mexico. Beginning the study in 1983, we chose an urban research site in order to ensure the availability of a sufficient number of women who had completed primary school. The medium-sized city of Cuernavaca (1980 population: about 200,000) in the state of Morelos 50 miles south of Mexico City was selected. Within Cuernavaca, we chose two low-income neighborhoods, an old inner-city section and a new squatter settlement, in which to conduct a census of women aged 15–35 with children under 4 years of age, restricting our sample to those with at least 1 and no more than 9 years of school. This educational range included the majority of child-bearing women in the neighborhoods (typical of urban Mexico in 1983) and eliminated the extremes of those who had never attended school and those who had completed high school, in order to focus on whether completing primary school (6 years of school) and obtaining postprimary education (*secundaria*

in the Mexican system, equivalent to junior high school) make a difference in maternal behavior. A sample of 333 mothers who met these criteria were interviewed concerning family life, reproductive history, and child care, and a subsample was chosen for the observational study on the basis of having a child approaching either 5 or 10 months of age; all such mothers in the larger sample were selected for home observation.

Subjects. A total of 72 mothers had babies available for home observation at 5 and 10 months. The average mother in this subsample was 23.4 years old (range = 14.9 to 35.6 years), had attended school for almost 7 years (range = 1 to 9 years), was married to a man with 7 years of education (range = 1 to 17 years), and had had 2 children (range = 1 to 8). The group of 72 was divided into two cohorts for purposes of the observational study: one of 30 infants that was observed at 5 and 10 months, and another of 42 infants observed at 10 and 15 months. In this article we focus on the 10-month data, which included the full sample of 72 and permits comparison with the Gusii and Boston data.

Procedure. Each mother – infant pair was observed by a Mexican field assistant in social interaction during four 20-min sessions over a 2-day period at each age point. The observer used an observational instrument consisting of 10 maternal behaviors (vocalize, hold, look, feed, physical, approach, caretaking, gesture, object-mediated, other action) and 10 infant behaviors (vocalize, look, cry, motor, physical, object-mediated, gesture, approach, explore, self-engaged), which approximated the collapsed categories derived from the earlier Gusii and American studies. The observer checked off the occurrence of any of the behaviors on an optical scanning sheet while an audio beeper signalled 8-s intervals to provide a timeline; coding was continuous. The procedure was designed to allow relatively easy, rapid, and reliable data collection without the use of automatic recording devices. The three observers were trained using videotapes of mother-infant pairs from the community. Interobserver reliability of at least 80% was achieved for each category before data collection began.

Results

The same eight behaviors presented for the Gusii and Boston samples are here examined for the Mexican sample at 10 months of age: look, talk, hold, touch, and feed for the mothers and vocalize, look, and distress for the infants. For the Mexican mothers interacting with 10-month-old infants, the rank order of frequency was look, talk, hold, touch, and feed. The infants were most frequently vocalizing, looking, and crying, in that order. These patterns are most similar to those of the Boston mothers at 10 months.

For purposes of examining maternal responsiveness in these data, we followed procedures identical to those used in the Gusii–Boston comparison. Table 13.4 shows the proportions of the five maternal behaviors as responses to infant vocalizing, looking, and distress. The Mexican mothers most often looked and talked in response to both vocalizing and looking from their infants and in response to crying. The next most frequent response to infant vocalizing and looking was maternal touch, followed by holding. In the case of infant distress, the next most frequent response was mother holding, followed by touch. Feeding was a rare response to any of these infant behaviors. These results from Mexico again appear most similar to the behavior of the Boston mothers with their 10-month-olds, with one difference. In the Boston sample, maternal rates of talking and looking in

response to infant behaviors were very similar. In Mexico, maternal looking was a much more frequent response than maternal talking (mothers looked in response to infant behaviors in approximately one half or more of the intervals). The Mexican mothers monitor their infants visually, intervening as the occasion requires with more active behaviors such as talking, touching, or holding.

To test Hypothesis 2, we examined the correlations of maternal schooling with four categories of maternal responsiveness at 10 months, as shown in Table 13.5. (Mother's touching has been dropped from the table because its correlations with schooling were consistently close to 0.) Although not all of the correlations are significant, it is clear that the more schooling a Mexican mother has had, the more she talks and looks, and the less she holds, in response to the three categories of infant behavior at 10 months. (A similar pattern of correlations was found for maternal response to infant motor behaviors [LeVine et al., 1991].) Mothers with more education are also significantly more likely to feed their crying infants.

These results suggest that underlying the pattern seen for the whole sample of Mexican mothers in Table 13.4 are two divergent, schooling-related patterns of maternal responsiveness at 10 months of age – one in which looking and talking, or carrying on conversational exchanges, has become an important part of maternal care (as in the Boston

Table 13.4 *Mean proportion of maternal behaviors in response to 10-month-old infant behaviors in the cuernavaca sample*

	Infant behavior					
	Vocalize		Look		Cry	
Maternal behavior	M	SD	M	SD	M	SD
Look	.46	.21	.59	.21	.60	.33
Talk	.19	.12	.27	.15	.31	.27
Hold	.12	.15	.14	.15	.21	.25
Physical	.14	.13	.16	.12	.17	.19
Feed	.02	.03	.06	.06	.04	.08

Note. n = 72.

Table 13.5 *Correlations of maternal schooling with four types of maternal responsiveness to infant behaviors at 10 months of age in the Cuernavaca sample*

	Infant behavior		
Maternal response	Vocalize	Look	Cry
Look	.21*	.22*	.25**
Talk	.29***	.28**	.18
Hold	−.15	−.28**	−.14
Feed	.09	−.15	.26**

Note. n = 72.
*p <.10. **p <.05. ***p <.01.

sample), and another one in which holding the infant is the predominant mode of responding to infant behaviors (as in the Gusii sample). Father's schooling has no effect on any of the maternal responsiveness variables, and birth order affects only a few (it is mainly negatively related to maternal responsiveness to crying).

We examined this finding across the three age points (5, 10, and 15 months), using simple regression to predict the logistically transformed probability of each maternal responsiveness variable with mother's schooling. With the obtained models, we then calculated "fitted logits" by substituting in two different levels of maternal education: 2 years and 9 years. The results of these calculations are shown in Figure 13.1. The steepness of the slope of the line connecting the predicted values indicates the strength of the relationship with maternal schooling at a particular age point. The relative height of the line reflects the probability of the behavior (lines that are higher reflect more probable behaviors).

At 5 months, when babies are being held much of the time, there is little difference in holding between the mothers with 2 years and those with 9 years of schooling. By 10 months, however, when the frequency of holding has dropped for the sample as a whole, the average level is much lower for mothers with 9 years of schooling. Mothers' verbal and visual responsiveness to three infant behaviors tends to show the opposite trend, although verbal response to infant vocalization is higher for the more educated mothers at all age points. By the time their infants are 10-months-old, the mothers with 9 years of education were more responsive verbally and visually. The 15-month data indicate that this general trend increases further for the older infants, indicating a greater trend toward conversational interaction among the more educated mothers with their infants. On the whole, the correlational analysis of the Mexican observations at 10 months (Table 13.5) and the regression analyses at 5 and 15 months as well as at 10 months (Figure 13.1) provide evidence supporting Hypothesis 2, that maternal responsiveness within a culturally similar population is affected by the mother's level of school attainment.

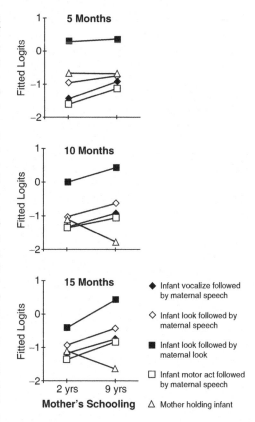

Figure 13.1 *Fitted logits, calculated from a regression analysis of mother's education on five types of maternal responsiveness at 5, 10, and 15 months.*

General Discussion

These two studies indicate that cultural and educational variations affect maternal responsiveness in specific ways, confirming and amplifying the two hypotheses formulated at the beginning of the article. The Gusii–Boston comparison showed that two groups of mothers differing by conventions of conversational interaction and norms of mother–infant interaction are both responsive to their infants, though differently. The Gusii are physically responsive, particularly to crying rather than nondistress vocalization; the Boston mothers are predominantly verbally and visually responsive, about equally to babbling and crying. These cultural differences are evident at 3–4 months but more pronounced at 9–10 months, partly because of the greater physical distance that Boston mothers put between themselves and their babies at the later age, when Gusii mothers retain the earlier pattern of close proximity and tactile contact. The increasing cultural divergence may also reflect the mutual establishment of a communicative pattern between infant and mother as the infant's capacities for social and communicative response continue to grow. We have interpreted this cultural difference in maternal style of responsiveness in terms of the Gusii mothers' goal of soothing and minimizing infant arousal, in contrast to the Boston mothers' goal of visual and vocal engagement, stimulation, and positive emotional arousal. Furthermore, the gaze aversion of Gusii mothers in the videotaped face-to-face situation when their babies were becoming positively excited was one of the distinctive findings of the microanalysis by Dixon et al. (1981). In short, the Gusii mothers, by comparison with the Boston sample, show a pattern of responsiveness that is strikingly designed to reduce distress and maintain calm in the infant during the 1st year of life.

These group differences in behavior reflect divergent cultural scripts for mother – infant interaction, one of which promotes conversational exchange as understood in the West, the other of which promotes a distinctly different model of maternal responsiveness that seems to be consistent with nonpathological development. This divergence can be explained in various ways, but no definitive explanation is possible in the context of a two-culture comparison with small samples.

It is possible to claim, however, that the fairly extreme deviation of Gusii mothers from the norms of maternal responsiveness prevalent in middle-class America raises fundamental questions about what is normal and pathogenic in responsiveness to infants. We see no indication in this evidence that one group of mothers is more responsive than the other, only that they are responsive in different ways to their infants' signals. The rarity among the Gusii of the kind of communicative engagement that has been held to be universally required for the healthy psychological development of human infants (Trevarthen, 1989)

underscores the necessity of conceptualizing the universal needs of infants in terms more open to cultural variation. These findings suggest that the Gusii and Boston infants begin participating during the first few months of life in conventionally organized patterns of communicative interaction, of which maternal responsiveness is a central part, and that these patterns provide an entry into the culture-specific systems of meaning that constitute the environment for their subsequent psychological development (Bruner, 1990). How the nonverbal communication and tactile responsiveness of Gusii mothers, and their greater responsiveness to the crying than to the babbling of their infants, affects the latter's psychological development, is a matter of speculation at this point but constitutes a challenge for future research.

The Mexican study was designed to test Hypothesis 2 by examining educational differentials in maternal responsiveness without concomitant variations in social stratification. The low-income neighborhoods of Cuernavaca, where female school attendance is relatively recent and where wide-ranging individual differences in school attainment occur among women of the same street, socioeconomic status, and culture, were well suited to this purpose. The correlations of maternal school attendance, which ranged from 1 to 9 years, with verbal and visual responsiveness to infants were strikingly and surprisingly similar to relationships found in the United States at much higher levels of maternal education. The relationships in the Mexican sample were found at 5, 10, and 15 months and were largely unrelated to husband's schooling or birth order of the child. Maternal schooling emerges from this study as an important influence on maternal responsiveness during infancy in and of itself, rather than as reflecting the social variables with which it is often associated.

The question of how schooling affects maternal responsiveness cannot be entirely answered on the basis of these Mexican findings. Nevertheless, the relationship of a mother's schooling to her verbal responsiveness strongly suggests that the school experience provides women with verbal skills and models of adult–child verbal instruction that they would not acquire without schooling and that are carried forward into the way they care for their infants as parents (LeVine et al., 1991). Thus schooling inadvertently constitutes socialization for a particular kind of mothering involving early reciprocal vocalization, that engages mother and infant in a long-term relationship based on verbal communication.

It should be noted that the findings from both studies involved a contrast between verbal and nonverbal forms of maternal responsiveness, partly because of the gross behavioral categories used and perhaps also because educational levels varied between the Gusii and Boston samples as well as within the Mexican sample. The determinants and consequences of verbal interaction during infancy remain promising topics for investigation, but an even greater challenge is presented by the description and analysis of nonverbal forms of maternal responsiveness.

REFERENCES

Ainsworth, M. D. S., Blehar, M. C., Waters, E., & Wall, S.
(1978) *Patterns of attachment.* Hillsdale, NJ: Erlbaum.

Bornstein, M. H. (Ed.)
(1989) *Maternal responsiveness: Characteristics and consequences. New Directions for Child Development, No. 43.* San Francisco: Jossey-Bass.

Bornstein, M. H., Tamis-LeMonda, C. S., Pecheux, M., & Rahn, C. W.
(1991) Mother and infant activity and interaction in France and the United States: A comparative study. *International Journal of Behavioral Development, 14*(1), 21–43.

Bruner, J.
(1990) *Acts of meaning.* Cambridge, MA: Harvard University Press.

Clarke-Stewart, K. A.
(1973) Interactions between mothers and their young children: Characteristics and consequences. *Monographs of the Society for Research in Child Development, 38*(6–7, Serial No. 153).

Cohen, E. S., & Beckwith, L.
(1976) Maternal language in infancy. *Developmental Psychology, 12,* 371–372.

Crockenberg, S.
(1983) Early mother and infant antecedents of Bayley Scale performance at 21 months. *Developmental Psychology, 19,* 727–730.

Dixon, S. D., LeVine, R. A., Richman, A. L., & Brazelton, T. B.
(1984) Mother–child interaction around a teaching task: An African-American comparison. *Child Development, 55,* 1252–1264.

Dixon, S. D., Tronick, E. Z., Keefer, C., & Brazelton, T. B.
(1981) Mother–infant interaction among the Gusii of Kenya. In T.M. Field, A. M. Sostek, P. Vietze, & P. H. Leiderman (Eds.), *Culture and early interactions* (pp. 149–170). Hillsdale, NJ: Erlbaum.

Feiring, C., & Lewis, M.
(1981) Middle class differences in the mother-child interaction and the child's cognitive development. In T. M. Field, A. M. Sostek, P. Vietze, & P. H. Leiderman (Eds.), *Culture and early interactions* (pp. 63–94). Hillsdale, NJ: Erlbaum.

Field, T. M., Sostek, A. M., Vietze, P., & Leiderman, P. H.
(1981) *Culture and early interactions.* Hillsdale, NJ: Erlbaum.

Field, T. M., & Widmayer, S. M.
(1981) Mother-infant interaction among lower SES Black, Cuban, Puerto Rican and South American immigrants. In T. M. Field, A. M. Sostek, P. Vietze, & P. H. Leiderman (Eds.), *Culture and early interactions* (pp. 41–62). Hillsdale, NJ: Erlbaum.

Keefer, C. H., Tronick, E. Z., Dixon, S., & Brazelton, T. B.
(1982) Specific differences in motor performance between Gusii and American newborns and a modification of the Neonatal Behavioral Assessment Scale. *Child Development, 53,* 754–759.

Konner, M.
(1977) Infancy among the Kalahari Desert San. In P. H. Leiderman, S. R. Tulkin, & A. Rosenfeld (Eds.), *Culture and infancy: Variations in the human experience* (pp. 287–328). San Diego, CA: Academic Press.

Laosa, L. M.
(1980) Maternal teaching strategies in Chicano and Anglo-American families: The influence of culture and education on maternal behavior. *Child Development, 51,* 759–765.

Laosa, L. M.
(1982) School, occupation, culture and the family: The impact of parental schooling on the parent–child relationship. *Journal of Educational Psychology, 74*, 791–827.

Leiderman, P. H., Tulkin, S. R., & Rosenfeld, A.
(1977) *Culture and infancy: Variations in the human experience.* San Diego, CA: Academic Press.

LeVine, R. A., Dixon, S., LeVine, S. E., Richman, A., Leiderman, P. H., & Brazelton, T. B.
(in press-a) *Omwana: Infants and parents in a Kenya community.* New York: Cambridge University Press.

LeVine, R. A., & LeVine, B.
(1966) *Nyansango: A Gusii community in Kenya.* New York: Wiley.

LeVine, R. A., LeVine, S. E., Richman, A., Tapia, F. M. U., Correa, C. S., & Miller, P. M.
(1991) Women's schooling and child care in the demographic transition: A Mexican case study. *Population and Development Review, 17*, 459–496.

LeVine, R. A., LeVine, S. E., Richman, A., Tapia Uribe, F. M., & Sunderland Correa, C.
(in press-b) Schooling and survival: The impact of women's education on health and reproduction in the third world. In L. Chen, A. Kleinman, J. C. Caldwell, & N. Ware (Eds.), *Health and social change.* New York: Oxford University Press.

LeVine, R. A., Miller, P. M., & West, M. M. (Eds.)
(1988) *Parental behavior in diverse societies. New Directions for Child Development, No. 40.* San Francisco: Jossey-Bass.

Martin, J. A.
(1981) A longitudinal study of the consequences of early mother – infant interaction: A microanalytic approach. *Monographs of the Society for Research in Child Development, 46*(3, Serial No. 190).

Ochs, E., & Schieffelin, B. B.
(1984) Language acquisition and socialization: Three developmental stories and their implications. In R. Shweder & R. A. LeVine (Eds.), *Culture theory* (pp. 276–322). New York: Cambridge University Press.

Richman, A. L.
(1983) *Learning about communication: Cultural influences on caretaker – infant interaction.* Unpublished doctoral dissertation, Harvard University.

Richman, A. L., LeVine, R. A., New, R. S., Howrigan, G. A., Welles-Nystrom, B., & LeVine, S.
(1988) Maternal behavior to infants in five cultures. In R. A. LeVine, P. M. Miller, & M. M. West (Eds.), *Parental behavior in diverse societies* (pp. 81–98). San Francisco: Jossey-Bass.

Schieffelin, B. B., & Ochs, E.
(1986) Language socialization. *Annual Review of Anthropology, 15*, 163–191.

Trevarthen, C.
(1989) Universal co-operative motives: How infants begin to know the language and culture of their parents. In G. Jahoda & I. M. Lewis (Eds.), *Acquiring culture* (pp. 37–91). London: Croom Helm.

Tulkin, S. R., & Kagan, J.
(1972) Mother-child interaction in the first year of life. *Child Development, 43*, 31–41.

14

Self-Construction through Narrative Practices: A Chinese and American Comparison of Early Socialization

Peggy J. Miller, Heidi Fung, and Judith Mintz

In recent years discourse-level language has emerged as an important locus of inquiry into a number of problems central to psychological anthropology (e.g., Lutz 1985; Shweder and Much 1987; White 1992). Prominent among them is the cultural constitution of self and personhood. In developmental psychology a similar trend is apparent, particularly with respect to processes of self-construction in early childhood (e.g., Bruner 1986, 1990; Miller, Mintz et al. 1992; Nelson 1989; Snow 1990). Thus the shift from a representational view of language to a broader discourse view is evident in the two subdisciplines that intersect in the problem of how children construct culture-specific selves. Instead of treating lexical items or utterance-level propositions as semantic encodings of self-referential categories, researchers have begun to examine how self-expressive talk is constructed with and responsive to others. In this view, language is not merely a methodological tool for revealing the categorical self: it is the means by which selves are created and transformed through the dual capacity of language to be both reflective of and embedded in interpersonal experience.

In this article we explore the process by which young children, in coordination with other social actors, reconstruct their personal experiences. Focusing on Chinese and American two-year-olds, we locate self construction within a discourse practices theory of childhood socialization. This framework derives from several powerful theoretical currents – Vygotsky's (1987[1934]) sociohistorical theory (Wertsch 1985, 1991), practice and performance approaches to language in linguistic anthropology and language socialization (e.g., Bauman and Briggs 1990; Duranti and Goodwin 1992; Ochs 1988; Schieffelin 1990), and Bourdieu's (1977, 1990) practice theory of social life – that have revitalized thinking about socialization. Taken together, these theories converge on a view of language as socially situated practices that are organized beyond the sentence level into genres, dialogues, and multichanneled performances. They share the premise that meaning is constituted through discursive practices, with the implication that an adequate model of socialization must incorporate talk in a principled way.

As applied to the problem of socialization in early childhood, a discourse practices model takes as its central task the identification of the communicative activities that occur routinely in the course of everyday life, mediating relations

Peggy J. Miller, Heidi Fung, and Judith Mintz, Self-Construction Through Narrative Practices: A Chinese and American Comparison of Early Socialization from *Ethos*, Vol. 24, No. 2 (June, 1996), pp. 237–280. © 1996 American Anthropological Association. Reprinted with permission of the American Anthropological Association.

between children and their caregivers and companions.[1] It posits that the social and psychological consequences of children's routine participation in these practices will depend on how messages are packaged in discourse. When messages are packaged in self-relevant ways, the consequences for the child include not only the acquisition of discursive skills but the creation of self or identity.

Although there are many types of everyday family discourse that have socializing implications for the self, we chose to study stories of personal experience – stories that people tell in ordinary conversation in which they relate past experiences from their own lives. Personal storytelling provides a fruitful focus for comparative analysis because it is widely practiced yet variably constituted in cultures around the world (Miller and Moore 1989). Moreover, several sources of narrative-self affinity – temporal, causal, evaluative, and conversational – converge in this narrative genre, providing a rationale for treating personal storytelling as an important locus for self-construction (Miller 1994; Miller, Potts et al. 1990). In addition, because it is now well established that children from a variety of cultural backgrounds are able to recount past experiences in conversation by two to two-and-a-half years of age (e.g., Eisenberg 1985; Heath 1983; Miller, Potts et al. 1990; Miller and Sperry 1988; Sperry 1991), personal storytelling affords the opportunity to study the beginnings of self-construction.

In this article we compare personal storytelling as practiced by Chinese families in Taipei and American families in Chicago. Our goal is to gain insight into the actual process of self-construction by examining how young children's past experiences are narrated in the two cultures. We ask how personal storytelling is practiced in the everyday settings that young children inhabit, what kinds of participant roles children and caregivers assume, which of the child's personal experiences are treated as reportable, and what kinds of interpretive frameworks are instantiated in narrations of young children's experiences.

A second goal is to demonstrate the usefulness of a discourse practices model for comparative inquiry into socialization and self-construction. There is strong consensus on the need to move beyond dichotomizing comparisons of psychological functioning in Western and non-Western cultures (e.g., Howard 1985; Kleinman and Kleinman 1989; Spiro 1993), and concrete proposals have been offered for achieving more adequate comparisons (e.g., Corsaro and Miller 1992; Gaskins 1994; Lucy 1992; Markus and Kitayama 1991; Shweder and Sullivan 1993; White 1992; Wierzbicka 1993). Thus, finding effective ways to represent the intricate patterning of similarities and differences among cultures – without subduing the complexity of particular meaning in each – poses a challenge of major importance.

A discourse practices perspective, as we envision it, has several key implications for how this challenge can be met. The first is that comparative study must be grounded in rigorous description of discourse practices, with their inherent systematicity and variability. A second implication is that there is a great deal more to stories (and other cultural "texts") than disembodied texts, and that cultural principles are expressed not just in the content of stories but in the way that narrative discourse is organized internally and in relation to larger events and sequences of talk. The unit of analysis is thus the entire event of narration rather than the isolated story. Still another implication is that any given practice carries with it multiple interpretive frameworks that coexist in complex relationship with one another. And, finally, a discourse practices approach acknowledges the individual variation within cultural groups and thus requires that the idiosyncratic and personal be taken into account (Miller and Mintz 1993).

The article is organized as follows. We begin with an introduction to the study and to the worlds in which the children live, and then describe how personal storytelling is made available to young children in the two cultural cases. In the second part we focus more directly on self-construction, situating our analysis within Lutz and White's (1986) comparative framework for studying emotional lives in cultural context. We show how two of the problems of social relationship they propose get played out similarly in some ways, differently in other ways, in Chinese and American narrations of personal experience. The most striking contrast between the two cases concerns how a child's violations of cultural codes are treated narratively.

Studying Personal Storytelling in Taipei and Chicago

The comparison reported here is part of a larger comparative project designed to investigate how personal storytelling is used to socialize young children within the family context (Miller, in press; Miller, Mintz et al. 1992). The Chinese study was done in Taipei, Taiwan; the American study in "Longwood," a middle-class European American community in Chicago. In keeping with standard research practice in the field of language socialization, we combined ethnographic fieldwork with extensive audio and video recording of naturally occurring talk. Each researcher spent at least two years in the field and collected both cross-sectional and longitudinal data, encompassing the period from two-and-a-half to five years of age.

The second author, a native speaker of Mandarin Chinese who was born and raised in Taipei, worked with the Chinese families. The third author, who grew up in middle-class European American communities in the United States, worked with the American families. We chose to assign researchers to cultures about which they had native intuitions, thereby enabling them to draw on their cultural expertise in custom-designing their interactions with children and their families. We also adopted the following general guideline: try to participate as a friend who has stopped by for a casual visit; at the same time, don't "push" narrative talk. Within these parameters, the ethnographers were left to their own ingenuity in negotiating a role with the families.

As it turned out, the two ethnographers negotiated roles that contrasted in an important way. The American researcher came to be treated as a family friend who was addressed by her first name. The Chinese researcher was granted fictive kin status; children were encouraged to call her "Auntie." She was introduced to the families' relatives and was frequently invited to family events, such as dinners or picnics. In parallel with these contrasting roles, the ethnographers participated differently in the families' narrative practices, as we shall see below (see also Miller, in press).

In this article we single out for scrutiny that moment in development when children have just begun to enter into the narrative life of their culture. Our corpus for the two-and-a-half-year-olds consists of four hours of recorded observations for each of nine children in each cultural group, for a total sample per group of 36 hours of home observation. The descriptions of the families and of personal storytelling as a routine practice, presented in the next two sections, are based on the full sample plus extensive field notes. Later in the article we examine more intensively the naturally occurring narrations produced by three families from each cultural group, with the aim of extracting the interpretive frameworks instantiated in personal storytelling. This analysis is based on verbatim transcriptions of more than 40 narrations per group (see Miller, Mintz et al. 1992 for description of procedures for transcribing speech and identifying co-narrations).

Both the Chinese and the American youngsters whom we studied came from two-parent families who lived in large cities, owned their own homes, and were economically secure. All but a few of the parents were college educated. Despite these similarities, the children were growing up in very different worlds.

Taipei

Taipei, the largest city in Taiwan, Republic of China, has undergone enormous change in the second half of this century, beginning with the imposition of Kuomintang (KMT) rule at the end of World War II and the transfer of the KMT government from mainland China to Taipei in 1949. When the Chinese nationalists arrived on the island, Taiwan was a rural society with a capital city of 200,000 inhabitants (Chang 1987). The second author's parents remember watching water buffalo graze in the fields outside their house in Taipei. Today more than 2.5 million people live in a city that has quadrupled in area (Taipei Municipal Government 1988). In what has come to be known as the "economic miracle," an agrarian economy was transformed into an industrialized economy in a matter of decades. By 1990 Taiwan had become a consumer society, with an average per capita income exceeding U.S.$8,000, a low rate of unemployment, a relatively equitable distribution of income, and a trade surplus envied by other nations (Simon and Kau 1992).

In parallel with economic development, social change has been rapid as well. Forty percent of the nation's workforce are high school graduates, the literacy rate exceeds that of the United States, and women are entering the workforce in record numbers (Cohen 1988). Inevitably, development has exacted its costs: severe noise and air pollution, nonstop traffic jams, and rising rates of violent crime (Simon and Kau 1992).

In comparison with the economic and social spheres, political life in Taiwan has been slow to change. Significant reforms have occurred in the last several years, however, marking a transition from the one-party dictatorship established by the KMT to a more democratic form of government (Simon and Kau 1992; Tien 1989). Martial law, in effect for 40 years, was lifted in 1987, and opposition parties have been legalized. The first presidential election was held in March 1996.

The families in our study are members of the first "middle-class" generation in Taiwan. Most of the parents were college educated, and the majority of fathers worked in white-collar jobs (e.g., physician, businessman, architect, engineer). Two of the parents received graduate degrees or job training in the West, and several had a close relative who was currently residing in the United States or Canada. All of the parents were born in Taiwan and had two children.

In counterpoint to these similarities, our sample also reflects the ethnic, linguistic, and religious diversity characteristic of contemporary Taipei. The sample included children whose grandparents were native-born Taiwanese as well as those whose grandparents came to Taiwan from mainland China after the Communist revolution. Indeed, several of the families were "mixed" in that one parent was a second-generation mainlander and one was Taiwanese. Although half of the parents spoke fluent Taiwanese, all used Mandarin Chinese,

the country's official language, with their children. Many parents in Taipei want their children to learn Mandarin early so that they will not be at a disadvantage in school (Farris 1988). The situation with respect to religious affiliation was especially complex. Folk religion provided a common thread that wove through the families in complex and subtle ways.[2] At the same time a variety of other religious traditions were represented both within and across families. For example, in one case the parents worshipped at folk temples, but the primary caregiver was a devout Protestant. In another family the grandmother worshipped daily at a Protestant church yet remained strongly committed to folk religious beliefs.

In contrast to Chicago, Taipei is not organized into distinct neighborhoods. There is little residential segregation by class and ethnicity; an engineer and a fruit vendor or a physician and a gas station attendant might live in the same apartment building. Geographical proximity seemed to play little part in the formation of social networks. Instead, the family and other social institutions, such as church or school, took precedence. In keeping with this pattern, families were recruited for the study through contacts provided by the second author's own family and friends and through the cooperation of a kindergarten. In the latter case, endorsement of the study by the school authorities was not sufficient to persuade families to participate; first-hand contact with the researcher was also necessary.

Owing to continuing migration from outlying areas, space is at a premium in Taipei. Nearly everyone lives in apartments, and housing accounts for the largest chunk of the family budget. The families in our study occupied living spaces that were remarkably similar in size and floor plan: about 1,200 square feet, divided into a living room, a dining area, a small kitchen, three bedrooms, and one or two bathrooms. Most households consisted of the immediate family: mother, father, and two children. This pattern departed from the traditional three-generation household, in which the married couple moved in with the husband's family and the grandmother, mother, and other female relatives shared domestic and child-care responsibilities.

Today, as an increasing number of women remain in the work force after their children are born, child-care support is needed more than ever, yet many young couples prefer to establish their own two-generation households. Our sample was divided between mothers who were full-time housewives and those who worked outside the home as teachers or clerks. For the latter, child-care arrangements varied widely. In one family the maternal grandmother lived in the household and took care of the children during the week. In another family the children lived with the maternal aunt and her teenage children while the parents worked, visiting their parents only on the weekend. Two families sent their children to a group day-care center from one year of age. The majority of families, however, entrusted their children to the care of the mother or an older female relative.

The early years of life were spent in close physical and emotional proximity to this caregiver, who supervised and nurtured the child. Even though there was extra space in the apartment and an individual bed for the child in a room shared with an older sibling, the caregiver slept with the young child. Except for excursions to the grocery store, visits with relatives in another part of the city, or trips to school to pick up an older sibling, two-year-olds stayed at home. Their days were punctuated by meals and by a long nap in the early afternoon. Within the constraints of their housekeeping responsibilities, caregivers found time to talk to their youngsters, pretend with them, help with puzzles, play board or card games, and otherwise focus attention on them, one or two at a time. When mothers were busy, youngsters played alone or with a sibling or watched television. The children had a modest number of play-things – stuffed animals, blocks, matchbox cars, cookware sets – that filled a shelf or two in a closet or fit neatly into a toy box.

Children saw their fathers in the evenings and on the weekends. After the family dinner, fathers might play or watch TV with the two-year-old, teach her some simple Chinese characters, or read classical poems to her. Bedtime for adults and children alike was 10:00–11:00 p.m. Weekends were a time for family activities such as picnics, going to the flower market or book exhibition, and visiting or dining out with grandparents and other relatives.

The children's social life thus revolved around the immediate and extended family. Apart from siblings or cousins, preschoolers had little experience with peers. Since families lived in apartment buildings in which neighbors were unacquainted, the children were restricted to their own apartment. Only those who attended day care had regular contact with non-kin of their own age.

Caregivers held high standards for their children's conduct. Two-year-olds were expected to successfully negotiate a home environment that was not child-proofed, offering the temptations of open cabinets and fragile objects. They were expected to listen attentively to their elders, comprehend what was said, and behave accordingly. Misdeeds were dealt with promptly, and rules of conduct were rehearsed. Caregivers also corrected grammar and mispronunciations and rehearsed rhymes and poems. They made sure that two-year-olds knew their full name, parents' names, address, and phone number. Literacy skills were actively cultivated. Parents read to the children and taught them to draw, and some used flash cards to teach Chinese characters or numbers. All of the children were toilet trained by 18 months, and several of the mothers reported that they had begun toilet training at 6 months. When the first author visited the families and gave each child a wrapped present decorated with small candies, she was astonished at their self-control. In keeping with proper etiquette, even the two-year-olds waited until the guests departed to open their gifts.

Longwood

The other children in our study lived halfway around the globe from their Chinese counterparts, in a predominantly Irish-Catholic neighborhood in Chicago. Longwood has been a home to Irish Americans for nearly a century, and many of its residents have deep roots in the community. Holidays such as St. Patrick's Day are observed with great enthusiasm and include an annual neighborhood parade. The neighborhood is known locally for the beauty of its streets and homes, several of which are on the national historic registry. Civic organizations have worked actively to preserve the special character and small-town ambience of the neighborhood. Many express disdain for a newly established shopping mall and feel that it is important to resist the homogenization they see in nearby suburbs. At the same time, Longwood has responded to demographic changes in the city, especially the expansion of an adjacent African American neighborhood. The community made a determined effort in the 1970s not to join the flow of "white flight" from the city and to work toward increasing ethnic integration. Although most families continue to praise the neighborhood and take tremendous pride in the continuity of their community, several have recently expressed doubts about its ability to sustain itself in the face of continuing diversification.

Most of the parents in the study had college or professional degrees from local universities or community colleges. Fathers' occupations varied: some were lawyers, several owned their own businesses, others worked for the city as policemen or firemen or held jobs in advertising or sales. In contrast to the Chinese families, none of the mothers worked full-time outside the home, but many had worked as social workers, clerks, or teachers prior to having children. A number of mothers participated in "babysitting coops," which allowed them to share child care, and some offered day care in their homes for other families in the community. Most of the families had three or four children; none had fewer than two. Many of the parents were natives of Longwood and had parents or siblings living nearby. Parents typically had at least five siblings, and it was not uncommon to meet those who had eight or nine.

Families were recruited for the project by word of mouth. The initial contact was made through the intervention of a friend who had grown up in Longwood. He introduced the researcher to a relative who referred her to friends and neighbors who had children in the desired age range. Recruitment was facilitated by the fact that Longwood's status as a community is based on much more than regional proximity or neighborhood boundaries. Many residents participate in a cohesive social network based on a common cultural heritage and active involvement in one of the three local Catholic churches. Most send their children to the local Catholic school that they themselves attended. Thus the Longwood families were tied by cultural tradition, religion, family history, and active commitment to a community that had a distinct identity within the larger urban environment. Unlike Taipei, where the extended family seemed to be the most vital unit of social organization beyond the immediate family, in Longwood the community and the extended family interlocked to form a level of organization that brought young children into extensive contact with both kin and non-kin.

The families in our sample lived in large, single-family homes located on quiet, exclusively residential, tree-lined streets. Built before World War II, the typical house had two stories, four bedrooms, a recreation room in the basement, and an expansive backyard. Houses in Longwood are almost never placed on the real estate market, being sold instead by word of mouth. Yards are manicured and well kept. A concerted effort is made to keep streets safe and clean to a degree that is unusual in urban environments in the United States. One community member explained that "keeping up the neighborhood" was an implicit expectation among Longwood inhabitants; if a new resident did not maintain his lawn to expected standards, neighbors would "drop by to see if everything was alright" and to offer their "help." Children are often seen riding bikes or tricycles on the sidewalks or playing out on the front lawn.

The interiors of the homes reflected an emphasis on family life. Virtually all the homes in our sample contained playrooms filled with toys. Basement family rooms also contained numerous items to encourage children's play and activities. In addition to rooms and objects that were specifically intended for children, the children generally had access to other parts of the house. The designation of specific portions of a home as children's or family space was not meant to restrict children. Instead, it served to index the high priority that families placed on attending to their young. In short, family and community life was very child centered and quite consciously designed to provide an "optimal" environment for children's perceived needs. At the same time, each member of the family, including the youngest, was provided with his or her own space and property. Children either had their own bedrooms, or two same-sex siblings shared a bedroom in which each had his or her own bed.

Most of the families in our sample expressed the belief that very young children should be cared for routinely by their own mothers. Several mothers also stated that they chose to stay home with their preschool children because they did not want to miss the opportunity to observe and influence their child's development. Thus very young children spent the majority of their time in the home environment under the supervision of their mothers. While children played with siblings or peers, mothers often attended to household chores, periodically checking on the child and engaging in play or bookreading with her. Children also watched videos or TV. Longwood mothers varied in the degree to which they provided structured activities (e.g., baking, doing a crafts project, having the child help with the laundry), but all allowed their children plenty of time for creative, self-initiated play. Aside from play, Longwood children's days were organized around informal meals, an afternoon nap, and often an outing of some sort (e.g., shopping; watching an older sibling's softball game; a trip to the park, the zoo, or a museum; a visit to a nearby relative's home). By the age of three, several of the children began to spend a few half-days per week at one of the local nursery school programs, two of which were church-affiliated.

Fathers spent time with their children in the evenings and on weekends. Many Longwood fathers also moonlighted as baseball and soccer coaches for local children's teams. Fathers interacted with preschoolers at dinner and afterwards by reading, playing, or watching videos with them. Fathers also helped with bath and bedtime. Most preschoolers were put to bed between 8:00 and 9:00 p.m. In households where there were older children, bedtimes were stratified by age, with older children having the privilege of a later bedtime.

In contrast to the Chinese, young children experienced a world that was heavily populated with other children both inside and outside the home. In addition to siblings and cousins, children made friends with their neighbors on the block. In several homes in Longwood, children ran in and out of each other's houses and yards on a casual and frequent basis. Preplanned play dates also took place. Birthday and other holiday parties were arranged for children, and visits to local parks provided another forum for children to meet and interact. Thus, early in their lives, Longwood children were initiated into a peer-based social life through several types of interactional activities and settings in their community.

Within this highly social environment Longwood youngsters were exposed to a great deal of talk in both multiparty and dyadic configurations. As in the "mainstream" case described by Ochs and Schieffelin (1984), mothers talked directly to their youngsters, accommodating to their perspective and language level by building upon and extending the child's semantic intent. This tendency to accommodate to the child was evident in a variety of other practices as well, including childproofing the environment, use of child-scaled objects and furniture, and abundant provision of toys, as indicated earlier. Talking and listening to children, reading to them, pretending with them, teaching them to play baseball were not just enjoyable experiences but ways in which parents could provide the kind of focused attention that they believed fostered healthy development. Several mothers expressed the view that children need a great deal of adult attention to feel happy and good about themselves. In discussing a popular preschool teacher, they spoke admiringly of her ability to foster the children's self-esteem.

Longwood preschoolers were taught and expected to follow rules of appropriate conduct. When children misbehaved in minor ways – refusing to share with a playmate, quarreling with a sibling, hanging on the dining room curtains – parents intervened promptly and repeatedly if necessary. At the same time, most parents expressed respect for young children's willfulness and appreciated the "clever" ways their youngsters attempted to get what they wanted. When a serious behavior problem occurred, such as hitting or biting another person or an uncontrollable temper tantrum, parents resorted to "time out" procedures or revoked a privilege or treat. For the most part, however, these incidents were not dwelled on by parents, and once settled, were no longer the focus of attention. When misdeeds were discussed, emphasis was placed on the rationale for the rule and on helping the child to understand the reasons why it is important to obey (e.g., if a child hit someone, "That hurts! Say you're sorry!").

In sum, the two groups of children whom we studied from 1988 to 1991 were not "typical" Taiwanese or "typical" Americans and should not be taken as such. They were members of families who occupied a relatively privileged position within their respective societies and created a particular cultural idiom at a particular moment in history. Although Longwood has changed over the past decades, what stands out is the extent to which its identity and continuity with the past have been preserved. Families take pride in their traditional values and family-centered way of life, rooted in long-term prosperity. In Taipei the balance between change and continuity is tipped in the other direction. The Chinese children inhabited a world that differed substantially from those in which their parents and grandparents grew up. We entered their lives at a time when the symptoms of modernization were blindingly obvious. Yet, as we shall see, traditional Chinese values were also visible, sturdy, and intricate in everyday narrative practices.

Personal Storytelling as Routine Practice

The first question we asked about personal storytelling was whether it was routinely available to young children in Taipei and Longwood, and, if so, how their narrative participation was structured. We found that personal storytelling occurred regularly as part of everyday family life in both cases. In addition, Chinese and American two-year-olds were exposed to

personal storytelling in three related ways. Stories about other people's past experiences were told *around* young children as co-present others. Stories of the young child's past experiences were told collaboratively *with* the child as co-narrator. And stories *about* the young child's past experiences were told in the child's presence, with the child assuming the participant role of co-present other or ratified participant.

In the practice of telling stories *around* the child, a family member narrated to another person a past experience from his or her life. The child was neither a protagonist in the story nor an addressee, but he or she was present during the narration and was free to listen or not, to contribute verbally or not. For example, a Chinese mother might tell her friend, a devotee of the stock market, a story about her successful transaction the week before, or an American mother might tell an older child a story about some mishap that occurred when she went on a camping trip. Young children thus had the opportunity to hear the people who were most important to them select reportable experiences from their lives and narrate them in their own words. We have discussed elsewhere the socializing power of this practice and its relevance to the child's understanding of self and other (see Miller and Moore 1989; Miller, Potts et al. 1990). This article is restricted to analysis of the two practices in which the *child's* past experiences were narrated.

In telling stories *with* young children, the child collaborated with one or more family members in jointly constructing stories about his or her own past experiences. The child spoke in the first person, coparticipants in the second person. Some of these co-narrations were initiated by the two-year-olds, others by caregivers or siblings. Co-narrators prompted, directed, edited, and elaborated on the child's contributions. For example, a Chinese child, Didi, co-narrated a story with his mother and older sister about an event in which he cried and made a scene at older sister's music lesson, causing his mother to lose face *(hao mei-you mianzi)*. The following is an excerpt from the beginning of a much longer co-narration.

Example 1

Mother: [Looks at child.] Eh, eh, you that day with Mama, with younger sister [pats sister's back], with older sister went to the music class. Was that fun?

Child: It was fun.

Mother: What didn't the teacher give you?

Child: Didn't, didn't give me a sticker.

Mother: Didn't give you a sticker. Then you, then what did you do?

Child: I then cried.

Sister: Cried loudly, "Waah! Waah! Waah!"

Mother: Oh, you then cried? Yeah, you constantly went: "Waah, didn't [gestures wiping eyes, makes staccato gesture of fists away from body], why didn't you give me a sticker? [whines] Why didn't you give me a sticker? [whines]," didn't you?

[Child looks up from book, gazes at mother, smiles, and looks down at book again.]

Sister: [To mother:] Yes, "Why didn't you give me a sticker?" [claps hand]

Mother: [To child:] Sticker. [sighs] Ai, you made Mama lose face [hao meiyou mianzi]. That, that, I wanted to dig my head into the ground. Right? [smiles, shakes head, smiles again]

[Child points to picture book and says something unintelligible.]

Sister: Almost wanted to faint [hun-dao]. Mommy almost began to faint [hun-dao].

In this example the mother initiated the narration by introducing the topic of the older sister's music lesson. She prompts Didi to recount what happened – that he cried when the teacher did not give him a sticker. (Stickers were rewards for good performance and were distributed only to the students in the music class.) Both mother and older sister elaborate on Didi's contributions to the narration by quoting what he said when denied a sticker and by reenacting his gestures and demeanor.[4] Later in this co-narration Didi and his mother assert conflicting versions of what happened in the past event.

Telling stories *about* young children resembled co-narrated storytelling in that the child

was again cast as a protagonist in the story. However, this practice differed in that the narrator addressed the story to a third party, referring to the child in the third person. For example, Didi's mother later renarrated the story of her son's misconduct, directing it to the researcher as Didi and his sister looked on: "Because at 3, at 4:00 [pause] there was no time, person to take care of him. So that I thought I for the first time might just take him. It turned out to be very very terrible!" In this narrative practice caregivers exercised more extensive control over the story than they did in co-narrations. At the same time, the young child's participant role also differed. Whereas young children were, by definition, verbal participants in co-narrated storytelling, they did not necessarily participate verbally in this narrative practice. They might watch and listen silently; become absorbed in some other activity, apparently tuning out what others said about them; or lend their own voices to the story as ratified participants.

In sum, these findings establish an important similarity between Longwood and Taipei, namely that two-year-olds had ready and varied access to personal storytelling on an everyday basis. In both Chinese and American families children were growing up amid a complex and shifting web of personal storytelling practices. These practices mediated relations between the child and significant others and defined and redefined the child's past experiences in terms of specific interpretive frameworks.

Interpretive Frameworks for Narrating Personal Experience

In their influential review of anthropological research on emotion, Lutz and White (1986) argue that a comparative framework for studying emotional lives in cultural contexts should begin not with biopsychological criteria but with problems of social relationship or existential meaning that cultures often present in emotional terms. They offer a partial list of such problems as "initial comparative reference points" (1986:428) that would shift comparative inquiry away from questions of decontexualized experience to questions about how people make sense of life events. We have found two of the problems that they propose especially useful as points of departure in identifying the interpretive frameworks instantiated in Chinese and American narrations of children's experiences. The first is what they call the "positive" problem of rewarding bonds with others. The second is ego's violation of cultural codes. In the next two sections we address each of these in turn, examining events of personal storytelling that arose within the flow of family interaction.

Narrated selves as relational selves

As applied to personal storytelling, the problem of rewarding bonds with others invites us to ask whether the past experiences of two-year-olds were rendered as interpersonal events. Note that it is possible to construct a perfectly intelligible and well-formed narration in which the child protagonist acts alone. This seldom happened, however, in either cultural case. The past experiences of both the Chinese and the American children were routinely narrated as interpersonal experiences. This was evident at two levels of analysis: the level of the narrated event and the level of the event of narration (see Miller 1994; Miller, Mintz et al. 1992 for further discussion of these analytic levels).

The Narrated Event. The narrated event refers to the child's past experience as it is re-created in the here and now. In the majority of narrations, child and family members constructed a rendition of the past experience in which the child protagonist was situated in a social nexus. The stories described above concerning Didi's experience at his older sister's music lesson provide good illustrations: Didi's transgression occurred in response to the teacher's action, and it caused his mother to lose face. In the following example from the American corpus, the participants co-construct an account in which some friends gave presents to Athena and her sister. Immediately prior to this co-narration, Athena's mother had been describing a present that she planned to give to a friend.

Example 2
Child: Did they give us a present?
Mother: Yes, they did give us a present for Christmas, that's right. What did they give you, Athena? Do you remember what Martha and Ken gave you guys for Christmas? Think about it, can you recall?
   Sister: We forgot.
Mother: You can't remember the art set with all the paints and crayons and markers? And she gave a little puzzle to Athena with all the stars and the little crescent moons? Remember that puzzle?
Child: It goes up the sky [points and looks upward]. Up, up, up.
Mother: What goes up in the sky?
Child: Moon.
Mother: Right, yes, you are right.
Child: Up in the, in the home, up in the home.

Further analysis of the narrations revealed that the participants, including the two-year-olds, linked self and other in specific ways in their narrative re-creations. They portrayed the child protagonist as simply sharing an activity or experience with another person (e.g., the child went to the zoo with a friend), as the recipient of help or benefit from another person (as in the example above), and they compared the child protagonist with others (e.g., the child was not afraid to go on the ride but his older brother was). These were the most frequent ways of linking self and other for both the Chinese and the American children.

A fourth way of linking self and other yielded an intriguing developmental pattern in relation to comparable data from five-year-olds in the two communities. This linkage, which we call "self apart from other," is similar to the dimension that Markus and Kitayama (1991) have called the "independent" self. The child explicitly said that he was not with another person, did not share an activity or experience with another person, or did some activity all by himself. In setting himself or herself apart, the child typically mentioned another person (e.g., Aunt wasn't holding my hand, Father let me drive the car by myself) and, in so doing, invoked a relational frame of reference while at the same time portraying the self as independent. Neither the Chinese nor the American two-year-olds linked self and other in this way; for five-year-olds, however, this linkage was made more frequently by the American children than by the Chinese children. If verified in subsequent analyses, these findings would suggest that a relational framework for interpreting personal experience emerges very early in narrative development for both the Chinese and the American children and that setting the self apart from others is a later elaboration of that framework for the American children. These findings leave open the questions of how relational interpretive frameworks get elaborated for the Chinese children and of how Chinese children come to differentiate themselves from others when narrating their past experiences.

The Event of Narration. So far we have described relatedness at the level of the narrated event. The child portrayed himself or herself as "being with" another person in some past event. But at the same time the child was "being with" another person in the present, that is, in the very act of narrating the past event. In other words, the event of narration was itself an interpersonal event, involving at least two persons. Moreover, we found that these levels of relatedness were connected. Children were more likely to compare the self-protagonist to another child in the past event when a peer was present in the event of co-narration (Miller, Mintz et al. 1992; Mintz 1993). In addition, children sometimes altered their version of a past experience in response to what co-narrators said. These findings suggest that two-year-old narrators were responsive to the particulars of the interpersonal event in which the story was told and expose the emergent nature of their constructions of their own past experiences. They show that interpretations of the child's past experiences arose as by-products of the social process of coordinating and negotiating narrative accounts. A child's interpretation of a past event and of herself as protagonist in that event was subject to repeated alteration and revision in

the here-and-now social activity of narrating and renarrating experience.

Another way in which self and other were related at the level of the event of narration was in terms of the distribution of storytelling rights. When caregivers collaborated *with* the child in relating the child's experience or told a story *about* the child in the child's presence, they were constructing stories that, strictly speaking, were stories of vicarious experience. These practices raise the Bakhtinian (1981) question: Whose story is it, the child's or the caregiver's? They suggest that while young children were granted rights as speaker, they were not granted full rights to author their own experience (Goffman 1981). The disparity in storytelling rights was especially wide in the practice of telling stories about the child in the child's presence. When caregivers and older siblings engaged in this practice they did more than direct or edit the child's contributions. They exercised their right as parent or older sibling to appropriate the young child's experience and to fashion a more unilateral, less negotiated narrative. In the process, they not only furnished the child with personalized models of how to organize and interpret particular past experiences, but indexed the asymmetrical power relations between caregiver and child.

In sum, these analyses suggest that the past experiences of two-year-olds, whether Chinese or American, were anchored to an interpersonal matrix through the construction of a continuing series of miniature interpersonal dramas. Although autobiographical, these dramatizations of the child's personal experiences were not created by the child alone; instead they were joint productions in which older family members often exercised more authority than the child in constructing relational interpretations of the child's past experiences.

Ego's violation of cultural codes

We turn now to the second problem from Lutz and White's comparative scheme, namely, ego's violation of cultural codes. Whereas an interpretive framework of relatedness of self and other was evident in the narrative constructions of two-year-olds from the two cultures, this second problem more strongly differentiated the narrative practices in which Chinese and American youngsters participated. The child as transgressor figured more prominently in Chinese than in American constructions of children's experience, and this finding applied to both co-narrated storytelling and to telling stories about the child in the child's presence.

Telling Stories with the Child. We were initially alerted to this contrast by Fung's (1987) analysis of the co-narrations of two Chinese children and their mothers. In these co-narrations moral and social rules were repeatedly invoked and the child was explicitly cast as a transgressor. Not only did the mothers guide their three-year-olds toward rule-centered accounts of experience, but the children themselves elaborated on their transgressions and even volunteered confessions.

Our analysis is consistent with these findings, showing that Chinese co-narrators were much more likely than their American counterparts to make explicit reference to code violations by the child. In addition, all of the most lengthy and elaborate Chinese stories but none of the most lengthy and elaborate American stories were structured so as to establish the child's rule violation as the point of the story. The co-narration above concerning Didi's misbehavior at the older sister's music lesson provides a good example. In another example, consisting of more than 50 turns, the caregiver directed the child to tell Auntie (the researcher) why she had gotten spanked the day before. Through a series of queries from caregiver and Aunty and responses from the child, it was established that the child interrupted a church meeting, the caregiver spanked her, she cried, and the other adults who were present "saved" her by allowing her to distribute snacks to them. The co-narration ended with an exchange in which the caregiver asked the child whether she still wanted to go to church meetings and the child responded by saying that she would not run around next time. Without specific prompting from the caregiver, the child thus volunteered that she would not repeat her misdeed in the future. The co-narration was bounded at the beginning by the caregiver's demand that the child confess her misdeed to Aunty and at the end by the child's explicit commitment not to transgress in the future. Such

symmetry makes one wonder whether the misdeed was a well-worked narrative topic that had undergone a degree of ritualization.

There is nothing comparable to this co-narration in the American corpus. Although caregivers intervened promptly when children misbehaved, they tended not to treat the child's past transgressions as storyworthy. When a rule violation was invoked it was peripheral to the main point of the story. For example, an American child initiated a story about going to the dentist to have her tooth pulled, resulting in a windfall from the tooth fairy. A code violation was implied only once, as the final contribution to the co-narration. An older sibling explained that the two-year-old had been "eating bad food" so she had to have her tooth pulled. Both the placement of this contribution and the fact that no one elaborated on it render the rule violation peripheral to the main action of the co-narration.

Lest we convey too stark a contrast between the Chinese and American co-narrations or leave the impression that Chinese caregivers invariably assumed the voice of authority toward their children's past experiences, we want to emphasize that in the majority of co-narrations for both the Chinese and American children rules were not invoked. Children and their families created joint accounts of holidays or family excursions – birthday parties, the fair, the zoo, McDonald's for the American children, the night market, the zoo, riding on trains and horses for the Chinese children. Both groups of children also talked about experiences of physical harm, such as illnesses and nosebleeds, and about times when they were afraid. Thus the striking cultural difference in the priority given to a transgressive interpretation of the child's experience must be seen against this backdrop of overlapping content between Chinese and American co-narrations.

Telling Stories about the Child. These patterns apply not only to telling stories with the child but to telling stories about the child. American stories about the child were less likely to invoke rule violations or to be structured so as to establish the child's transgression as the point of the story. Instead, narrators selected benign or entertaining events that illustrated how cute or smart or odd the child was. The following example is one of a chain of stories that an American mother told about her two-year-old daughter's language errors:

Example 3
[The child and her older sister are playing a board game.]
>Mother: You'll get a big kick out of this one. Friday night, we were just sitting around. Jim took Friday off, I don't know what we did but, we were just sitting here at night. Jim and I were sitting on the ground and Jack was [inaudible]. She puts her hand on me and says, "Me happy." And I'm like, "That's good, Mollie. You happy."
>Researcher: I love it, it sounds so cute.
>Mother: I said, "I don't think I ever heard anyone say that," and Jim says, "I know I never heard anyone come up with [inaudible]."
>Researcher: "Me happy."

There are two notable features of this narration. First, the story is structured around the child's funny pronoun usage, rendered in direct quotation, and the parents' response, which is quoted, recycled, and elaborated. The narrator thereby conveys the surprising and endearing quality of her child's expression. What is reportable is not only the unusual usage, but the sentiment that is expressed and the novel, unprecedented nature of the error. The child's act is represented in a manner that is consistent with the parents' view, articulated in other interactions, that this is their goofy child, the one who is "touched." Second, the researcher has a definite role to play as audience for and participant in this narration. The mother introduces the story with a comment about the story's anticipated impact on the researcher, "You'll get a big kick out of this one," and the researcher obligingly responds, "I love it, it sounds so cute."

This type of story about a child was common in the American middle-class corpus, as was the researcher's role of joining with the caregiver in appreciating the child's antics,

accomplishments, and enjoyable experiences. The Chinese corpus included some stories that were similar in that the caregiver and the researcher were aligned in taking an affirming stance toward the child's benign or decidedly positive experience – for example, a feat of memory or quick-wittedness. However, the Chinese stories about young children, in parallel with co-narrated stories, were much more likely than the American stories to be organized around the child's transgression. Thus the Chinese researcher often found herself in a somewhat delicate position: as party to accounts in which the caregiver assumed the voice of authority toward the child's misdeeds, she could side either with the caregiver or with the child.

We found that most of the time the researcher affirmed the caregiver's perspective, even going so far as to assume the caregiver's voice in relation to the child. For example, after a mother told a story about how her child had made a false accusation, the researcher said to the child, "You're young but tricky, aren't you?" At other times, however, the researcher took the child's perspective on the event, thereby mitigating the caregiver's interpretation of the child's wrongdoing. In the following example, which is the final segment of a longer narration, the researcher alternately sides with the child and with the aunt, who is the child's primary caregiver. At issue, from the aunt's standpoint, is the child's greediness, as exemplified in her demands to ride in a small mechanical car owned by a vendor in the neighborhood.

Example 4
>Aunt: Children are greedy by nature, you know? Really. So, one time she [the child] wants to ride in [the car], and then, she wants to buy stuff, and wants to ride again. How can this go on! This can't go on.
>Researcher: But she also knows it; she also knows –
>Aunt: It's because we never let ... I, I was very angry. Like this. Yeah.
>Researcher: [laughs]
>Aunt: On the one hand, on the one hand, she can go to the market and after buying everything, she turns around

and wants to ride again. She just wants everything, period.

Researcher: [To child:] Are you very greedy?

[Child nods and makes a face.]

Researcher: [To child:] Yeah? Oh, you want everything? [laughs] And, and you're still acting like a poor mistreated thing?

Aunt: [laughs]

The researcher's first response is a defense of the child: she refers back to earlier comments made by the child in which the child indicated that she understood and accepted her aunt's limits on bumper car riding. When the aunt recycles her claims about the child, however, the researcher turns to the child and directs several rhetorical questions to her that affirm the aunt's perspective on the child's greediness.

Two Transgression Stories Compared. Although this kind of story about the child was much more frequent in the Chinese families, we did find the rare American story in which the child was cast as transgressor. Such exceptions are important analytically, for they allow us to examine how caregivers in Longwood handle an interpretive task that caregivers from Taipei engaged in routinely. The question, then, is this: Given that the caregiver has selected the child's transgression as storyworthy, how does the transgression get narrated in the Chinese and American cases? The following story is the only one in our American corpus that "looks Chinese" in the sense that it is structured so as to establish the child's wrongdoing as the point of the story. As narrated by the mother, the story actually involved two transgressions. First, Mollie wrote on the wall, and then she tried to evade responsibility for her misdeed by falsely accusing her sister.

Example 5

Mother: [To child:] Did you tell Judy what you wrote on the dining room wall with?

Child: Ah … key.

Researcher: [To child:] You wrote on the dining room wall?

Mother: With a key, not even a pencil.

Researcher: [To mother:] You must have loved that!

Mother: A key, the front end of that key.

Sister: And behind a living room chair.

Mother: I was sort of napping in there and I saw this and I thought it was a pencil. And I woke up and said [whispering], "Mol, you didn't write on Mommy's wall with a pencil, did you?" Oh, she was so relieved, she said, "No! Me no use pencil, me use key!" and I was like, "OH, GOD! Not a key!" And she said, "No, no, ME no use key, Mom. Kara use key," and then I was even more upset.

Sister: I didn't even see her do it!

Mother: But it's so funny. You look at her and she's like, "I didn't use pencil."

Researcher: So, I'm in the clear.

Mother: Oh, yeah.

Sister: I didn't even see her do it. I was at school.

This story about the child is preceded by a co-narrated account initiated by the mother in which Mollie is prompted to confess her wrongdoing to the researcher. The child complies and the researcher invites further response. Several turns ensue in which the mother emphasizes that Mollie used a key to write on the wall, the researcher aligns herself with the mother through an ironic expression ("You must have loved that!"), and Mollie's older sister, Kara – who was falsely blamed by Mollie – contributes further information about the incident.

Having established Mollie's wrongdoing by eliciting supporting accounts from the parties involved, the mother then explains more fully to the researcher what happened. That is, she situates the wall-writing incident within the events that preceded and followed it, providing a story about the child. In this story the mother explains that she was napping when the transgression occurred. Her dawning realization that Mollie wrote on the wall while she napped is re-created in the narration through the mounting suspense of parallel, but increasingly damaging, admissions by the child. Mollie is represented as trying to mitigate her responsibility for wrongdoing, first, by explaining that she used a key instead of a pencil, and, second, by falsely blaming her sister. The humor lies in the fact that the child's inept and increasingly transparent attempts to explain away her misdeeds have exactly the opposite effect. Her mother's subsequent comment "But it's so funny" explicitly acknowledges that the narration is framed nonseriously. Note also that although the mother says that she was "even more upset" by the child's lie than by the misdeed that occasioned it, there is no further mention of the more serious transgression. Also, the interaction that preceded the story about the child, including the elicited confession from the child, includes no mention of Mollie's false accusation.

There are, of course, many Chinese stories about children's past transgressions that could be compared with this story from Long-wood. We have chosen the Chinese story that most closely resembles it. In this story, Angu, like Mollie, wrote on the wall and then tried to shift the blame to someone else. Angu lived with her aunt, who was her primary caregiver. She referred to her aunt as "Mama" and to her biological mother, who was a school teacher, as "Teaching Mother." According to the aunt's narration, after Angu wrote on the wall and was rebuked by her aunt, she called Teaching Mother on the phone and complained that her aunt had mistreated her. Although this sequence includes ten times as many turns as the American example and lasts for nearly six minutes, it too was prefaced by a prompted confession from the child.

Example 6
    Aunt: After you scribbled on my wall, how did you tell your mother? [pause] Tell me! [pause] Tell me!
[Child is silent, tries to get on sofa, gazes at aunt.]
    Aunt: Tell me! [louder]
Child: Hmm.
    Aunt: You tell Auntie [referring to the researcher], how did you accuse me? [pause] Hmm? [louder]
[Child is silent.]
    Aunt: [to researcher:] Has she said, have I said it before?
Researcher: No.
    Aunt: Oh.

[Aunt picks up the child and puts her next to herself on the sofa.]
    Aunt: [To child:] You, you made my wall, you used, you. ... At midnight before going to bed, and then you used a pen to scribble on my wall. And then how did you call Teaching Mother? Tell me. Tell Auntie. Tell, tell her how smart you are able to accuse. [turns her body to face child and makes child sit still] Hurry up.
[Child is silent, makes face and turns away.]

Eight additional turns follow in which Angu remains silent as her aunt continues to prod her into confessing to her false accusation. The aunt then escalates her efforts by threatening to leave.

    Aunt: You won't say, right? Good, we're leaving. Good-bye. [pretends to move away from sofa] We're leaving.
Researcher: Goodbye.
    Aunt: Goodbye.
[Child turns toward her aunt and seems ready to say something.]
    Aunt: Then what are you going to say? What are you going to say?
    Child: Go away!
    Aunt: Okay, I'm going away. You say it.
[Child turns away from her aunt and breathes heavily.]
    Aunt: How did you tell Teaching Mother?
    Child: [Lowers her head, displays a sad facial expression.] "Mama [referring to the aunt], I'm not going to come back to your home [whining]. I'm, I'm going to go to Teaching Mother's home [whining]." [looks at her aunt and enacts sobbing]
    Aunt: And then?
    Child: Then [lengthening the word], Mama [referring to her aunt] didn't talk. [sad face]
    Aunt: Mama didn't talk? I didn't scold you! You even called your mother to report it. How did you report? How did you report?

Although Angu finally provides a partial confession, quoting the complaint against her aunt that she had made in the phone call to Teaching Mother, her aunt continues to try to elicit from her a more detailed account of her transgression. The aunt shames the child through 72 additional turns, occasionally invoking the researcher's support against the child and repeatedly expressing her displeasure. The child continued to resist, saying at times, "I faint [hun-dao]."

In parallel with the American example, the sequence eventually evolves into a story about the child as the aunt shifts from the second to the third person and renarrates the story to the researcher, explaining more fully what happened:

> Aunt: [To researcher:] She is really bad. At that time, she told her mother [enacts crying, sobbing, and whining], "Ummmm, I don't want to live in Brother Mother's home.5 I want to go back to your home. I don't like Brother Mother's home." And then she cried. Wah, look, such a big deal. I didn't scold her at all [for writing on the wall]. I only looked at her. I was in a good mood. I didn't scold her. Yet she acted like this. Look, what a rascal.
>
> Researcher: [laughs]
>
> Aunt: If she were my sister [referring to the child's mother], were not my sister, ages ago we would already. … At midnight, after eleven o'clock [the child called her mother on the phone to complain], midnight after eleven o'clock, just before going to bed, at the head of the bed, she scribbled on the wall with chalk. We had already had our home painted again ages ago.
>
> Researcher: [laughs]

This narration resembles its American counterpart in several ways. In both accounts it is the child's deception after being discovered in an act of wrongdoing that the caregiver takes to be the more serious transgression. The nature of the deception is similar in that Mollie falsely blames her sister for the wall writing and Angu falsely accuses her aunt of mistreatment. Both accounts imply that the child realized she had done something wrong. In addition, the Chinese story, like the American, is structured around a quoted response from the child.

The difference is that in the Chinese story the quote serves to foreground the more serious transgression: not writing on the wall, but calling the mother on the phone to complain about the aunt. From the aunt's perspective, this behavior is even more unacceptable given the immediately preceding circumstances – that the child had written on the wall and that she had responded leniently to the misdeed. The foregrounding of the child's false accusation is also accomplished in the lengthy preceding interaction in which the aunt's efforts to draw a confession from the child remain steadfastly focused on the child's complaint to mother, not on the wall-writing incident. In this respect the Chinese story contrasts sharply with the American story, in which the lesser transgression of writing on the wall is foregrounded both in the story about the child and in the preceding interaction in which the child is prompted to confess to writing on the wall. This contrast is heightened by the parallel contrast in the keying of the narration (Goffman 1974; Hymes 1972), with the American story being told in a consistently humorous, nonserious manner. Thus, despite notable similarities of content, structure, and interpretation, the two wall writing stories differ qualitatively in the meanings that the caregivers assigned to the children's misdeeds.

However, there is another reading of this contrast that must be acknowledged. It is possible, even likely, that Angu's and Mollie's false accusations are ranked differently within the scale of values of their respective caregivers. To falsely accuse the aunt herself, as Angu did, is very serious from the aunt's perspective, for it is not only disrespectful and face-threatening but could sow dissension among the adults in the family ("See what a troublemaker she is. … If she were my sister, if she were not my sister, ages ago we would already …"). On the other hand, Mollie's attempt to fix blame on her sister is perhaps less serious from her mother's perspective because conflict among young siblings is expected. This may help to account for the contrast in length and keying of the two stories. The major point for our purposes, however, is that the story from the American corpus that most closely resembles the Chinese stories of children's transgressions – indeed, the only story in which an American caregiver constructs a story around a child's past transgressions – conveys a qualitatively different interpretation. Instead of creating an opportunity for remediation, the caregiver develops the amusing dimensions of the incident. She creates a mischief maker, not a transgressor.

Conclusion

In this article we set out to compare personal storytelling as it is practiced with very young children in Taipei and Longwood. We found that two-year-olds' past experiences were repeatedly narrated and renarrated in the course of everyday family life in both cultural cases, and that the youngsters themselves assumed a variety of participant roles. Each time a child heard her past actions narrated by a caregiver or contributed to a collaborative narration, she engaged in self-relevant interpretive activity.

In attempting to identify the interpretive frameworks instantiated in these narrative activities, we focused on two frameworks corresponding to Lutz and White's (1986) problems of bonds between self and other and ego's violation of cultural codes. We do not mean to imply that these frameworks are the only ones that are instantiated in the narrative practices described above. Given the contradictions inherent in any ideological system and the multiplicity of perspectives that can be taken toward any event, human experience is rarely describable in terms of one or two problems (Lutz and White 1986). Thus our analysis is quite clearly incomplete. Nonetheless, it does reveal something of the complexity of meaning conveyed through narrative practices and lays a foundation for future analyses.

With respect to bonds between self and other, we found that the children's past experiences were interpreted in terms of a relational

framework in both cultural systems. Acting in concert with other social actors in re-creating a past experience in the here and now, the *narrating self* constructed a version of the past experience in which the *narrated self* as protagonist was situated interpersonally. The children's experiences were thus doubly anchored, in the past and in the present, to relationships with other people. It is perhaps not surprising that the Chinese and American families shared a relational perspective. The children inhabited a rich social world, daily life was spent in close emotional proximity to significant others, and both cultural systems placed a high value on family relationships, however differently these were defined. This is not to say that the relational frameworks instantiated in Chinese and American narrative practices were identical. Our finding of increasing differentiation during the preschool years on a dimension of setting the self apart from others underscores this point. We expect that further analysis will reveal other differences, especially as we extend our analyses into later ages.

With respect to the second problem, we found that the personal experiences of two-year-old Chinese children were more likely than their American counterparts' to be interpreted within an explicitly evaluative, overtly self-critical framework. The primacy of this interpretive framework for the Chinese cut across co-narrated story-telling and caregivers' narrations about the child, and it was jointly maintained by the coordinated efforts of the several participants. It was maintained by caregivers as they invoked rules explicitly, structured stories so as to establish the rule violation as the point of the story, and recruited the researcher's support against the errant child. It was maintained by older siblings as they aligned themselves with the caregiver, speaking in the voice of authority. It was maintained by the children themselves as they confessed to misdeeds, kept silent, laughed, and expressed feelings of shame. And it was maintained by the ethnographer as she alternately aligned herself with the caregiver and with the child.

These findings support Wu's (1981) contention that discipline begins early in life for Chinese children and suggest that evaluation and criticism, identified as key cultural

constructs in early (Hu 1944) and contemporary accounts of Chinese cultures (Kleinman
1986; Schoenhals 1991), have their roots in
early socialization practices in the family.
Wang's (1992) study of young deaf children and
their mothers in Taipei is consistent with this
conclusion. Moreover, by following two of the
children from our sample longitudinally from
two to four years of age, Fung (1994) has shown
that Chinese notions of face and shame come
into play when children's experiences are narrated from an evaluative perspective and that
the repeated, negotiated application of this
framework through the medium of personal
storytelling is a major means by which the
socialization of shame is accomplished.
Committed to a moral ideology in which shame
is positively valued, the parents felt that they
would be remiss as parents if they did not raise
their children to know shame and to abide by
the rules of appropriate conduct. These findings
resonate strongly with Schoenhals's (1991)
study of a middle school in the People's Republic
of China, in which he found that evaluation,
criticism, face, and shame formed a major clus-
ter of values and that children prior to puberty
were openly criticized by parents and teachers.

In the American case, a different interpretive
framework was at work in personal storytelling
practices, one that we might call implicitly evaluative and overtly self-affirming. Observations of
nonnarrative activity in the American homes
suggest that the narrative practice of portraying
the child protagonist in a favorable light is part
of a wider network of practices that caregivers
use to protect their children's self-esteem – handling discipline in the here and now without
dwelling on the child's past misdeeds, conducting serious disciplining in private, putting the
best face on the child's shortcomings or even
recasting shortcomings as strengths. As with the
Chinese, this framework was maintained
through the active collusion of the several participants, including the researcher. Thus the contrast between the Chinese and American practices
reflects, in part, systematic differences in how
the researcher's role got defined in the two cases.
Whereas the Chinese researcher was enlisted as
judging witness to the child's past misdeeds, the
American researcher was cast as appreciative
audience to the child's benign experiences. From

the American standpoint, the Chinese practices
appear harsh; from the Chinese standpoint, the
American practices appear irresponsible.

In identifying contrasting interpretive frameworks in Taipei and Longwood, it is important
not to overstate these differences. The Chinese
families found ways to portray their children
favorably and to show their appreciation, and
the American families found ways to enforce
moral and social rules. Also, within each cultural group families differed among themselves
in the extent and manner in which they instan-
tiate particular frameworks. It is equally important not to treat these differences as though
they existed in isolation, unconnected to other
interpretive frameworks. Indeed, one of the
chief advantages of a practice perspective is
that it acknowledges that any given practice
carries a multiplicity of meanings simultaneously. Thus, when Chinese families narrated a
young child's transgression, they simultaneously situated the child in relation to others.
Were we to examine personal storytelling in
terms of the other social problems proposed by
Lutz and White (1986), still more interpretive
threads would come to light. The task for children, as for the rest of us, is to create meaning
by tracing through the variety and intercon-
nectedness of interpretive threads in "the tan-
gle of experience" (Briggs 1992:26).

These several findings, in conjunction with
the finding that personal storytelling practices
occurred routinely in the everyday home environments of both the Chinese and American
children, shed new light on the process of self-
construction. Personal storytelling emerged in
both cultural cases as an important means by
which young children, together with family
members, construct and reconstruct their experiences in culture-specific terms. Each co-
narrated story, each story that the caregiver tells
about the child, provides him with yet another
opportunity to hear how he is related to other
people, how he transgressed, or why a particular action was funny. Each story instantiates
these problems somewhat differently but always
in personally relevant terms, thereby inviting,
perhaps impelling, the child's emotional involvement (Briggs 1992). Our findings thus suggest
that self-construction is a highly dynamic process in the early years of life, a process that

encompasses not only the child's moment-by-moment interpersonal encounters but his or her participation in iterative narrations of those encounters, which are themselves embedded in moment-by-moment interpersonal encounters.

The dynamic nature of self-construction follows not only from the recurrent nature of narrative practices but from the variability inherent in the situatedness of narrative practices (Miller and Mintz 1993). This is most apparent when a narrator spontaneously retells a story (Miller, Hoogstra et al. 1993). Several of the examples we cited were told repeatedly. For example, the incident in which the Chinese child was described as interrupting a church meeting occurred first as a co-narration; later in the same video recording, the caregiver renarrated the incident, this time as a story about the child in the child's presence. Note also that the two stories about writing on the wall were prefaced by co-narrated stories on the same topic, without any obvious boundary between the two. This suggests an important property of narrative practices that should not be overlooked, namely, that the analytic distinction between types of practices (e.g., telling stories with the child, telling stories about the child), however useful, masks the interpenetration of types that occurs in everyday life, the seamless manner in which a co-narration merges, at times, with a story about the child. This complicates the researcher's task of identifying units of analysis that preserve the integrity of naturally occurring events (Watson-Gegeo 1988). But for the child, this higher-order packaging and repackaging, conveying both multiple perspectives on events and cross-cutting redundancies, provides yet another cultural resource for creating personal meaning.

NOTES

1 This model confers several important advantages for a theory of childhood socialization: (1) the actual processes of socialization are rendered accessible through analysis of the forms and functions of everyday discourse; (2) an active role is accorded to the child through a focus on child and caregivers' mutual, negotiated participation in discourse practices; and

(3) because language practices systematically index social statuses and ideologies, a discourse model helps to explain the variety of affective stances – eager acceptance, resistance, playfulness – that children assume as they attempt to invest cultural resources with meaning.

2 In a recent survey of religious affiliations in Taiwan (Chu 1991) conducted by the Academia Sinica in Taipei, only 35.8 percent of the respondents claimed folk religion as their religious affiliation. However, two-thirds expressed the hope that their descendants would worship them after death.

3 In all examples given, the child is identified as "Child," and siblings are referred to as "Sister" or "Brother." Chinese transcripts are provided in the Appendix.

4 Note that although the mother and older sister consistently focus on the inappropriateness of Didi's behaviors and the resultant loss of face to his mother, their narration is keyed nonseriously, as indicated by their smiles and laughter (see Fung 1994 for further discussion of this point).

5 In addition to referring to her aunt as "Mama," Angu also called her "Brother Mother," that is, mother of Angu's brother (or male cousin, in American terms).

REFERENCES

Bakhtin, Mikhail M.
    1981 The Dialogic Imagination. Austin: University of Texas Press.
Bauman, Richard, and Charles Briggs
    1990 Poetics and Performance as Critical Perspectives on Language and Social Life. Annual Review of Anthropology 19:59–88.
Bourdieu, Pierre
    1977 Outline of a Theory of Practice. New York: Cambridge University Press.
    1990 The Logic of Practice. Stanford: Stanford University Press.
Briggs, Jean L.
    1992 Mazes of Meaning: How a Child and a Culture Create Each Other. *In* Interpretive Approaches to Children's Socialization (New Directions for Child Development). William A. Corsaro and Peggy J. Miller, eds. Pp. 25–49. San Francisco: Jossey-Bass.
Bruner, Jerome
    1986 Actual Minds, Possible Worlds. Cambridge, MA: Harvard University Press.

1990 Acts of Meaning. Cambridge, MA: Harvard University Press.

Chang, Ying-hwa
1987 The International Structure of Taipei Municipality: An Ecological and Historical Analysis. Bulletin of the Institute of Ethnology, Academic Sinica, 63. pp. 1–62. (In Chinese.)

Chu, Hai-Yuan, ed.
1991 Executive Report, Social Change Basic Survey Project, Taipei, Taiwan: Institute of Ethnology, Academia Sinica. (In Chinese.)

Cohen, Marc J.
1988 Taiwan at the Crossroads. Washington, DC: Asia Resource Center.

Corsaro, William A., and Peggy J. Miller, eds.
1992 Interpretive Approaches to Children's Socialization (New Directions for Child Development). San Francisco: Jossey-Bass.

Duranti, Alessandro, and Charles Goodwin, eds.
1992 Rethinking Context: Language as an Interactive Phenomenon. New York: Cambridge University Press.

Eisenberg, Ann R.
1985 Learning To Describe Past Experiences in Conversation. Discourse Processes 8:177–204.

Farris, Catherine S. P.
1988 Language and Sex Role Acquisition in a Taiwanese Kindergarten: A Semiotic Analysis. Unpublished doctoral dissertation, University of Washington.

Fung, Heidi
1987 Early Talk about the Past: Some Sociocultural Reflections on Two Chinese Children's Narratives of Personal Experience. Trial research project submitted to the Committee on Human Development, University of Chicago.
1994 The Socialization of Shame in Young Chinese Children. Unpublished Ph.D. dissertation, University of Chicago.

Gaskins, Suzanne
1994 Integrating Interpretive and Quantitative Methods in Socialization Research. Merrill-Palmer Quarterly 40:313–333.

Goffman, Erving
1974 Frame Analysis: An Essay on the Organization of Experience. Cambridge, MA: Harvard University Press.
1981 Forms of Talk. Philadelphia: University of Pennsylvania Press.

Heath, Shirley Brice
1983 Ways with Words: Language, Life, and Work in Communities and Classrooms. New York: Cambridge University Press.

Howard, Alan
1985 Ethnopsychology and the Prospects for a Cultural Psychology. In Person, Self, and Experience: Exploring Pacific Ethnopsychologies. Geoffrey M. White and John Kirkpatrick, eds. Pp. 401–420. Berkeley: University of California Press.

Hu, Hsien Chin
1944 The Chinese Concepts of "Face." American Anthropologist 46:45–64.

Hymes, Dell
1972 Models of the Interaction of Language and Social Life. In Directions in Sociolinguistics: The Ethnography of Communication. John J. Gumperz and Dell Hymes, eds. New York: Holt, Rinehart and Winston.

Kleinman, Arthur
1986 Social Origins of Distress and Disease: Depression, Neurasthenia, and Pain in Modern China. New Haven, CT: Yale University Press.

Kleinman, Arthur, and Joan Kleinman
1989 Suffering and Its Professional Transformation. Paper presented at the meeting of the Society for Psychological Anthropology, San Diego.

Lucy, John
1992 Language Diversity and Thought: A Reformulation of the Linguistic Relativity Hypothesis. Cambridge: Cambridge University Press.

Lutz, Catherine A.
1985 Ethnopsychology Compared to What? Explaining Behavior and Consciousness among the Ifaluk. In Person, Self, and Experience: Exploring Pacific Ethnopsychologies. Geoffrey M. White and James Kirkpatrick, eds. pp. 35–79. Berkeley: University of California Press.

Lutz, Catherine A., and Geoffrey M. White
1986 The Anthropology of Emotions. Annual Review of Anthropology 15:405–436.

Markus, Hazel, and Shinobu Kitayama
1991 Culture and the Self: Implications for Cognition, Emotion, and Motivation. Psychological Review 98:224–253.

Miller, Peggy J.
1994 Narrative Practices: Their Role in Socialization and Self-Construction. In The Remembering Self: Construction and Accuracy in the Self-Narrative. Ulrich Neisser and Robyn Fivush, eds. pp. 158–179. Cambridge: Cambridge University Press.
In press Instantiating Culture through Discourse Practices: Some Personal Reflections on Socialization and How To Study It. In

Ethnography and Human Development: Context and Meaning in Social Inquiry. Richard Jessor, Anne Colby, and Richard A. Shweder, eds. Chicago: University of Chicago Press.

Miller, Peggy J., Lisa Hoogstra, Judith Mintz, Heidi Fung, and Kimberly Williams
1993 Troubles in the Garden and How They Get Resolved: A Young Child's Transformation of His Favorite Story. *In* Memory and Affect in Development. Minnesota Symposia on Child Psychology, Vol. 26. Charles Nelson, ed. pp. 87–114. Hillsdale, NJ: Eribaum.

Miller, Peggy J., and Judith Mintz
1993 Instantiating Culture: Socialization through Narrtive Practices. Paper presented at the biennial meeting of the Society for Research in Child Development, New Orleans, March.

Miller, Peggy J., Judith Mintz, Lisa Hoogstra, Heidi Fung, and Randolph Potts
1992 The Narrated Self: Young Children's Construction of Self in Relation to Others in Conversational Stories of Personal Experience. Merrill-Palmer Quarterly 38:45–67.

Miller, Peggy J., and Barbara B. Moore
1989 Narrative Conjunctions of Caregiver and Child: A Comparative Perspective on Socialization through Stories. Ethos 17:428–449.

Miller, Peggy J., Randolph Potts, Heidi Fung, Lisa Hoogstra, and Judith Mintz
1990 Narrative Practices and the Social Construction of Self in Childhood. American Ethnologist 17:292–311.

Miller, Peggy J., and Linda L. Sperry
1988 Early Talk about the Past: The Origins of Conversational Stories of Personal Experience. Journal of Child Language 15:293–315.

Mintz, Judith
1993 Self in Relation to Other: Preschoolers' Verbal Social Comparisons. Poster presented at the biennial meeting of the Society for Research in Child Development, New Orleans.

Nelson, Katherine
1989 Monologue as the Linguistic Construction of Self in Time. *In* Narratives from the Crib. Katherine Nelson, ed. pp. 284–308. Cambridge, MA: Harvard University Press.

Ochs, Elinor
1988 Culture and Language Development. New York: Cambridge University Press.

Ochs, Elinor, and Bambi B. Schieffelin
1984 Language Acquisition and Socialization: Three Developmental Stories and Their Implications. *In* Culture Theory. Richard A. Shweder and Robert A. LeVine, eds. Pp. 276–320. New York: Cambridge University Press.

Schieffelin, Bambi B.
1990 The Give and Take of Everyday Life: Language Socialization of Kaluli Children. New York: Cambridge University Press.

Schoenhals, Martin
1991 The Paradox of Power in a People's Republic of China Middle School. Unpublished doctoral dissertation, University of Pennsylvania.

Shweder, Richard A., and Nancy C. Much
1987 Determinations of Meaning: Discourse and Moral Socialization. *In* Moral Development through Social Interaction. William M. Kurtines and J. L. Gewirtz, eds. Pp. 197–244. New York: Wiley.

Shweder, Richard A., and Maria Sullivan
1993 Cultural Psychology: Who Needs It? Annual Review of Psychology 44:497–523.

Simon, Denis F., and Michael Y. M. Kau
1992 Taiwan: Beyond the Economic Miracle. Armonk, NY: M. E. Sharpe.

Snow, Catherine E.
1990 Building Memories: The Ontogeny of Autobiography. *In* The Self in Transition. Dante Cicchetti and Marjorie Beeghly, eds. Pp. 213–242. Chicago: University of Chicago Press.

Sperry, Linda L.
1991 The Emergence and Development of Narrative Competence among African-American Toddlers in a Rural Alabama Community. Unpublished doctoral dissertation, University of Chicago.

Spiro, Melford E.
1993 Is the Western Conception of the Self "Peculiar" within the Context of the World Cultures? Ethos 21:107–153.

Taipei Municipal Government
1988 The Statistical Abstract of Taipei Municipality. Taipei: Bureau of Budget, Accounting, and Statistics. (In Chinese.)

Tien, Hung-mao
1989 The Great Transition: Political and Social Change in the Republic of China. Stanford, CA: Hoover Institution Press.

Vygotsky, Lev S.
1987[1934] Thinking and Speech. New York: Plenum.

Watson-Gogeo, Karen A.
1988 Response to Schieffelin and Ochs' Paper on Language Socialization. Paper presented at American Anthropological Association Annual Meeting, Phoenix, November.

Wang, Xiao-Lei
1992 Resilience and Fragility in language Acquisition: A Comparative Study of the Gestural Communication Systems of Chinese and American Deaf Children. Unpublished doctoral dissertation, University of Chicago.

Wertsch, James
1985 Vygotsky and the Social Formation of Mind. Cambridge, MA: Harvard University Press.
1991 Voice of the Mind: A Sociocultural Approach to Mediated Action. Cambridge, MA: Harvard University Press.

White, Geoffrey M.

1992 Ethnopsychology. *In* New Directions in Psychological Anthropology. Theodore Schwartz, Geoffrey M. White, and Catherine A. Lutz, eds. pp. 21–46. New York: Cambridge University Press.

Wierzbicka, Anna
1993 A Conceptual Basis for Culture Psychology. Ethos 21:205–231.

Wu, David Y. H.
1981 Child Abuse in Taiwan. *In* Child Abuse and Neglect: Cross-Cultural Perspectives. Jill E. Korbin, ed. pp. 139–165. Berkeley: University of California Press.

APPENDIX

Each Chinese example that appears in the text is given here, with the Chinese on the left and the English translation on the right. The Chinese is rendered in *pinyin*, a standardized system for transcribing Chinese into the Roman alphabet. Each line in Chinese is followed immediately by its literal translation.

Example 1

Mother to Child:
  Ei, ei, ni no-tian
  Eh, eh, you that-day
  gen Ma, gen Mei,
  with mama, with younger-sister,
  gen Jiejie qu shang yinyue ke.
  with elder-sister go up music class.
  Hao-bu-heo wan?
  good-not-good play?

[Looks at child.] Eh, eh, you that day with Mama, with younger sister, with older sister went to the music class. Was that fun?

Child to Mother:
  Hao wan a.
  Good play a.

It was fun.

Mother to Child:
  Laoshi dou mei-you gei ni
  Teacher all not-exist give you
  shenme dongxi?
  what thing?

What didn't the teacher give you?

Child to Mother:
  Mei, mei-you gei wo tiezhi.
  not, not-exit give me sticker.

Didn't didn't give me a sticker.

Mother to Child:
  Mei-you gei ni tiezhi.Ranhou
  not-exist give you sticker. later
  ni jiu, ni jiu zenme la?
  you then, you then how la?

Didn't give you a sticker. Then you, then what did you do?

Child to Mother:
  Jiu ku le.
  then cry le.

I then cried.

Sister to Mother:
Da-sheng ku,
big-voice cry,
"*A! A! A*"
"waah! waah! waah!"   Cried loudly, "Waah! Waah! Waah!"

Mother to Child:
O, ni jiu ku la? Dui, jiu   Oh, you then cried? Yeah, you constantly went:
oh, you then cry la? correct, then   "Waah, didn't [gestures wiping eyes, makes staccato
          gestures of fists away from body], why didn't
yizhi: "A, mei-you,   you give me a sticker? [whines] Why didn't you
straight: "waah, not-exist,   give me a sticker?" [whines] Didn't you?
wei-shenme mei-you gei wo tiezhi?
for-what not-exist give me sticker?
Wei-shenme mei-you gei wo
for-what not-exist give me
tiezhi?" Dui-bu-dui?
sticker?" correct-not-correct?

[Child looks up from the book, gazes at mother, smiles, and looks down at the book again.]

Sister to Mother:
Dui ya, "wei-shenme mei-you gei   Yes, "Why didn't you give me a sticker?" [clap
correct ya, "for-what not-exist give *wo tiezhi?"*   hand]
me sticker?"

Mother to Child:
Tiezhi. Aya, hai de Mama   Sticker. [sighs] Ai, you made Mama lose face.
sticker. aya, harm de mama   That, that, I wanted to dig my head into the
hao mei-you mionzi. Na-ge, na-ge   ground. Right? [smiles, shakes head, smiles
very not-exist face, that-ge that-ge   again]
tou dou yao wang di-shang zuan
head all want into ground-up dig
le. Dui-bu-dui?
le. correct-not-correct?

[Child points to picture book and says something unintelligible.]

Sister to Mother:
Dou yao hun-dao le. Mama yao   Almost wanted to faint. Mommy almost began
all want faint-down le. mama want   to faint.
kai-shi hun-dao le.
open-begin faint-down le.

Example 4

Aunt to Researcher:
Xiaohaizi de benxing haishi hen   Children are greedy by nature, you know?
child de nature still very   Really. So, one time she wants to ride in [the
tanxin de, ni zhidao ba? Zhende.   car], and then, she wants to buy stuff, and wants
greedy de, you know ba? true de.   to ride again. How can this go on! This can't go
Suoyi yixiazi you yao wan,   on.
so suddenly again want play,
ranhou ne, you yao mai dongxi,
later ne, again want buy thing,
you xiang yao wan. Nali keyi
again think want play, how can
zhe-yang! Bu keyi zhe-yang.
this-mode! not can this-mode.

Researcher to Aunt:
Danshi ta ye zhidao a.
but she also know a.
Ta ye zhidao –
she also know –

But she also knows it. She also knows –

Aunt to Researcher:
Ye shi women yizhi bu gei,
also be we always not give,
wo, wo hen shengqi ya. Zhe-yang
I, I very angry ya. this-mode
de. Shi.
de. be.

It's also because we never let … I, I was very angry. Like this. Yeah.

Researcher: [laughs]
Aunt to Researcher:
Yi-mian, ta keyi yimian qu
one-side, she can one-side go
cai-shichang, zhe-ge shenme
vegetable-market, this-ge what
dou mai wan le, ta jiu
all buy finish le, she then
hui-tou you yao zuo.
back-head again want sit.
Ta sheme dou yao jiu dui
she what all want then correct
liao le.
liao le.

On the one hand, on the one hand, she can go to the market and after buying everything, she turns around and wants to ride again. She just wants everything, period.

Researcher to Child:
Ni shi-bu-shi hen tanxin?
you be-not-be very greedy?

Are you very greedy?

[Child nods and makes a face.]

Researcher to Child:
Shi o? O, ni sheme dou xiang yao
be oh? oh, you what all think want
a? Hai yao, hai yao ban
a? still want, still want act
hen kelian, hen weiqu de
very sympathy, very grievance de
yangzi.
appearance.

Yeah? Oh, you want everything? [laughs] And, and you're still acting like a poor mistreated thing?

Aunt: [laughs]

Example 6

[Note that the child lives with her aunt, who is her primary caregiver, and the aunt's teenage song. Her parents live in another household. The child calls her aunt "Mama." She calls her biological mother, who works as a teacher, "Teaching Mother." Sometimes her aunt is also referred to as "Brother Mother," meaning mother of the brother, although the "brother" is actually the child's cousin.]

Aunt to Child:
Ni gei wo-de qiangbi hua hei le
you to I-de wall draw black le

After you scribbed on my wall, how did you tell your mother? [pause] Tell me! [pause] Tell me!

yihou, ni zenme gen ni mama shuo
later, you how with you mama say
de? Ni shuo! Ni shuo!
de? you say! you say!

[Child is silent, tries to get on sofa, gazes at aunt.]

Aunt to Child:
Ni shuo a!   Tell me! [louder]
you say <u>a</u>!

Child to Aunt:
N.   Hmm.
hmm.

Aunt to Child:
Ni gaosu Ayi, shuo ni   You tell Auntie [refers to researcher], how did
you tell auntie, say you   you accuse me? [pause] Hmm? [louder]
zen-yang gaozhuang? N?
how-mode accuse? hm?

[Child is silent.]

Aunt to Researcher:
Ta shuo guo-le, wo shuo guo-le   Has she said, have I said it before?
she say <u>guo-le</u>, I say <u>guo-le</u>
mei-you?
not-exist?

Researcher to Aunt:
Mei-you.   No.
not-exist.

Aunt to Researcher:
O.   Oh.
oh.

[Aunt picks up the child and puts her next to herself on the sofa.]

Aunt to Child:
Ni, ni ba wo-de qiang, ni na,   You, you made my wall, you used, you. … At
you you ba; I-de wall, you take,   midnight before going to bed, and then you
ni … Ni sangenbanye yao   used a pen to scribble on my wall. And then
you. … you midnight want   how did you call Teaching Mother? Tell me. Tell
shuijiao de shihou, ranhou ni   Auntie. Tell, tell her how smart you are able to
sleep de time, later you   accuse. [turns her body to face child and makes
zenme da dianhua gei Jiao-shu   child sit still] Hurry up.
how call phone to teach-book
Mama de? Ni shuo, shuo gei Ayi
mama de? you say, say to auntie
ting. Shuo, shuo ni zen-yang
hear. say, say you how-mode
congming hui gaozhuang.
smart know accuse.
Gankuei shuo.
hurry say.

[Child is silent, makes face and turns away.]
[8 more turns]

Aunt to Child:
  Ni bu shuo, dui-bu-dui?   You won't say, right? Good, we're leaving.
  you not say, correct-not-correct?   Good-bye. [pretends to move away from sofa]
  Hao, na women zou le. Zai-jian.   We're leaving.
  good, then we go <u>le</u>.
  again-see.
  Women zou le.
  we go <u>le</u>.

Researcher to Child:
  Zai-jian.   Good-bye.
  again-see.

Aunt to Child:
  Zai-jian.   Good-bye.
  again-see.

[Child turns toward her aunt and seems ready to say something.]

Aunt to Child:
  Na ni shuo shenme?   Then what are you going to say? What are you
  Na ni shuo   going to say?
  then you say what? then you say
  shenme?
  what?

Child to Aunt:
  Zou-hai!   Go away!
  go-apart!

Aunt to Child:
  Hao, wo zou-kai.   Okay, I'm going away. You say it.
  Ni shuo.
  good, I go-apart. you say.

[Child turns away from her aunt and breathes heavily.]

Aunt to Child:
  Ni zenme gen Jiao-shu Mama shuo de?   How did you tell Teaching Mother?
  you how with teach-book mama say <u>de</u>?

Child to Aunt:
  "*Mama, wo bu-yao hui nimen jia*   [lowers her head, displays a sad facial expres-
  "mama, I not-want return   sion] "Mama, I'm not going to come back to
  your home   your home. [whining] I'm, I'm going to go to
  le. Wo yao gen, wo yao dao   Teaching Mother's home." [whining] [looks at
  <u>le</u>. I want with, I want go   her aunt and enacts sobbing]
  Jiao-shu Mama tjia la."
  teach-book mama home <u>la</u>."

Aunt to Child:
  Ranhou na?   And then?
  later na?

Child to Aunt:
  Jiu, Mama bu jianghua.   Then [lengthening the word], Mama didn't talk
  then, then mama not talk.   [sad face].

Aunt to Child:

Mama bu jianghua? Wo mei-you
mama not talk? I not-exist
ma ni a! Ni hai da dianhua
scold you <u>a</u>! you even call phone
gao ni mama. Yenme gao?
report you mama. how report?
Zenme gao?
how report?

Mama didn't talk? I didn't scold you! You even called your mother to report it. How did you report? How did you report?

[72 more turns]

Aunt to Researcher:

Ta hao huai o! Ta na shihou
she very bad <u>o</u>! she that time
gen ta mama shuo,
with she mama say,
"N n n, wo bu-yao hui nimen
"ummm, I not-exist return your
jia. Wo bu xihuan Gege Mama jia."
home. I not like brother mama home."
Ranhou jiu ku le. Wa, ni kan
later than cry <u>le</u>. wah, you look
bu-de-liao. Wo genben mei ma ta.
not-get-<u>liao</u>. I root not scold her.
Wo xinqing hen hao. Wo mei-you
I mood very good. I not-exist
ma ta. Ta jiu zhe-yang.
scold her. she this-mode.
Ni kan, hao huai-dan.
you look, very rotten-egg.

She is really bad! At that time, she told her mother [enacts crying, sobbing, and whining], "Ummm, I don't want to live in Brother Mother's home. I want to go back to your home. I don't like Brother Mother's home." And then she cried, Wah, look, such a big deal. I didn't scold her at all [for writing on the wall]. I only looked at her. I was in a good mood. I didn't scold her. Yet she acted like this. Look, what a rascal.

Researcher: [laughs]

Aunt to Researcher:

Ruguo shi ziji meimei a, bu-shi
if be own sister a, not-be
meimei a, zao ba-beizi
sister a, early eight-generation
bei ta, bei ta shuo. ...
by she, by she say. ...
Sangenbanye, shiyi-dian duo,
midnight, eleven-o'clock over,
yao shuijiao le. Jiu zai
want sleep le. then at
chuang-tou, na fenbi jiu
bed-head, take chalk then
hua qiangbi a. Women jia zao
draw wall a. we home early
ba-beizi you yijing
eight-generation again already
fenshua guo yi-ci le.
paint guo one-time le.

If she were my sister [referring to child's mother], were not my sister, ages ago we would already. ... At midnight, after eleven o'clock, midnight after eleven o'clock, just before going to bed, at the head of the bed, she scribbled on the wall with chalk. We had already had our home painted again ages ago.

Researcher: [laughs]

Parent–Child Communication Problems and the Perceived Inadequacies of Chinese Only Children

Vanessa L. Fong

Soon after China's one-child policy was implemented in 1979, the Chinese media was filled with discussions of how children born under that policy had failed to develop the obedience, caring/sociableness, independence, and excellence their parents, teachers, and society demanded. These discussions were echoed in complaints I frequently heard from parents during my research among Chinese single-child families. What I found particularly striking was how parents often gave their children seemingly contradictory and inconsistent directives about what values they should abide by. The Chinese singletons I knew often told me that the mixed messages they felt they were receiving from their parents caused them stress and confusion.[1] In this article, I argue that Chinese singletons' tendency to behave in ways their parents considered unsatisfactory was not merely because of the singleton status often blamed for the younger generation's failings but also to the difficulty of teaching children to abide by different values in different contexts. Although the singleton status of most urban Chinese children was integral to the rapid and dramatic social, political, economic, and demographic transformations China experienced in the final decades of the 20th century, the problems Chinese parents experienced while trying to socialize their children resulted mainly from

the difficulty of constantly adjusting to those changes, rather than from the children's singleton status per se.[2] I analyze the case studies of five teenagers and their parents to shed light on the misunderstandings and miscommunications that occurred when parents tried to teach their teenagers to become independent agents able to excel in a competitive global capitalist economy, and to mature as caring, sociable friends, family members, and employees in a Chinese society that still values obedience and the cultivation of social relationships.[3] Although modernization policies have hastened China's upward mobility in the capitalist world system in ways that most Chinese people consider highly desirable, these policies have also created significant moral conflicts (Kleinman and Kleinman 1999). This article examines how a combination of rapid child–adolescent development and rapid social, political, economic, and demographic change exacerbate the tensions resulting from those conflicts.

Research Setting and Methods

This article is based on 32 months of longitudinal research (1997, 1998–2000, 2002, 2004, 2005, and 2006) conducted in Dalian, a

Vanessa L. Fong, Parent–Child Communication Problems and the Perceived Inadequacies of Chinese Only Children from *Ethos*, Vol. 35, Issue 1, pp. 85–127. © 2007 American Anthropological Association. Reprinted with permission of the American Anthropological Association.

large coastal city in Liaoning Province, northeastern China, where I conducted participant-observation and a survey of 2,273 students in a junior high school, a vocational high school, and a college-prep high school.[4] I lived in the homes of six different families and visited the homes of 101 other families that invited me to tutor the children in English or provide information about going abroad. I established long-term relationships with 31 of the families I met, participated in their social lives, leisure time, and everyday activities, and kept in touch with them by phone and e-mail when I was not in China. In addition, I interacted with thousands of other people I met in public places, in the schools I studied, or during activities with the families I visited. Although the present article focuses on case studies of five families (selected because their children were the youngest among the families that invited me to their homes regularly over the course of my research, thus providing the richest data on changes that occurred in the transition from adolescence to adulthood), my description of the values of independence, excellence, obedience, and caring/sociableness and of parents' efforts to get their children to conform to those values is based on participant observation among my much larger total sample, as well as on the scholarly literature on Chinese parenting. My survey of 2,273 students did not ask questions about the specific values I describe here, so I use my survey data mainly to describe the broader social milieu from which the families I describe were drawn.

Values, Cultural Models, and Chinese Discourses about Unsatisfactory Singletons

Soon after China's one-child policy was implemented in 1979, Chinese media and academic discourses started emphasizing how the singletons born under that policy were timid, uncooperative, careless about others' property, hostile to others, unable to care for themselves, disrespectful to elders, and poorly mannered (Shanghaishi Youerjiaoyu Yanjiushi [Shanghai Preschool Education Study Group] 1980, 1988). Many Chinese scholars and journalists

also claimed these children were moody, bad tempered, self-aggrandizing, delinquent, neurotic, and emotional (Kuo-Tai Tao et al. 1995; Kuotai Tao and Chiu 1985; Tseng et al. 1988); eccentric, offensive, selfish, dependent, willful, delicate, weak willed, lazy, and dishonest (Chen Kewen 1988; Wu 1986); egocentric, uncooperative, incompetent, and unpopular (Jiao et al. 1986); finicky, selfish, jealous, complacent, petty, obstinate, vain, aloof, conceited, unscrupulous, hostile, and psychologically disturbed (Tang 2001).

A particularly influential critique cited by many parents I knew in China was the one made by Sun Yunxiao, Deputy Director of *Zhongguo Qingshaonian Yanjiuzhongxin* (the China Youth and Children Research Center) in Beijing. In the laments about the flaws of the single-child generation that he frequently broadcast on television and wrote about in newspapers, Sun often cited his observation of 30 Chinese children and 77 Japanese children who went on a camping trip together in the Chinese province of Inner Mongolia in 1992 (1993a, 1993b). Both groups of children were between the ages of 11 and 16. Sun detailed many examples of how Chinese children were alarmingly more flawed than the Japanese children. When confronted with illness or discomfort, the Chinese children cried and complained, while the Japanese children continued hiking with determination. The Japanese children were competent at bringing, rationing, and preparing food, while the Chinese children did not know what to do and wanted adults to prepare food for them. The Japanese children worked together to deal with problems, while the Chinese children either hung back passively or, in the case of one Chinese child with a leadership title, stood back while telling others to work harder. The Chinese parents rushed to assist whenever their children had problems, while the Japanese parents stood back and let their children learn independence. "The Japanese have already publicly stated, 'your current generation of children is no match for ours!'" Sun warned (1993b:15). "All the world is competing, and education is key; if Chinese children have no ability to compete in the world, can China not fall behind?" Sun's critique was widely cited by the Chinese media, although it was also criticized for drawing unfair comparisons: after all, the camping trip was organized by Japanese camping enthusiasts for a largely Japanese group with much more camping experience than their Chinese counterparts (He Pingping et al. 1994). Still, Sun's exaggerated praise of Japanese children and harsh critique of Chinese children was often mentioned to me by Dalian parents when they discussed the flaws of the single-child generation, or of specific singletons. Because they viewed Japanese people as rivals, role models, former colonizers, and potential future aggressors, people I knew in Dalian were especially fearful and angry about the charge that Chinese children could not compete against their Japanese counterparts. Sun had succeeded in using the common journalistic strategy (Boyer 2000) of highlighting deeply felt social concerns by exaggerating cultural differences about which audiences were already sensitive.

The Chinese parents I knew generally agreed with media discourses about the singleton generation's failure to behave in accordance with the values Chinese society wanted them to live by. I often heard them scolding their own children for this kind of failure. During my research in Dalian homes and schools, I noticed that the terms *tinghua* (obedience), *zhaogu/guanxin/hui jiao pengyou* (caring/sociableness), *zili/duli* (independence), and *youxiu* (excellence) were commonly used by parents when they talked about values that their children should learn. These values were key to Chinese parents' aspirations for and complaints about their own children and about the singleton generation in general. Although these values were not the only ones promoted by Chinese parents, I have chosen to focus on them because they were the most prominent ones I heard parents discuss. These four values are also prominent in previous studies of Chinese childrearing (Chao 1994, 1995, 2000, 2001; Li 2001; Lieber et al. 2001; Lieber et al. 2004; Xiao 2001).[5] Though independence and excellence were more necessary than caring/sociableness and obedience for upward mobility, parents I knew in Dalian from a wide range of socioeconomic positions all considered it important for their children to internalize all four of these values.[6]

Although these values have many nuanced meanings, I refer to them by the simple terms *obedience, caring/sociableness, independence,* and *excellence* for the sake of conciseness. Although these values refer not to discrete objects but, rather, to wide ranges of beliefs and perceptions, I use discrete terms as heuristic shorthand. I call these ideas "values" to distinguish them from "cultural models," the complex network of many connected cognitive schemas and scripts that exist in the minds of individuals but are often too complex, tacit, and taken for granted to be fully recognized or articulated (D'Andrade 1995; D'Andrade and Strauss 1992; Strauss and Quinn 1997). Cultural models include values, but are far more complex and flexible, and, thus, difficult for individuals to recognize and discuss. Values are the simple heuristic terms that people often use when discussing aspects of cultural models that they consider good, important, and worthy of emulation.

The need to use simple terms to represent complex values exists not only in scholarly arguments like my own but also in the ways Chinese parents talked to their children about how their children should behave. Indeed, as I will argue below, children's failure to behave in the ways their parents desired resulted less from their singleton status per se than from the fact that much detail and nuance was lost when parents translated the complex cultural models in their minds into simple terms, expecting that these simple terms would enable children to (re)construct the much more complex cultural models their parents wanted them to develop.

Unlike the discourses popular in the Chinese media and among the Chinese parents I knew in Dalian, much of the recent scholarship on the personalities of singletons in China (Davis and Sensenbrenner 2000; Falbo and Poston 1993; Falbo et al. 1989; Feng 1992, 2005; Fong 2004a) and in the West (Falbo 1984a, 1984b; Laybourn 1994) has suggested that singleton status per se is not actually the causal factor underlying many of the social, psychological, and moral failings attributed to it. Here, I suggest an alternative explanation for these failings, by examining the values Chinese parents want their children to appropriate and the reasons most Chinese singletons seem unable to do so.

Obedience

While Chinese parents expect their children to bring their families and society the benefits of modernization, they also want their children to internalize the longstanding Chinese value of obedience to parents, teachers, elders, employers, and the state. This value has its roots in the Confucian ideology that was promoted by the Chinese state from the Sui Dynasty (581–618) until the fall of the Qing Dynasty in 1911. The civil service exams that structured the education of the elite in imperial China were based primarily on state interpretations of Confucianism that emphasized the importance of the *sangang* (Three Bonds): analogous hierarchical relationships in which subjects must obey rulers, sons must obey fathers, and wives must obey husbands (De Bary and Chaffee 1989; Elman 1990). The value of obedience was also promoted by socialization experiences in the patriarchal, high-fertility families of prerevolutionary China, in which Confucian ideology, parental control of property, the limited availability of schooling, and competition among siblings for parental favor ensured that children were powerless and responsive to authority (Hsiao-Tung Fei 1992; Lan and Fong 1999; Watson 1980, 1984, 1985, 1992; Wolf 1972; Wolf and Huang 1980).

The generation that grew up under Maoism had fewer reasons to obey their elders, since the Maoist government had discredited Confucianism, confiscated elder-controlled property, and expanded schooling (thus allowing children to form horizontal peer bonds that rivaled their bonds to adults).[7] Some Red Guard teenagers even participated in the denunciation and torture of teachers, cadres, and other authority figures during the Cultural Revolution (1966–76). Yet their perpetration of political violence could also be seen as the result of a powerful sense of obedience to Mao Zedong and to local Red Guard leaders they perceived as advocating the true path of Maoism, which enforced a political culture of total obedience to the state. Moreover, most parents I knew

told me that they had been obedient to their parents despite the Cultural Revolution because they had to compete with siblings for their parents' favor. Despite the Maoist state's attempts to usurp the role of the family, parents still had the power to allocate affection, attention, praise, scoldings, and beatings, as well as chores, wedding expenses, opportunities for further education, opportunities for inheriting a parent's job in a state enterprise, and opportunities for staying in the city rather than being sent to the rural areas, to which most urban youth were exiled during the Cultural Revolution (Davis and Harrell 1993; Jankowiak 1993; Whyte and Parish 1984).

After 1978, the Chinese government rehabilitated certain aspects of Confucianism (particularly those that promoted filiality, education, and obedience) and continued to demand obedience to the state, although not as strictly as under Maoism. Parents I observed in Dalian still considered obedience very important and tried to promote it by using the same shame training techniques observed by Heidi Fung among families in Taiwan (Fung 1999; Miller et al. 1999; Miller et al. 2001).

Parents were especially likely to tell daughters to be obedient, saying that women lacking in this regard were likely to be seen as unpleasant by husbands, parents-in-law, and employers. Although they were seen as naturally less obedient than girls, boys were also encouraged to be obedient because defiance could hinder their success in the educational system and in their future careers. Although they encouraged children to be ambitious agents in the pursuit of academic and socioeconomic achievement, parents hoped that children's ambitions would be channeled into a kind of "docile agency" similar to that described by Saba Mahmood (2001), who argued that the religiously devout Muslim Egyptian women she studied expressed their agency through self-discipline and cultivated obedience.

Caring/Sociableness

Parents I knew in Dalian often tried to remind their children that they should care for others and know how to make friends (zhaogu/ guanxin/hui jiao pengyou). While imperial

Chinese cultural models of Confucianism emphasized obedience to authority, they also promoted the reciprocal responsibilities exemplified by the Five Relations (*wulun*) between father and son, ruler and subject, husband and wife, older brother and younger brother, and friend and friend (De Bary and Chaffee 1989; Tu 1998). The overwhelming importance of caring/sociableness continued to be deeply embedded in Chinese society well into the early 20th century (Hsiao-Tung Fei 1992) and remained highly salient under Maoism as well as during the post-Mao era, as an organizing schema for the *renqing* (human feelings) and *guanxi* (connections) that structured China's political economy (Fei 1982; Gold et al. 2002; Hwang 1987, 2000; Kipnis 1997; Yan 1996; Kuo-Shu Yang 1995; Mayfair Mei-Hui Yang 1994), for the heavy parental investment that fueled singletons' achievements and opportunities, and for the *xiaoshun* (filiality) that was supposed to ensure social security for the elderly even as the Chinese state dismantled its social welfare system. The emphasis on caring/sociableness seemed to be an aspect of Chinese culture that transcended citizenship and geography: In a comparison with childrearing values of Euro-American mothers and immigrant Chinese mothers (most of whom were from Taiwan) in Los Angeles, Ruth Chao found that the Chinese mothers were more likely than the Euro-American mothers to emphasize interdependence rather than independence (Chao 1994, 1995, 2000, 2001). In prerevolutionary, Maoist, and post-Mao periods alike, success at any endeavor in China depended on the creation and maintenance of elaborate social networks in which gifts and favors were exchanged, as well as on the art of knowing how to help other people avoid losing face, and discern others' needs, desires, alliances, and enmities in complex social situations.

Parents I knew in Dalian told me they were worried that, having missed out on experiencing the reciprocities of sibling relationships, their children would be poorly prepared to deal with the web of social relationships they were supposed to cultivate once they reached adulthood. Moreover, because the exchange of gifts, loans, and favors among siblings was a key element of adult social networks, parents worried that their children would be deprived of the social relationships vital to economic as well as emotional well-being. In the 1990s and early 2000s, siblings were the main source of loans and gifts that enabled unemployed parents to pay living and medical expenses and even send their children to schools they could not otherwise afford. The availability of many siblings who could offer financial assistance was key to maintaining social stability during the economic restructuring that caused 25 percent of survey respondents' mothers ($N = 2,190$) and 12 percent of their fathers ($N = 2,190$) to be laid off or given early retirement even though the average age of survey respondents' mothers was 43 ($N = 2,125$), and the average age of their fathers was 45 ($N = 2,128$). Siblings were also key for helping one and one's children get new employment or promotions (Bian 1994).

Parents were especially concerned when their children seemed to want to avoid forming the family ties that produced the strongest relationships of all. The importance of marriage and childrearing (which were key to creating and maintaining the bonds that would produce caring/sociableness) was supposed to be universally practiced in China. As of 1987, less than one percent of Chinese women had remained single through age 50 (Zeng 2000:93), and an analysis of China's 1982 one-per-thousand fertility survey showed that the median annual period parity progression for the decade 1972–81 was 0.986, suggesting that only 1.4 percent of married women did not end up having children (Feeney and Wang 1993:71; Feeney and Yu 1987:81). Among respondents to my survey, however, 86 percent ($N = 1,144$) of girls and 73 percent ($N = 834$) of boys indicated that they wanted to live neolocally after marriage; 18 percent of girls ($N = 1,239$) and 10 percent of boys ($N = 870$) indicated that they did not want to eventually marry; and 32 percent of the girls ($N = 1,215$) and 16 percent of the boys ($N = 853$) indicated that they did not want to eventually have children. The higher proportion of girls who indicated that they preferred neolocality, marriage avoidance, and childlessness was probably because of recognition that family ties imposed especially heavy responsibilities on women. Because the socialization of male and female singletons was very similar (Fong 2002), many girls felt uncomfortable about the extra responsibilities that were expected of women in family relationships.

Independence

While the terms *zili* and *duli* (independence) could be found in writings on self-cultivation in the Confucian tradition (Pei-Yi Wu 1990), they acquired new prominence as part of Chinese discourses of nationalism in the 19th century, when, beginning with China's defeat in the Opium War (1839–42), the imperial Chinese government made a series of concessions of money, territory, sovereignty, and trade rights to a variety of foreign countries, including Austria, England, France, Germany, Italy, Japan, Russia, Spain, and the United States. The problems caused by these concessions created a new class of Chinese reformers and revolutionaries distressed by China's low position within the world system and convinced that both Chinese individuals and the Chinese nation-state needed to build independence to avoid falling victim to conquest and colonization. The tendency to relate national to individual independence was exemplified by the revolutionary activist Ou Qujia, who published an article in 1902 lamenting Cantonese merchants' lack of personal and political independence from foreigners, colonizers, and government officials (Ou 1971:18). As Prasenjit Duara noted, "Ou used *zili* creatively to forge a link between political or national independence and the character or spirit of independence" (1997:55). The Maoist government strongly promoted the value of independence as an antidote both to China's submissive relationship with foreign powers and to the complex webs of "feudal" social relationships that interfered with the Chinese state's attempts to establish direct relationships with individual citizens. *Fulian* (The All-China Women's Federation) promoted the slogan *zili, zixin, ziqiang* (independence, self-confidence, self-strengthening) as a key prescription for women's liberation from feudal patriarchy. Parents in Dalian also told me that

parental neglect, political instability, economic hardship, and compulsory migration taught them independence while they were growing up in large, poor families, facing political violence, and forced to live in impoverished rural areas during the Cultural Revolution (1966–76). They worried that their children lacked these toughening hardships, even though independence would be particularly important for those upwardly mobile members of the single-child generation who would have neither sibling support nor the assistance of parents or other relatives experienced in the educational and professional arenas of upward mobility.

Independence is an important theme in child socialization in many societies. Adrie Kusserow (1999, 2004) found that lower-class and lower-middle-class New York parents counseled their children to develop independence to protect them from being dragged into the underclass and to help them claw their way into the middle class, and Caroline Bledsoe (1990) found that Sierra Leone parents claimed that having their children live in foster homes in which they were mistreated would strengthen children's character. Similarly, parents in Dalian considered independence both a product of hardship and a quality that would enable one to endure hardship. Yet, despite their desire for children to develop independence, parents also wanted to spare their children from hardship, invest heavily in their physical, emotional, and academic well-being, and foster powerful relationships of mutual dependence similar to the mother–child bonds found by Margery Wolf (1972) in 1960s Taiwan and by Anne Allison (1996) in 1980s Japan. Although such intense parental involvement could persuade children to be obedient and help them excel, it could also cause children to rely on parental investment rather than their own initiative and ability.

Excellence

The Chinese value of youxiu (excellence) has its roots in the stratification system of imperial China, especially the ostensibly meritocratic imperial civil service exam system, which began under the Han Dynasty (202 BCE to CE 220), became the main path to elite status under the Song Dynasty (960–1279), and lasted until 1905, when it was abolished as part of the Qing Dynasty's last-ditch efforts at reform. The value of excellence was powerful in this system, but it was largely confined to elite male gentry and often relevant only for a few especially talented sons in each family (Elman 1990, 1991; Esherick and Rankin 1990; Hsiao-Tung Fei 1953; Hymes 1987; Waltner 1983). The Maoist government attacked the value of excellence by promoting egalitarianism, persecuting intellectuals, and severely limiting the socioeconomic rewards of academic achievement (Pepper 1996). The Maoist state tried to redefine excellence in terms of political loyalties and revolutionary zeal. However, political definitions of *excellence* were so unstable and dependent on dangerous power struggles that parents who grew up under Maoism told me that they learned to focus on avoiding trouble rather than on trying to excel. The post-Mao government revived the prerevolutionary value of excellence, which fit well with the competitive structure of global neoliberal capitalism. Stratification became increasingly severe and meritocratic, and the value of excellence became increasingly salient. Lower fertility forced parents to invest more heavily in making sure that their singletons excelled. Unlike children of the large sibsets common among previous generations, post-Mao singletons were their parents' sole source of pride, hope, and old-age insurance. In large sibsets, daughters and less-talented sons could be excused from parental demands for excellence; after the one-child policy, however, almost every urban child was a singleton whose parents desperately hoped for excellence. The educational system and the job market became increasingly competitive, as every child tried to reach the top of a political economy that was becoming increasingly pyramidal. As the number of job seekers with higher education rose, employers raised the bar of minimum educational qualifications. Excellence became increasingly important as well as expectations and hiring standards rose.

Two* Case Studies of Parents' Efforts to Teach Their Children Excellence, Independence, Obedience, and Caring/Sociableness

I heard frequent complaints from parents in Dalian about their own children's inability to live up to values of excellence, independence, obedience, and caring/sociableness, as well as about the prevalence of such inability among the single-child generation in general. In this section, I examine the miscommunications and misunderstandings that caused these complaints in five families I observed over the course of eight years. I have chosen to focus on these five families as case studies because their children were the youngest among the families that invited me to their homes regularly over the course of my research. Most of the other families I knew in Dalian either met me after their children were already in their late teens, or did not invite me to their homes frequently enough to enable me to observe their parent-child interactions over the course of their adolescence. Though these five families were unique (in the same way that every family is unique), they were not unusual, either in the terms of their socioeconomic characteristics (which were similar to those of most of my survey respondents) or in terms of their personalities or family dynamics. The conflicts I observed among these family members were common, and I observed similar conflicts between parents and children over similar issues among most of the other families I knew in Dalian.

Xu Qun: Not caring/sociable enough, not obedient enough, or not excellent and independent enough?

When I first met Xu Qun in 1998, she was a 16-year-old singleton vocational high school student whose parents often praised her for her resistance to peer pressure. "Her high school is chaotic, with lots of little hoodlums, but she

*Five case studies are reported in original paper.

doesn't pay any attention to them," her father told me proudly. "My daughter doesn't need to play around with others, and she's happy to just stay home when she's not at school." "My daughter knows her study time is precious, so she doesn't waste time playing around," Xu Qun's mother told me happily. Xu Qun was not a particularly outstanding student, and she spent most of her after-school time watching TV instead of studying. Still, her parents encouraged her social aloofness because they thought it would keep her out of trouble and free up more time that could potentially be devoted to study.

At the same time, Xu Qun's parents also criticized her for not caring enough about others, particularly family members. Once, in 1999, Xu Qun's parents were preparing food for a large group of Xu Qun's mother's relatives who had come for a Spring Festival family reunion. They called for Xu Qun to help them, but Xu Qun ignored them because she wanted to finish watching a soap opera. Xu Qun's mother grabbed her and pulled her into the kitchen, telling her to help cut vegetables. Xu Qun complained that she was missing one of her favorite soap operas, but her mother insisted, saying that "a girl needs to learn to care for others." Xu Qun slowly and reluctantly cut the vegetables, but tears started flowing down her face. Her mother snapped at her for "crying over such a small thing" and said it would "look bad in front of the others." Xu Qun's father was more sympathetic and said she could go back to watching her soap opera, but Xu Qun said it was over anyway and continued to cut the vegetables slowly, as tears streamed down her face. "My parents are always saying my time is precious, but they keep making me do chores and don't let me have my own time," Xu Qun later complained to me.

On another occasion in 1999, when Xu Qun said she preferred to watch TV rather than go shopping with her 11-year-old maternal cousin, Xu Qun's mother scolded her for not caring about her cousin. "Why don't you want to go shopping with your cousin?" Xu Qun's mother demanded. "Cousins should always care for each other. Someday when we're gone, your cousins will be all you have left!" Xu Qun replied that shopping was too exhausing, and spending time with her cousin was "not interesting" because they did not have much in common.

"How can you say that?" Xu Qun's mother demanded. "What kind of girl are you, without even a bit of a loving heart?"

Xu Qun relented and took her cousin shopping but later told me she resented having to do it. "My parents are always telling me that my time is precious, and that I shouldn't waste it, but they keep wanting me to waste time doing boring things like this."

Xu Qun's parents wanted Xu Qun to practice independence only when it was necessary for attaining excellence through studying and for avoiding the mischief that might result from socializing with "hoodlum" classmates; they did not want her to isolate herself from social activities in favor of solitary leisure activities that would not lead to excellence, such as watching TV. They wanted her to show less caring/sociableness toward those her parents considered unworthy (such as classmates) while prioritizing caring/sociableness with others (such as relatives) deemed worthy by her parents. What Xu Qun internalized, however, were the aspects of the values of excellence and independence that defined her own time (regardless of whether it was spent on leisure or studying) as so valuable that it should not be wasted on anyone else, including relatives. She therefore felt hurt and confused when her parents wanted her to waste time on family social activities that she did not enjoy.

In 2000, Xu Qun's social aloofness waned as she started dating Sun Hang, a handsome but academically average male classmate whose parents were both factory workers. She increasingly spent most of her after-school time with him and his friends, none of whom were very studious. When she invited him to her home, she eagerly cooked an unusually elaborate and delicious meal for him. After he left, her mother asked her coldly why she was usually unwilling to cook for her own parents or relatives, but so eager to cook for her boyfriend. Xu Qun was hurt because she had assumed her parents would be proud of her for cooking such a large, delicious meal. "You always tell me to care for others, but now you're saying this!" she said with exasperation.

Xu Qun's parents disapproved of her relationship with Sun Hang and tried to get her to end it. "Don't look at him as so important,"

Xu Qun's mother told her. "Your time is valuable. You should be studying, instead of wasting time with him."

"Why do you want to hang around with a little hoodlum like him?" Xu Qun's father demanded. "A boy like him has no future. He's no use at all!"

"I like him!" Xu Qun replied. "I like being with him! Don't manage my affairs!" Xu Qun continued to date Sun Hang despite her parents' misgivings. When she failed to pass the adult education college entrance exam, her parents blamed her failure on the time she wasted on dating rather than studying. Xu Qun, however, claimed that she failed the exam because she "just wasn't made of studious material," and that she would have spent her time on other leisure activities if she had not dated Sun Hang. After graduating from vocational high school, Xu Qun spent most of her time with Sun Hang and other friends. Xu Qun spent even less time than before with her parents and relatives. Her parents frequently scolded her for caring so much for Sun Hang and other friends they considered unworthy.

At the same time, however, Xu Qun's parents continued to encourage her to be sociable with those they considered worthy of her time. In 2002, when Xu Qun got her first job as a salesclerk, she came home crying after just a few weeks. "I can't stand how the girls at work gossip and conspire against me!" she sobbed. "Their relationships are complicated, but the boss always takes good care of them because they flatter the boss."

She wanted to quit, but her parents advised against it. "Social relationships will be difficult wherever you go," her father said. "You can't expect to do well at your job just because you have ability. You have to learn to get along with your coworkers and flatter your supervisors as well."

"They've been working together for a long time, so of course they're going to care for each other more than they care for you," her mother said. "You should try to get along with all of them, and care for them, and do extra work even when they don't ask you to. Eventually you'll have good relations with them too."

Xu Qun did as her parents said, and tried to befriend coworkers and supervisors. By 2006, she had become such good friends with them that she spent much of her free time with them. Her parents were pleased that she got along with her coworkers and supervisors, but they scolded her when she refused to look for better jobs because she now enjoyed working with her coworkers and supervisors and did not want to be disloyal to them. She even broke up with Sun Hang and began dating a coworker. Her parents were dismayed because this coworker's family background and career prospects put him in an even lower socioeconomic status than that occupied by Sun Hang. Although their efforts to get her to care for others had succeeded in some ways, they were still dissatisfied because Xu Qun often focused her care on people her parents deemed unworthy and failed to put aside these social ties even when they hindered her pursuit of excellence.

Chen Sheng: Not independent and excellent enough or not caring/sociable enough?

When I first met Chen Sheng in 1998, he was a 15-year-old singleton junior high school student whose parents often exhorted him to sacrifice caring/sociableness to pursue excellence. "Your time is precious," Chen Sheng's mother told when he asked for permission to go to the mall with his lower-achieving friends. "You should be spending all your time on studying."

"You shouldn't play with classmates who don't love to study," Chen Sheng's father added. "Your goal is to get into a keypoint high school, but they just want to hang out in society. You'll leave them behind soon, so you might as well stay away from them now."

"Not everyone can be good at studying, but their characters are good," Chen Sheng protested. "I think it's good to play with them." His parents relented and let him go to the mall that time but continued to discourage him from spending too much time with less studious friends. Because it was difficult to secure his parents' permission to spend time with them outside of school, Chen Sheng increasingly limited his social activities to school time and spent most of his time outside of school studying by himself.

As Chen Sheng and his friends entered their final year of junior high school in 1999, Chen Sheng spent less time with his friends, even at school. Instead of playing basketball with them during lunch breaks, he stayed in the classroom and continued to study. "I want to play with them, but I don't have time," Chen Sheng told me in 1999. "Our thinking is different. I know the high school entrance exam is important, but they don't."

In 2000, Chen Sheng's less studious friends entered vocational high schools while Chen Sheng entered a keypoint high school that kept him so busy that he almost never had time to visit his less studious friends from junior high school.[8] Chen Sheng at first told me that he missed spending time with them. As he made new, equally studious friends at his keypoint high school, however, Chen Sheng mentioned prior friendships less and less. Chen Sheng's parents liked Chen Sheng's new friends much better than the old cohort and did not deter Chen Sheng from visiting his new friends outside of school. Unlike his old friends, however, Chen Sheng's new friends seldom spent time together engaging in leisure activities after school because they were all too busy studying in their respective homes. Their social activities together consisted mainly of helping each other with schoolwork during study hall at school, and sometimes calling each other for further help. Although Chen Sheng sometimes spoke with nostalgic fondness about the fun he had playing with less studious friends during junior high school, he was increasingly comfortable with the values of excellence and independence his parents tried to inculcate in him. "What my parents said was right," Chen Sheng told me in 2002. "I enjoyed playing with my friends, but if I had played too much with them, I would not have got into this high school. If I want to succeed, I have to rely on my own ability."

Although Chen Sheng's parents were pleased at Chen Sheng's increasing excellence and independence, they were dismayed when his focus on these values caused him to care less for relatives than they felt he should. In 2002, when Chen Sheng's father wanted to take him to his paternal relatives' Spring Festival family reunion feast, Chen Sheng wanted to stay at home and study instead. "If

I go, I'll spend the whole night playing poker and chatting idly!" Chen Sheng protested. "That's such a waste of time! You always tell me to study, but now you're telling me to play. What if this keeps me from getting into college?"

"How can you be so lacking in family sentiments?" Chen Sheng's father demanded. He made Chen Sheng go to his family reunion, but Chen Sheng returned home to study after just a few hours instead of staying to play poker all night as his parents did.

Chen Sheng's dedication to his studies paid off in 2003 when he was admitted to a good four-year university program. When I visited him and his parents in 2004, however, his father complained to me that Chen Sheng had so much trouble getting along with his college roommates that he lived at home and commuted to his university classes, wasting the dormitory rent that his parents had paid for him. "He studies well, but he isn't good at social relations," Chen Sheng's father complained to me. "Society is too complicated, and I fear he will not have the ability to adjust." Chen Sheng's parents succeeded in getting Chen Sheng to prioritize excellence and independence over caring/sociableness, but they also considered Chen Sheng's resulting aloofness unsatisfactory.

Discussion

I have presented the dilemmas faced by Chen Sheng, and Xu Qun, as examples of contradictions between the values of obedience, caring/sociableness, independence, and excellence their parents encouraged them to follow. Most parents I knew in Dalian wanted their children to adhere to the desirable aspects and avoid the undesirable aspects of all four of these values. Although children tried to do so, they found it tremendously difficult and were often criticized for failing to live by one or another aspect of at least some of these values. The desirable aspect of each value was often inseparable from its undesirable side. The undesirable aspects of a given value could often conflict with the desirable aspects of another. The flip side of obedience was the kind of passivity demonstrated by lack of initiative and ambition; the flip side of caring/sociableness was the kind of dependence that made them too eager to socialize instead of studying and too comfortable with coworkers and boyfriend to pursue better jobs and boyfriends; the flip side of independence was a kind of isolation; and the flip side of excellence was an arrogance toward family members that their parents thought deserved more obedience, care, and sociableness. As the experiences of these families suggest, it was difficult for children to consistently abide by all the values their parents promoted because these were often mutually contradictory.

Recognizing that their society was an uneasy mixture of Confucianism, socialism, and capitalism, parents I knew in Dalian tried to teach their children values that would enable them to fulfill all the roles that would be expected of them. They would have to be excellent and self-reliant enough to make their way to the top of the neoliberal world system, but still sufficiently devoted to their duty to bring their families and society with them in their uphill march. They would have to rely on themselves alone to excel in a competitive stratification system, but they would also have to remain responsible to their families and social networks and obedient to their elders and superiors. What parents feared, however, was that their children would also learn the undesirable aspects of all of these values: Obedience could stifle their excellence; caring/sociableness could limit their ambition; independence could encourage them to refrain from creating and maintaining family ties and social networks; excellence could encourage them to assert their own superiority and distance themselves from peers, parents, teachers, employers, and state authorities that they deemed inferior. It was difficult for children to develop only the desirable aspects of the values their parents promoted, as these desirable aspects were inextricably connected with undesirable consequences.

The values of independence, excellence, obedience, and caring/sociableness are used heuristically by Chinese and Western psychologists, as well as by the Chinese media and by the Chinese parents and children I knew, to refer to the desired outcomes of behaving in accordance with cultural models held in mind but too complex to be adequately referenced or communicated in simple terms. As Roy D'Andrade, Naomi Quinn, Dorothy Holland, Michael Cole, and Claudia Strauss have argued, an individual's emotions and actions are motivated by interactions between countless cultural models with varying degrees of psychological force (D'Andrade 1995; D'Andrade and Strauss 1992; Holland and Cole 1995; Holland and Quinn 1987; Strauss and Quinn 1997). Cultural models are cognitive schemas that can be embodied and taken for granted, but they can also be consciously perceived and expressed, in whole or in part. A cultural model can also be seen as a "script" that individuals try to follow as they "perform" their lives (Kohrman 1999; Townsend 2002). Cultural models are interlinked networks of cognitive schemas "shaped by the learner's specific life experiences" and sensitive to context. Such models tend to be shared by many (though not all) people who have had similar experiences (Strauss and Quinn 1997:52). Though individuals use cultural models to "reconstruct . . . memories of past events, determine the meanings . . . [of] ongoing experience, [provide] . . . expectations for the future," and "fill in missing or ambiguous information" (Strauss and Quinn 1997:49), these models are also flexible enough to be adapted to new or ambiguous situations through "regulated improvisation" (Bourdieu 1977:11).

Because talk about the values of independence, excellence, obedience, and caring/sociableness is much simpler than the complex, flexible, interconnected cultural models held in mind by parents, many of the nuances of the parents' cultural models were lost in the process of transmission to their children, who, in the course of maturing, developed practices and rationales that differed significantly from those that would ideally be generated by the cultural models of their parents. This resulted in parental dissatisfaction with their children's attitudes and behaviors. Exacerbating this dissatisfaction was the fact that parents not only wanted their children to replicate the cultural models they held in mind, they also wanted their children to improve on these cultural models in ways that would make them better adjusted to contemporary socioeconomic conditions than their parents were. The contradictions inherent in parents' dual desires for replication and improvement made it even more difficult for children to understand and fulfill their parents' wishes.

Claudia Strauss outlined multiple strategies (sometimes conscious, sometimes unconscious) that a person could use to deal with contradictory cultural models: choosing one and rejecting the rest; selectively choosing parts from each of several contradictory cultural models and integrating them in a new, internally consistent one; compartmentalizing contradictory cultural models so that expressions of one are unrelated to expressions of the other; following one cultural model on certain occasions and another on other occasions; and simply living with the discomfort of ambivalence (1990, 1997a, 1997b:213–214). As children in my study matured into adults, they became more skilled and sophisticated at practicing strategies for dealing with contradictions in ways that would allow them to attain social and economic success while minimizing psychological discomfort. Parents wanted their children to become skilled at these strategies, but they did not necessarily agree with their children about how to do so. As children became young adults, they eventually developed complex integrative cultural models just as their parents had. These models did not reproduce those of their parents but were constructed anew by the younger generation.

Unlike the complex, context-sensitive cultural models held in mind by parents, the values of excellence, independence, caring/sociableness, and obedience were discussed in simple and seemingly inflexible terms. Like the Pakistani woman Katherine Ewing saw as maintaining "an experience of wholeness in the face of radical contradictions, by keeping only one frame of reference in mind at any particular moment" (1990:274), and the U.S. men whose experiences of their cultural models Claudia Strauss saw as "partially fragmented, partially integrated" (1997a), the parents I knew in Dalian talked as if they always lived by the same set of values, even though they

actually followed different, often contradictory principles in different contexts. Parents' tendency to claim wholeness and integration despite the contradictions and fragmentation in their child socialization practices resulted in inconsistencies that children found frustrating.

Individuals tend to adhere to different, often mutually contradictory, values in different contexts, even while believing that their values are integrated, stable, and noncontradictory. Children started out unable to recognize which values should be applied in which contexts and, thus, tried to apply the same value to every situation. When this caused problems, parents scolded children for failing to abide by appropriate values. Because parents themselves had the "illusion of wholeness" Ewing described, parents at any given moment thought the values they wanted their children to follow were consistent and did not explain to children that what was needed was better judgment about which values fit which context. Believing, based on the "illusion of wholeness" perpetuated by parents, that values can and should be applied consistently across contexts, and unable (at first) to recognize salient differences between different contexts, children became frustrated at contradictions between what parents said in one context and what they said in another, and feared that parents would find reasons to scold them no matter what they did. Parents, meanwhile, were frustrated by children's inability to live up to whatever values the parents thought most important on any given occasion.

As the parent–child interactions described in my case studies suggest, parental socialization consisted primarily of scolding children for failing to adhere to one value or another and, less frequently, of praising children for adhering to one value or another. Parents seldom talked to children about generalizable metastrategies for deciding which value to match to which context. Children were usually left to develop their own metastrategies based on trial and error, with parental scoldings and undesirable social consequences serving to show when they were in error. Parents themselves did not consciously think about complex guidelines because matching values to contexts was part of their taken-for-granted habitus

(Bourdieu 1977, 1998). The "illusion of wholeness" prevented parents from emphasizing the context-sensitive quality of valued practices and prevented parents from teaching their children appropriate guidelines.

The difficulties of teaching the subtleties of context sensitivity were exacerbated by the rapidity of social and economic change that made it difficult for parents to figure out what kinds of metastrategies would enable their children to attain socioeconomic success while still abiding by values the parents considered important. Frequent changes in the costs and benefits of following any given value in any given context (because of constantly changing individual and family situations and the dramatic social, political, and economic changes China was experiencing) made it hard for parents themselves to figure out what optimal guidelines were, and, thus, even less able to articulate them. Moreover, parents were usually not aware of the metastrategies they themselves used. As taken-for-granted parts of habitus, such metastrategies were difficult to recognize, conceptualize, or articulate. Even when parents tried to articulate aspects of these metastrategies to their children, it was difficult to do so in ways that children could understand, internalize, and apply.

Moreover, by the time children were mature enough to discuss and understand metastrategies their parents might articulate to them, cultural models they had developed earlier in childhood – including the metastrategies they unconsciously developed as part of their own habitus, which usually differed from the metastrategies their parents wanted them to develop – were already ingrained and difficult to change. As Strauss and Quinn argue, cultural models people develop during childhood are especially durable and likely to have motivational force because they tend to be reinforced by associations with parental love or disapproval that have particular power because of children's emotional vulnerability, and because they can become self-reinforcing as the lens through which future experiences are interpreted (1997:90–94). As the first schemas to become imprinted in a person's mind, values and cultural models learned during childhood are hard to erase entirely, even though they may be altered or overwritten by later experiences. In addition, parents also had difficulty adjusting their own cultural models of child socialization quickly enough to keep pace with their children's cognitive, social, and emotional development. When children were small, they could only understand simple talk about simple values, so parents learned to express their desired for children's behavior in terms of these values. As they grew up and encountered more complex situations and expanded their cognitive abilities, however, children gradually, unconsciously, and habitually developed more complex cultural models that included their own metastrategies for matching different values to different contexts. This was part of the process of becoming an adult. As adults, parents likewise behaved in accordance with complex cultural models, and indeed wanted their children to develop similar models that would help them cope with the complex, changing situations they would increasingly encounter.

Children ultimately did so, but their cultural models developed from newer baselines that included the simple values their parents had articulated to them, as well as inferences based on other experiences, but did not typically replicate the unarticulated cultural models actually held in mind by parents. Because complex cultural models are constructed in response to experiences, and experiences vary widely among individuals, it was unlikely for any two individuals to develop identical cultural models. While individuals may share values, each individual is likely to develop a unique set of cultural models to determine how they should selectively apply these values in context.

NOTES

1 I use the term *singleton* to refer to an "only-child" or a "person without siblings."

2 Part of China's modernization strategy was the enforcement of a one-child policy designed to concentrate parental resources and expectations on each child and, thus, create a generation of ambitious, well-educated children who would lead their country into the First World (Anagnost 1997; Fong 2004a, 2004b, 2006; Greenhalgh 2003a, 2003b, 2005;

Greenhalgh and Winckler 2005; Murphy 2004). The social, economic, and demographic changes associated with this modernization strategy prevented any one set of consistent ideals from becoming dominant in Chinese culture, and made the means to attain success so variable and unpredictable over time that parents and children had difficulty developing consistently effective guidelines for successful behavior.

3   All names in this article (besides those of cited authors) are pseudonyms. Some of the Chinese people described in this article have been mentioned under other pseudonyms in previous publications based on my longitudinal research, but I have given them new pseudonyms in this article to avoid revealing their identities with too many cumulative details in my published work.

4   This survey was administered in 1999 to most of the students in grades 8–9 at the junior high school, grades 10–11 at the vocational high school, and grades 10–12 at the college-prep high school. Of the 2,273 respondents, 738 were from the junior high school, 753 were from the vocational high school, and 782 were from the college-prep high school. The junior high school and college-prep high school had balanced gender ratios, while respondents from the vocational high school were 71 percent ($N = 752$) female because their school specialized in female-dominated majors such as business and tourism. All respondents were between the ages of 13 and 20, 94 percent ($N = 2,167$) of them had no siblings, 5 percent ($N = 2,167$) had one sibling, and 98 percent ($N = 2,171$) were Han, the ethnic group that comprised 92 percent of the Chinese population (Guojia Tongji Ju [National Bureau of Statistics] 2001:93, 100) in 2000. The average age of survey respondents was 16 ($N = 2,253$).

5   Other researchers have sometimes classified what I refer to as the values of excellence, obedience, independence, and caring/sociableness differently. Still it is clear that we are all discussing the same complex of values. For instance, the value I call "independence" encompasses what Ruth Chao calls "the importance of independence, or self-reliance"; what Hong Xiao calls "autonomy," the value I call "obedience," encompasses what Chao calls "balance of choices with obedience and

parental respect"; what Hong Xiao calls "obedience," and what Lieber et al. call "obedience" and "respect for elders and authority," the value I call "excellence," encompasses what Chao calls "the importance of education," what Jin Li calls "the Chinese cultural model of learning," what Hong Xiao calls "hard work," and what Lieber et al. call "excellence and achievement striving, responsibility, and work ethic;" and the value I call "caring/sociableness" encompasses what Chao refers to as "mentioning love and sacrifice: fostering a good relationship with the child," "balance of choices with obedience and parental respect," "respect and concern for other children or others in general," "a good personality and adaptability," "good character, morals, and ethics," what Hong Xiao calls "care orientation," and what Lieber et al. call "caring for others" (Chao 1995; Li 2001; Lieber et al. 2004; Xiao 2001).

6   Although it is possible that certain socioeconomic characteristics correlated with the parenting practices and beliefs I discuss here, such correlations were not noticeable or widely discussed enough for me to make arguments about them based on qualitative data alone. The families I got to know in Dalian included those from many different urban socioeconomic levels (ranging from those of unemployed former factory workers to those of company managers), but I did not know any families from the tiny top (e.g., high-level officials and owners of large corporations) or the large bottom (e.g., farmers and rural migrants lacking urban residency rights) of Chinese society, whose cultural models may have been distinct from those of the less internally differentiated group of working-class and middle-class urban residents in my study. Despite significant differences in their current socioeconomic statuses, the families I knew in Dalian had chaotic stratification histories because of multiple, mutually contradictory destratification and restratification processes that resulted from the Communist takeover of China (1949), the Cultural Revolution (1966–76), and the post-Mao economic reforms (1976–present). I was thus not able to observe the kinds of correlations between class status and childrearing goals that have been observed in Western capitalist societies with more entrenched class systems (Bourdieu

1984; Kusserow 2004; Willis 1977). Although such correlations may exist in China, their analysis would require quantitative data correlating socioeconomic variables with parental beliefs and practices. My survey collected quantitative data about socioeconomic, demographic, and attitudinal variables, but not about the four values I discuss here.

7 Although respondents to my survey indicated that 26 percent ($N = 7,606$) of their grandparents were illiterate, they also indicated that 99 percent of their parents ($N = 4,349$) had at least graduated primary school, and that 96 percent of their parents had at least graduated junior high school.

8 Performance on the citywide high school entrance exam was the main determinant of which kind of high school a student could attend. On the high school application form for 1999 graduates, school types were ranked by selectivity in the following order: (1) keypoint college-prep high schools (*zhongdian gaozhong*); (2) ordinary college-prep high schools (*putong gaozhong*); (3) private college-prep high schools (*minban gaozhong*); (4) professional high schools (*zhongdeng zhuanye xuexiao*); and (5) vocational high schools, adult education professional high schools (*zhiye gaozhong, zhiye zhongzhuan, chengren zhongzhuan*) and technical high schools (*jigong xuexiao*). Students indicated their school preferences prior to taking the entrance exam, and were admitted on the basis of their exam scores.

REFERENCES

Allison, Anne
1996 Producing Mothers. *In* Re-Imaging Japanese Women. A. E. Imamura, ed. Pp. 135–155. Berkeley: University of California Press.
Anagnost, Ann
1997 National Past-Times: Narrative, Representation, and Power in Modern China. Durham, NC: Duke University Press.
Bian, Yanjie
1994 Work and Inequality in Urban China. Albany: State University of New York Press.
Bledsoe, Caroline
1990 "No Success without Struggle": Social Mobility and Hardship for Foster Children in Sierra Leone. Man (n.s.) 25(1):70–88.

Bourdieu, Pierre
1977 Outline of a Theory of Practice. Richard Nice, trans. Cambridge: Cambridge University Press.
1984 Distinction: A Social Critique of the Judgement of Taste. Cambridge, MA: Harvard University Press.
1998 Practical Reason: On the Theory of Action. Cambridge: Polity.
Boyer, Dominic
2000 On the Sedimentation and Accreditation of Social Knowledges of Difference: Mass Media, Journalism, and the Reproduction of East/West Alterities in Unified Germany. Cultural Anthropology 15(4):459–491.
Chao, Ruth K.
1994 Beyond Parental Control; Authoritarian Parenting Style: Understanding Chinese Parenting through the Cultural Notion of Training. Child Development 45:1111–1119.
1995 Chinese and European American Cultural Models of the Self Reflected in Mothers' Childrearing Beliefs. Ethos 23(3): 328–354.
2000 The Parenting of Immigrant Chinese and European American Mothers: Relations between Parenting Styles, Socialization Goals, and Parental Practices. Journal of Applied Developmental Psychology 21(2):233–248.
2001 Extending Research on the Consequences of Parenting Style for Chinese Americans and European Americans. Child Development 72:1832–1843.
Chen Kewen
1988 Dushengzinü Yu Feidushengzinu Xingwei Tedian He Jiating Jiaoyu De Bijiao Yanjiu: Dui Beijing Shichengxiang Qianming Ertong De Diaocha Baogao (Comparative research on the behavior particularities and family education of singletons and non-singletons: A report on 1000 children from rural and urban areas of Beijing). *In* Dushengzinü De Xinli Tedian Yu Jiaoyu (Singletons' psychological particularities and education). Beijing Shifan Daxue Jiaoyu Kexue Yanjiusuo (Beijing Normal University Educational Science Research Center), ed. Pp. 133–148. Beijing: Nongcun Duwu Chubanshe (Rural reading materials publisher).
D'Andrade, Roy
1995 The Development of Cognitive Anthropology. Cambridge: Cambridge University Press.

D'Andrade, Roy G., and Claudia Strauss
1992   Human Motives and Cultural Models. Cambridge: Cambridge University Press.

Davis, Deborah, and Stevan Harrell
1993   Chinese Families in the Post-Mao Era. Berkeley: University of California Press.

Davis, Deborah, and Julia S. Sensenbrenner
2000   Commercializing Childhood: Parental Purchases for Shanghai's Only Child. In The Consumer Revolution in China. Deborah Davis, ed. Berkeley: University of California Press.

De Bary, William Theodore, and John W. Chaffee
1989   Neo-Confucian Education: The Formative Stage. Berkeley: University of California Press.

Duara, Prasenjit
1997   Nationalists among Transnationals: Overseas Chinese and the Idea of China, 1900–1911. In Ungrounded Empires: The Cultural Politics of Modern Chinese Transnationalism. Aihwa Ong and Donald M. Nonini, eds. Pp. 39–60. New York: Routledge.

Elman, Benjamin A.
1990   Classism, Politics, and Kinship: The Ch'ang Chou School of New Text Confucianism in Late Imperial China. Berkeley: University of California Press.
1991   The Journal of Asian Studies. Political, Social, and Cultural Reproduction via Civil Service Examinations in Late Imperial China 50(1):7–28.

Esherick, Joseph, and Mary Rankin
1990   Chinese Local Elites and Patterns of Dominance. Berkeley: University of California Press.

Ewing, Katherine P.
1990   The Illusion of Wholeness: Culture, Self, and the Experience of Inconsistency. Ethos 18(3):251–271.

Falbo, Toni
1984a   Only Children: A Review. In The Single-Child Family. Toni Falbo, ed. Pp. 1–24. New York: Guilford.

Falbo, Tony, ed.
1984b   The Single-Child Family. New York: Guilford.

Falbo, Toni, and Dudley L. Poston Jr.
1993   The Academic, Personality, and Physical Outcomes of Only Children in China. Child Development 64(1):18.

Falbo, Toni, Dudley L. Poston, G. Ji, S. Jiao, Q. Jing, S. Wang, Q. Gu, H. Yin, and Y. Liu
1989   Physical, Achievement and Personality Characteristics of Chinese Children. Journal of Biosocial Science 21(4):483–495.

Feeney, Griffith, and Feng Wang
1993   Parity Progression and Birth Intervals in China; The Influence of Policy in Hastening Fertility Decline. Population and Development Review 19(1):61–101.

Feeney, Griffith, and Jinyuan Yu
1987   Period Parity Progression Ratio Measures of Fertility in China. Population Studies 41(1):77–102.

Fei, Hsiao-Tung
1953   China's Gentry: Essays on Rural-Urban Relations. Chicago: University of Chicago Press.
1992   From the Soil: The Foundations of Chinese Society. Gary G. Hamilton and Wang Zheng, trans. Berkeley: University of California Press.

Fei, Xiaotong
1982   On Changes in Chinese Family Structure. Tianjin Social Science 3:2–5.

Feng, Xiaotian
1992   Dusheng Zinu: Tamen De Jiating, Jiaoyu, He Weilai (Only children: their families, education, and future). Pei-ching: Shehuikexue Wenxian Chubanshe (Sociological contributions publisher).
2005   Guanyu Yihun Dushengzinu Duli Shenghuo Nengli De Shizhengyanjiu (An empirical study of independent living ability in married only children). Zhongguo Qingnian Yanjiu (China youth study) 9:32–36.

Fong, Vanessa L.
2002   China's One-Child Policy and the Empowerment of Urban Daughters. American Anthropologist 104(4):1098–1109.
2004a   Only Hope: Coming of Age under China's One-Child Policy. Stanford: Stanford University Press.
2004b   Filial Nationalism among Chinese Youth with Global Identities. American Ethnologist 31(4):629–646.
2006   Chinese Youth between the Margins of China and the First World. In Chinese Citizenship: Views from the Margins. Vanessa L. Fong and Rachel Murphy, eds. Pp. 151–173. London: Routledge.

Fung, Heidi
1999   Becoming a Moral Child: The Socialization of Shame among Young Chinese Children. Ethos 27(2):180–209.

Gold, Thomas B., Doug Guthrie, and David Wank

2002 Social Connections in China: Institutions, Culture, and the Changing Nature of Guanxi. Cambridge: Cambridge University Press.

Greenhalgh, Susan
2003a Planned Births, Unplanned Persons. American Ethnologist 30(2):196–215.
2003b Science, Modernity, and the Making of China's One-Child Policy. Population and Development Review 29(2):163–196.
2005 Globalization and Population Governance in China. In Global Assemblages: Technology, Politics, and Ethics as Anthropological Problems. Aihwa Ong and Stephen J. Collier, eds. Pp. 354–372. Malden, MA: Blackwell.

Greenhalgh, Susan, and Edwin A. Winckler
2005 Governing China's Population: From Leninist to Neoliberal Biopolitics. Stanford: Stanford University Press.

Guojia Tongji Ju (National Bureau of Statistics)
2001 Zhongguo Tongji Nianjian (China Statistical Yearbook), 2001. Beijing: Zhongguo Tongji Chubanshe (China Statistics Press).

He Pingping, Zhang Aixue, and Chang Hong
1994 Duzhuan De "Jiaoliang" Suowei Riben Haizi Dabai Zhongguo Haizi De Shenhua (Exaggerated "lessons": the myth of Japanese children defeating chinese children). Beijing Qingnian Bao (Beijing Youth News), 1.

Holland, Dorothy
1992 The Woman Who Climbed up the House: Some Limitations of Schema Theory. In New Directions in Psychological Anthropology. Theodore Schwartz, Geoffrey M. White, and Catherine Lutz, eds. pp. 68–79. Cambridge: Cambridge University Press.

Holland, Dorothy C., and Naomi Quinn
1987 Cultural Models in Language and Thought. Cambridge: Cambridge University Press.

Holland, Dorothy, and Michael Cole
1995 Between Discourse and Schema: Reformulating a Cultural-Historical Approach to Culture and Mind. Anthropology and Education Quarterly 26(4):475–489.

Holland, Dorothy, William Lachiotte, Jr., Debra Skinner, and Carole Cain
1998 Identity and Agency in Cultural Worlds. Cambridge, MA: Harvard University Press.

Hwang, Kwang-kuo
1987 Face and Favor: The Chinese Power Game. American Journal of Sociology 92(4): 944–974.

2000 Chinese Relationalism: Theoretical Construction and Methodological Considerations Journal for the Theory of Social Behaviour 30(2):155–178.

Hymes, Robert
1987 Statesmen and Gentlemen: The Elite of Fu-Chou, Chiang-Hsi, in Northern and Southern Sung. Cambridge: Cambridge University Press.

Jankowiak, William R.
1993 Sex, Death, and Hierarchy in a Chinese City: An Anthropological Account. New York: Columbia University Press.

Jiao, Shulan, Guiping Ji, and Qicheng Jing
1986 Comparative Study of Behavioral Qualities of Only Children and Sibling Children. Child Development 57(2):357–361.

Kipnis, Andrew B.
1997 Producing Guanxi: Sentiment, Self, and Subculture in a North China Village. Durham, NC: Duke University Press.

Kleinman, Arthur, and Joan Kleinman
1999 The Transformation of Everyday Social Experience: What a Mental and Social Health Perspective Reveals About Chinese Communities under Global and Local Change. Culture, Medicine, and Psychiatry 23(1):7–24.

Kohrman, Matthew
1999 Grooming Que Zi: Marriage Exclusion and Identity Formation among Disabled Men in Contemporary China. American Ethnologist 26(4):890–909.

Kusserow, Adrie Suzanne
1999 De-Homogenizing American Individualism: Socializing Hard and Soft Individualism in Manhattan and Queens. Ethos 27(2): 210–234.
2004 American Individualisms: Child Rearing and Social Class in Three Neighborhoods. New York: Palgrave MacMillan.

Lan, Hua R., and Vanessa L. Fong, eds.
1999 Women in Republican China. Armonk, NY: M. E. Sharpe.

Laybourn, Ann
1994 The Only Child: Myths and Reality. Edinburgh: HMSO.

Li, Jin
2001 Chinese Conceptualization of Learning. Ethos 29(2):111–137.

Lieber, Eli, Dorothy Chin, and Kazuo Nihira
2001 Holding on and Letting Go: Identity and Acculturation among Chinese Immigrants. Cultural Diversity and Ethnic Minority Psychology 7(3):247–261.

Lieber, Eli, Kazuo Nihira, and Iris Tan Min
2004 Filial Piety, Modernization, and the Challenges of Raising Children for Chinese Immigrants: Quantitative and Qualitative Evidence. Ethos 32(3):324–347.

Mahmood, Saba
2001 Feminist Theory, Embodiment, and the Docile Agent: Some Reflections on the Egyptian Islamic Revival. Cultural Anthropology 16(2):202–236.

Miller, Peggy J., Heidi Fung, and Judith Mintz
1999 Self-Construction through Narrative Practices: A Chinese and American Comparison of Early Socialization. Ethos 24(2):237–280.

Miller, Peggy J., Todd L. Sandel, Chung-Hui Liang, and Heidi Fung
2001 Narrating Transgressions in Longwood: The Discourses, Meanings, and Paradoxes of an American Socializing Practice. Ethos 29(2):159–186.

Murphy, Rachel
2004 Turning Peasants into Modern Chinese Citizens: "Population Quality" Discourse, Demographic Transition and Primary Education. China Quarterly 177:1–20.

Ou, Qujia
1971[1902] Xin Guangdong (New Guangdong). In Wan Qing Geming Wenxue (Revolutionary literature from the late Qing). Yufa Zhang, ed. pp. 1–49. Taipei: Xinzhi Zazhishe.

Pepper, Suzanne
1996 Radicalism and Education Reform in 20th-Century China: The Search for an Ideal Development Model. Cambridge: Cambridge University Press.

Quinn, Naomi
1996 Culture and Contradiction: The Case of Americans Reasoning about Marriage. Ethos 24(3):391–425.

Shanghaishi Youerjiaoyu Yanjiushi (Shanghai preschool education study group)
1980 Dushengzinü De Jiatingjiaoyu (Family education of only children). Zhongguo Funü (Chinese women) 5(17):12–35.
1988 Wu Zhi Liu Sui Dushengzimü De Zhishi Mian Renshi Nengli Ji Jiating Jiaoyu De Diaocha (Investigation of the knowledge, understanding, and family education of single-tons between ages five and six). In Dushengzinü De Xinli Tedian Yu Jiaoyu (Singletons' psychological particularities and education). Beijing Shifan Daxue Jiaoyu Kexue Yanjiusuo (Beijing Normal University Educational Science Research Center), ed. pp. 148–165. Beijing: Nongcun Duwu Chubanshe (Rural reading materials publisher).

Strauss, Claudia
1990 Who Gets Ahead? Cognitive Responses to Heteroglossia in American Political Culture. American Ethnologist 17(2):312–328.
1997a Partly Fragmented, Partly Integrated: An Anthropological Examination of "Postmodern Fragmented Subjects." Cultural Anthropology 12(3):312–328.
1997b Research on Cultural Discontinuities. In A Cognitive Theory of Cultural Meaning. Claudia Strauss and Naomi Quinn, eds. pp. 210–251. Cambridge: Cambridge University Press.

Strauss, Claudia, and Naomi Quinn
1997 A Cognitive Theory of Cultural Meaning. Cambridge: Cambridge University Press.

Sun, Yunxiao
1993a Women De Haizi Shi Ribenren De Duishou Ma (Are our children a match for the Japanese?). Huangjin Shidai (Golden Age) 7:50–51.
1993b Xialingying Zhong De Jiaoliang (Evaluations from summer camp). Duzhe (Reader) 11:14–15.

Tang, Yuankai
2001 The "Unbearable" Examination. Beijing Review 30(2):12–20.

Tao, Kuo-Tai, Jing-Hwa Qiu, Bao-Lin Li, Wen-Shing Tseng, Hsu Jing, and Dennis G. McLaughlin.
1995 One-Child-Per-Couple Family Planning and Child Behaviour Development: Six-Year Follow-up Study in Nanjing. In Chinese Societies and Mental Health. Tsung-Yi Lin, Wen-Sheng Tseng, and Ying-K'un Yeh, eds. pp. 341–374. Oxford: Oxford University Press.

Tao, Kuotai, and Jing-Hwa Chiu
1985 One-Child-Per-Family Policy: A Psychological Perspective. In Chinese Culture and Mental Health. Wen-Sheng Tseng and David Y. H. Wu, eds. pp. 153–165. Orlando: Academic Press.

Townsend, Nicholas W.
2002 The Package Deal: Marriage, Work, and Fatherhood in Men's Lives. Philadelphia: Temple University Press.

Tseng, Wen-shying, Kuotai Tao, Hsu Jing, and Jinghua Chiu

1988 Family Planning and Child Mental Health in China: The Nanjing Survey. American Journal of Psychiatry 145(11):1396–1403.

Tu, Wei-ming
1998 Probing the "Three Bonds" and "Five Relationships" in Confucian Humanism. *In* Confucianism and the Family in an Interdisciplinary, Comparative Context. Walter H. Slote and George DeVos, eds. pp. 121–136. Albany: State University of New York Press.

Waltner, Ann
1983 Building on the Ladder of Success: The Ladder of Success in Imperial China and Recent Work on Social Mobility. Ming Studies 17:30–36.

Watson, James L.
1980 Transactions in People: The Chinese Market in Slaves, Servants, and Heirs. *In* Asian and African Systems of Slavery. James L. Watson, ed. pp. 223–250.

Watson, James L., ed.
1984 Class and Social Stratification in Post-Revolution China. Cambridge: Cambridge University Press.
1992 Chinese Kinship Reconsidered: Anthropological Perspectives on Historical Research. China Quarterly 82(December):589–622.

Watson, Rubie S.
1985 Inequality among Brothers: Class and Kinship in South China. New York: Cambridge University Press.

Whyte, Martin, and William Parish
1984 Urban Life in Contemporary China. Chicago: University of Chicago Press.

Willis, Paul
1977 Learning to Labor: How Working Class Kids Get Working Class Jobs. New York: Columbia University Press.

Wolf, Arthur P., and Chieh-Shan Huang
1980 Marriage and Adoption in China, 1845–1945. Stanford: Stanford University Press.

Wolf, Margery
1972 Women and the Family in Rural Taiwan. Stanford: Stanford University Press.

Wu, Naitao
1986 Dealing with the Spoiled Brat. Beijing Review 29(12):26–28.

Wu, Pei-Yi
1990 The Confucian's Progress: Autobiographical Writings in Traditional China. Princeton: Princeton University Press.

Xiao, Hong
2001 Childrearing Values in the United States and China: A Comparison of Belief System and Social Structure. Westport: Praeger.

Yan, Yunxiang.
1996 The Flow of Gifts: Reciprocity and Social Networks in a Chinese Village. Stanford, Calif.: Stanford University Press.

Yang, Kuo-Shu
1995 Chinese Social Orientation: An Integrative Analysis. *In* Chinese Societies and Mental Health. Tsung-Yi Lin, Wen-Shing Tseng, and Eng-Kung Yeh, eds. pp. 19–39. Hong Kong: Oxford University Press.

Yang, Mayfair
Mei-Hui 1994 Gifts, Favors, and Banquets: The Art of Social Relationships in China. Ithaca, NY: Cornell University Press.

Zeng, Yi
2000 Marriage Patterns in Contemporary China. *In* The Changing Population of China. Peng Xizhe and Guo Zhigang, eds. pp. 91–100. Malden, MA: Blackwell.

Part V

The Self in Everyday Life, Ritual, and Healing

Introduction

Cultural Narratives of Self: Strategies, Defenses, and Identities

Hallowell's concept of the self as a set of universal categories of human experience with culturally variable orientations (Chapter 3 of this book) had an important long-term influence on psychological anthropology, pointing to ways in which fieldworkers could make ethnography serve goals they had formerly sought in personality tests – a description of the motives driving, and concepts framing, observable social behavior – but formulated in the terms of a particular culture. The idea of a focus on the self was not original with Hallowell, as he acknowledges in citing philosophers, psychologists, and the anthropologist Marcel Mauss (1938), but in synthesizing their contributions he confronted in a new way the reality that the self (as cultural representation and moral ideal) is part of the "objective" environment individuals confront and also (as concept and motive) part of the "subjective" mental agency with which they confront it. By the time he wrote on the self in 1954, Hallowell had had long experience with personality testing, using the Rorschach test extensively in Ojibwa communities (which made it possible to describe a distribution of psychological characteristics within a population as well as differences across populations), but his work on the self shows a search for improving the psychological assessment itself through ethnographic investigation of the *contexts* in which individuals perceive themselves.

This ethnographic turn in psychological anthropology inspired by Hallowell and represented in the selections on the self in Part V of this volume had its parallel in a cultural turn in psychology starting in the late 1980s that gave rise to the cultural psychology movement – which is equally focused on variations in the self across cultures but uses psychological methods of assessment (see Markus and Kitayama, 1991; Kitayama and Markus, 1994; Kitayama and Cohen, 2007). Both movements represent a deliberate move away from the concept of personality (as trait or system) that had prevailed in social psychology until the mid-1960s and had influenced culture and personality studies. The movements in anthropology and psychology can be seen as complementary, in that one is primarily concerned with the cultural terms that set the context for experience of self, while possibly sacrificing or at least postponing knowledge of the distribution of self-experiences, whereas the other is willing to sacrifice a deep description and analysis of context in favor of data enabling quantitative comparisons of self across populations. Psychocultural research as an interdisciplinary field needs both perspectives, and in the long run they will be brought together.

The newfound interest in the self in psychological anthropology and cultural psychology during the second half of the 20th century was part of a larger trend in the social sciences toward conceptualizing the contents of conscious experience (emphasized in phenomenological philosophy) in both cultural and psychological terms. This trend included Erik Erikson's (1950, 1959) concept of *identity*, Erving Goffman's (1959, 1963, 1972) exposition of *self-presentation in social interaction*, George Lakoff's (1987) studies of *metaphor*, Roy D'Andrade's (1992, 1995) conception of *schema*, Eliot Mishler's (1999) and Jerome Bruner's (1990) proposal of *narrative* as a focus for cultural psychology, and Walter Goldschmidt's (1990) concept of *career* as a category for comparison in anthropology. Thus from 1950 to the end of the century some social scientists (the aforementioned and many others) have sought to move beyond the formal assessments of personality psychology to treat the individual's experience, behavior and motives as a field for exploration in everyday life, natural language and clinical interaction. Armed with concepts designed to capture the contents of personal experience in social and cultural context, their studies permitted us to approach mental processes as they occur in the actual settings of diverse cultures. This trend enriched psychological anthropology with views of the psyche not bound by the pre-formed categories of psychoanalysis and personality theory, views grounded in categories used by the humans whose minds are the subject of investigation.

Ethnopsychology, that is, the folk categories of behavior and psychological process used within a culture, became an important topic of investigation in psychological anthropology during this period. Jean Briggs (1970) published a 55-page glossary of Inuit emotion terms as an appendix to her book on her field experience in an Inuit community (Chapter 4 in this reader.) Robert Levy (1973) published a full-length monograph on Tahitian "mind and experience" that approached those topics through the terms Tahitians have available to talk about feelings, thoughts, and actions. There were thereafter numerous ethnopsychological studies, limited only by the realization that in many cultures the phenomena of personal experience categorized as "psychological" in our own culture are conceptualized in terms of bodily or spiritual experience; that is, there is no separate realm equivalent to our "psychology" (Lutz, 1988). So ethnopsychology became part of the toolkit of psychocultural research, a necessary, but by itself insufficient, ethnographic method in any research program designed to probe individual experience.

Gender identity became a focus in psychological anthropology during this time. Anthropologists had always taken more interest in gender than other social scientists, and Margaret Mead (1935, 1949) formulated this interest in psychological and developmental as well as cultural terms, including the problem she perceived of American boys growing up with both an envy of the female reproductive role and anxiety about their masculinity. In 1958 John W. M. Whiting initiated a series of cross-cultural studies of male sex identity that attempted to account for the distribution of male initiation ceremonies across the world in terms of cultural variations in the experience of boys and the demands of their environments (Whiting, Kluckhohn and Anthony, 1958). As his research program continued, he and his collaborators found that the initiation ceremonies were institutionalized in societies where boys were raised by their mothers but had to become warriors at or after puberty. The hypothesis was that, beginning in early childhood, they acquired a female identity (through envy of the mother's status) that the ceremonies were designed to reverse, masculinizing the "feminine" boys into tough warriors ready to fight. In societies where the demands of warfare were absent, their female identity was permitted to express itself in customs like the *couvade*, involving male pregnancy symptoms and a cultural script in which husbands play the role of a child-bearing woman (Munroe and Munroe, 1973; Munroe, Munroe and Whiting, 1981). Psychological anthropologists working in Spain (Brandes, 1980; Gilmore, 1987) and Italy (Parsons, Chapter 10 in this reader) as well as elsewhere (Gilmore, 1990) have also noted the identity conflicts of males in a cultural context where masculinity is not only valued but heavily dramatized in cultural narratives. Chapter 17 in this reader by Herdt provides a vivid example from New Guinea.

Many outstanding ethnographies of the self have been published over the last 25 years, and only a small sample could be published in this section of the reader. The selections represent four areas of investigation:

Chapter 16: Gregor describes the presentation of self in the narratives of everyday social interaction among people of the Brazilian Amazon.

Chapter 17: Herdt describes narratives embedded in ritual performances by men.

Chapter 18: Hollan distinguishes between person-centered ethnography and the assessment of individual selves, showing how the latter can be achieved through a culturally based clinical interview and exploring the problem of individualism vs. collectivism in Sulawesi, Indonesia.

Chapter 19: Calabrese describes conflicting therapeutic practices and narratives in a Navajo context.

Each of these research areas has generated an extensive research literature, and the study of healing and illness narratives is a major topic in medical anthropology, now a large part of cultural anthropology.

REFERENCES

Brandes, Stanley
  1980   Metaphors of Masculinity: Sex and Status in Andalusian Folklore. Philadelphia: University of Pennsylvania Press.
Briggs, Jean
  1970   Never in Anger. Cambridge, MA: Harvard University Press.
Bruner, Jerome
  1990   Acts of Meaning. Cambridge, MA: Harvard University Press.
D'Andrade, Roy G.
  1992   Schemas and Motivation. In R. G. D'Andrade and Claudia Strauss, eds., Human Motives and Cultural Models. New York: Cambridge University Press.
  1995   The Development of Cognitive Anthropology. New York: Cambridge University Press.

Erikson, Erik H.
   1950   Childhood and Society. New York: W. W. Norton.
   1959   Ego Identity and the Life Cycle. New York: International Universities Press.
Gilmore, David D.
   1987   Aggression and Community: Paradoxes and Andalusian Culture. New Haven: Yale
   University Press.
   1990   Manhood in the Making: Cultural Concepts of Masculinity. New Haven: Yale
   University Press.
Goffman, Erving
   1959   The Presentation of Self in Everyday Life. New York: Doubleday.
   1963   Behavior in Public Places. New York: The Free Press.
   1972   Relations in Public: Microstudies of the Public Order. New York: Basic Books.
Goldschmidt, Walter
   1990   The Human Career: The Self in the Symbolic World. Malden, MA: Blackwell.
Kitayama, Shinobu and Dov Cohen, eds.
   2007   The Handbook of Cultural Psychology. New York: Guilford Press.
Kitayama, Shinobu and Hazel Rose Markus, eds.
   1994   Emotion and Culture: Empirical Studies of Mutual Influence. Washington, DC:
   American Psychological Association.
Lakoff, George
   1987   Women, Fire, and Dangerous Things. Chicago: University of Chicago Press.
Levy, Robert I.
   1973   Tahitians: Mind and Experience in the Society Islands. Chicago: University of Chicago
   Press.
Lutz, Catherine
   1988   Unnatural Emotions: Everyday Sentiments on a Micronesian Atoll and their
   Challenge to Western Theory. Chicago: University of Chicago Press.
Markus, Hazel and Shinobu Kitayama
   1991   Culture and the Self: Implications for Cognition, Motivation and Emotion.
   Psychological Review 98: 224–253.
Mauss, Marcel
   1938   Une Categorie de l'esprit humaine: La notion de personne celle de "moi". Journal
   of the Royal Anthropological Institute. 58: 263–281.
Mead, Margaret
   1935   Sex and Temperament in Three Primitive Societies. New York: William Morrow.
   1949   Male and Female. New York: William Morrow.
Mishler, Eliot
   1999   Storylines: Craftartists Narratives of Identity. Cambridge, MA: Harvard University
   Press.
Munroe, R. Lee and Ruth H. Munroe
   1973   Psychological Interpretation of Male Initiation Rites: The Case of Male Pregnancy
   Symptoms. Ethos 1: 490–498.
Munroe, R. Lee, Ruth H. Munroe and John W. M. Whiting
   1981   Male Sex-Role Resolutions. In Ruth H. Munroe, R. Lee Munroe and John W. M.
   Whiting, eds. Handbook of Cross-Cultural Human Development (pp. 611–632). New
   York: Garland STPM Press.
Whiting, John W. M., Richard Kluckhohn and Albert Anthony
   1958   The Function of Male Initiation at Puberty. In T. Newcomb, E. Maccoby and
   E. Hartley, eds. Readings in Social Psychology. New York: Appleton-Century-Crofts.

16

The Self in Daily Dramas

Thomas Gregor

Greetings and Goodbyes

"Where are you going?"
"I'm going bathing."
"Well; then go."

Heard many times each day on the path to the river

In "every culture known to history or ethnography" there are regular ways for greeting and taking leave of one's fellows (Murdock 1945: 123). The reason for this universality is that actors cannot engage and withdraw haphazardly like billiard balls caroming against each other on a pool table. Interaction, like all social life, is governed by rules, and the way in which the process begins and ends is apparently too vital to leave to chance or individual predilection. The cultural recognition of the significance of properly initiating and terminating an interactional sequence is institutionalized in patterns of greetings and farewells. Among the Mehinaku these patterns furnish us with clues to the relationship of the actors, their definition of the situation, and the course that their interaction will take. Greetings and farewells are not simply a minor part of a system of etiquette but a significant chapter in the ethnography and theory of Mehinaku social relations.

Greetings

Following the Mehinaku classification of greetings, there are four ways of opening interaction with fellow villagers. The method of choice depends on the setting, the relationship, and the definition of the situation. The first method is the most formal and stereotyped, "to greet formally" (*yukapu*).

Formal greetings consist of a set pattern of words and gestures. The greeter looks up, raises his eyebrows, smiles, and says, "You are (here)" (*pitsupai*). The response is to nod the head and say, "I am (here)" (*natupai*). This pattern is reserved for Mehinaku who are socially distant from the speaker. A villager who enters his neighbor's house, for example, is likely to be greeted in this fashion. I have noticed that this greeting is sometimes used as a polite veneer that masks a considerable amount of hostility. Ipyana, the alleged Mehinaku witch, was often formally greeted in this fashion by many of his fellow villagers before his execution in 1971.

A second method of opening interaction is simply to "call" the other person (*atakutapu*). Mehinaku call each other under both formal and informal circumstances, the nature of the situation being indicated by the modulation of

Thomas Gregor, *Mehinaku: The Drama of Daily Life in a Brazilian Indian Village.* © 1977 by The University of Chicago, The University of Chicago Press, Chicago, The University of Chicago Press, Ltd., London, pp. 177–223. Reprinted with permission.

the voice and the choice of words. The formal method of calling is used on the central plaza to recruit participants in rituals and collective labor projects. The caller steps into the plaza, faces the house of the person he is addressing, and calls in a long drawn-out voice: "My son, Kupatekuma ... come here!" Invariably this formal pattern begins with a kinship term and then adds a personal name if the term is ambiguous. Calling the name alone is not appropriate in this public setting.

The informal method of calling is less stereotyped and uses different language. It occurs between individuals who are on more or less friendly terms and who share a relationship based on close association. The setting for this kind of interactional opening can be anywhere in the village or around it, though never during a ceremony or other formal occasion. Kuyaparei is being called to the men's bench where his cross-cousins plan to joke with him: "Kuyaparei! Get over here!" (*tswi kwa*!) Kuyaparei responds: "What's up?" (*natsi*?)

Or, a woman inside her house calls her sister-in-law: "Come here, pregnant one!" (*ama kana itsukuyalu*). Kin terms are frequently used in situations similar to these: My son! My sister's child's father! My brother-in-law!, and so on.

A third technique of opening interaction is to ask a question (*aiyapυ*). This kind of greeting is informal and varies widely in the information requested, the setting in which it appears, and the relationship of the actors. For example, a close relative entering the house may be greeted with, "What's up?" (*natsi*?). Often as not the response is, "Nothing!" (*aitsa wa*). Questions are the most frequently used interactional openers, and we will return to their description and analysis after examining one more class of greetings.

The fourth and last category of greeting is simply "to speak to" (*akaiyakátapυ*). This type of greeting often uses a special set of words which approach kin terms in their meaning, although they have no genealogical implication. Table 16.1 summarizes the variables that determine the choice of a particular term.

The table shows that the greetings *hai ja*, *hai ju*, and *hai* code consanguinity, affinity,

Table 16.1 *Terms used in greeting kinsmen and in-laws*

	Consanguineal relatives (roughly of ego's generation)	Affinal relatives
Male to male	*Hai ja*	*Hai*
Female to female	*Hai ju*	*Hai*

and sex. In practice they are used in informal contexts and between the speakers of roughly equal status. Thus children do not "*hai ja*" their parents or others who are clearly of the older generation. A listener is most likely to hear these terms where the general atmosphere is one of informal equality, as in the men's house. Interaction between men and women, between persons of different generations, and between parents and children-in-law are opened by using either a kin term or a personal name.

"Greeting," "Calling," "Questioning," and "Speaking" are the approved methods of initiating interaction among the Mehinaku. Each of these opening gambits codes the relationship and the nature of the social situation. The choice of greeting, however, is determined by still another factor: the setting in which the contact occurs.

Some greetings and their stereotyped responses are setting specific, occuring only in certain regions, such as the paths around the village. According to proper etiquette, no one can be passed on a public path without some kind of recognition or display of affinal respect. The only persons who are not expected to greet each other are villagers living in the same household, for as one man put it, "Why bother? You see them all the time anyway." All others, however, must be pleasantly recognized. To fail to do so is to brand oneself as angry or sullen.

Let's listen as the villagers greet Kuyaparei as he goes to bathe.

The first person he meets on the path is an older distant kinsman who lives in another house. They do not get along well but conduct themselves courteously in each other's presence. The correct formula for a polite greeting on the way to the bathing area is to ask, "Where are you going?" (*atenäi pyala?*). The man returning to the village always is the one who asks this question first, since his own destination is obvious. And so Kuyaparei is questioned:

"Where are you going?"

"I'm going bathing."

"Well, then go."

Neither of the two men has slowed his pace on the path, and each continues on his way. No information has been communicated other than their mutual recognition of the respect that each owes the other.

A bit further down the path Kuyaparei passes his crosscousin, with whom he is obliged by the rules of kinship to tease and joke. His cousin immediately throws his arms about him and demands:

"Where are you going?"

"Nowhere. To bathe."

"Ha! You are going to 'alligator'" (look for women to have sexual relations).

"No, to bathe!"

"You sex fiend!" (*aintyawaka nitséi*).

The next person along the path is one of the oldest women in the village. She is not a close relative of Kuyaparei's, but she addresses him as grandson, as she does most of the village men:

"Where are going, grandson?"

"To bathe, old woman" (*aripi*, old woman, not a pejorative term).

"Then go."

"Be careful, grandmother; there is a slippery place on the path. Don't fall and break a bone!"

The last person Kuyaparei meets on the way to the stream is his girl friend. He casts a quick glance over his shoulder to make sure that they are unobserved. If she had been with her husband, or if he was nearby, he would have completely ignored her and she him. To do otherwise would have been an affront to her husband, for if they speak to each other at all, it is assumed that the subject is an assignation. Kuyaparei hurriedly approaches her:

"I'll wait for you behind your house in the woods."

"Yes!"

Without pausing each continues on, she to the village, he to the river.

All of these exchanges, except for the last, have followed roughly the same form. The person leaving the village is questioned about his destination, he responds in the expected way, and the exchange is capped with a joke, a pleasantry, or a conversational remark. In every instance the dialogue just takes a few moments, and the speakers barely slacken their pace. When the dialogue fails to follow this pattern, it is usually because the speakers are transacting some kind of tangible business, as in the last encounter, rather than merely saluting each other as kinsmen, friends, or in-laws.

Goodbyes

Disengaging from interaction does not require that the actors explicitly recognize each other's social status. The greetings and the course of the interaction have already established these facts, and it only remains for the participants in the encounter to withdraw in some orderly fashion. There are several basic rules, the most important of which is that something must be said. No one can legitimately walk away from a social engagement or out of a house without some kind of leave-taking. The only exceptions to this rule occur between affinal relatives who are honoring an avoidance taboo or close kinsmen who live together. Everyone else must be recognized as he leaves.

The second rule is that the person taking his leave speaks first, unless his intentions are obvious (he is collecting his gear, rolling up his hammock, and saying goodbye to everyone else). Finally, the content of the farewell usually offers some indication of when the person leaving will return. At times this information is built into the structure of the verb:

"I'm going (far off and won't return soon)" (*Niyaneleigu*), or "I'm going (and will be back soon)" (*Niyatekeigu*). The response may simply be, "You are going."

On occasion a leave-taking is a little more elaborate, as when a man gets up to leave the men's house where he has been talking with a friend:

"I'm going (and will return)."

"Don't leave!"

"I'm lazy. I'm getting into my hammock; I'll be back soon."

"Then go."

The importance of Mehinaku greetings and goodbyes

Mehinaku greetings and farewells are more complicated and convey more information than we might have thought necessary in a small society. After all, there are only seventy-seven people living in an open community and they see each other many times during the course of the day. Why burden ordinary social business with the freight of such stereotyped gestures? Nothing tangible is exchanged in these social engagements, and yet the Mehinaku regard those who ignore them as boors, angry men, and worse. To approach the problem of why the Mehinaku are so punctilious about how social encounters are opened and closed, look at Table 16.2, a summary of some of the data presented above.

Though greetings and farewells take only a few seconds, the chart shows that a great deal of information is packed into them. The few words of a greeting may state both the speaker's personal feelings towards the villagers addressed as well as the shared social relationship. Information about friendship, hostility, kinship, age, common residence, formality of relationship, and sexual activity is all compressed into a few words.

The richness of greetings in social information is a puzzle, given that this information is available from many other sources and is well known to the Mehinaku. Erving Goffman, in an elegant paper called the "Nature of Deference and Demeanor," suggests that little "rituals" such as greetings and farewells are a vital constituent of the social order:

The rules of conduct which bind the actor and the recipient together are the bindings of society. But many of the acts which are guided by these rules occur infrequently or take a long time for their consummation. Opportunities to affirm the moral order and the society could

Table 16.2 *The meaning of Mehinaku greetings*

Greetings	The participants and the implication of the greeting or goodbye
No greeting	
1. Avoidance behavior	Parents and children-in-law
2. No avoidance behavior	A. close relatives who live in the same house, suggesting close familiarity.
	B. potential sexual partners who are maintaining proper appearances.
Greetings	
1. *Hai, Hai ja, Hai ju*	The choice of greeting may reveal whether the speakers are affinal or consanguineal kinsmen, the sex of the speaker and the person spoken to, and the relative age of speakers.
2. Kin term	Kin relationship specified.
3. Personal name	Informal relationship specified; nonaffinal relationship asserted.
4. Formal greeting (*yucapu*; "*pitsupai*")	Speakers socially distant, possibly hostile.
5. Ribaldry, sexual joking	Cross-cousins
Goodbyes	
No formal leave-taking	A. Kinsmen who live together
	B. Mutual hostility
Leave-taking	Suggests polite or friendly relationship

therefore be rare. It is here that ceremonial rules play their social function, for many of the acts which are guided by these rules last but a brief moment, involve no substantive outlay, and can be performed in every social interaction (Goffman 1956: 496).

Goffman thus would argue that the Mehinaku reaffirm the order of their society each time they greet and take leave of one another. I would take an even stronger position. In greeting and taking leave of each other the villagers not only affirm the structure of their society but assure their fellows of their location within it. Why do the Mehinaku require such assurances? This is a question that must be held in abeyance, for an answer requires that we consider the extraordinary flexibility in the definition and allocation of Mehinaku social roles, a subject to be considered in detail in part 4 of this book. For the moment, let us move deeper into the process of interaction. We will bring two Mehinaku into social contact. They greet each other in a friendly way. What happens next? What will they say to each other? How will they conduct themselves in each other's presence? We next consider the content of informal interaction.

Portraits of Self

Look at me. I paint-up nearly every afternoon. I joke in the men's house. I wrestle and dance. I'm no "trash yard man."

Shumōi, explaining the difference between himself and his less sociable kinsmen

The analogy between life and theater must never be taken too literally. In the conventional theater, the actor's lines are specified so precisely that there is very little room for improvisation or any other significant departure from the script. In life, however, relatively few roles are so inflexibly defined that knowledge of the norms is all that is required to predict behavior. Among the Mehinaku only in the acting out of certain ceremonial and affinal relationships are the behavioral possibilities so stereotyped that real-life interaction begins to approach a staged scene.

Most other conduct, even though it occurs in a normative framework, is not so limited. Companions who sit in front of the men's house, walk along a trail, or fish together are participating in a very loosely defined social engagement where there is a great deal of room for variation. In this chapter I plan to explore how the Mehinaku conduct themselves when interaction is not clearly bounded by the constraints of social roles or the guidelines of well-defined social settings.

A useful concept for understanding encounters of this kind is the notion of the "presentation of self" as developed primarily by Erving Goffman (1959). In every social engagement, Goffman argues, the actors are in an unspoken and often unconscious collusion to maintain the definition of the situation and their position in it. Two businessman who come together to conclude a deal, for example, have a mutual interest in conducting themselves as if each man's competency and integrity were unquestionable. While behind the scenes they may be checking each other's credit rating and character, up front each man offers assurances that the other is honest, trustworthy, efficient, and businesslike. To do otherwise could turn a "high level" commercial transaction into a brawl between street peddlers, doing violence to both the social value of the encounter and the image of the characters engaged in it. Since the result can be bad business and worse etiquette, both parties are constrained to sustain each other's position in the performance and the image of self they choose to present.

The strength of this approach to encounters is that it can take us beyond the role framework. Actors not only perform "selves" that are bound to specific social statuses, such as that of "businessman," but are constantly offering more general presentations that simply identify them as good men. They represent themselves as cooperative, friendly, generous, and trust-worthy participants in social engagements. These are the fundamental messages transmitted in the casual and "purposeless" interaction that makes up most of our social day. A description of the basic characters performed in such informal social encounters ought to be a part of the standard ethnography.

We may think of two ways of ferreting out the kind of character a people ascribe to the good citizen. One is to examine the qualities of self that are attributed to such a person. Numerous ethnographies make an effort in this direction, tying a people to a list of adjectives. Ruth Benedict's classic *Patterns of Culture* is an exercise in this kind of description. We are told that the Pueblos of New Mexico are "ceremonious ... of yielding discription ... generous ... never violent ... realistic ... apollonian" (1934).

A second approach is to find out what constitutes a bad citizen. Ethnographies that include such information often fail to explain in sufficient detail just what the bad apples are like. More crucially, the description is usually based on the observer's assessment rather than a people's own concepts of what constitutes the good citizen or the reprobate. It is these native concepts we are after, for they are the guideposts by which each individual directs his conduct and finds his way through the course of informal interaction. Let us examine how the Mehinaku mete out praise and abuse as a means of defining the characters they strive to emulate or reject. The conceptual portraits produced by this method should take us a long way toward understanding social engagements not governed by clearly defined social roles.

The Sociable Man

The basic requirement in Mehinaku social relationships is a willingness to respond to others in a warm and positive manner. The word for this quality is *ketépepei*, a term that also refers to the kind of beauty and balance found in a well-made artifact, such as a basket. An additional linguistic clue to the meaning of *ketépepei* is that it has the same root as the verb "to be happy" (*eketepemunapai*). I gloss *ketépepei* as "sociable" because most of the virtues of the man who is labeled by this term are social ones. He speaks well, he never grows angry, he laughs and smiles often, he has an open and attractive face, he does not avoid others, he is cooperative and generous. These are the qualities that the Mehinaku cite when discussing this kind of individual or when they – as they do more frequently – point out someone who is not sociable.

Conversation and good humor

The first quality associated with the sociable man is the ability to "speak well." Whenever two persons are together and their attention is not focused on a particular task, the general rule is that they should enter into conversation. The subjects vary, though they are usually quite commonplace. Men sitting on the bench in front of the men's house may discuss the need for a new men's house, the women's latest ceremonial activity, the likelihood of success on a fishing trip, or the weather – topics that are mulled over again and again among the same participants. The willingness and ability to participate is an attribute of the man who "speaks well." On the other hand, a man who is close-mouthed and sullen is not only socially undesirable but potentially dangerous: "Do you see old 'Rotten Fish' over there?" my friend Kuyaparei once asked me. "When he sits on the men's bench he never says anything. He's angry because we had sex with his wife. If he bewitches me or my son I may kill him!"

While Mehinaku men keep up the expected conversational patter, they should give evidence of a sense of humor. In ordinary interaction, one jokes a little (*metalawatãi*) in a restrained and inoffensive way. For example, one may tease a child who happens to be standing nearby: "The neck of your penis is small!" (meaning you are immature). This sort of jest gets a sure-fire laugh and at the same time avoids offense since it is not directed at adults. Other humorous sallies involve plays on language. A favorite is to imitate Brazilians or other Xingu tribesmen, some of whom, notably the Trumaí, are said to have the ugliest speech conceivable. On my visit in 1974 some of the villagers were calling each other by the Auití tribe's term for brother-in-law, a word which sounded funny to the Mehinaku ear. A month or so later this fad had died out and everyone was using the Txicão tribe's interrogative (*wa*?) as a new source of amusement.

Joking between men, unless they happen to be cross-cousins, must be practiced with discretion. A few Mehinaku, however, will engage in the broadest kind of humor with virtually everyone. Called *metalawaitsi* (jokers, wise guys), they are a continual source of irritation to the more sober-minded. My friend and informant, Kupate, is a *metalawaitsi*, and though his father has publicly warned him that "wise guys" die young because they arouse the antagonism of witches, he seems irrepressible.

Restraining anger

The ability to speak well and a proper sense of humor are two of the important attributes of the sociable man. A third is the ability to contain negative emotions, especially anger and hostility. A display of anger is a disturbing and even frightening experience for the Mehinaku. The word for being angry (*japujapai*) is applied metaphorically to things that are completely out of control, such as a fire raging in a dry garden or a species of pepper (*japujaitsi*) so hot that it leaves any man foolish enough to eat it writhing on the ground in agony. Similarly, thunderstorms, powerful winds, and stinging ants are all *japujapai*. Open anger is associated with unpredictability and violence, characteristics said to be typical of non-Xingu tribes (*wajaiyu*), who are avoided and despised for this reason. Anger is also dangerous to the man who nurses the emotion "in his belly," for he then courts serious illness and becomes undersirable to his wife, friends, and fellow villagers. An angry child is sternly rebuked by his parents and ridiculed as a *japujaitsi* (angry one, "hot pepper").

Although there are occasions when a Mehinaku may legitimately express his anger, such as when discovering his wife *inflagrante*, serious quarrels are rare. In over eighteen months of residence in the Mehinaku village, I never saw any violent expressions of interpersonal hostility except between husbands and wives. Even children feel sufficiently constrained to refrain from real fighting. It is true that the Mehinaku do become angry at times, for there are numerous sources of irritation and antagonism within the society – conflicts aroused by gossip and scandal, jealousies inspired by extramarital affairs, tensions of living in close quarters, fear of witchcraft, and envy over possessions, to name a few. According to the Mehinaku image of the sociable man, however,

hostility must not be expressed directly. An unabashed display of anger must be reserved for only the most extreme circumstances.

Generosity

One of the outstanding characteristics of the sociable man is that he is generous. Although there is no word in Mehinaku for "generous" other than "not stingy" (*aitsa kakaianúmapai*), the concept is well-defined by specific acts and obligations and is of great importance to the villagers as a guide to daily conduct. The hallmark of the generous man is that he eats with his kinsmen and friends and shares his food. The man who is stingy with food (*kanahiri*) eats alone. He sneaks back from a fishing trip and enters the village unseen to avoid sharing his catch. When he has to share, he gives up only the poorest fish and keeps the most delectable portions for himself.

Mehinaku women are often regarded as stingy, perhaps because of their key role in the distribution of food. Ijau, though many years dead, is still remembered for her technique of short-changing her residence mates. After cooking fish stew for the entire household, she would spoon out meager portions onto slabs of manioc bread. Then having made certain that everyone had heard her scraping the pot, she would announce that there was none left. But it turned out that there was a great deal left; the noise of the spoon scraping the bottom of the pot was really the noise of the spoon scraping the side of the pot. The name Ijau is now synonymous with stinginess among the Mehinaku, and I was occasionally called "Ijau" when I refused to share some of my own reserves of food.

A sociable person, unlike Ijau, is not stingy with food. Indeed, he is conspicuously generous with it. On a fishing trip he yields part of his catch to his less successful comrades. On his return he walks through the center of the village so that everyone may see how much he has caught. A short time later he dispatches his children with substantial gifts of fish to kinsmen in other houses. He distributes part of his catch in the men's house and tells the men exactly where he was fishing so that they will be successful the next day.

A generous man is willing to part with valuable possessions. It may be a painful decision since prestige is accorded those who accumulate shell belts, collars, feather headdresses, Brazilian trade goods, and other high status property. A villager nevertheless must be prepared to give away or trade much of his wealth if he is to avoid the stigma of stinginess. He must reward his in-laws with valuable gifts after the birth of a child. He must participate in rituals during which he gives away precious possessions. And, unlike the stingy man who avoids barter sessions on some flimsy pretext, he must always be ready to trade.

One way a villager can remind the community of his generous nature is to grow corn. Planted in September at the beginning of the rainy season, corn reaches maturity by January at the time of a calendrical festival (Amairi) associated with fertility and a short midwinter dry season. In the evening at harvest time a farmer will announce to the entire village that his corn is ripening. The next morning everyone descends on his field and quickly strips away every last ear. The farmer is left with the satisfaction of having been a generous man and the knowledge that his generosity has been unmistakably communicated to the entire community.

Working hard and appearing energetic

A villager not only must share with his comrades, but he must also be hard working. If, for example, he is lounging about the men's house he must be ready to assist anyone who wants help to carry a heavy canoe to the water, lug a newly fallen log from a trail, or prop up a fallen *pequi* tree in a nearby orchard. Unlike the lazy man who conveniently leaves the village "to defecate" when he sees work ahead, the sociable man participates in collective labor with spirit and enthusiasm.

A man's industry may be judged by the frequency of his fishing trips. Fish is the preeminent food for the villagers and, given its role in their diet as the principal source of animal protein, it is not surprising that going fishing is regarded as evidence of good citizenship. Normally, all men fish for their household, but instead of a set schedule or formal system of taking turns, there is a general expectation that one man's contribution today will be reciprocated

by another man's tomorrow. During the wet season, however, when fishing becomes frustrating and uncertain, this formal arrangement tends to break down. Relationships among the men in a house become tense as each waits for the other to go first. The war of nerves ends only when someone, driven by annoyance or hunger, finally gives in, packs his gear, and goes off to fish. Such confrontations, however, are rare, largely because the ethic demands that the men work hard and give freely of their services.

No less important than being a hard worker is giving the appearance of being a hard worker. At all times a man should look energetic. In the men's house he is spirited and boisterous. He is the first one up in the morning, blowing on his fire, rousing his children from their hammocks, and marching them down to the stream for cold baths. While other villagers are still asleep, he has already left to clear a distant garden, to hunt monkey along trails miles from the village, or to fish on a hard-to-reach lake. He keeps a rooster or two on a perch near his house to awaken him (and the rest of the village) at four in the morning with their raucous crowing. "Sleep," he loves to explain, "weakens a man and saps his strength. Only a dog or a 'hammock lover' sleeps during the day when he should be fishing, hunting, of clearing land."

Although this work ethic is vigorously promoted by the chief in his evening speeches, it is in reality pursued only by a very few of the younger men. The village is no beehive of productive activity, and it requires little searching to find both the old and the young snoozing in their hammocks or lazing about the men's house. Nevertheless, being vigorous, energetic, and hardworking is one of the "presentations of self" that the Mehinaku deliberately foster; it is part of the portrait of the "good man" by which they guide their conduct and evaluate their fellows.

The Rich and the Poor

Sharing food, work, and possessions are the hallmarks of a good man. Paradoxically, however, the ideal villager not only manages his property and labor generously but profitably as well. He does so because he knows that his

Table 16.3 *Inventory of the possessions of one of the wealthiest villagers*

1. Valuables (*apapalaiyaja*, literally, "true possessions") and other itmes of considerable worth
    - 7 shell belts
    - 4 shell necklaces
    - 5 stone ornaments for belts
    - 10 lbs. beads (estimated)
    - 2 bows
    - 2 .22 rifles
    - 1 feather headdress
    - 1 woven hammock
    - 1 canoe
    - 1 dog
    - 2 large racks for drying manioc
    - 1 large bamboo barrier for seclusion
    - 3 gardens
2. Ordinary and lesser possessions (*apapalai, apapalaimalú*; literally, possessions, worthless possessions)
    - 35 lbs. salt (estimated) in a large bag; a year's supply for personal use and trade
    - 30 arrows
    - 3 small suitcases
    - 2 small aluminum pots
    - 1 large ball of palm fiber cord
    - 5 balls of wool (Brazilian manufactured)
    - 1 large ball of native cotton thread
    - 50 feet of nylon parachute cord
    - 3 spools of nylon fishing line and hooks Various tools of Brazilian manufacture: pliers, machete, ax, plane, chisel drill, pocket knife
    - 1 flashlight without a bulb or batteries
    - 1 large box of matches

wealth is a measure of his worth as an individual and a basis for the respect and esteem of his comrades.

Given our own standards of wealth and poverty, the reader may well wonder just what kind of social distinctions the Mehinaku can draw on the basis of the ownership of material goods. Table 16.3, which lists every possession of one of the wealthiest men in the village, hardly solves the puzzle. In our society few have less than this "Croesus." Among the Mehinaku, however, the concept of "true or valuable possessions" (*apapálaiyaja*, see chapter 8) helps distinguish two loosely designated but significant economic divisions within the village – the "rich" (*kapapálapai*, having many

possessions) and the "poor" (*mapapalawa*, having few possessions). A poor man may have nearly as many possessions as the well-to-do, but he crucially lacks the belts, collars, headdresses, ceramic pots, guns, and other valuables that enrich the wealthy man.

Although a wealthy Mehinaku never brags about his possessions (he usually professes his poverty), the villagers have a fairly accurate idea of the extent of his property. Many of his valued possessions are worn in public and others are easily visible both inside and around his house. The poor man's status is equally conspicuous, revealed by his shabby ornaments, his low status bead belts, and his efforts to borrow headdresses and shell collars for public ceremonies.

The rich man is respected because it is supposed that he has attained his status through hard work. The villagers understand how valued objects – with the exception of Brazilian trade goods – are made and judge their worth by the work that has gone into them. A man examining a feather headdress fully appreciates the skill and labor of the craftsman who put it together. It follows that all one need do to become wealthy is to apply oneself assiduously. He who will not work is deservedly poor, a lazy fellow without any regard for his appearance minus shell belts and necklaces. I frequently pointed out that a man could be poor because of ill luck, because his parents never taught him to make valued objects, because he was not fortunate enough to have married a skilled Waura ceramicist, or because he was not a shaman who could charge high medical fees. No matter – for all this there were any number of quick retorts. Any man who wants to own valuable property can acquire it through trade. He can cultivate additional gardens, gather salt, or build many canoes and exchange them for belts and necklaces. A man incapable of making a feather headdress or a black bow deserves no one's sympathy. He is a "trash yard man" of the worst sort.

The Skillful and the Knowledgeable

The Mehinaku do not overlook the superb musician, the great raconteur, or the maker of well-balanced arrows. Men may excel in as

Table 16.4   *Age and craft skills*

Individual's Estimated Age	Canoe Making	Bench Carving	Mask Carving	Fishtrap Making	Basket Making	Percentage Skills Known
61	+	+	+	+	+	100
55	–	+	+	+	+	80
45	+	+	+	+	+	100
45	+	–	+	+	+	80
45	+	+	+	+	+	100
45	+	+	+	+	+	100
41	+	–	–	+	+	60
41	+	+	+	+	+	100
36	+	+	+	+	–	80
35	+	+	+	+	–	80
31	–	–	+	–	–	20
31	+	+	+	+	+	100
28	–	–	–	+	–	20
28	–	+	+	+	+	80
23	–	–	–	–	+	20
23	–	–	+	–	–	20

+ individual possesses skill
– individual lacks skill

many ways as there are crafts. A visitor need only ask "Who makes the most beautiful baskets?" to be immediately directed to a select number of villagers who are best in their skill. The best bowmakers, bench carvers, headdress fashioners, flutemakers, and canoe builders are all equally identifiable and accorded respect as *katámapapai* (intelligent, skillful, knowledgeable), a term always applied with a tone of admiration and deference.

In theory, the villagers' skills could all be mastered by one man, but in practice there is considerable variation in knowledge and ability. Just as material wealth is unevenly distributed among the community, so knowledge and skills tend to become the monopoly of a few. Only one of the Mehinaku, for example, knows how to carve the sacred flutes stored in the men's house. Only three are really expert musicians. These monopolies are maintained by the conscious efforts of those who benefit from them as well as by inefficient teaching methods. Methods of teaching are inefficient by our standards because they are limited to a small circle of kin and are primarily imitative. A novice learns by watching an expert, usually his father, perform a task and subsequently repeating what he has seen. There is little questioning or explanation involved in the procedure. Verbal skills such as ritual songs are taught more formally. The singer takes his pupil aside and has him perform the song line by line until he has committed it to memory. Jealous of their knowledge, singers of ritual songs often demand a fee from their apprentices. I was repeatedly urged not to play certain songs I had taped lest someone acquire them without paying the singers.

Less exotic skills also have only a limited distribution in the community. Table 16.4 documents the men's knowledge of five important craft skills – bench carving, fishtrap making, basket weaving, canoe building and ritual mask making. Although these skills are relatively simple and are economically and socially significant, only five men seem to have mastered them all. On the average, men over forty know 90 percent of the listed skills. Men under forty are familiar with only half the listed skills. Education is a continuing process among the Mehinaku, and the community is far from homogeneous in possession of craft knowledge.

The Mehinaku contradict the customary picture of the technologically primitive community in which every man is supposed to be a jack of all trades.

Knowledge of crafts, myths, and tribal lore has an observable effect on informal interaction when it is either grossly deficient or outstanding. Itsa commands so few skills that he seems culturally impoverished. Regarded as a village fool, he is frequently teased in the course of the banter and high jinks that go on in the men's house. Kuya, on the other hand, is a master craftsman and spellbinding raconteur, a man who tells a story so well that no one seems to care whether it is true or not. Respect for his skills is so great that he is accorded deference he would otherwise never receive, for he is far from being an ideal citizen.

Physical Attractiveness

The good man is not only generous, wealthy, skilled, and sociable; he is also attractive. Although ornaments and paints can enhance his looks, the basic measure of attractiveness is physical appearance. For men, the principal requirement of a good appearance is height. Respectfully referred to as *wékepei* (tall, big) and commanding the deference and respect of his comrades, the tall man is an unbeatable wrestler, a successful fisherman, a powerful man of political importance. During an earthly golden age in the mythic past, all the Mehinaku fit that mold. Today such a man is *káukapapai*, a deferential term applied to those worthy of fear and respect. In reality, height, strength, and success as a hunter, wrestler, and politician are not necessarily linked. The Mehinaku stereotype of the ideal man, however, has them intimately connected.

A different portrait emerges of the short man. He is *peritsi*, an abusive term connoting ugliness that is seldom uttered without a sneer or laugh. Scorned by women and rejected by prospective parents-in-law, the *peritsi* is a feeble wrestler, an improvident fisherman, an ineffective leader. He certainly is not *káukapapai* since he lacks those qualities that inspire fear and esteem. Consider Itsa, the village fool, who is one of the shortest men in the community and who is continually teased about his

appearance. Itsa has internalized the prevailing attitude toward him by acting the part. When he wrestles, he mimics the style of successful wrestlers while the men laugh and shout mock advice. Often addressed as "Penis," he is teased about the size and shape of his genitals and ribbed about his amorous adventures – for which he must usually bribe the village girls.

Ahira is also considered a *peritsi*. The shortest man in the village, less than five feet tall and shorter than many of the women, he is teased less than Itsa but abused behind his back. Many of the men conduct affairs with his wife and show contemptuously little concern about hiding their indiscretions. They not only make passes at her when her husband is nearby but flirt with her in his presence. To them, a very short man does not merit respect. His size is a justification for taking advantage of him; not only is it safe to abuse him and have relations with his wife, it is also what he deserves.

Judgments based on stature also influence the villagers' allocation of prestigious statuses. Table 16.5 indicates the close association between a man's height and the number of his mistresses, his wealth, his sponsorship and participation in rituals, and his chiefly status. Most remarkably, the three tallest men in the village have nearly twice as many mistresses as the three shortest men even though their average ages are greater.

To the Mehinaku, height and attractiveness are not simply a matter of genetics and good luck. Being *peritsi* is a moral failing, for the short man could have grown up tall and strong if he had taken the trouble to follow all the rules associated with adolescent seclusion – taking his medicines, winding his biceps and calves with cotton ligatures, and refraining from excessive contact with women. This last restriction is particularly important, because the loss of seminal fluid (*yaki*) saps a man's strength and stunts his growth. In this connection, it is interesting to note that *peritsi* rhymes with *itsi* (penis). In derisive jokes and puns the *peritsi* is mocked as one whose *itsi* is "too hungry" for sex. Lacking the self-discipline required to comply with the rules of adolescent seclusion or to curb his excessive sexual appetite, he grows up ridiculously short and he has no one to blame but himself.

Table 16.5   *Height and social participation of the adult Mehinaku men*

Individual's height in feet and inches from medical records	Estimated age	Number of mistresses	Rich or poor	Sponsorship of important rituals (#)	Participation in important rituals (#)	Chief, "C", or Nonchief, "N" or Trash yard man, "T"
5'9¼"	55	6	R	1	1	C
5'5"	23	10	R	1	3	C
5'4½"	35	7	R	1	3	N
5'4¼"	28	7	R	2	1	C
5'4¼"	28	6	?	1	2	N
5'4¼"	45	3	?	0	2	N
5'4¼"	31	3	P	1	0	N
5'3¾"	45	4	?	0	0	N
5'3¾"	45	3	P	1	0	N
5'3¾"	36	2	P	0	0	T
5'3"	41	4	?	0	1	C
5'2¾"	41	2	P	0	1	N
5'¾"	45	3	P	0	0	T
5'¼"	31	6	P	0	1	N
4'11¾"	23	3	P	0	0	T

The Mehinaku bias for tall men is shared by many other societies, including our own. The sociologist Saul Feldman (1975) reports that "heightism" affects our interpersonal judgments, courtship patterns, job opportunities, and earnings. It should also be pointed out that neither among the Mehinaku nor among ourselves does short stature invariably doom a man to ridicule or failure in sexual or social relations. Pitsa, though just over five feet tall, has six mistresses. Ipyana, a very short man, was held in awe as a witch before his violent death in 1971. And Kuya, one of the shortest men in the village, is an honored storyteller. Build is only one of the factors in evaluating a man's worth. Let those who cannot achieve the desired physical standards strive to be generous, controlled, well-spoken, skilled, and sociable, and they may yet be well-regarded by their fellows.

Spoiled Identities

The Mehinaku sum up the constituent characteristics of social identity by labeling one another as good men or as failures. The *awujitsi*, or good man, meets all the tests of sociability, generosity, wealth, knowledgeability, and physical attractiveness. At present, however, the village has no one who measures up to this ideal image. "In the days of our grandfathers," as the chief frequently puts the matter in his evening lectures, "there were many truly good-men who were generous, hardworking, and sociable. They have all died. The rest of us are not good men; we are bare shadows of our grandfathers, the real *awujitsi*." Although this speech is partly good-old-days rhetoric, it also reflects the fact that it is extremely difficult to be a good man. Some of the requirements are contradictory, simultaneously enjoining a man to accumulate possessions and to give them away. Others are unattainable; not everyone is physically attractive. Given the inflexibility of the critics and the rigor of the standards, it becomes far easier to be a flop than a hit in the theater of Mehinaku social life.

Let us look at several of these failures: the trash yard man, the freeloader, and the witch.

The Trash Yard Man

A visitor walking through the village at almost any hour in the day will encounter many of the adult males in the public areas of the community, chatting, working on crafts, or just observing the daily routine. In Mehinaku, sitting idly with others and watching the passing scene is called "facing" (*upawakatapai*), and it is one of the hallmarks of the sociable man. A rich vocabulary of abuse is applied to the villager who will not "face" his comrades. The *metanaka* (literally "backs" or "back persons"), for example, is always seen from the rear as he flees his more social comrades. Other derisive words and nasty nicknames label the chronically grumpy, sullen, and cold. The significance of the code of sociability and the pejorative terms that back it up becomes clear when we examine one of its most flagrant violators, the *miyeipyenuwanti*, or "trash yard man."

"Trash yard man" is an apt title for one who avoids others, since the trash yards are among the less visible regions of the village. There the trash yard man spends most of his time, working by himself rather than in the men's house.

"Look at old 'Rotten Fish,'" Kuyaparei said one day. "He is a *real* trash yard man. He never gets up to bathe at dawn like the rest of us, and he sleeps all day in his hammock. He doesn't own any *urucu* pigment and never paints himself up in front of the men's house. When he isn't sleeping he is moping around the trash yard or the back door of his house. He doesn't even know how to play the sacred flutes. He has no friends and goes fishing by himself. Last month he went on a two-day fish poisoning trip all by himself."

To my knowledge Kuyaparei's complaints are essentially just. I have never heard "Rotten Fish" make a joke in public or participate in the banter of the men's house. A dour and close-mouthed individual, he probably knows less than any other villager about crafts and traditional myths and lore.

Trash yard men like "Rotten Fish" are unloved. They are gossiped about and pointed out to children as the kind of people one should not grow up to be. Yet they are tolerated, and their presence in the village is testimony to the Mehinaku's willingness to put up with a diverse range of human types. Nevertheless, considering the contempt in which they are held and the rewards of conforming to the ethic of social participation, how can the existence of marginal characters like "Rotten Fish" and the two other notorious trash yard men be explained?

"Rotten Fish" was orphaned at such an early age that he remembers neither his father nor his mother. Without close kinsmen he was brought up in a family where he was always an outsider. The two other trash yard men have a similar background. As a child one lost close relatives in an epidemic, the other in a witch killing at an equally young age. A child cut off from kinsmen is at an enormous disadvantage in Mehinaku society. He tends to be mistreated by the other children and receives little attention from villagers who could teach him basic crafts and skills. As an adult he is condemned to remain outside a vital network of reciprocal gifts of food and labor and therefore has few opportunities to participate in the practice of generosity. An alienated individual, he can never achieve the image of the enthusiastic, social, and extraverted man admired by the Mehinaku.

The Freeloader

The trash yard man's failing is social: he does not hold up his end of the interactional dialogue that makes everyday life pleasant and spirited. Given the ethic of sociability and a community "traffic pattern" that makes encounters inevitable, his sullenness leaves a trail of resentment that follows him through the day. Nevertheless, as long as his delicts are purely social, the villagers try to receive him with a veneer of their customary good humor. As soon as he begins to shortchange them in the give and take of reciprocal obligations, however, their resentments surface in the form of definite sanctions.

The villagers linguistically recognize several types of freeloaders: those who take advantage of their fellow tribesmen in the areas of production, distribution, or consumption. The lazy man (*miyeikyawairi*) conveniently makes himself scarce when it is time to assist his comrades. He announces he must attend to another errand or slips off when no one is looking. The stingy man (*kakaianumairi*) hoards his possessions and refuses to trade when called upon. Finally, the glutton (*kanahiri*) not only eats more than his share but eats alone, a sure sign of his intention to eat too much. The terms labeling a man "lazy," "stingy," or "gluttonous" are loaded with intense negative feelings. Such men are ungenerous, a serious failing since the economic system depends on generosity, and they are mendacious and furtive as well. The lazy man complains of a sore back when it is time to lift a heavy canoe; the stingy man hides his possessions in the woods to conceal his true wealth; the glutton smuggles fish into the village unseen and then sneaks off to eat by himself. Such abusive terms, as well as the portraits of self they suggest, act as sanctions to encourage generosity throughout the society.

When gossip and abuse are insufficient to bring a miscreant into line, his female residence mates may apply heavier pressure. Each fine evening in the dry season, for example, one of the women prepares a hot drink made from manioc. She calls to each of her residence mates to join her: "Kama, come and drink nukaiya!" Stepping out to the back yard, Kama is presented with a gourd dipper brimming with the beverage. He takes his drink and chats awhile with his housemates before leaving. If Kama has been marked as "lazy," "stingy," or "gluttonous," however, he will not be called to join the others. No one will stop him from doing so on his own, but the fact that he has not been invited will rankle.

If he still does not get the message, it will be repeated in another guise. When fish is distributed Kama will get the driest, boniest, and meanest portions. Worse, the women who prepare the fish may wait until he steps out before they decide that the fish is properly cooked and ready to serve. On his return he may find that no one has saved him anything. If he persists in his ways, the pressure will increase. His in-laws will ask his wife to withdraw her sexual and domestic services. She may refuse to go bathing with him, build a fire between her hammock and his, or sleep with her feet on a line with his head. Each of these gestures is a symbolic denial of the marital relationship (see Gregor 1974). Should such sanctions fail to move him, an elder male kinsman may publicly deliver a stern lecture warning him that no woman will ever have anything to do with him unless he reforms and that in addition he risks arousing the rancor of witches.

Kama, who is in fact the most notorious of the Mehinaku freeloaders, has at various times been subject to these measures and yet has not wholly reformed his ways. On my most recent trip to the village (1976) his behavior had become a community concern. Angered by his stinginess and emboldened by his isolated status (Kama has few close kinsmen in the village), practical jokers (*metalawaitsi*) had ripped up portions of his garden and looted his fish traps with such regularity that he had abandoned them. Focusing their attention on Kama's one odd physical feature, an extrawide mouth, the jokers had carved his caricature around the village. Trees, charred logs, cleared ground, and termite hills leered at the passerby in a grotesque parody of Kama's enormous grin.

In a small community like the Mehinaku village these sanctions have tremendous leverage. Kama himself has become somewhat more generous, and certainly no one else so little values his good name and his position in the network of reciprocity that he can be described as incorrigibly lazy, stingy, or gluttonous. On the contrary, the villagers by and large strike the observer as remarkably willing to share their labor, possessions, and food – a pattern that is best explained by the positive ethic of sociability and generosity. The sanctions I have described, and the portraits of self suggested by stinginess, laziness, and gluttony, provide strong additional motivation for striving to become a good citizen, an *awujitsi*.

The Witch

The trash yard man is a villager who has lost his good name. No matter how much effort he may put into being sociable, he brings to each encounter the dead weight of a spoiled identity. The case of the witch, however, is somewhat different. Unlike the trash yard man, he usually is a full participant in the ebb and flow of daily interaction. And yet just beneath the normal courtesy accorded him lie fear, hostility, and often murderous intent.

The villagers believe that human actions are responsible for events we would regard as matters of chance or nature. Children grow into adulthood as a consequence of going into seclusion and taking the proper medicines.

Table 16.6 *Witches and some of their methods*

1. *ipyanawekehe* (literally, *ipyana*, "wood master")

   The *ipyanawekehe* is the witch par excellence. Using slivers of *ipyana* wood (a dark, heavy wood, probably of the genus *Tecoma*), he shoots his victims with magic darts or, more commonly at present, "ties them" with cord by wrapping some thread tightly around a wooden splinter. The term *ipyana* is used generally to refer to all kinds of witchcraft and *ipyanawekehe* loosely designates a witch using any of the techniques listed below.

2. *itsítyawekehe* (literally, "tie master")

   The "tying witch" casts his spells by stealing his victim's armbands and tightly tying them up. The victim sickens and eventually dies. The *itsítyawekehe* may also be a sorcerer who practices revenge witchcraft for paying clients

3. *ejáiwekehe* (literally, "blood master")

   The "blood witch" kills by introducing poisonous animal blood into his victim's food.

4. *majajáiwekehe* (translation unknown)

   A ball of waxy *majajái* is shot at the victim with a tiny slingshot. His face turns red, his hair falls out, he gradually dies.

5. *eíyuwekehe* (literally, mosquito master")

   The "mosquito witch" torments the entire community by generating mosquitoes from wax pellets that he surreptitiously seeds about the village.

6. *ejekekíwekehe* (literally, "breath master")

   The "breath master" is only marginally a witch, since blowing can cure as well as harm. Just as a fire can be started by blowing on it, so a man can be restored to health by puffs of breath. Malevolent witches, however, can kill their victims by blowing in their direction.

7. *kurítsiwekehe* (literally, "love wax master")

   The *kurítsiwekehe* makes women sexually aggressive by secretly applying *kuritsi* wax to their bodies. He is tolerated as long as he confines his magic to this one technique.

Physical attractiveness is no roll of the genetic dice but a result of self-discipline and again, conformity to the rules of seclusion. Health, success in fishing, fertility of orchards, and a happy afterlife at least partly depend on the performance of rituals and self-limitations on sexuality. It follows that life's misfortunes may also be the responsibility of individual Mehinaku. Thunderstorms, invasions of ants, depredations of wild pigs, house-demolishing winds, female sexual aggressiveness, sickness, death, and other mysterious phenomena can all be attributed to witches.

The first witch was the Sun. Plucking a few of his wife's pubic hairs, he fashioned the first *kaukí*, or disease-causing objects that are shot into a person's body. The Sun taught his methods to his children and they to theirs, with ever new elaborations and techniques. The process of transmission continues today as parent witches train their sons for the profession. "Making" a witch requires a kind of black seclusion during which a young boy is initiated into witchcraft as well as adulthood. He is scarified as in ordinary seclusion, but the scarifier is made not of fish teeth but of snake's teeth, spider mandibles, or stingers from the ferocious *tocandira* ant. After being thoroughly scraped, venomous compounds and smoke are introduced into the wounds to make the novice's magic powerful. At first, the young witch experiments with his new power by inducing a mild illness in his victims or pestering the village with a modest plague of mosquitoes. In the fullness of time, however, he is capable of killing by a variety of magical techniques such as I have noted in Table 16.6. Listed in rough order of importance in the present (1974) culture of witchcraft, these methods are faddish and change with time.

In 1967 virtually all allegations of witchcraft mentioned tiny invisible arrows described as invariably fatal. In 1974 this technique, while still significant, was on the wane as others came into vogue.

Witches resort to deadly magic because of a desire for revenge. The jealous lover, the cuckolded husband, the envious, the robbed, and the slighted are therefore likely targets for accusations of witchcraft. In normal times such accusations may be secretly muttered in the course of malicious gossip. Once a death has occurred, however, they become the basis for action. The deceased's relatives may publicly denounce the witch; they may shoot volleys of arrows and bullets through the roof of his house; or they may attempt to kill him magically using the "grilling" method. On occasion they murder the witch, especially if he is an individual who has no kinsmen to defend or avenge him. The last thirty years have seen four such killings, a rate undoubtedly inflated by the fears aroused by epidemics of measles and influenza.

A witch killing is a grisly affair, the details of which are told and retold by the villagers. The victim's last words, his dying shrieks, his groans as he is clubbed or shot are as much a part of Mehinaku oral history as the description of the activities of a great chief. In 1972, for example, Keje told me how he had killed Ipyana the year before.

I didn't want to kill Ipyana, but all my kinsmen told me I had to, and I *was* angry. My stepfather asked some of the villagers if we could go ahead, and word of our intentions got back to Ipyana. He was afraid to leave his house. One day he went to the Post and we were on the trail to ambush him. He tried to run, but I grabbed him from behind. The others held back. I shouted, "Are you women? Kill him!" They clubbed him on the head with sticks and machetes until he fell down groaning. We buried him nearby. No one dares go along the trail to the Post, for his soul (ĩyeweku, literally, shadow) still roams about, moaning and shrieking in pain.

This description is typical of others for, like Ipyana, the victims of witch killings are usually men who are socially estranged and lack the protection of male kin. As in this case, the victim is ambushed and outnumbered, unable to protect himself against his assailants. The unusual element of Ipyana's slaying was the effort to seek some consensus in the village before the killing took place. Wide agreement is not usually sought because communication networks are far too open to conceal preliminary deals. Unlike other tribal societies where a killing may be a community-approved execution (compare Hoebel's [1970: 89] account of the execution of Eskimo recidivist murderers), the Mehinaku witch killing is the action of a tight handful of aggrieved individuals.

Despite the killings, the accusations, and the belief that misfortune is caused by magic, there are few, if any, practitioners of witchcraft present in the community. Some of the villagers may have tried out a few of the simpler techniques to work off a grudge, but no evidence suggests that the institution is as elaborate or entrenched as the Mehinaku would have it. The evil intentions attributed to witches and their fanciful methods seem to be a projection of the villagers' own hostility and fear. The best evidence for this point, the sociology of allegations of witchcraft, will also take us into the effect of witchcraft beliefs on informal encounters.

Table 16.7 lists accusations of witchcraft by approximately half the adults in the tribe. All the suspects named are men because the villagers believe that only males can be witches. The thirteen persons questioned offered eighty-nine allegations of witchcraft, nearly seven accusations per individual. Every Mehinaku male was regarded as a witch by at least one informant, and two men were named as witches by every informant. As the table shows, accusations of witchcraft are most often directed against persons who are neither relatives nor residence mates of the informant. Unlike other South American tribes (such as the Mundurucú as reported by Murphy 1960), the Mehinaku have no tendency to accuse shamans of witchcraft nor do they link a shaman's and a witch's magic.

Village life is not as grim as the data in Table 16.7 suggests. Though each man believes his neighbor is capable of bewitching him, this does not mean he will actually do so. The witch may be out of practice, his magic may be weak, he may even be a friend. The chief puts the matter in this fashion: "Yes, I think Yuta is a

Table 16.7 *Accusations of witchcraft by thirteen Mehinaku adults*

Accusation, assertion of innocence, or denial of knowledge	Relationship of informant and suspect		Residence of informant and suspect		
	Kinsmen	Not kinsmen	Coresidents, or coresidents prior to marriage	Not coresidents	Totals
Suspect guilty of witchcraft	9	80	6	83	89
Suspect innocent	52	25	37	40	77
Informant unsure of suspect's innocence	8	20	8	20	28

little bit of a witch. But it has been a long time since he made anyone sick, and I know he never would hurt me. He is my friend." The truly dangerous witches apparently number only one or two individuals, their identity depending on who is asked and changing as new tales are churned out by the everactive gossip mill.

Although the villagers are not continually fearful, reminders of their uneasiness are always visible. During a recent visit, the doors to my house were tied shut at night to keep out prowling witches. A cautious householder patched up the holes in the thatch wall near his hammock so that he would not be shot with magic arrows. An older woman constructed an alarm system of old pot lids to alert her to nocturnal intruders. One of my companions took special pains to keep his clothes, arm bands, hair clippings, chewed fishbones, and other effluvia well away from neighbors he distrusted.

Casual interaction is also marked by anxiety about witchcraft. I have already noted how Ipyana was treated with deference and formality by villagers fearful of his power. Other suspected witches receive courteous or seemingly friendly treatment for the same reason. Kuyaparei explains his special greeting and a big smile for Yuma: "He nearly killed my son last year because he was jealous of my new gun. If I were not afraid of him, I would not treat him so sociably." And Shumõi, a compul-

sive practical joker, never dares to pull a prank on a suspected witch. His interactional style is far more muted and respectful in the presence of a villager he fears: "Did you see me with Yuta? I never play around with him. I pay him respect. Whenever we wrestle I let him win. I make absolutely sure he does not find out when I have sexual relations with his wife." If Shumõi's and Kuyaparei's restraint is typical, then one of the effects of belief in witches is to give community life a veneer of courtesy and affability it otherwise might not have. Each villager is motivated to be sociable not only by the carrot of community acceptance but also by the stick of witchcraft.

Portraits of Self

A villager's identity is largely comprised of the roles he acts within the community. His position as a kinsman, chief, or shaman, for example, affects the way others form judgments about him and interact with him. Cutting across a man's social positions, however, are the attributes of self I have described in this chapter. All of a man's roles will be affected by his sociability, his generosity, his riches, his knowledge, and his physical attractiveness. In the course of casual social engagements not clearly governed by well-defined social roles, these characteristics may become crucial. Taken together they help to determine who a man is within the community. They identify him to his fellows and allow them to evaluate his moral worth, to predict his conduct, and to respond to his overtures.

The theater of Mehinaku social life, unlike the legitimate stage, is a theater of improvisation. Actors do not bring scripts to their informal engagements, merely rough guidelines of how they ought to act. A scene may occasionally surprise us with an unexpected turn or a trick ending. Nonetheless, the portraits of self I have described impose a regularity on such encounters, providing a basis for understanding the course of informal interaction and the motives of the participants. They are, in effect, the unwritten lines that give direction, purpose, and predictability to everyday life.

Withdrawal and Disengagement

I'm going for a stroll. I'll be back later.
Kuyaparei, to his wife

In my description of Mehinaku interaction, I have been concerned with how the villagers prepare for interaction, how they greet each other, and how they present themselves once they are engaged in informal social situations. A full description of interaction, however, requires attention to the values and institutions that separate people and disengage them from social contact. Patterned methods of withdrawal and disengagement are in fact prerequisites for a society. If individuals are to come together in an orderly way, there must be times when they stay apart. The shape of interactional patterns in a society is determined by rules of separation as well as rules of engagement.

The ability to break off and withdraw from social engagements appears to be intertwined with personality and the emotional perception of one's fellows. Constant engagement is de-selfing and a possible threat to the differentiation of the ego. The psychological realization of one's self as a unique entity requires some means of social separation. It is only during moments of isolation that we can integrate and reflect on our experiences and return to new

encounters with a sense of our own history and an awareness of ourselves as individuals.

Although withdrawal and disengagement help to determine the total pattern and rate of interaction, the topic has attracted little ethnographic attention. Anthropologists have usually focused on the bizarre examples of institutions that facilitate social separation, as in the case of patterns of affinal avoidance. In this chapter I plan to examine some of the problems posed by the frequent interaction that arise out of daily living and the techniques by which the Mehinaku manage to hold themselves aloof from social contact.

There are relatively few shelters from social engagement available within the Mehinaku community, and strong sanctions prevent a villager from making too much use of them. The reader can get a rough idea of the extent of the Mehinaku's exposure to one another by reconsidering the social events that can occur on the short walk to the bathing area described earlier. In a brief ten-minute walk a young man had to act virtually his entire repertory of social characters – the respectful son-in-law, the sober brother-in-law, the concerned grandchild, the joking cross-cousin, and the desirous lover. Even on a very personal errand, a villager is continually open to social engagement.

Shumõi is on his way out of the village. As he leaves his house, his wife questions him: "Shumõi, where are you going?" He answers with the apparent indifference of a husband: "Nowhere, just to defecate." "Oh." As he passes a neighboring house, his uncle spots him through a tiny window in the thatch wall: "Nephew!" (the voice emerges through the wall) "Where are you going?" "To defecate." "Then go." Finally, on the path he meets his cross-cousin who is returning to the village with firewood: "Hai ja! Where are you going? Are you alligatoring the girls again?" "No, you vagina lover, I'm just carrying my egg" (that is, going to defecate). "Ha! Go ahead then!" And so it goes. A walk through the village is a journey through Mehinaku social structure, an unending series of social encounters from which there is no apparent escape.

Although I have no statistical information on precisely how often the Mehinaku are engaged with each other, the actual rate of interaction is less important than the fact that the Mehinaku sometimes find exposure to social contact abrasive and unwanted. The source of this attitude is that many of the persons with whom the villagers must interact are feared as witches, thieves, and gossips. To these fears must be added all the disagreements and antagonisms that are probably inevitable in any small human community. The Mehinaku therefore regard much of the courteous interaction that occurs in the men's house and on the public paths as something of a conscious presentation for the sake of social appearances. Repeated day after day, such presentations become habitual but, according to some of my informants, are nonetheless burdensome.

Several of the Mehinaku trash yard men seem to have given up the burden entirely. "Rotten Fish" not only avoids social contact as often as he can, but when greeted by others, responds with an unsmiling dour expression. Although only a few villagers conduct themselves like "Rotten Fish," many others are sullen from time to time. On such occasions their bad temper and rudeness generate waves of irritation and hostility among those who must deal with them. Admittedly sullenness and irritability are human universals, but the openness of the Mehinaku community to social engagement and the ethic that encourages men to initiate social encounters makes such moods unusually abrasive. There are devices, however, which enable the villagers to disengage themselves from unwanted social involvements.

Spatial Methods of Disengagement

The man who wants to avoid his comrades simply packs his bags and leaves the tribe. His destination is either another tribe, the Indian Post, a dry season village, or just the forest, where he can wander about.

Visits to other tribes

The Mehinaku, like other Xinguanos, are inveterate travelers. As Robert Carneiro rightly notes, "A common sight in the Upper Xingu is a traveling family: the man with his bow and arrows in his hand, the woman with a gourd or basketful of flour on her head, and their children carrying a few odds and ends" (1957: 242). Although there are many motives for these trips, some are clearly attributable to disaffection with local village life. There is no better antidote to the pressures or the occasional slow pace of community activities, for example, than a trip to another tribe. Normally these visits are short and informal, ending after the visitor has participated in his hosts' rituals or arranged to trade a shell belt or ceramic pot. On occasion, however, the intertribal visit is a method of leaving the home community on a permanent or semi-permanent basis. One of the few Mehinaku to embrace this strategy is Kua. Regarded as a malevolent gossip, he is almost always seething with anger over some slight or other. After the death of both his parents in a measles epidemic, he went to live with an American missionary along the Batovi River, where he spent almost all of his growing-up years.

After the missionary left the Xingu region, Kua (now with the new name of Carlos) returned to the Mehinaku but found himself unable to get along with the villagers. He felt persecuted by the men whose wives and mistresses became his girl friends and by the chief who, so he believed, begrudged him the fact that he was also of a chiefly line. Stories kept circulating through the village that he was a magician skilled in love magic and in the production of stinging ants.

Kua has told me of his feelings:

When I greet everyone on the path and smile, don't think that I am happy here. At night, after the fires have died down and everyone is sleeping, I cry in my hammock. I know what everyone says about me, but I will not confront them. I am a great chief. When I am dying everyone will come to me in my hammock and I will say: "Look what you and your malicious gossip have done." And then *they* will be sad.

Kua's problems have driven him from one village to another in the course of which he has mastered all of the Upper Xingu languages but Trumaí. Leaving a trail of stories behind him alleging that he beat children and practiced witchcraft, he was never able to find a welcome in any tribe. He is now considering giving up his own people and going to live for good at the Batovi Post of the Indian service.

Despite Kua's unhappy experience, the Xingu tribes are not always unreceptive to long-term visitors. As we shall see in chapter 18, the Xinguanos' formal pattern of hospitality ensures that virtually any visitor can count on a friendly reception. An unwanted guest finds that this welcome quickly wears thin, but in some cases he can integrate himself in his host's community on a long-term basis. In the course of most of my field work, for example, there was at least one family from another Xingu tribe living with their Mehinaku kinsmen. The motives for these extended stays were usually based on accusations or fear of witchcraft in the visitors' home village. At present (1976), two Mehinaku are living outside their own community and are unlikely to return. Ukalu, for example, lives among the Waura partly because the Mehinaku still recall the disgraceful years in which she incestuously cohabited with her father. Mutu lives a marginal existence shuttling between several of the neighboring tribes, ever fearful that he will be slain as a witch if he returns to the Mehinaku village.

The Indian Post

A man who moves from house to house is a bad sort, a man on his way out of the community. A man who shifts from village to village is said to be just like the man who cannot get along with his residence mates. He, however, is not just on the way out of his home community; he is on the way out of the traditional social world. His destination is a life of exile along the margins of Brazilian civilization. He may, for example, go to work as a temporary laborer earning only his keep at one of the ranches now located along the boundaries of the Xingu reservation. None of the Mehinaku other than Kua have considered this alternative, for leaving the reservation is social suicide, a renunciation of one's entire previous life.

A less extreme and more common refuge from social pressures can be found at the Indian Post, Posto Leonardo Villas Boas, an agency of Brazil's Indian Foundation (Fundação Nacional do Indio). At present the Post consists of an air strip, a small clinic and dispensary, a guest house, and several homes for the Foundation's employees. In addition, each of the Xingu tribes has built a house at the Post to use during their visits to receive medical aid, to trade with the crews of air force planes, and to learn the latest news about the white man. The tribal houses continue to serve these functions as well as an unanticipated one: sheltering villagers marked as witches who cannot return to their own homes. At home they would be killed as soon as the next epidemic provided their accusers with a motive. Ipyana, for example, had lived for a considerable time at the Post before his death at the hands of some of the Mehinaku in 1971. He occasionally returned to the village, but there he remained in fear of his life. So afraid was he of an ambush that each time he went on an errand he carried his small son on his shoulders to discourage and shame would-be assailants. Whenever anyone in the village became ill during his stay, he promptly rolled up his hammock, shouldered his fishing gear and rifle, and left for the Post.

Ipyana would probably be alive today had he stayed at Posto Leonardo. To date the Xinguanos have had the temerity to kill only one witch at the Post ("the white man's village") and then only under extraordinary circumstances. Three alleged witches remain there, including one Mehinaku, all living rather marginal lives away from the ceremonial and social activities that make village life exciting and worthwhile. Most of them have exhausted their welcome in all the Xingu tribes, and spend much of their time hanging about the Post buildings, cadging gifts from visitors, and (when hunger and their families drive them to it) going on short fishing trips. Their presence is an embarrassment for the Post personnel, who are appalled at witch killings but who also respect the autonomy and traditions of the Xingu tribes. The dilemma is compounded by the Xinguanos' fear of the witches, sometimes leading them to put off going to the clinic when they badly need medical treatment. From the point of view of the accused witches, however, the Post offers an opportunity that had never previously existed. If village life becomes intolerable, if one is hated and feared by his comrades, there is at least an alternative; a final sanctuary for the outcasts of Xingu village society.

The dry season village

A less radical alternative to permanent departure from the home community is to establish a dry season village (*uleinejepu*). At present two Mehinaku families and their dependent relatives regularly leave the community to cut new gardens near their dry season villages, each of which consists of a shabbily constructed house in a clearing near the Culiseu River. During the months that a family spends in the dry season village, the men clear new fields and the women harvest the old ones, building up a large surplus of manioc flour for the coming rainy season. Shortly before the first rains, the villagers return home with their flour.

One of the questions that puzzled me when I began my research was Why do the Mehinaku bother to make dry season villages? The gardener can plant his manioc in the ample land still surrounding the main village and spare himself the arduous task of transporting the flour home over a long distance. A partial explanation of the pattern is related to warfare. In the 1950s the Mehinaku were the victims of a series of raids by the Carib-speaking Txicão. At one point, fearing for their lives, the tribe broke into its constituent house groups and moved to a number of dry season villages hidden away in the forest. Having a second home and a garden ready to harvest was a form of survival insurance in the days when the Xingu peoples were preyed upon by "wild Indians" from beyond their borders.

How can we, however, account for the persistence of dry season villages today? I believe that one of their attractions is that they offer the Mehinaku a legitimate way of leaving the village for a prolonged period. When community tensions mount, that is the time to move to a dry season village. My friend Shumõi explained one man's departure: "Whenever he gets mad at the men for having sexual relations with his wife, that's when he decides to go to his dry season village." Shumõi, who is himself planning to clear a dry season garden site, says that he is doing so to get away from village gossip. At the dry season village there are no accusations of witchcraft, no invidious gossip, no intrigues between adulterous lovers, nor any of the other potentially abrasive situations that mar life back home.

Wandering

The dry season village and relocating in another tribe help the Mehinaku to withdraw from unwanted social contact. Still another shelter from unwanted engagements is the pattern of "strolling" or "wandering" (*etunauwakátapai*, derived from the verb *etúnapai*, to walk).

Wandering is such an entrenched institution among the Xingu tribes that the observer who is accustomed to it must make a deliberate effort to see its significance. Exclusively a male activity, it is usually done alone, although on occasion two men may go out together. Often the wanderer has some vague purpose in mind. I have strolled through the forest with Mehinaku who were ostensibly looking for root medicines, reeds suitable for flutes, or birds with feathers for decorating headdresses. Invariably they carried guns just in case they ran across a jaguar, a monkey, or an edible bird. Sometimes we would go out to the gardens in the hope of finding a ripe pineapple or a tree full of edible locusts. Once we went on a half-hearted jaguar hunt in which neither of my companions seemed to have much interest in tracking down the animal (fortunately!). Although it was usually not what we were seeking, we almost always brought back something useful: a fledgling bird to give to the children as a pet, edible wild fruit, or at least bark fiber for making ankle bands.

Although these strolls allow the Mehinaku to scan their environment and its potential resources, I am convinced that there is something else that sends them out on such excursions. The trips are far too frequent (a man is apt to be off wandering every two or three days for two to three hours at a time) to explain them as merely subsistence activities. At least some of the "walk abouts" have to be understood in the light of what is happening in the village. My impression is that the men go strolling under two conditions, the first of which is stress. Men who quarrel with their wives are especially likely to go wandering. The second condition is boredom. Whenever there is very little happening in the village, men will go for a stroll. The forests and streams are potentially exciting places where men may have chance meetings with animals and even spirits. In short, wandering through the woods enables the Mehinaku to make short-term adjustments to unsatisfactory patterns of interaction. When relationships become particularly difficult or uninteresting, a stroll though the forest provides welcome relief.

Symbolic Methods of Disengagement

The techniques of withdrawal I have just described are primarily spatial. A man simply rolls up his hammock, shoulders his rifle, and leaves the village. There are communities, however, where it is possible to secure privacy simply with gestures or other conventionalized signals. Consider the elegant method of social disengagement used by the Yagua, as described by Paul Fejos:

Although an entire Yagua community lives and sleeps in one large house devoid of partitions or screens, its members, nevertheless, are able to obtain perfect privacy whenever they wish it simply by turning their faces toward the wall of the house. Whenever a man, woman, or child faces the wall, the others regard that individual as if he were no longer present. No one in the house will look upon, or observe, one who is in private facing the wall, no matter how urgently he may wish to talk to him. I observed this custom for the first time at the Ant settlement when I entered the house to question the chief. As the chief was unable to answer some of my questions, I asked him to call over the shaman who was sitting nearby on his hammock facing the wall. The chief declined to call him and seemed astonished at my ignorance in wishing to disturb a person who was in private and therefore not "at home." We waited for almost an hour until the shaman turned toward the center of the house and only then did the chief call him over. At first I thought that this rule applied

only to the shaman, but later I discovered that all members of the clan, even children, possessed this privilege (Fejos 1943: 87).

The Mehinaku, however, have not developed any comparable method of symbolically isolating themselves except when they are emotionally unprepared for interaction, as when a villager feels shame.

The relationship of interactional withdrawal to the personal feeling of shame (*iaipiripyai*) is a healthy reminder to us that, unlike actors on the legitimate stage, the real life actors in the Mehinaku community are fully engaged in their roles. They not only appear as kinsmen, shamans, and chiefs, they are kinsmen, shamans, and chiefs. A corollary is that interaction, for them, unlike theatrical interaction, is psychologically real. They are not simply concerned with how their performance looks but how it is personally experienced. When the Mehinaku discuss their experience they employ a small number of descriptive words that summarize a complex pattern of emotions and attitudes, including "sociability," "respect," and "shame." One or more of these terms applies to every Mehinaku relationship, labeling a continuum of attitudes that we would call openness at one end, and withdrawal and disengagement at the other. We are already well-acquainted with the importance of sociability, a term suggesting a cheerful receptiveness to others, enjoyment of interaction, and warmth of disposition. Respect suggests the less spontaneous feelings associated with deference and is appropriate for the unequal or opposed relationships of in-laws and tribal chiefs. Shame is the extreme end of the continuum, a feeling associated with disengagement and retreat.

Shame

The Mehinaku feel shame in a wide variety of circumstances. Shumōi tells me that he feels shame in predictable situations, such as when he visits another tribe, when he speaks a foreign language, when he enters someone else's house, and when he speaks as a chief on the plaza at night. On the other hand, Ulawalu, an attractive adolescent girl, feels shame in virtually any public situation, such as appearing on the main plaza.

The experience of shame appears to be associated with misconduct, uncertainty about what is expected, or inability to carry off a role performance. A visit to another tribe, for example, is an uncomfortable experience, given the ambivalent relationship of the Xingu villages, the lack of familiarity with the language, and the proximity of many persons with whom there is no established basis for interaction. Entering another person's house, usually considered a violation of privacy, places the visitor in a socially anomalous position. So far as public oratory is concerned, Shumōi is unused to speaking on the plaza, feels unprepared for his chiefly role, and experiences shame when he tries to carry it off. Ulawalu's chronic sense of shame in public situations has a similar source. Only recently emerged from adolescent seclusion, she is now of sexual interest to many men who had previously been indifferent to her. She is exposed to a great deal of sexual joking from her cross-cousins. Conscious of the glances and laughter of the men seated on the bench in front of the men's house, she suspects that some of them will remark about her obvious comeliness and gossip about her affairs. Unprepared for this kind of attention and unused to her new role as a woman, she is understandably in a state of shame.

Whatever the source of shame, the villager who experiences it separates himself from his comrades. "When you are ashamed it hurts to be seen," the Mehinaku say, so the shamed man keeps out of the public eye. He may spend the day wandering through the forest or working in his garden. On his return he sits for hours on a bench staring out of a small hole he has made in the thatch wall of the house. When he goes to the river, he will use the alternate bathing areas and hidden paths that lead from the back door of each house. At night he ties his hammock between two trees in the forest to pass the night far from his family and neighbors. On his return to his house in the morning, he takes to his hammock again, lying on his side with his knees pulled up to his chest. He is said to be "curled up" with shame, just as a caterpillar curls up when held in the hand. If a kinsman or friend makes an effort to humor him out of his withdrawal, he places both hands over his eyes to communicate his unwillingness to be engaged.

Only the grossest mismanagement of affinal taboos or the exposure of serious misconduct would lead a villager to retreat so far. Less grave sources of shame, however, also make him avoid his fellows. To communicate his isolated status, he may discard feather ornaments and body paints or go about naked, without even a shell belt. Like a man in seclusion he keeps off the plaza in daylight hours, avoids the companionship of the men's house, and keeps to himself when his housemates assemble to drink tapica (*nukaiya*) in the early evening. In these ways the shamed person physically and symbolically establishes a private world for himself. Ordinarily he will not have to live in this world for very long, for he gradually allows his friends and kin to woo him back to his normal routine. When he at last begins to feel a whole social person, he rubs his body with red *urucu* body paint and reenters the public life of the community.

Shame is thus an antisocial emotion, the antithesis of sociability. The shamed man strips himself of the paints, costumes, and other accoutrements of interaction and retreats from his comrades. In acute form, the emotion forces him into a presocial state, his eyes hidden from the "painful gaze" of his comrades, his body curled up into a fetal position, wrapped unseen in his hammock.

Disengagement and the Dramaturgical Perspective

The dramatist does not always bring his characters onto the scene; at times he must make sure they are kept well in the wings and hidden from the audience. In real life the divisions between actors and audience or stage and green room cannot always be neatly drawn. Nonetheless, the members of a small community like the Mehinaku must take care not to clutter up the action when they are ill-prepared to participate in it. Chronic public sullenness like that of "Rotten Fish" or anger like that of Kua is intolerable when the script calls for courtesy and good humor. For them and for others who are not up to participating in the drama, there are techniques of disengagement – visits to other tribes, wandering in the forest, and respites in the dry season village. If they choose to remain in the community and are still badly prepared for their performance, they may feel shame. From our perspective this emotion is the personal experience of a dramaturgical imperative: the play cannot be staged by amateurs just learning their lines or even by experienced actors who muff their cues. Shame drives such performers into the wings as effectively as the yank of the classic shepherd's crook.

Leaving the community and exhibiting signs of shame may well be employed as techniques of disengagement by all peoples. The Mehinaku have other methods of social withdrawal that undoubtedly are equally widely distributed, such as the short periods of avoiding others associated with sullenness or "feeling blue." A man who is sad withdraws from the public life of the community. Being sad (*amakanatúapai*) literally means to "place oneself in one's hammock" and, like the shamed man, the sad man spends much of his day sleeping, thereby avoiding his companions.

Sadness, shame, and the other techniques we have examined, are all informal and noninstitutionalized methods of separating oneself from one's community.

REFERENCES

Goffman, E.
  1956   The nature of deference and demeanor. American Anthropologist 58: 473–502.
Hoebel, E. A.
  1970   The Law of Primitive Man. New York: Atheneum.
Murdock, G. P.
  1945   The Common Denominator of Culture. *In* R. Linton (ed.), The Science of Man in World Crisis. New York: Columbia University Press, pp. 123–42.

17

Sambia Nose-Bleeding Rites and Male Proximity to Women

Gilbert H. Herdt

Since the early work of Bateson (1936) and Mead (1935), New Guinea cultures – especially in the Eastern Highlands studied by Read (1951, 1952) – have been identified with various initiatory rituals, among which none have proved as symbolically complex or theoretically controversial as those of bloodletting. In spite of considerable cross-cultural variation in the practices, researchers have not only drawn on these data, but have also reached divergent conclusions about their meaning. Furthermore, each of the proposed interpretations implied different slants on the developmental context of the rites that were seldom explicated, let alone demonstrated. It is remarkable, then, that after these many years of theoretical interest no ethnographer since Read (1965:127–133) had published detailed observations of these ritual behaviors until recently (cf. Lewis 1980; Poole 1982; Tuzin 1980:72–78), and none has systematically described the behavioral experience or cultural context of bloodletting in the male life cycle of a Highlands people. It is these problems – in relation to the cultural structure of nosebleeding and the ritualization of proximity to women throughout the developmental cycle – that I shall examine among the Sambia, a hunting and horticultural people of the Eastern Highlands.

New Guineasts have tended to view bloodletting rites from several analytic perspectives.

Read's (1952) emphasis on the social solidarity effected by the cult context of such rites has been widely supported (Berndt 1962; Newman 1965; Strathern 1969). Others have also concurred with Read (1952:13) that bloodletting is a form of "psychological conditioning" associated with the male warrior ethos (Allen 1967; Hogbin 1970; Mead 1935; Tuzin 1980; Whiting 1941). Meggitt (1964) saw consistent correlations between types of sexual activity (e.g., "lechers" and "prudes"), purificatory cults, and intergroup hostility vis-à-vis affines (cf. Allen 1967:11–12, 52–53). Langness (1967) went further, arguing that "sexual antagonism" – within the warring Highlands environment – arose as a culturally constituted response to deny men's dependence upon women. Lindenbaum (1972, 1976) contended that rites like male bloodletting operate as systemic ecological controls on women and their productivity (cf. Chowning 1980). Langness (1974) further added that the secrecy of cult rituals affects *male* solidarity and power in regulating strategic female domains in which male social control needs "supernatural" aids. Moreover, many New Guineasts have emphasized native ideas that expurgations of maternal substance or "pollution" are needed to develop and maintain masculinity (Bateson 1936:130ff.; Berndt 1965:92–94; Herdt 1981; Hogbin 1970:103ff.; Lewis 1980; Mead

Gilbert H. Herdt, Sambia Nosebleeding Rites and Male Proximity to Women from *Ethos*, Vol. 10, No. 3 (Autumn, 1982), pp. 189–231. Published by Blackwell Publishing on behalf of the American Anthropological Association, © 1982 by the Society for Psychological Anthropology. Reprinted with permission of the American Anthropological Association.

1935:85; Meigs 1978; Newman 1964; Poole 1982; Read 1951, 1965; Whiting 1941:64ff.). In sum, however, these studies have taken a synchronic viewpoint which stresses the *adult outcome* of ritual experiences for the functioning of social groups and institutions.

Here I take a diachronic perspective on Sambia sexual polarity and ritual that will, I hope, offer fresh questions and answers about ritual bloodletting by attending to the developmental context in which it emerges. Let me begin by stating several analytic points about the Sambia sociocultural system (see Herdt 1981, 1982). The first point concerns a societal imperative: before pacification (1964–1965), Sambia communities needed to create tough, aggressive fighters to fill and replenish the ranks of their warriorhood. Next, I believe that the production of this type of "warrior personality" among males anywhere was not easy or "natural" (Mead 1935 and Schwartz 1973); moreover, its difficulties were exacerbated by the Sambia developmental cycle that results in the presence of too much mother and too little father, thus stunting the male's early separation from his mother in childhood. Last, the accommodation of these early childhood experiences, and core gender identity (see Stoller 1968), to the demanding behavioral environment of adult male character structure, established special, enduring, psychosocial needs for autonomy that could be symbolically sustained through ritual mechanisms – e.g., nosebleeding behaviors – enabling competent adjustment to, and performance of, the adult masculine gender role throughout life. Although these psychosocial needs arose as unintended social consequences of Sambia socialization, their symbolic expression has been culturally transmitted and reproduced to filter those needs. The symbolic structure specifically "filtered out" mother and all that she stood for, and "filtered in" father, aggressivity, and ritualized proximity to women; and these "symbolic filters" (Herdt 1981) came to take on a life of their own – as "internal discourses" for the institution and audiences (Foucault 1980:28) of bloodletting. Viewed in this way, the experience of nosebleeding binds the ideological and sensory poles of meaning to the *designata* of dominant symbols (Turner 1967) in Sambia ritual, making the male warrior ethos and world view (Geertz 1973) a dynamic product of a developmental context.

It is obvious and has been well reported (see below) that cutting the body in bloodletting is painful. It is also known that these "mutilation rites" are, throughout New Guinea, first administered forcibly by elders on groups of boys in collective initiation. Bloodletting is often said to be necessary for "male growth," so one can understand, in terms of the native model, why bloodletting should be done until maturity has been achieved. But what motivates those ritual behaviors afterwards, on into old age? Unless one assumes (as I do not) that these painful operations are *intrinsically* pleasurable or satisfying, we must examine the cultural and social psychological factors that compel subsequent adult operations: beliefs, self experiences, and ever present audiences that are sufficiently approving or fearsome to result in the painful repetition of such self-inflicted acts. Here, I think, we anthropologists have still not met the challenge of Bettelheim's (1955:14) old question: What is "the function of mutilations regularly inflicted"? The Sambia material is helpful.

The Sambia ritual cycle of initiations emphasizes four broad developmental themes in males' relationships to women that define the context of nosebleeding throughout the life cycle. They emerge as follows: (1) Boys must be physically separated from their mothers, and then nosebled, to rid them of female pollutants that block "male growth" (a concept that is, however, complex). (2) The behavioral and cultural content of secret rites, especially nosebleeding, is organized violently so as to effect psychological detachment of boys vis-à-vis their mothers and avoidance of all females. (3) This ritual aggressiveness, furthermore, effects attachment to masculine figures through obedience to them as authorities, who train the boys to become warriors – social outcomes that help explain, but also require changes in – the cultural context of nosebleeding ritual following the initiates' social elevation into the upper ranks of the ritual cult hierarchy. (4) After marriage, nosebleeding acts are transformed from being involuntary public rituals to voluntary private events: men must (while alone) induce nosebleeding on each occasion of their wives' menstrual periods, into old age. And they also become initiators. Thus, initiation nosebleed-ings are a social control mechanism of the male cult which effects the *collective regulation* of boys; whereas among adult men, private nose-bleedings become a means of one's autonomous *self-regulation* in contacts with women. The meaning of nosebleeding thus changes with successive ritual initiations; and, among adult men, those layers of meaning (concepts of man-hood) are fixed within the developmental transformations in male character structure that enable one's self-regulation to come about. From these points there follows my thesis: psy-chosocial (and physical) *proximity to women* is the key variable in predicting the occurrence of nosebleeding behavior; changes in the cultural definitions of proximity, at different points in the male life cycle, precisely regulates the shift-ing temporal sequence, ideological teachings, sociocultural context, and the affective inten-sity of the bloodletting experience.

Each one of these developmental themes bearing on nosebleeding and proximity to women shall be examined in turn. A related and somewhat disconcerting pattern in the Sambia system will also be tackled. Sambia believe that a boy must be nosebled to "grow" and attain reproductive competence. But once married and fully initiated, men no longer offer that rationale for the private practices – not until middle age, that is. Among those older men, who have long since married once, twice, or more, and reared families, many again begin offering the pat statement that unless they nosebleed themselves they will "stop grow-ing." The thick connotations of that sense of "growth" must be interpreted, since they involve the end point of psychosocial auton-omy and contacts with women.

The Cultural Context

Sambia are a mountain people inhabiting iso-lated river valleys of the remote Eastern Highlands. They number some 2,000 people dispersed in clusters of small hamlets over a wide region. Men hunt and both sexes garden. Descent is patrilineally based; residence is pat-rilocal. Marriage is arranged through infant betrothal or sister exchange. Warfare was endemic and destructive among Sambia. It had two forms: the stylized bow-fight among neighboring hamlets and the inter-hamlet war party sent to raid and kill neighboring tribes. Propinquitous hamlets thus inter-married and sometimes warred (cf. Meggitt 1964:219ff.). And every three or four years they joined together in building a great collective cult house to stage bachelorhood initiation (see Herdt 1981).

Relationships between the sexes are sharply polarized along the lines of a misogynist male belief system depicting women as polluting, depleting inferiors a man should distrust and keep distant. Most unrelated, sexually mature women are regarded as potentially contaminat-ing relative to their menstrual and vaginal flu-ids. But these ideological stereotypes (see M. Strathern 1972) do shift somewhat, according to particular individuals and situations. For example, men fear contamination mostly from their wives, not their sisters. Like Tuzin (1982), I have noted a disparity between male ritual rhetoric and the more steady domestic relation-ships among the sexes, including spouses. Sambia customarily expect the spouses to cohabit within a single domicile, and this pat-tern also affects men's ritually constituted misogyny. Nevertheless, one should not wish to push the significance of these constraints too far: men are in full charge of public affairs; women are relegated to heavy, dirty garden work and the polluting business of childbear-ing; ritual secrecy remains an enduring political and psychological force that suppresses women and children; most men are constantly mindful of female contamination and semen depletion through sexual intercourse; and abusive lan-guage, squabbling, and wife-beating, as well as suicides resulting from some such incidents, are pervasive in Sambia life.

The developmental cycle of children thus occurs in the context of open hostility, or at the least, ambivalence, in men's behavior toward their wives. Children are involved in this famil-ial conflict. By custom, infants are exclusively cared for by their mothers; other female care-takers later help out. Fathers remain aloof since both mother and child are regarded as one in their polluting potential, especially fol-lowing birth; and also because postpartum taboos strictly forbid close interaction among the spouses, since that would lead to sexual intercourse, harming both mother and infant. Boys and girls remain closely attached to their mothers until two or three years of age (and sometimes longer, according to particular circumstances, e.g., widowhood). Girls become their mother's companions, and they continue residing with their parents until marriage, usually around the time of the menarche (about 15–17 years of age). Thereafter, the young women reside with their husbands or parents-in-law, which often removes them to another hamlet. Boys spend more time with their mothers and playmates than they do with their fathers. This style of maternal attachment continues relatively unchanged until first-stage initiation. But boy-initiates are thereafter sanctioned for *any* contact (e.g., talking, looking at, or eating) with women, including their mothers. They reside exclusively in the men's clubhouses with other unmarried initiates and bachelors. Not until ten years and more later, after marriage and the strict deritualization of these avoidance taboos, may youths begin interacting with women again.

Men worry over the effects of the mother's prolonged contact with children, but especially with their sons. This concern is more than ideological rationalization, as one sees in actual case studies (see Herdt 1981). Stated briefly, men regard the attainment of adult reproductive competence as far more problematic for males than females. Maleness is thought to depend on the acquisition of semen – the stuff of "biological" maleness – for precipitating male anatomic traits *and* masculine behavioral capacities (e.g., prowess). Femaleness rests on the creation and circulation of blood, which is held, in turn, to stimulate the production of menstrual blood, the menarche, and final reproductive competence. A girl's menarche is celebrated in secret events that simply recognize socially her "natural" achievements. In girls, who possess a self-activating and functional menstrual-blood organ (*tingu*), maturation is thus viewed as an unbroken process leading from birth and maternal bonding into adulthood. In boys, however, two obstacles block male growth: their mother's pollution, food, and overall caretaking, which at first

nurtures but then stifles growth; and their innate lack of semen, since the semen organ (*kereku-kereku*) can only store, not manufacture, sperm – the key precipitant of manly reproductive competence. In the native model, then, femaleness is a natural development leading into feminine adulthood; maleness is not a naturally driven process but rather a personal achievement of which men wrest control through ritual initiations to ensure that boys attain adult masculine competence.

The Sambia ritual cult channels male development through six successive stages of initiation. The first three initiations are collectively performed by the regional confederacy of hamlets noted above. The cycle begins by constructing the cult house, quickly followed by third-stage initiation, a puberty rite (youths, ages 14–16). These graduated bachelors then assist in the staging of second-stage initiation (boys 11–13 years). Last, both these elevated age-grades join adult men in staging first-stage initiation (boys 7–10 years), creating a new regional set of age-mates. Following third-stage initiation, youths are eligible for marriage; within a year or more, fourth-stage initiation – a marriage ceremony and associated secret rites – can be held inside the hamlet. Later, at the menarche of a particular youth's wife, his fifth-stage initiation will be performed. (Until now and for some months afterwards, the youth continues residing in the clubhouse. Later, the couple will build a separate house, cohabit, and may then engage in coitus.) Finally a year or two later, at the birth of his first child, he is initiated and attains sixth-stage ritual status. After two children are born, he is accorded the cultural status of full manhood (*aatmwunu*). What distinguishes Sambia ritualized masculine development from that of other Highlands initiatory cults is the prolonged institutionalization of secret homosexual fellatio, which is believed vital to the boy's maturation. Men hold that oral insemination is the only means of creating the "biological" changes needed to masculinize boys. It continues for many years, boys being first fellators then fellateds, and later, bisexuals. But, following marriage, custom decrees that homosexual activity halt and that men become exclusively heterosexual (see Herdt 1980, 1981).

The Belief System

How shall we take cognizance of the male belief system surrounding blood and female pollution in understanding the significance of secret nosebleeding? Here I wish to simply summarize a larger body of data to orient the following material on ritual behavior.

At various levels of meaning, blood and its secular and ritual *designata* are identified with the vitality and longevity of women and femaleness. Females, unlike males, are believed to be gifted with an endogenous means of producing blood that hastens the development of female growth, the menarche, and the menses; it is also the provider of womb life for the fetus. The male and female parts in reproduction are clearly defined: a man's semen enters the womb and becomes a pool that eventually coagulates into fetal skin and bone tissue, set within the female blood of the womb. Fetal blood, supplied only by the mother's womb, becomes the circulatory blood needed by all babies and adults.

For all humans, circulatory blood is thought to be an elixir – within limits – that stimulates body functioning and growth, and the ability to withstand sickness or injury. The limits of this idea are embedded in several constructs through which Sambia perceive blood. First, there is a tacit distinction that amounts to the difference between circulatory blood and menstrual-womb blood. Both males and females possess circulatory blood (*menjaaku*); but only females have menstrual blood (*chenchi*), categorized with all female contamination (*pulungatnyi*). Second, Sambia speak of reproductively competent humans (and also trees and animals) as being fluid or "watery" (*wunyu-tei*), not "dry" (*yaalkoogu*), that is, either sexually mature or old and "used up." In females, fluidity stems from having circulatory and menstrual blood, vaginal fluids, and that part of her husband's semen a woman "ingests" through sexual intercourse. Males, by contrast, are fluid only through their original circulatory blood, and later (artificially ingested), semen. Children and old people are "dry" but girls are more fluid than boys; adults – unless sickly or sexually depleted – are fluid. Third, blood is

said to be "cold," whereas semen is "hot." Since Sambia see sickness and plagues (*numbu-lyu-oolu*: "pathway of sickness") as incorporeal active agents attracted to "heat" and repelled by "cold," this temperature difference counts heavily in body functioning: the more blood, the less sickness; the more semen, the greater chance of illness and debilitation. Fourth, menstrual periods are likened to a periodic sickness that rids female bodies of excess *tingu* blood and any sickness that manages to penetrate them. Ironically, then, women bounce back from their periods with greater vitality vis-à-vis this "natural" expurgative function males lack (cf. Mead 1935:106). The female capacities to create and discharge blood are thus *designata* of the structure and functioning of women's bodies, the embodiments of birth-giving, procreative fluidity, and health, so men reckon that these mechanisms account for why women typically outlive men.

Now what matters for ritual nosebleeding is that menstrual-womb blood, although a life-giving female elixir, also represents the sine qua non of lethal fluids for male body functioning. By implication, all male circulatory blood originates from the mother's womb, so the collective initiatory nosebleedings try to purge it. Other female substances like skin flakes, saliva, sweat, and especially vaginal fluids, are also classified as *pulungatnyi* and are felt to be inimical to men. (Male illness resulting from female sorcery usually hinges on the conviction that a man has incorporated menstrual or vaginal fluids.) But menstrual blood is dreaded most. Children take in these substances through birth, and later, through feeding and touching. Women definitely evince concern not to contaminate themselves or others, especially their children, with menstrual fluids during their periods. Neither their public statements nor activities, however, reveal the intense anxiety easily aroused in men. Contrary to girls, boys are definitely at risk: menstrual-womb blood can thwart the "biological" push into masculine maturity. Men are even at greater risk since menstrual blood, in particular, can penetrate the urethra during coitus, bringing sickness and turning back the manliness that has been so hard won. For this reason, men say, they must remain cautious about contact with their children, too, since the latter may unwittingly transmit (cf. Meigs 1976) and infect men with the traces of their mother's body products.

The most harmful effect of women's *verbal behavior* during child-bearing is pinpointed on the boy's nose which is, next to the mouth, the body's main port of entry. Here, mother's speech and harangues have a lethal power. A woman's airstream emitted while speaking is thought to emerge from her blood-filled caverns. If it is directed – particularly at close range during anger – toward boys, the boys are believed harmed: simply by inhaling those insults and air (cf. Meigs 1978:305), a boy is defiled: the nasal orifice absorbs and stores the contaminants, henceforth blocking the free movement of circulatory blood and other fluids from the nose throughout the body. (Likewise, women pollute boys simply by lifting their legs in proximity to them, emitting vaginal smells that boys can breathe in; and, for this reason, men keep their noses plugged during coitus, avoiding incorporation of the vaginal smell they describe as most harmfully foul (see also Devereux 1937:515). Nosebleeding is *the* critical means of egesting these incorporated materials from the male body, since Sambia practice no other form of bloodletting.

Despite these necessary expurgations, however, nosebleeding is unmistakably risky, even dangerous. The reason is simple: blood loss from cuts or wounds in general is dangerous, a process that, if left unchecked, would rob one of circulatory blood and of life itself. Large cuts are handled as quickly as possible; and even with minor scrapes men are squeamish about placing bindings to stop any blood loss. (The greatest single expense in my fieldwork medical budget was for bandages – for which people constantly asked.) Blood is "vital stuff" (Lewis 1975:203): like ourselves, Sambia view the containment of blood-loss as a critical symptom of life-risk and a prognostic indicator for recovery. Birth giving and menstrual bleeding also carry a risk, but one of a different sort, since the female body is thought to "naturally" control blood flow. Thus, even though women use native medicines to reduce menstrual flows, they appear to be relatively

unconcerned about their periods. Male nosebleeding is another matter. Nosebleeding is painful and the blood-loss disliked: it is done to remove female contaminants. Indeed, it is unlikely that Sambia would ever use medicinal bloodletting as did our ancestors, or as do other New Guineans (Barth 1975:139; Williams 1936:342). Here, I think, is a major clue as to the psychosocial difference between nosebleeding, and menstrual periods or medicinal bleeding: one initiates a temporary bleeding inside a ready orifice to remove poisonous female matter, and it is he who rather precisely controls the amount of blood loss (cf. Lindenbaum 1976:57).

These elements of belief, namely women's innate production of blood, its association with reproduction, the contaminating potential of female blood for males, and the riskiness of blood-loss, are the background factors that generally influence – color, crystallize, constrain – the actual experience of secret nosebleeding. In their particulars, however, secular beliefs combine with subsequent ritual teachings that are introduced through transitions in the ritual lifecycle. Successive stages of initiation teaching draw on more secret, explicitly sexual elements, that reinforce the aggressive ethos of the Sambia warriorhood. It is to the system of ritual nose bleeding behaviors that I now turn, describing the emerging contexts of ritual belief in sequence.

Ritual Nosebleeding Behavior

The nosebleeding (*chemboo-loruptu: chembootu*, nose; *loropina*: a verb meaning to "cleanse and expand") act is the single most painful ritual technique, by common assent of initiates and men alike. (In contrast, mere piercing of the nasal septum is a benign secular ceremony occurring in childhood for both sexes.) That feeling is understandable. Physically, nosebleeding is a penetrating trauma of the nasal mucous membranes. The psychological effect of nosebleeding is enhanced by secrecy; so its forcible administration by men upon boys – and by surprise, at that – turns into a violent assault having effects probably close to producing authentic trauma.

Boys themselves often hark back to the nose-bleeding with expressions such as "I feared they were going to kill me." The ritual efficacy and subjective dynamics of collective nose-bleeding are highly focused on the actual blood flow. The body of assembled initiators *always* concentrate on a generous but controlled blood flow – the sight of which is greeted triumphantly with a unified ritual/war chant. That collective action amounts to a forcible penetration of a boy's body boundaries, for, aside from its surprise and ostentatious context, the psychological impact of nosebleeding assumes greater power when it is understood that Sambia place tremendous personal emphasis on the nose, second only to the genitals: the nose is second to none in matters of body appearance, notions of beauty, and their manifestations in gender symbolism.[1]

Sambia recognize two different procedures for nosebleeding that are associated with phratry affiliation. These techniques are hidden from all women and children, and from younger initiates until their ritual revelation at successive initiations. Traditionally, knowledge of the different practices was partially hidden from men of the two opposing phratries of the Sambia Valley, since the procedures are incorporeal property: ritual customs – trademarks – of the respective groups. Following pacification, however, these practices were shared with the opposite sides. Nowadays, men have some choice in the type of nosebleeding utilized in collective or private ritual.[2] The most common technique consists simply of thrusting stiff, sharp cane grasses into the nose until blood flows (cf. Langness 1974:194; Read 1965:131). The other technique, forcing extremely salty liquid down the nose, is also painful, but there is less severe penetration since no hard projectile is involved. In the latter instance a beastly saline solution is made from soaking water in native vegetal salt that is sponged into the nostrils as the face is held upwards. Blood instantly flows following that action most times, and profusely so, in some cases.

The cane-grass technique was used in the first-stage and third-stage collective initiations by all the Sambia groups in which I observed nosebleeding. That practice is regarded as more dangerous than the water technique, largely due to men's perception that there is always a chance that the cane-grasses might break off and lodge in one's nose, risking death – the prime reason men offer in explaining why Sambia themselves abandoned cane swallowing before pacification. Following third-stage initiation, the choice of bloodletting technique is made on the basis of phratry membership in individually oriented fifth- and sixth-stage initiations. In private nosebleeding, however, personal needs and public glory are also involved; for example, the cane-grass technique is the riskier, more daring routine, and is identified as among the most masculine of activities. Here, men's subjectivity seems to be pinpointed on the need – and pseudorisk – of a physical, hard projectile actually penetrating the nostrils to achieve the painful and desired inward-to-outward effect of blood release. And, to reiterate, that penetrating thrust of cane-grass seems to be necessary for culturally accomplishing the first acts of efficacious nosebleeding within collective initiations.

With this background, I shall describe field observations on the first-stage nosebleeding behavior in detail; because of limited space I will then summarize the data pertaining to later initiatory nosebleeding contexts.

First-stage initiation

Nosebleeding occurs on the third day of first-stage initiation as but one part of a longer sequence of manly ordeals. It is preceded by purificatory rites, collective dancing, fasting, beating rites, and a state of fatigue born of sleeplessness and constant, frighteningly unpredictable surprises. On the morning of its occurrence, the novices' mothers are sarcastically informed that their sons are to be killed, so women begin a sorrowful wailing – that is genuinely tearful or ritually stylized – according to their personal situations. The novices, too, are threateningly warned to watch out because of what lies in store. Here, the mysterious power of the flutes (heard, not yet seen) comes into play, building on and enfusing the novices' growing expectations about the elders' authority over the supernatural and themselves (see Herdt 1982). The initiates are first taken from their mothers and lodged in the ritual cult-house: several hours later they are removed to the edge-land forest where the unexpected nosebleeding occurs.

Initially, the boys confront a massive vibrating wall of thick green foliage, a fence of young saplings tightly woven together. Pieces of red headband (a ceremonial garment) are tied up in the green mass, while inside (unseen to the novices) a chorus of bachelors shakes the trees, emitting an eerie sputtering sound associated with ritual ordeals. The effect is calculatedly bizarre: from the approaching distance one is made to experience the green mass itself as if blood were dripping from the branches. The novices plunge into that disturbing morass literally tied to the backs of their ritual sponsors, through a small opening at its center. Some scream and cry; some try to escape. But all are carried through the barricade into a muddy inner chamber, that leads only one way – into a cagelike passage-way of naked saplings, tied together like a fence on both sides.[3] (The passage space was barely wide enough for me to walk through.) Lined up, outside and next to the passageway, are numerous warriors holding wild ginger stalks; and as the sponsor/initiate pairs walk the gamut of the enclosure they are pounded on their legs and backs. Most of the boys cry; indeed, by the time they exit into the forest clearing (20 feet away), many look terrified. Several cry out for their mothers as the all-male audience looks on.

The initiates are then grouped around the ritual site of a small brook flowing down from a thicket. A huge crowd of men assemble, fencing in the initiates. The nosebleeders themselves take center-stage: several of them are wearing upturned pig's-tusk noseplugs (worn with the tusk points turned upwards only at war and during these rites). The men are serious; and even as their tense bodies strain forward to convey that posture some of the men actually grimace. A "strong" man, a former war-leader, steps forward and silently plunges cane-grasses down his own nose: in full view of the initiates blood streams down his face into the water. Somewhere, still out of sight, the flutes hauntingly serenade his feat. The men all respond with a piercing ritual/war chant: a signal that they want more.

The first boy is quickly grabbed. He struggles and shouts but is held down by three men. None of us can catch his breath before the initiator rolls up cane-grasses and, as the novice's head is held back, pushes them down repeatedly into the boy's nose. Tears and blood flow as the boy is held, and relaxed forward, over the water. Next, one and then another boy is grasped and bled. One lad tries to run away but is grabbed: as a punishment he is next bled harder and longer than the others. The next initiate resists fiercely, so four men lift him up off the ground and, while there suspended, he is nosebled. Another boy is penetrated until blood flows profusely; and after each instance of this, the collectivity of men raise the ritual/war chant time and again.

Many of the previous first-stage initiates (from an initiation held several months earlier) were also nosebled again. They stood in the wings of the group. Some resisted; others did not. But few of them resisted as fiercely as the new novices. Soon the act became almost mechanical for the initiators – the boys' clansmen, cross-cousins, and matrilateral kin.

The reactions of the boys, however, are the opposite. At first the new novices do not resist much. But after several boys defied the bleeders, others resist more. Some struggle and cry; some must be forcibly bled. The men have little pity for the lads. Those who resist are even more severely dealt with by prolonging the action and thereby brutalizing it. All of the novices (they numbered 42) are bled. Afterwards, the boys remain standing over the stream to let the blood flow. The water ensures that women will not later discover any signs of blood, and it also allows the boys to wash themselves off. Then sponsors (who did not serve as bleeders) dab the boys' noses with ferns wiping the face clean of any remaining traces of blood. An elder collects the leaves.[4]

Following the bleeding, the boys were lined up by the stream for the ritual teaching. The rhetoric described the nosebleeding as punishment for the insubordination of novices toward their fathers and elders. Pollution was also mentioned. Merumie (a respected fight leader and shaman) did the rhetorical teaching; he began by telling the novices that they must learn hospitality:

If a man visiting your hamlet comes and asks you for water, you must offer him some. You must not hide your water vessels. He ought to be given water; if there is none, you must go and fetch some, even if it is dark and raining.

Next he reprimanded the boys, saying that when they were children they made "bad talk," sassing ritual initiates. He further asserted that if the boys defied or disregarded their elders' instructions to fetch water or betel nut, they would be nosebled again, as punishment. For those acts, Merumie said, "We now pay you back." The boys are told they must "change their ways."

Merumie then lectured the boys on their mothers' harmful effects and the value of letting blood:

You [novices] have been with your mothers ... they have said "bad words" to you; their talk has entered your noses and prevented you from growing big. Your skins are no good. Now you can grow and look nice.

A teaching about warrior aggressiveness was also performed until the first-stage initiation in 1973, at which time it was abandoned.[5] Elders stressed that nosebleeding could help novices become more fearless during warfare. Boys were told to be "strong" and unafraid on the battlefield. They were upbraided: having been nosebled themselves, henceforth they must not fear the sign of their agemates' or comrades' spilled blood on the battlefield. In fact, elders stressed, the sight of blood itself was to have been regarded as a challenge – to seek revenge against the responsible enemies for the loss of blood on one's own side.

Second-stage initiation

Nosebleeding is not performed at this event, several years later. (Likewise, no nosebleeding occurs at fourth-stage initiation.) Boys do not know that, of course, until afterwards: in each subsequent initiation they are always left wondering about that fearsome possibility until the last. Men say that the initiates, having been bled once and long separated from their mothers, are protected by other external "cleaning" rites, like those which painfully scrub the body through use of stinging-nettles. However,

individual second-stage initiates may be bled at the behest of their clansmen during subsequent first-stage nosebleeding rites. In addition, and somewhat inexplicable at that, men say that the boys, who are fed pandanus fruit (ending a taboo imposed earlier at first-stage initiation), are spurred enough by its ingestion and the smearing of its crimson juice on their skins to further "grow them." Women are expressly forbidden to see those events – which secrecy also seems to help offset the need for another nosebleeding till the following initiation.

Third-stage initiation

This event is the last collective initiatory performance of nosebleeding performed on boys as a regional set of age-mates. Later instances are individually oriented rites. This may be one reason the context is severe, almost cruel, in its violence and physical threats. This time, however, there is a greater element of voluntary action on the part of the youths, who, having attained puberty, are accorded the status of "young men" to be betrothed. As new warriors they are expected to be brave, self-disciplined, and emotionally steadfast, even though some cannot live up to that demand. After two days of the initiation (which lasts a week), youths are assembled on a signal (not dragged into line on their ritual sponsors' backs as occurred the first time). Many of them (they told me later) suspected they were to be nosebled. While lined up, military fashion, they are thus "attacked" by older men. A line of warriors, soot-blackened and garbed "like ghosts, like enemies," encircle them, plucking bows and arrows, hooting, shouting, and feigning an ambush. There, on a hidden hillside (away from the hamlet women), without a stream, they are grasped by sponsors and men and forcibly nosebled again (cf. Newman and Boyd 1982; Tuzin 1980). Although youths are not supposed to flinch, struggle, or cry, some of them do: the terror of the experience is greater than the stamina of certain individuals to passively submit to nasal penetration. (See Table 17.1 on the bilaterality of choice in this situation.) No stream should be needed for that reason: if the youths are "manly enough" they will effortlessly and with sober-faced calm

Table 17.1 Cultural and behavior characteristics of nosebleeding rites in the male life cycle*

Initiation stage	Focus of ritual teachings				Behavioral context: Audience			Physical and societal constraints			
	Physical growth	Mother's pollution of ego	Warrior's aggressiveness ethos	Wife's pollution of ego	The directing authorities	Collective ritual	Solitary (private ritual)	Voluntary nose bleeding	Involuntary nose bleeding	Other induced bleeding	Self induced bleeding
First stage (7–10 years)	x——x	x	x——x		Elders	x			x——x	x	
Second stage (11–13 years)											
Third stage (13–16 years)			x		Elders	x		x——x (Bilateral)	x——x	x	
Fourth stage (16 years +)											
Fifth stage (16–20 years)			x——x	x	Elders Peers	x		x		x	
Sixth stage (20–30 years)			x——x	x	Elders Peers	x		x		x——x (Optional)	x
Wife's menses	X (Old Age)		x——x	x	Self		x	x			x

*Please note fourth stage is not covered in original paper.

allow themselves to be neatly nosebled. Their blood should carefully fall into leaves provided for their own cleansing and disposal.

The teachings of third-stage nosebleeding convey to youths, for the first time, some dangers of sexual contact – physical intimacy – with women. But that is *not* why elders tell them they were bled: after all, initiates must strictly avoid women, so the thought of illicit heterosexual intercourse is not even mentioned. Instead, youths are warned about three things: first, they must be vigilant and always ready for enemy attack; second, sexual contact with women will debilitate and make them vulnerable to death in battle; and third, they must avoid women and know that death from the angry husband and his cohorts awaits adulterous transgressors. The first element is graphically impressed on the novices by the mock attack of men posing as tribal "enemies" who administered the nosebleeding. The second element is left ominously vague, for the future. The third aspect is sanctioned by, and indexed toward, the flutes, whose cries – during the ritual – are said to represent a woman's sensuous moans as she adulterously copulates with an unwary youth. The unsuspecting youth will be killed by the cuckold and his age-mates, elders warn: obey us or suffer that fate. In other words, nosebleeding is here explicitly used as a powerful social sanction to constrain the youths' sexuality, ruling out premarital heterosexuality and ruling in homosexual activities. Indeed, it is the youths' first act of being a homosexual inseminator, at the conclusion of third-stage initiation, that is culturally regarded as an essential confirmatory act towards attaining manhood.

Fifth-stage initiation

These events are triggered by the occurrence of menarche for the youth's young wife. Nosebleeding is its final ritual. The novice and his married age-mates engage in days of collective hunting in the forest (for possum-meat prestations bestowed on the wife's cognatic kin) while adhering to strict ingestion taboos. Bloodletting then becomes the focus of essential teachings that finally reveal the full dangers of genital-to-genital intercourse, vaginal

pollution, and the subsequent dangers of wives' menstrual periods.

The novice himself is first to be nosebled as his elders and cohort look on. There is absolutely no question here of voluntary submission to the act: the youth is expected to be willing, even eager to be bled; most youths remained unflinching and frozen during the actual procedure. Any sign of fear or reticence is regarded as unmanly and inappropriate, and my observations have revealed no visible reticence. Either cane-grasses or the saline solution are acceptable techniques depending on one's phratry identification; but that decision is a matter for elders, not youths, to decide. Older men actually nosebleed the youth. Afterwards, when blood flows, the characteristic ritual/war chant is raised by the whole chorus of men. The novice's age-mates are then bled too. Older men may choose to bleed themselves or to be bled. (Younger initiates, of course, are excluded from this secret ritual advancement.) Older middle-aged men, particularly graying elders, do not usually take part, and nothing is said about this. (I have, however, seen several such men on occasion spontaneously ask to be bled.)

Elders emphasize the youth's erotic/procreative relationship to his newly menstruating wife in the following teachings. More than at fourth-stage initiation, ritual knowledge of purificatory techniques is taught so youths can protect themselves against the lethal effects of female sexual contact. Examples: special leaves may be eaten and muds smeared on the skin to strengthen the body; other leaves can be used to plug the nose; and tree bark can be chewed (and later spit out) during coitus to eliminate from one's mouth traces of female body odors and breath. The youths are especially warned to be conservative in all ways about heterosexual intercourse, and they are taught how to replace depleted semen "lost" to their wives (see Herdt 1981:249). Once again, the youths are enjoined not to be adulterous and they are warned of the fatal consequences if that rule is broken. And all of these warnings are set within the ritual prescription that, henceforth, the young man must take personal responsibility for privately nosebleeding himself alone in the forest after each of his wife's menses (regardless of whether he recently had coitus): that deadly blood must be avoided and eliminated at all costs, with scrupulous measures taken before and after each menses to avoid its contagious power.

Fifth-stage teachings also explicate a theme of hostility to women that was earlier implicit. This theme concerns making men responsible, autonomous warriors, by re-directing onto women some responsibility for the "pain of nosebleeding." It is an unmanly sign of weakness (*wogaanyu*) for the youth to sit idly by while his wife menstruates. Since she is "reproductively active," elders say, a man must be "ritually active" in a way germane to her body's release of menstrual blood into his world. Men add that *they* have no other orifice with which to bleed except that of the nose. Elder authorities challenge that since the youth now has (a sexual relationship with) a wife, he must prove himself stronger, manlier, on the battlefield. That message is then referred back ominously to domestic life: since it was *because* of the wife's harmful menses that the youth had to "feel pain," he must never forget his suffering on her account. She must bear responsibility for his pain; she must learn to respect him for the warriorhood ordeals he has endured to be fully masculine for her. So, if a wife is sassy or insubordinate, or under any hint of suspicion that she is being unfaithful, a man must not spare the rod in demonstrating his ownership and power over this creature who is responsible for his smarting nose.

Sixth-stage initiation

This nosebleeding occurs in conjunction with the birth of a man's first child. The rite again follows ceremonial hunting and other purificatory rites. It confirms final initiation into the male cult hierarchy, although the rites and feasting are repeated again for the next birth or two – confirming full status as a masculine person. The teachings center on the birth fluids and their polluting potential, and a man's need to adhere to postpartum taboos by keeping distant from the mother/infant pair. The nosebleeding behavior is somewhat different: as competent manly adults, men are now autonomous and responsible for the maintenance of

their own health. Indeed, the behavioral shift from being bled by others to bleeding oneself may actually occur in this initiation since novices have a choice with regard to nosebleeding themselves. (This choice also applies to the initiate's age-mates, who are also bled.) What matters is the greater stoic demand to self-consciously nosebleed oneself as a secret masculine response in defending against the immediate danger at hand: one's own wife's birth contaminants released into the close quarters of the hamlet environs. Following this initiation, most men do not nosebleed themselves again until (some two to two and one-half years later) they resume coitus with their wives following the child's breast-weaning. Whether induced by oneself or others, then, this nosebleeding is a "voluntary" act applauded again by the ritual/war chant accompanying the released blood.

Private nosebleeding acts

I have already mentioned the normative injunction that a man is personally responsible for "cleansing" his body through nosebleeding after each of his wife's periods. Here I shall simply sketch the context of those private rites that follow after fifth-stage initiation and into old age.

Private nosebleedings are highly personal acts performed alone. The morning on which a man's wife disappears to the menstrual hut (and she will never even mention this to her husband or other men), the husband also quietly leaves the hamlet compound for his own forest preserve. There he nosebleeds himself with respect to the ritual procedure of his phratry. He ingests certain leaves and tree "milk-saps," and also rubs the "milk-saps" on his body to "strengthen" it at those points he contacted his wife (i.e., penis, abdomen, navel, etc.) during coitus. Then he smears red mud on his torso and limbs. This oddly sympathetic body-painting obviously communicates to the community that he has done *something secret* in the forest; men themselves say the red mud merely "hides" the underlying white tree-sap smeared on the skin from the probing eyes of women and children. (The full significance of meaning surrounding that egested blood, the white "milk-sap" and red ochre, is complex and will be examined elsewhere.) Here, of course, we have arrived at the final regime of bloodletting behavior, and one in which the action *is* completely private, is "voluntary," self-induced, and is performed – or so one thinks – for the independent audience of oneself. At the same time, though, private nosebleeding depends on personal initiative and is publicly unobserved, so we should thus expect individual variation in its behavior and experience.

This latter point raises difficult questions about the experience of adult bloodletting – a subject that constitutes a fascinating "internal discourse" in male life precisely because it is so much avoided. Most men are timid and tight-lipped about private nosebleeding, even among their peers. Younger men even evince some embarrassment about it. Such reticence seems striking and puzzling, for among their cronies men will sooner or later touch on their night's dreams, and wet dreams, body fluids (both male and female), sexual conquests or needs and even, with repugnance, female contaminants – all ritual domains except personal bleeding. (To get detailed information, I had to elicit personal accounts from informants, and usually while alone with them.) The silent message seems to be that a powerful, but vulnerable, piece of the self is secreted in that private act – an idea to which I shall later return.

What emerges from ritual rhetoric and private conversations is the view that private nosebleeding is both burdensome and painful, necessary and cathartic. All adult men are believed to regularly let blood as described above, but their emotionality differs somewhat. The fight leaders and self-conscious elders are undemonstrative and matter-of-fact about their bleedings; younger newlyweds are more exuberant, but also more squeamish. Weiyu, a close, married informant in his early 20s, deplores the fierce pain of nosebleedings; grudgingly submits to it only when absolutely unavoidable, in public, where he uses cane-grass on himself; but in private he uses the salt solution because it is less dangerous. Imano, an older, quieter, comfortable man, about 30 years old, who has two wives and definitely enjoys coitus with them, is also known as a faithful nosebleeder; he feels that the bloodlettings keep him healthy, and he generously lets blood in regular

synchrony with his wives' periods. Sambia men thus engage in private bleeding for many years, till they halt coitus or their wives undergo menopause and stop having periods. In between, one hears many comments about the value of nosebleeding, but the earlier idioms about "male growth" disappear. Then, among seniors in their late 30s and 40s, men again offer, in explanation of their own continuing bloodletting, the pat remark: "I am still growing."

Men are quite explicit about the conscious intent of that idea. My informant, Tali, for instance, has said: "The woman expels her blood and you, her husband, must also expel it. If you do't, your stomach will become no good, it will swell up …" (cf. Meigs 1976). For that reason, he noted, "Old men continue nosebleeding until their wives stop menstruating." Unless they do, he said, they "won't grow anymore." And here is Weiyu:

It's [menstrual blood] not men's blood, but the bad talk and menstrual blood of a man's "sickly" wife. It [blood] doesn't belong to us, it belongs to the women. …

We say their [women's] blood and bad words enter our skin and lodge their, so we expel it [blood] from the nose.

G.H.H.: But what can you replace the blood with?

Weiyu: Nothing. We don't replace it. It's the contamination (*pulungatunyi*) of women, we expel it, that's all; it shouldn't be replaced.

But eventually, as Tali said elsewhere, "Old [i.e., senile] men don't [need to] perform nosebleedings on themselves; his [sic] skin is fastened to his bones; [He thinks to himself:] 'I won't grow anymore.'" To understand that belief and the developmental transformations that lead to its expressions in adult behavior, I must interpret the whole system of ritual nosebleedings that shape male character.

Ritual Transformations in Male Character Structure

Although it seems clear that forcible bloodletting – administered collectively on boys – eventuates in the adult social outcome that men will voluntarily and, in private, let their own blood, the psychosocial mechanisms underlying this shift remain implicit. Nor is it clear why ceremonial bloodlettings throughout New Guinea involve extensive "ritual violence" (Tuzin 1982), "male dominance" (Langness 1974), or "ritual aggression" (Berndt 1962), and even, as among the Gahuku (Read 1965:129), "ritual exhibitionism ... of the sexual aspects of male strength." To understand these issues in the Sambia material I shall analyze the above data with reference to several theoretical perspectives that help account for the influence of forcible nosebleeding on male personality development. Four developmental themes involving nosebleeding as cultural and behavioral controls on proximity to women (see Table 17.1) will be examined: (1) maternal detachment, (2) ritual aggression and obedience, (3) ritual reversals, and (4) heterosexual autonomy.

Maternal Detachment

The great impetus of Sambia initiation concerns the physical separation of boys from women and children, followed by their irreversible insertion into exclusive male associations. This dual process is well-known from the literature (Allen 1967; Poole 1982; Whiting, Kluckhohn, and Anthony 1958). But, with few exceptions (Roheim 1942; Tuzin 1980), writers have tended not to view the behavioral experience of initiation in the context of the nature of the boy's tie to his mother (Bowlby 1958). In New Guinea societies like that of the Sambia this tie amounts to an "exclusive attachment" (Bowlby 1969) to mother and the female domain. Initiation is the most radical means of breaking that bond in order to subjectively create a new identity in the boy. This conclusion – which is no news to New Guineasts – is novel only in its psychosocial stress: boys must be traumatically detached from their mothers and kept away from them at all costs, otherwise the desired identity transformation cannot take place.

The severity of this ritual detachment remains a measure of the qualitative strength of the mother/child bond in traditional Sambia

life before pacification. Admittedly, the data to support this view are retrospective and, at best, thin (but see Mead 1935; Whiting 1941). Nor does space allow an extended presentation of ethnographic material on post-pacification Sambia (cf. Herdt 1981). But even today, from birth on, Sambia infants still experience profound and constant sensual involvement with their mothers, not their fathers, for several years and more. Babies are attached to their mothers, who meet their basic biosocial needs – food, warmth, cleanliness, stimulation, quieting, protection. In the warring environment, fathers were removed from their infants for long periods. They are still weakly involved in infant-caretaking, on an hour-by-hour basis, compared to mothers or older siblings. The polarity of the sexes – in the division of labor, domestic discord, and in ritual arenas – exacerbates the struggle for security in the child's developing sense of self. Were this a different historical tradition the outcome might be left to chance. But not so for Sambia who believed – can it be felicity? – that boys do not "naturally" mature, become manly, unless powerful collective responses place boys into firm masculine gender roles that deny and override mother's influence, feminine attributes, and identity-signs in the boy (see Stoller and Herdt 1982).

Initiation begins with boys being taken from their mothers in a way that guarantees anxiety in the novice. They are kept in the dark about whether or not they will be initiated. It is true that most boys "know" (at some level of awareness) that they will be initiated eventually. It is also true that initiation is associated with male pride and glory, that is, parading in ritual regalia, and that it is boys' only means to "grow up": parents and others communicate attitudes of this sort, overtly or covertly, according to the family situation. But remember that Sambia boys are only 7–10 years old, that initiation is designed as a surprise, and that its symbolic messages are coded to create anxiety in the boy's wrenching from hearth and family: feelings of loss arising from the irreversible awareness that the initiate may never again "be with" – touch, hold, talk to, eat with, or look at – his mother.

First-stage rituals make use of this traumatic reaction in precise ways designed to radically resocialize the boy. Both parents are removed from the scene; a substitute ritual sponsor is introduced; boys undergo days of ordeals, hunger, thirst, sleeplessness, fatigue, and alarming surprises – including great revelations (e.g., about the flutes and ritual fellatio). Thus, following physical separation, a different form of attachment – "anxious attachment," in Bowlby's (1971:196–197, 201–203) terms – is stimulated. It arises from fear and inability to predict what will happen next, while being denied access to one's protective attachment figure, mother. *Detachment* results: despair, crying, searching behavior, including depression or its suppressed counterpart, anger (see Poole 1982). Sambia rituals play upon such feelings by making familiar persons or surroundings seem alien, bizarre, and even terrifying. (Róheim [1945: 249] referred to such a process as "separation anxiety.") In the wake of these experiences new *male* attachment figures and sentimental bonds are introduced. The ritual sponsor, for instance, is the primary guardian and maternal substitute; and boys who called for the parents, who sobbed or clung to their sponsors, for example, in nosebleeding, were carried, and offered solace and comfort, by their sponsors. Sharing in ordeals also forges lasting ties between novices as age-mates (Turner 1967), and this peer group identification also tends to mitigate maternal loss and detachment.

Forcibly inserted into secret male rites – in this mood state – nosebleeding thus becomes a most powerful means for penetrating inside a boy's body and identity. Mother is removed; blood becomes a sign *of* and *for* her, in the all-male context. Further, cutting the nose releases *mother's* blood: in ritual experience this blood is not simply a "symbol" of female essence – it *is* isomorphic with one's (incorporated) femaleness and what that means – womb, nurturance, mother's goodness, softness and curses, and the femaleness that cannot become maleness. Ritual attempts to identify all those aspects as contained within the part of self which is removed with the blood. For as Marilyn Strathern (1979) has argued, New Guinea societies often make the body/skin surface an analog of what we call the "self." Nosebleeding violates one's body boundaries, removing the "female" blood, so that one's body (self) literally becomes an object of reclamation by the ritual cult. It is only the completion of this act that paves the way for appropriate homosexual fellatio, which "fills up" boys' insides with semen – "biological maleness" – "displacing" the female essences.

But the critical experiential precedent is this: a male learns to nosebleed in order to eliminate femaleness from his body – an act which for boys separates "me" from mother and all femaleness – and this act in time becomes a sign to the self that one's identity is clearly male.

Ritual Aggression and Obedience

Forcible nosebleeding belongs to a power play. Viewed in developmental perspective, nosebleeding is one of many social control mechanisms used to create and maintain the social hierarchy of the ritual cult. The hamlet-based warriorhood, into which boys are conscripted, supports this cult hierarchy. Elders are at the top of the ritual status ladder. Fully initiated married men dominate over bachelors, who dominate initiates. Women and children are excluded from cult rites, to which they are nonetheless politically subordinated. Men (including the boys' fathers) utilize initiation to separate boys from their mothers and natal households, thereafter ensuring masculine gender differentiation, conformity to adult male gender role norms, and the maintenance of cult secrets. Initiation thus effects immediate and total *physical separation* from all females. But what about the latter nosebleedings, for example, those at third-stage initiations? Why is it necessary to violently nosebleed youths years after they have been detached from their mothers, have avoided women, and have conformed to ritual conventions as residents of the men's clubhouse?

To answer this question we must understand the political context of ritual domination. The presence of a cult-based warriorhood in every Sambia hamlet is a function of certain societal imperatives that clan elders direct. These imperatives can be briefly stated as follows: (1) perpetuation of socioeconomic stability in the community; (2) requiring control and expropriation of the products of women's bodies and labor, that is, sexual services, babies, breast milk, garden food, and domestic services (cooking, baby-sitting); (3) authority over sons, whose allegiance as ritual supporters and young warriors is vital for the maintenance of elders' authority and hamlet defense; and (4) control over female children – daughters, sisters, nieces, cousins, granddaughters – who are needed as a commodity to obtain future wives for the bachelors, whom elders control further by abrogating all responsibility for exchanging these females and arranging marriages for youths. The eventual success of all these political moves, however, is bound up with first separating boys from the female realm, and making them dependably fierce warriors – obedient to "the cult" – in the persons of the elders: "agents of external authority" (Milgram 1974:62).

Seen in symbolic terms, this latter requirement is by no means easy or "natural." If we cast Sambia relationships in the conceptual paradigm of Bateson's (1936, 1972) ideas about "complementary" versus "symmetrical" ties, elders are faced with a dilemma that initiation resolves. As uninitiated boys, males are in complementary relationships to their mothers, who are their primary superordinates. Initiation transfers this relationship to elders and bachelors: boys become their subordinates. Initiates are removed from direct interaction with females. Age-mates take up symmetrical relationships with one another, matching masculine performances in hunting and fighting. Even ingesting semen becomes a "race" between initiates to see who grows faster. By puberty, then, bachelors are superordinates of initiates but subordinates of elders. Women are tantalizingly nearby but still stringently roped-off and out of reach. Here is where ritual violence is reintroduced and must be perpetuated.

Nosebleeding, periodically performed as a secret surprise of later initiations, is the most powerful social sanction for reinforcing boys' obedience to authority. Next to threats of death (which are also used), nosebleeding can be seen as an act of raw aggression (Tuzin

1980:74) over budding youths.[6] This domination comes first in late childhood, when boys would be prone to sexual experimentation; it comes next at puberty – when a powerful inhibitor is again needed to ensure heterosexual repression. As a kind of "symbolic castration" (or perhaps even "phallic aggression": Vanggaard 1972:101–112) violent bloodletting is a very efficient but traumatic means of funnelling youths' sexual and aggressive impulses along a particular developmental line – away from women, and elders, respectively – toward initiates (fellators) and enemies. Adjustment to ritual cult life takes that form: being involved only in homosexual relationships, avoiding all heterosexual impulses and contacts with women until marriage; and performing as efficacious hunter-warriors, directed by war leaders and elders. Ritual beliefs about the deadly contaminating power of women's bodies, with their greater depleting power compared to boy-fellators, further rationalizes youths' fears and avoidance of women.

In short, under the most powerful conditions of collective initiation, ritual aggression is used to instill fear and obedience of male authorities and cult conventions, bravado in fighting performance, and avoidance and fear of women.

Ritual Reversals

A dramatic transformation occurs in nosebleeding behavior between first initiation and the attainment of adulthood years later: the shift from being forcibly nosebled to "voluntarily" bleeding oneself. This reversal involves many other changes – psychosexual and cultural, as well as sociopolitical advancements in ritual roles and statuses. On the surface, this shift suggests fundamental alterations in one's behavior, from being a helpless (not passive) victim of violent nosebleeding assaults, to becoming a victorious initiator fully in charge of his own ritual actions and bodily functioning. Psychodynamically, however, self-bleeding requires developmental changes in character structure that Sambia identify with the esteemed traits of the proven warrior. Being a trustworthy cult member and being self-controlled in proximity to women are among these traits. Here, we must be chiefly concerned with identity transformations that are psychologically entailed by cultural and contextual shifts in the performance of nosebleeding itself. (The gross characteristics of these changes are represented in Table 17.1.)

First there are changes in the societal constraints governing the cultural context of nosebleeding. The general rule is: the more immature and less obedient the initiate is to male authority, the more violence accompanies bloodletting. At the start of the ritual cycle, the greatest force is used, implying that only males who must be forcibly separated from women require physical assaults. Thereafter "voluntary" choice enters into bleeding. From third-stage initiation on, one *should* stoically submit to the ordeal others perform on oneself. The cult standard is clear: the *manliness* of one's identity is judged by the initiate's willingness and capacity to be bled without fear or other "female" emotions. This reversal occurs simultaneously with performative acts that signify one's accountability to all ritual conventions – and without others having to regulate the initiate's activities – as, for instance, with new novices who are distrusted. From the start to the finale of ritual transitions it is the initiate's relationships to women that are most visible and scrupulously monitored in this respect. A novice's avoidance of all females is watched at first. The youth's continuing avoidance, his abstinence from premarital heterosexual contacts, and his patient obeisance to his elders in regard to his eventual marriage contract are next. Later, the signs of self-accountability in a married man are judged by his ritual regulation of sexual relations with his wife, and by his adherence to postpartum taboos, purifications, nosebleedings following coitus, and refraining from adultery.

Second, there are changes in the cultural beliefs surrounding nosebleeding. The general theme of ritual rhetoric stresses the dual ideas that the creation and preservation of maleness ("growth") goes hand in hand with becoming an aggressive warrior. Ideologically, first-stage nosebleeding is a punishment for boys' childish insolence to men; represents the idea that mothers' blood has blocked boys' masculiniza-

tion; and embodies the notion that boys must become tough and learn to master their fear of blood on the battlefield. Initiates, here as always, are made beholden to their elders for ensuring their masculine "growth." Following puberty, however, the concern with "growth" turns upon the fear of menstrual contamination. Rhetoric about "mother" is dropped. Instead, from fourth-stage until old age, beliefs about female contamination are transferred from mother onto men's wives, only sexual intercourse – not mere nurturance – becomes the perceived danger that thwarts maleness.

Throughout this transformation the only elements that remain constant are women as dangerous and the cultural beliefs about the aggressive warrior's ethos. Repeated nosebleedings not only condition one to the sight of blood, but their initial traumas are supposed to be converted into bold prowess – leading and killing in battle without compunctions. The social significance of this aggressive stance is, without doubt, later inserted into domestic life too: one who is an accomplished killer is to be feared by his wife and respected by peers. Consequently, elders constantly stress the initiates' obedience to authorities as well. Nosebleedings are chronologically timed in the life cycle to ensure that elders retain social control over bachelors – after puberty – until such time that youths are married and thereby become adult members invested in the cult. Then, of course, they can be relied upon for perpetuation of established controls over women and initiates.

Third, a number of highly structured and ritually organized reversals in sexual behavior are correlated with the meaning of bloodletting acts at various levels of significance. Ultimately, all these transformations bear upon physical proximity to women. Sexually, these changes issue from first being a passive homosexual fellator to being a dominant fellated; thereafter sexual behavior switches from exclusive homoerotic contacts to brief bisexual encounters – secret fellatio with boys and private fellatio with one's bride – and then, finally, to exclusive heterosexual relationships in marriage. (For details, see Herdt 1981. Some rather complex symbolic interchanges of blood and semen, also involved in this structure, are examined elsewhere.) Moreover, several important symbolic attachments to ritual agents – such as the fantasied female hamlet-spirit animating the ritual flutes – are fostered as transitional objects in boys' identity changes from childhood to manhood, which attachments lend transitional homosexual practices their own excitement (cf. Herdt 1982). Changes in nosebleeding behavior then, from one ritual stage to the next, are followed by new sexual rights and duties – the final form of which I set out below.

Last, the composition of the nosebleeding ritual audience undergoes symbolic changes of various sorts. At first-stage initiation, novices are classed together against all older males. As age-mates, these boys are placed in symmetrical relationships with one another, nosebleeding and doing other acts with which their masculine performance is compared and judged. They are made subordinates of all elder males, who substitute for the boys' superordinate mothers in complementary relationships to initiates. Boys' fathers are in the audience of initiators; physical presence here counts as a primary sign of the politico-ritual division between fathers and sons. Nevertheless, both generations are made privy to the all-male secret rites, compared to the mothers – who are left wailing helplessly behind in the village. But mother is symbolically inserted into the context – through the *designata* of nose blood, "female contamination" – which invidiously links boys and women. Never again is that comparison made. In subsequent nosebleedings, then, mother is a part of the distant background whereas father becomes an emerging ritual teacher; and one's peers and adult men emerge as the key audience. The ritual sponsor's role declines after marriage until it is perfunctory. Elders remain prominent until adulthood, since they sanctify ritual teachings, but they, too, increasingly take a back seat as their physical power wanes. After puberty, moreover, the frightening attacks halt: no reason to remind bachelors who are one's enemies, for they are identified with other groups who kill (whose initiates drain off one's semen and whose women – potential wives – can pollute and sorcerize), not just nosebleed bachelors, as their elders do to "help" them.

The final transformations occur following marriage and fatherhood. One's wife now displaces mother as the focus of contaminated blood that must be expelled due to sexual contacts. But the blood-lettings are self-induced and private, acknowledging the marital bond and the particular periodicity of men's wives. Men do not perform for their peers or compete with them in bloodletting. They are, obviously, competing now with their wives, but this symmetrical "contest" is solitary and secreted in a very special sense. That mode of self-control concerns my final argument.

Heterosexual Autonomy

Sambia manhood rests on the above ritual transformations – the fusion of which is necessary for, and "carried" in, the psychosocial elements of painfully performing private bloodlettings on oneself. That act, to reiterate, represents marriage and fatherhood: full manhood. It signals also the "acceptance" (socialization, internalization, habitualized reinforcements, etc.) of masculine rhetoric, secret beliefs, and comportment regarding self and significant others; in a word: self-autonomy. Two pervasive cultural assumptions must be kept in mind. First, it is in a man's own willingness to bleed himself that Sambia recognize the finishing-off of the phallic warrior. Second, only men who are married and having sex with their wives privately bleed themselves. (Analogically, then, Sambia "read" private bloodletting as meaning that one is engaging in heterosexual coitus, the most privileged sexual act.) Most of all, we must analytically underline the context of these assumptions: once again – for the first time in years following maternal separation – the individual man is placed alone in an intimate relationship with a woman.

Contained within the passages leading to this heterosexual union we can see several remarkable contradictions in masculine experience. Full masculine adulthood is denied without marriage. Children – heirs – are necessary for full personhood. Cohabitation and coitus are thus necessary for social esteem and the "reproduction" of the family and society. Ironically, physical and especially sexual proximity to women is the key threat to masculine health and vitality: it saps one's semen and "paints the penis" with female contaminants. And what about heterosexual pleasure? While most men regard coitus with some trepidation, and the act itself is laden with shame (see Herdt 1981:164ff.), Sambia men generally regard it as intensely exciting and pleasurable (and no less so *because* it is dangerous).[7] Mixed in all these contradictions is also the great imperative that one must not become too intimate for fear of revealing ritual secrets – including previous homosexual activities – and of losing control over one's wife and children.

There is another dynamic which we can see as a dilemma but which Sambia themselves unself-consciously act upon. The ritual rhetoric regards women as men's inferiors. Men are supposed to be "on top" – in complementary dominating relationships with women – in domestic interaction, in economic routines, in ritual, and in sex. (Never mind that women don't always or easily bow to men in public.) However, after marriage, men's private nosebleeding acts amount to quite a different symbolic pattern: symmetrical responses to their wives' periods. On the one hand, men define the husband/wife relationship as complementary: men hunt, women garden; the more *womanly* a wife becomes – producing babies and garden food – the more *manly* the husband is perceived (as genitor). But, on the other hand, ritual convention requires that a man match his wife's "natural periods" with "cultural periods" of nosebleeding. Otherwise, he is seen as *wogaanyu* (weak, feminine). The implicit idea is that a woman's periods are evidence that she is still growing, is still fluid, not dry or "used up." She must not "win" over her husband, Sambia say. As an instance of the "Jones effect," private nosebleeding matches female with male "growth" in terms of an equivalent (not identical) act. (Sambia do not say nosebleeding is the same as menstruation: cf. Bettelheim 1955:177–178; Hogbin 1970; Lewis 1980:128–131; Lidz and Lidz 1977; Róheim 1945: 169–171; 1949:321–322.) Regular nosebleedings thus ritually frame the marital relationship as special compared to symmetrical peer ties or other complementary relationships (subordination to elders; dominance over initiates, and dominance over wives

in public). In short, the marital bond is the one enduring relationship that has both symmetrical and complementary aspects because of regular "bleedings" in both spouses.

My point is that private nosebleeding is the key ritual context in which men live these contradictions. Custom demands that men live with their wives, have sex, rear children, and yet avoid interpersonal closeness, that is, they should stay aloof (Whiting and Whiting 1975). In both public and private situations, in sex and in battle, the ritual cult depends upon a man's personal control – autonomy, vigilence, self-regulation – as well as hostility (aggressiveness) toward wife and enemies, real or potential. Of course men do not treat their wives as real enemies; and in some Sambia marriages one finds expressions of care, respect, and, in this sense, love. But the rhetoric of ritual discourse ignores these complications (Faithorn 1976) by expecting visible aggressiveness in one's stance towards the world. By culturally structuring proximity to women in terms of systematic bleeding, the ritual cult has ensured that even in adulthood men will sustain these expectable contradictions. Privately, men nosebleed to eliminate their wives' femaleness from their bodies. This act compulsively repeats, time after time, the separation of the male "me" from other aspects of self (conscious, unconscious): mother, wife, father, elders, one's earlier identities. Its affects – fear, disgust phobic reactions to red fluids, shame – suggest that bloodletting experience has unconscious elements that utilize "conversion-reaction" as a culturally constituted defense mechanism (Spiro 1965) in the service of ego. Its solitariness (Freud 1907:19) also allows for the ripe experience of personal, not just collective, fantasies. For instance: that one's noseblood (can it be otherwise?) contains some part of mother (circulatory blood). Private nosebleeding signifies to the self that one is still male and masculine despite heterosexual union. It thus aids heterosexual virility and maintains controlled proximity in a double sense: to one's wife and to one's secret ritual (secret identity).

But what about the anomaly of old men still "growing"? This complex problem requires an answer that is both symbolic and psychological. First there is a semantic point: what does the native concept of "growth" mean? I hope it is clear that for Sambia its connotations extend beyond mere physical maturation (though the natives often couch their answers in this form when responding to elicited questions).[8] *Male* "growth" entails "strength" (*jerungdu*: another thick idea), personality traits such as aggressiveness and autonomy, as well as attitudes and behavioral acts involving interpersonal ties. On these grounds "growth" has a psychological sense that is similar to our own concept of "separateness" (see Mahler 1963 on separation-individuation). We must remember that boys' first experience with "growth" is what *elders* collectively teach. So when men say, in middle age, that they are now *privately* nosebleeding because they are still growing – and their situation involves physical, erotic, and psychological proximity to their wives – then we may postulate a psychosocial conflict requiring painful ritual acts which relieve that conflict. Psychologically, I think, the resurrection of the notion of "growth" to account for their bloodletting, despite their age, social respect, wives and children, seems to suggest there is a characterological identity conflict in Sambia males that never really goes away, it just lies dormant for a time. Symbolically, growth-through-nosebleeding is always available as a sign for elders to again clarify the separateness of their body boundaries and sense of self as being clearly masculine.

From this viewpoint there is no puzzle about why elders say they must still nosebleed to "grow." Their own physical powers are waning. Death is ahead. They have outlived some of their peers and enemies, but their wives are still there. And they still menstruate until menopause. They still engage in sex and perhaps – as some of them say – they enjoy it more. (Hors d'affaire?) But their fighting days are long gone and their hunting is negligible. They garden, visit, spin tales, and still direct ritual. In short, their phallicness is defused, they are more with their wives – upon whom they become increasingly dependent – and the old boundary between masculinity and femininity in the marital bond grows fuzzy. The main result is that they may slip into a new complementary relationship, subordinated to their wives as they were once dominated by their mothers.

Nosebleeding is still a ready means to defend against this loss of autonomy in old age, for it is the best revitalizing act available. It also serves as a sign – to self and community – that the elder is still sexually active and is symmetrically matching his wife's periods.

Conclusion

The violence of Sambia initiation is tied to the exigencies of its behavioral environment, which was defined by constant war. Nosebleeding, regularly inflicted, is but one of the mechanisms that requires and creates an especially aggressive kind of masculinity, whose model – the idealized phallic warrior – was suited to this environment. Moreover, the rites are the most powerful regulator of male interaction with females. Consecutive initiations effect both these outcomes: males begin as infants long sheltered in their mother's world, but they must wind up as warriors capable of killing, perpetuating painful initiations, and living and copulating with potentially hostile women. The contrast between those two countervailing developmental epochs is the difference between being traumatically conscripted into the ritual cult versus internalizing its "inalienable" fierce temperament (Mead 1936:265); between being forcibly bled versus painfully bleeding oneself. However much boys resist this psychosocial transformation, they cannot be allowed to circumvent it, for individual and community survival depended upon its successful outcome.

The degree of ritual violence and radical resocialization which characterizes Austro-Melanesian cults like that of Sambia are measures of the profound psychosocial obstacles against which men must work to initiate boys. The scale of institutionalization and affective intensity of bloodletting rites are correlated with a configuration of fragile family dynamics virtually unmatched elsewhere in the tribal world (except, perhaps, the Amazon basin: see Murphy 1959). The effects of warfare arrangements on the family can be seen in intense, prolonged maternal attachment, and distance from father. And too little father and too much mother inhibit a boy's easy, rapid, conflict-free transition into the warrior mold (Read [1952] was correct: aggressiveness is not an easy condition for humans to *create and sustain*. Freud [1930:34, 50] should have visited New Guinea.)

The corresponding developmental issues are twofold. First, how to check boys' earliest pre-Oedipal identifications and wishes to merge with, and depend upon, their mothers (Mahler 1963). Thus, the "primary femininity" in a boys' core gender identity (Money and Ehrhardt 1972; Stoller 1977) must be drastically halted, for Sambia scarcely allow softness in men. Second, how to get boys to *primarily* identify with their fathers, with masculinity and the cult at large, thereby forcing them to conform to the psychosocial (and Oedipal) demands of war, ritual, and "hostile" women. No exceptions to universal initiation are allowed (cf. Barth 1975:47), which mocks the naïveté of early armchair writers regarding personal choice in ritual.[9] In short, a fierce "push" and a pride-filled "pull" by the men's organization are needed to effect maternal detachment and masculinization in boys (Lidz and Lidz 1977; Stoller and Herdt 1982). Repeated nosebleeding is essential to the culturally desired outcome.

It is the precise psychocultural definition of proximity to women, at each point in the life-cycle, that governs the vicissitudes of Sambia nosebleeding. Let us accord full recognition to the native point of view: being in closeness to women is a social problem of magnitude at various levels – political, sexual, psychological, ritual. For males, female proximity always remains a power-laden issue; it embodies the culture dilemma mentioned before; it involves conflict, domestic and ritual, intrapsychic and interpersonal – as seen most dramatically in initiations – where nosebleeding mediates between individual "life crises" and the social order.

How does nosebleeding regulate proximity? There are four domains of constraints based on ritual custom and belief. (1) *Symbolic identifications*: nearness to women is believed always to impart femaleness to males, and hence, pollution (demasculinization). In ritual, boys are identified with mothers, and husbands with wives. The rule is: female contacts make one less masculine, so avoid them. Later, symbolically, one must match one's wife's periods

with private bleedings to ensure that he is as clearly male and as productively masculine as she is productively feminine. (2) *Cultural timing*: enforced nosebleeding checks personal choice at critical junctures in attachments to women: separation from mother; puberty and sexual maturation; marriage and cohabitation; birth and postpartum "distance"; and encroaching agedness, which threatens overdependence on one's wife. (3) *Sexual access*: nosebleeding is the greatest sanction supporting boys' female avoidance behavior, youths' taboos on premarital heterosexuality and adultery, homosexual practices, and men's self-regulation in sexual activities with their wives. (4) *Secret identity*: nosebleeding experience, concealed by ritual secrecy, appropriates a vulnerable piece of the self that is primarily feminine and thus must be bounded and kept hidden from women. This last point means that nosebleeding is not only a culturally constituted bundle of defense mechanisms (cf. Bettelheim 1955; Stephens 1961; Whiting, Kluckhohn, and Anthony 1958). It is also a creator of that complex experience: selfhood.

Seen this way, nosebleeding is a *system of identity contexts* which layer upon one another in the life cycle. Each successive initiation introduces changes in the bloodletting act – roles, scripts, signs, and audiences which unfold and transform the social organization of experience. To balance childhood experience against the demands of adult roles (with all that entails) constitutes the "internal discourse" of private nosebleeding for men. This discourse concerns the objective dilemma that one live and be sexually intimate with a woman while staying aloof from her, being secretive, fierce, and manipulative, according to warfare and ritual designs (initiate sons, trade daughters in marriage). The formula of self-bleeding ensures this touchy holding pattern. That solitary act subsumes layer upon layer of past experience and identity. Its audiences include the inner representations or fantasied "voices" of mother and father, one's earliest objects; as well as one's elders and peers present through memories of past initiations, with their trauma, separations, violence, cutting of flesh, manly pride, respect, and autonomy. The ritual cult thus reinserts itself, time and again, into the self and the marital relationship. And this is how it must be: enjoying women and sexual release in coitus is a self-initiated threat to manhood. Bloodletting becomes a habitualized style for checking one's affections and lust, one's self-doubts about being alone with, and inside of, a woman again. It is humanly impossible for men, without coitus, to create children and reap the rewards of hard-won sexual access and manhood, but they take their lives into their own hands each time they do so. Private nosebleeding therefore enables a man to maintain lifelong proximity to his wife – with some intimacy – by serving as a sign that he is separate and potent (it keeps him "heterosexually masculine") and a vigorous warrior. This thick compound of meanings is embodied in the adult sense: "I am still growing."

If my interpretation is correct, than we should expect that the end of warfare will bring an end to nosebleeding. As a system of identity contexts, bloodletting is a part of the behavioral environment that included war and other material consequences on the sociocultural system and family arrangements. Pacification has indeed changed the whole system; but the parts of the system are not changing in equal measure. In fact, cane-swallowing was abandoned first, the warriorhood aspect of nosebleeding teachings was halted in 1973, and finally, nosebleeding itself was entirely dropped from the most recent Sambia initiations in the late 1970s. Family arrangements are changing slowly, although there are no longer the tremendous pressures on males to always be seen as fierce warriors. Initiation persists (cf. Gewertz 1982). Men, reared with war, still privately bleed themselves. But, in another generation, nosebleeding will only be known as social history to the Sambia.

NOTES

1   The generic term for nose is *chembootu*; the penis is called *laakelu*; the glans penis is *laakelu chembootu* – which male idiom jokingly labels "that no good man down there (i.e., the pubic area) without teeth." Nose and penis associations like this one are not only consciously generized in everyday discourse (see Herdt

1980:61–62) but unconsciously elaborated in individual dreams and cultural products like ritual symbolism and folklore.

2   This report represents the ethnographic present of 1974–1976, when these data were mostly collected. Sambia say that they stopped practicing cane-swallowing (cf. Berndt 1965: 84: Salisbury 1976:62) of their own volition shortly before pacification (about 1964–1965). Pacification has brought formerly hostile Sambia hamlets close together, social changes that have also resulted in sharing certain clan or phratry ritual secrets (e.g., about nosebleeding) with affines or age-mates, creating more choice in these matters. During fieldwork in 1979, I noted that most Sambia men still privately nosebled, according to their own self-reports. In contrast, however, those same men say that cane-swallowing was simply *too* dangerous, painful, and messy (they feared that the canes would break off in their stomachs and kill them); nosebleeding is much preferred.

3   It is with the imagery of ritual paraphernalia like this – "blood raining down," a dark cavernous entrance, and a tight narrow passageway leading into a flowing stream (where blood is expelled) – that Jungians delight in interpreting womb and birth symbolism: "unconscious universal archtypes." But notice, too, that the ritual site, like a good Hollywood director's stage set, is constructed so that its subliminal perceptual effects build mystery, sanctity (Freud 1964:67), and fear, experiences that heighten and funnel subjective excitement along this particular line to a psychosocial outcome: trauma (for the novice) or triumph (for the initiator). I am indebted to Robert J. Stoller for this suggestion.

4   These bloodied leaves have but one, dramatic use, vis-à-vis older men's harangues of women somewhat later, back at the dance-ground site. The initiates' mothers are cursed for their "bad" treatment (e.g., cursing) of the boys, which is said to have thwarted masculine growth and required that men "kill" the boys. The red-stained leaves are held up as evidence of the boys' deaths. On one occasion I witnessed a remarkable display at this time: a young man, holding some of the bloody leaves, became excited and agitated and, quite beside himself, ran up to and assaulted one of the mothers nearby, forcibly stuffing some of the leaves in her mouth. He fled, and immediately a large group of women turned on the men

denouncing the assault. This anecdote graphically illustrates how the nosebleeding context – for one adult initiator, at least – precipitated a flurry of aggressive behavior that was permitted to be directed towards a boy's mother.

5 Elders say that this warriorhood aspect of first-stage nosebleeding teaching was abandoned in the early 1970s because it was anachronistic. Its counterpart in third-stage rites, however, is still taught. This seeming descrepancy involved the fact that third-stage initiates are older – they still remembered warfare – and, moreover, the bachelors are required to socially perform as warriors, even though war is gone.

6 I think that workers have tended to play down the subjective terror of this experience, for, Sambia males are virtually unanimous in expressing the feeling that they believed they were to be killed on the spot at nose-bleeding, and one finds similar reports elsewhere, spread between Australia (for example, Howitt 1884: 451n.) and New Guinea (cf. Read 1965:132; Watson 1960:144–145). Tuzin's (1980:74ff.) important work is the best and most recent exception to this omission.

7 Here are several clues about why men avoid discussing private nosebleeding. Private bleeding means you are engaging in coitus. Since coitus is shameful (even when men privately discuss sex with their cronies they tend to intellectualize, rather than refer to personal experience) private bleeding is tinged with shame. (See Whiting's [1941:64] related anecdote.) I suspect that men's heterosexual excitement is another factor, since sexual desire for women implicates loss of control, and intimacy, two areas that I have stressed above. (See also Tuzin 1980:76.)

8 Perhaps we should carefully examine again the connotations and contexts in which ideas about male "growth" are cited in Highlands societies (cf. Meigs 1976:399; Read 1951:162; Salisbury 1965:61).

9 "Teenagers in pre-literate societies are probably relatively more able to meet adult tasks than are adults in our society; hence they feel less dependent on or overawed by adults. These adolescents would certainly be able to resist rites inflicted on them by the old men if they wanted to do so" (Bettelheim 1955:92). Clearly, we can see Oedipal dynamics at work in the fierceness of initiation, both for fathers and sons. Indeed, it could be argued (Róheim 1942) that it is not until men fully act as initiators for their sons that they have attained the status of manly persons. How valid is Reik's (1946) contention that these fathers are mainly motivated to traumatize their sons out of hostile, Oedipal wishes? We still do not know, of course; though whatever their intrapsychic motives, there remains plenty of other, socially sanctioned reasons, for allowing men to believe they are acting out of necessity for the welfare of themselves and their sons. Nevertheless, there is far too much violence, trauma, and even genital threats in penis bleeding (see, for instance, Salisbury 1965:56ff.; Tuzin 1980:69–70) such that we should dismiss the Oedipal argument out of hand (cf. Bettelheim 1955; Langness 1974; 204–205; Lidz and Lidz 1977:29; Stephens 1961; Young 1965).

REFERENCES

Allen, Michael R.
1967 *Male Cults and Secret Initiations in Melanesia.* Melbourne: Melbourne University Press.

Barth, Frederik A.
1975 *Ritual and Knowledge Among the Baktaman of New Guinea.* New Haven: Yale University Press.

Bateson, Gregory.
1936 (1958) *Naven.* Stanford: Stanford University Press.

Bateson, Gregory.
1972 *Steps to an Ecology of Mind.* Scranton, Pa.: Chandler.

Berndt, Ronald M.
1962 *Excess and Restraint.* Chicago: University of Chicago Press.

Berndt, Ronald M.
1965 The Kamo, Usurufa, Jate and Fore of the Eastern Highlands. *Gods, Ghosts and Men in Melanesia* (P. Laurence and M. J. Meggitt, eds.), pp. 78–194, Melbourne: Melbourne University Press.

Bettelheim, Bruno.
1955 *Symbolic Wounds, Puberty Rites and the Envious Male.* New York: Collier Books.

Bowlby, John.
1958 The Nature of the Child's Tie to His Mother. *International Journal of Psychoanalysis* 39:350–373.

Bowlby, John
1969 *Attachment and Loss*, Vol. 1: New York: Basic Books.

Bowlby, John
1971 *Attachment and Loss*, Vol. 2: New York: Basic Books.

Chowning, Ann
1980 Culture and Biology Among the Sengseng of New Britain. *Journal of the Polynesian Society* 89:7–31.

Devereux, George
1937 Institutionalized Homosexuality of the Mohave Indians. *Human Biology* 9:498–527.

Faithorn, Elizabeth
1976 Women as Persons: Aspects of Female Life and Male-Female Relations Among the Kafe. *Man and Woman in the New Guinea Highlands* (P. Brown and G. Buchbinder, eds.), pp. 86–95. Washington, D.C.: American Anthropological Association.

Foucault, Michel
1980 *The History of Sexuality* (Robert Hurley, trans.) New York: Vintage Books.

Freud, Sigmund
1907 (1963) Obsessive Acts and Religious Practices. *Character and Culture*, pp. 17–33. New York: Collier Books.

Freud, Sigmund
1930 *Civilization and Its Discontents* (J. Strachey, trans.) New York: Norton.

Freud, Sigmund
1964 *The Future of an Illusion*. Garden City: Doubleday/Anchor Books.

Geertz, Clifford
1973 Ethos. World View, and the Analysis of Sacred Symbols. *Interpretation of Cultures*, pp. 126–141. New York: Basic Books.

Gewertz, Deborah
1982 The Father Who Bore Me. The Role of the *Tsambunwuro* During Chambri Initiation Ceremonies. *Rituals of Manhood: Male Initiation in Papua New Guinea* (G. H. Herdt, ed.), pp. 286–320. Berkeley: University of California Press.

Herdt, Gilbert H.
1980 Semen Depletion and the Sense of Maleness. *Ethnopsychiatrica* 3:79–116.

Herdt, Gilbert H.
1981 *Guardians of the Flutes: Idioms of Masculinity*. New York: McGraw Hill.

Herdt, Gilbert H.
1982 Fetish and Fantasy in Sambia Initiation. *Rituals of Manhood: Male Initiation in Papua New Guinea* (G. H. Herdt, ed.), pp. 44–98. Berkeley: University of California Press.

Hogbin, Ian
1970 *The Island of Menstruating Men*. Scranton, Pa.: Chandler.

Howitt, A. W.
1884 On Some Australian Ceremonies of Initiation. *Journal of the Royal Anthropological Institute* 13:432–459.

Langness, L. L.
1967 Sexual Antagonism in the New Guinea Highlands: a Bena Bena Example. *Oceania* 37:161–177.

Langness, L. L.
1974 Ritual Power and Male Domination in the New Guinea Highlands. *Ethos* 2:189–212.

Lewis, Gilbert
1975 *Knowledge and Illness in a Sepik Society*. London: Athlone Press.

Lewis, Gilbert
1980 *Day of Shining Red*. Cambridge: Cambridge University Press.

Lidz, Ruth W., and Theodore Lidz
1977 Male Menstruation: A Ritual Alternative to the Oedipal Transition. *International Journal of Psychoanalysis* 58:17–31.

Lindenbaum, Shirley
1972 Sorcerers, Ghosts, and Polluting Women: an Analysis of Religious Belief and Population Control. *Ethnology* 11:241–253.

Lindenbaum, Shirley
1976 A Wife is the Hand of Man. *Man and Woman in the New Guinea Highlands* (P. Brown and G. Buchbinder, eds.), pp. 54–62. Washington, D.C.: American Anthropological Association.

Mahler, Margaret S.
1963 Thoughts About Development and Individuation. *Psychoanalytic Study of the Child* 18:307–327.

Mead, Margaret
1968 (1935) *Sex and Temperament in Three Primitive Societies*. New York: Dell.

Meggitt, Mervyn J.
1964 Male-Female Relationships in the Highlands of Australian New Guinea. *American Anthropologist* 66:204–224.

Meigs, Anna.
1976 Male Pregnancy and the Reduction of Sexual Opposition in a New Guinea Highlands Society. *Ethnology* 25:393–407.

Meigs, Anna
1978 A Papuan Perspective on Pollution. *Man* 13:304–318.

Milgram, Stanley
1974 *Oedience to Authority, An Experimental View*. London: Tavistock.

Money, John, and Anke Ehrhardt
1972 *Man, Woman, Boy, Girl*. Baltimore: John Hopkins University Press.

Murphy, Robert F.
1959 Social Structure and Sex Antagonism. *South-western Journal of Anthropology* 15:89–98.

Newman, Philip
1964 Religious Belief and Ritual in a New Guinea Society. *American Anthropologist* 66:257–272.

Newman, Philip
1965 *Knowing the Gururumba*. New York: Holt, Rinehart & Winston.

Newman, Phillip, and David Boyd
1982 The Making of Men: Ritual and Meaning in Awa Male Initiation. *Rituals of Manhood: Male Initiation in Papua New Guinea* (G. H. Herdt, ed.), pp. 239–285. Berkeley: University of California Press.

Poole, John Fitz P.
1982 The Ritual Forging of Identity: Aspects of Person and Self in Bimin-Kuskusmin Initiation. *Rituals of Manhood: Male Initiation in Papua New Guinea* (G. H. Herdt, ed.), pp. 99–154. Berkeley: University of California Press.

Read, Kenneth E.
1951 The Gahuku-Gama of the Central Highlands. *South Pacific* 5:154–164.

Read, Kenneth E.
1952 Nama Cult of the Central Highlands, New Guinea. Oceania 23:1–25.

Read, Kenneth E.
1965 *The High Valley*. London: George Allen and Unwin Ltd.

Reik, Theodore
1946 *Ritual: Four Psycho-Analytic Studies*. New York: Grove Press.

Roheim, Geza
1942 Transition Rites: *Psychoanalytic Quarterly* 2:336–374.

Roheim, Geza
1945 *The Eternal Ones of the Dream*. New York: International University Press.

Roheim, Geza
1949 The Symbolism of Subincision. *American Imago* 6:321–328.

Salisbury, Richard F.
1965 The Siane of the Eastern Highlands. *Gods, Ghosts and Men in Melanesia* (P. Lawrence and M. Meggitt, eds.), pp. 50–77. Melbourne: Melbourne University Press.

Schwartz, Theodore
1973 Cult and Context: the Paranoid Ethos in Melanesia. *Ethos* 1:153–174.

Spiro, Melford E.
1965 Religious Systems as Culturally Constituted Defense Mechanisms. *Context and Meaning in Cultural Anthropology* (M. E. Spiro, ed.), pp. 100–113. New York: Free Press.

Stephens, W. N.
1961 A Cross-Cultural Study of Menstrual Taboos. *Genetic Psychology Monographs* 64:385–416.

Stephens, W. N.
1962 *The Oedipus Complex: Cross-Cultural Evidence*. New York: The Free Press.

Stoller, Robert J.
1968 *Sex and Gender, Volume I: On the Development of Masculinity and Feminity*. New York: Science House.

Stoller, Robert J.
1977 *Perversion: The Erotic Form of Hatred*. London: Quartet Books.

Stoller, Robert J., and Gilbert H. Herdt
1982 The Development of Gender Identity: A Cross-Cultural Contribution. *Journal of the American Psychoanalytic Association* 30:29–59.

Strathern, Andrew J.
1969 Descent and Alliance in the New Guinea Highlands: Some Problems of Comparison. *Proceedings of the Royal Anthropological Institute of Great Britain and Northern Ireland for 1968*, pp. 37–52.

Strathern, A. Marilyn.
1972 *Women in Between*. London: Seminar Press.

Strathern, A. Marilyn
1979 The Self in Self-Decoration. *Oceania* XLIX: 241–257.

Turner, Victor
1967 Betwixt and Between: the Liminal Period in Rites de Passage. *The Forest of Symbols*, pp. 93–111. Ithaca: Cornell University Press.

Tuzin, Donald F.
1980 *The Voice of the Tamberan*. Truth and Illusion in Ilahita Arapesh Religion. Berkeley: University of California Press.

Tuzin, Donald F.
1982 Ritual Violence among the Ilahita Arapesh: The Dynamics of Religious and Moral Uncertainty. *Rituals of Manhood: Male*

Initiation in Papua New Guinea (G. H. Herdt, ed.), pp. 321–355. Berkeley: University of California Press.

Vanggaard, Thorkil.
1972. *Phallos*. New York: International Universities Press.

Watson, James B.
1960. A New Guinea 'Opening Man.' *The Company of Man* (J. B. Casagrande, ed.), pp. 127–173. New York: Harper and Row.

Whiting, John W. M.
1941. *Becoming a Kwoma: Teaching and Learning in a New Guinea Tribe*. New Haven: Yale University Press.

Whiting, John W. M., R. Kluckhohn, and A. Anthony
1958 The Function of Male Initiation Ceremonies at Puberty. *Readings in Social Psychology* (E. E. Maccoby, T. M. Newcomb, and E. L. Hartley, ed.), pp. 359–370. New York: Henry Holt.

Whiting, John W. M., and Beatrice B. Whiting.
1975 Aloofness and Intimacy of Husbands and Wives: a Cross-Cultural Study. Ethos 3:183–207.

Williams, F. E.
1936. *Papuans of the Trans Fly*. Oxford: Clarendon Press.

Young, Frank W.
1965 *Initiation Ceremonies: A Cross-Cultural Study in Status Dramatization*. Indianapolis: Bobb-Merrill.

18

Cross-Cultural Differences in the Self

Douglas Hollan

Marsella, DeVos, and Hsu (1985:ix) note a renewed interest in the study of the self. While such interest is evident in psychology and philosophy, it seems to be especially strong in anthropology, where recent work on the self includes ethnographies (e.g., Rosaldo 1980; Myers 1979; Keeler 1987), collections of articles (e.g., Heelas and Lock 1981; Marsella, DeVos, and Hsu 1985; White and Kirkpatrick 1985; Carrithers, Collins, and Lukes 1985; Lee 1979; Levy and Rosaldo 1983; Shweder and LeVine 1984; Dieterlen 1973; Stigler, Shweder, and Herdt 1990), chapters in texts or books (e.g., Bock, 1988; LeVine 1982; Crapanzano 1990), and at least one extensive review of the literature (Fogelson 1979).[1]

As Howard points out for the collection edited by White and Kirkpatrick (1985), much of the recent anthropological work on person, self, and other aspects of ethnopsychology has been in the revisionist vein of Mead (1928) and Malinowski (1951): it purports to demonstrate the culture-boundedness of Western conceptions and theories of person, self, and emotion by presenting data from around the world which appear to contradict them. "The aim is to release 'scientific' psychology, which should be universal, from the shackles imposed on it by Western 'folk' psychology, which is culturally constricted" (Howard 1985:403).

Anthropologists have argued, for example, that Western conceptions of the person as a discrete, autonomous, and individuated locus of personal will and responsibility – an "egocentric reductionist" view of the individual-in-society (Shweder and Bourne 1984) – misrepresent notions of the person in many non-Western societies. Geertz (1984:126), for instance, has noted:

The Western conception of the person as a bounded, unique, more or less integrated motivational and cognitive universe, a dynamic center of awareness, emotion, judgment, and action organized into a distinctive whole and set contrastively both against other such wholes and against a social and natural background is, however incorrigible it may seem to us, a rather peculiar idea within the context of the world's cultures.

In many non-Western societies, it has been argued, views of the person are much more "sociocentric organic" in nature (Shweder and Bourne 1984:193). The person is seen as so inextricably woven into a fabric of culturally prescribed social roles, patterns of interpersonal behavior, and corporate identities that it is more appropriate to speak of the person as the "person-in-relationships," rather than as a discrete, well-bounded unit (cf. Howard 1985:414).

Geertz and Shweder and Bourne use the term "person" in the work cited above to refer, at least in part, to a locus of subjective

Douglas Hollan, Cross-Cultural Differences in the Self from *Journal of Anthropological Research*, Vol. 48, No. 4 (Winter, 1992), pp. 283–300. Published by University of New Mexico. Reprinted with permission of the *Journal of Anthropological Research*.

experience. Used in this way, the concept closely resembles what Hallowell refers to as "self." According to Hallowell (1959:52), the self is that part of consciousness that comes into play when a human being begins to take him- or herself as an object. As such, it is an *experiential* datum that, unlike the Freudian "ego," can be directly described and talked about by actors, not merely deduced or postulated from psychological or cultural theory. In this paper, I limit my focus to anthropological studies of "self" in Hallowell's sense of the word.[2]

The notion that concepts of the self vary by culture is now accepted by many, if not most, social and cultural anthropologists. Yet the theoretical and methodological implications of such a finding remain obscure. For example, when we say that concepts of the self vary by culture, do we mean only that different cultures have different ways of conceptualizing and talking about the self, or do we mean something more: that aspects of subjective experience also vary considerably?[3]

Anthropologists are often not explicit on this issue. They frequently fail to clearly and unequivocally address such questions as: To what extent are selves culturally constituted? If selves are only partially constituted by culture, what other factors play a part in their makeup? Are those other factors – social, biopsychological, etc. – universal in nature? Even if all selves are at least partly culturally constituted, are some selves more culturally constituted than others? Some researchers have argued that the experiential self must vary as much as the cultural models within which it is embedded, because the latter largely constitute the former. According to this position, since "the metaphors by which people live and the world views to which they subscribe mediate the relationship between what one thinks about and how one thinks" (Shweder and Bourne 1984:189) and since "cultural models … provide a basis for the organization of activities, responses, perceptions, and experiences by the conscious self" (Rosaldo 1984:140), it is reasonable to assume that (usually) there is little or no distance between cultural models or theories of selfhood and the experiential self. Indeed, Lutz (1987:308) has argued that such questions as "Does any particular ethnotheoretical model

have an effect on the way people feel and behave?" and "How does the structure of ethnotheory acquire direction and force?" – which presuppose some gap between cultural conceptions and the self, emotions, and other psychological processes – are both unanswerable and culture-bound. They are, according to Lutz, suggested by our own Western theories of the mind, based on Cartesian dualisms, which emphasize, among other things, a split between self and social persona.

While the above position aptly points out how Western conceptions may distort cross-cultural research, other anthropologists have cautioned that the relationship between cultural conceptions of the self and "actual" subjective experience may be highly problematic. Howard (1985) notes, for example, that despite our American model of the self as separate, independent, and autonomous, experientially we seem to extend ourselves beyond the boundaries of the skin through such processes as empathy, identification, and personal space extension. Furthermore, he asks, despite evidence that many non-Westerners

do not normally distinguish themselves as individualized entities in ordinary discourse, does this mean that they do not have a clear conception of themselves as unique individuals? If so, how do they deal with the corporal reality of the body – the fact that it urinates and defecates and experiences hunger, thirst, and sexual urges? (Howard 1985:414)

Howard is arguing here that the sharp contrasts which are often drawn between Western and non-Western experiential selves have probably been exaggerated. I would agree and suggest that this occurs, in part, because some researchers (e.g., Dumont 1970; Geertz 1973) may too readily assume a close correspondence, or even identity, between cultural models or theories and subjective experience. There are at least three problems with this assumption.

The first concerns "cultural models," the presupposed, taken-for-granted, commonsensical, and widely shared assumptions which a group of people hold about the world and its objects (see Holland and Quinn 1987 for an excellent general discussion). Cultural models (of selves or anything else) present a simplified and often idealized conception of objects and processes in which much of the blooming, buzzing complexity of phenomena is either suppressed or ignored. Such models are often implicit, rather than explicit, and may be partial, situational, ad hoc, or inconsistent in nature (Keesing 1987). If cultural models of the self, like most other types of cultural models, are simplified and/or idealized, then we should not mistakenly assume that they encompass all aspects of the experiential self or that they alone should serve as the basis for a comparison of the self.

Second, by too readily assuming the cognitive and emotional "saliency" (Spiro 1984) of cultural discourse and conceptions, one may fail to recognize that cultural models are merely "ideas, *premises* by which people guide their lives, *and only to the extent a people lives by them do they have force*" (Shweder and Bourne 1984:193; second emphasis added). One way people actually "live by" a cultural model of the self is by maintaining childrearing practices which result in deep intuitions about the model's inherent truth and correctness. Consider, for example, socialization for autonomy in the United States. By extending the rights of privacy to even very young children, American parents repeatedly assert, through concrete interactions, the value of autonomy and independence.

And, where are these "assertions" redundantly (even if tacitly) reiterated? Well, the assertion is there in the respect shown by a parent for a child's "security blanket." It's there as well when an adult asks a three-year-old "What do you want to eat for dinner?" and again in the knock on the door before entering the child's personal space, his private bedroom, another replica of the assertion. (Shweder and Bourne 1984:194)

The extent to which a people actually "lives by" or practices a given model of the self is a question that should be investigated empirically, since the possibility exists that the model or some part of it will *not* be integrated into everyday experience.

Third, by emphasizing a one-to-one correspondence between cultural models and the experiential self, one underplays the extent to which aspects of subjective experience are also a product of psychobiological propensities (Hallowell 1955, 1959) and social encounters (G.H. Mead 1934; Cooley 1922; Blumer 1969) which may actually run counter to, or contradict, ideal cultural representations. For example, a child raised in an ostensibly "egocentric" society may yet be treated in such a way as to deny or discourage the emergence of a sense of initiative and autonomy. This, in turn, may lead to the development of individually constituted self-concepts which are at odds with the ideal sense of self promoted by the culture at large. Thus, cultural discourse and ideal conceptions "may not coincide neatly with personal experience and may ignore, obscure, and even misrepresent aspects of experience" (Wellenkamp 1988a:488; see also Levy 1984:218–28).

The position I am developing here is based on the view that while cultural and linguistic categories provide one important means by which the self is conceptualized and talked about and must surely influence the way the self is constructed (see, e.g., Hallowell 1955; Lakoff and Johnson 1980; Lutz 1982, 1985; Rosaldo 1980, 1984), cultural models and conceptions of the self should not be conflated with the experiential self.[4] Self-concepts may also be derived from one's own personal and social experience. Such individually constituted self-concepts may or may not be widely shared and they may or may not coincide with or reinforce self-concepts which are culturally constituted. Just as one cannot assume that cultural models of the self are merely projections of individual phenomenology, one cannot assume that an individual's experiential self can be reduced to the concepts and terms which are used to talk about it (cf. Bock 1988:199). While the two are no doubt intimately and dynamically related, the extent to which they influence and shape one another should remain an empirical question (cf. Wellenkamp 1988a). This teasing apart of culture and subjective experience is fraught with difficulty (e.g., How is the report of an experience related to the experience reported upon?). Yet I agree with Keesing (1982:31) that "with strategic interviews, projective tests, dreams,

and other psychological methods, we *can* separate out the strands of individual experience
from the cultural designs into which they are
woven."

This distinction between cultural concepts
or theories of the self and aspects of subjective
experience which may escape such models is
often lost or confused in recent discussions, yet
it is not without precedent. Mauss, for example, in his article "A Category of the Human
Mind: The Notion of Person; The Notion of
Self" (1985), made clear that he was concerned
with examining cultural variations in the *concept* of the self, not the experiential self, which
he believed to be much less culturally variable:

> I shall leave aside everything which relates to
> the "self" (moi), the conscious personality as
> such. Let me merely say that it is plain, at least
> to us, that there has never existed a human
> being who has not been aware, not only of his
> body, but also at the same time of his individu-
> ality, both spiritual and physical. ...
>   My subject is entirely different, and
> independent of this. It is one related to social
> history. Over the centuries, in numerous socie-
> ties, how has it slowly evolved – not the sense
> of "self" (moi) – but the notion or concept
> that men in different ages have formed of it?
> (Mauss 1985:3; cf. Theodore Schwartz's com-
> ments quoted in Shweder 1984:13–14)

In the next two sections, I illustrate some of
these methodological and theoretical points by
examining some discrepancies between ideal
cultural models and aspects of subjective experience in both Toraja (South Sulawesi,
Indonesia) and the United States. My intent
here is to illustrate, in programmatic fashion,
the complexity of the relationship between cultural models and the self as a locus of subjective experience, not to develop a comprehensive
or conclusive analysis of either the Torajan or
American experiential self.

Much of the data I present comes from the
use of open-ended interviews conducted with a
select group of American and Torajan respondents.[5] In a review of three recent works based
on in-depth interviewing,[6] Marcus and Fischer
(1986:54) note that the mark of such
contemporary approaches is the "display of
discourse – self-reflective commentaries on

experience, emotion, and self; on dreams,
remembrances, associations, metaphors, distortions, and displacements; on transferences
and compulsive behavior repetitions – *all of
which reveal a behaviorally and conceptually
significant level of reality reflecting, contrasting with, or obscured by public cultural forms*"
(emphasis added). The following passage from
Levy and Wellenkamp (1989) provides further
elaboration of this point. What they have to
say about the advantages of the open interview
in the anthropological investigation of emotional experience also applies to the study of
subjective experience in general.

> Such interviews provide two kinds of infor-
> mation about emotion. Individuals being
> interviewed are used in part as *informants*,
> providing their own interpretations of phe-
> nomena related to emotion. At the same time
> they may serve as *respondents*, objects of sys-
> tematic study in themselves, in which their
> discourse – and in particular the *forms* of that
> discourse and their behavior as they talk –
> indicates something about the organization of
> emotion in that particular individual. ...
> Many aspects of form can be put to analytic
> use here – facial expression and body lan-
> guage (capable of being recorded by video
> tape) as well as paralinguistic features, and a
> rich field of thematic clumpings, distortions,
> evasions, hesitations, slips of the tongue, and
> confusions, all amply illustrated and easily
> discernible in a close listening to tape record-
> ings of interviews. (Levy and Wellenkamp
> 1989:223–24)

While Abu-Lughod (1986) has recently
demonstrated that different aspects of the self
may be culturally elaborated in different contexts, my point in this paper is somewhat different: that aspects of the experiential self are
sometimes left undeveloped and unelaborated
because they are only poorly understood or
because they directly contradict other, more
highly valued experiences. The open interview
data I present should make clear that while
there are significant differences between Toraja
and American experiential selves, the differences are not of the magnitude that one might
suppose from an examination of ideal cultural
models alone.

Throughout my discussion I focus on the individuated/relational dimension of the experiential self: that is, the extent to which the self is clearly individuated and distinguished from others in the behavioral environment or identified and merged with them. There are two reasons for this. First, the "self" is a global term that refers to several aspects or dimensions of subjective experience (Gergen 1971). For example, one could focus on the self's orientation in space and time, the evaluation of self, the sense of being "in control" as opposed to being "under control" (Heelas 1981; Lock 1981), the differences in what is considered "inside" the self or "outside" the self, etc. The failure to clearly specify which aspect of the self one is concerned with is yet another source of confusion in the contemporary literature. Thus, "self" is a term that gains analytical utility only to the extent that its referents are carefully specified and delimited. Second, the individuated/relational dimension of the self is most frequently described and commented upon in the anthropological literature and is the aspect of self for which comparable data are most readily available. Both the American and Toraja data sets illustrate the complexities of the self/other relationship, though both were originally collected for other purposes.[7]

The Relational Self in the United States

In research Jane Wellenkamp and I conducted some years ago (1981), we attempted to elicit salient aspects of middle-class American beliefs regarding death and bereavement by interviewing undergraduate students who had recently experienced a death in their families. Among other things, we were struck by the extent to which students relied upon notions of self-sufficiency, autonomy, and independence to cope with the experience of grief and loss. For example, each of our respondents believed that it was important to show "strength" in the wake of a death. To be "strong," one had to control the public display of one's emotions as well as actively master or resolve one's private sense of grief so that a normal lifestyle could be resumed as quickly as possible. According

to one woman, even the death of a very close relative cannot be allowed to threaten one's sense of self-sufficiency and autonomy:

> Well, it's like our family is a boat. We've made a flotilla. And we've tied up to each other. And then these ties are all cut off [by a death in the family]. ... But you just have to say that I don't need any of these ties at all. I can stand on my own.

Later in the same interview, she goes on to assert that in order to "stand on one's own," one has to develop "spine," so that one can avoid positions of dependency vis-à-vis other people.

Similar sentiments were voiced by another woman who argued that one has a duty to oneself to carry on after the death of a relative. Others may die and fade away, but oneself must and should persevere:

> Go on and keep your life rolling. Don't let it stand still because of that [a death in the family]. *Your* life is still there. And you should always watch out for yourself. When something like that happens [the death], it also makes you appreciate yourself more. At least you have yourself. That's what you'll always have. And you should never forfeit it.

Such statements about the need for strength and self-control in the face of a relative's death were complemented by negative evaluations of those who did not show such "spine." One respondent concluded a moving description of her mother's emotionally volatile reaction to the death of the respondent's sister by saying, "She really wasn't that strong."

Thus, according to the cultural model articulated by our undergraduate students, the self should be "strong" and independent and should not be compromised by the deaths of other people. And indeed, our respondents had actively sought to comply with such expectations when faced with a death in their own families. Yet other interview data clearly suggest that such losses did in fact present a strong challenge to the integrity and independence of our respondents' selves. They also indicate that Americans experience themselves to be more intertwined with one another, and so less impermeable, than the cultural model would suggest. For example, students occasionally displayed a fleeting recognition, cultural models to the contrary notwithstanding, that the death of a significant other also involved a partial "death" of one's own self:

You think about your time with them [the dead person] and what you'll miss about them. Like I think about going to the beach and playing tennis with her [a recently dead sister]. And gossiping with her. And that's the part I miss because it makes me sad. Because I think everyone has a tendency to think about what they'll miss from that person [the one who has died]. You realize that they're gone and that a part of you had gone with them. And that can hurt.

Similarly:

You're stripped of a certain role [when someone dies]. One of the people you relate with is gone. And so that side of you is gone. And you're kind of empty and reaching out for something.

Musings such as these seek to describe and articulate subjective experiences which are only poorly understood and conceptualized. The nature of these experiences is given more exact formulation by the sociologist Vernon (1970:133):

We are speaking here not of biological death, but rather of the death or cessation of behavior patterns – of a social death. Without doubt, part of one's way of behaving dies, or is no longer possible, when another individual with whom the behavior has been integrated is no longer there to react. Part of one's self, or his self-definition, dies when the other with whom one has been interacting dies. A particular reflected or mirror image is no longer there to receive.

It appears, then, that feelings of loss and emptiness during periods of bereavement betray aspects of the American experiential self which are only poorly accounted for, if not actually denied, by the ideal cultural model: namely, that the self is at least partly constituted by the "others" with whom it interacts

and that the boundaries between self and other may remain somewhat fluid and indistinct. This is, of course, a point that G.H. Mead (1934) and the symbolic interactionists (e.g., Blumer 1969) have made repeatedly.

Autonomous Aspects of the Toraja Self

The Sa'dan Toraja (henceforth called the "Toraja") number approximately 350,000 and live in the interior mountainous regions of South Sulawesi, Indonesia. They are primarily wet-rice farmers who also cultivate small gardens of sweet potatoes, cassava, and assorted vegetables. Traditionally, Toraja society was stratified into three primary groups: nobles, commoners, and slaves or dependents. Although one's position within this hierarchy was theoretically ascribed at birth, status and prestige could also be achieved by slaughtering livestock at community feasts. Since the development of a cash economy, however, even former dependents are now heavily involved in the competitive slaughter of livestock. The traditional religion of the Toraja, *Alukta*, is based on the veneration and propitiation of spirits and deceased ancestors. Yet at least 50 percent of older adults and almost all Toraja under the age of twenty have now converted to Christianity.[8]

The Toraja are a strongly "sociocentric" people. Like many other Austronesian-speaking groups, they place a high value on affiliation and alliance within the community and strongly criticize self-serving, boasting, "pushy" behavior. The statuses and identities of individual villagers are not only tied to generations of ancestors who have preceded them, but also, through a system of teknonymy, to the generations of children and grandchildren that follow. The belief that the sins and "mistakes" of individuals may be visited upon the family or community as a whole, or on the generations to follow (Hollan 1988a), also serves to link the fate and prosperity of one to the moral behavior of all.

Toraja notions of the ideal person also reflect a concern with community and relatedness. People with *penaa melo*, "good breath," are said to be sensitive to the needs and concerns of others. They give generously and willingly – within the bounds of reciprocity – when asked for help, and they are at pains to avoid giving offense. Should disagreements arise, they strive for consensus and shun confrontational behavior. They are though scrupulously honest in economic affairs, but they quite properly dissemble when brute facts and "sharp" words would serve only to embarrass or anger. Above all else, people with penaa melo are said to recognize that the peace and well-being of the community must come before individual interests; identity and self-esteem are affirmed within the community not apart from it.

Open interview data[9] confirm that the interrelatedness of Toraja selves is often experientially "real" as well as culturally valued. For example, many of my respondents found it difficult to make evaluations of their own behavior without at the same time analyzing its effects on neighbors and kin. When Ambe'na ("Father of") Patu is asked what part of his character or behavior he would change if he could, he replies:

> [beginning to laugh] It depends on other people. If other people want us to change, we can change. … We may feel that our behavior/attitudes are good, but if other people don't like them they may say, "Don't act like that. …" How are we ourselves to know how to change? Only other people can know that, you know? So if other people don't like us, we can try to change. We can try to change whatever behavior/attitudes are not liked.

This concern with, and openness to, others' opinions of oneself is also suggested by Indo'na ("Mother of") Rante:

> With regard to one's behavior/attitudes, it changes everyday. (Is that easy or difficult?) Easy! We think to ourselves, "Don't act like this or that [in ways people disapprove of], act like this [in ways people approve of]." It is the same when we instruct our children: "Don't act like that [inappropriately], act like your mother and father." That way, people don't criticize. That's how we maintain good behavior/attitudes.

Such statements suggest the extent to which the individual's sense of conscience and moral awareness are directly linked to the evaluations and opinions of others (cf. Levy 1973; Shore 1982).

Yet while Toraja culture and society clearly encourage the interrelatedness and identification of self with others, such embeddedness is not always sought or achieved. In the following pages I discuss a number of contexts in which respondents express, directly or indirectly, a sense of their own autonomy or protest vigorously when that autonomy is challenged. While such expressions are partially supported by a general understanding that it is wrong to coerce people to do things against their will (Hollan 1990:372–76), they are usually limited to relatively private settings, and they are less clearly articulated, and more morally ambiguous, than expressions of the sociocentric self.

(1) One such expression involves occasional resistance to requests for aid or assistance. On the one hand, the Toraja are fond of saying that maturity and proper "understanding" necessarily eventuate in cooperative, unselfish, compliant behavior. Children are not always cooperative and compliant, and are often selfish, because they do not yet "know" the rules of proper behavior. The notion is, if one understands that relationships within the village are reciprocal and interdependent, then one *will be* responsive to the needs of others. Yet respondents also state that others cannot, and should not, take their cooperation and compliance for granted. They often asserted in the open interviews that they cannot be forced to do that which they do not wish to do. Such feelings of self-assertive defiance are especially evident when respondents imagined themselves replying to a request for assistance with a resounding "I don't want to!"[10]

The point here is not that the Toraja merely *claim* to identify with the needs of others. In fact, the Toraja *are* extremely cooperative and compliant. And when they do, rarely, refuse the requests of others, they do so in a culturally appropriate, nonconfrontational manner: they assiduously avoid the person asking for aid or assistance until the request is dropped or forgotten. The point, rather, is that when the Toraja *do* respond to the wishes and requests of others, as they usually do, they do so, in their own minds, because they *choose* to cooperate – not because they are incapable of resistance, self-assertion, or autonomy (cf. Levy 1973:460).

(2) Respondents also express a sense of autonomy when they state that they have extensive knowledge of the nature of the relationships, both human and supernatural, in which they are embedded. By claiming, as they frequently did in private contexts, that they "know everything" about politics, religion, customs, etc., they sought to *use* these relationships to satisfy their own personal needs and desires, rather than to be submerged and dominated by them. Several men, for example, claimed that their knowledge of omens, dream interpretation, astrology, and special magical amulets called *balo'* enabled them to manipulate the life-enhancing powers of the gods and ancestors to insure the fertility of their crops and livestock. They were thus capable of feeling *in* control, not just *under* control (cf. Heelas 1981; Lock 1981).

(3) Open interview data indicate that the botanical metaphors which the Toraja often use to suggest that a group of people have mutual interests and a common identity may also be employed to *deny* how separate and autonomous the interests and identities of that group may actually be. In the passage below, Nene'na ("Grandfather of") Tandi uses a conventional metaphor in an effort to convince his parents that they cannot disinherit him simply because he chooses to exercise his independence and become a member of the Christian church:

> There is not a person in the world who can be separated from his parents. Just like trees. There is not a leaf that can be separated from the tree [it grew from]. All of them, even if they fall, fall beneath the tree. They do not fall away from the tree. I [the leaf] am the same to you [his parents, the tree].

(4) Aspects of an autonomous self are also evident during certain dream experiences in which respondents envision themselves looming above and dominating those around them.[11] While some such dreams are culturally prescribed ways of validating claims to positions of power and influence, they also may be inter-

preted as expressions of an individual, autonomous self which stands apart from the crowd.

Nene'na Limbong reported two such dreams. In one, he found himself high atop a mountain. As he raised his arms perpendicular to his body, he discovered that he loomed above the landscape and that his hands reached to the farthest corners of Tana Toraja, dominating all those around him. In the second dream, an important government official asks several men to prove their worthiness to lead the village by climbing to the top of a tall pole. Nene'na Limbong watches other men try and fail in this task before he himself successfully reaches the top and is given the leadership of the village. Here, quite graphically, Nene'na Limbong asserts a dominant, commanding self.

As in the United States case, aspects of the Toraja experiential self – in this case autonomous aspects – are not readily inferred from an analysis of ideal cultural models alone. Such discrepancies suggest that the relationship between ideal cultural conceptions and subjective experience is complex and problematic and requires active investigation.

Discussion and Conclusion

I have argued that by too readily assuming a close correspondence between ideal cultural conceptions of the self – which are often simplified and idealized – and subjective experience, some researchers have tended to exaggerate the differences between a closed, individuated, autonomous, egocentric, "Western" self and an open, relational, interdependent, sociocentric, "non-Western" self (cf. Kleinman 1986; Carucci 1987; Mines 1988; McHugh 1989; Rosenberger 1989; Stephenson 1989; Ewing 1990, 1991). Using nondirective interview techniques which allow one to explore both valued and disvalued aspects of the experiential self, I have shown that one can find evidence, *in some contexts*, of an independent, autonomous self among the "sociocentric" Toraja of Indonesia and of an interdependent, relational self among "egocentric" Americans in the United States.

Rather than continue to focus on broad contrasts between "Western" and "non-Western" selves, I suggest, first, that we begin to examine in greater detail *degrees* of egocentrism or sociocentrism, openness or closedness, individuation or relation, etc., *within specific contexts* in both Western and non-Western societies. We might also begin to analyze more closely the different ways in which societies develop or fail to develop different aspects of the experiential self, for example, through such processes as "hypocognition" or "hypercognition" (Levy 1973, 1984). Only by making more subtle and detailed analyses of regional and intraregional variation will we begin to discern the ways in which different types of human reflexivity are related to different types of sociocultural systems.[12]

Second, partly as a result of the tendency to confuse ideal-typical models and theories of the self with the experiential self, current research often focuses on culturally valued dimensions of the self to the exclusion of those dimensions that are disvalued or those that are valued, or tolerated, only in narrowly defined contexts. This constricted focus not only oversimplifies the complexity of the human self, which is often characterized by multiple and contradictory facets (Gergen 1971), but it also leaves unexamined a fascinating area of research: the differential manner in which disvalued or disapproved dimensions of the self, some of which may be unconscious,[13] are culturally organized, expressed or suppressed, and managed. Closer examination of culturally disvalued dimensions of the self would also demand that we begin to analyze the ways in which different dimensions of the self, both valued and disvalued, are mutually defined and interrelated.[14]

Anthropologists have clearly demonstrated that cultural models of the self may vary significantly from culture to culture. The task now is to investigate both the manner and the extent to which these various models are actually "lived by" and thereby to ascertain the range of the experiential self as well.

NOTES

1   Funding for parts of this research was provided by the National Science Foundation; the National Institute for Mental Health; The Wenner-Gren Foundation for Anthropological Research; Sigma Xi, The Scientific Research Society; and the Office of Graduate Studies and Research, University of California, San Diego. Sponsorship in Indonesia was provided by Lembaga Ilmu Pengetahuan Indonesia in Jakarta and by Universitas Hasanuddin in Ujung Pandang. Jane Wellenkamp's comments and suggestions have been invaluable. I have also benefited from the comments of Robert Levy, anonymous JAR reviewers, and the editor.

2   The inconsistent and imprecise use of terminology has been one of the banes of ethnopsychological research (see Harris 1989).

3   The relationship between cultural variation and individual psychology has been critical to the cross-cultural study of cognition and emotion as well. As Cole and Scribner (1974:172) note, for example:

So long as we are concerned with demonstrating that human cultural groups differ enormously in their beliefs and theories about the world and in their actual products and technical accomplishments there can be no question: there are marked and multitudinous differences. But are these differences the result of differences in basic cognitive processes or are they merely the expressions of the many products that a universal human mind can manufacture, given variations and conditions of life and culturally valued acts?

And Wellenkamp (1988a:487) has observed:

Even preliminary work in the ethnopsychology of emotion reveals the wide diversity in ways of talking about emotions. When the Javanese say that a group of villagers beat to death a reckless driver because they were "startled" by his behavior or when an Ilongot says, "[Since] I couldn't kill my wife, I just decided to forget my anger," are we to conclude that their emotional lives are very different from our own?

4   See Spiro (1984:324–25) for a more detailed discussion of the problems which result from conflating culture and phenomena which are partially constituted by culture and partially constituted by noncultural processes.

5   All of the interviews in both the United States and Indonesia were tape-recorded and transcribed. The quotations that follow are direct quotes taken from these interviews.

6 These are Levy (1973), Kracke (1978), and Obeyesekere (1981). Levy interviewed rural and urban Tahitians, Kracke interviewed Kagwahiv political leaders and their followers, and Obeyesekere interviewed religious specialists in Sri Lanka.

7 The American data were collected during a study of loss and bereavement in the United States. The Toraja data were collected for the purpose of writing a "personcentered" ethnography.

8 For a more comprehensive description of Toraja life, see Bigalke (1981), Hollan (1984, 1988a, 1988b), Nooy-Palm (1979, 1986), Volloman (1985), and Wellenkamp (1984, 1988a, 1988b).

9 All of the quotations in this section are taken from a series of in-depth, openended life history interviews that Jane Wellenkamp (1984, 1988a, 1988b, 1991, 1992) and I (Hollan 1984, 1988a, 1988b, 1989, 1990, 1992) conducted with eleven Toraja of varying social and economic backgrounds. Wellenkamp interviewed the women and I interviewed the men. For a profile of individual respondents and a description of the interviewing techniques and procedures, see Hollan and Wellenkamp (n.d.).

10 I want to emphasize that this is a response that informants *imagine* themselves making. In fact, I never saw anyone blatantly and rudely reject a request for assistance in this way. Yet even if such feelings of defiance are not openly expressed, they obviously belie the assertion that members of "organic cultures" must necessarily "feel at ease in regulating and being regulated" (Shweder and Bourne 1984:194). It is probably more accurate to say that they feel at ease being regulated in certain contexts and at certain times.

11 For a brief ethnography of Toraja dreams, see Hollan (1989).

12 Gaines (1984) has shown, for example, that within "the West," there are significant differences between the "referential" self-concepts of the Northern European culture areas and the "indexical" self-concepts of the Latin Mediterranean culture areas. It remains to be seen whether such cultural differences also reflect significant differences in individual phenomenology.

13 It is, of course, awkward to speak of unconscious aspects of the self, since reflexive awareness implies consciousness. Yet we know that representations of the self and other which are out of awareness *do* shape human behavior in important ways. The challenge, then, is to develop a model of mind and consciousness which integrates various aspects of the self, those that are conscious and at least partly culturally constituted and those that may be individually constituted (though perhaps widely shared) and out of awareness. Unfortunately, neither anthropologists nor psychoanalysts have responded to this challenge. The former deal almost exclusively with culturally constituted aspects of the self, while the latter spend most of their time investigating aspects of self which are unconscious or out of awareness.

14 Melford Spiro has addressed such issues in several places (e.g., 1965, 1978, 1984). See also Thomas Hay (1977:78), who has argued that among the Ojibwa, a "conscious self-concept of helplessness is derived from the unconscious self-concept [of anger and hostility] through repression and projection"; Abu-Lughod (1986), who shows how the Bedouin come to value both the vulnerability and invulnerability of the self in different contexts; and Rosenberger (1989), who analyzes the bipolar nature of the Japanese self.

REFERENCES

Abu-Lughod, L.
   1986   Veiled Sentiments: Honor and Poetry in a Bedouin Society. Berkeley: University of California Press.

Bigalke, T.
   1981   A Social History of "Tana Toraja," 1870–1965. Ph.D diss., University of Wisconsin, Madison.

Bock, P.
   1988   Rethinking Psychological Anthropology: Continuity and Change in Human Action. New York: W.H. Freeman and Company.

Blumer, H.
   1969   Symbolic Interactionism. Englewood Cliffs, N.J.: Prentice-Hall, Inc.

Carrithers, M., S. Collins, and S. Lukes, eds.
   1985   The Category of the Person. Cambridge, Eng.: Cambridge University Press.

Carucci, L.M.
1987 The Person as an Individual in the Pacific. Paper presented in the symposium "Cultural Meaning and Self Representation" at the 86th Annual Meeting of the American Anthropological Association, November 18–22, Chicago, III.

Cole, M., and S. Scribner
1974 Culture and Thought: A Psychological Introduction. New York: Wiley.

Cooley, C.H.,
1922, Human Nature and the Social Order. New York: Scribner's.

Crapanzano, V.
1990 On Self Characterization. Pp. 401–23 in Cultural Psychology: Essays on Comparative Human Development (ed. by J.W. Stigler, R.A. Shweder, and G. Herdt). Cambridge, Eng.: Cambridge University Press.

Dieterlen, G., ed.
1973 La notion de la personne en Afrique noire. Paris: CNRS.

Dumont, L.
1970 Homo Hierarchicus. Chicago: University of Chicago Press.

Ewing, K.P.
1990 The Illusion of Wholeness: Culture, Self, and the Experience of Inconsistency. Ethos 18:251–78.

Ewing, K.P.
1991 Can Psychoanalytic Theories Explain the Pakistani Woman? Intrapsychic Autonomy and Interpersonal Engagement in the Extended Family. Ethos 19:131–60.

Fogelson, R.D.
1979 Person, Self, and Identity: Some Anthropological Retrospects, Circumspects, and Prospects. pp. 67–109 in Psychological Theories of the Self (ed. by B. Lee). New York: Plenum Press.

Gaines, A.D.
1984 Cultural Definitions, Behavior, and the Person in American Society. pp. 167–92 in Cultural Conceptions of Mental Health and Therapy (ed. by A.J. Marsella and G.M. White). Dordrecht, Neth.: D. Reidel Publishing Co.

Geertz, C.
1973 Person, Time, and Conduct in Bali. pp. 360–411 in The Interpretation of Cultures (by C. Geertz). New York: Basic Books.

Geertz, C.
1984 From the Native's Point of View: On the Nature of Anthropological Understanding.

Pp. 123–36 in Culture Theory: Essays on Mind, Self, and Emotion (ed. by R.A. Shweder and R.A. LeVine). Cambridge, Eng.: Cambridge University Press.

Gergen, K.J.
1971 The Concept of Self. New York: Holt, Rinehart and Winston, Inc.

Hallowell, A.I.
1955 The Self and Its Behavioral Environment. Pp. 75–110 in Culture and Experience (by A.I. Hallowell). Philadelphia: University of Pennsylvania Press.

Hallowell, A.I.
1959 Behavioral Evolution and the Emergence of the Self. pp. 36–60 in Evolution and Anthropology: A Centennial Appraisal (ed. by B.J. Meggars). Washington, D.C.: Anthropological Society of Washington.

Harris, G.G.
1989 Concepts of Individual, Self, and Person in Description and Analysis. American Anthropologist 91:599–612.

Hay, T.
1977 The Development of Some Aspects of the Ojibwa Self and Its Behavioral Environment. Ethos 5:71–89.

Heelas, P.L.F.
1981 The Model Applied: Anthropology and Indigenous Psychologies. pp. 39–63 in Indigenous Psychologies (ed. by P.L.F. Heelas and A.J. Lock). New York: Academic Press.

Heelas, P.L.F., and A.J. Lock, eds.
1981 Indigenous Psychologies: The Anthropology of Self. New York: Academic Press.

Hollan, D.
1984 "Disruptive" Behavior in a Toraja Community. Ph.D. diss., University of California, San Diego.

Hollan, D.
1988a Pockets Full of Mistakes: The Personal onsequences of Religious Change in a Toraja Village. Oceania 58:275–89.

Hollan, D.
1988b Staying "Cool" in Toraja: Informal Strategies for the Management of Anger and Hostility in a Nonviolent Society. Ethos 16:52–71.

Hollan, D.
1989 The Personal Use of Dream Beliefs in the Toraja Highlands. Ethos 17:166–86.

Hollan, D.
1990 Indignant Suicide in the Pacific: An Example from the Toraja Highlands of

Indonesia. Culture, Medicine, and Psychiatry 14:365–79.

Hollan, D.
1992 Emotion Work and the Value of Emotional Equanimity among the Toraja. Ethnology 31:45–56.

Hollan, D., and J.C. Wellenkamp, n.d. Contentment and Suffering: Culture and Experience in Toraja. Unpub. ms.

Holland, D., and N. Quinn, eds.
1987 Cultural Models in Language and Thought. Cambridge, Eng.: Cambridge University Press.

Howard, A.
1985 Ethnopsychology and the Prospects for a Cultural Psychology. pp. 401–20 in Person, Self, and Experience (ed. by G.M. White and J. Kirkpatrick). Berkeley: University of California Press.

Keeler, W.
1987 Javanese Shadow Plays, Javanese Selves. Princeton, N.J.: Princeton University Press.

Keesing, R.
1982 Prologue: Toward a Multidimensional Understanding of Male Initiation. pp. 2–43 in Rituals of Manhood (ed. by G.H. Herdt). Berkeley: University of California Press.

Keesing, R.
1987 Models, "Folk" and "Cultural": Paradigms Regained? pp. 369–93 in Cultural Models in Language and Thought (ed. by D. Holland and N. Quinn). Cambridge, Eng.: Cambridge University Press.

Kleinman, A.
1986 Social Origins of Distress and Disease: Depression, Neurasthenia, and Pain in Modern China. New Haven, Conn.: Yale University Press.

Kracke, W.
1978 Force and Persuasion: Leadership in an Amazonian Society. Chicago: University of Chicago Press.

Lakoff, G., and M. Johnson
1980 Metaphors We Live By. Chicago: University of Chicago Press.

Lee, B., ed.
1979 Psychosocial Theories of the Self. New York: Plenum Press.

LeVine, R.
1982 Culture, Behavior, and Personality. 2nd ed. Chicago: Aldine.

Levy, R.I.
1973 Tahitians: Mind and Experience in the Society Islands. Chicago: University of Chicago Press.

Levy, R.I.
1984 Emotion, Knowing, and Culture. Pp. 214–37 in Culture Theory (ed. by R.A. Shweder and R.A. LeVine). Cambridge, Eng.: Cambridge University Press.

Levy, R.I., and M.Z. Rosaldo, eds.
1983 Special Issue Devoted to Self and Emotion. Ethos 11(3).

Levy, R.I., and J.C. Wellenkamp
1989 Methodology in the Anthropological Study of Emotion. Pp. 205–32 in Emotion: Theory, Research, and Experience, vol. 4: The Measurement of Emotions (ed. by R. Plutchik and H. Kellerman). New York: Academic Press.

Lock, A.J.
1981 Universals in Human Conception. pp. 19–36 in Indigenous Psychologies (ed. by P.L.F. Heelas and A.J. Lock). New York: Academic Press.

Lutz, C.
1982 The Domain of Emotion Words on Ifaluk. American Ethnologist 9(1):113–28.

Lutz, C.
1985 Ethnopsychology Compared to What? Explaining Behavior and Consciousness among the Ifaluk. pp. 35–79 in Person, Self, and Experience: Exploring Pacific Ethnopsychologies (ed. by G.M. White and J. Kirkpatrick). Berkeley: University of California Press.

Lutz, C.
1987 Goals, Events, and Understanding in Ifaluk Emotion Theory. pp. 290–312 in Cultural Models in Language and Thought (ed. by D. Holland and N. Quinn). Cambridge, Eng.: Cambridge University Press.

McHugh, E.L.
1989 Concepts of the Person among the Gurungs of Nepal. American Ethnologist 16:75–86.

Malinowski, B.
1951 Sex and Repression in Savage Society. New York: Humanities Press.

Marcus, G.E., and M.M.J. Fischer
1986 Anthropology as Cultural Critique: An Experimental Moment in the Human Sciences. Chicago: University of Chicago Press.

Marsella, A.J., G. DeVos, and F.L.K. Hsu, eds.
1985 Culture and Self: Asian and Western Perspectives. New York: Tavistock Publications.

Mauss, M.
1985 A Category of the Human Mind: The Notion of Person; The Notion of Self. pp. 1–25 in The Category of the Person (ed. by M. Carrithers, S. Collins, and S. Lukes). Cambridge, Eng.: Cambridge University Press.

Mead, G.H.
1934 Mind, Self, and Society. Chicago: University of Chicago Press.

Mead, M.
1928 Coming of Age in Samoa. New York: Morrow.

Mines, M.
1988 Conceptualizing the Person: Hierarchical Society and Individual Autonomy in India. American Anthropologist 90:568–79.

Myers, F.
1979 Pintupi Country, Pintupi Self: Sentiment, Place, and Politics among Western Desert Aborigines. Washington, D.C.: Smithsonian Institution Press.

Nooy-Palm, H.
1979 The Sa'dan Toraja: A Study of Their Social Life and Religion, vol. 1: Organization, Symbols, and Beliefs. The Hague: Martinus Nijhoff.

Nooy-Palm, H.
1986 The Sa'dan Toraja: A Study of Their Social Life and Religion, vol. 2: Rituals of the East and West. Dordrecht, Neth.: Foris Publications.

Obeyesekere, G.
1981 Medusa's Hair: An Essay on Personal Symbols and Religious Experience. Chicago: University of Chicago Press.

Rosaldo, M.
1980 Knowledge and Passion: Ilongot Notions of Self and Social Life. Cambridge, Eng.: Cambridge University Press.

Rosaldo, M.
1984 Toward an Anthropology of Self and Feeling. Pp. 137–57 in Culture Theory (ed. by R.A. Shweder and R.A. LeVine). Cambridge, Eng.: Cambridge University Press.

Rosenberger, N.R.
1989 Dialectic Balance in the Polar Model of Self: The Japanese Case. Ethos 17:88–113.

Shore, B.
1982 Sala'ilua: A Samoan Mystery. New York: Columbia University Press.

Shweder, R.A.
1984 Preview: A Colloquy of Cultural Theorists. pp. 1–24 in Culture Theory (ed. by R.A. Shweder and R.A. LeVine). Cambridge, Eng.: Cambridge University Press.

Shweder, R.A., and E.J. Bourne
1984 Does the Concept of the Person Vary Cross-Culturally? pp. 158–99 in Culture Theory (ed. by R.A. Shweder and R.A. LeVine). Cambridge, Eng.: Cambridge University Press.

Shweder, R.A., and R.A. LeVine, eds.
1984 Culture Theory: Essays on Mind, Self, and Emotion. Cambridge, Eng.: Cambridge University Press.

Spiro, M.E.
1965 Religious Systems in Culturally Constituted Defense Mechanisms. pp. 100–13 in Context and Meaning in Anthropology (ed. by M.E. Spiro). New York: The Free Press.

Spiro, M.E.
1978 Burmese Supernaturalism. Expanded ed. Philadelphia: Institute for the Study of Human Issues.

Spiro, M.E.
1984 Some Reflections on Cultural Determinism and Relativism with Special Reference to Emotion and Reason. pp. 323–46 in Culture Theory (ed. by R.A. Shweder and R.A. LeVine). Cambridge, Eng.: Cambridge University Press.

Stephenson, P.H.
1989 Going to McDonald's in Leiden: Reflections on the Concept of Self and Society in the Netherlands. Ethos 17:226–47.

Stigler, J.W., R.A. Shweder, and G. Herdt, eds.
1990 Cultural Psychology: Essays on Comparative Human Development. Cambridge, Eng.: Cambridge University Press.

Vernon, G.
1970 Sociology of Death. New York: Ronald Press.

Volkman, T.
1985 Feasts of Honor: Ritual and Change in the Toraja Highlands. Chicago: University of Illinois Press.

Wellenkamp, J.C.
1984 A Psychocultural Study of Loss and Death among the Toraja. Ph.D. diss., University of California, San Diego.

Wellenkamp, J.C.
1988a Notions of Grief and Catharsis among the Toraja. American Ethnologist 15:486–500.
Wellenkamp, J.C.
1988b Order and Disorder in Toraja Thought and Ritual. Ethology 27:311–26.
Wellenkamp, J.C.
1991 Fallen Leaves: Death and Grieving in Toraja. pp. 113–34 in Coping with the Final Tragedy (ed. by D. Counts and D. Counts). Amityville, NY.: Baywood Publishing Co.
Wellenkamp, J.C.
1992 Variations in the Social and Cultural Organization of Emotions: The Meaning of Crying and the Importance of Compassion in Toraja, Indonesia. Pp. 189–216 in Social Perspectives on Emotion (ed. by D.D. Franks and V. Gecas). Greenwich, Conn.: JAI Press.
Wellenkamp, J.C., and D. Hollan
1981 The Influence of American Concepts of the Self on the Experience of Bereavement. Paper presented at the Kroeber Anthropological Society, Spring 1981, Berkeley, California.
White, G.M., and J. Kirkpatrick, eds.
1985 Person, Self, and Experience: Exploring Pacific Ethnopsychologies. Berkeley: University of California Press.

19

Clinical Paradigm Clashes

Joseph D. Calabrese

This article focuses on a basic question in the study of culture and mental health: what is psychotherapeutic intervention? Is it the modern psychotherapeutic office session in which a client agrees to rationally discuss his or her most private emotions and experiences with a professional stranger in regular office visits? Is effective psychotherapeutic intervention something that was invented by Western European doctors? Is it something owned and regulated by the American Psychological Association? Increasingly, this is the case for clinical psychologists and other practitioners of psychotherapeutic intervention in the United States. Psychotherapeutic intervention is increasingly seen as something that can be standardized, manualized (encoded in the instructions of a "how-to" manual), and regulated. However, this article aims to remind us of an important fact: psychotherapeutic intervention is a basic human activity, and it was a basic human activity long before clinical psychologists and psychotherapeutic office sessions existed. It is not owned by any particular cultural group or professional organization but is a generic activity of humankind. Claims that Freud or whoever else "invented" psychotherapeutic intervention are similar to claims that Columbus "discovered America": they are insulting to members of other cultural traditions who have also "discovered" the phenomenon in question for themselves.

Note here that I am talking about "psychotherapeutic intervention," a broader concept than that referred to by the term *psychotherapy* as usually understood. The term *psychotherapy* is, today, typically used to refer to the tradition of rational talk therapy practiced by professional "psychotherapists." This has not always been the case, even within the European tradition. For example, if one consults historic definitions of *psychotherapy* in the *Oxford English Dictionary*, one finds that early definitions (ca. 1900) were very broad, including mesmerism, hypnotism, and, as Kellogg stated in 1897, "every means and every possible agency which primarily affects the psychical rather than the physical organization of the patient in a curative direction" (Simpson and Weiner 1989). By 1976, definitions were narrower and saturated with particular cultural and theoretical ideologies, such as that of Smythies and Corbett: "Psychotherapy consists very largely in helping people to grow up, to exchange the egocentric child's role for the mature role of the adult" (Simpson and Weiner 1989:771). The typical contemporary definition of *psychotherapy* as rational talk therapy itself reflects the increasing standardization of this activity.

In any case, given that the relevant professional guilds involved have claimed the word *psychotherapy*, in this article I instead use "psychotherapeutic intervention" to refer to

Joseph D. Calabrese, Clinical Paradigm Clashes: Ethnocentric and Political Barriers to Native American Efforts at Self-Healing from *Ethos*, Vol. 36, No. 3, pp. 334–353. © 2008 by the American Anthropological Association. Reprinted with permission of the American Anthropological Association.

the full range of psychological and relational (as opposed to purely biomedical) methods of healing the mind or soul. My aim is to draw attention to the existence and importance of a more inclusive category, referencing all behaviors and meaning structures that support mental health, including not only psychotherapy but also hypnosis, mutual help organizations, support groups, religious or spiritual explanatory systems, faith healing, and the traditional healing rituals of indigenous peoples. I treat psychopharmacology as a separate category here, although I discuss a Native American tradition in which psychopharmacology supports the patient's emplotment in a structure of meaning. I use the word *psychiatry* to refer to a broader category still, encompassing both a given society's psychopharmacological and psychotherapeutic forms of intervention as well as its diagnostic systems and definitions of the normal or healthy.

A corollary of the view that European doctors invented psychotherapeutic intervention is the view that ritual interventions of premodern societies are "precursors" that merely reflect the ignorance of people who still believe in magic rather than science (Frazer 1998). However, effective psychotherapeutic intervention is actually something that exists across a diverse range of human cultures, although its forms differ radically. If psychotherapists and clinical scholars are serious about culturally relevant treatments and multicultural competency, a broader understanding of therapeutic processes and practices is needed. This will involve an increased awareness and questioning of Euro-American ideological and cultural commitments.

In human cultures, including modern Euro-American culture, systems of clinical knowledge and systems of ideological and metaphysical assumptions are not distinct but tend to interrelate and structure one another (Good 1992, 1994; Gone 2004). This is most apparent in the domain of mental health, in which it is often hard to separate behavior that is "healthy" from behavior that is merely in line with social conventions. Systems of psychotherapeutic knowledge typically contain tacit cultural commitments (e.g., to individualism, to rationalism, to what is locally considered "normal" sexuality, to tolerance of only culturally familiar intoxicants and medicines, to the primacy of the male sex, to particular cultural views of childrearing or maturity or healthcare, etc.). Examples of commitments to cultural ideology in Western clinical sciences include the classification (until recently) of homosexuality as a mental illness, the individualist emphasis on intrapsychic causal explanations of distress, and the equally individualist assumption that autonomy or "individuation" is the ultimate goal of development.

The interrelationship of clinical knowledge and cultural ideology is revealed by the fact that, as society changes, psychiatric knowledge changes with it. Consider the cultural values encoded in the third edition of the *Diagnostic and Statistical Manual of Mental Disorders* (*DSM–III*; American Psychiatric Association 1980). The diagnostic criteria for Antisocial Personality Disorder include "repeated sexual intercourse in a casual relationship" (American Psychiatric Association 1980). Whoever wrote this criterion had a cultural value system that identified casual sex as diagnostic of an antisocial personality. But by 1994, repeated sexual intercourse in a casual relationship had become more of a cultural norm than a deviance and, as such, the criterion was dropped from *DSM–IV* (American Psychiatric Association 1994). One wonders how consensual sexual intercourse in a relationship could medically be considered antisocial behavior in the first place, when it is so obviously the opposite. Here we clearly see the influence of moral ideologies on medical diagnosis.

In spite of these historical shifts, many Euro-American clinicians continue to believe that their understandings are culture free. Intelligence tests in particular are interpreted as scientific measures of inherited biological potential or neuropsychiatric integrity. This naive interpretation facilitates the use of these tests in supporting misleading racist and ethnocentric arguments (Hernstein and Murray 1994). As a practicing clinician, I have administered these tests many times. However, I often felt silly asking several of the items on the most widely used IQ test to an immigrant from a non-European country. To my amazement, the subject's IQ score decreases if he or she does not know the author of a particular centuries-old German or English novel. One's "intelligence" decreases if one cannot identify the main theme of a particular chapter of the Judeo-Christian bible, or the meaning of narrowly local colloquial (and outdated) English language expressions, or the distance between a particular large American city and a particular large European city. In addition, the whole activity of completing geometric puzzles as quickly as possible is probably unique to a narrow group of cultures and assumes a particular level of motivation in the subject.

This relatedness of clinical understanding and cultural ideology (including the naive scientific ideology discussed in the previous paragraph) becomes problematic because of the fact of human cultural diversity. The societies of the world do not agree on fundamental issues of personhood, sexuality, health, consciousness alteration, religion, or childrearing. Instead, human societies have developed unique and heterogeneous ways of understanding and adapting to local environments, maintaining relationships among consociates, and sustaining mental health. As such, a society's members are likely to respond more to therapeutic interventions that are appropriate to their unique histories of adaptation.

In this article, I describe differences between modern Euro-American understandings of psychotherapeutic intervention and understandings of psychotherapeutic intervention prevalent in many Native American communities. In particular, I focus on the Navajo communities in which I have done ethnographic field research as well as clinical practice. My contention is that the deep cultural differences between Euro-American and Native American cultures constitute a paradigm clash in which the psychotherapeutic interventions of Native American cultures are not recognized as therapeutic interventions by members of Euro-American cultures but are, rather, seen as mere aesthetic performance, religious tradition, superstitions, even drug abuse or manifestations of mental illness. For this reason, as well as for political reasons involving the hegemony of Euro-American clinical disciplines and culturally favored psychoactive substances (among other factors), Native American and other traditional forms of intervention have not been taken seriously by most Euro-American clinicians or by the U.S. population at large. This lack of cultural awareness has resulted in a situation in which Euro-American interventions may function as forms of cultural proselytization (Gone 2005, this issue) in Native American communities. Among the various ritual interventions used by the Navajos, I pay special attention to one in which the clinical paradigm clash and resulting level of intercultural misunderstanding are especially intense: the Peyote Meeting of the Native American Church (NAC; Calabrese 1994, 1997, 2001).

Field Research

The Navajos or, as they call themselves, the *Diné* (meaning "the People"), are an Athabaskan-speaking people who have a matrilineal clan-based system of descent. The Navajo Nation comprises a large area of semi-arid land in the states of Arizona, New Mexico, and Utah. The ancestors of the Navajos are believed to have migrated to their present territory between the four Sacred Mountains from Alaska and Western Canada in the 15th or 16th century (Kunitz and Levy 1994). The Navajos learned agriculture from their new Pueblo Indian neighbors and, by 1800, sheep herding had become the dominant subsistence activity (Hester 1962). Today, members of the community are engaged in a variety of occupations as a wage-labor economy continues to develop. Other Athabaskan-speaking groups have settled in areas to the south and east of the Navajos and have become the peoples we refer to as the various Apache tribes.

I conducted a total of two years of clinical ethnographic research within the Navajo Nation between 1990 and 1998. During my first summer, I lived with the rural family of an elderly Road Man (as ritual leaders of the NAC are called), herding their 150 sheep and goats in exchange for meals (mostly mutton) and a cot in the hogan (the circular log cabin that is the traditional Navajo dwelling). Subsequent summers were spent increasing my contacts in other communities and building rapport with individuals there. The project culminated in a full year combining fieldwork with a clinical placement at a treatment facility accredited by the Joint Commission on Accreditation of Healthcare Organizations (JCAHO), run by a Navajo Road Man, and administered by the Navajo tribe.[1]

My Navajo fieldwork was stimulated by an interest in traditional healing systems that are especially well preserved among the Navajos as compared to other Native American societies. It was also stimulated by a specific interest in the NAC given the Supreme Court case of *Employment Division of Oregon v. Smith*, 494 U.S. 872 (1990). In their decision in this case, the Supreme Court abandoned the view that the burden of proof rests with the government to demonstrate a compelling interest in denying religious freedom. Members of the NAC were judged to be "guilty of a Class B felony" (see Calabrese 2001).

The Peyote Meeting

The Peyote Meeting of the NAC is among the most misunderstood rituals within the contemporary United States. It has been mischaracterized as everything from an invocation of the Devil to a sexual orgy to "drug use in the guise of religion" (Stewart 1987:17–30, 128–147; see also Aberle 1991:205–223). But the all-night Peyote Meeting is actually a very formal and controlled ritual with a beautiful symbolic structure (see Calabrese 1994). It is also a form of therapeutic intervention that can be analyzed using anthropological and clinical concepts.

The claim that ritual peyote use is a treatment modality will appear controversial to those who have not immersed themselves in Native American clinical contexts and in the lives of those recovering from alcoholism in Native American communities. However, a situation of confusion reflecting a paradigm clash between two cultural traditions of clinical interpretation is suggested by the fact that the same U.S. government that classifies peyote as a Schedule I drug (defined as dangerous and with no therapeutic uses) also classifies the Peyote Meeting as an accepted intervention for substance abuse in Native American communi-

ties. The Peyote Meeting has its own "client service code" on the U.S. Indian Health Service's code list 13. This code list is used for reporting provision of services to the Indian Health Service. The entry for NAC treatment in the IHS document reads as follows:

04: Native American Treatment: Participation in Native American Church Ceremonies (Peyote Church) led by a Road Man, who has been recommended by a local NAC chapter, and conducted primarily for the purpose of treating persons with alcohol and drug problems. This code should not be used for those Native American Church services conducted for general prayer service, birthdays, or other purposes. [Kunitz and Levy 1994:202]

This contradiction within the U.S. federal government structure itself calls for a questioning of the validity of peyote's Schedule I status. In addition, a recent study by Halpern and colleagues (2005), researchers at McLean Hospital-Harvard Medical School, compared mental health and neuropsychological test results of three groups of Navajos: one group of NAC members who regularly use peyote; one group of Navajos with a past alcohol dependence but currently sober at least two months; and one group reporting minimal use of peyote, alcohol, or other substances. Results of this study, which used the Rand Mental Health Inventory (RMHI) and a battery of standard neuropsychological tests, indicated that the peyote group showed no significant differences from the abstinent comparison group on most scales and scored significantly better on two scales of the RMHI. Furthermore, among NAC members, greater lifetime peyote use was associated with significantly better RMHI scores on five of the nine scales including the composite Mental Health Index.

Peyote Meetings are called for the purpose of healing a patient ("doctoring meetings") as well as for expressing thanks and for supporting continued health ("appreciation meetings"). The Peyote Meeting takes place in a circular enclosure, usually a tipi but sometimes a hogan open to the east. Inside the enclosure, a crescent mound of earth is constructed and a line drawn along the top to represent the "Peyote Road."

Participants enter the tipi at sundown. The Road Man places an especially fine peyote cactus, most often called "Mother Peyote" or "Father Peyote," on top of the moon altar. Peyotists are taught to maintain focus on this peyote, sending their prayers through it. After an opening prayer, which states the purpose of the meeting, peyote is passed around and drumming and singing of peyote songs begins. The ritual continues until dawn of the following day, when there is a ceremonial breakfast of corn, meat, fruit, and water, and the participants go outside to greet the sun. Healing experiences reported after these rituals include impressive visions interpreted as divine messages or warnings, important new insights about one's life, feelings of rejuvenation or holiness, and desires to transform one's behavior (Aberle 1991; Calabrese 1994).

I argue that the ritual process of the Peyote Meeting involves a dialectical relationship between two practices often encountered in cultural psychiatries: therapeutic emplotment and consciousness modification. The term *emplotment* concisely captures the ritual-based symbolic or rhetorical approach to shaping consciousness studied by anthropologists and often referred to as "symbolic healing" (Dow 1986) or "the effectiveness of symbols" (Lévi-Strauss 1963). Emplotment is a familiar term both in narrative studies and in medical anthropology (Ricoeur 1984; Good 1994:144; Obeyesekere 1990:267). *Therapeutic emplotment*, as defined in this article, refers to interpretive activity or application of a preformed cultural narrative placing events into a story that is therapeutic, either in that it supports expectations of a positive outcome, makes illness or treatment comprehensible, discourages unhealthy behaviors, or otherwise supports health. In the Peyote Meeting, emplotment of the patient in a therapeutic narrative structure is aided by a technique of consciousness modification. The term *consciousness modification* refers to any cultural technology used to alter the consciousness state of self or others. This includes pharmacological techniques and behavioral techniques such as fasting, ritual ordeals, or prolonged dancing.

A dialectic between a structure of meaning (e.g., a myth) and a technology of consciousness modification is found in many initiation rites and healing ceremonies in which society has an important message to "implant" in the mind of the individual. In initiation rites, these messages focus on a change of one's social status and the rights and responsibilities that go with it, for example "you are now an adult" or "you are a warrior" (see Herdt 1987; Turner 1967; Van Gennep 1960). Secret or otherwise vital teaching is often presented after an exhausting ritual ordeal or after ingestion of a psychoactive substance. Healing ceremonies aim for a change in the health status of the person and are typically characterized by transformation symbolism and messages such as "you are healed." The consciousness modification technology in such rituals makes the mind more malleable – in other words, more open to social messages – by altering the individual's attention and suggestibility. This is an effect noted for various hypnotic induction methods as well as for certain psychoactive substances and painful or exhausting ritual ordeals (Grob and Dobkin de Rios 1994; Sjoberg and Hollister 1965).

The ritual symbolism of the Peyote Meeting depicts the human self or life course in the arc of the crescent moon altar and symbolically embeds this depiction of the self in natural transformative processes of gestation, birth, and the dawning of a new day. The message is one of a natural transformation and renewal of the self to facilitate the goal of living harmoniously into old age. This is an emotionally potent message for Navajo Peyotists and its form somewhat resembles the central mystical formula of the traditional Navajo religion, *Sa'ah naghái bik'eh bózhó*. This Navajo phrase is not easily translated but it conveys the sense of a beautiful, harmonious condition arising out of the natural completion of the human life course in old age (see Witherspoon 1974).[2]

Ten Areas of Cultural Difference Contributing to the Paradigm Clash

In what follows, I will highlight various areas of cultural difference in basic approaches to psychotherapeutic intervention that contribute to the paradigm clash between Euro-American and Native American interventions. These distinctions are listed with particular Native American contexts in mind, specifically the Navajo communities in which I lived and worked. However, these areas of cultural psychiatric difference would also be applicable to many other cultural contexts in which ideological and clinical assumptions differ from those of contemporary European and Euro-American cultures.

1 Individualist dyad versus communal group process

The most typical contrast drawn between modern Euro-American cultures and many non-European cultures is that between an individualist ideology and more communal or collectivist ideologies (e.g., Shweder and Bourne 1984). The distinction is often overemphasized, as any society has its own individualist elements and modern Euro-American culture has its own communalist elements. However, this difference in cultural emphasis is helpful for understanding differences in therapeutic systems. When one thinks of psychotherapeutic intervention, what typically comes to mind in the Euro-American context is the therapeutic dyad: a patient (often reclining on a couch) and a therapist (often taking notes or calmly probing with questions). The model is that of a conversation or cooperative relationship. Working with the adolescent clients I treated on the Navajo reservation convinced me that individual therapy sessions were not very useful. Clients were typically unwilling to adopt the role of a cooperative therapy patient. My identity as a Euro-American undoubtedly played a role. However, I had much more success in my group therapy sessions and with milieu interventions.

A cursory glance at the ethnographic literature reveals that the calm, rational discussions characteristic of Euro-American talk therapy are not the approaches to healing used by the majority of human societies (e.g., see Dobkin de Rios 1972; Katz 1982; Kennedy 1967; Lévi-Strauss 1963).[3] Anthropological research reveals the centrality of ritual approaches to healing in many cultures outside the industrialized West. In these traditions, a technique of emplotment of the patient in ritual symbols, songs, and myths is typical, often in connection with a technique of consciousness modification. Ecstatic emotions and liminal symbolism predominate. From one perspective, Euro-American talk therapy may be seen as more decentered from a particular cultural tradition than these ritual forms (being more secular and cosmopolitan and less explicitly based in cultural myths). But talk therapy can also be considered a very modernist, Euro-American enterprise in that it tends to limit itself to calm, rational argumentation within individual-to-individual relationships and discussions. This second perspective characterizes Euro-American talk therapy as following its own deeply ingrained cultural templates.

Psychotherapeutic process, for most psychotherapy researchers, refers to elements of verbal interaction and interpersonal relationship between a therapist and a client in one-to-one settings. However, psychotherapeutic intervention in many cultural traditions is not a dyadic conversation but rather a dramatic communal ritual. Rather than being excluded from the dyad for reasons of privacy, a patient's significant others are present and participating. Victor Turner even argued that among the Ndembu of Zambia healing was actually aimed at the group rather than the individual. Turner writes that "the patient will not get better until all the tensions and aggressions in the group's interrelations have been brought to light" (1967:392). This is also true to some extent for the NAC rituals that I have studied in that healing is not limited to the patient but is also aimed at relationships and is ultimately available to anyone attending the ritual. This is similar to some of the ideas of family systems and group therapy approaches to psychotherapeutic intervention in the Euro-American tradition, although the central paradigm of psychotherapy remains the individualist dyadic one.

2 The role of the healer

Another difference between Navajo and Euro-American psychotherapeutic healing approaches has to do with the role of the healer. Many Western theories of psychotherapeutic efficacy focus on personal properties of the therapist. The most familiar example is probably Carl Rogers's (1995) emphasis on the therapist's empathy, warmth, and genuineness. Even anthropological theories of therapeutic process such as the influential theory of James Dow (1986) are healer-centered. In Dow's model, (1) the experiences of healers and healed are generalized with culture-specific symbols in cultural myth, (2) a suffering patient comes to a healer who persuades the patient that the problem can be defined in terms of the myth, (3) the healer attaches the patient's emotions to transactional symbols particularized from the general myth, and (4) the healer manipulates the transactional symbols to help the patient transact his or her own emotions. Note that the healer is central to each of these stages.

However, Dow's model may still be too tied to Euro-American psychotherapeutic assumptions to be applicable across cultures. This is because, in many healing traditions, the healer's role is less central. For example, in the Peyote Meeting, the Road Man's role seems less important than the nature of the milieu that he manages. He is a role model, leads the ceremony, prays for the patient with the other participants, and may administer specially blessed medicine to the patient. But there is little direct verbal interaction. It is often said that the patient is responsible for his or her own healing, that one does the ceremony for or on oneself, or that the real healer is the Peyote spirit present in the sacramental medicine. The most important therapeutic communications are often those that come to the patient not from the healer but directly from God or the Peyote spirit in the form of visions or other sacred experiences.

Western mainstream psychotherapy research approaches tend to have little to say about such experiences. In the Peyote Meeting, it seems that therapeutic messages are implicit in the symbolism of the ritual and have already been "implanted" in the mind of the patient through socialization. The healing ceremony "activates" these messages in an impressive way that, in combination with other ritual alterations of consciousness and the supportive presence of the community, may lead to cognitive and behavioral change in the patient.

3 The expectation of calm self-disclosure to a professional stranger

One critique of scientist approaches to psychological assessment and intervention is that they too often take the client's motivation for granted (the motivational interviewing approach of Miller and Rollnick 1991 is a notable exception). Just as neuropsychological testing assumes that the client is motivated to construct puzzles as quickly as possible (which they often are not), psychotherapy often assumes that the client is willing to disclose and rationally discuss his or her deepest emotions to a professional stranger in therapy sessions.[4] However, this sort of disclosure seems specific to Euro-American psychotherapy. Some Native American healing rituals, such as the sweat lodge or Peyote Meeting, involve expression of emotion but this expression occurs in an emotionally charged group context involving a supportive gathering of family and friends. Other rituals, such as the traditional Navajo healing ceremonies called "sings," do not focus on disclosure or emotional expression.

As a clinician working on the Navajo Reservation with Native American adolescents who had very severe problems with alcoholism and substance abuse, I found that individual therapy sessions and Alcoholics Anonymous were not appealing to the majority of these young people. However, most had some interest in Native American ceremonies, and it was standard practice for me to attend a weekly sweat lodge ritual with my patients. Self-disclosure in the sweat lodge was not a personal choice but a spiritual duty, and a lot of useful clinical information was made available that could be discussed later in an individual session or in milieu interactions. Clinically relevant information derving from these rituals was summarized in a therapy note added to the patient's chart.

4 The time factor

This brings to mind another difference in approach: the temporal duration of the intervention. In the Euro-American situation, patients (or outpatients, at least) tend to be straightjacketed into the professional office hour. They are assumed to be ready to self-disclose within this period of time and it is assumed that their problems can be addressed effectively (at least for the current session) within an hour. This contrasts strongly with Native American forms of intervention that seem, in some cases at least, more realistic. In the Navajo context, for example in the sweat lodge or Peyote Meeting, six or seven hours of ritual ordeal may elapse before the patient is ready to disclose or express feelings. The duration of traditional Navajo healing rituals may extend to five or even nine nights. From a comparative perspective, this is a huge dose of psychotherapeutic intervention.

Secular versus spiritual intervention

This brings us to another aspect of difference between modern and traditional forms of psychotherapeutic intervention that may result in misunderstandings reflecting paradigm clash: secular intervention versus spiritual intervention. When one begins to study psychotherapeutic intervention across cultures, one is immediately led into the study of religious or spiritual systems. Likewise, when one begins to study comparative religion, one finds that the religious leader – the shaman – is also frequently the psychiatric and psychotherapeutic practitioner. A separation of these two roles only occurred late in social divisions of labor, and in many societies did not occur at all.

A particularly vexing question for psychotherapists and psychotherapy researchers alike is the role of spiritual or supernatural beings. Modern secular clinical approaches tend to see talk of spiritual beings as diagnostic of psychotic disorder. However, for most of human history, spiritual beings have been an intimate part of how people healed. This heritage continues in many traditions that were never secularized. Within the NAC tradition I have studied, peyote is believed to facilitate a direct communication with divinity and this sort of ritual experience can be the foundation stone on which a recovery process is built.

I have done research on the role of the Peyote spirit in child development, specifically superego formation and parental control of children (Calabrese 1997, 2006). Children are taught that Peyote is an omniscient being that knows "if you are good or bad." The fact that one's visions, which are typically interpreted as divine communications, contain material from one's most intimate thoughts, guilt feelings, or memories experientially confirms Peyote's omniscience. Peyotist children told me that Peyote comes to "know who you are." One child told me that the Father Peyote "knows if you have smoked or drunk." Peyote is referred to as "Mother Peyote" or "Father Peyote" and it acts as a sort of parental figure, enforcing moral prohibitions (esp. against alcohol consumption) when parents are not present. Because it is seen as an omniscient spirit, it is believed that Peyote knows when children are misbehaving (e.g., drinking or using drugs of abuse) no matter where they are.

According to the anthropologist Paul Radin, "If a person eats Peyote and does not repent openly, he has a guilty conscience, which leaves him as soon as the public repentance has been made.... If a Peyote-user relapses into his old way of living, then the Peyote causes him great suffering" (1914:5–6). Peyote is thus experienced as a spiritual entity, a relationship is established, and the omniscient gaze of the morally evaluative divinity becomes present in the subjectivity of the worshipper, facilitating social control. So we can see peyote as helping in the creation of the "panoptical gaze," a system of social control as Michel Foucault (1979) wrote about it, or, to be more psychological, a culturally structured superego or conscience. This is just one of the aspects of spirituality in the NAC that can be considered therapeutically and developmentally useful.

Change as rational decision versus ecstatic experience or hypnotic suggestion

There is another contrast concerning the mechanism of therapeutic change. The dyadic model of rational discussion of one's problems tends to imply a model of change as a rational decision. Thus, Western therapists engage in "collaborative empiricism" and may use "cost – benefit analysis" and other rational methods to help patients achieve insight into their problems. Here I just want to point out that in more traditional approaches, therapeutic change may involve ecstatic emotions, visions, conversion experiences, feelings of religious significance, relationships with divinities, and various forms of suggestion.

With the cases I worked with on the Navajo reservation, where substance abuse problems were often very severe, standard rational approaches were not very useful. In many cases, a radical transformation involving a shift in consciousness, and often a shift toward spiritual life, seemed the only way to interrupt dangerous behaviors and initiate change. This sort of shift was facilitated by ritual interventions. In addition, these rituals could also provide an ongoing aftercare program in areas of the reservation where there were no twelve-step meetings.

Individualized narratives versus preformed narratives

This leads to another difference between Navajo and classically Western approaches to psychotherapeutic intervention: whether therapeutic narrative structures are collaboratively constructed in an ongoing therapeutic conversation and individualized for a specific patient or preformed by cultural tradition (as in ritual symbolism or sacred songs). A good modern psychotherapist is most often nondirective. He or she tends to elicit and work with the significant narratives of the patient or at least works collaboratively to fashion a unique therapeutic story that is carefully tailored to the individual patient's life history. In contrast, traditional healing more often embeds the patient in preformed narrative structures that are implicit in myths and ritual symbolism. I think of this in terms of the "laying on of narratives." A vivid example of this occurs in traditional Navajo sings, in which a sand painting depicting a particular myth is created and the patient is literally placed on top of this narrative-laden mythic depiction. Some common therapeutic plot structures of this sort include death and rebirth as in the symbolism of the Peyote

Meeting (Calabrese 1994), a journey to retrieve a lost soul, sucking out of a malevolent object (or similar purifying rituals), a historic victory over evil, ingestion of a medicinal or magical substance, and the rite of passage. When these therapeutic plot structures help form basic cultural structures (e.g., Christ's death and rebirth in Christianity), I refer to this as "culturally embedded therapeutic emplotment," in which an enculturated person is always emplotted.

An intermediate category between individualized and preformed narratives involves stereotypical formulas for ritualistically telling one's own story according to a predetermined cultural pattern. These also facilitate therapeutic emplotment. Consider the personal narratives ritualistically repeated by members of Alcoholics Anonymous and other self-help groups: "Hi. I'm Bob and I'm an alcoholic" (after which the crowd says "Hi Bob" and Bob launches into a description of his disease and then moves to a description of his recovery). This ritual performance resembles the common death–rebirth narrative structure. The actively drinking self is shifted into the past tense (and, thus, rhetorically nullified) and the narrative of a recovered Bob is fashioned in the present tense (a revised self). Those who have converted to the NAC or have had a life-changing vision tell similarly structured stories, as do "Born Again Christians," "GROWers" (Corrigan et al. 2002), and others. This situation may be considered a hybrid of therapeutic self-emplotment and culturally embedded therapeutic emplotment: the actual narrative is constructed by the individual but it follows a preformed cultural template very closely. This approach is not characteristic of psychotherapy, which suggests that Alcoholics Anonymous and other mutual help organizations are, in some ways, closer in structure to traditional healing than to modern clinical services.

Psychotherapeutic intervention as remedial–stigmatized versus preventative–valorized

In the Western mode, psychotherapeutic intervention tends to be remedial and stigmatized. Most Euro-Americans do not see a therapist unless something is wrong and even then, going to see a therapist may be seen as a personal failure. This relates to the stigma generally associated with mental illness in U.S. society (Corrigan and Calabrese 2005; Link and Phelan 2001). The ideological roots of the Euro-American view in this case may be the optimistic view of normality or mental health as a biological given rather than a social or personal construction, which in turn accounts for the view of all psychiatric problems as invading disease entities rather than possibly being problems intrinsic to the human condition (see Calabrese 1997:251–252). In contrast, for Navajo members of the NAC and in many other Native American healing practices, psychotherapeutic intervention is seen as preventative and growth-oriented as well as remedial. Stigma connected with ritual treatment is not as apparent. In fact, the person who actively seeks psychological harmony through ritual is valorized rather than stigmatized.

Dualist separation of meaning-centered and pharmacological interventions versus integration

The example of the Peyote Meeting also illustrates another difference: that between the Cartesian mind–body split typically underlying modern clinical approaches and the treatment of the whole individual in many Native American community based approaches. The biomedical clinical approach involves a dualist separation of mind and body and a division of clinical labor that separates psychopharmacological intervention from meaning-centered intervention. A dialectic between emplotment and consciousness modification lies at the heart of many cultural psychiatries, including Euro-American psychiatry and Navajo Peyotist psychiatry. However, given a dualist philosophical base, the psychotherapeutic and psychopharmacological interventions in the Euro-American system tend to be institutionally separated (into clinical psychology vs. psychiatry) rather than integrated. This tends to mask their interaction at the level of the lived experience of patients.

A dialectical relationship between mind and body, emplotment and consciousness modifi-

cation is more apparent in Navajo Peyotist cultural psychiatry, in which emplotment and consciousness modification occur simultaneously and work together as parts of the same ritual intervention. Psychopharmacology is employed to achieve insight as well as emplotment in a socially desired and health-facilitating narrative of transformation and relationship with Peyote (psychedelic substances are known to alter suggestibility as well as insight). In contrast, Euro-American psychotherapies (aside from hypnosis, which itself is dyadic and talk-based) tend to eschew radical modifications of consciousness and rely on rational discussions.

Psychopharmacology in the Euro-American context aims at correcting a malfunctioning biochemical mechanism, whereas psychopharmacology in the NAC aims at interrupting the addiction process, reawakening spirituality, supporting emplotment, and facilitating the patient's insight. Psychopharmacological intervention to facilitate radical shifts in perspective, therapeutic emplotment, or insight is not standard in Euro-American psychiatry. We may call the NAC's approach a semiotic–reflexive paradigm of psychopharmacology in contrast to the rather limited agonist–antagonist (materialist) paradigm of Euro-American psychiatry, which focuses on fixing discrete neurochemical imbalances at the molecular level. In the absence of serious research on both traditions, it is not acceptable to assume that the molecule-focused Euro-American psychiatric paradigm is the only valid approach and that the higher order semiotic–reflexive paradigm is ignorant or mistaken. The safest assumption is that this is a psychopharmacological paradigm clash and, thus, interesting for cross-cultural research.

Clashing psychopharmacologies: synthetic–processed versus natural plant forms

Dominant Euro-American norms limit psychoactive substance use to only a few culturally familiar substances: mass-produced tobacco products, alcohol, caffeine, and various approved psychiatric medications. Another U.S.

cultural norm is abstinence from consciousness-altering substances often denounced in moral terms as "evil" or "sinful." Clinical psychopharmacology is limited to the exclusive use of lab-created psychological medicines that are profitable for drug companies and that are rationalized scientifically (although they often have significant negative side effects of their own). The psychoactive plant medicines of other societies have been labeled in classic Western biomedicine as drugs of abuse or are assumed to be inferior to lab-created medicines, ensuring the hegemony of the Euro-American cultural norms and the incomes of drug companies. However, members of the NAC and many other Native Americans and other cultural minorities continue to trust their sacred plant medicines precisely because they are culturally familiar products of the natural environment rather than inventions of the Euro-American scientist.[5]

Conclusion

The paradigm clash between Euro-American and Navajo Peyotist traditions of psychotherapeutic intervention is profound and multifaceted. The generative sources of these contradictions are differences in basic cultural orientations to epistemology, the person in social context, the role of spirituality in healing, and the separation or integration of mind and body. These differences derive from particular social histories and adaptations over time to unique local contexts. The analysis presented here illustrates the complex relationship of clinical understanding and cultural ideology and contributes to critiques of biomedical hegemony and the view that the cultural Other holds culturally determined and often erroneous "beliefs" whereas medical science provides "straightforward, objective depictions of the natural order" (Good 1994:22).

This article contributes to a psychiatric anthropology of therapeutic process and therapeutic response through a detailed consideration of the therapeutic event from the perspectives of Navajo Peyotist and Euro-American cultures. This analysis demonstrates the diversity of cultural paradigms of psycho-

therapeutic intervention and the close fit of cultural formations and therapeutic practice in each context. Many studies of therapeutic process across cultures search for "common factors" in psychotherapy (e.g., Frank and Frank 1993), possibly following the assumptions of the psychic unity doctrine (Stocking 1982:115–123). My analysis suggests that healing traditions may approach intervention using structurally dissimilar and philosophically opposed rather than common factors. We need to study "uncommon factors" in therapeutic intervention, those that are unique to particular cultural traditions or groups of traditions.

Euro-American psychotherapy derives from a cultural orientation that can be described as individualist, positivist, rationalist, secular, and mind – body dualist. It emphasizes the dyadic (one-to-one) healer–patient relationship within a positivist approach that emphasizes the single patient as a source of data to be collected in isolation from the patient's social contexts, sequestered within a private office and within the one-hour time slot. Therapeutic change is typically characterized as a rational decision arrived at through cost-benefit analysis or weighing of evidence. There is an expectation of calm self-disclosure and rational discussion of one's deepest emotions to a professional stranger in hour-long therapy sessions in which an individualized health-facilitating narrative is collaboratively constructed by therapist and patient. A form of mind–body dualism is revealed in the Euro-American approach to psychopharmacology. Euro-American culture has divided into separate clinical disciplines the psychopharmacological approaches to mental health intervention (psychiatry) and the semiotic and behavioral approaches (clinical psychology). The interventions in each of these disciplines have become increasingly polarized and autonomous.

In contrast, Native American traditions of intervention and especially the practices of Navajo members the NAC tend to be communal, focused on experiences rather than reasoning and conversation, and embedded in a system of spiritual understandings and practices. Healing may involve ecstatic experiences or hypnotic suggestions forged in a symbolically structured ritual context that may extend for many hours or days (unlike the rather limited psychotherapeutic office hour). This process involves an integrated understanding of mind and body and a more meaningfully integrated approach to psychopharmacology. Although Euro-American psychopharmacological intervention has followed a very materialist agonist–antagonist paradigm, paying the bulk of its attention to effects at the molecular level, psychopharmacological intervention in Native American rituals like the Peyote Meeting tends to follow what may be called a semiotic – reflexive paradigm. This approach emphasizes the ability of certain psychoactive plants (working in close coordination with structures of meaning and behavior) to facilitate therapeutic emplotment, meaningful emotional experiences, and insight. Rather than being institutionally separated, psychopharmacology and meaning are aspects of the same intervention. Use of psychoactive medicines is aimed at higher-order mental processes and transformative experiences rather than micromanagement of a person's mood state and level of arousal.

Cheryl Mattingly (1994) and Mary-Jo DelVecchio Good and colleagues (1994) have provided sophisticated anthropological analyses of the collaborative creation and negotiation of plot structures by Euro-American clinician and patient dyads. The study presented here begins to consider how different this process may be in cultural psychiatric contexts that are less dyadic, in which therapeutic plot structures are more fixed by cultural tradition, and in which the presence of a healer may not even be necessary for a therapeutic process to occur. Such an expanded approach to therapeutic emplotment would encompass collective cultural processes in which therapeutic structures are built into shared meaning systems that continually emplot individuals and groups and that are activated by ritual.

The analysis presented here suggests that future research on psychotherapeutic intervention in diverse cultural contexts or with minority communities within multicultural democracies should do more to take such fundamental differences into account. It is vital that Euro-Americans become more aware of the particular cultural orientations that help form modern clinical disciplines. Without an understanding of such contrasts, researchers and policy makers may succumb to the paradigm clash and judge the healing modalities of other cultures to be ineffective superstitions, pathological drug use, or mere cultural performances. In the realm of clinical services, therapeutic interventions that have evolved over centuries and are uniquely compatible with local cultural orientations and expectations may be replaced by Euro-American interventions of questionable compatibility or therapeutic value but with considerable colonizing power.

There is a growing debate in the clinical disciplines about pluralism in the context of the increasing standardization of psychotherapeutic intervention (e.g., see Chambless and Ollendick 2001; Elliott 1998; Henry 1998; Silverman 1996; Westen et al. 2004). Much of this debate centers on the so-called "empirically validated treatments" (American Psychological Association Division of Clinical Psychology 1995). It is often assumed that if a particular treatment has some empirical support, then it should work for anyone. This ignores the issue of cultural and individual differences in what works therapeutically. Because patients are not homogeneous, neither should psychotherapeutic intervention be reduced to a "one size fits all" therapy manual. Human diversity includes deep cultural psychiatric differences, often requiring therapeutic pluralism rather than standardization of treatment options.

In conclusion, dealing with cultural issues is often intimidating for Western clinicians trained to rely on implicit and unexplored cultural values or for Navajo of the NAC whose healing practices similarly rely on cultural presuppositions seldom explicitly reflected on. In fact, any traditional practice can be considered vital and necessary by the people who perform it. Faced with a diversity of claims, each nation fashions its own balance of pluralistic tolerance and forced assimilation. However, a special ethical issue is raised by traditional practices that can be shown to support health or effective socialization for members of the social group in question. My year of clinical experience working with Native American clients has convinced me that, for many Native

Americans and especially the Navajo of the NAC, Euro-American psychotherapeutic interventions are often irrelevant and useless, if not harmful. The data, including the reports of Aberle and many other ethnographers, the Indian Health Service coding of the NAC ritual as a reimbursable therapy, the study by Halpern and colleagues (2005), and my own relationships with many Navajos who recovered from alcoholism using the NAC, suggest that the NAC's ritual intervention is safe and successful in fostering abuse-free lifestyles in Native American clients. Yet paradigm clashes associated with this tradition have resulted in the Supreme Court's decision that the practice can be prosecuted as a "Class B felony."

An attack on non-Western community based approaches to intervention that can be shown to work in favor of classic Western techniques that do not work amounts to an attack on the very mental stability of Navajo and other Native American individuals and families. This sort of psychiatric imperialism is not the role of clinicians and clinical researchers. Instead, the full range of human psychotherapeutic interventions requires critical study. Therapeutic practitioners need to work to support all peoples in their efforts at self-healing.

NOTES

1 This project was established under the guidance of the leadership of the Four Corners Chapter of the NAC and with the permission of the clinical facility mentioned based on a vote of its Board. IRB approval was obtained from the Social and Behavioral Sciences Institutional Review Board at the University of Chicago. This project was initiated years before the Navajo IRB came into existence and overlapped minimally beyond its establishment. The author is seeking retroactive approval of the project from the Navajo IRB. However, the present publication is a reflection on data already published elsewhere as permitted by the Four Corners Chapter of the NAC and the clinical facility (Calabrese 1994, 1997, 2001).
2 This comparison raises the question of the relationship between the NAC and the older religious traditions among the Navajos.

Although this similarity in symbolism may resonate in syncretic ways for some Navajos, it must be emphasized that the NAC and traditional Navajo religion are distinct traditions. The NAC derived from Plains traditions that were considered unwelcome foreign influences by many Navajos and Navajo NAC members faced intense opposition from traditionalist and Christian members of the tribe. In fact, I interviewed Navajo NAC members who had been jailed by their own tribe for practicing this religion.
3 It should be pointed out here that the ethnographic literature also contains a few accounts (e.g., Edgerton 1971) of traditional healers who take a more empirical, quasi-scientific approach to healing even within cultures that emphasize witchcraft or ritual impurity in their understandings of illness. There are also, of course, dyadic therapeutic encounters that take place within traditional healing contexts. I am discussing a paradigmatic approach in a particular tradition that has been targeted by the U.S. Supreme Court as illegal rather than exploring the full range of Navajo or Native American healing practices.
4 Of course, sensitive psychotherapists may have a talent for reading beneath the patient's words, going beyond the explicit content of the communication.
5 The herbal industry may be considered a sort of middle ground between the two.

REFERENCES

Aberle, David F.
  1991[1966] The Peyote Religion Among the Navajo. Chicago: University of Chicago Press.
American Psychiatric Association
  1980 Diagnostic and Statistical Manual of Mental Disorders, 3rd edition. Washington, DC: American Psychiatric Association.
American Psychiatric Association
  1994 Diagnostic and Statistical Manual of Mental Disorders, 4th edition. Washington, DC: American Psychiatric Association.
American Psychological Association Division of Clinical Psychology
  1995 Training in and Dissemination of Empirically-Validated Psychological Treatments: Report and Recommendations. The Clinical Psychologist 48: 3–27.

Calabrese, Joseph D.
1994 Reflexivity and Transformation Symbolism in the Navajo Peyote Meeting. Ethos 22(4): 494–527.
1997 Spiritual Healing and Human Development in the Native American Church: Toward a Cultural Psychiatry of Peyote. Psychoanalytic Review 84(2): 237–255.
2001 The Supreme Court versus Peyote: Consciousness Alteration, Cultural Psychiatry and the Dilemma of Contemporary Subcultures. The Anthropology of Consciousness 12(2):4–19.
2006 Mirror of the Soul: Cultural Psychiatry, Moral Socialization and the Development of the Self in the Native American Church. Ph.D. dissertation, Committee on Human Development, the University of Chicago.

Chambless, Dianne L., and Thomas H. Ollendick
2001 Empirically Supported Psychological Interventions: Controversies and Evidence. Annual Review of Psychology 52: 685–716.

Corrigan, Patrick W., and Joseph D. Calabrese
2005 Strategies for Assessing and Diminishing Self-Stigma. In On the Stigma of Mental Illness: Practical Strategies for Research and Social Change. P. Corrigan, ed. Washington, DC: American Psychological Association.

Corrigan, Patrick W., Joseph D. Calabrese, Sarah E. Diwan, Cornelius B. Keogh, Lorraine Keck, and Carol Mussey
2002 Some Recovery Processes in Mutual-Help Groups for Persons with Mental Illness I: Qualitative Analysis of Program Materials and Testimonies. Community Mental Health Journal 38(4): 287–301.

Dobkin de Rios, Marlene
1972 Visionary Vine: Hallucinogenic Healing in the Peruvian Amazon. Prospect Heights, IL: Waveland Press.

Dow, James
1986 Universal Aspects of Symbolic Healing: A Theoretical Synthesis. American Anthropologist 88(1): 56–69.

Edgerton, Robert
1971 A Traditional African Psychiatrist. Southwestern Journal of Anthropology 27(3): 259–278.

Elliott, Robert
1998 Editor's Introduction: A Guide to the Empirically Supported Treatments Controversy. Psychotherapy Research 8(2): 115–125.

Foucault, Michel
1979 Discipline and Punish. New York: Vintage Books.

Frank, Jerome D., and Julia B. Frank
1993 Persuasion and Healing: A Comparative Study of Psychotherapy. Baltimore: Johns Hopkins University Press.

Frazer, James George
1998[1890] The Golden Bough: A Study in Magic and Religion. Oxford: Oxford University Press.

Gone, Joseph P.
2004 Mental Health Services for Native Americans in the 21st Century United States. Professional Psychology: Research and Practice 35(1): 10–18.
2005 "This life you gave me, and the power to heal and cure": Ethnotherapeutics among the Gros Ventre. Paper presented at the 36th Annual Meeting of the Society for Psychotherapy Research, Montreal, Quebec, June 22–25

Good, Byron J.
1992 Culture and Psychopathology: Directions for Psychiatric Anthropology. In New Directions in Psychological Anthropology. T. Schwartz, G. White, and C. Lutz, eds. Pp. 181–205. Cambridge: Cambridge University Press.
1994 Medicine, Rationality and Experience: An Anthropological Perspective. Cambridge: Cambridge University Press.

Good, Mary-Jo DelVecchio, Tseunetsugu Munakata, Yasuki Kobayashi, Cheryl Mattingly, and Byron J. Good
1994 Oncology and Narrative Time. Social Science & Medicine 38(6): 855–862.

Grob, Charles S., and Marlene Dobkin de Rios
1994 Hallucinogens, Managed States of Consciousness, and Adolescents: Cross-Cultural Perspectives. In Psychological Anthropology. P. K. Bock, ed. Westport, Connecticut: Praeger.

Halpern, John H., Andrea R. Sherwood, James I. Hudson, Deborah Yurgelun-Todd, and Harrison G. Pope Jr.
2005 Psychological and Cognitive Effects of Long-Term Peyote Use among Native Americans. Biological Psychiatry 58: 624–631.

Henry, William P.
1998 Science, Politics, and the Politics of Science: The Use and Misuse of Empirically Validated Treatments. Psychotherapy Research 8(2): 126–140.

Herdt, Gilbert
1987 The Sambia: Ritual and Gender in New Guinea. New York: Holt, Rinehart and Winston.

Hernstein, Richard J., and Murray Charles
1994 The Bell Curve: Intelligence and Class Structure in American Life. New York: Free Press.

Hester, James J.
1962 Early Navajo Migrations and Acculturation in the Southwest. Papers in Anthropology No. 6 Santa Fe: Museum of New Mexico.

Katz, Richard
1982 Boiling Energy: Community Healing among the Kalahari Kung. Cambridge, MA: Harvard University Press.

Kennedy, John G.
1967 Nubian Zar Ceremonies as Psychotherapy. Human Organization 26(4): 185–194.

Kunitz, Stephen J., and Jerrold E. Levy
1994 Drinking Careers: A Twenty-Five Year Study of Three Navajo Populations. New Haven: Yale University Press.

Lévi-Strauss, Claude
1963 The Effectiveness of Symbols. In Structural Anthropology. Pp. 186–205. New York: Basic Books.

Link, Bruce G., and Jo C. Phelan
2001 Conceptualizing Stigma. Annual Review of Sociology 27: 363–385.

Mattingly, Cheryl
1994 The Concept of Therapeutic Emplotment. Social Science & Medicine 38(6): 811–822.

Miller, William R., and Stephen Rollnick
1991 Motivational Interviewing: Preparing People to Change Addictive Behavior. New York: Guilford Press.

Obeyesekere, Gananath
1990 The Work of Culture: Symbolic Transformation in Psychoanalysis and Anthropology. Chicago: University of Chicago Press.

Radin, Paul
1914 A Sketch of the Peyote Cult of the Winnebago: A Study in Borrowing. Journal of Religious Psychology 7(1): 1–22.

Ricoeur, Paul
1984 Time and Narrative. Chicago: University of Chicago Press.

Rogers, Carl
1995 On Becoming a Person: A Therapist's View of Psychotherapy. New York: Mariner Books.

Shweder, Richard, and Edmund Bourne
1984 Does the Concept of the Person Vary Cross-Culturally? In Culture Theory: Essays on Mind, Self, and Emotion. R. Shweder and R. LeVine, eds. Pp. 158–199. Cambridge: Cambridge University Press.

Silverman, W. H.
1996 Cookbooks, Manuals, and Paint-by-Numbers: Psychotherapy in the 90's. Psychotherapy 33: 207–215.

Simpson, J. A., and E. S. C. Weiner
1989 The Oxford English Dictionary, 2nd Ed. Oxford: Oxford University Press.

Sjoberg, B. M., and L. E. Hollister
1965 The Effects of Psychotomimetic Drugs on Primary Suggestibility. Psychopharmacologia 8: 251–262.

Stewart, Omer C.
1987 Peyote Religion: A History. Norman: University of Oklahoma Press.

Stocking, George W. Jr.
1982 Race, Culture, and Evolution: Essays in the History of Anthropology. Chicago: University of Chicago Press.

Turner, Victor
1967 The Forest of Symbols: Aspects of Ndembu Ritual. Ithaca: Cornell University Press.

Van Gennep, Arnold
1960 The Rites of Passage. Chicago: University of Chicago Press.

Westen, Drew, Catherine M. Novotny, and Heather Thompson-Brenner
2004 The Empirical Status of Empirically Supported Psychotherapies: Assumptions, Findings, and Reporting in Controlled Clinical Trials. Psychological Bulletin 130(4): 631–663.

Witherspoon, Gary
1974 The Central Concepts of the Navajo World View (I). Linguistics 119:41–59.

Part VI

Psychosocial Processes in History and Social Transformation

Introduction

Culture Change: Psychosocial Processes in Social Transformation

All cultures are changing all the time, regardless of how stable they might appear to their bearers or to outside observers. An ethnographic description of a culture is like a snapshot that freezes the action at a particular moment, losing its validity – except as an historical record – as time goes on. Anthropologists have recognized this fact and, increasingly, return to their field sites after years and decades to record cultures over time, obtaining a more accurate picture than the single snapshot by adding an historical perspective to their descriptions and analyses.

For psychological anthropology, culture change presents valuable opportunities to observe persons and their social and cultural environments when their adaptive relationships no longer hold. When persons and environments are well adapted to each other, it is difficult for the researcher to separate the contributions of individual dispositions and cultural scripts to observable behavior: How can you tell the dancer from the dance? When the scripts or the institutional structures controlling them change, however, or when there is widespread change among the persons in a population, the chance arises to identify the roles that individual dispositions play in maintaining and changing scripts and to observe the psychosocial processes accounting for historical change.

Consider the three kinds of change illustrated in the chapters of this final section:

1 **Immigration.** Individuals and families leave home to move to a different place with a different institutional and/or cultural environment. Immigration was part of the intellectual matrix from which psychological anthropology emerged, in Boas's (1911, 1912) studies of physical growth in New York and Thomas and Znaniecki's (1918) studies of Polish immigrants to Chicago. By the late 20th century, immigration to the United States had resumed on an even larger scale, which is outlined in Chapter 20 by C. Suárez-Orozco and M. Suárez-Orozco. Their account presents the contexts for change in family relationships and other aspects of psychosocial adaptation; in other parts of that book and its successor

(Suárez-Orozco and Suárez-Orozco, 2001; Suárez-Orozco, Suárez-Orozco and Todorova, 2008) the psychological consequences are shown in detail.

2 **Institutional diffusion.** Individuals remain at home, but their environment changes due to the borrowing of institutions and cultural scripts from elsewhere. An example that applies to most of the world in the last 50 years is the international spread of Western bureaucratic institutions including schools, hospitals, police, and armies. In Chapter 21, LeVine and LeVine describe the spread of schooling to women in the less developed countries where it was formerly unknown and the consequences for child health, family life, and the rearing of children.

3 **Revitalization and religious change.** Having become dissatisfied with and emotionally detached from the institutions and culture of their home environment, individuals are attracted to leaders who promise a more satisfying life through renewed commitment to cultural traditions or a radical change in behavior. In Chapter 22, Anthony F. C. Wallace presents his theory of "revitalization movements", still a bold and promising proposal more than 50 years after its original publication. Wallace includes in a single formula, which draws upon the concepts of Max Weber, the tendencies to change and preserve traditional cultural symbols that often coexist in religious and political movements. But Charles Lindholm in Chapter 23 argues with an American example, and also invoking Weber, that the social and emotional processes powerfully involved in leader–follower relations are not bound to traditional cultural symbols and their vicissitudes but can create new bonds to novel and exotic symbols and scripts.

This is not an exhaustive list of psychosocial change processes, which would include conquest, cultural drift and others. But it is an introduction to the ways in which psychological anthropology contributes to the analysis of social change. It is poised to make many more such contributions in the future.

REFERENCES

Boas, Franz
    1912   Instability of Human Types. In Gustave Spiller, ed., Papers on Interracial Problems Communicated to the First Universal Races Conference held at London University, 1911. Boston: Ginn and Co.
Suárez-Orozco, Carola and Marcelo Suárez-Orozco
    2001   Children of Immigration. Cambridge, MA: Harvard University Press.
Suárez-Orozco, Carola, Marcelo Suárez-Orozco and Irina Todorova
    2008   Learning in a New Land: Immigrant Students in American Society. Cambridge, MA: Harvard University Press.
Thomas, W. I. and Florian Znaniecki
    1918   The Polish Peasant in Europe and America, Vols. 1–5. Boston: Gorham Press.

20

The Psychosocial Experience of Immigration

Carola Suárez-Orozco and Marcelo M. Suárez-Orozco

Families migrate to improve their lives. For many, immigration results in opportunity, and personal growth. But there are costs involved in all immigrant journeys. Immigration is a transformative process with profound implications for the family. Immigrant children experience a particular constellation of changes that have lasting effects upon their development. And yet surprisingly little systematic research has focused on the psychological experiences of immigrant children.[1] Much of the work to date has either emphasized the adult immigrant experience or has examined the physical rather than psychological health of children. What do we really know about what it is like to be a child in a new country?

Separations and Reunification

Many new immigrants migrate primarily to be reunited with family members who emigrated earlier. Family networks generate – and sustain – substantial migratory flows. Indeed, transnational family reunification continues to be a critical factor in immigration today.[2] While a number of studies have examined how transnational family chains generate a powerful momentum of their own, we know little about how children manage the complex social and psychological experiences that come under the rubric of "family reunification."

For many immigrant children today, family reunification is a long, painful, and disorienting ordeal. Only 20 percent of the children in our sample came to the United States as a family unit. Most of the children were separated from one or both parents for a few months to a few years. Figure 20.1 includes the various ways that immigrant children are separated from their parents during the family's migration.

Immigrant children respond in a variety of ways to their separations from loved family members. For some, not surprisingly, it is a traumatic process. Others find it stressful but not traumatic. How the children experience the separation, their social conditions back home, and their perceptions of what is going on plays a critical role in their subsequent adaptations in the new land.

The cultural frame for the separation will influence how the child internalizes and responds to the experience. For example, in Caribbean countries there is a long-standing cultural practice of "child fostering." Children are sent to live with relatives either purposefully (as in when a mother has a live-in work position or when educational opportunities are better near a relative) as well as in response to a family crisis. In that social context,

Carola Suárez-Orozco and Marcelo M. Suárez-Orozco, The Psychosocial Experience of Immigration reprinted by permission of the publisher from *Children of Immigration*, ed. Carola Suárez-Orozco and Marcelo M. Suárez-Orozco, pp 66–86, 173–174, 185–201, Cambridge, MA: Harvard University Press.

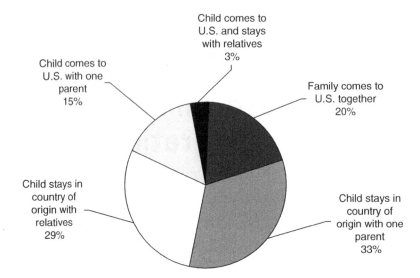

Figure 20.1 *Immigration and separation from parents. Such separations may not be harmful if they are considered normal in the child's native culture and if the child has healthy relationships with the parents and family members providing care*

the separation is often *not* experienced as abandonment. When international separations occur, however, expectations in the host culture are likely to have important repercussions – especially when children enter a new social context where such separations are viewed as a symptom of a pathological family situation.[3] Teachers, administrators, physicians, and other professionals often misinterpret the social meanings of these separations and are quick to label absent parents as not caring about or being properly attached to their children. Receiving such social signals may complicate the child's interpretations and psychological responses to the separation. The child may begin to doubt that her parents had her best interests in mind.

When the separation is not protracted, is carefully planned, and when the child has a clear understanding of what will happen next, the process may be not harmful to the child. This certainly is true if the child is well cared for by loving relatives during the separation. It is also important that the parents maintain regular communication and give frequent updates about the anticipated reunification. Communication can take the form of phone calls, letters and postcards, audio or videotapes,

photographs, and gifts. Children reported feeling touched and "special" when they received precious gifts from their parents prior to joining them. Haitian novelist Edwidge Danticat reveals how the packages sent to children carry emotions as well as gifts: "Around us were dozens of other people trying to squeeze all their love into small packets to send back home."[4]

Even under the best of conditions, however, there will be losses and ambivalence. If the child was left with a loving caretaker for an extended period of time, she will become attached to that caretaker. The beloved aunt or grandmother may assume the role of symbolic mother. Danticat, who was left behind by her mother with her loving aunt in Haiti, recalls how she felt that she was "my mother's daughter and Tante Atie's child."[5] When a child leaves to join the parents, she will probably feel both happy about the prospect of "regaining" them and disappointed about losing close contact with her beloved caretakers.

For children who are left for long periods with more ambivalent relatives who are neglectful or even abusive, there are more serious problems. This situation is exacerbated if the child has no clear timetable or sense of what will happen next, and little or no communication with parents.

Once the child does migrate to reunite with her family, all kinds of delicate psychological adjustments will be required. If the separation was long, the reunited family must first get reacquainted. And when the reunification involves children who were left behind when very young, the child will in essence be "meeting" her parents.

If new younger siblings are born during the separation, the older child who was "left behind" will almost inevitably have to contend with feelings of jealousy and disconnection with the family unit. In many cases, too, parental authority needs to be renegotiated – before, grandma and grandpa were the disciplinarians, and now the child may have to deal with a new set of rules. Indeed, many immigrant children reported to us that with the move they experienced a significant loss of freedom because immigrant parents are often very concerned about crime in their new neighborhoods.

Much will depend on whether the child left behind felt neglected and abandoned or, conversely, viewed the separation as necessary to the future well-being of the family. If a child felt neglected, "acting out" upon reunification may be a way to "punish" parents for leaving him behind. While most children are happy to be reunited with their families, they are also likely to feel disoriented and even depressed while they mourn their lost attachments: their best friends, beloved grandparents, or a favorite aunt left behind. For these children, the gains of immigration are tainted by loss.

The Stresses of Immigration

Transitions are always stressful. Social scientists and mental health professionals have long regarded events like moves, job changes, and ruptures in social relations as highly disruptive.[6] Transitions can trigger a variety of reactions, including excitement, anticipation, and hope as well as anxiety, anger, depression, somatic complaints, and illness.[7]

Transitions become particularly stressful when people are both unable to draw on their usual resources and coping strategies and are conscious of just how much is at stake.[8] Immigration often captures both of these elements. It is a major life transition where the stakes are high. Because families consciously choose to invest precious resources in the move, failure to adapt in the new setting can lead to serious consequences.

Indeed, by any measure, immigration is one of the most stressful events a family can undergo.[9] It removes family members from many of their relationships and a predictable context: community ties, jobs, customs, and (often) language. Immigrants are stripped of many of their significant relationships – extended family members, best friends, and neighbors. They also lose the social roles that provide them with culturally scripted notions of how they fit into the world. Initially, without a sense of competence, control, and belonging, many immigrants will feel marginalized. These changes in relationships, contexts, and roles are highly disorienting and nearly inevitably lead to a keen sense of loss.[10]

At the most dramatic end of the stress spectrum are the events that result in post-traumatic stress disorder (PTSD). Experiencing or witnessing killing, rape, or torture often leads to transient as well as long-term symptoms.[11] Asylum seekers from Kosovo, Bosnia, Somalia, Central America, Vietnam, and Haiti have often escaped from highly traumatic situations. PTSD symptoms include recurrent traumatic memories, a general numbing of responses, as well as a persistent sense of increased arousal leading to intense anxiety, irritability, outbursts of anger, difficulty concentrating, and insomnia.[12] New arrivals who have experienced trauma will often suffer recurring waves of symptoms and remain preoccupied with the violence they left behind. In addition to recurring thoughts, images, and nightmares of painful past events, they may feel guilty about having escaped when loved ones remain behind.[13]

These symptoms add significantly to the stresses of immigration. To complicate matters, traumatized new arrivals in need of counseling can seldom communicate with ease in the new language. They must face a whole array of challenges in the new setting often without cultural competence or the necessary social supports. The severity of the symptoms will in many ways depend on the extent of the trauma as well as the psychological, social, and material resources available to the victims in the new setting.

Other immigrants face a different form of violence as they cross the border. The actual border crossing is often extremely frightening and upsetting for adults and children alike. Undocumented crossers at the U.S.-Mexican border are subject to a variety of dangers including exposure to heat exhaustion as well as violence at the hands of border agents, "coyotes" (paid crossing guides), and others. Girls and women face additional risks. According to a recent disturbing Amnesty International report, "women are at particular risk of being physically abused, raped, robbed, or murdered on their journey."[14]

Our own interviews with immigrant children reveal that many of them experience the crossing of the border as highly traumatic. Some were detained, deported, beaten, or humiliated. Others sensed potential danger. A nine-year-old Mexican boy with fear in his voice told us of his crossing: "I had to be careful of where I put my feet. My parents told me that the *migra* [slang term for the INS] had put piranhas in the river to keep us away."[15]

Immigrant families who survive the violence of their countries and the crossing ironically often find a new form of violence as they settle in their American neighborhoods. New arrivals today, especially those from Latin America and the Caribbean, tend to settle in highly segregated neighborhoods where violence is an everyday occurrence.[16] All too many immigrant children experience disconcertingly high levels of violence in their new neighborhood and school settings. Of our informants, 36 percent indicated that violence was the thing they liked least about living in the United States. An eleven-year-old Mexican girl told us: "There is a lot of violence here in the United States. They kill people in the streets." A thirteen-year-old Mexican girl said: "There I was freer. Here there are bad people who hurt children." A twelve-year-old Haitian girl recounted: "I don't like the neighborhood where I live. There is a lot of crime in the neighborhood. One day, we were sleeping and the police came and opened the door. There was a

man in the apartment above us who had killed his wife ... I was scared because he could have come and killed us too." A ten-year-old Mexican boy reported a frightening incident: "I saw a man lying out in front of my house with blood on his legs and stomach. I think someone shot him." Another child, a thirteen-year-old Chinese girl, told us: "I have seen gang activities near my house ... I am afraid to go out – I don't feel safe."

Surely not all immigrants experience violence or trauma either in their homeland or in their new land. Many fly in comfortable airplanes, are politely received by INS officers, and move into safe middle-class neighborhoods. Nonetheless, it is important to bear in mind that for a significant number of immigrant children, violence has been and continues to be a part of their lives.

Even when violence is not a defining feature of the immigrant experience, immigrant families endure other forms of stress. While anticipating the migration and during the first weeks in the new country, many experience a sense of euphoria.[17] Expectations are often high; for many the anticipated possibilities seem boundless. Upon arrival, immigrants focus their energies on attending to the immediate needs of settling into the new environment. The priorities include finding a place to live, securing employment, and enrolling the children in schools. There is little time for the family to process psychologically many aspects of their new experiences.

After taking care of the essential needs, immigrants will begin to confront some unanticipated realities. Many will experience a variety of psychological problems.[18] Most frequently, the cumulative losses of loved ones and familiar contexts will lead to a range of feelings, from mild sadness to depression to "perpetual mourning."[19] For others, the general dissonance in cultural expectations and the loss of predictable context will be experienced as anxiety and an acute disorientation.[20] Many immigrants who arrive with exaggerated expectations of opportunity and wealth must come to terms with a starker reality. Disappointed aspirations, when coupled with a hostile reception in the new environment, may lead some to feelings of distrust, suspicion, anger, and even paranoia.[21] While some immigrants will display acute symptoms that should be treated, others – perhaps most – feel only transient discomfort and adapt to their circumstances with relative ease.

Learning the New Rules

A form of stress specific to immigration is referred to as "acculturation stress."[22] Acculturation is the process of learning new cultural rules and interpersonal expectations. Language is not the only form of communication that immigrants must learn. Social interactions are culturally structured. A Middle Eastern immigrant will need to learn that in the United States, most people stand farther apart when speaking than in her native country. Argentines will need to learn that Americans will interpret their normal volume in discussion as near shouting. A Haitian child will sooner or later find out that politely averting her eyes while her teacher is scolding her (as her parents taught her) will only anger her American teacher more. A Brazilian immigrant will need to learn the culture of "appointments" – in her new country, a nine o'clock appointment does not mean arriving anytime between nine and eleven. All immigrants must learn the new rules of engagement.

Such cultural practices are first learned in childhood as part of socially shared repertoires that make the flow of life predictable. The social flow changes in dramatic ways following immigration. As Polish immigrant Eva Hoffmann describes in her exquisitely written memoirs, immigration causes people to fall "out of the net of meaning into the weightlessness of chaos."[23] Without a sense of cultural competence, control, and belonging, immigrants are often left with a keen sense of loss and disorientation. A twenty-three-year-old Mexican informant summed up the experience: "I became an infant again. I had to learn all over again to eat, to speak, to dress, and what was expected of me."

Immigrant children typically come into contact with American culture sooner and, indeed more intensely, than their parents do. Schools are an important site of cultural con-

tact for immigrant children. It is where they meet teachers (who are often members of the dominant culture) as well as children from other backgrounds. For many immigrant children today, peers will be members of other ethnic and racial minorities.[24] In schools they must contend quickly and intensively with the new culture. Their parents, however, may be more removed from mainstream American culture, particularly if they work, as many do, in jobs with other immigrants and those of the same ethnic background.[25] The child's fast absorption into the new culture will create particular conflicts and tensions.[26] Children may have feelings ranging from vague to intense embarrassment in regard to aspects of their parents' "old country" and "old-fashioned" ways. Parents may try to slow down the process by warning children not to act like other children in the new setting.

As a result of their greater exposure to the new culture, children often learn the new language more quickly than do their parents. Though the child may continue to speak the home language, the level of fluency is likely to atrophy over time. Without a concerted effort by both parents and children, the vocabulary and literacy level of the language of origin usually lags far behind that of the new language. While the child may easily communicate about basic needs in her language of origin ("What is for dinner?"), she is likely to have more difficulty communicating subtleties of thought and emotion in that language.[27] Parents, however, often continue to communicate more effectively in the language of origin. Hence in complex discussions between parents and children, subtleties of meanings are likely to be missed and miscommunication may result. It is not uncommon to overhear discussions in which parents and children switch back and forth between languages and completely miss one another's intent. Esmeralda Santiago recalls the special linguistic bond she developed with her siblings – and how her mother and grandmother were excluded: "Slowly, as our vocabularies grew, it became a bond between us, one that separated us from Tata and from Mami, who watched us perplexed, [their] expression changing from pride, to envy to worry."[28] The worry may not be misplaced. Children are not above deliberately using their linguistic edge to mislead their parents. A thirteen-year-old Mexican boy admitted to us that he had told his parents that the *F* on his report card stood for "fabulous."

Family Roles

Migration tends to have a destabilizing effect on the family.[29] It creates particular stresses on the family system that may translate into conflict between family members, particularly if there were tensions prior to migration. For example, migration often reduces the amount of time that parents and children spend together. Many immigrant parents (particularly those coming from poorer backgrounds) work several jobs. These and other obligations make them less available. Immigrant parents often tell us that working hard is the best way they can help their children, yet these long work hours leave many children unattended. This physical absence compounds the psychological unavailability that often accompanies parental anxiety and depression.[30] These two forms of absence all too frequently leave immigrant children to their own devices long before they are develpmentally ready. While in some cases this leads to hyper-responsible children, in other cases it leads to depressed kids who are drawn to the lure of alternative family structures such as gangs.[31]

Migration creates other changes within the structure of the family. Children who learn English more quickly than their parents are placed in situations where they must advocate for them. They may become privy to "family secrets" in their new roles as translators in medical, legal, and other social settings. Roles are often reversed, turning culturally scripted dynamics of parental authority upside down. Lan Cao, a Vietnamese refugee who arrived as a child, captures these dynamics poignantly:

The dreadful truth was simply this: we were going through life in reverse, and I was the one who would help my mother through the hard scrutiny of ordinary suburban life. I would have to forgo the luxury of adolescent experiments and temper tantrums, so that

I could scoop my mother out of harm's way and give her sanctuary. Now, when we stepped into the exterior world, I was the one who told my mother what was acceptable and unacceptable behavior ... And even though I hesitated to take on the responsibility, I had no choice. It was not a simple process, the manner in which my mother relinquished motherhood. The shift in status occurred not just in the world but in the safety of our home as well, and it became most obvious when we entered the realm of language.[32]

More than simple issues of relative linguistic competence are at work in the complex mutual familial calibrations that immigration requires. Former family leaders may be "demoted."[33] A wise grandfather who in Hong Kong is the source of guidance may now be unable to give meaningful practical advice to his granddaughter. Because immigrant parents "have no map of experience" before them, their self-assurance and authority can be undermined both in the outside world as well as in the more intimate world of the family.[34]

Parental loss of status in the new society has profound effects on the morale of the parent and hence the child. Luis Alberto Urrea describes the collapsing status his father experienced as he moved from the upper echelons of Mexican politics and power to the demeaning role of "greaser" in San Diego, California: "Nothing broke my father. Except for the U.S. He couldn't find his footing here. He couldn't rise again, and he knew it. He tried many jobs – busboy, cannery worker, bakery truck driver. I often think that he settled on bowling alleys because he was the most erudite man there, even if he was a greaser."[35]

Within the intimacy of the family, "the worm of self-doubt that undermines basic certitude" likewise subverts parental authority.[36] Eva Hoffman recalled about her parents following the family's migration from Poland: "They don't try to exercise much influence over me. 'In Poland, I would have known how to bring you up, I would have known what to do,' my mother says wistfully, but here she has lost her sureness, her authority."[37]

While some parents may quietly relinquish their authority, others resist doing so and may become severe disciplinarians. But the ways that immigrant parents discipline their children also may have to do with child-rearing practices in their country of origin. Withholding a meal, spanking a child, or pulling a child's ear are not uncommon techniques found in many countries, but they are dissonant with mainstream American ideals of the proper disciplining of a child. As parents discipline their children in ways approved of in their country of origin, they may come into conflict with U.S. Child Protective Services.[38]

In other cases, disciplinary practices seem to be secondary to the stresses generated by the migration itself. As parents are frustrated and feel increasingly threatened by the encroachment of new cultural values and behaviors among their children, they often attempt to "tighten the reins." But the children, wise to the ways of the new land, may use against their parents the threat of reporting them to state agencies. This further debilitates parental authority. In the Haitian community, it is said that "the first thing a child learns in the United States is to dial 911." In another folkloristic story, it was said that as soon as a Salvadorian father returned to the Central America for a visit with his family, he spanked his son "for all the times I could not spank you in the United States." While these stories probably contain only a grain of truth, during the course of our research many parents indeed reported to us their frustrations and fears of state encroachment into their basic parental authorities. Many fear that in the new country, laws and customs will prevent them from ensuring that their children behave in ways they deem appropriate.

Gender and the New Culture

Immigrant families are often caught in powerful and contradicting social currents, which result in both radical change and regidification. In the realm of gender relations, many of the paradoxes created by immigration appear with clarity and force. Immigration sets in motion certain forces that draw women away from the inner world of the family. Economic necessity dictates that women venture (in many cases for the first time) into the world of work outside of the home.[39] By venturing out of the world of the family and into the world of work and the new culture, immigrant women often adapt more quickly in subtle ways that have important implications for family life.

At the same time, a powerful counterforce gives immigrant women the responsibility for maintaining the traditions, values, and norms of the country of origin. In the upheaval of immigration, women typically emerge as the keepers of culture and family traditions. While some women become the self-appointed guardians of tradition, others may feel that this role is imposed upon them by their husbands and other members of the community.[40] Many immigrant families fear the detrimental affects of "Americanization" should the mother fail to act as cultural guardian. Rumors and other informal and formal social sanctions will be levied against women who fail to control the influences of Americanization on, for example, their sons' or daughters' style of dress, dating, and progress in school.

These pervasive dynamics generate their own opportunities and tensions. In the long term, many women come to experience immigration as liberating. It may result in more equitable gender relations, social freedom, and empowerment. Indeed, researchers have found that immigrant women are more likely than their husbands to feel content with their new situations and are less likely to say that they wish to return to their homeland.[41]

Recently arrived women often work in jobs that place them in intimate and sustained contact with members of the dominant society. They may find employment as child-care workers, in elderly care, and as housekeepers. As such, many enter the homes of members of the dominant society and become privy to different gender relations, child-rearing techniques, and expectations about the future. As they observe and evaluate new cultural models and social practices, they may subtly act as catalysts to change within their own families. In the long term, women must strike a balance between promoting certain forms of change they find desirable and guarding against those forms of change they perceive as harmful.

As immigrant women craft new roles and enjoy newfound independence, tensions within the husband-wife relationship may occur. For men, the adjustments can be difficult. Conflicts are most likely to occur when the wife's gains coincide with a social demotion for the husband – for example, when he is unemployed or can only find work beneath his qualifications and skills. As a result, spousal abuse is an issue in some immigrant families.[42]

Immigrant families make a Faustian bargain. While the longterm goal of immigration is greater opportunity for the children, parents often panic when their children begin to show the first signs of Americanization. Many immigrant families encourage their children to pick up certain cultural competencies (such as the English language) while fiercely resisting others. They come to see certain American attitudes and behaviors as a threat to family unity. They often view American popular culture as wanting in such realms as dating, respect of elders, and peer relations. Immigrant parents view with suspicion even such cultural icons as slumber parties; many of our informants reported that their parents would never allow them to sleep over at a friend's house.

Esmeralda Santiago recalls her mother's ambivalence: "The way she pronounced *Americanized*, it sounded like a terrible thing, to be avoided at all costs, another *algo* to be added to the list of 'somethings' outside the door ... It was good to be healthy, big, and strong like Dick, Jane, and Sally. It was good to learn English and to know how to act among Americans, but it was not good to behave like them."[43]

Nowhere are the anxieties around Americanization more clearly articulated than in parental concerns about their daughters' exposure to the cultural repertoire of the American peer group. In some immigrant communities, becoming "Americanized" is synonymous with becoming sexually promiscuous.[44] Often significant family tensions emerge around the dating of adolescent girls. As a result, the activities of girls outside the home tend to be heavily monitored and controlled. While boys may be encouraged to venture into the new world, girls and young women are more likely to be kept close to the family

hearth. Because girls tend to value social and family ties more than their brothers, they may be reluctant to struggle to separate from the family.[45] Adolescent girls often experience the burden of being torn between the pursuit of romantic love and the role of dutiful daughter.[46]

Immigrant girls have far more responsibilities at home than do their brothers.[47] Their roles include translating; advocating in financial, medical, legal transactions; and acting as surrogate parents with younger siblings. Eldest children in particular are expected to assist with such tasks as babysitting, feeding younger siblings, getting siblings ready for school in the morning, and escorting them to school.[48]

As a result of the concerns around dating and the heavy family responsibilities at home, activities of immigrant girls outside the home are heavily restricted. These restrictions are often experienced by adolescent girls as "unfair" and "oppressive" and may be the focus of family conflict. Immigration researcher Rob Smith and his team at Columbia University, however, note that these restrictions seem to protect girls somewhat from violence or gang-related activities. Indeed, several researchers have found that girls are less likely to be involved in gangs, and when they are, their involvement is more symbolic and less intense.[49] Girls who flirt with gang activities are more likely to remain in school and to transition relatively smoothly out of gangs and into the labor market.[50] A major related finding indicates that substance abuse is substantially lower in immigrant girls than boys.[51] Immigrant girls are also less likely than their nativeborn counterparts to engage in substance abuse and other risky behaviors.[52]

In schools, immigrant girls tend to outperform immigrant boys. Since the beginning of this century, among most ethnic groups, immigrant girls tended to complete more years of school than their male counterparts.[53] An analysis of census data found that Asian American females reach higher levels of educational attainment than males.[54] In a study of Caribbean-origin youth in New York City, the eminent Harvard immigration scholar Mary Waters found that girls are more likely than boys to complete high school.[55]

While immigrant girls tend to outperform their brothers in school, there are some exceptions.[56] Religion and culture have a tremendous influence on the experiences of immigrant girls. Girls of Hindi Indian or Muslim Afghani backgrounds face very different issues than do Catholic Mexican, or Buddhist Chinese, girls. Arranged marriages are the norm in some cultures – for a girl raised in a postindustrial culture steeped in media images of what life should be like in the new society, this practice will cause much more emotional conflict than if she had been raised in her country of origin.[57] Among those immigrant families that discourage their daughters from remaining in school past marriageable age (which may be in their mid-teens), educational pursuits for girls will be cut short.

On aggregate, however, immigrant girls tend to have more successful educational careers than boys do. Why? Several reasons are at work. Because immigrant girls are more restricted by their parents than are boys, "time at school … becomes a precious social experience."[58] They tend to view their time in school as a period of relative freedom (in contrast to mainstream American teenagers, who tend to talk about school as a "prison experience.")[59] They may feel more positive about school and therefore may be more seriously engaged in learning.

Girls and boys seem to respond somewhat differently to cultural and racial stereotypes. As eminent anthropologists George De Vos and John Ogbu have noted, academic engagement is compromised for youth coming from stigmatized backgrounds.[60] But boys from these groups have even more problems performing in school than do the girls. This seems to be the case, for example, among Caribbean-origin youth in Britain, Canada, and the United States, among North African males in Belgium, and among Moroccan and Algerian boys in France.[61]

In addition, Harvard psychiatrist Felton Earls has persuasively argued that familial and community control play a significant role in the well-being (including academics) of youth.[62] Furthermore, teachers' expectations for minority boys are quite different than those for girls. Teachers and administrators often perceive adolescent minority and immigrant boys as

threatening. Another contribution to the gender gap may be the strong peer pressure for boys to reject school.[63] Behaviors that gain respect with peers often bring boys in conflict with their teachers.

Influences on Successful Long-Term Adaptation

In all social systems, the family is a basic structural unit, the most significant emotional foundation in the lives of individuals. This is especially so for immigrants who may not have other social networks immediately available to them. Understanding family-level factors is indeed critical for evaluating the long-term adaptations of immigrant children. In looking at the role of immigrant families, however, we must be cautious. Immigrant families are structured in a variety of culturally relative ways. In some cases, the nuclear family (father-mother-children) is the ideal type. In other cases, however, matrifocal patterns (where women are at the center of family life) are the norm. In still other immigrant families, extended members such as grandparents, aunts, and uncles are integral to the system. It is therefore always risky to apply mainstream, middle-class standards to immigrant family dynamics.[64]

Family cohesion and the maintenance of a well-functioning system of supervision, authority, and mutuality are perhaps the most powerful factors in shaping the well-being and future outcomes of all children – immigrant and non-immigrant alike. Because no family is an island, family cohesion and healthy dynamics are enhanced when the family is part of a larger community that displays effective forms of what Felton Earls has termed "community agency."[65]

Patterns of social cohesion and belonging can be assessed by a variety of social indicators. Perhaps the most important of these is: Who is in charge in the life of a child? Are the parents and other responsible adults in control of children's activities, or are the peers most influential? Do the adults know what the children are up to? Does information about potential trouble travel through the community network before it is too late and the police become involved? Do parents know the parents of their children's friends?

Factors relating to parents' socioeconomic and educational background also influence the adaptations of immigrant families: they play a decisive role in determining the kinds of neighborhoods that families settle into, the kinds of schools that children attend, and the ability to maintain contact with loved ones back home by making regular visits.[66] On the whole, upper-middle-class immigrants are able to retain much of their prestige and offer their children better opportunities. Individuals and families of middle- and lower-class backgrounds are likely to face more adverse circumstances, to settle into less desirable neighborhoods, and to enroll their children in schools with fewer resources. They will also have fewer opportunities to visit their country of origin and so may suffer from being cut off from their loved ones.

Middle-class immigrants often experience significant losses in prestige: they frequently find employment in positions far below their training and qualifications because of language difficulties, lack of connections, or lack of certification in certain professions. The high school teacher from Moscow becomes a babysitter; the Indian doctor a preschool teacher; the Haitian lawyer a cab driver. In addition, middle-class immigrants may suffer for the first time the painful experience of prejudice and discrimination in the new country.

The poorest immigrants, who are largely members of the lower classes in their country of origin, often suffer tremendous adversity as a result of immigration. In spite of these difficulties – which may include xenophobia, racism, and fierce competition for the least desirable jobs – they often improve their economic and social circumstances. In addition, while they certainly suffer from discrimination in the new country, social disparagement may not necessarily be a new experience. As members of the lower socioeconomic class, they are likely to have suffered such treatment in their country of origin. They have less to lose and less far to fall. Those with little or no education, however, find themselves at a great disadvantage in guiding their children through the complex educational maze in the new land.

While the family is extremely important to how the child adapts to the new land, a number of other factors significantly shape how children respond to the transitions and stresses of immigration.[67] Some of these factors involve characteristics that immigrant families bring with them, and others involve variables they encounter in the new land.

The circumstances surrounding the migration can play a key role. Was the family pushed or pulled out of the country of origin? If the family was lured out of the homeland by the promise of opportunity and adventure, its members are likely to be more positively disposed to the experience than if they were pushed out by ethnic, religious, or political conflict, chronic hardship, or famine. By the same token, at least initially, the individual initiating the migration is likely to be more enthusiastic about the experience than a reluctant spouse, elderly parent, or child.[68] We have found that children in particular often have only a vague understanding of why the family is migrating. As a result, they may not look forward to the migration and may experience the move as an imposition from which they have little to gain.

Personality and temperamental factors make a great difference too.[69] A healthy response to dramatic change requires the ability to adapt to new circumstances. Individuals who are rigid in their views, or who have a high need for predictability, are likely to suffer.[70] Those who are particularly shy, proud, or sensitive to outside opinions are also at higher risk, as are those who are highly suspicious of the motivations of others. Being able to draw upon a variety of coping strategies is certainly an important asset.[71]

By the same token, psychological and physical health prior to migration will also aid or impede the ease of the response to immigration. Children who are suffering from posttraumatic stress (as discussed earlier) are of course highly at risk. So too, are immigrants who suffer from depressive tendencies as well as any number of other psychiatric disorders. Physical health may also play a role, particularly if an illness or disability interferes with either maintaining gainful employment or with general quality of life.

Speaking the language of the new country clearly is an asset. Religiosity and connection with a church may also play a positive role. On the other hand, moving from a village to a major city (a common pattern for many immigrants) may complicate the transition. Many immigrant children in our study report to us that they find it very difficult to adjust to the *encerramiento* (Spanish for being "shut in"). While they may have had considerable freedom to play and roam their neighborhoods in their place of origin, they often lose such freedoms when moving to an urban environment.

Once in the new setting, the network of social relations is important. Nothing is better for one's mental health than having friends and family. The relative absence of social support has been linked to disease, mortality, slowed recovery, and mental illness. The presence of a healthy social support network has long been regarded as a key mediator of stress.[72]

Interpersonal relationships are important in several ways.[73] Immigrants, disoriented in the new land, rely on friends and relatives to provide them with tangible aid (such as running an errand or making a loan) as well as guidance and advice (including job and housing leads). The companionship of these friends and relatives also helps maintain and enhance self-esteem and provides much needed acceptance and approval. A well-functioning social support network, quite predictably, is closely linked to better adjustment to the new environment. Of course, in part, the availability of an effective social support structure will be influenced by the individual's preexisting social competence. Individuals with highly developed social skills are likely to be better able to establish and draw upon interpersonal relationships.[74]

A number of other factors in the new setting must be considered in understanding the adaptation of the immigrants. Whether or not the immigrant is "documented" or "undocumented" will affect his or her access to opportunities and general quality of life.[75]

For adults the availability of jobs will be key. Here, social networks will be important because employers often rely on migrant networks to provide them with referrals to potential new employees.[76] Features of the job

itself – wages, seasonal availability, safety, and pleasantness of the work – will also play a role in the employee's adjustment.

For children, the quality of their schools will ease or complicate the transition. Unfortunately, many immigrant children find themselves in segregated, poor, and conflict-ridden schools.[77] In our sample of schools, several administrators have reported high crime rates. In one of our participating middle schools, a student was raped and murdered; a high school principal told us of approximately thirty murders during the previous year within the immediate neighborhood; and many other school officials and students complained of significant gang activity on school property and in the surrounding neighborhood. A middle school student told us that a security guard, who had supposedly been hired to protect the students, was the main dealer of drugs on campus. During focus groups we conducted with Mexican immigrant students in a San Francisco Bay Area school, students said that only a few days earlier an escaped prisoner had barricaded himself during school hours on the school grounds, leading to an exchange of gunshots between him and the police.[78]

Obviously, neighborhood safety will do much to influence the quality of life for children and adults alike. Many immigrants move to inner-city areas in search of housing that they can afford. Unfortunately, affordable urban housing is often located in areas that are virtual war zones.

Finally, the way that immigrant children are received plays a critical role in their adaptation. As we outlined, discrimination against many new immigrants is widespread, and social scientists have established that prejudice and exclusion are traumatic.[79] Exclusion can be structural (such as when individuals are kept from jobs or housing) or attitudinal (as when new arrivals are treated with disparagement and public hostility). It impinges upon the daily quality of life of its victims and interferes with their emotional health and social adaptation.[80] In the long term, xenophobia and exclusion can deeply undermine the immigrant child's trust in equal opportunity and hope for the future.

Immigrant families and their children face multiple challenges. While the special problems we have delineated in this chapter are part of their daily lives, most immigrant families cope well with the stresses. For most, the acute phase of distress is limited in severity and short-lived. Over time, as these immigrants become more acclimatized and less disoriented – a task that is easier for those who are able to settle in well-functioning close-knit communities – many will thrive. Most immigrants will find that overall, their gains out-weigh their losses.

NOTES

1 Garcia-Coll and Magnuson 1998.
2 In 1996, 915,900 immigrants were formally admitted to the United States. Among them, 596,264 were family-sponsored immigrants – most of them the children and spouses of those already here. Likewise, in Europe family reunification is one of the few formal ways to migrate to the continent.
3 M. Waters 1999.
4 Danticat 1994, p. 51.
5 Ibid., p. 49.
6 Schlossberg 1984.
7 Dohrenwend 1986.
8 House 1974, pp. 12–27.
9 Falicov 1998.
10 See Ainslie 1998; L. Grinberg and R. Grinberg 1989.
11 Somach 1995.
12 See Horowitz 1986; Smajkic and Weane 1995.
13 M. Suárez-Orozco 1989.
14 Eschbach, Hagan, and Rodriguez 1997; Amnesty International 1998, p. 24.
15 All quotations from our informants are translations from their native languages.
16 Orfield 1998.
17 Sluzki 1979, pp. 379–390.
18 Ainslie 1998; Arrendondo-Dowd 1981, pp. 376–378; L. Grinberg and R. Grinberg 1989; Rumbaut 1977; Sluzki 1979; M. Suárez-Orozco 1998.
19 Volkan 1993, pp. 63–69. For a brilliant analysis of the psychodynamics of loss among immigrants, see Ainslie 1998.
20 L. Grinberg and R. Grinberg 1989.
21 Ibid.
22 See Berry 1998; Flaskerud and Uman 1996, pp. 123–133; J. F. Smart and D. W. Smart 1995, pp. 390–396.
23 Hoffmann 1989, p. 151.
24 Orfield and Yun 1999.
25 M. Suárez-Orozco 1998.
26 Falicov 1998.
27 Wong-Fillmore 1991, pp. 323–346.
28 Santiago 1998, p. 18.
29 Sluzki 1979; Falicov 1998.
30 Ahearn and Athey 1991.
31 Vigil 1988.
32 Cao 1997, p. 35.
33 Shuval 1980.
34 Hoffman 1989, p. 159.
35 Urrea 1998, p. 41.
36 Hoffman 1989, p. 128.
37 Ibid., p. 145.
38 *New York Daily News*, April 1, 1999.
39 See *American Behavioral Scientist* 1999.
40 Espin 1987, esp. p. 493.
41 Hondagneu-Sotelo 1994.
42 Min 1998.
43 Santiago 1998, pp. 12 and 25.
44 Espin 1999; Olsen 1998.
45 Goodenow and Espin 1993, pp. 173–184.
46 Olsen 1988.
47 Valenzuela 1999, pp. 720–742; Waters 1997; Smith 1999.
48 Valenzuela 1999.
49 Vigil 1988; Smith 1999.
50 Smith 1999.
51 Khoury et al. 1999, pp. 21–40.
52 Hernandez and Charney 1998.
53 Olneck and Lazerson 1974, pp. 453–482.
54 Brandon 1991, pp. 45–61.
55 Waters 1997.
56 Gibson 1997, pp. 431–454.
57 Olsen 1998.
58 Ibid., p. 125.
59 Ibid.
60 De Vos 1992a; De Vos 1992b; Ogbu and Simons 1998, pp. 155–188.
61 Gibson 1997.
62 See Earls 1997.
63 Fordham 1996; Gibson 1988; Smith 1999; Waters 1999.
64 Falicov 1998; J. F. Smart and D. W. Smart 1995.
65 Earls 1997.
66 Flaskerud and Uman 1996; C. Suárez-Orozco 1998.
67 Garcia-Coll and Magnuson 1998; Laosa 1989; Rumbaut 1997.
68 Shuval 1980.
69 Garcia-Coll and Magnuson 1998; ibid.

70 Wheaton 1983, pp. 208–229.
71 Lazarus and Folkman 1984; Pearlin and Schooler 1978, pp. 2–21.
72 Cobb 1988, pp. 300–314; Cohen and Syme 1985.
73 Wills 1985.
74 Heller and Swindle 1983.
75 Chavez 1992; J. F. Smart and D. W. Smart 1995.
76 Waldinger 1997; Cornelius 1998.
77 Orfield and Yun 1999.
78 School authorities and news reports substantiated this finding. Alex Stepick and his team of researchers at Florida International University are currently doing important research on violence and immigrant children in American schools.
79 Garcia-Coll and Magnuson 1998, p. 119; Adams 1990.
80 Adams 1990.

REFERENCES

Adams, P. L.
1990 "Prejudice and Exclusion as Social Trauma." In J. D. Noshpitz and R. D. Coddington, eds., *Stressors and Adjustment Disorders*. New York: John Wiley and Sons.

Ahearn, Jr., Frederick L., and Jean L. Athey
1991 *Refugee Children: Theory, Research, and Services*. Baltimore, Md.: Johns Hopkins University Press.

Ainslie, Ricardo
1998 "Cultural Mourning, Immigration, and Engagement: Vignettes from the Mexican Experience." In Marcelo M. Suárez-Orozco, ed., *Crossings: Mexican Immigration in Interdisciplinary Perspectives*. Cambridge, Mass.: David Rockefeller Center for Latin American Studies and Harvard University Press.

American Behavioral Scientist
1999 Issue devoted to "Gender and Contemporary U.S. Immigration" 42, no. 4.

Amnesty International
1998 "From San Diego to Brownsville: Human Rights Violations on the USA-Mexico Border." *New Release*, May 20, 24.

Arrendondo-Dowd, P.
1981 "Personal Loss and Grief as a Result of Immigration." *Personnel and Guidance Journal* 59: 376–378.

Berry, John W.
1998 "Psychology of Acculturation." In Nancy Goldenberg and Judy B. Veroff, eds., *The Culture and Psychology Reader*. New York: New York University Press, 1998.

Brandon, P.
1991 "Gender Differences in Young Asian Americans' Educational Attainment." *Sex Roles* 25, nos. 1/2: 45–61.

Cao, Lan
1997 *Monkey Bridge*. New York: Penguin.

Chavez, Leo R.
1992 *Shadowed Lives: Undocumented Immigrants in American Society*. Fort Worth, Tex.: Harcourt Brace.

Cobb, S.
1988 "Social Support as a Moderator of Life Stress." *Psychosomatic Medicine* 3, no. 5: 300–314.

Cohen, S., and S. L. Syme
1985 "Issues in the Study and Application of Social Support." In S. Cohen and S. L. Syme, eds., *Social Support and Health*. Orlando, Fla.: Academic Press.

Cornelius, Wayne A.
1998 "The Structural Embeddedness of Demand for Mexican Immigrant Labor," in Marcelo M. Suárez-Orozco, ed., *Crossings: Mexican Immigration in Interdisciplinary Perspectives*. Cambridge, Mass.: David Rockefeller Center for Latin American Studies and Harvard University Press, pp. 113–155.

Danticat, Edwidge
1994 *Breath, Eyes, Memory*. New York: Vintage Press.

De Vos, George
1992a "The Passing of Passing." In George De Vos, *Social Cohesion and Alienation: Minorities in the United States and Japan*. Boulder, Colo.: Westview.
1992b *Social Cohesion and Alienation: Minorities in the United States and Japan*. Boulder, Colo.: Westview.

Dohrenwend, B. P.
1986 "Theoretical Formulation of Life Stress Variables." In A. Eichler, M. M. Silverman, and D. M. Pratt, eds., *How to Define and Research Stress*. Washington, D.C.: American Psychiatric Press.

Earls, Felton.
1997 As quoted in "Tighter, Safer Neighborhoods." *Harvard Magazine* November/December.

Eschbach, K., Jaqueline Hagan, and Nestor Rodriguez
1997   *Death at the Border.* Houston: Center for Immigration Research.

Espin, Olivia
1987   "Psychological Impact of Migration on Latinas: Implications for Psychotherapeutic Practice." *Psychology of Women Quarterly* 11: 489–503.

Falicov, Celia Jaes
1998   *Latino Families in Therapy: A Guide to Multicultural Practice.* New York: Guilford Press.

Flaskerud, J. H., and R. Uman
1996   "Acculturation and Its Effects on Self-Esteem among Immigrant Latina Women." *Behavioral Medicine* 22: 123–133.

Fordham, Signithia
1996   *Blacked Out: Dilemmas of Race, Identity, and Success at Capital High.* Chicago: University of Chicago Press.

Garcia-Coll, Cynthia, and K. Magnuson
1998   "The Psychological Experience of Immigration: A Developmental Perspective." In A. Booth, A. Crouter, and N. Landale, eds., *Immigration and the Family: Research and Policy on U.S. Immigrants.* Mahwah, N.J.: Lawrence Erlbaum, pp. 91–131.

Gibson, Margaret.
1988   *Accommodation without Assimilation: Sikh Immigrants in an American High School.* Ithaca, N.Y.: Cornell University Press.

Gibson, Margaret
1997   "Complicating the Immigrant / Involuntary Minority Typology." *Anthropology and Education Quarterly* 28, no. 3: 431–454.

Goodenow, C., and O. Espin.
1993   "Identity Choices in Immigrant Adolescent Females." *Adolescence* 28, no. 109: 173–184.

Gordon, Milton
1964   *Assimilation and American Life.* New York: Oxford University Press.

Grinberg, Leon, and Rebeca Grinberg,
1989   *Psychoanalytic Perspectives on Migration and Exile.* New Haven: Yale University Press.

Heller, K., and R. W. Swindle
1983   "Social Networks, Perceived Social Support, and Coping with Stress." In R. D. Felner, ed., *Preventative Psychology: Theory, Research, Practice in Community Intervention.* New York: Penguin.

Hernandez, D., and Evan Charney, eds.
1998   *From Generation to Generation: The Health and Well-Being of Children in Immigrant Families.* Washington, D.C.: National Academy Press.

Hoffmann, Eva
1989   *Lost in Translation: A Life in a New Language.* New York: Penguin.

Hondagneu-Sotelo, Pierrete
1994   *Gendered Transitions: Mexican Experiences of Immigration.* Berkeley: University of California Press.

Horowitz, Ruth
1986   *Honor and the American Dream: Culture and Identity in a Chicano Community.* New Brunswick, N.J.: Rutgers University Press.

House, J. S.
1974   "Occupational Stress and Coronary Heart Disease: A Review." *Journal of Health and Social Behavior* 15: 12–27.

Khoury, Elizabeth, George Warheit, Rick Zimmerman, William Vega, and Andres Gil
1999   "Gender and Ethnic Differences in the Prevalence of Alchohol, Cigarette, and Illicit Drug Use over Time in a Cohort of Young Hispanic Adolescents in South Florida." *Women and Health* 24, no. 1: 21–40.

Laosa, L.
1989   *Psychological Stress, Coping, and the Development of the Hispanic Immigrant Child.* Princeton, N.J.: Educational Testing Service.

Lazarus, R. S., and S. Folkman
1984   *Stress, Appraisal, and Coping.* New York: Springer.

Min, Pyong Gap
1998   *Changes and Conflicts: Korean Immigrant Families in New York.* Boston: Allen and Bacon.

Ogbu, John, and Herbert Simons
1998   "Voluntary and Involuntary Minorities: A Cultural-Ecological Theory of School Performance with Some Implications for Education." *Anthropology and Education Quarterly* 29: 155–188.

Olneck, M. R., and M. Lazerson
1974   "The School Achievement of Immigrant Children: 1899–1930. *History of Education Quarterly* 14: 453–482.

Olsen, Laurie
1988   *Crossing the Schoolhouse Border: Immigrant Students in the California Public Schools.* Oakland: California Tomorrow.

Olsen, Laurie
1998 *Made in America: Immigrant Students in Our Public Schools*. New York: New Press.
Orfield, Gary
1998 "Commentary." In Marcelo M. Suárez-Orozco, ed., *Crossings: Mexican Immigration in Interdisciplinary Perspectives*. Cambridge, Mass.: David Rockefeller Center for Latin American Studies and Harvard University Press.
Orfield, Gary, and John T. Yun
1999 *Resegregation in American Schools*. Cambridge, Mass.: Civil Rights Project, Harvard University.
Pearlin, L. I., and C. Schooler
1978 "The Structure of Coping." *Journal of Health and Social Behavior* 19, no. 3: 2–21.
Rumbaut, Ruben
1977 "Life Events, Change, Migration and Depression." In W. E. Fann, I. Karocan, A. D. Pokorny, and R. L. Williams, eds., *Phenomenology and Treatment of Depression*, New York: Spectrum.
Santiago, Esmeralda
1998 *Almost a Woman*. Reading, Mass.: Perseus Books.
Schlossberg, Nancy K.
1984 *Counseling Adults in Transition: Linking Practice with Theory*. New York: Springer.
Shuval, J.
1980 "Migration and Stress." in I. L. Kutasshm, L. B. Schlessinger, et al., *Handbook on Stress and Anxiety: Contemporary Knowledge, Theory, and Treatment*. San Francisco: Jossey-Bass.
Sluzki, Carlos
1979 "Migration and Family Conflict." *Family Process* 18, no. 4: 379–390.
Smajkic, A., and S. Weane
1995 "Special Issues of Newly Arrived Refugee Groups." In Susan Somach, ed., *Issues of War Trauma and Working with Refugees: A Compilation of Resources*. Washington, D.C.: Center for Applied Linguistics Refugee Service Center.
Smart, J. F., and D. W. Smart
1995 "Acculturation Stress of Hispanics: Loss and Challenge." *Journal of Counseling and Development* 75: 390–396.
Smith, Robert
1999 "The Education and Work Mobility of Second-Generation Mexican Americans in New York City: Preliminary Reflections on the Role of Gender, Ethnicity, and School Structure." Paper presented at the Eastern Sociological Society Meeting, Boston. March.
Somach, Susan
1995 *Issues of War Trauma and Working with Refugees: A Compilation of Resources*. Washington, D.C.: Center for Applied Linguistics Refugee Service Center.
Suárez-Orozco, Carola
1998 "The Transitions of Immigration: How Are They Different for Women and Men?" *David Rockefeller Center for Latin American Studies News*, Harvard University. Winter.
Suárez-Orozco, Marcelo M.
1989 *Central American Refugees and U.S. High Schools: A Psychosocial Study of Motivation and Achievement*. Stanford, Calif.: Stanford University Press.
Suárez-Orozco, Marcelo M.
1998 *Crossings: Mexican Immigration in Interdisciplinary Perspectives*. Cambridge, Mass.: David Rockefeller Center for Latin American Studies and Harvard University Press.
Urrea, Luis Alberto
1998 *Nobody's Son*. Tuscon: University of Arizona Press, p. 41.
Valdéz, Guadalupe
1998 "The World Outside and Inside Schools: Language and Immigrant Children." *Educational Researcher* 27, no. 6: 9.
Valenzuela, A.
1999 "Gender Roles and Settlement Activities among Children and Their Immigrant Families." *American Behavioral Scientist* 42, no. 4: 720–742.
Vigil, Diego
1988 *Barrio Gangs: Street Life and Identity in Southern California*. Austin: University of Texas Press.
Villareal, José A., *Pocho*.
1959 New York: Anchor Books, pp. 149–150.
Volkan, V. D.
1993 "Immigrants and Refugees: A Psychodynamic Perspective," *Mind and Human Interaction* 4, no. 2: 63–69.
Waldinger, Roger
1997 "Social Capital or Social Closures? Immigrant Networks in the Labor Market." Working Paper Series 26. Lewis Center for Regional Policy Studies, University of California, Los Angeles.

Waters, Mary. C.
1997 "The Impact of Racial Segregation on the Education and Work Outcomes of Second-Generation West Indians in New York City." Paper presented to the Levy Institute Conference on the Second Generation, Bard College. October 25.

Waters, Mary
1999 *Black Identities: West Indian Dreams and American Realities.* Cambridge, Mass.: Harvard University Press.

Waters, Tony
1999 *Crime and Immigrant Youth.* Thousand Oaks, Calif.: Sage.

Wheaton, B.
1983 "Stress, Personal Coping Resources, and Psychiatric Symptoms: An Investigation of Interactive Models." *Journal of Health and Social Behavior* 24, no. 9: 208–229.

Wills, T. A.
1985 "Supportive Functions of Interpersonal Relationships." In S. Cohen and S.L. Syme, eds., *Social Support and Health.* Fla.: Academic Press.

Wong-Fillmore, L.
1991 "When Learning a Language Means Losing the First." *Early Childhood Research Quarterly* 6: 323–346.

21

The Schooling of Women: Maternal Behavior and Child Environments

Robert A. LeVine and Sarah A. LeVine

Our ongoing research project on maternal schooling follows directly from an insight Beatrice Whiting published in 1977, when she pointed out that much research linking social variables with psychological ones (as independent and dependent variables, respectively) was woefully unbalanced: The psychological side was conceptualized in specific terms and measured with sophisticated care, while the social side was treated as a series of standard categories like age, sex, culture, socioeconomic status, and urbanization. These social categories had proven to be potent predictors of psychological or behavioral variation, but they remained mysterious "packaged variables," particularly in comparative research – opaque and possibly misleading labels representing unknown processes of uncertain variability. It was time, she argued, to "unwrap" the packages through serious research on their specific contents as environmental factors. This meant identifying their component parts in different contexts and studying the processes by which these features of the social environment become psychologically salient to individuals. Addressing developmental psychologists, she exhorted them to undertake this kind of research and gave examples from her own studies with Thomas Weisner on urban – rural variations and Carolyn Edwards on sex differences.

Our project has focused on women's schooling as a possible determinant of variations in childbearing, child health care, and demographic change. The project was initiated about twenty years ago as an attempt to explain a finding from comparative studies that was exciting interest in demography and international public health research at the time: that the schooling of women, measured simply as years attended or highest level attained, was the most consistent and robust household-level predictor of reduced fertility and child mortality in developing countries. It had been known previously that women's schooling was associated with variations in birth and death rates, but many had assumed it was a "proxy" for the economic or social status of the household. Only in the late 1970s was it demonstrated that when household socioeconomic status – a classic packaged variable, particularly when used across cultures – was unwrapped statistically, the effects of women's schooling were independent of husband's schooling and his occupational status and of measures of household wealth or income. Leading demographers and health researchers recognized the potential importance of this finding, but perceiving that school attainment was itself a package in need of unwrapping, they called for empirical research into the intervening processes of this apparent cause–effect relationship.

Robert A. LeVine and Sarah E. LeVine, The Schooling of Women: Maternal Behavior and Child Environments from *Ethos*, Vol. 29, No. 3, pp. 259–270. © 2002 by the American Anthropological Association. Reprinted with permission of the American Anthropological Association.

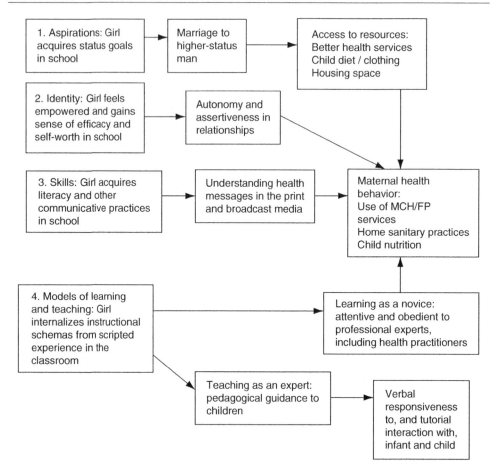

Figure 21.1 *Hypothetical pathways from women's schooling to health behavior.*

We answered that call and have spent two decades in the unwrapping process. With our students and colleagues we have conducted research in six sites: two in Mexico, two in Nepal, one in Zambia and one in Venezuela. We adopted the method of intracommunity replication recommended by Bea Whiting in her Editor's Notes in the SCS *Field Guide* (Whiting et al. 1966) and in the article on the packaged variable (1977), and we learned from problems she encountered in analyzing the SCS that our samples of mothers must be relatively large (usually at least 100). The findings to date are summarized in an article in the *Harvard Educational Review* (LeVine et al. 2001), but the research goes on, supported by the W. T. Grant Foundation.

Women's schooling has proved a difficult packaged variable to unwrap adequately, in part because it is so closely related conceptually and empirically to so many other variables. There is some empirical support for many plausible rival hypotheses about the processes involved. We have classified these as four pathways from schooling during childhood and adolescence to altered reproductive and health behavior during the childbearing years: status aspirations, identity (including empowerment), skills, and models of learning and teaching (Figure 21.1). Each of these pathways is a plausible mediator of the influence of schooling on reproductive and health behavior. They may be acting together or separately and may be of variable influence in different populations or even different cohorts within the same population.

Our first study, in a working-class population in the Mexican city of Cuernavaca, revealed evidence of all of the pathways (LeVine 1993; LeVine et al. 1991). In addition to interviewing more than 300 mothers, we conducted home observations of 72 women with their infants and young children (up to 15 months) that indicated that the mothers with more formal education were more verbally responsive to their infants from five months of age onwards and were much more so at 15 months – a finding consistent with a substantial body of observational literature on American mothers (Richman et al. 1992) and that has since been replicated in another cross-cultural study by Rogoff et al. (1993). We interpreted this to mean that women who had spent more time in school were more likely to have internalized the model of learning and teaching (i.e., the teacher–pupil instructional schema) embedded in heavily scripted classroom interaction. As a consequence, we argued, they were more likely to act like *pupils* in relation to the medical authorities of the media and the clinic – thus obediently following medical advice; but also more inclined to act like *teachers* in relation to their own young children – infusing child care with verbal communication and pedagogical interaction. From the point of view of demographic change, this meant an intensification of maternal attention that could result in improved child survival in the short run and, through the child's expectations for prolonged attention, in the mother's bearing fewer children. We were suggesting, in other words, that formal education was leading to the greater labor intensity of childcare, which in turn led eventually to lower rates of child mortality and fertility. But preliminary results from our studies in *rural* Mexico and Nepal did not show the expected correlations between schooling and mother–child verbal communication, leading us to believe that the impact on early interaction might be specific to the advanced stage of demographic transition of the urban Mexican sample.

Our early research, then, generated even more plausible hypotheses than we had started with but did not result in the disentangling of one pathway from the others. Although we were prepared to believe that it might be impossible to disentangle the pathways, we decided to see if we could decisively falsify one of them, namely, skills, particularly literacy skills, as a link between schooling and maternal health behavior. We consulted a literacy expert, Patricia Velasco, then finishing her doctorate at the Harvard Graduate School of Education, who brought the thinking and assessment methods of our colleagues Jeanne Chall and Catherine Snow into our studies in rural Mexico, rural Nepal and urban Zambia. To our surprise, literacy and language skills were highly correlated with mothers' years of schooling and with mothers' comprehension of health messages in print and on the radio, in these three very diverse samples (Dexter et al. 1998; Joshi 1994; LeVine et al. 1994a; Stuebing 1997). This finding caused us to turn completely around and focus our research on the skill pathway, looking specifically at literacy and language skills as links between maternal schooling and the utilization of health and reproductive services, in new studies conducted in a low-income barrio of Caracas, Venezuela, and in two sites (urban and rural) in the Kathmandu Valley of Nepal (Figure 21.2).

Moving into the literacy field, we learned that it had advanced far beyond the conventions by which a population is divided into literates and illiterates. Indeed, the concept of literacy had been unwrapped and reconceptualized as numerous skills varying across cultures and historical periods and involving a variety of cognitive processes. From Chall's (1983) work we learned that the ability to read in school, far from being limited to a mechanical decoding of script acquired during the first years, refers to a cognitive process of comprehension that improves with the complexity of written texts mastered throughout the school experience. Thus, reading proficiency should be seen as a continuous variable that might differentiate those who terminated their schooling at different levels from first grade to university. This is important when attempting to relate this literacy variable to the reproductive and health behavior of mothers varying widely in years of school attendance.

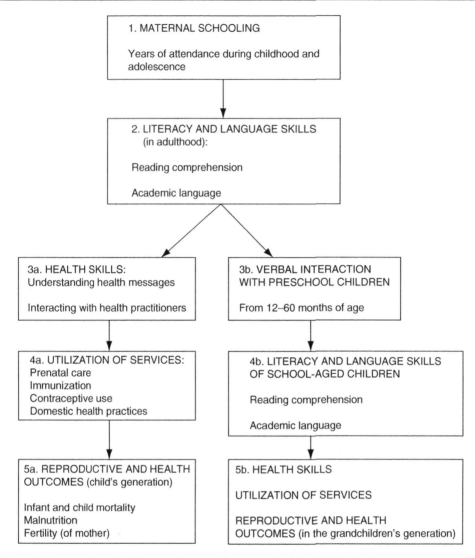

Figure 21.2 *Hypothetical influences of maternal literacy on health and child development.*

From Snow's (1990) work we learned that a certain way of using the language of written texts, in oral discourse or written form, is fundamental to school performance. She calls it decontextualized language ability. Others call it context-reduced or synoptic communication or the academic register. It is a type of discourse or speech register that contrasts sharply with everyday vernacular conversation in its use of abstract nouns and explicit descriptions that assume no prior shared knowledge of particulars. Proficiency in this impersonal form of communication that assumes no sharing of knowledge of particulars but does assume mastery of superordinate relationships among words (that a dog is an animal and a clock a machine) can be assessed by means of Snow's noun definitions test in which the respondent is asked to define simple nouns. Definitions are coded for the use of superordinate and other features characteristic of this form of discourse. We decided to assess literacy through the noun definitions and a measure of reading comprehension based as much as possible on school texts varying in complexity. Our theory is that schools are training grounds for participation in bureaucratic organizations and that their training is in the communicative code of such bureaucracies, namely, the academic language proficiency measured by the noun definitions test, which enables a woman to use bureaucratic health and contraceptive services more effectively. In school, girls from agrarian communities undergo a communicative socialization that gives them the literacy skills for bureaucratic participation involved in the demographic transition.

The new research has enabled us to look more closely at literacy and language skills as children learn them in school and as they may influence mothers' access to health messages in the media and their interactions with health practitioners. Our studies in Nepal and Venezuela show that mothers – even those who attended low-quality schools and did not complete primary school – retain some literacy skills in adulthood that may help them comprehend the instructional messages of public health authorities and interact more effectively with health practitioners. Our regression analyses have shown, furthermore, that a composite measure of the two academic-literacy skills best represents the probable pathway between schooling and health comprehension in both sites (LeVine et al. 2001; LeVine et al. n.d.). It is particularly noteworthy that these findings have been replicated in the extremely diverse settings of Nepal, a poor South Asian country where only about 15 percent of adult women have attended school, and Venezuela, an oil-producing Latin American country where primary schooling for women is virtually universal and child-survival rates are far higher than in Nepal.

In the next phase of our research we shall explore the intergenerational transmission of literacy skills, which we believe to be crucial in the long-term process by which schooling facilitates demographic transition, by examining the links between mother's literacy and the literate environments and skills of their children in Nepal, Venezuela, and the United States. This will also enable our data from developing countries to be connected with research on maternal schooling and its psychological consequences in the United States. In addition, having helped plan a UNICEF survey of literacy and health care (larger than anything we have done) in two districts of Nepal outside the Kathmandu Valley, we are looking forward to having an impact on demographic and health surveys there and in other parts of the world.

All of this may seem to have taken us far from Beatrice Whiting's research on the social lives of children and her interests, Freudian and otherwise, in the connections between culture and psychological development. We are certain she does not see it that way, and not only because of the roots we have shown of our current project in her concepts and methods. As a psychological anthropologist trained at Yale in the 1930s and a social scientist deeply interested in the processes of change and the problems of women everywhere, she has provided us with an enduring model of social and psychological research that recognizes no boundaries in the search for knowledge of human development.

REFERENCES

Barker, Roger, and Herbert Wright
    1954 Midwest and its Children: The Psychological Ecology of an American Town. Evanstown, IL: Row, Peterson, and Company.
Chall, Jeanne C.
    1983 Stages of Reading Development. New York: McGraw-Hill.
Dexter, Emily, Sarah E. LeVine, and Patricia Velasco
    1998 Maternal Schooling and Health-Related Literacy and Language Skills in Rural Mexico. Comparative Education Review 42(2):139–162.
Haggard, Ernest
    1960 On the Reliability of the Anamnestic Interview. Journal of Abnormal and Social Psychology 61(3):311.
Joshi, Arun
    1994 Maternal Schooling and Child Health: Preliminary Analysis of the Intervening Mechanisms in Rural Nepal. Health Transition Review 4(1):1–28.
LeVine, Sarah E.

1993 Dolor y Alegria: Women and Social Change In Urban Mexico. Madison: University of Wisconsin Press.

LeVine, Robert A., Emily Dexter, Patricia Velasco, Sarah LeVine, Arun Joshi, Kathleen Stuebing, and Medardo F. Tapia Uribe
1994a Maternal Literacy and Health Care in Three Countries: A Preliminary Report. Health Transition Review 4(2):186–191.

LeVine, Robert A., Suzanne Dixon, Sarah E. LeVine, Amy Richman, P. Herbert Leiderman, Constance H. Keefer, and T. Berry Brazelton
1994b Child Care and Culture: Lessons from Africa. New York: Cambridge University Press.

LeVine, Robert A., Sarah E. LeVine, Amy Richman, Medardo F. Tapia Uribe, Clara Sunderland Correa, and Patrice Miller
1991 Women's Schooling and Child Care in the Demographic Transition: A Mexican Case Study. Population and Development Review 17(3):459–496.

LeVine, Robert A., Sarah E. LeVine, and Beatrice Schnell
2001 "Improve the Women": Mass Schooling, Female Literacy, and Worldwide Social Change. Harvard Educational Review 71(1):1–50.

LeVine, Robert A., Sarah E. LeVine, Beatrice Schnell, and Meredith Rowe
N.d. Maternal Literacy and Demographic Change in the Kathmandu Valley.

Richman, Amy, Patrice Miller, and Robert A. LeVine
1992 Cultural and Educational Variations in Maternal Responsiveness. Developmental Psychology 28:614–621.

Robbins, John
1963 The Accuracy of Parental Recall of Aspects of Child Development and of Child Rearing Practices. Journal of Abnormal and Social Psychology 66(3):261.

Rogoff, Barbara, Jyanthi Mistry, Artin Goncu, and Christine Mosier
1993 Guided Participation in Cultural Activity by Toddlers and Caregivers. Monographs of the Society for Research in Child Development, 58 (Serial No. 236).

Snow, Catherine E.
1990 The Development of Definitional Skill. Journal of Child Language 17(3):697–710.

Stuebing, Katherine
1997 Maternal Schooling and Comprehension of Health Information in Urban Zambia. Health Transition Review 7(2):151–172.

Whiting, Beatrice B.
1963 Six Cultures: Studies of Child Rearing. New York: John Wiley and Sons.
1976 The Problem of the Packaged Variable. In The Developing Individual in a Changing World, vol. 2. pp. 303–309. K. F. Riegel and J. A. Mesoham, eds. The Hague: Mouton.

Whiting, Beatrice B. and Carolyn Pope Edwards
1988 Children of Different Worlds. Cambridge, MA: Harvard University Press.

Whiting, Beatrice B. and John W. M. Whiting
1975 Children of Six Cultures. Cambridge, MA: Harvard University Press.

Whiting, J. W. M., Irvin L. Child, William W. Lambert, Ann M. Flscher, John L. Fischer, Corinne Nydegger, William Nydegger, Hatsumi Maretski, Thomas Maretski, Leigh Minturn, A. Kimball Romney, and Romain Romney
1966 Field Guide for a Study of Socialization. New York: John Wiley and Sons.

22

Revitalization Movements

Anthony F. C. Wallace

Introduction

Behavioral scientists have described many instances of attempted and sometimes successful innovation of whole cultural systems, or at least substantial portions of such systems. Various rubrics are employed, the rubric depending on the discipline and the theoretical orientation of the researcher, and on salient local characteristics of the cases he has chosen for study. "Nativistic movement," "reform movement," "cargo cult," "religious revival," "messianic movement," "utopian community," "sect formation," "mass movement," "social movement," "revolution," "charismatic movement," are some of the commonly used labels. This paper suggests that all these phenomena of major cultural-system innovation are characterized by a uniform process, for which I propose the term "revitalization." The body of the paper is devoted to two ends: (1) an introductory statement of the concept of revitalization, and (2) an outline of certain uniformly-found processual dimensions of revitalization movements.

The formulations are based in major part on documentary data, mostly published. Library research on the project began in 1951 with a study of the new religion initiated by Handsome Lake, the Seneca prophet, among the nineteenth century reservation Iroquois. The Handsome Lake materials being unusually ample (a number of manuscript journals and diaries were found) provided a useful standard with which to compare the various other movements which have since been investigated. Our files now contain references to several hundred religious revitalization movements, among both western and nonwestern peoples, on five continents. These represent only a small portion, gathered in a quick preliminary survey of anthropological literature. An earnest attempt to collect all revitalization movements described in historical, anthropological, and other sorts of documents, would without question gather in thousands. Movements on which we have substantial data include: in North America, the Handsome Lake case (the Seneca, 1799–1815), the Delaware Prophet (associated with Pontiac, 1762–1765), the Shawnee Prophet (associated with Tecumseh, 1805–1814), the Ghost Dance (1888–1896), and Peyote; in Europe, John Wesley and early Methodism (1738–1800); in Africa, Ikhnaton's new religion (ancient Egypt), the Sudanese Mahdi (the Sudan, 1880–1898), and the Xosa Revival (South Africa, 1856–1857); in Asia, the origin of Christianity, the origin of Mohammedanism (c610–650), the early development of Sikhism (India, c1500–c1700), and the Taiping Rebellion (China, 1843–1864); in Melanesia, the Vailala Madness (New Guinea, c1919–c1930); in South America, a series of *terre sans mal* movements among the forest tribes, from early contact to recent times.[1]

Anthony F. C. Wallace, Revitalization Movements from *American Anthropologist*, New Series, Vol. 58, No. 2 (April 1956), pp. 264–281.

Accordingly, the formulations presented here are in an intermediate stage: a species has been recognized and certain characteristics (selected, of course, in the light of the author's theoretical interests) described, after the fashion of natural history. More abstract descriptions, in terms of the interaction of analytic variables, can only be suggested here, and other papers will present details of the dynamics of the revitalization process.

The Concept of Revitalization

A revitalization movement is defined as a deliberate, organized, conscious effort by members of a society to construct a more satisfying culture. Revitalization is thus, from a cultural standpoint, a special kind of culture change phenomenon: the persons involved in the process of revitalization must perceive their culture, or some major areas of it, as a system (whether accurately or not); they must feel that this cultural system is unsatisfactory; and they must innovate not merely discrete items, but a new cultural system, specifying new relationships as well as, in some cases, new traits. The classic processes of culture change (evolution, drift, diffusion, historical change, acculturation) all produce changes in cultures as systems; however, they do not depend on deliberate intent by members of a society, but rather on a gradual chain-reaction effect: introducing A induces change in B; changing B affects C; when C shifts, A is modified; this involves D . . . and so on *ad infinitum*. This process continues for years, generations, centuries, millennia, and its pervasiveness has led many cultural theorists to regard culture change as essentially a slow, chain-like, self-contained procession of superorganic inevitabilities. In revitalization movements, however, A, B, C, D, E . . . N are shifted into a new *Gestalt* abruptly and simultaneously in intent; and frequently within a few years the new plan is put into effect by the participants in the movement. We may note in passing that Keesing's assessment of the literature on culture change (1953), while it does not deal explicitly with the theoretical issue of chain-effects versus revitalization, discusses both types. Barnett (1953) frankly confines his

discussion to innovations of limited scope in the context of chains of events in acceptance and rejection. As Mead has suggested, cultures *can* change within one generation (Mead 1955); and the process by which such transformations occur is the revitalization process.

The term "revitalization" implies an organismic analogy.[2] This analogy is, in fact, an integral part of the concept of revitalization. A human society is here regarded as a definite kind of organism, and its culture is conceived as those patterns of learned behavior which certain "parts" of the social organism or system (individual persons and groups of persons) characteristically display. A corollary of the organismic analogy is the principle of homeostasis: that a society will work, by means of coordinated actions (including "cultural" actions) by all or some of its parts, to preserve its own integrity by maintaining a minimally fluctuating, life-supporting matrix for its individual members, and will, under stress, take emergency measures to preserve the constancy of this matrix. Stress is defined as a condition in which some part, or the whole, of the social organism is threatened with more or less serious damage. The perception of stress, particularly of increasing stress, can be viewed as the common denominator of the panel of "drives" or "instincts" in every psychological theory.

As I am using the organismic analogy, the total system which constitutes a society includes as significant parts not only persons and groups with their respective patterns of behavior, but also literally the cells and organs of which the persons are composed. Indeed, one can argue that the system includes nonhuman as well as human subsystems. Stress on one level is stress on all levels. For example, lowering of sugar level (hunger) in the fluid matrix of the body cells of one group of persons in a society is a stress in the society as a whole. This holistic view of society as organism integrated from cell to nation depends on the assumption that society, as an organization of living matter, is definable as a network of intercommunication. Events on one subsystem level must affect other subsystems (cellular vis-à-vis institutional, personal vis-à-vis societal) at least as information; in this view, social organization exists to the degree that events in one subsystem are information to other subsystems.

There is one crucial difference between the principles of social organization and that of the individual person: a society's parts are very widely interchangeable, a person's only slightly so. The central nervous system cells, for example, perform many functions of coordinating information and executing adaptive action which other cells cannot do. A society, on the other hand, has a multiple-replacement capacity, such that many persons can perform the analogous information-coordination and executive functions on behalf of society-as-organism. Furthermore, that regularity of patterned behavior which we call culture depends relatively more on the ability of constituent units autonomously to perceive the system of which they are a part, to receive and transmit information, and to act in accordance with the necessities of the system, than on any all-embracing central administration which stimulates specialized parts to perform their function.

It is therefore functionally necessary for every person in society to maintain a mental image of the society and its culture, as well as of his own body and its behavioral regularities, in order to act in ways which reduce stress at all levels of the system. The person does, in fact, maintain such an image. This mental image I have called "the mazeway," since as a model of the cell-body-personality-nature-culture-society system or field, organized by the individual's own experience, it includes perceptions of both the maze of physical objects of the environment (internal and external, human and nonhuman) and also of the ways in which this maze can be manipulated by the self and others in order to minimize stress. The mazeway is nature, society, culture, personality, and body image, as seen by one person. Hallowell (1955) and Wallace (1955 and 1956) offer extended discussions of the mazeway and the related concepts of self, world view, and behavioral environment.

We may now see more clearly what "revitalization movements" revitalize. Whenever an individual who is under chronic, physiologically measurable stress, receives repeated information which indicates that his mazeway does not lead to action which reduces the level of stress, he must choose between maintaining his present mazeway and tolerating the stress, or changing the mazeway in an attempt to reduce the stress. Changing the mazeway involves changing the total *Gestalt* of his image of self, society, and culture, of nature and body, and of ways of action. It may also be necessary to make changes in the "real" system in order to bring mazeway and "reality" into congruence. The effort to work a change in mazeway and "real" system together so as to permit more effective stress reduction is the effort at revitalization; and the collaboration of a number of persons in such an effort is called a revitalization movement.

The term revitalization movement thus denotes a very large class of phenomena. Other terms are employed in the existing literature to denote what I would call subclasses, distinguished by a miscellany of criteria. "Nativistic movements," for example, are revitalization movements characterized by strong emphasis on the elimination of alien persons, customs, values, and/or materiel from the mazeway (Linton 1943). "Revivalistic" movements emphasize the institution of customs, values, and even aspects of nature which are thought to have been in the mazeway of previous generations but are not now present (Mooney 1892–93). "Cargo cults" emphasize the importation of alien values, customs, and materiel into the mazeway, these things being expected to arrive as a ship's cargo as for example in the Vailala Madness (Williams 1923, 1934). "Vitalistic movements" emphasize the importation of alien elements into the mazeway but do not necessarily invoke ship and cargo as the mechanism.[3] "Millenarian movements" emphasize mazeway transformation in an apocalyptic world transformation engineered by the supernatural. "Messianic movements" emphasize the participation of a divine savior in human flesh in the mazeway transformation (Wallis 1918, 1943). These and parallel terms do not denote mutually exclusive categories, for a given revitalization movement may be nativistic, millenarian, messianic, and revivalistic all at once; and it may (in fact, usually does) display ambivalence with respect to nativistic, revivalistic, and importation themes.

Revitalization movements are evidently not unusual phenomena, but are recurrent features in human history. Probably few men have lived who have not been involved in an instance of the revitalization process. They are, furthermore, of profound historical importance. Both Christianity and Mohammedanism, and possibly Buddhism as well, originated in revitalization movements. Most denominational and sectarian groups and orders budded or split off after failure to revitalize a traditional institution. One can ask whether a large proportion of religious phenomena have not originated in personality transformation dreams or visions characteristic of the revitalization process. Myths, legends, and rituals may be relics, either of the manifest content of vision-dreams or of the doctrines and history of revival and import cults, the circumstances of whose origin have been distorted and forgotten, and whose connection with dream states is now ignored. Myths in particular have long been noted to possess a dream-like quality, and have been more or less speculatively interpreted according to the principles of symptomatic dream interpretation. It is tempting to suggest that myths and, often, even legends, read like dreams because they *were* dreams when they were first told. It is tempting to argue further that culture heroes represent a condensation of the figures of the prophet and of the supernatural being of whom he dreamed.

In fact, it can be argued that all organized religions are relics of old revitalization movements, surviving in routinized form in stabilized cultures, and that religious phenomena per se originated (if it is permissible still in this day and age to talk about the "origins" of major elements of culture) in the revitalization process – i.e., in visions of a new way of life by individuals under extreme stress.

The Processual Structure

A basic methodological principle employed in this study is that of event-analysis (Wallace 1953). This approach employs a method of controlled comparison for the study of processes involving longer or shorter diachronic sequences (vide Eggan 1954 and Steward 1953). It is postulated that events or happenings of various types have genotypical structures independent of local cultural differences; for exam-

ple, that the sequence of happenings following a severe physical disaster in cities in Japan, the United States, and Germany, will display a uniform pattern, colored but not obscured by local differences in culture. These types of events may be called behavioral units. Their uniformity is based on generic human attributes, both physical and psychological, but it requires extensive analytical and comparative study to elucidate the structure of any one. Revitalization movements constitute such a behavioral unit, and so also, on a lower level of abstraction, do various subtypes within the larger class, such as cargo and revival cults. We are therefore concerned with describing the generic structure of revitalization movements considered as a behavioral unit, and also of variation along the dimensions characteristic of the type.

The structure of the revitalization process, in cases where the full course is run, consists of five somewhat overlapping stages: 1. Steady State; 2. Period of Individual Stress; 3. Period of Cultural Distortion; 4. Period of Revitalization (in which occur the functions of mazeway reformulation, communication, organization, adaptation, cultural transformation, and routinization), and finally, 5. New Steady State. These stages are described briefly in the following sections.

I. *Steady State.* For the vast majority of the population, culturally recognized techniques for satisfying needs operate with such efficiency that chronic stress within the system varies within tolerable limits. Some severe but still tolerable stress may remain general in the population, and a fairly constant incidence of persons under, for them, intolerable stress may employ "deviant" techniques (e.g., psychotics). Gradual modification or even rapid substitution of techniques for satisfying some needs may occur without disturbing the steady state, as long as (1) the techniques for satisfying other needs are not seriously interfered with, and (2) abandonment of a given technique for reducing one need in favor of a more efficient technique does not leave other needs, which the first technique was also instrumental in satisfying, without any prospect of satisfaction.

II. *The Period of Increased Individual Stress.* Over a number of years, individual members of a population (which may be "primitive" or "civilized," either a whole society or a class, caste, religious, occupational, acculturational, or other definable social group) experience increasingly severe stress as a result of the decreasing efficiency of certain stress-reduction techniques. The culture may remain essentially unchanged or it may undergo considerable changes, but in either case there is continuous diminution in its efficiency in satisfying needs. The agencies responsible for interference with the efficiency of a cultural system are various: climatic, floral and faunal change; military defeat; political subordination; extreme pressure toward acculturation resulting in internal cultural conflict; economic distress; epidemics; and so on. The situation is often, but not necessarily, one of acculturation, and the acculturating agents may or may not be representatives of Western European cultures. While the individual can tolerate a moderate degree of increased stress and still maintain the habitual way of behavior, a point is reached at which some alternative way must be considered. Initial consideration of a substitute way is likely, however, to increase stress because it arouses anxiety over the possibility that the substitute way will be even less effective than the original, and that it may also actively interfere with the execution of other ways. In other words, it poses the threat of mazeway disintegration. Furthermore, admission that a major technique is worthless is extremely threatening because it implies that the whole mazeway system may be inadequate.

III. *The Period of Cultural Distortion.* The prolonged experience of stress, produced by failure of need satisfaction techniques and by anxiety over the prospect of changing behavior patterns, is responded to differently by different people. Rigid persons apparently prefer to tolerate high levels of chronic stress rather than make systematic adaptive changes in the mazeway. More flexible persons try out various limited mazeway changes in their personal lives, attempting to reduce stress by addition or substitution of mazeway elements with more or less concern for the *Gestalt* of the system. Some persons turn to psychodynamically regressive innovations; the regressive response empirically exhibits itself in increasing incidences of such things as alcoholism, extreme passivity and indolence, the development of highly ambivalent dependency relationships, intragroup violence, disregard of kinship and sexual mores, irresponsibility in public officials, states of depression and self-reproach, and probably a variety of psychosomatic and neurotic disorders. Some of these regressive action systems become, in effect, new cultural patterns.

In this phase, the culture is internally distorted; the elements are not harmoniously related but are mutually inconsistent and interfering. For this reason alone, stress continues to rise. "Regressive" behavior, as defined by the society, will arouse considerable guilt and hence increase stress level or at least maintain it at a high point; and the general process of piecemeal cultural substitution will multiply situations of mutual conflict and misunderstanding, which in turn increase stress-level again.

Finally, as the inadequacy of existing ways of acting to reduce stress becomes more and more evident, and as the internal incongruities of the mazeway are perceived, symptoms of anxiety over the loss of a meaningful way of life also become evident: disillusionment with the mazeway, and apathy toward problems of adaptation, set in.

IV. *The Period of Revitalization.* This process of deterioration can, if not checked, lead to the death of the society. Population may fall even to the point of extinction as a result of increasing death rates and decreasing birth rates; the society may be defeated in war, invaded, its population dispersed and its customs suppressed; factional disputes may nibble a way areas and segments of the population. But these dire events are not infrequently forestalled, or at least postponed, by a revitalization movement. Many such movements are religious in character, and such religious revitalization movements must perform at least six major tasks:

1. *Mazeway reformulation.* Whether the movement is religious or secular, the reformulation of the mazeway generally seems to depend on a restructuring of elements and subsystems which have already attained currency in the society and may even be in use, and which are known to the person who is to become the prophet or leader. The occasion of

their combination in a form which constitutes an internally consistent structure, and of their acceptance by the prophet as a guide to action, is abrupt and dramatic, usually occurring as a moment of insight, a brief period of realization of relationships and opportunities. These moments are often called inspiration or revelation. The reformulation also seems normally to occur in its initial form in the mind of a single person rather than to grow directly out of group deliberations.

With a few exceptions, every religious revitalization movement with which I am acquainted has been originally conceived in one or several hallucinatory visions by a single individual. A supernatural being appears to the prophet-to-be, explains his own and his society's troubles as being entirely or partly a result of the violation of certain rules, and promises individual and social revitalization if the injunctions are followed and the rituals practiced, but personal and social catastrophe if they are not. These dreams express: 1. the dreamer's wish for a satisfying parental figure (the supernatural, guardian-spirit content), 2. world-destruction fantasies (the apocalyptic, millennial content), 3. feelings of guilt and anxiety (the moral content), and 4. longings for the establishment of an ideal state of stable and satisfying human and supernatural relations (the restitution fantasy or Utopian content). In a sense, such a dream also functions almost as a funeral ritual: the "dead" way of life is recognized as dead: interest shifts to a god, the community, and a new way. A new mazeway *Gestalt* is presented, with more or less innovation in details of content. The prophet feels a need to tell others of his experience, and may have definite feelings of missionary or messianic obligation. Generally he shows evidence of a radical inner change in personality soon after the vision experience: a remission of old and chronic physical complaints, a more active and purposeful way of life, greater confidence in interpersonal relations, the dropping of deep-seated habits like alcoholism. Hence we may call these visions "personality transformation dreams." Where there is no vision (as with John Wesley), there occurs a similarly brief and dramatic moment of insight, revelation, or inspiration, which functions in most respects

like the vision in being the occasion of a new synthesis of values and meanings.

My initial approach to the understanding of these visions was by way of psychoanalytic dream theory. This proved to be of some use in elucidating the meaning of the vision. From an analysis of its manifest content and from the circumstances of the dreamer's history and life situation, it is possible to make more or less plausible interpretations of the nature of the prophet's personal preoccupations and conflicts. But conventional dream theory was designed to explain the conflicts represented in ordinary night dreams. Prophetic visions, while essentially dream formations, differ in several respects from ordinary symptomatic dreams: they often occur during a waking state as hallucinatory experiences, or in an ecstatic trance rather than in normal sleep; they impress the dreamer immediately as being meaningful and important; the manifest content is often in large part rational and well considered intellectual argument and cogent moral exhortation; and recollection of them is in unusually rich detail. This brings to mind Fromm's position (1951), that many dreams are not so much symptomatic of unconscious neurotic conflict as insightful in a positive and creative sense. But this additional consideration did not seem adequately to account for the most remarkable feature of all: the transformation of personality, often in a positive therapeutic sense, which these dreams produced. Prophetic and ecstatic visions do express unconscious conflict; they sometimes reveal considerable insight, but they also work startling cures.

We therefore became interested in pursuing the dynamics of personality transformation dreams. As a type of event, they would seem to belong to a general clinical category of sudden and radical changes in personality, along with transformations occurring in psychotic breaks, spontaneous remissions, narcosynthesis, some occasions in psychotherapy, "brainwashing," and shock treatments. There are, incidentally, some interesting similarities between the physical state of prophets and converts in the vision-trance, and patients undergoing shock (Sargant 1949, 1951). Physical stress and exhaustion often seem to precede the vision-trance type of transformation, and it seems probable that chemical substances produced in the body under stress may be important in rendering a person capable of this type of experience (Hoffer, Osmond, and Smythies, 1954). The relationship of this sort of sudden personality change to slower maturational processes, on the one hand, and to what happens in rites of passage, on the other, should be points of interest to social scientists generally.

Nonclinical analogues of the prophet's personality transformation vision appear in several contexts: in accounts of individual ecstatic conversions and experiences of religious enthusiasm; in the guardian spirit quest among American Indians and elsewhere; and in the process of becoming a shaman, which is similar in many cultures all over the world. Conversion, shamanism, and the guardian-spirit vision seem to be phenomena very similar in pattern. All three of these processes are distributed globally; in many cultures all three are normal phenomena; all involve persons who are faced with the opportunity (if not necessity) of assuming a new cultural role and of abandoning an earlier role in order to reduce stress which they will not be able to resolve if they stand pat. A precipitating factor in many cases is some sort of severe physical stress, such as illness, starvation, sleeplessness, or fatigue. After the vision experience, the individual is often able to assume a new role requiring increased or differently phrased emotional independence. In the vision experience, he has invented a fictitious, nurturing, parent-like supernatural figure who satisfies much of his need for authority and protection; thus he is presumably able to loosen emotional ties to certain cultural objects, roles, and persons, and to act without undue inhibition and anxiety. Inconvenient wishes are displaced onto a fictitious but culturally sanctioned supernatural pseudo-community, leaving the personality free for relatively healthy relationships to the real world. An essential function of the vision is that the demands for energy made by transference wishes are minimized by displacement onto supernatural objects which can in fantasy be perceived as uniformly supporting and protective.

Inasmuch as many prophets were suffering from recognizable and admitted mental disorders before their transformation, which they achieved by means of a type of experience (hallucination) that our culture generally regards as pathological, the relevance of psychopathology to the vision experience needs to be explored. We have under way some observations on the case histories of a series of persons in a state mental institution who have been known to attendants for their excessive religiosity.[4] This survey, which we hope to extend to include interview materials, is not complete, but I can summarize our initial impressions. Chronic schizophrenics with religious paranoia tend to believe that they are God, Jesus, the Virgin Mary, the Great Earth Mother, or some other supernatural being. Successful prophets, on the other hand, usually do not believe that they are the supernatural, only that they have communicated with him (although their followers may freely deify them). Prophets do not lose their sense of personal identity but psychotics tend to become the object of their spiritual longing.

There are in this institution several persons who were hospitalized during the course of an experience which resembles in many respects the process of becoming a prophet. A man, burdened with a sense of guilt and inadequacy, and sensible of the need to reform his life, has a religious conversion in which he sees God or hears his voice; thereafter he displays a changed and in some ways healthier (or at least less rapidly deteriorating) personality; he undertakes an evangelistic or prophetic enterprise which is socially inconvenient to spouse, relatives, employer, warden, or other closely associated persons; he is thereupon certified as insane and hospitalized. Such frustrated prophets, being unable any longer to satisfy important human needs and suffering the obvious disapproval of the community, may also lose confidence in their relationship to the supernatural pseudo-community. They cannot return to their preconversion state because the hospital situation makes anything remotely approaching normal cultural and social participation impossible. Many therefore take the emotionally logical but unfortunate next step, and become the guardian spirit.

At this time, then, we would tentatively conclude that the religious vision experience per se is not psychopathological but rather the reverse, being a synthesizing and often therapeutic process performed under extreme stress by individuals already sick.

2. *Communication*. The dreamer undertakes to preach his revelations to people, in an evangelistic or messianic spirit; he becomes a prophet. The doctrinal and behavioral injunctions which he preaches carry two fundamental motifs: that the convert will come under the care and protection of certain supernatural beings: and that both he and his society will benefit materially from an identification with some definable new cultural system (whether a revived culture or a cargo culture, or a syncretism of both, as is usually the case). The preaching may take many forms (e.g., mass exhortation vs. quiet individual persuasion) and may be directed at various sorts of audiences (e.g., the elite vs. the down-trodden). As he gathers disciples, these assume much of the responsibility for communicating the "good word," and communication remains one of the primary activities of the movement during later phases of organization.

3. *Organization*. Converts are made by the prophet. Some undergo hysterical seizures induced by suggestion in a crowd situation; some experience an ecstatic vision in private circumstances; some are convinced by more or less rational arguments, some by considerations of expediency and opportunity. A small clique of special disciples (often including a few already influential men) clusters about the prophet and an embryonic campaign organization develops with three orders of personnel: the prophet; the disciples; and the followers. Frequently the action program from here on is effectively administered in large part by a political rather than a religious leadership. Like the prophet, many of the converts undergo a revitalizing personality transformation.

Max Weber's concept of "charismatic leadership" well describes the type of leader-follower relationship characteristic of revitalization movement organizations (1947). The fundamental element of the vision, as I have indicated above, is the entrance of the visionary into an intense relationship with a supernatural being. This relationship, furthermore, is one in which the prophet accepts the leadership, succor, and dominance of the supernatural. Many followers of a prophet, especially the disciples, also have ecstatic revelatory experiences; but they and all sincere followers who have not had a personal revelation also enter into a parallel relationship to the prophet: as God is to the prophet, so (almost) is the prophet to his followers. The relationship of the follower to the prophet is in all probability determined by the displacement of transference dependency wishes onto his image; he is regarded as an uncanny person, of unquestionable authority in one or more spheres of leadership, sanctioned by the supernatural. Max Weber denotes this quality of uncanny authority and moral ascendency in a leader as charisma. Followers defer to the charismatic leader not because of his status in an existing authority structure but because of a fascinating personal "power," often ascribed to supernatural sources and validated in successful performance, akin to the "mana" or "orenda" of ethnological literature. The charismatic leader thus is not merely permitted but expected to phrase his call for adherents as a demand to perform a duty to a power higher than human. Weber correctly points out that the "routinization" of charisma is a critical issue in movement organization, since unless this "power" is distributed to other personnel in a stable institutional structure, the movement itself is liable to die with the death or failure of individual prophet, king, or war lord.

Weber, however, is essentially discussing a quality of leadership, and one which is found in contexts other than that of revitalization movements. In consequence, his generalizations do not deal with the revitalization formula itself, but rather with the nature of the relationship of the early adherents to their prophet. Furthermore, there is a serious ambiguity in Weber's use of the charisma concept. Weber seems to have been uncertain whether to regard it as an unusual quality in the leader which is recognized and rationalized by his adherents, or whether to regard it as a quality ascribed to the leader by followers and hence as being a quality of their relationship to him, determined both by the observed and the observer in the perceptual transaction. We have used it to denote the libidinal relationship which Freud described in *Group Psychology and the Analysis of the Ego* (1922).

It would appear that the emotional appeal of the new doctrine to both the prophet and his followers is in considerable part based on its immediate satisfaction of a need to find a supremely powerful and potentially benevolent leader. For both the prophet and his followers, this wish is gratified in fantasy (subjectively real, of course); but the follower's fantasy is directed toward the person of the prophet, to whom are attributed charismatic properties of leadership (Weber 1946, 1947).

4. *Adaptation.* The movement is a revolutionary organization and almost inevitably will encounter some resistance. Resistance may in some cases be slight and fleeting but more commonly is determined and resourceful, and is held either by a powerful faction within the society or by agents of a dominant foreign society. The movement may therefore have to use various strategies of adaptation: doctrinal modification; political and diplomatic maneuver; and force. These strategies are not mutually exclusive nor, once chosen, are they necessarily maintained through the life of the movement. In most instances the original doctrine is continuously modified by the prophet, who responds to various criticisms and affirmations by adding to, emphasizing, playing down, and eliminating selected elements of the original visions. This reworking makes the new doctrine more acceptable to special interest groups, may give it a better "fit" to the population's cultural and personality patterns, and may take account of the changes occurring in the general milieu. In instances where organized hostility to the movement develops, a crystallization of counterhostility against unbelievers frequently occurs, and emphasis shifts from cultivation of the ideal to combat against the unbeliever.

5. *Cultural Transformation.* As the whole or a controlling portion of the population comes to accept the new religion with its various injunctions, a noticeable social revitalization occurs, signalized by the reduction of the personal deterioration symptoms of individuals, by extensive cultural changes, and by an enthusiastic embarkation on some organized program of group action. This group program may, however, be more or less realistic and more or less adaptive: some programs are literally suicidal; others represent well conceived and successful projects of further social, political, or economic reform; some fail, not through any deficiency in conception and execution, but because circumstances made defeat inevitable.

6. *Routinization.* If the group action program in nonritual spheres is effective in reducing stress-generating situations, it becomes established as normal in various economic, social, and political institutions and customs. Rarely does the movement organization assert or maintain a totalitarian control over all aspects of the transformed culture; more usually, once the desired transformation has occurred, the organization contracts and maintains responsibility only for the preservation of doctrine and the performance of ritual (i.e., it becomes a church). With the mere passage of time, this poses the problems of "routinization" which Max Weber discusses at length (Weber 1946, 1947).

V. *The New Steady State.* Once cultural transformation has been accomplished and the new cultural system has proved itself viable, and once the movement organization has solved its problems of routinization, a new steady state may be said to exist. The culture of this state will probably be different in pattern, organization or *Gestalt*, as well as in traits, from the earlier steady state; it will be different from that of the period of cultural distortion.

Varieties and Dimensions of Variation

I will discuss four of the many possible variations: the choice of identification; the choice of secular and religious means; nativism; and the success-failure continuum.

1. *Choice of Identification.* Three varieties have been distinguished already on the basis of differences in choice of identification: movements which profess to *revive* a traditional culture now fallen into desuetude; movements which profess to *import* a foreign cultural system; and movements which profess neither revival nor importation, but conceive that the desired cultural endstate, which has never been enjoyed by ancestors or foreigners, will be realized for the first time in a future *Utopia*. The

Ghost Dance, the Xosa Revival, and the Boxer Rebellion are examples of professedly revivalistic movements; the Vailala Madness (and other cargo cults) and the Taiping Rebellion are examples of professedly importation movements. Some formulations like Ikhnaton's monotheistic cult in old Egypt and many Utopian programs, deny any substantial debt to the past or to the foreigner, but conceive their ideology to be something new under the sun, and its culture to belong to the future.

These varieties, however, are ideal types. A few movements do correspond rather closely to one type or another but many are obvious mixtures. Handsome Lake, for instance, consciously recognized both revival and importation themes in his doctrine. It is easy to demonstrate that avowedly revival movements are never entirely what they claim to be, for the image of the ancient culture to be revived is distorted by historical ignorance and by the presence of imported and innovative elements. Importation movements, with professed intentions to abandon the ancestral ways, manage to leave elements of the ancestral culture intact, if unrecognized, in large areas of experience. And movements which claim to present an absolutely new conception of culture are obviously blinding themselves to the fact that almost everything in the new system has been modeled after traditional or imported elements or both. Although almost every revitalization movement embodies in its proposed new cultural system large quantities of both traditional and imported cultural material, for some reason each movement tends to profess either no identification at all, a traditional orientation, or foreign orientation. This suggests that the choice of identification is the solution of a problem of double ambivalence: both the traditional and the foreign model are regarded both positively and negatively.

Culture areas seem to have characteristic ways of handling the identification problem. The cargo fantasy, although it can be found outside the Melanesian area, seems to be particularly at home there; South American Indian prophets frequently preached of a migration to a heaven-on-earth free of Spaniards and other evils, but the promised-land fantasy is known elsewhere; North American Indian prophets most commonly emphasized the revival of the old culture by ritual and moral purification,

but pure revival ideas exist in other regions too. Structural "necessity" or situational factors associated with culture area may be responsible. The contrast between native-white relationships in North America (a "revival" area) and Melanesia (an "importation" area) may be associated with the fact that American Indians north of Mexico were never enslaved on a large scale, forced to work on plantations, or levied for labor in lieu of taxes, whereas Melanesians were often subjected to more direct coercion by foreign police power. The Melanesian response has been an identification with the aggressor (vide Bettelheim 1947). On the other hand, the American Indians have been less dominated as individuals by whites, even under defeat and injustice. Their response to this different situation has by and large been an identification with a happier past. This would suggest that an important variable in choice of identification is the degree of domination exerted by a foreign society, and that import-oriented revitalization movements will not develop until an extremely high degree of domination is reached.

2. *The Choice of Secular and Religious Means.* There are two variables involved here: the amount of secular action which takes place in a movement, and the amount of religious action. Secular action is here defined as the manipulation of human relationships; religious action as the manipulation of relationships between human and supernatural beings. No revitalization movement can, by definition, be truly nonsecular, but some can be relatively less religious than others, and movements can change in emphasis depending on changing circumstances. There is a tendency, which is implicit in the earlier discussion of stages, for movements to become more political in emphasis, and to act through secular rather than religious institutions, as problems of organization, adaptation, and routinization become more pressing. The Taiping Rebellion, for instance, began as religiously-preoccupied movements; opposition by the Manchu dynasty and by foreign powers forced it to become more and more political and military in orientation.

A few "purely" political movements like the Hebertist faction during the French Revolution, and the Russian communist movement and its derivatives, have been officially atheistic, but the quality of doctrine and of leader-follower relationships is so similar, at least on superficial inspection, to religious doctrine and human-supernatural relations, that one wonders whether it is not a distinction without a difference. Communist movements are commonly asserted to have the quality of religious movements, despite their failure to appeal to a supernatural community, and such things as the development of a Marxist gospel with elaborate exegesis, the embalming of Lenin, and the concern with conversion, confession, and moral purity (as defined by the movement) have the earmarks of religion. The Communist Revolution of 1917 in Russia was almost typical in structure of religious revitalization movements: there was a very sick society, prophets appealed to a revered authority (Marx), apocalyptic and Utopian fantasies were preached, and missionary fervor animated the leaders. Furthermore, many social and political reform movements, while not atheistic, act through secular rather than religious media and invoke religious sanction only in a perfunctory way. I do not wish to elaborate the discussion at this time, however, beyond the point of suggesting again that the obvious distinctions between religious and secular movements may conceal fundamental similarities of socio-cultural process and of psychodynamics, and that while all secular prophets have not had personality transformation visions, some probably have, and others have had a similar experience in ideological conversion.

Human affairs around the world seem more and more commonly to be decided without reference to supernatural powers. It is an interesting question whether mankind can profitably dispense with the essential element of the religious revitalization process before reaching a Utopia without stress or strain. While religious movements may involve crude and powerful emotions and irrational fantasies of interaction with nonexistent beings, and can occasionally lead to unfortunate practical consequences in human relations, the same fantasies and emotions could lead to even more unfortunate practical consequences for world peace and human welfare when directed toward people improperly perceived and toward organs of political action and cultural ideologies. The answer would seem to be that as fewer and fewer men make use of the religious displacement process, there will have to be a corresponding reduction

of the incidence and severity of transference neuroses, or human relationships will be increasingly contaminated by character disorders, neurotic acting out, and paranoid deification of political leaders and ideologies.

3. *Nativism.* Because a major part of the program of many revitalization movements has been to expel the persons or customs of foreign invaders or overlords, they have been widely called "nativistic movements." However, the amount of nativistic activity in movements is variable. Some movements – the cargo cults, for instance – are antinativistic from a cultural standpoint but nativistic from a personnel standpoint. Handsome Lake was only mildly nativistic; he sought for an accommodation of cultures and personalities rather than expulsion, and favored entry of certain types of white persons and culture-content. Still, many of the classic revivalistic movements have been vigorously nativistic, in the ambivalent way discussed earlier. Thus nativism is a dimension of variation rather than an elemental property of revitalization movements.

A further complication is introduced by the fact that the nativistic component of a revitalization movement not uncommonly is very low at the time of conception, but increases sharply after the movement enters the adaptation stage. Initial doctrinal formulations emphasize love, co-operation, understanding, and the prophet and his disciples expect the powers-that-be to be reasonable and accepting. When these powers interfere with the movement, the response is apt to take the form of an increased nativistic component in the doctrine. Here again, situational factors are important for an understanding of the course and character of the movement.

4. *Success and Failure.* The outline of stages as given earlier is properly applicable to a revitalization movement which is completely successful. Many movements are abortive; their progress is arrested at some intermediate point. This raises a taxonomic question: how many stages should the movement achieve in order to qualify for inclusion in the category? Logically, as long as the original conception is a doctrine of revitalization by culture change, there should be no requisite number of stages. Practically, we have selected only movements which passed the first three stages (conception, communication, and organization) and entered

the fourth (adaptation). This means that the bulk of our information on success and failure will deal with circumstances of relatively late adaptation, rather than with such matters as initial blockage of communication and interference with organization.

Two major but not unrelated variables seem to be very important in determining the fate of any given movement: the relative "realism" of the doctrine; and the amount of force exerted against the organization by its opponents. "Realism" is a difficult concept to define without invoking the concept of success or failure, and unless it can be so defined, is of no use as a variable explanatory of success or failure. Nor can one use the criterion of conventionality of perception, since revitalization movements are by definition unconventional. While a great deal of doctrine in every movement (and, indeed, in every person's mazeway) is extremely unrealistic in that predictions of events made on the basis of its assumptions will prove to be more or less in error, there is only one sphere of behavior in which such error is fatal to the success of a revitalization movement: prediction of the outcome of conflict situations. If the organization cannot predict successfully the consequences of its own moves and of its opponents' moves in a power struggle, its demise is very likely. If, on the other hand, it is canny about conflict, or if the amount of resistance is low, it can be extremely "unrealistic" and extremely unconventional in other matters without running much risk of early collapse. In other words, probability of failure would seem to be negatively correlated with degree of realism in conflict situations, and directly correlated with amount of resistance. Where conflict-realism is high and resistance is low, the movement is bound to achieve the phase of routinization. Whether its culture will be viable for long beyond this point, however, will depend on whether its mazeway formulations lead to actions which maintain a low level of stress.

Summary

This programmatic paper outlines the concepts, assumptions, and initial findings of a comparative study of religious revitalization movements. Revitalization movements are defined as deliberate, conscious, organized efforts by members of a society to create a more satisfying culture. The revitalization movement as a general type of event occurs under two conditions: high stress for individual members of the society, and disillusionment with a distorted cultural *Gestalt*. The movement follows a series of functional stages: mazeway reformulation, communication, organization, adaptation, cultural transformation, and routinization. Movements vary along several dimensions, of which choice of identification, relative degree of religious and secular emphasis, nativism, and success or failure are discussed here. The movement is usually conceived in a prophet's revelatory visions, which provide for him a satisfying relationship to the supernatural and outline a new way of life under divine sanction. Followers achieve similar satisfaction of dependency needs in the charismatic relationship. It is suggested that the historical origin of a great proportion of religious phenomena has been in revitalization movements.

NOTES

1 The Handsome Lake project, supported largely by a Faculty Research Fellowship of the Social Science Research Council, with supplemental funds from the Behavioral Research Council and Committee for the Advancement of Research of the University of Pennsylvania, has served as a pilot study, and the larger investigation is now largely financed by the National Institute of Mental Health (U. S. Public Health Service), Grant M-883, with supplemental funds from the American Philosophical Society and the Eastern Pennsylvania Psychiatric Institute. I should like to express my appreciation to Sheila C. Steen (who has been the "field director" of the project, responsible for much of the empirical research and participant in conceptual formulation), and to research and clerical assistants Josephine H. Dixon, Herbert S. Williams, and Ruth Goodenough. Persons whose comments and suggestions on the first draft of this paper

have been of value in its revision include Margaret Mead, Theodore Schwartz, Walter Goldschmidt, A. I. Hallowell, David F. Aberle, Betty S. Wallace and Ward Goodenough. The Handsome Lake movement will be described in detail in a book the writer is now preparing. For other treatments now in print, see Parker, 1913; Deardorff, 1951; Voget, 1954; and Wallace, 1952a and 1952b.

2 This article is not the place to present a general discussion of the notions of order and field, function and equilibrium, the organismic analogy, the concept of homeostasis, and certain ideas from cybernetics, learning and perception, and the physiology of stress, which would be necessary to justify and fully elucidate the assumptions on which the revitalization hypothesis is based. See however, Wallace 1953, 1955, and 1956 for further development of the holistic view and more extended discussions of the mazeway concept.

3 After we had coined the term "revitalization movement," we discovered that Marian Smith in an article on the Indian Shakers (Smith 1954) uses the closely related term "vitalistic movements" ("a vitalistic movement may be defined as 'any conscious, organized attempt on the part of a society's members to incorporate in its culture selected aspects of another culture in contact with it'"). However, she uses this term for what I would call nonnativistic revitalization movements with importation (rather than revivalistic) emphasis.

4 I should like to express my appreciation to Dr. Arthur P. Noyes, Superintendent, and Drs. Warren Hampe and Kenneth Kool of the staff of Norristown (Pa.) State Hospital, for their assistance in making this survey possible.

REFERENCES

Barnett, H. G.
1953 Innovation: The Basis of Culture Change. New York.

Bettelheim, B.
1947 Individual and Mass Behavior in Extreme Situations. In Newcomb, Hartley, et al., eds., Readings in Social Psychology. New York.

Cantril, Hadley
1941 The Psychology of Social Movements. New York.

Deardorff, M. H.
1951 The Religion of Handsome Lake: Its Origin and Development. In Symposium on Local Diversity in Iroquois Culture, edited by W. N. Fenton, Bureau of American Ethnology Bulletin 149:79–107. Washington.

Eggan, Fred
1954 Social Anthropology and the Method of Controlled Comparison. American Anthropologist 56:743–63.

Freud, Sigmund
1922 Group Psychology and the Analysis of the Ego. London: International Psycho-Analytic Press.

Fromm, Erich
1951 The Forgotten Language. New York.

Hallowell, A. L.
1955 The Self and Its Behavioral Environment. In A. I. Hallowell, Culture and Experience. Philadelphia.

Hoffer, A., H. Osmond, and J. Smythies
1954 Schizophrenia: A New Approach. II. Result of a Year's Research. Journal of Mental Science, 100:29–45.

James, William
1902 Varieties of Religious Experience. New York.

Keesing, Felix M.
1953 Culture Change: An Analysis and Bibliography of Anthropological Sources to 1952. Stanford.

Knox, R. A.
1950 Enthusiasm: A Chapter in the History of Religion, with Special Reference to the XVII and XVIII Centuries. Oxford.

Linton, Ralph
1943 Nativistic Movements. American Anthropologist 45:230–40.

Lowe, Warner L.
1953 Psychodynamics in Religious Delusions and Hallucinations. American Journal of Psychotherapy 7:454–62.

Mead, Margaret
1954 Nativistic Cults as Laboratories for Studying Closed and Open Systems. Paper read at annual meeting of the American Anthropological Association.
1955 How Fast Can Man Change? Address presented to Frankford Friends Forum, Philadelphia, 4 Dec. 1955.

Mooney, James
1892–93 The Ghost Dance Religion. Bureau of American Ethnology Annual Report. Washington.

Parker, Arthur
 1913 The Code of Handsome Lake, the Seneca Prohbet. New York State Museum Bulletin 163. Albany.
Sargant, William
 1949 Some Cultural Group Abreactive Techniques and Their Relation to Modern Treatments. Proceedings of the Royal Society of Medicine 42:367–74.
 1951 The Mechanism of Conversion. British Medical Journal 2:311 et seq.
Schwartz, Theodore
 1954 The Changing Structure of the Manus Nativistic Movement. Paper read at annual meeting of the American Anthropological Association.
Smith, Marian
 1954 Shamanism in the Shaker Religion of Northwest America. Man, August 1954, 181.
Steward, Julian N.
 1953 Evolution and Process. In A. L. Kroeber, ed., Anthropology Today. Chicago.
Voget, Fred W.
 1954 Reformative Tendencies in American Indian Nativistic Cults. Paper read at annual meeting of the American Anthropological Association.
 1952a Handsome Lake and the Great Revival in the West. American Quarterly, Summer: 149–65.
 1952b Halliday Jackson's Journal to the Seneca Indians, 1798–1800. Pennsylvania History 19: Nos. 2 and 3.

 1953 A Science of Human Behavior. Explorations No. 3.
 1955 The Disruption of the Individual's Identification with His Culture in Disasters and Other Extreme Situations. Paper read at National Research Council, Committee on Disaster Studies, Conference on Theories of Human Behavior in Extreme Situations, Vassar College.
 1956 The Mazeway. Explorations No. 6. In press.
Wallis, Wilson D.
 1918 Messiahs – Christian and Pagan. Boston.
 1943 Messiahs – Their Role in Civilization. Washington.
Weber, Max
 1930 The Protestant Ethic and the Spirit of Capitalism. Translated by Talcott Parsons. New York.
 1946 From Max Weber: Essays in Sociology. Translated and edited by H. Gerth and C. W. Mills, New York.
 1947 The Theory of Social and Economic Organization. Translated and edited by A. M. Henderson and Talcott Parsons. New York.
Williams, F. E.
 1923 The Vailala Madness and the Destruction of Native Ceremonies in the Gulf Division. Port Moresby: Territory of Papua, Anthropology Report No. 4.
 1934 The Vailala Madness in Retrospect. In Essays Presented to C. G. Seligman. London.

23

Culture, Charisma, and Consciousness

Charles Lindholm

Charisma, Common Sense, and Culture

American social science has great difficulty understanding why others should give up their own desires, ambitions, families, careers, and even lives, in service to charismatic leaders and their causes. Commitment to figures such as Jim Jones or, more recently, to Osama bin Laden, is usually taken as madness at worst, delusion at best. This attitude reflects our taken-for-granted manner of conceptualizing sanity as the capacity to calculate our acts to gain personal advantage. Subordination to the will of another when that may mean one's own death is impossible to grasp from within this utilitarian perspective. Nonetheless, charismatic movements have been the engines of social change in the past and will remain a challenge in the future. What role can anthropology have in developing a paradigm for these extraordinary states of mind?

Up to now, anthropologists have contributed very little. We have generally been satisfied to demonstrate that assumptions about normal consciousness vary according to cultural context: what is madness here is reckoned to be sensible there, and vice versa. But although the anthropological analysis of meaning systems assumes that rational behavior is not the same everywhere, the underlying paradigm for understanding action still rests on the postulate that human beings are rational free agents capable of calculating how to maximize their self-interests; the only difference is that these interests are now reckoned to be culturally variable. Although it has its virtues, this paradigm is not adequate to grasp the self-sacrifices and irrationality that occur in charismatic relationships. Another model of consciousness is required (Lindholm 1990, 1992).

Charisma in Classical Social Theory Weber, Durkheim, and Freud

The theoretical armature of such a model already exists within the canon of Western social thought, though mostly in highly abstract form. It begins with the work of Max Weber, which is still unsurpassed in its sophistication and breadth (1968, original German publication 1921). As is well-known, Weber's work is based on the interpretive method of "verstehen," that is, taking the point of view of others in order to grasp the meaning systems that motivate them. This is the side of Weber that has inspired anthropologists. But while he devoted himself to explicating the types of rationality that make sense of human action in other cultures and historical epochs, Weber

Charles Lindholm, Culture, Charisma, and Consciousness: The Case of the Rajneeshee from *Ethos*, Vol. 30, No. 4, pp. 357–375. © 2003 by the American Anthropological Association . Reprinted with permission of the American Anthropological Association.

also realized that people are very often motivated by two types of action orientation that are without any conscious purpose or meaning whatsoever. These types are tradition, motivated by inertia, and charisma, motivated by emotion.

Here I will discuss only charisma, leaving an inquiry into habit and tedium for another time. In its simplest ideal typical form, charisma is defined by Weber as "a certain quality of an individual personality by virtue of which he is considered extraordinary and treated as endowed with supernatural, superhuman or at least specifically exceptional powers or qualities" (Weber 1968:242). Individuals possessing charisma are portrayed by Weber as above all else passionate and intrinsically compelling; to the followers, whatever the charismatic leader says is right not because it makes sense or because it coincides with what has always been done but because *the leader says it*. Orders can be, and often are, completely whimsical and self-contradictory, but the devotee obeys automatically and unquestioningly without regard for either coherence or consequence.

Although Weber places charisma outside the realm of meaning, it nonetheless does have a certain structure and trajectory. In particular, in its ideal form, charisma completely repudiates the past and overturns all rational organizational principles: spiritual calling, not technical training, is what is required of members; salaries and systematic organization are despised; hierarchy is fluid and is determined by the leader's intuition. Love, not reason, is at the core of the movement. Yet this primary form of charisma cannot last. If it is to survive, it must be rationalized and rigidified into a new tradition, based on the followers' interpretations of the leader's original message. The visionary must be replaced by the bureaucrat; the priest must take the place of the prophet. If this does not occur, the movement is sure to collapse, a victim of its own unrealized cosmic ambitions and the inevitable processes of delegitimization, as the prophet's world-transforming mission meets its limits.

According to Weber, the prototypical charismatic can be the inspired demagogue or the berserker who awes others by his "spells of maniac passion" (1968:242). But the ancestor figures of all charismatics are the magician-shamans who reveal divine powers in their ecstatic and dramatic enactments of death and rebirth. The shaman serves both as an exemplar of ecstasy and as the leader in the rituals of communal intoxication and orgiastic merger that Weber took as the original sacred experience (Weber 1968:242, 400–403, 535–536, 554, 1112, 1115; for more recent studies of the shaman's enactment of death and rebirth, see Lewis 1971; Wallace 1970).

Weber's picture of the charismatic was drawn from theorists of mass hypnosis and crowd psychology (for an outline of this material see Darnton 1968; Lindholm 1990). According to this now almost forgotten paradigm, the psychic influence of the hypnotist undermined rationality and permitted powerful spiritual/emotional forces to dominate the entranced subjects; these forces were likely to spread contagiously through the audience, drawing them also into trance states of diminished autonomy and enhanced emotionality. According to Weber, the shaman's dramatic performance exerted a similar fascination on audiences who were drawn into imitative states of ecstasy. Superhuman powers were attributed to the shaman-hypnotist who kindled these vitalizing and otherworldly sensations (Greenfield 1985).

Influenced by the same studies of crowd psychology that inspired Weber, his contemporary Emile Durkheim argued that an extraordinary state of irrational excitement (which he called "collective effervescence") was likely to occur spontaneously "whenever people are put into closer and more active relations with one another" (1965:241, original French publication 1912). Using ethnographic material from Australia, Durkheim argued that within an excited crowd, powerful emotions were intensified through automatic processes of imitation and amplification. Participants' egos disintegrated as they merged in ecstatic communion with the surrounding throng. This extraordinary state served, Durkheim thought, as the founding impetus for all religion and, in fact, for all civilization and all thought. For Durkheim, then, charisma (a term he never used) exists only in states of collective effervescence; the charismatic leader who is Weber's hero is merely a "crowd crystal" around whom the ecstatic collective can solidify and resonate (Canetti 1978). It is for this reason that Durkheim can make the seemingly paradoxical claim that "despotism is nothing more than inverted communism" (1984:144, original French publication 1893).

But even though Durkheim downplayed the part of the leader while Weber focused on leadership, both agreed that what is essential and compulsive in charisma is not its meaning, though explanatory meaning systems are inevitably generated after the fact. What is crucial instead is the collective ecstasy that experientially and immediately dissolves the individual ego into the group.

The same point was made by Sigmund Freud, though with a very different explanatory model and moral attitude. Unlike Durkheim and Weber, who had generally positive views of charisma and the crowd, for Freud elimination of the rational self in the collective allowed people to "throw off the repression of the unconscious instinctual impulses" and to revel in "all that is evil in the human mind" (1959:10, original German publication 1921). In the Freudian paradigm, the crowd consists of "many equals, who can identify with one another, and a single person superior to them all" (1959:53). The leader is a narcissistic primal father figure "who loved no one but himself, or other people only in so far as they served his needs" (Freud 1959:55). Under his orders, forbidden desires and passions are released with impunity.

Vastly simplified, Freud's group psychology is based on his belief that we are all products of Oedipal family constellations that leave us burdened with guilt over our own irreconcilable and unrealizable impulses to both love and hate those closest to us. We experience this fundamental tension in intimate relationships throughout our lives and continually seek to escape the pain it causes. Losing the self in a crowd united in worship of a self-absorbed leader offers relief from our existential quandary. Within the embrace of the group, ambivalence is alleviated by adoration of the leader who channels rage outward. As Freud remarks, "it is always possible to band together a considerable number of people in love, so long as

there are other people left over to receive the manifestations of their aggressiveness" (1962:61, original German publication 1930). But this psychic stratagem is never completely successful, and internal scapegoats are often required to absorb the group's excess hostility.

Freud's emphasis on the fundamental ambiguity of followers' attitudes toward charismatic power and collective participation was an original contribution. In Weber's actor-centered theory, there was no notion that the irrational intensity of the charismatic relationship could evoke hatred as well as attraction. Durkhelm too disallowed conflict, since for him collective effervescence served only to disintegrate the individual into the ecstatic crowd. But in Freud's theory, the band of brothers was united not only by love but also by loathing.

To conclude: according to Weber, Durkheim, and Freud, individuals are drawn to charismatic groups because such groups stimulate powerful and intoxicating states of dissociation and self-loss. These ecstatic states occur as the crowd unites in its shared love for the posturing and dramatic leader who is at its center and who directs its fears and aggression outward. Yet beneath the delirious surface, deep ambivalence remains, stimulating polarization, denial, and scapegoating.

Although this synthesis offers a theory that does some justice to the actual inner experience of charisma, it does so in a way that is blind to the tones of context and culture. For Weber, charisma in its ideal form was outside meaning; culture entered only with rationalization. Durkheim was interested solely in universal aspects of collective exhilaration, while Freud was concerned with equally universal psychic processes. Obviously, there is a great need for anthropological clarification of the roots and vectors of real charismatic movements. Such research could do much to bridge the gap between culture and the individual that has so plagued anthropological theory; it could also offset the unfortunate tendency of anthropologists to discount the dynamics of group consciousness and to assume that people are always rational actors seeking culturally validated benefits.

Sociologists, as the direct descendants of Weber and Durkheim, have devoted considerable energy to describing the dynamics of charismatic groups (c.f. Kephart 1987; Wallis 1984; Zablocki 1980); psychologists too have had their say about charisma (characteristic examples are to be found in Halperin 1983), but for whatever reasons, only a few anthropologists have even referred to charisma in their writing (examples are Csordas 1994; Kracke 1978; Lewis 1986; Willner 1984). Yet the dialectical sociopsychological framework outlined above, when applied in tandem with in-depth anthropological fieldwork and historical research, offers the possibility of gaining new insight into some of the most puzzling, disturbing, and threatening events and social movements of our time.

Rajneeshism as an Example of Charisma

To illustrate this possibility, the following pages provide a very rapid and preliminary analysis of Rajneeshism, the charismatic religious movement created by Bhagwan Shree Rajneesh, whose colorful devotees, clad in the colors of the sunset, were a familiar sight in the United States until the group disintegrated in 1985. Unfortunately, the Rajneeshee are not the best subject for stimulating an anthropological approach to charisma, since, although Indian in origin, Rajneeshism flourished mostly in the United States and strongly reflected American spirituality. Furthermore, the material to be reviewed here is all secondary; neither I nor any anthropologist (as far as I know) undertook extensive participant-observation among the Rajneeshee, though the sociologist Marion Goldman spent some time with the group in its last phases. Nonetheless, the trajectory of Rajneesh and his cult has been very well documented by members and former members, and by many other qualified observers.

The texts of these authors naturally reflect their varied perspectives. For example, those who actually participated in the movement are usually either apostates or enthusiasts, and their work has to be appraised accordingly. Among the apostates are Milne (1987), Belfrage (1981), Strelley and San Souci (1987), and Franklin (1992), who all present a rela-

tively dark picture of the movement. However, Franklin wrote two propagandistic tracts about Rajneesh under her *sannyasi* (devotee) name of Satya Bharti (1980, 1981) that offer a valuable corrective to her post-Rajneesh attitude. The Bhagwan's personal physician also wrote a sympathetic book (Meredith 1988) outlining the inner workings of the group at its peak, and Rajneesh himself published many books on his own life and philosophy (those most referred to by devotees are Rajneesh 1974, 1976, 1977). More distanced analyses of Rajneesh include Fitzgerald (1986), Carter (1990), Gordon (1987), and Goldman (1999). This wealth of material, despite its inevitable biases and second-hand character, provides enough data to allow me to undertake "anthropology at a distance" and to sketch the dynamics of this extraordinary movement.

Bhagwan Shree Rajneesh (originally named Mahan Chandra Rajneesh) was born to a Jain family in India in 1931. After taking a degree in philosophy, he taught at the University of Jabalpur and also gave lectures throughout India, debunking all accepted truths and calling for a new kind of awareness, more life-affirming than customary Indian asceticism and more open to change. His eclectic, secular approach won him an enthusiastic following of heterodox, socially concerned middle-class Indians, who found Rajneesh's spiritual message of worldly antitraditionalism appealing. In 1966 he resigned his university post to devote himself to full-time spiritual teaching. In 1970 he settled in Bombay and began advertising his own unique brand of "dynamic meditation," which was geared to provide speedy enlightenment. In 1971, he designated himself Bhagwan, the incarnation of the deity, revealing that he had gained this exalted status 20 years previously after the death of his ego. His new aim, he said, was to lead others through the experience he had painfully undergone on his own. Soon many Westerners were drawn to this sophisticated, humorous, and educated guru who promised them immediate transcendence.

To accommodate his growing following, Bhagwan Shree Rajneesh, as he was now known, founded a hugely successful Ashram (temple) in Poona, India, where he enlisted

Western therapists to lead workshops and groups that made use of contemporary psychological techniques to achieve spiritual transformation. Poona became a psychic carnival of multiple modes of altering awareness and rapidly grew into the center of a world-wide network of at least 40 thousand, and perhaps as many as 300 thousand, initiates, many of them successful, well-to-do, and highly educated.

However, despite his great success, Bhagwan feared that treacherous followers were planning to betray him and that a jealous Indian government intended to attack Poona. Therefore, he suddenly uprooted his Ashram from India and transplanted it to a new massive commune outside the small town of Antelope in Oregon, which he renamed Rajneeshpuram in his own honor. He also proclaimed himself founder of a messianic religion, Rajneeshism, which he claimed would destroy illusions and lead believers to union with the infinite. In this paradisiacal state, families and politics would become obsolete: the believers would live together in absolute unity and harmony. According to Bhagwan, Rajneeshpuram would serve as the cradle for a new cosmic race after the rest of the world was destroyed in a gigantic nuclear holocaust.

Adhering to its world-transforming mission and its polarized view of humanity, the commune felt justified in riding roughshod over its neighbors. Lying to and insulting local residents were excused as exercises designed to "awaken" them. Meanwhile, within the commune itself paranoia steadily increased: weapons were hoarded, obsessional hygienic measures were initiated to protect against infection by AIDS, listening devices were planted to spy on suspect members. Some of Bhagwan's closest disciples, including Sheela, his all-powerful personal secretary, began a campaign of systematically poisoning people both inside and outside the group whom they suspected as traitors. Luckily no one was killed.

In late 1985, these illegal activities came to light, and the commune was shut down by local authorities. Bhagwan himself was arrested trying to flee the country but was finally allowed to leave the United States after pleading guilty to two felony counts. Sheela and some other close disciples were jailed. The multimillion dollar enterprise of Rajneeshpuram was completely abandoned. Nonetheless, many of the Rajneeshee continued to revere their exiled leader, arguing that the Rajneeshpuram debacle was Bhagwan's way of teaching his disciples a necessary lesson in nonattachment. Meanwhile, Bhagwan returned to Poona, changed his name to Osho, and renamed his much diminished Ashram the "Osho Commune International." Disciples who visited him there described him as at peace with himself. He "left his body" on January 19, 1990, but about 20,000 of his devotees worldwide remain loyal to his teachings and memory, though there are few, if any, new converts. This lingering group can be reached at http://osho.org.

The Construction of Charismatic Commitment

We can begin to understand the power and longevity of Rajneeshism by looking at the way the Rajneeshee freed themselves from what they saw as the distorting conditioning of society. As mentioned above, the central ritual of the movement was "dynamic meditation," which involved blind-folded free-form dancing, shouting, and hyperventilating. This progressed to a coordinated climax. The group then joined together in postcoital collective meditation under the leadership of a disciple represented as an emanation of Rajneesh. I use sexual imagery here advisedly, since the ritual quite consciously replicated a sexual orgy. For devotees the movement from frantic free-form paroxysms, to rhythmic communal breathing exercises, to lulled group trance, had a powerful effect, producing the physical and psychic sensations of self-loss and expansion that are typical of charismatic group ritual. The catalytic figure of the leader served as the totem around which generalized collective excitement could coalesce and be intensified.

Similar techniques for disintegration of social constraints and personal identity, along with the stimulation of ecstatic communion in the group and around the leader, were initiated by the psychotherapists, Gestalt practitioners, Reichians, graduates of Esalin, humanistic psychologists, and others who followed Rajneesh. Given permission by their guru to search for ways to attain permanent states of ecstasy, these therapeutic idealists formed the core of activists in the movement and were the creators of what was probably one of the most effective set of procedures for altering human consciousness ever devised.

Transformation began as visitors were intuitively screened by the therapeutic inner cadre and sorted according to their supposed psychic capacities; they were then placed in various groups oriented toward "centering," that is, at finding their "natural" cores through meditative reflection and through dynamic meditation, which many had already practiced in Rajneeshee centers in their home countries. New recruits were enrolled as well in "self-awareness" groups that used more confrontational techniques to challenge the individual's sense of self. The standard form was described by one initiate as follows: "Two people would sit, and one would say, 'Who are you?' The other would speak for five minutes. Then it would reverse, and the second would say, 'Who are you?' And the first one would speak for five minutes. You sat with three people an hour, and you basically did that for eight hours a day, interspersed with some meals, some exercises, some music" (quoted in Goldman 1999:148). Naturally enough, participants in this process found themselves questioning their identities, while also experiencing strong surges of emotional energy and connection with their ever-changing partners.

Afterward, suitable recruits were shuttled into far more strenuous group exercises that occupied their every waking hour. Techniques that challenged self-esteem, personal identity, and logic were used in concordance with highly charged cathartic confrontations, "tantric" group sexuality, and overt violence, in alternation with periods of contemplative communal meditation. Individuals were often required to act out their fears, hostilities, and past traumas in a public arena, and to confess their deepest anxieties and sins. Leaders also used imitation and mirroring to reflect the devotees back to themselves in order to allow them to discover their true inner natures beneath social conditioning. Pervasive self-questioning prepared

the way for self-doubt and self-loss by subjecting all feelings, thoughts, and intuitions to disintegrative analysis within the critical and encompassing collective framework.

In this charged environment, group leaders were regarded by the trainees, and by themselves, as divinely inspired emanations of Bhagwan; they therefore could do no wrong. Any demands that seemed excessive were automatically defined as lessons in devotion and personal surrender. Those who held back were singled out for the group's sometimes abusive attention. The participants were told over and over again that whatever happened in the group, even if violent or humiliating, was only for their own enlightenment. Any resistance demonstrated "hang-ups" preventing illumination. The whole process served to distance the individual from the critical self and to instill new and powerful collective identifications under Rajneesh's auspices.

These methods could cause agony, but torment was regarded as the necessary precondition for separation from the ego and ecstatic communion with the group. This desired disjuncture was marked as the devotees took on new names, donned their orange robes, and celebrated their "sannyas birthdays" in replacement of personal birthdays. Henceforth, all personal pronouns were eliminated; the members spoke only of "we" and used the third person when obliged to refer to themselves as individuals. The only personal pronouns generally permitted were those referring to Rajneesh himself. In writing about the guru, it was always "He" with a capital letter.

Bhagwan was cuite aware of the powerful effects he was orchestrating. He had studied mass psychology and hypnotism and knew the importance of promoting and creating disquiet and uncertainty among the following to generate an amblance favoring his charismatic domination. As he said, "confusion is my method. The moment I see you accumulating something, creating a philosophy or theology, I immediately jump on it and destroy it" (Bhagwan quoted in Gordon 1987:58). As we shall see, he carried this policy of confusion through in all aspects of actual administration of the community, leaving himself as the sole source of meaning and identity for his followers.

Another factor in gaining the followers' commitment was the change in consciousness engendered by physical strain and disease. Since the acolytes were working as enlightened beings, they had no days off, nor were there vacations; work was strenuous, and made more so by the linkage of labor with spiritual perfection. Sickness was considered a "meaningful" experience that should be "lived through"; hospitalization was a sign of imperfection, and those who were sick too often were dismissed from the commune. General fatigue functioned to lower the devotees' physical resistance to potent experiences of self-loss in the collective. In turn, from these vitalizing experiences the acolytes learned that the energy of Rajneesh and the commune could sustain them, however great their personal pain and fatigue.

A characteristic and indicative way in which confusion, self-doubt, and increased devotion to the center were created and intensified was through Bhagwan's policy of permitting only certain disciples to participate in his lectures. His personal guards stood at the door, turning back those whose odor might offend Bhagwan's sensitive nose. Hopeful devotees spent hours obsessively washing themselves, but were likely to be rejected over and over again. In fact, this restrictive policy had little to do with Bhagwan's sense of smell and everything to do with escalating the anxiety and anticipation of the followers. When a disciple, after weeks of nervous scrubbing, finally was deemed pure enough to enter Bhagwan's sacred presence, he or she was strongly inclined to be overwhelmed. Not to find the experience sublime would be a repudiation of all the sacrifices that had been already made.

Once a devotee finally gained entry into the favored inner circle, Bhagwan's will became ever more pervasive and intrusive, both indicating and increasing his influence. Extensive files were kept on the private sexual relations of group members, which were regulated by Rajneesh and his close associates. Bhagwan's personal permission was required for any intimate relationships; on his word, people were assigned new lovers, or a couple could be broken up by sending one partner out of the commune. Letting a lover go was a laudable act of surrender to Bhagwan. Sexuality itself was reconfigured within the commune, where the ideal was to maintain a sexual plateau without orgasm. Intercourse without climax turned the fusion of eroticism into a kind of solitary spiritual discipline, a mystical revelation of one's own essential transpersonal being – which led, in turn, to merger in the collective, where that transpersonal core was embodied by the guru.

Sexual union was not the only intimacy controlled within the commune. In fact, all relations that might counter unity with Rajneesh were discouraged. For example, Bhagwan "suggested" that his faithful disciples give up their ties with children and parents. He also "suggested" abortions and sterilization for his followers, since children were considered a distraction from total commitment to Bhagwan. These irrevocable sacrifices disconnected the followers from any external loyalties, bound them closer together, and drew them more deeply into Rajneesh's embrace.

As Rajneeshpuram became increasingly successful, the organization of the Ashram settled into a pattern that also helped to increase the dependence of the following and augment Bhagwan's charismatic domination. Within each task group, secrecy came to be strictly enforced, and communication among workers of different departments was forbidden. In this fragmented charismatic organization, individuals were merged together during Bhagwan's performances and in group exercises, but in the mundane world they were kept isolated in segmented factions continually struggling for attention in a fluid environment. Without any standardized chain of command, each faction anxiously looked to Bhagwan to validate its power, thereby escalating his importance. Tensions were increased because of the commune's ideological premise of absolute unity and harmony that made followers unable to confront and discuss the hierarchies and hostilities that actually surrounded them. Malcontents were accused of "taking the game too seriously" and of being "unaware" of the true nature of Rajneeshpuram. This too led to greater dependence on the leader, who was the only sure source of knowledge and support (for a rare analysis of the use of factionalism to maintain a charismatic group, see Nyomarkay 1967).

The erosion of any space for personal reflection and autonomy was furthered by a doctrine of absolute obedience. The Rajneeshee were obliged to follow all instructions to the letter, no matter how absurd or counter-productive these orders seemed. The same directions for mundane, repetitive tasks were reiterated every day, establishing a ritualized atmosphere that denied the worker's capacity for memory and initiative. Each task had to be done perfectly, regardless of the cost or the difficulty, as a proof of spiritual awakening and as a sign of devotion to Bhagwan. Since any error might mean expulsion, and expulsion meant losing touch with the infinite, obsessive attention to detail was a major element in the lives of the disciples and was considered a path to dissolution of the ego.

Personal judgment or criticism was prohibited within the communal world, since it was defined as projecting one's own inner incapacity outward and demonstrated that one had not yet gained enlightenment. At the same time, since Bhagwan vacillated and changed his mind continuously, absolute rules might be suddenly overthrown at a whim, and devotees were expected to adapt immediately to rapid and unexplained changes. When his orders proved too difficult, Rajneesh was likely to laugh and counter them, but only after the disciples had struggled mightily to obey. Even more confusing, the rules themselves were often hard to discover, so that converts could be expelled precipitously for violation of a regulation they did not know existed. The consequences of rule breaking were also arbitrary and varied according to how the inner cadre functionary in charge of discipline reacted to the "aura" of the person accused of wrongdoing. Similar techniques are common in other charismatic groups and mystical orders. The expressed idea is to break the disciple from being bound by rules, but by increasing confusion and anxiety, this method vastly increases the acolyte's focus on the leader as the sole source of meaning and safety.

The Bhagwan's followers had to learn to live in a world in which complete capriciousness was combined paradoxically with compulsive rigidity. As one disciple put it: "Ashram life continually forces us to live in a state of insecurity. ... All kinds of crisis-situations are

created, until finally there's an explosion. And in its wake, a transformation" (Ma Satya Bharti quoted in Fitzgerald 1986:94). This transformation was one of a deep identification with Bhagwan as the only point of orientation in a world of high demands and total uncertainty (see Kanter 1972 for a comprehensive list of commitment mechanisms commonly utilized in charismatic groups).

In compensation for their loyalty and labor, the elite of the Ashram were designated by Rajneesh as Boddhisattvas, enlightened ones. It was believed that they had dropped their personal identities and had been absorbed into Bhagwan's essence. And, indeed, they did feel that they had assimilated some of his extraordinary powers, though, of course, they still remained far below him in the spiritual hierarchy. These powers were manifested in achieving seemingly impossible tasks with ease, in working harder than anyone, in succeeding at whatever they attempted. They also felt themselves to have certain paranormal abilities, such as telepathic communion with others in the group; an intuitive facility to "read" other people; a capacity to reach into a mystical source to achieve sudden synthetic conclusions; the ability to alter identities like a chameleon changes colors, taking on roles and shifting personalities according to the need of the moment. Having eliminated the programming of the past, buoyed by the expansive power of the group and without any encumbering personal identities of their own, they now could manipulate their emotions and empathetically reflect whomever faced them. They could dance freely where unenlightened people saw only limits and boundaries. And at the center of it all, giving form to their formlessness, was Rajneesh, whose enigmatic wishes they sought to intuit and carry out, regardless of the consequences.

Bhagwan's Charismatic Character

For the devotees, Bhagwan was truly God on earth, with the power to give his followers a transcendent sense of self-loss, expansion, and empowerment. As we have seen, this state was actually achieved via techniques that combined fragmentation of the individual with immersion in the group consciousness. But from the beginning the group was a creation of Bhagwan. It was he who inspired the *sannyasin* by his presence. How did this occur?

Hypnosis is used again and again by disciples and nonbelievers alike to describe the way Rajneesh affected those around him. Whether Rajneesh was consciously trying to mesmerize his audience, it is clear that he had an amazing theatrical capacity for enchantment. His performances were expressive improvisations that moved, without pause or doubt, from highly abstract philosophical reflections to obscene jokes and racist remarks that were designed to shock his audience, who were caught up in the exhilaration of his rapidly changing moods, his intonations and dramatic pauses, his potent rhetoric. Rajneesh himself said his sermons were "like the acting of an actor" (quoted in Fitzgerald 1986:77), and like an actor his vast range of expression never escaped his control. His audience was entranced by the excitement of witnessing intense emotions and extreme opinions that challenged their ordinary sense of reality and focused them on the supernatural presence of Bhagwan.

The appeal of Rajneesh was showcased, as with all charismatics, within a self-conscious theatrical context that framed and heightened his performance. His appearances were carefully constructed to set him off to best advantage and to increase his mystery and the audience's sense of awe. Later in his career he began wearing robes that would emphasize his broad shoulders, makeup to improve his complexion, and so on. Other props and techniques were used as well to heighten the disciples' experience. But these dramatic stagings and costumes were simply frosting on the cake. As he caressed the audience with his voice, shifted emotions and rhetoric with fluidity, and used his expressive hands to counterpoint his remarks, Bhagwan gave the faithful a sense of being carried onto a higher level of existence, both immediate and transcendent. For the devotees, being close to Bhagwan was ineffable.

Devotees likened the experience of being with Bhagwan to the experience of romantic love. As one disciple said, "I love the man no matter what he does" (quoted in Gordon

1987:225). Or, as Goldman puts it, "He was the sannyasins' fairy-tale prince, rescuing maidens who were imprisoned by their own emotional fragility" (1999:244). As in romantic love, the believers felt they were in a direct, intimate, and passionate relationship with Rajneesh. Drawing close to him was likened to a moth flying into a flame, a burning that both energizes and immolates. His love was visualized and experienced as so great the follower could never hope to match it. The extravagant donations of the followers, including dozens of Rolls Royces, expressed their recognition of the guru's superiority and their own abject dependence.

The inequality of the relationship correlated with Bhagwan's characteristic personal stance of disconnection and remoteness. Bhagwan was clear about his lack of involvement with his disciples. They needed him, he did not need them; he could touch them at will, but they could never touch him. As Richard Sennett has argued, this in itself is a crucial factor in gaining power over a following, since "someone who is indifferent arouses our desire to be recognized. ... Afraid of his indifference, not understanding what it is which keeps him aloof, we come to be emotionally dependent" (Sennett 1981:86). Yet Sennett's picture is too simple to wholly account for Bhagwan Shree Rajneesh, who combined distance with great empathy, who shifted from remoteness to complete involvement in a moment, and who was capable of inspiring his followers to transformative experiences of merger and ecstasy.

Fluid, ungraspable, full of life but without substance, absolutely loving yet ultimately detached, Rajneesh's extraordinary personality reflected exactly the sort of disintegrative psychic crisis that is commonly found in the life histories of shamans as well as contemporary charismatic figures (see Lindholm 1990 for more cases). At the age of 21 he suffered a year-long depression in which he felt himself lost in a "bottomless abyss." The Ayurvedic doctor who treated him diagnosed his malady as divine intoxication. And indeed Rajneesh was cured in a way that is familiar from shamanistic and mystical texts. Overwhelmed by an explosion of bliss, he lost his personal identity and gained a new transpersonal self: "That night I died and was reborn. But the one that was reborn has nothing to do with that which died, it is a discontinuous thing. ... The one who died, died totally; nothing of him has remained" (Bhagwan Shree Rajneesh quoted in Fitzgerald 1986:87).

As mentioned, the techniques used to bring the Rajneeshee devotees into awareness of and communion with their leader were consciously designed to replicate Bhagwan's own shamanlike fragmentation, death, and transfiguration. Through his performances, he aroused the audience members into ecstatic states of self-loss and merger with the group and with himself, giving them a transformative experience that was similar to his own deification. Yet there remained an essential difference. For the disciples the spiritual capacity to transcend the self was reliant on continuing support and mirroring from Bhagwan and from the community, while Bhagwan's condition derived from his own psychic state or, as he would say, from the universal Godhead whose vehicle he had became. His was the original light, and the followers merely dancing shadows, their experiences a pale reflection of his.

Rajneesh's evolution from human being to depersonalized deity cannot be reduced to childhood traumas, but we can nonetheless recognize typical influences in the process that led to his metamorphosis. He was raised by his grandparents, to whom he was greatly attached, but his grandfather died when he was seven, and according to his own memoirs, it was then that he began to feel a deep sense of estrangement: "Whenever my relationship with anyone began to become intimate ... death stared at me. ... For me the possibility of anyone else becoming my center was destroyed at the very first steps of my life" (Bhagwan Shree Rajneesh quoted in Gordon 1987:22). Later, when he was a teenager, his first, and last, beloved died. After these deaths, he could no longer find his "center" anywhere outside of himself, and when he searched within he found nothing to sustain him.

What did remain in his emptiness was a pleasure in manipulating death and suffering. Rajneesh wrote in 1979 that watching people die was his longtime hobby. "The moment

I would hear that somebody was on his deathbed, I would be there ... and I would sit and watch" (quoted in Milne 1986:96). Along with pleasure in watching death, Rajneesh enjoyed frightening and controlling others. As a youth he also showed a strong desire to come close to death through risky adventures that made him a hero to his school friends. Nonetheless he could not keep anxiety at bay, and every seven years after the death of his grandfather, he underwent a period of deep depression, withdrawal, paranoia, and psychosomatic illness. At the age of 21, the worst such episode culminated in the revelation outlined above in which he felt himself disintegrated, reconfigured, and deified as Bhagwan. However, the cycle did not stop but returned again and again throughout his life. Rajneesh coped by projecting his paranoia outward, staging attacks on himself when necessary to validate the reality of his anxieties. One such cycle occurred before he moved to Poona; another, seven years later, initiated his departure from India; a third preceded the disintegration of Rajneeshpuram.

In sum, according to his own account, from an early age Rajneesh felt an inner vacuity and emotional detachment and was plagued by recurring experiences of fragmentation and depression. His condition was partially resolved by his experience of personal disintegration and merger with a transpersonal deity, which left him beyond connections with others, isolated in a realm where death and life are coterminous. As a result, he could reinterpret his inner void as an identification with the cosmos. His internal life was now the same as the life of the universe. Whatever he felt or thought arose from a source outside of the personal self, which had been obliterated. Because of his transubstantiation, he could awe and inspire others with abreactive performances that expressed his struggle with and transcendence over death. Existence was, he knew, a cosmic joke, and he had the punch line.

But the joker requires an appreciative audience. Bhagwan, though presenting himself as beyond all desire, actually had a powerful need to construct a total universe where he could be protected from the fears that constantly threatened to destroy him. This could only be accomplished by absorbing those around him into relationships of complete dependency. To this end, Rajneesh created a symbiotic family of helpless children who loved him unconditionally. From his lonely height and out of his divine compassion, he was willing to remain with them and teach them to dance in the void. In return, they must trust him, depend on him, adore him, become him.

Bhagwan's sexuality, according to most accounts, was primarily voyeuristic and was symptomatic of his complex relationship with his disciples. Isolated in his icy cold sanctuary, purified and protected from all germs and pollutants, he found satisfaction in fondling his "mediums" and watching them have sexual intercourse in front of him, encouraging them to lose their boundaries, to melt into one another. While remaining detached from human intimacy, pure, cold, and unreachable, Bhagwan inspired his followers to banish any trace of their own autonomy in states of absolute dependency and merger.

But this could not last. As the collective grew in power and complexity, participants were able to attain ecstatic moments and succeed in community enterprises that were not under Bhagwan's direct command. Efforts to create greater centralization and control led only to increasing fears of betrayal and more oppressive rigidity. Furthermore, Rajneesh's own recurring depressive tendencies made him increasingly dissatisfied with his human toys and prey to darker and darker moods. More and more often, he withdrew into isolation, silence, drugs, and insatiable viewing of bombastic videocassettes. His favorites were *Patton* and *The Ten Commandments*. Meanwhile, his circle of lieutenants, under his second-in-command Sheela, tried to hold the group together by paranoid and arrogant acts of violence, intimidation, and subterfuge.

His ordinary followers also had a crucial role in the downward cycle; they wanted Bhagwan to fulfill their own dreams of absolute power and purity; their hopes and fears encouraged him to indulge himself in the grandiose and fearful visions that lay beneath his surface of detachment and heedlessness. The more these fantasies were enacted, the more schizoid and paranoid the community became

and the more inevitable its collapse. Unhappily for the devoted and idealistic spiritual seekers of Rajneeshpuram, their faith in complete love and harmony conjured up hatred and factionalism; their hope for absolute freedom ended in repression; their pursuit of transcendence led to poisonous betrayal. This is a pattern that is all too familiar in the West, and one that I have traced in detail in numerous other charismatic movements (Lindholm 1990).

Conclusion

I began this article remarking on the difficulty Western social science has in conceptualizing the experience of charisma. In its demand for self-sacrifice and absolute devotion to an apparently irrational leader, it seems to stand at right angles to our common sense understandings of human motivation. Yet Western social theory has developed a set of theoretical approaches to charisma that, taken together, offer a way of grasping what seems, on the surface at least, to be wholly outside normal experience. To reiterate: Weber imagined the leader as the animating center who brings the collective into being; Durkheim saw the leader as an emblem or totem representing the energy of the group; Freud revealed the inner tensions of the leader – follower relationship. Together, they provide a paradigm we can apply to actual cases of charisma.

From the example of Rajneeshism, we see that individuals are drawn into charismatic groups because participation in those groups gives them a sense of vitality and commitment, albeit at the cost of autonomy. In fact, immersion coincides with and is facilitated by the systematic undermining and breakup of the psychic structure of the individual; taken-for-granted reality is thereby replaced by a new cosmic emotional truth – one that is seen to emanate from the extraordinary personality of the shamanlike charismatio leader. This new world is mutually constructed in a dialectical process that unites leader and follower in an ongoing psychological dynamic of desire, hope, and fear.

The case of Rajneesh is only one of a number I have analyzed at second hand (for a look at some others, see Lindholm 1990, 1992).

Unfortunately, most have been within the Western context, where charisma is subdued and repressed. What is required is more field-work on charismatic movements in different cultural contexts, to see how much the frame-work I have outlined is transferable and how charisma is attenuated, maintained, legitimized, and challenged under other cultural conditions (see Chien-yu 2001; Kakar 2001; Pinto 2002 for recent examples). This effort is not of purely academic interest. Those fanatics who destroyed themselves and thousands of others on September 11th were, it should be recalled, dedicated followers of a charismatic leader.

REFERENCES

Belfrage, Sally
1981   Flowers of Emptiness: Reflections on an Ashram. New York: Dial Press.
Bharti (Franklin), Satya
1980   Drunk on the Divine: An Account of Life in the Ashram of Bhagwan Shree Rajneesh. New York: Grove Press.
1981   Death Comes Dancing: Celebrating Life with Bhagwan Shree Rajneesh. London: Routlege and Kegan Paul.
Canetti, Elias
1978   Crowds and Power. New York: Seabury.
Carter, Lewis
1990   Charisma and Control in Rajneeshpuram. New York: Cambridge University Press.
Chien-yu, Julia Huang
2001   Recapturing Charisma: Emotion and Rationalization in a Globalizing Buddhist Movement from Taiwan. Ph.D. dissertation, Department of Anthropology, Boston University.
Caordas, Thomas
1994 The Sacred Self: A Cultural Phenomenology of Charismatic Healing. Berkeley: University of California Press.
Darnton, Robert
1968   Meamerism and the End of the Enlightenment in France. New York: Schocken Books.
Durkheim, Emile
1965[1912]   The Elementary Forms of the Religious Life. New York: Free Press.
1984[1893]   The Division of Labor in Society. New York: Free Press.

Fitzgerald, Frances
1986   Rajneeshpuram. New Yorker, September 22: 46–96.
Franklin, Satya Bharti
1992   The Promise of Paradise: A Woman's Intimate Story of the Perils of Life with Rajneesh. New York: Station Hill Press.
Freud, Sigmund
1959[1921]   Group Psychology and the Analysis of the Ego. New York: Norton.
1962[1930]   Civilization and Its Discontents. New York: Norton.
Goldman, Marion
1999   Passionate Journeys: Why Successful Women Joined a Cult. Ann Arbor: University of Michigan Press.
Gordon, James
1987   The Golden Guru. Lexington: Stephen Grenne Press.
Greenfield, Lish
1985   Reflections on the Two Charismas. British Journal of Sociology 36:117–132.
Halperin, David, ed.
1983   Psychodynamic Perspectives on Religion, Sect and Cult. Boston: John Wright.
Kakar, Sudhir
2001   Ecstasy. London: Viking.
Kanter, Rosabeth Moss
1972   Commitment and Community: Communcs and Utopies in Sociological Perspective. Cambridge: Harvard University Press.
Kephart, William
1987   Extraordinary Groups. New York: St. Martin's Press.
Kracke, Waud
1978   Force and Persuasion: Lendership in an Amazonian Society. Chicago: University of Chicago Press.
Lewis, I. M.
1971   Ecstatic Religion: An Anthropological Study of Spirit Possession and Shamanism. Harmondsworth, England: Penguin.
1986   Religion in Context: Cults and Charisma. Cambridge: Cambridge University Press.
Lindholm, Charles
1990   Charisma. Oxford: Basil Blackwell
1992   Crowds, Charisma, and Altered States of Consciousness. Culture, Medicine and Psychiatry 16: 287–310.
Meredith, George
1988   Bhagwan: The Most Godless yet the Most Godly Man. Poona: Rebel Publishing House.

Milne, Hugh
  1986   Bhagwan: The God That Failed. New York: St. Martin's Press.
Nyomarkay, Joseph
  1967   Charisma and Factionalism in the Nazl Party. Minnespolis: University of Minnesots Press.
Pinto, Paulo
  2002   Mystical Bodies: Ritual, Experience and the Embodiment of Sufism in Syria. Ph.D. dissertation, Department of Anthropology, Boston University.
Rajneesh, Bhagwan Shree
  1974   The Book of Secrets. Poona: Rajneesh Foundation.
  1976   Meditation: The Art of Ecstasy. Poona: Rajneesh Foundation.
  1977   I Am the Gate. New York: Harper and Row.
Sennett, Richard
  1981   Authority. New York: Vintage.

Strelley, Kate, with Robert San Soucl
  1987   The Ultimate Game: The Rise and Fall of Bhagwan Shree Rajneesh. New York: Harper and Row.
Wallace, Anthony F. C.
  1970   The Death and Rebirth of Seneca. New York: Knopf.
Wallis, Roy
  1984   The Elementary Forms of the New Religious Life. London: Routledge and Kegan Paul.
Weber, Max
  1968[1921]   Economy and Society: An Outline of Interpretive Sociology. I. Roth and C. Wittich, eds. Berkeley: University of California Press.
Willner, Ann Ruth
  1984   The Spellbinders: Charismatic Political Leadership. New Haven: Yale University Press.
Zablocki, Benjamin
  1980   Alienation and Charisma. New York: Free Press.

Index